Monographs in Theoretical Computer Science
An EATCS Series

Editors: W. Brauer J. Hromkovič G. Rozenberg A. Salomaa

On behalf of the European Association
for Theoretical Computer Science (EATCS)

Advisory Board:
G. Ausiello M. Broy C.S. Calude A. Condon
D. Harel J. Hartmanis T. Henzinger T. Leighton
M. Nivat C. Papadimitriou D. Scott

T0137182

Monographs in Theoretical Computer Science
An EATCS Series

Dines Bjørner · Martin C. Henson
Editors

Logics of
Specification Languages

 Springer

Prof. Emeritus, Dr. Dines Bjørner
Informatics and Mathematical Modelling
Technical University of Denmark
2800 Kgs. Lyngby
Denmark
bjorner@gmail.com

Prof. Martin C. Henson
University of Essex
Department of Computer Science
Wivenhoe Park
CO4 3SQ Colchester
United Kingdom
hensm@essex.ac.uk

Series Editors

Prof. Dr. Wilfried Brauer
Institut für Informatik der TUM
Boltzmannstr. 3
85748 Garching, Germany
brauer@informatik.tu-muenchen.de

Prof. Dr. Juraj Hromkovič
ETH Zentrum
Department of Computer Science
Swiss Federal Institute of Technology
8092 Zürich, Switzerland
juraj.hromkovic@inf.ethz.ch

Prof. Dr. Grzegorz Rozenberg
Leiden Institute of Advanced
Computer Science
University of Leiden
Niels Bohrweg 1
2333 CA Leiden, The Netherlands
rozenber@liacs.nl

Prof. Dr. Arto Salomaa
Turku Centre of
Computer Science
Lemminkäisenkatu 14 A
20520 Turku, Finland
asalomaa@utu.fi

ISBN 978-3-642-09345-6   e-ISBN 978-3-540-74107-7

DOI 10.1007/978-3-540-74107-7

ACM Computing Classification (1998): F.4, F.3, D.1, D.2, D.3

Monographs in Theoretical Computer Science. An EATCS Series. ISSN 1431-2654

© 2008 Springer-Verlag Berlin Heidelberg
Softcover reprint of the hardcover 1st edition 2008

This work is subject to copyright. All rights are reserved, whether the whole or part of the material is concerned, specifically the rights of translation, reprinting, reuse of illustrations, recitation, broadcasting, reproduction on microfilm or in any other way, and storage in data banks. Duplication of this publication or parts thereof is permitted only under the provisions of the German Copyright Law of September 9, 1965, in its current version, and permission for use must always be obtained from Springer. Violations are liable to prosecution under the German Copyright Law.

The use of general descriptive names, registered names, trademarks, etc. in this publication does not imply, even in the absence of a specific statement, that such names are exempt from the relevant protective laws and regulations and therefore free for general use.

Cover Design: KünkelLopka, Heidelberg

Printed on acid-free paper

9 8 7 6 5 4 3 2 1

springer.com

The editors dedicate this book to:

ASM : Yuri Gurevich
B : Jean-Raymond Abrial
CASL : Peter D. Mosses
CafeOBJ : Joseph A. Goguen, 1941–2006
DC : Zhou Chaochen
RAISE : Søren Prehn, 1955–2006
VDM : Peter Lucas
TLA+ : Leslie Lamport
Z : Jean-Raymond Abrial

Preface

1 Specification Languages

By a specification language we understand a formal system of syntax, semantics and proof rules. The syntax and semantics define a language; the proof rules a proof system. Specifications are expressions in the language — and reasoning over properties of these specifications is done within the proof system.

This book [2] will present nine of the current specification languages (ASM [40], B [5], CafeOBJ [8], CASL [33], Duration Calculus [14], RAISE (RSL) [12], TLA$^+$ [32], VDM (VDM-SL) [11] and Z [22]) and their logics of reasoning.

1.1 Specifications

Using a specification language we can formally describe a domain, some universe of discourse "out there, in reality", or we can prescribe requirements to computing systems that support activities of the domain; or we can specify designs of computing systems (i.e., machines: hardware + software).

A specification has a meaning. Meanings can be expressed in a property-oriented style, as in ASM, CafeOBJ, CASL and Duration Calculus, or can be expressed in a model-oriented style, as in B, RAISE/RSL, TLA, VDM or Z. RAISE/RSL provides a means for "slanting" a specification either way, or some "compromise" in-between. In the property-oriented style specifications emphasise properties of entities and functions. In the model-oriented style specifications emphasise mathematical values like sets, Cartesians, sequences, and maps and functions over these. (The above "compartmentalisation" is a very rough one. The nine language chapters of this book will provide more definitive delineations.)

Descriptions

Descriptions specify an area of, say, human activity, a domain, as it is, with no reference to requirements to computing systems that support activities of the domain. Usually the domain is "loose", entities, functions, events and behaviours of the domain are not fully understood and hence need be loosely described, that is, allow for multiple interpretations. Or phenomena of the domain are non-deterministic: the value of an entity, the outcome of a function application (i.e., an action), the elaboration of an event, or the course of a behaviour is not unique: could be any one of several. We take behaviours to be sets of sequences of actions and events — or of behaviours, that is multiple, possibly intertwined behaviours.

Hence we find that some specification languages allow for expressions of looseness, underspecification, non-determinism and/or concurrency. Since phenomena of domains are usually not computable the specification language must allow for the expression of non-computable properties, values and functions.

Prescriptions

Prescriptions are also specifications, but now of computable properties, values, functions and behaviours. Prescriptions express requirements to a computing system, i.e., a machine, that is to support activities (phenomena: entities, functions, events and behaviours) of a domain. Thus prescription languages usually emphasise computability, but not necessarily efficiency of computations or of representation of entities (i.e., data).

Designs

On the basis of a requirements prescription one can develop the design of a computing system. The computing system design is likewise expressed in a specification language and specifies a machine: the hardware and software that supposedly implement the requirements and support desired activities of the domain. The machine, once implemented, resides in the (previously described) domain and constitutes with that prior domain a new domain. (Usually we think of requirements being implemented in software on given hardware. We shall, accordingly, just use the term software design where computing systems is the more general term.)

1.2 Reasoning

In describing domains, in prescribing requirements and in designing software we may need to argue that the specification possess certain not immediately obvious (i.e., not explicitly expressed) properties. And in relating requirements prescriptions to the "background" domain, and in relating software designs to the "background" requirements and domain, one may need to argue that the requirements prescription stands in a certain relation to a domain description or that the software design is correct with respect to "its" requirements under the assumptions expressed by a domain description.

For this we need resort to the proof system of the specification language — as well as to other means. We consider in this prelude three such means.

Verification

Verification, in general terms, is a wide and inclusive term covering all approaches which have the aim of establishing that a system meets certain properties. Even a simple *test case* demonstrates a, perhaps limited, fact: that in *this* case (though maybe no others) a given system achieves (or does not) a desirable outcome.

More specifically and usually, we use the term *verification* for more elaborate and systematic mathematical techniques for establishing that systems possess certain properties. Here, the *system* might be a more-or-less abstract description (a specification) or a concrete realisation in hardware or software. The *properties* may be specific emergent properties of abstract specifications; they include general statements of, say, *liveness, safety* and/or *termination*; and they cover the *correctness* of realisations or implementations of given system specifications. In all the cases of interest to us, the system description and the properties to be determined will be couched in a precise formal mathematical language. As a consequence, the results of such a verification will be correspondingly precise and formal.

There are three forms of formal verification that are relevant to the material covered in this book and that are, therefore, worth describing in just a little more detail.

Inferential Verification

This approach is often simply referred to as *verification* despite the fact that other approaches, such as model checking, are also such methods. Here, we have at our disposal logical principles, a logic or proof system, which correctly captures the framework within which the system is described. This framework might be a programming or specification language with a semantics which lays down, normatively, its meaning. The logical principles will (at the very least) be *sound* with respect to that semantics; thus ensuring that any conclusions drawn will be correct judgements of the language in question.

The logical principles, or fully-fledged logic, will provide means that are appropriate for reasoning about the techniques and mechanisms that are available in the language of description. For example, many frameworks provide a means for describing recursive systems, and appropriate induction principles are then available for reasoning about such systems.

Inference-based methods of verification allow us to make and support general claims about a system. These may demonstrate that an implementation is *always* guaranteed to meet its specification; that it *always* possesses certain characteristic properties (for example, that it is *deadlock-free* or maybe that it *terminates*); or that an abstract specification will always possess certain implicit properties (which will, in turn, be inherited properties of *any* (correct) implementation).

Model Checking

This approach to verification (see, for example, [6]) aims to automatically establish (or provide a counterexample for) a property by direct inspection of a model of the system in question. The model may be represented (explicitly or implicitly) by a directed graph whose nodes are states and whose edges are legitimate state transitions; properties may be expressed in some form of temporal logic.

Two key issues are *finiteness* and the potential *combinatorial explosion* of the state space. Many techniques have been developed to minimise the search. In many cases it is not necessary to build the state graph but simply to represent it symbolically, for example by propositional formulae, and then, using techniques such as SAT-solvers, to mimic the graph search. Partial order reductions, which remove redundancies (in explicit graphs) arising from independent interleavings of concurrent events can also be employed to significantly reduce the size of the search space. It is also possible to simplify the system, through abstraction, and to investigate the simpler model as a surrogate for the original system. This, of course, requires that the original and abstracted systems are related (by refinement) and that the abstracted system is at least *sound* (if not *complete*) with respect to the original: that properties true of the abstracted system are also true of the original, even if the abstracted system does not capture *all* properties of the original.

Model checking has been a spectacularly successful technology by any measure; the model checker SPIN [23], for example, detected several crucial errors in the controller for a spacecraft [21]. Other important model checkers are SMV [31] and FDR, based on the standard *failures-divergencies* model of CSP [42].

Formal Testing

Dijkstra, in his ACM Turing Lecture in 1972, famously said: "*... program testing can be a very effective way to show the presence of bugs, but is hopelessly inadequate for showing their absence*" [9]. A correct contrast between informal testing (which might demonstrate a flaw in a system) and a formal verification (which might make a general correctness claim) was established by this remark. More recently, however, it has become clear that there is something to be gained by combining variations on the general theme of testing with formal specifications and verifications. Indeed, the failure of a *formal* test is a *counterexample*, which is as standard a mathematical result as could be wished for (and potentially as valuable too); the problem is that when testing without a theoretical basis (informal testing), it is often simply unclear what conclusion can and should be drawn from such a methodology.

A portfolio approach, in which a variety of verification methods are used, brings benefits. In the case of *formal* testing, there is an interplay between test (creation, application and analysis) and system specification: a formal description of a system is an excellent basis for the generation (possibly automatically) of test cases which, themselves, have precise properties regarding coverage, correctness and so on. In addition, the creation of adequate test suites is expensive and time-consuming, not to say repetitious if requirements and specifications evolve; exploiting the precision implicit in formal specification to aid the creation of test suites is a major benefit of formal testing technologies.

1.3 Integration of Specification Languages

Domains, requirements or software being described, prescribed or designed, respectively, usually possess properties that cannot be suitably specified in one language only. Typically a variety, a composition, a "mix" of specification notations need be deployed. In addition to, for example, either of ASM, B, CafeOBJ, CASL, RAISE/RSL, VDM or Z, the specifier may resort to additionally using one or more (sometimes diagrammatic) notations such as Petri nets [27, 35, 37–39], message sequence charts [24–26], live sequence charts [7, 19, 28], statecharts [15–18, 20], and/or some textual notations such as temporal logics (Duration Calculus, TLA+, or LTL — for linear temporal logic [10, 29, 30, 34, 36]).

Using two or more notations, that is, two or more semantics, requires their integration: that an identifier a in one specification (expressed in one language) and "the same" identifier (a) in another specification (in another language) can be semantically related (i.e., that there is a 'satisfaction relation').

This issue of integrating formal tools and techniques is currently receiving high attention as witnessed by many papers and a series of conferences: [1, 3, 4, 13, 41]. The present book will basically not cover integration.[1]

2 Structure of Book

The book is structured as follows: In the main part, Part II, we introduce, in alphabetic order, nine chapters on ASM, event-B, CafeOBJ, CASL, DC, RAISE, TLA+, VDM and Z. Each chapter is freestanding: It has its own list of references and its own pair of symbol and concept indexes. Part III introduces just one chapter, Review, in which eight "originators" of respective specification languages will comment briefly on the chapter on "that language".

---

[1] TLA+ can be said to be an integration of a temporal logic of actions, TLA, with set-theoretical specification. The RAISE specification language has been "integrated" with both Duration Calculus and concrete timing.

3 Acknowledgements

Many different kinds of institutions and people must be gratefully acknowledged.

CoLogNET: Dines Bjørner thanks the 5th EU/IST Framework Programme (http://www.cordis.lu/fp5/home.html) of the European Commission, Contract Reference IST-2001-33123: CoLogNET: Network of Excellence in Computational Logic: http://www.eurice.de/colognet for support.

CAI: Dines Bjørner thanks the editorial board of the Slovak Academy Journal for giving us the opportunity to publish the papers mentioned on Pages 4–5.

Stara Lesna: We both thank Dr. Martin Pěnička of the Czech Technical University in Prague and Prof. Branislav Rovan and Dr. Dusan Guller of Comenius University in Bratislava, Slovakia for their support in organising the Summer School mentioned on Pages 5–6.

Book Preparation: We both thank all the contributing authors for their willingness to provide their contributions and their endurance also during the latter parts of the editing phase.

Springer: We both thank the editorial board of the EATCS Monographs in Theoretical Computer Science Series and the Springer editor, Ronan Nugent, for their support in furthering the aims of this book.

Our Universities: Last, but not least, we gratefully acknowledge our universities for providing the basis for this work: the University of Essex, UK and the Technical University of Denmark (DTU).

Martin Henson
University of Essex
Colchester, UK
April 4, 2007

Dines Bjørner
Technical University of Denmark
Kgs. Lyngby, Denmark
April 4, 2007

References

1. K. Araki, A. Galloway, K. Taguchi, editors. *IFM 1999: Integrated Formal Methods*, volume 1945 of *Lecture Notes in Computer Science*, York, UK, June 1999. Springer. Proceedings of 1st Intl. Conf. on IFM.

2. Edited by D. Bjørner, M.C. Henson: *Logics of Specification Languages* (Springer, 2007)

3. E.A. Boiten, J. Derrick, G. Smith, editors. *IFM 2004: Integrated Formal Methods*, volume 2999 of *Lecture Notes in Computer Science*, London, UK, April 4–7 2004. Springer. Proceedings of 4th Intl. Conf. on IFM.
4. M.J. Butler, L. Petre, K. Sere, editors. *IFM 2002: Integrated Formal Methods*, volume 2335 of *Lecture Notes in Computer Science*, Turku, Finland, May 15–18 2002. Springer. Proceedings of 3rd Intl. Conf. on IFM.
5. D. Cansell, D. Méry. *The event-B Modelling Method: Concepts and Case Studies*, pages 33–138. Springer, 2007. See [2].
6. E.M. Clarke, O. Grumberg, D.A. Peled: *Model Checking* (MIT Press, 2000)
7. W. Damm, D. Harel: *LSCs: Breathing Life into Message Sequence Charts*. Formal Methods in System Design **19** (2001) pages 45–80
8. R. Diaconescu. *A Methodological Guide to CafeOBJ Logic*, pages 139–218. Springer, 2007. See [2].
9. E.W. Dijkstra: *The Humble Programmer*. Communications of the ACM **15**, 10 (1972) pages 859–866
10. B. Dutertre: Complete Proof System for First-Order Interval Temporal Logic. In: *Proceedings of the 10th Annual IEEE Symposium on Logic in Computer Science* (IEEE CS, 1995) pages 36–43
11. J.S. Fitzgerald. *The Typed Logic of Partial Functions and the Vienna Development Method*, pages 427–461. Springer, 2007. See [2].
12. C. George, A.E. Haxthausen. *The Logic of the RAISE Specification Language*, pages 325–375. Springer, 2007. See [2].
13. W. Grieskamp, T. Santen, B. Stoddart, editors. *IFM 2000: Integrated Formal Methods*, volume of *Lecture Notes in Computer Science*, Schloss Dagstuhl, Germany, November 1–3 2000. Springer. Proceedings of 2nd Intl. Conf. on IFM.
14. M.R. Hansen. *Duration Calculus*, pages 277–324. Springer, 2007. See [2].
15. D. Harel: *Statecharts: A Visual Formalism for Complex Systems*. Science of Computer Programming **8**, 3 (1987) pages 231–274
16. D. Harel: *On Visual Formalisms*. Communications of the ACM **33**, 5 (1988)
17. D. Harel, E. Gery: *Executable Object Modeling with Statecharts*. IEEE Computer **30**, 7 (1997) pages 31–42
18. D. Harel, H. Lachover, A. Naamad et al.: *STATEMATE: A Working Environment for the Development of Complex Reactive Systems*. Software Engineering **16**, 4 (1990) pages 403–414
19. D. Harel, R. Marelly: *Come, Let's Play – Scenario-Based Programming Using LSCs and the Play-Engine* (Springer, 2003)
20. D. Harel, A. Naamad: *The STATEMATE Semantics of Statecharts*. ACM Transactions on Software Engineering and Methodology (TOSEM) **5**, 4 (1996) pages 293–333
21. K. Havelund, M.R. Lowry, J. Penix: *Formal Analysis of a Space Craft Controller Using SPIN*. Software Engineering **27**, 8 (2001) pages 1000–9999
22. M.C. Henson, M. Deutsch, S. Reeves. *Z Logic and Its Applications*, pages 463–565. Springer, 2007. See [2].
23. G.J. Holzmann: *The SPIN Model Checker: Primer and Reference Manual* (Addison-Wesley Professional, 2003)
24. ITU-T. CCITT Recommendation Z.120: Message Sequence Chart (MSC), 1992.
25. ITU-T. ITU-T Recommendation Z.120: Message Sequence Chart (MSC), 1996.
26. ITU-T. ITU-T Recommendation Z.120: Message Sequence Chart (MSC), 1999.

27. K. Jensen: *Coloured Petri Nets*, vol 1: Basic Concepts (234 pages + xii), Vol. 2: Analysis Methods (174 pages + x), Vol. 3: Practical Use (265 pages + xi) of *EATCS Monographs in Theoretical Computer Science* (Springer–Verlag, Heidelberg 1985, revised and corrected second version: 1997)

28. J. Klose, H. Wittke: An Automata Based Interpretation of Live Sequence Charts. In: *TACAS 2001*, ed by T. Margaria, W. Yi (Springer-Verlag, 2001) pages 512–527

29. Z. Manna, A. Pnueli: *The Temporal Logic of Reactive Systems: Specifications* (Addison-Wesley, 1991)

30. Z. Manna, A. Pnueli: *The Temporal Logic of Reactive Systems: Safety* (Addison-Wesley, 1995)

31. K. McMillan: *Symbolic Model Checking* (Kluwer, Amsterdam 1993)

32. S. Merz. *The Specification Language TLA*$^+$, pages 377–426. Springer, 2007. See [2].

33. T. Mossakowski, A.E. Haxthausen, D. Sannella, A. Tarlecki. *CASL – The Common Algebraic Specification Language*, pages 219–276. Springer, 2007. See [2].

34. B.C. Moszkowski: *Executing Temporal Logic Programs* (Cambridge University Press, UK 1986)

35. C.A. Petri: *Kommunikation mit Automaten* (Bonn: Institut für Instrumentelle Mathematik, Schriften des IIM Nr. 2, 1962)

36. A. Pnueli: The Temporal Logic of Programs. In: *Proceedings of the 18th IEEE Symposium on Foundations of Computer Science* (IEEE CS, 1977) pp 46–57

37. W. Reisig: *Petri Nets: An Introduction*, vol 4 of *EATCS Monographs in Theoretical Computer Science* (Springer, 1985)

38. W. Reisig: *A Primer in Petri Net Design* (Springer, 1992)

39. W. Reisig: *Elements of Distributed Algorithms: Modelling and Analysis with Petri Nets* (Springer, 1998)

40. W. Reisig. *Abstract State Machines for the Classroom*, pages 1–32. Springer, 2007. See [2].

41. J.M. Romijn, G.P. Smith, J.C. van de Pol, editors. *IFM 2005: Integrated Formal Methods*, volume 3771 of *Lecture Notes in Computer Science*, Eindhoven, The Netherlands, December 2005. Springer. Proceedings of 5th Intl. Conf. on IFM.

42. A.W. Roscoe: *The Theory and Practice of Concurrency* (Prentice Hall, 1999)

Contents

The event-B Modelling Method: Concepts and Case Studies
Dominique Cansell and Dominique Méry 47

A Methodological Guide to the CafeOBJ Logic
Răzvan Diaconescu 153

CASL – the Common Algebraic Specification Language
T. Mossakowski, A. Haxthausen, D. Sannella and A. Tarlecki 241

Part III   Postludium

Reviews

List of Contributors

Jean-Raymond Abrial
Department of Computer Science
Swiss Fed. Univ. of Technology
Haldeneggsteig 4/Weinbergstrasse
CH-8092 Zürich
Switzerland
jabrial@inf.ethz.ch

Dines Bjørner
Informatics
and Mathematical Modelling
Technical University of Denmark
DK-2800 Kgs. Lyngby
Denmark
bjorner@gmail.com

Dominique Cansell
LORIA
Campus scientifique, BP 239
F-54506 Vandœuvre-lès-Nancy
France
cansell@loria.fr

Moshe Deutsch
Hagefen 45
Moshav Liman
22820 Israel
Moshe.Deutsch@Alvarion.com

Răzvan Diaconescu
Inst. of Math. "Simion Stoilow"
PO Box 1-764
Bucharest 014700
Romania
Razvan.Diaconescu@imar.ro

John Fitzgerald
Centre for Software Reliability
School of Computing Science
Newcastle University
Newcastle upon Tyne, NE1 7RU, UK
John.Fitzgerald@ncl.ac.uk

Kokichi Futatsugi
Japan Adv. Inst. of Sci. & Techn.
1-1 Asahidai, Nomi,
Ishikawa, 923-1292 Japan
kokichi@jaist.ac.jp

Chris George
United Nations University
Intl. Inst. for Software Technology
Casa Silva Mendes
Est. do Engenheiro Trigo No. 4
P.O. Box 3058
Macau, China
cwg@iist.unu.edu

Yuri Gurevich
Microsoft Research
One Microsoft Way
Redmond, WA 98052, USA
gurevich@microsoft.com

Michael R. Hansen
Informatics
and Mathematical Modelling
Technical University of Denmark
DK-2800 Kgs. Lyngby
Denmark
mrh@imm.dtu.dk

Klaus Havelund
Lab. for Reliable Software
Jet Propulsion Laboratory (JPL)
4800 Oak Grove Drive
M/S 301-285
Pasadena, CA 91109
USA
havelund@gmail.com

Anne E. Haxthausen
Informatics
and Mathematical Modelling,
Technical University of Denmark
DK-2800 Kgs. Lyngby
Denmark
ah@imm.dtu.dk

Martin C. Henson
Department of Computer Science
University of Essex
Wivenhoe Park
Colchester
Essex CO4 3SQ
UK
hensm@essex.ac.uk

Cliff Jones
School of Computing Science
Newcastle University
Newcastle upon Tyne, NE1 7RU
UK
cliff.jones@ncl.ac.uk

Leslie Lamport
Microsoft Corporation
1065 La Avenida
Mountain View, CA 94043
USA
lamport@microsoft.com

Dominique Méry
LORIA
Campus scientifique, BP 239
F-54506 Vandœuvre-lès-Nancy
France
Dominique.Mery@loria.fr

Stephan Merz
INRIA Lorraine
Equipe MOSEL
Bâtiment B
615, rue du Jardin Botanique
F-54602 Villers-lès-Nancy
France
Stephan.Merz@loria.fr

Till Mossakovski
DFKI Lab Bremen
Robert-Hooke-Str. 5
DE-28359 Bremen
Germany
till@informatik.uni-bremen.de

Peter D. Mosses
Dept of Computer Science
Swansea University
Singleton Park
Swansea SA2 8PP
UK
P.D.Mosses@swansea.ac.uk

Steve Reeves
Computer Science Department
Computing
& Mathematical Sciences
University of Waikato
Private Bag 3105
Hamilton
New Zealand
stever@cs.waikato.ac.nz

Wolfgang Reisig
Institut für Informatik
Math.-Nat. Fakultät II
Humboldt-Universität zu Berlin
Unter den Linden 6, DE 10099 Berlin
Germany
reisig@informatik.hu-berlin.de

Donald Sannella
LFCS, School of Informatics
University of Edinburgh
King's Buildings
Mayfield Road
Edinburgh EH9 3JZ
UK
dts@inf.ed.ac.uk

Andrzej Tarlecki
Institute of Informatics
Warsaw University
ul. Banacha 2
PL 02-097 Warsaw
Poland
tarlecki@mimuw.edu.pl

Zhou Chaochen
Institute of Software
Chinese Academy of Sciences
P.O. Box 8718
100080 Beijing
China
zcc@ios.ac.cn

Part I

Preludium

An Overview

Dines Bjørner and Martin C. Henson

[1] Department of Informatics and Mathematical Modelling, Technical University of Denmark, DK-2800 Kgs. Lyngby, Denmark (`bjorner@gmail.com`)
[2] Department of Computer Science, University of Essex, Wivenhoe Park, Colchester, Essex CO4 3SQ, UK (`hensm@essex.ac.uk`)

Before going into the topic of formal specification languages let us first survey the chain of events that led to this book as well as the notions of the specific specification languages and their logics.

1 The Book History

Four phases characterise the work that lead to this book.

1.1 CoLogNET

CoLogNET was a European (EU) Network of Excellence. It was funded by FET, the Future and Emerging Technologies arm of the EU IST Programme, FET-Open scheme. The network was dedicated to furthering computational logic as an academic discipline.

We refer to `http://newsletter.colognet.org/`.

One of the editors (DB) was involved in the CoLogNET effort. One of his obligations was to propagate awareness of the logics of formal specification languages.

1.2 CAI: Computing and Informatics

One of the editors of this book (DB) was also, for many years, an editor of CAI, the Slovak Academy journal on Computing and Informatics (http://www.cai.sk/). The chief editors kindly asked DB to edit a special issue. It was therefore quite reasonable to select the topic of the logics of formal (methods') specification languages and to invite a number of people to author papers for the CAI.

The result was a double issue of CAI:

CAI, Volume 22, 2003, No. 3

⋆ **The Expressive Power of Abstract State Machines**
W. Reisig [7]

Abstract: Conventional computation models assume symbolic representations of states and actions. Gurevich's "Abstract State Machine" model takes a more liberal position: Any mathematical structure may serve as a state. This results in "a computational model that is more powerful and more universal than standard computation models".
We characterize the Abstract State Machine model as a special class of transition systems that widely extends the class of "computable" transition systems. This characterization is based on a fundamental Theorem of Y. Gurevich.

⋆ **Foundations of the B Method**
D. Cansell, D. Méry [1]

Abstract: B is a method for specifying, designing and coding software systems. It is based on Zermelo–Fraenkel set theory with the axiom of choice, the concept of generalized substitution and on structuring mechanisms (machine, refinement, implementation). The concept of refinement is the key notion for developing B models of (software) systems in an incremental way. B models are accompanied by mathematical proofs that justify them. Proofs of B models convince the user (designer or specifier) that the (software) system is effectively correct. We provide a survey of the underlying logic of the B method and the semantic concepts related to the B method; we detail the B development process partially supported by the mechanical engine of the prover.

⋆ **CafeOBJ: Logical Foundations and Methodologies**
R. Diaconescu, K. Futatsugi, K. Ogata [2]

Abstract: CafeOBJ is an executable industrial-strength multi logic algebraic specification language which is a modern successor of OBJ and incorporates several new algebraic specification paradigms. In this paper we survey its logical foundations and present some of its methodologies.

⋆ **CASL — The Common Algebraic Specification Language:**
      Semantics and Proof Theory
T. Mossakowski, A.E. Haxthausen, D. Sannella, A. Tarlecki [6]

Abstract: CASL is an expressive specification language that has been designed to supersede many existing algebraic specification languages and provide a standard. CASL consists of several layers, including basic (unstructured) specifications, structured specifications and architectural specifications (the latter are used to prescribe the structure of implementations). We describe a simplified version of the CASL syntax, semantics and proof calculus at each of these three layers and state the corresponding soundness and completeness theorems. The layers are orthogonal in the sense that the semantics of a given layer uses that of the previous layer as a "black box", and similarly for the proof calculi. In particular, this means that CASL can easily be adapted to other logical systems.

CAI, Volume 22, 2003, No. 4

⋆ **The Logic of the RAISE Specification Language**
C. George, A.E. Haxthausen [3]
Abstract: This paper describes the logic of the RAISE Specification Language, RSL. It explains the particular logic chosen for RAISE, and motivates this choice as suitable for a wide spectrum language to be used for designs as well as initial specifications, and supporting imperative and concurrent specifications as well as applicative sequential ones. It also describes the logical definition of RSL, its axiomatic semantics, as well as the proof system for carrying out proofs.

⋆ **On the Logic of TLA+**
S. Merz [5]
Abstract: TLA+ is a language intended for the high-level specification of reactive, distributed, and in particular asynchronous systems. Combining the linear-time temporal logic TLA and classical set-theory, it provides an expressive specification formalism and supports assertional verification.

⋆ **Z Logic and Its Consequences**
M.C. Henson, S. Reeves, J.P. Bowen [4]
Abstract: This paper provides an introduction to the specification language Z from a logical perspective. The possibility of presenting Z in this way is a consequence of a number of joint publications on Z logic that Henson and Reeves have co-written since 1997. We provide an informal as well as formal introduction to Z logic and show how it may be used, and extended, to investigate issues such as equational logic, the logic of preconditions, the issue of monotonicity and both operation and data refinement.

1.3 The Stara Lesna Summer School

The preparation of the many papers for the CAI lead to the desire to "crown" the achievements of the many authors by arranging the Logics of Specification Language Summer School at the Slovak Academy's conference centre in Stara Lesna, the High Tatras.

We refer to http://cswww.essex.ac.uk/staff/hensm/sssl/.

One of the editors of the present volume (MH) coordinated with the seven sets of authors of the CAI double issue as well as with Drs. John Fitzgerald (VDM: The Vienna Development Method) and Michael Reichhardt Hansen (DC: Duration Calculi) on the schedule of nine sets of lectures of 90 minutes each during the two-week event.

The other editor (DB) was the primary organiser of the event: soliciting funds, participants, and communicating with the local organiser Prof. Branislav Rovan at the Comenius University in Bratislava.

The event took place June 6–19, 2004 at the Slovak Academy's ideally located conference centre in Stara Lesna, the High Tatras.

Besides being substantially sponsored by the EU's CoLogNET effort, much-needed support also came from UNU-IIST, the United Nations University's International Institute for Software Technology (http://www.iist.unu.edu) (located in Macau, China) and Microsoft Research (http://research.microsoft.com/foundations/).

Forty-four young researchers from 22 countries in Asia and Europe took part in this seminal event.

1.4 Book Preparation

The success, so we immodestly claim, of the Summer School then lead to the proposal to rework the CAI papers and the Summer School lecture notes into a book. MH coordinated the first phase of this endeavour, summer 2004 to February 2006. DB then followed up and is responsible for the minute style editing, indexing, etc., and the compilation of the nine individual contributions into this volume.

2 Formal Specification Languages

Here we cull from the introductions to the chapters covering respective languages — and edit these "clips".

2.1 ASM: Abstract State Machines

ASM is a technique for describing algorithms or, more generally, discrete systems. An abstract state machine [specification] is a set of conditional assignment statements. The central and new idea of ASM is the way in which symbols occurring in the syntactic representation of a program are related to the real-world items of a state. A state of an ASM may include *any* real-world objects and functions. In particular, the ASM approach does not assume a symbolic, bit-level representation of all components of a state. ASM is "a computation model that is more powerful and more universal than standard computation models", as Yuri Gurevich, the originator of ASM, claims.

2.2 B

Classical B is a state-based method for specifying, designing and coding software systems. It is based on Zermelo–Fraenkel set theory with the axiom of choice. Sets are used for data modelling. Generalised substitutions are used to describe state modifications. The refinement calculus is used to relate models at varying levels of abstraction. There are a number of structuring mechanisms (machine, refinement, implementation) which are used in the organisation of a development.

Central to the classical B approach is the idea of a software operation which will perform according to a given specification if called within a given precondition. A more general approach in which the notion of *event* is fundamental is also covered. An event has a firing condition (a guard) as opposed to a precondition. It may fire when its guard is true.

2.3 CafeOBJ

CafeOBJ is an executable algebraic specification language. CafeOBJ incorporates several algebraic specification paradigms.

Equational specification and programming is inherited from OBJ and constitutes the basis of CafeOBJ, the other features being somehow built "on top" of it.

Behavioural specification characterises how objects (and systems) behave, not how they are implemented. This form of abstraction is used in the specification and verification of software systems since it embeds other useful paradigms such as concurrency, object-orientation, constraints, nondeterminism, etc.

Preorder algebra (abbreviated POA) specification (in CafeOBJ) is based on a simplified unlabelled version of Meseguer's rewriting logic specification framework for concurrent systems. POA gives a non-trivial extension of traditional algebraic specification towards concurrency. POA incorporates many different models of concurrency, thus giving CafeOBJ a wide range of applications.

2.4 CASL

The basic assumption underlying algebraic specification is that programs are modelled as algebraic structures that include a collection of sets of data values together with functions over those sets. This level of abstraction is commensurate with the view that the correctness of the input/output behaviour of a program takes precedence over all its other properties. Another common element is that specifications of programs consist mainly of logical axioms, usually in a logical system in which equality has a prominent role, describing the properties that the functions are required to satisfy.

Basic specifications provide the means for writing specifications in a particular institution, and provide a proof calculus for reasoning within such unstructured specifications.

The institution underlying CASL, together with its proof calculus, involves many-sorted basic specifications and subsorting.

Structured specifications express how more complex specifications are built from simpler ones.

The semantics and proof calculus is given in a way that is parameterized over the particular institution and proof calculus for basic specifications.

Architectural specifications, in contrast to structured specifications, prescribe the modular structure of the implementation, with the possibility of enforcing a separate development of composable, reusable implementation units.

Finally, libraries of specifications allow the (distributed) storage and retrieval of named specifications. Since this is rather straightforward, space considerations led to the omission of this layer of CASL in the present work.

2.5 DC: The Duration Calculi

Duration Calculus (abbreviated DC) is an interval logic. DC was introduced to express and reason about models of real-time systems. A key issue in DC is to be able to express the restriction of durations of certain undesired but unavoidable states.

By a duration calculus we shall understand a temporal logic whose concept of time is captured by **Real**, whose formula connectives include those of $\Box$ ($\Box P$: always P), $\Diamond$ ($\Diamond P$: sometimes P), $\rightarrow$ ($P \rightarrow Q$: P implies Q [Q follows logically from P]), and the chop operator, ';' ($P; Q$: first P then Q); whose state duration terms, P, include those of $\int P$ (duration of P), $o(t_1, ..., t_n)$, and ℓ; and whose formulas further include those of $\lceil\rceil$ (point duration) $\lceil P \rceil$ (almost everywhere P).

2.6 RAISE and RSL

The RAISE method is based on stepwise refinement using the invent and verify paradigm. Specifications are written in RSL. RSL is a formal, wide-spectrum specification language that encompasses and integrates different specification styles in a common conceptual framework. Hence, RSL enables the formulation of modular specifications which are algebraic or model-oriented, applicative or imperative, and sequential or concurrent.

A basic RSL specification is called a class expression and consists of declarations of types, values, variables, channels, and axioms. Specifications may also be built from other specifications by renaming declared entities, hiding declared entities, or adding more declarations. Moreover, specifications may be parameterized.

User-declared types may be introduced as abstract sort types, as known from algebraic specification. In addition RSL provides predicative subtypes, union and short record types, as known from VDM, and variant type definitions similar to data type definitions in ML.

Functions may describe processes communicating synchronously with each other via declared channels, as in CSP.

2.7 TLA and TLA+

TLA is a variant of linear-time temporal logic; it is used to specify system behaviour. TLA+ extends TLA with data structures that are specified in (a variant of) Zermelo-Fraenkel set theory. TLA+ does not formally distinguish between specifications and properties: both are written as logical formulas, and concepts such as refinement, composition of systems, or hiding of internal state are expressed using logical connectives of implication, conjunction, and quantification.

2.8 VDM

VDM can probably be credited as being the first formal specification language (1974).

Classical VDM focuses on defining types over discrete values such as numbers, Booleans, and characters — as well as over sets, Cartesians, lists, maps (enumerable, finite domain functions), and functions (in general); and defining applicative ("functional style specification programing") and imperative ("assignment and state-based specification programing") functions over values of defined types, including pre-/post-based function specifications. Set, list and map values can be comprehended, as in ordinary discrete mathematics. Logical expressions include first-order predicate (quantified) expressions.

2.9 Z

Z could be said to be rather close in some aspects to VDM-SL. A main — syntactically — distinguishing feature is, however, the schema. Schemes are usually used in two ways: for describing the state space of a system and for describing operations which the system may perform. From that follows a schema calculus. Another difference from VDM is the logics.

3 The Logics

The nine main chapters of this book comprise a dazzling, and even possibly intimidating, range of approaches; and it will be clear that the work on which this collection is based owes a debt to many researchers, over many years, who have struggled to find appropriate concepts, together with their formalisation, suitable for the task of tackling issues in the general area of system specification.

There are two perspectives which are useful to bear in mind when reading this book in its entirety, or more likely in selecting chapters to study in depth. The first is that these are studies in *applied mathematics*; the second that these are *practical methods in computer science*.

Applied mathematics is a term with a long pedigree and it has usually been identified with applications in, for example, physics, economics and so forth. A naive separation would place topics such as algebra and formal logic in the realm of *pure mathematics*; however it is not the *content* but the *motivation* that differentiates applied from pure mathematics, and the chapters of this book illustrate many areas in which more traditionally pure topics are set to work in an applied setting. ASM, CafeOBJ and CASL are based within algebra, the latter two securely located within category theory, an almost quintessential example of purely abstract mathematics; DC and TLA+ make use of modal logic; B, VDM and Z make use of set theory and (versions of) predicate logic; RAISE draws on ideas from set theory, logic, algebra and beyond. In all these too, the underlying formal structures are drawn from traditional pure mathematics, much of it from developments during the early part of the last century in the introspective realm of metamathematics: initially introduced in order for mathematics to take a closer look at itself.

It may have come as something of a surprise to early pioneers in algebra, set theory and logic to see how such abstract topics could be usefully harnessed to an applications area; but work over the last 30 years or so has demonstrated beyond question that these have become an appropriate basis for formal computer science. These chapters are a testament to, and further stage in, that developing history.

Excellent applied mathematics, however, does not come for free: one cannot simply select existing mathematics *off the shelf* and expect it to be fit for purpose. It is necessary to combine mathematical competence with a high level of conceptual analysis and innovation. In this book there are numerous examples of mathematical developments which have been necessary in order to model what have been identified as the fundamental concepts in the applications' areas, and one might select single examples from hosts of others in the various chapters. For example:

- in ASM one notes the analysis of *states as algebras* and then program statements as transformations of algebras;
- in B one notes the central concept of *generalized substitution* and its interpretation within a calculus of *weakest preconditions*;
- in CafeOBJ ones notes the introduction of *behavioural specification* based on *coherent hidden algebra*;
- in CASL one notes the use of the *institution* of *many-and-sub-sorted algebras*;
- in DC one notes the development of *continuous-time interval temporal logic* and the introduction of the concept of *durations*;

- in RAISE one notes the development of *the logic RSL* with its treatment of undefined terms, imperative and concurrent features;
- in TLA+ one notes the integration of set-theoretic notions with a version of temporal logic which includes *action formulae* and *invariance under stuttering*;
- in VDM one notes the development of the *logic of partial functions* allowing reasoning in the presence of *undefined terms*;
- in Z one notes the analysis of *refinement* and how it is analysed with respect to the *schema calculus*.

These very few observations barely scratch the surface of the wealth of conceptual novelty present within these nine frameworks, but serve to illustrate the way in which they each introduce new conceptual zoology suitable for tackling the issues they aim to address. In doing so, they must, and do, extend the mathematical framework on which they are based, whether that be set theory, some variety of formal logic or a framework of algebraic discourse. And the corollaries of that, of course, are developments of new mathematics.

Turning now to the second key point. However sophisticated the formal treatment, these are intended to be practical methods for the specification and development of systems. The chapters each address examples and applications in various ways and to differing extent. There are, here, a wealth of case studies and examples, both of practical applications and of theoretical infrastructure, all of which shed light on the applicability and fecundity of the frameworks covered. It may be worth remembering that once a perfect tool is developed, it will certainly stand the test of time. For example, consider a *chisel*: it is an ancient and very simple tool; moreover, despite centuries of technological development elsewhere, it is still in use today, essentially unchanged, because of that simplicity and its fitness for purpose. It has, quite simply, never been bettered. It is also a sobering experience to compare the simplicity of the chisel with the complexity and beauty of the wood-carvings which are possible when the tool lies in skilled and experienced hands. This is a good analogy: we will want to show that our specification frameworks are as simple and straightforward as possible, and develop skills in using them which result in applications that are significantly more complex (at least combinatorially) than the frameworks themselves. Have we yet, as a community, achieved that? Almost certainly not – but the challenge is there, and current work is mindful of these considerations. System specification is a truly monumental topic; it is very unlikely we can ever achieve the simplicity of the chisel for our frameworks, but we aim for the contrast: that we can employ them to rigorously, securely and dependably design the large and complex systems which are increasingly required of us. And surely, in that complexity, is there also a certain beauty.

How this area of formal specification will further develop in the future is a very interesting question. One imagines *and hopes* that the readers of this very volume will be among those making significant contributions towards answering that. Even if those future frameworks little resemble the ones presented here, we can be sure of one thing: their development will require the good taste, conceptual innovation and mathematical sophistication that we see exemplified in this volume.

References

1. Dominique Cansell and Dominique Méry. Logical Foundations of the B Method. *Computing and Informatics*, 22(1–2), 2003. This paper is one of a series: [2–7] appearing in a double issue of the same journal: *Logics of Specification Languages* — edited by Dines Bjørner.
2. Ražvan Diaconescu, Kokichi Futatsugi, and Kazuhiro Ogata. CafeOBJ: Logical Foundations and Methodology. *Computing and Informatics*, 22(1–2), 2003. This paper is one of a series: [1, 3–7] appearing in a double issue of the same journal: *Logics of Specification Languages* — edited by Dines Bjørner.
3. Chris W. George and Anne E. Haxthausen. The Logic of the RAISE Specification Language. *Computing and Informatics*, 22(1–2), 2003. This paper is one of a series: [1, 2, 4–7] appearing in a double issue of the same journal: *Logics of Specification Languages* — edited by Dines Bjørner.
4. Martin C. Henson, Steve Reeves, and Jonathan P. Bowen. Z Logic and Its Consequences. *Computing and Informatics*, 22(1–2), 2003. This paper is one of a series: [1–3, 5–7] appearing in a double issue of the same journal: *Logics of Specification Languages* — edited by Dines Bjørner.
5. Stephan Merz. On the Logic of TLA+. *Computing and Informatics*, 22(1–2), 2003. This paper is one of a series: [1–4, 6, 7] appearing in a double issue of the same journal: *Logics of Specification Languages* — edited by Dines Bjørner.
6. Till Mossakowski, Anne E. Haxthausen, Don Sanella, and Andrzej Tarlecki. CASL — The Common Algebraic Specification Language: Semantics and Proof Theory. *Computing and Informatics*, 22(1–2), 2003. This paper is one of a series: [1–5, 7] appearing in a double issue of the same journal: *Logics of Specification Languages* — edited by Dines Bjørner.
7. Wolfgang Reisig. The Expressive Power of Abstract State Machines. *Computing and Informatics*, 22(1–2), 2003. This paper is one of a series: [1–6] appearing in a double issue of the same journal: *Logics of Specification Languages* — edited by Dines Bjørner.

Part II

The Languages

Abstract State Machines for the Classroom
– The Basics –

Wolfgang Reisig

Institut für Informatik, Math.-Nat. Fakultät II, Humboldt-Universität zu Berlin,
Unter den Linden 6, DE 10099 Berlin, Germany,
`reisig@informatik.hu-berlin.de`

> ... we should have achieved a mathematical model of computation,
> perhaps highly abstract in contrast with the concrete nature of paper
> and register machines, but such that programming languages are merely
> executable fragments of the theory ...
>
> Robin Milner [16]

Summary. Abstract State Machines (hencefort referred to as just ASM) were introduced as "a computation model that is more powerful and more universal than standard computation models" by Yuri Gurevich in 1985.

Here we provide some intuitive and motivating arguments, and characteristic examples for (the elementary version of) ASM. The intuition of ASM as a formal framework for "pseudocode" algorithms is highlighted. Generalizing variants of the fundamental "sequential small-step" version of ASM are also considered.

Introduction

Many people find ASM difficult to understand. Most of these people are conventionally educated computer scientists, and hence have ba set of implicit or explicit assumptions and expectations about "yet another" specification language or computation model. ASM challenge some of those assumptions and expectations. It is this aspect that makes people struggle when trying to understand ASM. If computer science education start out with ASM (and there are many good reasons to do so), people would see the basic ideas of ASM as the most simple and natural approach to the notion of "algorithm".

This chapter addresses the conventionally educated computer scientist. To meet his or her implicit and explicit assumptions, Part I of this presentation addresses the intuition and foundations of ASM in great detail and various aspects. Part II then focuses technical details of the most elementary class of ASM. Part III considers various variants and extensions.

I: Intuition and Foundations of ASM

Section 1 addresses the fundamental aspects that make ASM a technique quite different from other techniques, to describe algorithms or, more generally, discrete systems. Without going into detail, the central idea is highlighted, and the ASM approach is embedded into the context of first-order logic and computable functions.

Section 2 is devoted to some small examples. As the central idea of ASM is, to some extent, independent of concrete syntactical representations, we represent each example in a pseudocode notation, in a form that is particularly intuitive for the respective algorithm. The translation of pseudocode to a "syntactically correct" ASM is postponed to Sect. 5. This translation can itself be conceived as part of the ASM formalism, because ASM can be considered as a formal basis for pseudocode. As we restrict ourselves in this chapter to a version of ASM that can be described by *transition systems*, we start the section with this fundamental notion.

Section 3 starts with the motivation behind the semantic aspects of states. The algorithms of Sect. 2 are used to exemplify how a pseudocode program is applied to a state. Section 3 finishes with the problem of characterizing the expressive power of pseudocode programs.

1 What Makes ASM so Unique?

1.1 A Basic Question

At first glance, an abstract state machine is just a set of conditional assignment statements. Several extensions of the basic version of the ASM have been suggested, including parallel, distributed and reactive ones. These concepts are likewise not too new. Some versions use quantified variables, essentially "$\forall x \ldots$" and "$\exists x \ldots$". Quantified variables usually do not appear in programming languages, but specification languages such as Z use quantification very well. What, then, makes ASM so unique? In what sense are ASM "a computation model that is more powerful and more universal than standard computation models", as Yuri Gurevich wrote in 1985 [12]?

1.2 The Central Idea of ASM

The central and new idea of ASM is easily described: it is the systematic way in which symbols occurring in the syntactic representation of a program are related to the real-world items of a state. In fact, a state of an ASM may include *any* real-world objects and functions. In particular, the ASM approach does not assume a symbolic, bit-level representation of all components of a state. Herein it differs from standard computational models – and most obviously to Turing Machines – where a state is a (structured) collection of symbols. The designer or user of a Turing Machine or any (more involved) programming or specification language may very well have in mind a particular meaning of a symbol. Examples of such symbols include "1", "∈", "init" and "millisecond". And a model usually makes little sense without this kind of interpretation. But conventional computation concentrates on the *transformation* of symbols, not dwelling too deeply on what they stand for.

1.3 ASM in the Context of Set Theory and Logic

The manner in which ASM relate symbols to their interpretation is not new at all. One may read the ASM approach as a recommendation just to take seriously, what formal logic has revealed in the last century. Since Cantor's definition of a set as "any collection into a whole M of definite and separate objects m of our intuition or our thought" [4], sets have entered mathematics in a clear and simple way. Tarski, in [20] suggested *structures*, including functions and predicates over real world items, as the most general mathematical framework. First-order logic has been developed as a language to define and to analyze such structures. In close correspondence to this line of development, Gurevich suggested a further step, introducing *algorithms* over real world items.

1.4 ASM and Computable Functions

The above considerations rose the question of *implementation*: in fact, many algorithms are definable by ASM, but cannot be implemented. Furthermore, many of them are not even intended to be implemented. Rather, they describe procedures involving real-world items. Examples include the algorithms for using a teller machine to withdraw money from one's bank account, and the procedure of pressing buttons on the walls and inside the lifts in a high-rise building, in order to be transported to another floor.

From this perspective, ASM can be conceived of as the theory of pseudocode. In any case, ASM provide a specification language to describe the steps of dynamic, discrete systems. Those systems include, in particular, implementable systems.

Computability theory characterizes the computable functions as a subset of *all* functions over the integers. Can the ASM-specifiable algorithms likewise be described as a subset of a potentially larger class of candidates? In fact, Gurevich [13] provided such a characterization for the most elementary class of ASM. Intuitively formulated, a discrete system can be represented as a "sequential small-step ASM", if the system exhibits global states and proceeds in steps from state to state, and if, for each step $S \to S'$, the following holds: to derive S' from S, it suffices to explore a bounded amount of information about S. (Details follow in Sect. 6.3.) For other classes of ASM, similar characterizations are under investigation.

1.5 The Future Role of ASM

In the above perspective, the theory of ASM contributes to the foundations of informatics as a scientific discipline. At the end of the day it may turn out that ASM will (together with various, so far unknown equivalent notions) provide an adequate notion of "algorithms" (with the important subclass of the "implementable" algorithms, i.e. the computable functions).

2 What Kind of Algorithms Do ASM Cover?

2.1 Transition Systems

Classical models of discrete systems assume global states and describe dynamic behaviour as steps

$$S \rightarrow S' \tag{1}$$

from a state S to its successor state S'. We restrict ourselves in this chapter to systems with this kind of behaviour. In technical terms, we consider (initialized) *transition systems*.

A transition system

$$A = (states, \textbf{init}, F) \tag{2}$$

consists of a set *states* of "states", $\textbf{init} \subseteq states$ of "initial states", and a "next state function" $F : states \rightarrow states$.

A *run* of a transition system is a sequence

$$S_0 S_1 S_2 \ldots \tag{3}$$

of states S_i with S_0 an initial state and $S_i = F(S_{i-1})$ $(i = 1, 2, \ldots)$.

One might suggest that one should reduce the set *states* to the reachable states, i.e. to those occurring in runs. But this set may be difficult to characterize. As a matter of convenience, it is frequently useful to allow a larger set of states.

The general framework of transition systems requires no specific properties of the states. In particular, it is not required to represent all components of a state symbolically. The forthcoming examples of – admittedly quite simple – algorithms yield transition systems that dwell on this aspect.

This general version of transition systems is not new at all: in the first volume of his seminal opus [14], Don Knuth introduced the notion of *algorithms*. As a framework for the semantics of algorithms, Knuth suggested *computational methods*. A computational method is essentially what we have called a transition system in (2). Knuth additionally assumed *terminal states* t with $F(t) = t$, and called a transition system A an *algorithm* if each run of A reaches a terminal state. The interesting aspect in Knuth's definition is that it comes without the requirement of F being "effective". Quoting [14, p 8]: "F might involve operations that mortal man can not always perform". Knuth defined *effective* computational methods as a special case: a computational method is effective iff it is essentially equivalent to a Turing Machine or to any other mechanism for the computable functions. Nowadays, the term "algorithm" is usually used to denote what Knuth called an "effective computational method".

As we have already done above, we shall use the term "transition system" instead of "computational method", and "effective transition system" instead of "effective computational method".

Transition systems have been generalized in several directions: non-terminating computation sequences adequately describe the behaviour of reactive systems; the next-state function F has been generalized to a relation $R \subseteq Q \times Q$, with computation sequences $x_0 x_1 \dots$ where $(x_i, x_{i+1}) \in R$. This represents non-determinism. Additionally, one may require a choice of x_{i+1} such that it follows a stochastic distribution or is fair. Some system models describe a single behavior not as a sequence of states, but as a sequence of actions. The sequence orders the actions along a time axis. One may even replace the total order by a partial order, representing the cause–effect relations between actions.

All these generalizations of effective transition systems can be reduced to equivalent conventional effective transition systems by reasonable notions of reduction and equivalence. Generalizations of this kind are intended to express algorithmic ideas more conveniently. They are not intended to challenge the established notion of effective computation.

We study non-effective transition systems in this chapter. The reader may wonder whether there is anything interesting "beyond" the computable functions. In fact, there is an exciting proper subclass of all transition systems, called 'Sequential Abstract State Machines', that in turn properly contains the effective transition systems.

Yet, to communicate algorithms, we have to *represent* them somehow. We may allow any kind of pseudocode notation, whichever is most intuitive for the respective algorithm. This kind of representation is related to the pseudocode approach in Sect. 3.

Distributed systems do not, canonically, exhibit global states and steps. Consequently, transition systems do not adequately represent their behaviour. This kind of system will be glanced at in Part III of this chapter, together with some other extensions of the basic formalism.

The rest of this section describes a series of algorithms, none of which is implementable, but each will turn out to be representable in the framework of ASM.

2.2 Set Extension

Let *augment* be a function with two arguments: the first argument is a set
and the second argument is *any* item. The function *augment* then extends the
set by the item. More precisely, for a set M and an item m, define

$$augment(M, m) =_{def} M \cup \{m\}. \tag{4}$$

Now we intend to construct an algorithm that extends any given set M
by *two* elements m and n, using the function *augment*. The idea is obvious:
in a sequence of two steps, we augment one element in each step. We write
this idea down in the usual style of "pseudocode". To this end we introduce
three variables X, x and y, which in the initial state S_0 are evaluated as M,
m and n, respectively. Then, the pseudocode algorithm

$$
\begin{aligned}
P_0: \textbf{begin} & \\
& X := \text{augment}(X,x); \\
& X := \text{augment}(X,y); \\
\textbf{end.} &
\end{aligned}
\tag{5}
$$

applied to S_0 terminates in a state S in which X isevaluated as $M \cup \{m, n\}$.
Notice that this algorithm can be applied to *any* set M and *any* elements m
and n. A bit-level representation of M, m and n is not required.

2.3 The Tangent Algorithm

In the geometrical plane assume a circle C with centre p, and let q be a point
outside C (see Fig. 1).

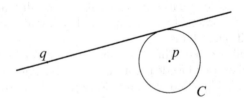

Fig. 1. The problem of the tangent algorithm

We have to design an algorithm to construct one of the tangents of C
through q . Such an algorithm is well-known from high school. First, construct
the point halfway between p and q. Call it r. Then, construct a circle D
with centre r, passing through p (and, by construction, through q). The two
circles C and D intersect in two points. Pick out one of them; call it "s". The
wanted tangent is the line through q and s. Figure 2 outlines this construction.
Figure 3 shows a corresponding pseudocode program.

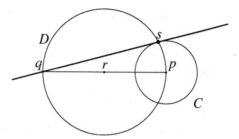

Fig. 2. The solution of the tangent algorithm

This algorithm employs three sets of data items, namely POINTS, CIRCLES and LINES, and five basic operations,

$$\text{halfway: POINTS} \times \text{POINTS} \rightarrow \text{POINTS},$$
$$\text{circle: POINTS} \times \text{POINTS} \rightarrow \text{CIRCLES},$$
$$\text{intersect: CIRCLES} \times \text{CIRCLES} \rightarrow \mathcal{P}(\text{POINTS}), \qquad (6)$$
$$\text{makeline: POINTS} \times \text{POINTS} \rightarrow \text{LINES},$$
$$\text{pick: } \mathcal{P}(\text{POINTS}) \rightarrow \text{POINTS}.$$

The tangent algorithm does not specify how points, circles and lines are represented, and how the operations produce their result. One choice was to represent a point as a pair of real numbers $\binom{x}{y}$, a circle by its center and its radius, and a line by any two points on it. In this case, the above four operations (6) can be defined by well established formulas, e.g.

$$\text{halfway}\left(\binom{x_1}{y_1}, \binom{x_2}{y_2}\right) = \binom{(x_1+x_2)/2}{(y_1+y_2)/2}. \qquad (7)$$

The choice from high school was to represent a point as a black dot on a white sheet of paper, a circle by its obvious curved line and a (straight) line by one of its finite sections. Each of the four above operations (6) can then be performed by pencil, rulers and a pair of compasses.

```
input(p, C, q);
if q outside C then
    r := halfway(p, q);
    D := circle(r, p);
    M := intersect(C, D);
    {|M| = 2}
    s := pick(M);
    I := makeline(q, s);
    output(I);
```

Fig. 3. The tangent algorithm

Observe that the above algorithm likewise applies to three-dimensional points, with spheres replacing the circles.

2.4 The Bisection Algorithm

For continuous functions $f : \mathbb{R} \to \mathbb{R}$, the *bisection algorithm* approximates zeros, i.e. finds arguments x_0 such that $|f(x_0)| < \varepsilon$ for some given bound ε. This algorithm starts with two real numbers a and b such that $f(a)$ and $f(b)$ are different from 0 and have different leading signs.

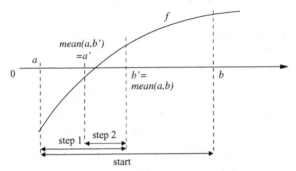

Fig. 4. Step of bisection algorithm

When $|f(a) - f(b)| > \varepsilon$, two actions are executed. Firstly, the mean m of a and b is computed. Secondly, if $f(a)$ and $f(m)$ have different leading signs, a is set to m, otherwise b is set to m. Figure 4 outlines a typical step, and Fig. 5 shows a pseudocode program for this algorithm.

> *while* |f(a) − f(b)| ≥ ε *do*
>   m := mean(a,b);
>   *if* sign(a) ≠ sign(m) *then* b := m
>   *else* a := m

Fig. 5. Pseudocode program for the bisection algorithm

2.5 The Halting-Problem Decision Algorithm

Let $\mathcal{T}$ be the set of all Turing machines. It is well known that $\mathcal{T}$ can be enumerated, i.e. the sets $\mathcal{T}$ and $\mathbb{N}$ correspond bijectively. Now let $f : \mathbb{N} \to \{0, 1\}$ be defined by $f(i) = 0$ iff the ith Turing Machine terminates when applied to the empty tape. It is well known that f is not computable (and this is the only reason for selecting f; any other non-computable function would likewise do the job). Nevertheless, the pseudocode program

$$input(i);$$
$$b := f(i); \tag{8}$$
$$output(b).$$

"computes" the function f.

2.6 A Cooking Recipe

As an – admittedly extreme – case, a cooking recipe may be considered as an algorithm, too. An example is the following recipe for pasta carbonara:

A: Fry the pancetta bacon in the butter over medium-high heat until it browns.
B: Heat the milk in a small saucepan.
C: Cook the pasta until 'al dente'. Drain well, then return pasta to pot.
D: Upon termination of A and B, add the bacon and butter to the saucepan. Stir well. Add the vinegar. Reduce heat to low and cook the sauce gently for about 15 minutes.
E: Upon termination of C and D, add the sauce, the beaten eggs, and the cheese to the pot. Stir well and serve.

The algorithm starts with three parallel branches A, B, C. A and B are single actions and C is a sequence of three actions. Upon termination, A and B trigger D. Finally, C and D trigger E.

2.7 Some General Observations

The reader may prefer a notion of an "algorithm" that would exclude some of the behaviours described above, for various reasons. Certainly, none of these algorithms is implementable. For example, the bisection algorithm of Sect. 2.4 applies to any continuous function f and any real numbers a, b and ε. But only rare cases of f, a, b and ε are representable in a real computer without causing precision problems. Yet, all of them can be handled in a formal setting. Part II will provide the details of how this is done.

3 Pseudocode Programs and Their Semantics

The term "pseudocode" usually denotes a description of an algorithm, composed of conventional keywords of programming languages such as the assignment symbol ":=", "if then" and "while", and symbols (mostly self-explanatory) for actions and conditions. A number of examples of pseudocode programs have been discussed in Sect. 2. Pseudocode programs allow one to engagewith objects, functions and predicates on a level of detail and precision freely chosen by the modeller. This makes pseudocode programs particularly understandable and simple.

In this section, we first discuss requirements for "faithful" models of algorithms. Then we see that pseudocode programs – in whatever form – meet these requirements. This is due to the particular style of formal semantics use as argued in the rest of this section.

3.1 Faithful Modelling

When we are bound to concrete examples, we usually have a clear understanding of what an "adequate" description of an algorithm could be: it should cover all aspects we would like to emphasize and it should hide all aspects we would prefer not to mention. Formulated more precisely, a really "faithful" modelling technique represents

- each elementary object of the algorithm as an elementary object of the formal presentation,
- each elementary operation of the algorithm as an elementary operation of the formal presentation,
- each composed object of the algorithm as a formal composition of the formal presentations of the corresponding objects,
- each composed operation of the algorithm as a formal composition of the formal presentations of the corresponding operations,
- each state of the algorithm as a state of the formal presentation, and
- each step of the algorithm as a step of the formal presentation.

Formulated comprehensively, elementary and composed objects and operations, as well as states and steps of an algorithm and of its model should correspond bijectively. This is the tightest conceivable relationship between intuitive and formal presentations of algorithms.

Can this kind of faithful modelling be conceived of at all? Is there a modelling technique that would achieve this goal for at least some reasonable class of algorithms? Are there any general principles for constructing such models? These are the questions to be discussed in the rest of this section.

3.2 Symbols and Their Interpretation in a State

The pseudocode programs in (5) and in Figs. 3 and 5 employ symbols that stand for various items and functions. For example, X in (5) stands for any initially given set, x and y stand for any items and "augment" for a function. The algorithm is executable only after interpreting the symbol "X" by a concrete set, M, the symbols "x" and "y" by concrete items m and n and "augment" by the function $augment$ that augments an element to a set. Hence, each *initial state* of an algorithm must provide an interpretation of all symbols, except the key symbols such as begin, if etc. For example, let $\Sigma = \{X, x, y, \text{augment}\}$ be a set of symbols and let S be a state with

$$X_S = M, \ x_S = m, \ y_S = n \text{ and augment}_S = augment \tag{9}$$

as defined in (4). The program (5) is applicable to this state. The first assignment statement of (5), $X := augment(X, x)$, then updates S, thus yielding a new state, S'. This state differs from S only with respect to the interpretation of X:

$$X_{S'} = X_S \cup \{m\} = M \cup \{m\}. \tag{10}$$

Then the second assignment statement, $X := augment(X, y)$, is executed, yielding a state S'' with

$$X_{S''} = X_{S'} \cup \{n\} = M \cup \{m\} \cup \{n\} = M \cup \{m, n\}. \tag{11}$$

3.3 Examples: the Bisection and Tangent Algorithms Revisited

The bisection algorithm of Sect. 2.4 can be understood according to the above schema. On the basis of the symbol set $\Sigma = \{a, b, \varepsilon, m, f, mean, sign, <\}$, assume an initial state S where a_S, b_S, ε_S and m_S are any real numbers, $f_S : \mathbb{R} \to \mathbb{R}$ any function, $mean_S : \mathbb{R} \times \mathbb{R} \to \mathbb{R}$ with $mean_S(x, y) = (x + y)/2$, $sign_S : \mathbb{R} \to \{+, -\}$, with $sign_S(x) = +$ iff $x > 0$, and $<_S \subseteq \mathbb{R} \times \mathbb{R}$ as usual. Assuming an initial state S_0, the program of Fig. 5 generates a sequence $S_0 S_1 S_2 \ldots S_k$ of states, iteratively updating m, a and b, with finally $|f_{S_k}(a_{S_k}) - f_{S_k}(b_{S_k})| < \varepsilon_{S_k}$. Note that this holds for *any* real numbers a_{S_0} and ε_{S_0} and *any* unary function f_{S_0} over the real numbers.

The same procedure applies to the tangent algorithm of Sect. 2.3. Given the symbol set $\Sigma = \{C, p, q, r, s, D, M, outside, halfway, circle, intersect, pick, makeline\}$ assume an initial state S such that C_S is any circle with centre p_S, and q_S is a point outside C_S. Furthermore, for points a, b and circles A, B, let $outside_S(a, A) = true$ if a lies outside of A, let $halfway_S(a, b)$ return the point halfway between a and b, let $circle_S(a, b)$ be the (unique!) circle, that has a as its centre and b on its circumference, let $intersect_S(A, B)$ be the set of intersecting points of A and B, and let $makeline_S(A, B)$ be the (unique!) line through a and b. For a set M of elements, let $pick_S(M)$ be a non-deterministically chosen element of M. The symbols q, r, s, D, M may be interpreted freely in the initial state S.

3.4 Applying a Pseudocode Program to a State

The above examples reveal a very simple schema: a pseudocode representation P of an algorithm M consists of two kinds of symbols:

1. Key symbols such as begin, :=, end, ;, input, if, then, output, while, do, and else (in the order of their occurrence in Sect. 2).
2. Constant and function symbols such as X, x, y in (5) and $C, p, r, q, \ldots$ in Fig. 3.

P can be *applied* to a *state* S, where S provides an interpretation σ_S for each constant and each function symbol σ of P. Applying P to S produces a state $P(S)$, where the interpretations of some symbols σ have been updated.

The notion of *a state of* M deserves closer investigation: each constant symbol and each function symbol can be interpreted by any item; virtually "everything" may serve as an interpretation. The only restriction is the *arity* of symbols: a constant symbol must be interpreted by an item, and a function symbol with arity n must be interpreted by a function of arity n. For example, in (5) the symbol "augment" has arity 2 and so every state S of this algorithm must provide a function $augment_S$ which requires two arguments. This restriction does not unduly limit the formalism: a state S (i.e. an interpretation of the constant and function symbols) that violated this restriction would spoil any attempt to define the application of P to S.

3.5 Pseudocode Algorithms

Every pseudocode program P has a finite set Σ of symbols to be interpreted in a state and, vice versa, a state of P is an interpretation of all symbols in Σ. Hence, there is an infinite set of states of P. An algorithm is not intended to run on *all* states. The designer of an algorithm is free to choose the states which the algorithm is intended for. In addition, the designer is free to choose the *initial* states. In Sect. 6 we shall describe the motivation for some restricting requirements on the set of states and of initial states. For the time being, we define a *pseudocode algorithm* M to be a triple

$$M = (states, \mathbf{init}, P) \tag{12}$$

where P is a pseudocode program, applicable to each state $S \in states$ and returning a state $P(S) \in states$, and $\mathbf{init} \subseteq states$.

For the sake of technical simplicity, we assume that the final states S can be be modelled as fixed-point states, i.e., $P(S) = S$.

As P defines a function over the set *states*, the algorithms M of Sects. 2.2–2.6 essentially define transition systems, as in (2), which is the *transition system of* M, $tr(M)$.

Summing up, the notions of *pseudocode programs* and *pseudcode algorithms* remain deliberately vague: assuming a set Σ of symbols, a *state* is fixed by interpreting all symbols in Σ, and the steps are described with the help of key words and the symbols in Σ.

A class of pseudocode algorithms, called *sequential small-step* algorithms, has been characterized by Gurevich [13]. Details will be given in Sect. 5.

II: The Formal Framework

The ASM approach is based on a few notions that were identified by Tarski [20] as providing a most useful general conceptual basis for mathematics: the notions of *structures*, *signatures* and their combination in Σ-*structures*. Any formalism employs symbols to represent objects that, in general, are not symbols. Σ-structures provide a means to perform this kind of representation. Section 4 presents the details. Σ-structures are the formal basis for Σ-programs, i.e. pseudocode programs over a signature Σ, as will be defined in Sect. 5, including the important subclass of sequential small-step ASM programs. Algorithms based on such programs are investigated in Sect. 6.

4 Signatures and Structures

4.1 Structures

As explained above, a state S of a pseudocode program is a *structure* (sometimes also called an *algebra*), consisting of

- a set U, the *universe* of S,
- finitely many *constants*, namely the elements of U, and
- finitely many functions over U, of the form $\phi : U^n \to U$; n is the *arity* of ϕ.

Constants can be conceived of as degenerate functions, with arity *zero*. So, a *structure* S is usually written

$$S = (U, \phi_1, \ldots, \phi_k). \tag{13}$$

If n_i is the arity of the constant or function ϕ_i, the arity tuple $(n_1, \ldots, n_k)$ is the *type* of S.

4.2 Homomorphism and Isomorphism

Some fundamental relationships among structures are *homomorphisms* and *isomorphisms*.

Assume two structures $R = (U_R, \psi_1, \ldots, \psi_k)$ and $S = (U_S, \phi_1, \ldots, \phi_k)$, both of the same type $(n_1, \ldots, n_k)$. Assume furthermore a mapping $h : U_R \to U_S$ such that for all $i = 1, \ldots, k$ and all $u_1, \ldots, u_{n_i} \in U_R$, the following holds:

$$h(\psi_i(u_1, \ldots, u_{n_i})) = \phi_i(h(u_1), \ldots, h(u_{n_i})). \tag{14}$$

Then h is a *homomorphism* from R to S, written $h : R \to S$.

Figure 6 shows the property of homomorphism in a diagrammatic form.

Now let R and S be structures of the same type, and let $h : R \to S$ be a bijective homomorphism. Then h is called an *isomorphism*.

It is not difficult to show that the reverse function $f^{-1} : U_S \to U_R$ of an isomorphism $f : R \to S$ is again a homomorphism, $f^{-1} : S \to R$. Hence, it is reasonable to declare two structures R and S to be *isomorphic*, written $R \simeq S$, if there exists an isomorphism $h : R \to S$.

$$(u_1, \ldots, u_{n_i}) \xrightarrow{\psi_i} \psi_i(u_1, \ldots, u_{n_i})$$

$$\downarrow h \quad \cdots \quad \downarrow h \qquad\qquad\qquad \downarrow h$$

$$(h(u_1), \ldots, h(u_{n_i})) \xrightarrow{\phi_i} \begin{array}{l} h(\psi_i(u_1, \ldots, u_{n_i})) = \\ \phi_i(h(u_1), \ldots, \phi_i(h(u_{n_i})) \end{array}$$

Fig. 6. The homomorphism property

4.3 Signatures and Ground Terms

The symbols occurring in a pseudocode program can be collected in a *signature*. Each function symbol is associated its arity and each constant symbol is given an arity 0. A signature Σ with symbols $f_1, \ldots, f_l$ is usually written

$$\Sigma = (f_1, \ldots, f_l, a_1, \ldots, a_l) \tag{15}$$

whwew a_i is the arity of f_i $(i = 1, \ldots, l)$. $(a_1, \ldots, a_l)$ is the *type* of Σ.

A signature Σ yields, canonically, the set T_Σ of *ground terms over* Σ: T_Σ is the smallest set of sequences of symbols in Σ such that

- each constant symbol in Σ is an element of T_Σ
- if $t \in \Sigma$ with arity n and if $t_1, \ldots, t_n \in T_\Sigma$ then $f(t_1, \ldots, t_n) \in T_\Sigma$. $\tag{16}$

T_Σ is apparently infinite iff Σ contains at least one constant symbol and one symbol with arity $n \geq 1$.

Ground terms typically occur on the right-hand side of an assignment statement, such as in "$x := x + 1$". In the context of ASM, "x" is a constant symbol and "$+$" a function symbol of arity 2. The ground term "$+(x, 1)$" is written in the more convenient infix form "$x + 1$". First order logic employs terms with additional symbols, called *variables*. The basic version of ASM, considered here, does without variables. We shall see later that ground terms, in their general form, may also occur as the left-side of an assignment statement, i.e. an assignment may be of the form

$$f(t_1, \ldots, t_n) := \ldots .$$

This may be conceived of as an update of any array.

4.4 Σ-Structures

A structure $S = (U, \psi_1, \ldots, \psi_k)$ of type $(n_1, \ldots, n_k)$ as in (13), "fits" to a signature $\Sigma = (f_1, \ldots, f_l, a_1, \ldots, a_l)$ as in (17) if both have the same type, i.e. if $k = l$ and $(n_1, \ldots, n_k) = (a_1, \ldots, a_l)$. In this case, S is a Σ-*structure*. The function ϕ_i is the *interpretation* of ϕ_i in S and we frequently write ϕ_i as f_{i_S}. Hence, S can be written

$$S = (U, f_{1_S}, \ldots, f_{k_S}). \tag{17}$$

Each term $t \in T_\Sigma$ canonically denotes an element t_S of the carrier of each Σ-structure S, defined by induction over the structure of T_Σ:

$$t_S = f_{i_S} \text{ if } t = f_i \text{ and } n_i = 0, \tag{18}$$

$$t_S = f_{i_S}(t_{1_S}, \ldots, t_{n_S}) \text{ if } t = f(t_1, \ldots, t_n). \tag{19}$$

A signature Σ yields the set $str(\Sigma)$ of all Σ-*structures*. This is a rich set, including a variety of quite different structures. Vice versa, if S is a Σ-structure as well as a Σ'-structure, the two signatures Σ and Σ' are identical up to bijective renaming of their symbols.

4.5 Two Lemmata on Σ-Structures

The following two lemmata will help us to characterize the expressive power of ASM algorithms. The first lemma states that the homomorphism property of Σ-structures extends to terms:

Lemma 1 (Homomorphism)
Let Σ be a signature, let R and S be two Σ-structures, and let $h : R \to S$ be a homomorphism. Then holds $h(t_R) = t_S$ for all $t \in T_\Sigma$.

Proof
By induction over the structure of T_Σ.

First case: t is a constant symbol. In this case the property holds according to the definition of homomorphism (see (14) in Sect. 4.2).

Second case: $t = f(t_1, \ldots, t_n)$. The inductive hypothesis implies $h(t_{i_R}) = t_{i_S}$ for $i = 1, \ldots, n$. Then, again by definition of homomorphism,

$$
\begin{aligned}
h(t_R) &= h(f(t_1, \ldots, t_n)_R) \\
&= h(f_R(t_{1_R}, \ldots, t_{n_R})) \\
&= f_S(h(t_{1_R}), \ldots, h(t_{n_R})) \\
&= f_S(t_{1_S}, \ldots, t_{n_S}) \\
&= f_S(t_1, \ldots, t_n) = t_S.
\end{aligned}
$$
□

The second lemma states that isomorphic Σ-structures can not be distinguished with the help of terms:

Lemma 2 (Indistinguishability)
Let Σ be a signature, let R and S be two Σ-structures, and let $R \simeq S$. Then, for all $t, u \in T_\Sigma$, we have $t_R = u_R$ iff $t_S = u_S$.

Proof
Let $h : R \to S$ be an isomorphism. According to the above lemma on homomorphism $t_R = u_R$ iff $h(t_R) = h(u_R)$ iff $t_S = u_S$.
□

5 Sequential Small-Step ASM Programs

Part I provided the intuition and Sect. 4 the formal means to define the syntax and semantics of a special kind of pseudocode program P: given a signature Σ, each state S of P is just a Σ-structure. The step function of P, providing for each state S a successor state $P(S)$, is syntactically represented with the help of terms in T_Σ, together with some key symbols such as $\texttt{if}$, $\texttt{then}$ and $\texttt{:=}$.

In this section we define a particularly simple version of such pseudocode programs. We start with assignment statements that update constants and functions. Then we proceed to sets of consistent statements and to conditional statements, and finish with sequential, small-step ASM programs. The semantics of such programs is rigorously defined in a mathematical setting.

5.1 Simple Assignment Statements

The simplest form of a program over a signature Σ is just an assignment statement, of the form

$$f := t \tag{20}$$

where f is a constant symbol in Σ and $t \in T_\Sigma$.

Applied to a Σ-structure S, (20) yields the step

$$S \xrightarrow{f:=t} S', \tag{21}$$

where S' updates the value of f: the constant symbol f gains t_S as a new value in S', i.e.

$$f_{S'} = t_S, \tag{22}$$

and the semantics of all other symbols remains untouched, i.e. $g_{S'} = g_S$ for each $g \in \Sigma$, $g \neq f$. For example, for the signature

$$\Sigma = (c, f, 0, 1) \tag{23}$$

and the Σ-structure

$$S = (\mathbb{N}, 0, suc), \tag{24}$$

we have $c_S = 0$ and $f_S = suc$. The step

$$S \xrightarrow{c:=f(c)} S' \tag{25}$$

yields $c_{S'} = 1$ and $f_{S'} = suc$.

As an exercise, the reader may show that (27) updates the value of *each* term $t \in T_\Sigma$; more precisely,

$$t_S = n \text{ iff } t_{S'} = n + 1. \tag{26}$$

5.2 Updates of Functions

The general form of the updates over a signature Σ is of the form

$$f(t_1, \ldots, t_n) := t, \tag{27}$$

with $f \in \Sigma$ and $t_1, \ldots, t_n, t \in T_\Sigma$; (20) is the special case for $n = 0$. f_S may be conceived of as a n-dimensional array, to be updated for one argument tuple. A step

$$S \xrightarrow{f(t_1, \ldots, t_n) := t} S' \tag{28}$$

updates f_S at $(t_{1S}, \ldots, t_{nS})$ by t_S, yielding

$$f_{S'}(t_{1S}, \ldots, t_{nS}) = t_S. \tag{29}$$

Hence, the right-hand side and the terms $t_1, \ldots, t_n$ denoting the arguments of the array on the left-hand side are evaluated in the initial state, S. The function f remains untouched for all other arguments, i.e.

$$f_{S'}(u_1, \ldots, u_n) = f_S(u_1, \ldots, u_n) \tag{30}$$

for all $(u_1, \ldots, u_n) \neq (t_{1S}, \ldots, t_{nS})$. Likewise, the semantics of all other function symbols remains, i.e.

$$g_{S'} = g_S \tag{31}$$

for all $g \in \Sigma$, $g \neq f$. As an example, we consider the signature Σ and the Σ-structure S given in (23) and (24). The step

$$S \xrightarrow{f(c) := c} S' \tag{32}$$

yields $c_S = 0$, and, hence, with (25),

$$f_{S'}(0) = f_{S'}(c_S) = 0. \tag{33}$$

For all $i \geq 1$, $f_S(i)$ remains untouched, i.e.

$$f_{S'}(i) = f_S(i) = suc(i) = i + 1. \tag{34}$$

Therefore, the functions f_S and $f_{S'}$ differ only for the argument 0.

As an exercise, the reader may show that (34) updates the value of all terms t (except $t = c$):

$$t_{S'} = 0 \tag{35}$$

holds for *all* terms $t \in T_\Sigma$.

Summing up, in a step $S \to S'$, an assignment statement selects in S *one* constant, or *one* function for *one* argument tuple, and in S' replaces it by a new value from the universe of S. In particular, the universe of S' must coincide with the universe of S.

From the point of view of the terms, an update $S \xrightarrow{f(t_1, \ldots, t_n) := t} S'$ potentially yields fresh values for all terms u which include as a subterm any term of the form $f(v_1, \ldots, v_n)$ with $(v_{1S}, \ldots, v_{nS}) = (t_{1S}, \ldots, t_{nS})$.

5.3 Consistent Assignment Statements

A step $S \rightarrow S'$ of an ASM program in general executes more than one assignment statement. This is easily achieved, provided every two such assignments are *consistent*, i.e. they do not try perform different updates of the same constant, or of the same function at the same argument tuple. More precisely, two assignment statements $f(t_1, \ldots, t_n) := t$ and $f(u_1, \ldots, u_n) := u$ are *consistent at a state S* if

$$(t_{1S}, \ldots, t_{nS}) = (u_{1S}, \ldots, u_{nS}) \text{ implies } t_S = u_S. \tag{36}$$

(This includes the case of (20) with $n = 0$.)

This definition is easily generalized: a set Z of assignment statements is *consistent at a state S* if the elements of Z are pairwise consistent at S.

To define the semantics of assignment statements formally, let Σ be a signature and let Z be a set of assignment statements with terms in T_Σ. Furthermore let S be a Σ-structure and assume that Z is consistent at S. Then S and Z together define a step

$$S \xrightarrow{Z} S' \tag{37}$$

where S' is a Σ-structure, too, and the universe U of S' is identical to the universe of S.

For an n-ary symbol $f \in \Sigma$ and an argument $\mathbf{u} \in U^n$, we give the following

Definition: in a state S, Z *updates* f_S at $\mathbf{u}$ by v if Z includes an assignment statement of the form $f(t_1, \ldots, t_n) := t$ with $\mathbf{u} = (t_{1S}, \ldots, t_{nS})$, and $v = t_S$. For S' as in (37), the value of $f_{S'}(\mathbf{u})$ is now given by

$$f_{S'}(\mathbf{u}) = \begin{cases} v & \text{if } Z \text{ at } S \text{ updates } f_S(\mathbf{u}) \text{ by } v, \\ f_S(\mathbf{u}) & \text{otherwise.} \end{cases} \tag{38}$$

5.4 Guards and Conditional Assignment Statements

ASM employ *conditional* assignment statements, of the form

$$\text{if } \alpha \text{ then } r, \tag{39}$$

where r is an assignment statement and α is a Boolean expression. The term α plays the role of a *guard* of R.

For a signature Σ, the *guards over Σ* are symbol sequences such that

- for all $t, u \in T_\Sigma$, "$t = u$" is a guard over Σ and
- if α and β are guards over Σ, so are "$\alpha \wedge \beta$" and "$\neg \alpha$".

Hence, we assume that each signature Σ is extended by the symbols $=$, $\wedge$, $\neg$, true and false. Each Σ-structure S is expected to interpret these symbols as usual. This implies, for each guard α over Σ and each Σ-structure S,

$$\alpha_S \in \{true, false\}. \tag{40}$$

Equation (39) is a *conditional assignment statement over a signature* Σ iff

- α is a guard over Σ and
- for r of the form $f(t_1, \ldots, t_n) := t$, the following holds: $f \in \Sigma$, and $t_1, \ldots, t_n, t \in T_\Sigma$.

5.5 Sequential Small-Step ASM Programs and Semantics

A *sequential small-step ASM program* P *over a signature* Σ is a set of conditional assignment statements over Σ, as defined in Sect. 5.4. For each Σ-structure S, the program P defines a *successor structure* S', usually written $P(S)$, by a step

$$S \xrightarrow{P} S'. \tag{41}$$

To define S', let $Z =_{def} \{r|$ ex. "if α then r" $\in P$ and $\alpha_S = true\}$ and construct S' according to (38).

The term "sequential" maz be bewildering in the face of concurrently executed statements; the term *"lock step"* was perhaps more intuitive. Furthermore, "small-step" refers to the limited number of updates during a step: the number of updates is bounded by the number of conditional statements. Hence, the term *"bounded"* was perhaps more accurate. We shall, however, follow tradition.

5.6 Simulation of Conventional Control Structures

The usual forms of pseudocode differ from sequential small-step ASM mainly with respect to control: sequences, alternatives and iterations are eliminated in ASM in favour of parallel execution of a set of conditional assignment statements. That ASM can simulate conventional control structures is fairly obvious; Sect. 5.7 will show some examples. Vice versa, some additional constant symbols can help us to simulate the ASM control structure by conventional means.

This kind of simulation comes however with a price: one step of an ASM program usually requires a sequence of steps in terms of conventional control structures. This price is quite high in the context of ASM, because a decisive aspect of ASM is the expressive power of their single steps, as discussed in Sect. 3.1: a sequence $S \rightarrow S'' \rightarrow S'$ of two steps from S to S' is not "as good as" the single step $S \rightarrow S'$.

5.7 Examples

Section 2 presented some pseudocode programs. We may wonder how they can be represented as ASM programs.

The set extension program of Sect. 2.2 is not an ASM program at first glance: an ASM program cannot express sequential composition. This deficit is easily overcome, however, by a well-known "trick": we extend the initial state by a fresh variable, l, and evaluate l as 0 in the initial state S_0. We reformulate (5) as

$$P_2 : \textbf{par} \quad \begin{array}{l} \text{if } l = 0 \text{ then } X := g(X, x); \\ \text{if } l = 0 \text{ then } l := 1; \\ \text{if } l = 1 \text{ then } X := g(X, y); \\ \text{if } l = 1 \text{ then } l := 2 \end{array}$$

$$\textbf{endpar}.$$

The same technique can be applied to get rid of the sequential composition in the tangent algorithm of Sect. 2.3.

The bisection algorithm of Sect. 2.4, formulated as an ASM, reads

```
if stop(a,b)=true then result:=a,
if ¬(stop(a,b)=true) ∧ f(mean(a,b))=0 then
    result:=mean(a,b),
if ¬(stop(a,b)=true) ∧ ¬(f(mean(a,b))=0)
    ∧ eqsign(f(a),f(mean(a,b)))=true then a:=mean(a, b),
if ¬(stop(a,b)=true) ∧ ¬(f(mean(a,b))=0)
    ∧ eqsign(f(b),f(mean(a,b)))=true then b:=mean(a, b)
```

As a final example consider a system composed of four components:

prod: a *producer* to produce items,
send: a *sender* to send produced items to a buffer,
rec : a *receiver* to take items from the buffer,
cons: a *consumer* to consume items provided by the receiver.

We base the model of this system on a signature including the 0-ary symbols x, y and buffer. Their values may represent items to be processed by the system. Furthermore, the values of x and y may be undefined (represented by x_undef and y_undef, respectively), and the buffer may be empty (represented by b_empty).

The components interact as follows: if the value of x is undefined, a fresh value item is assigned to x (by prod), then forwarded to the empty buffer (by send), removed from the buffer and assigned to y (by rec), and finally consumed (by cons).

Applied to an initial state S_0 with $x_{S_0} = \text{x\_undef}_{S_0}$, $y_{S_0} = \text{y\_undef}_{S_0}$ and $\text{buffer}_{S_0} = \text{b\_empty}_{S_0}$, the following components define a sequential ASM program with the behaviour described:

```
prod  =def  { if x=x_undef then x := item }

send  =def  if ¬(x=x_undef) ∧ buffer=b_empty then
                { buffer := x, x := x_undef }

rec   =def  if ¬(buffer=b_empty) ∧ y=y_undef then
                { y := buffer, buffer := b_empty }

cons  =def  { if ¬(y=y_undef) then y := y_undef }
```

Then

$$\Gamma = \text{prod} \cup \text{send} \cup \text{rec} \cup \text{cons} \tag{42}$$

is the required sequential ASM. Its behaviour is

$$S_0 \xrightarrow{\text{prod}} S_1 \xrightarrow[\text{rec}]{\text{send}} S_2 \xrightarrow{\text{prod}} S_3 \xrightarrow[\text{cons}]{\text{send}} S_4 \xrightarrow[\text{rec}]{\text{prod}} S_5 \quad \ldots, \tag{43}$$

where each step is labelled by the components that have guards that evaluate to *true*. For reasons that will become clear later on, we emphasize the order of occurrence of the components, and thus write (43) as

$$\text{prod} \rightarrow \text{send} < \begin{array}{c} \text{prod} \rightarrow \text{send} \rightarrow \text{prod} \\ \times \quad \times \\ \text{rec} \longrightarrow \text{cons} \longrightarrow \text{rec} \end{array} \quad \ldots \tag{44}$$

6 Properties of Sequential Small-Step ASM Programs

The semantics of the programs defined in Sect. 5.5 implies a series of properties of steps, to be considered here. Two of these properties ("steps preserve universes" and "steps respect isomorphism") are quite obvious. The third one, "exploration is bounded", is intuitively also simple, but requires a bit of formalism.

In this section, we assume a sequential small-step ASM program P over a signature Σ, and a Σ-structure S.

6.1 Steps Preserve Universes

The semantics of sequential small-step ASM programs, as defined in Sect. 5.5, is based on (38) and (37). There, it is explicitly specified that

$$\text{The universes of } S \text{ and } P(S) \text{ coincide.} \tag{45}$$

6.2 Steps Respect Isomorphism

Let R be a Σ-structure, and let $h : S \to R$ be an isomorphism. The definitions in Sect. 5.3, and, in particular, Sect. 3.5 imply, for a set Z of assignment statements, that Z is consistent at S iff Z is consistent at R. Furthermore, for each k-ary $f \in \Sigma$ and each argument tuple $(u_1, \ldots, u_k)$ for f_S, the set Z updates $f_S(u_1, \ldots, u_k)$ by v iff Z updates $f_R(h(u_1), \ldots, h(u_k))$ by $h(v)$. Consequently, referring to (38), $f_{P(S)}(u_1, \ldots, u_k) = v$ iff $f_{P(R)}(h(u_1), \ldots, h(u_k)) = h(v)$. Taking this together with (41), it now follows that

$$\text{If } R \simeq S \text{ then } P(R) \simeq P(S). \tag{46}$$

6.3 Exploration Is Bounded

To properly understand the last property, we now reconsider the semantics of ASM programs, as given in (37) and (38): P describes only the *updates* of a state S, and does not care about the rest of S. In fact, the rest of S is just adopted in $P(S)$. Technically, an update of a step $S \to P(S)$ is given by three parameters: a function symbol $f \in \Sigma$, an n-tuple $\mathbf{u}$ of arguments for f_S, and the new value, v. Formulated more formally, let Σ be a signature, let f be a function symbol in Σ with arity n, let U be a universe, let $\mathbf{u} \in U^n$ and let $v \in U$. Then

$$(f, \mathbf{u}, v) \tag{47}$$

is a Σ-*update over* U. For a step $S \to P(S)$, the triple (47) may be used to indicate that $f_S(\mathbf{u})$ is updated by v.

Each step of P yields a *set* of updates. This motivates the following definition: a Σ-update $(f, \mathbf{u}, v)$ over the universe U of S is a P-*update* of S iff

$$f_S(\mathbf{u}) \neq f_{P(S)}(\mathbf{u}) = v. \tag{48}$$

Let

$$\triangle(P, S) \tag{49}$$

denote the set of all P-updates of S. Now, let $T_0 \subseteq T_\Sigma$ be the set of all terms occurring in P. Let T be the subterm closure of T_0, i.e. the terms in T_0 together with all their subterms. Let R and S be two Σ-structures that T cannot distinguish, i.e., for all $t \in T$

$$t_R = t_S. \tag{50}$$

Then P inevitably yields the same updates for both states:

$$\triangle(P, R) = \triangle(P, S). \tag{51}$$

7 Gurevich's Theorem

We now search for a characterization of the expressive power of sequential small-step ASM. We state this problem as a question about transition systems, as considered in (2) and (12).

7.1 A Question and a Partial Solution

What requirements on a transition system $A = (states, \textbf{init}, F)$ would guarantee that F can be represented as a sequential small-step ASM program P as defined in Sect. 5.5? It will turn out that, essentially, the properties discussed in Sect. 6 provide such a set of requirements.

The first requirement for the above question is obvious: there must exist a signature Σ such that $states$ (and hence $\textbf{init}$) is a set of Σ-structures. The properties of sequential small-step ASM, as discussed in Sect. 6, must hold for F, and hence they provide another three requirements for the above question: F preserves universes, i.e., for each state $S \in states$, the domains of S and $F(S)$ coincide. Furthermore, F respects isomorphisms, i.e., for each $S \in states$ and each $R \simeq S$, $F(R) \simeq F(S)$. This requires F be well defined for each R isomorphic to some $S \in states$. Consequently, we require $states$ to be closed under isomorphism, i.e. if $S \in states$ and $S \simeq R$, then $R \in states$. The last requirement starts from the obvious observation that the required program P essentially makes use of finitely many terms $t \in T_\Sigma$. Together with (50) and (51), this implies that there exists a finite set $T \subseteq T_\Sigma$ of terms such that two states evolve with the same updates if they interpret all $t \in T$ alike.

7.2 Some Properties of Transition Systems

The above informal discussion, together with Sect. 6, will now be rephrased in a more formal setting. To this end, let $A = (states, \textbf{init}, F)$ be a transition system.

A is *signature-based* iff there exists a signature Σ such that $states$ is a set of Σ-structures. If Σ is known, A is denoted as Σ-*based*.

In the rest of this section, we assume A to be Σ-based.

A *preserves universes* if, for each $S \in states$, the universes of S and of $F(S)$ coincide.

A is *isomorphism-closed* if, for each $S \in states$ and each structure $R \simeq S$, $R \in states$.

A *respects isomorphism* iff, for each $S \in states$ and each $R \simeq S$, $F(R) \simeq F(S)$.

The last property requires the following definition: for a state $S \in states$, an *update of A at S* is a triple $(f, \mathbf{u}, v)$ with $f \in \Sigma$, $\mathbf{u} \in U^k$ and $v \in U$, where k is the arity of f, U is the carrier of S and $f_S(\mathbf{u}) \neq f_{F(S)}(\mathbf{u}) = v$. Let $\triangle(S)$

denote the set of all updates at a state $S \in$ *states*. The last property now reads as follows:

A *bounds exploration* iff there exists a finite set $T \subseteq T_\Sigma$ of terms, such that for all $R, S \in$ *states*, the following holds: if $t_R = t_S$ for all $t \in T_\Sigma$, then $\triangle(R) = \triangle(S)$.

A is *ASM-adapted* iff A is signature-based, A preserves universes, A is isomorphism-closed, A respects isomorphism and A bounds exploration.

7.3 Gurevich's Theorem

It is intuitively quite obvious that the properties of Sect. 7.2 provide necessary conditions for the question of Sect. 7.1: F can be represented as a sequential small-step ASM program only if A is ASM-adapted.

As an amazing and beautiful result, Gurevich in [13] has proven that this property is also sufficient! Hence we have the following theorem.

Theorem 1
*Let $A = ($states, **init**,$F)$ be an ASM-adapted transition system. Then there exists a sequential small-step ASM program P such that*

$$F = P|_{states} \ . \tag{52}$$

The proof of this theorem is far from trivial. It has been examined critically in [19].

III: Extensions

Not every algorithm is sequential or small-step. There are distributed, reactive, and large-step algorithms. The ASM approach covers those algorithms as generalizations of the version presented in Part II. We glance at some of those versions in this part.

8 Sequential Large-Step ASM Algorithms

As explained in Sect. 5.5, the term "small-step" refers to the limited number of updates in each step of an ASM program P: this number is bounded by the number of assignment statements in P. Of course, there are algorithms without such a bound. We present an example of such an algorithm and show its representation in an extended version of an ASM program.

8.1 An Example: Node Reachability

Let G be a directed graph and let *root* be a distinguished node of G. We seek for an algorithm that computes a unary predicate R on the nodes of G, to discern the nodes reachable from *root*.

Intuitively, this algorithm operates as follows. Initially, $R(x)$ holds if and only if x is the root. The following step is iterated until a fixed-point is reached (i.e. a state identical to its successor state): for all arcs $x \to y$ with $R(x)$ and $\neg R(y)$, extend R by y.

The amount of work executed in one step is unbounded: in a state S, the number of arcs $x \to y$ in G with $R(x)$ and $\neg R(y)$, is not limited. The algorithm can therefore not be represented by a small-step ASM program.

8.2 Quantified Variables

The above node reachability algorithm can be presented with a standard technique of formal logic, namely quantified variables. The steps of the algorithm can then be described by the program

$$\text{do for all } x, y, \text{ with } \text{Edge}(x, y) \wedge R(x) \wedge \neg R(y)$$
$$R(y) := true. \tag{53}$$

Equation (53) is a *large-step* ASM program.

An algorithm is large-step not only if the amount of change fails to be bounded. A step is also *large* if the number of items involved is bounded. An example of an unbounded number of items involved is the following ASM program that checks whether a given graph has isolated points:

$$\text{if } \forall x \, \exists y \, Edge(x, y) \text{ then } output := false$$
$$\text{else } output := true \tag{54}$$

9 Non-deterministic and Reactive ASM

So far, we have assumed an ASM program P over a signature Σ to define a unique successor state $P(S)$ for each state, i.e. each Σ-structure S. This generalizes to a *set* $P(S)$ of successor states for non-deterministic programs P. Non-determinism can be caused by various means, considered below.

9.1 Non-deterministic Semantics

One may change the semantic rule (38): in a state where more than one assignment statement's guard is evaluated as *true*, one may select one or a subset of them for execution. Though possible in principle, this idea is fairly bewildering for the reader used to the conventional approach and has therefore rarely been used.

9.2 The Operator "choose"

The *"choose"* operator is frequently useful. For example, let $A = \{a_1, \ldots, a_k\}$ be a set of symbols. We require an algorithm to produce all symbol sequences $u \in A^*$ such that, for $v, w \in \Sigma^*$,

$$u = vw, \ v \neq w \ \text{and} \ |v| = |w|. \tag{55}$$

The ASM program in Fig. 7 (with "choose" and "for all") does the job, provided the "choose" operator is *fairly* applied, i.e., every candidate value is eventually chosen.

```
choose n, i with i < n
    choose a, b ∈ Σ with a ≠ b
        v(i) := a
        w(i) := b
    forall j < n, j ≠ i
        choose a, b ∈ Σ
            v(j) := a
            w(j) := b
```

Fig. 7. Application of *choose* operator

9.3 The Reactive Case

The last source of non-determinism is the case where the environment updates a constant f_S or a function f_S for some argument tuple $\mathbf{u}$, at a state S. This is the case of *reactive* systems.

From the perspective of a program P, a step $S \rightarrow S'$ then includes a spontaneous change of the value of f_S or $f_S(\mathbf{u})$, respectively, not caused by P. Technically, this is a non-deterministic choice from a set of alternatives, in general infinite: an elegant method to construct reactive ASM programs. Details of this topic can be found in [2, 1], for example, and many other papers published mainly by Blass and Gurevich.

9.4 Turbo Algorithms

As is frequently mentioned, the faithful-modelling requirement as discussed in Sect. 3.1 is sensitive to the atomicity of steps. There are good reasons to squeeze more than one action, in particular communicating actions of reactive algorithms, into one step. This aspect has been addressed in many contributions, including [11, 3].

10 Distributed ASM

Both small-step and large-step ASM algorithms describe a single *run* of an algorithm, as a sequence $S_0 S_1 \ldots$ of states S_i. This is not adequate for *distributed* algorithms. As discovered by Petri in the 1960s [17] and discussed later also by Pratt [18], Lamport [15] and Gurevich [11], a run of a distributed algorithm is a partially ordered set of events, with $a > b$ iff a is causally necessary for b.

10.1 Distributed ASM Programs

This gives rise to the idea of a distributed version of ASM: a *distributed ASM* is just a non-empty, finite set of ASM programs, all over the same signature Σ. The programs are then called *components* of the distributed ASM, and every Σ-structure forms a *state* of the distributed ASM. The components may be executed concurrently if they involve stores with separate locations.

    A proper definition of small-step distributed ASM can be found in [10] . The general case of distributed ASM is discussed in [11].

10.2 An Example of a Distributed ASM

As an example, consider the producer/consumer system of Sect. 5.7:

$$D = \{\text{prod}, \text{send}, \text{rec}, \text{cons}\} \tag{56}$$

is a distributed ASM. Notice that (56) differs decisively from the sequential ASM in (42): a sequential ASM is a single set of conditional assignment statements, while a distributed ASM is a family of sets of conditional assignment statements. This implies a notion of *distributed runs*. The ASM program D in (56) yields a partially ordered run of occurrences of its four components, shown in Fig. 8.

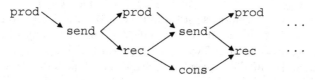

Fig. 8. Partial order of component occurrences of a distributed run of the producer/consumer ASM

It is illuminating to compare the partial order of the component occurrences, as outlined in Fig. 8, with the partial order of (44): in fact, the latter is unnecessarily strict. This is due to the lockstep semantics of a sequential ASM: a run is a sequence of steps, and its action occurrences are unordered if they belong to the same step. This yields partial orders with a transitive non-order relation, such as (44). Figure 8 shows that, for a distributed run of a distributed ASM, non-order of action occurrences is not necessarily transitive: the second production occurs unordered with the first consumption, which in turn occurs unordered with the second send. But the second production is causally before the second send. This example shows that distributed ASM in fact provide a substantial generalization of sequential ASM.

11 ASM as a Specification Language

In this chapter, we shall not evenattempt to glance at the large number of application projects of ASM. Nor shall we discuss all the tools and techniques, for example, for refinement and simulation, that support ASM as a specification language. We concentrate on one fundamental aspect only, i.e., the role plazed by constants and functions for various purposes in an algorithm.

11.1 Static Constants and Functions

Theory does not prevent any state S from interpreting the constant symbol "2" by the Boolean value "true", or the function symbol "$\sqrt{}$" as a function that assigns each employee of a company his or her salary. But this is not what the reader expects. There are a number of symbols with unique worldwide-accepted interpretations, including the integer symbols "0", ..., "9", used to construct representations of integers and rational numbers, and function symbols such as $+$, $-$, $\sqrt{}$ and $^{-1}$, used to denote the corresponding wellknown functions. Some symbols have a generally agreed denotation only in specific communities. It is of course reasonable to require the initial state S of an algorithm to interpret such symbols according to their conventional denotation and never to update them. In Sect. 5.4 we remarked that the symbols for propositional logic such as "$\neg$" and "$\wedge$" must be interpreted as usual, in order to construct reasonable guards. A set of constants and functions is made available this way and is denoted as *static* for obvious reasons.

More generally, we denote as "static" also constants and functions that are fixed in the initial state and are never updated. They typically play the role of an input to the algorithm. Typical examples are f and ε in the bisection algorithm, C and p in the tangent algorithm and f in the halting-problem decision algorithm.

Notice the generalized concept of "input" here: it may include entire functions, such as f in Fig. 5 and (8), and hence, in general, infinite structures.

11.2 Constant Symbols as "Program Variables"

The non-static constants include, in particular, symbols which in conventional programming languages would play the role of variables: such a symbol, x, gains some irrelevant value in the initial state. x is updated before being read, i.e. an assignment statement with x on the left side is executed before an assignment statement with x occurring in the term on its right side is executed. Consequently, a constant symbol frequently plays the role of a program variable, a frequent source of confusion for ASM beginners. In particular the reader must not confuse this kind of constant with a quantified variable, as introduced for large-step ASMs in Sect. 7.

11.3 Further Roles of Constants and Functions

A constant symbol occurring on the left but never on the right side of an assignment statement may be used as an output variable for a reactive algorithm. More generally, for the sake of clarity, one may explicitly declare a constant symbol as an "output variable" if it is assumed to be read by the environment.

12 Conclusion

This chapter is intended to show that the ASM approach indeed suggests a reasonable notion of an "algorithm", that is very adequate as a framework for the modelling of systems. Implementable systems arise as the special case of states with a bit-level representation for all components.

Two aspects in particular motivate the choice of ASM. Firstly, ASM fit perfectly into the framework of general algebra and logic. The use of the notion of structures, signatures, and Σ-structures to describe system states in an abstract way is well established. Computer science employs those notions in the context of algebraic specifications, to abstractly describe states. As a (sequential) behaviour is a sequence of Σ-structures, it is very natural to describe steps in terms of Σ-structures too.

Secondly, the definition of a sequential small-step ASM as a set of simultaneously executed set of conditional statements is motivated very well by Gurevich's theorem, as described in Sect. 7.3.

The idea of employing mathematical structures as components of states was advocated in [5]: data spaces such as stacks, trees and all forms of data structures in Algol, Lisp and Fortran, together with corresponding operations, define *virtual machines*. ASM generalizes this to *any* kind of data space, via algebras; [5] is restricted to structures that are implementable in a canonical way.

Ganzinger [7] suggested that the state of a program $\mathcal{P}$ should be defined as Σ-algebras, exactly as done in ASM. Ganzinger formally defines the semantics of $\mathcal{P}$ to be a free construct, i.e. a mapping from a set of Σ-algebras to a set of Σ-algebras. Reference [8] expands on this idea; it may be likewise applied to ASM.

The "state-as-algebra" paradigm [8] has been a basis for various lines of research. Categorical constructs, as employed in [7], were also used in [21]. In [9], it was shown that the "state-as-algebra" paradigm was useful for describing the semantics of specification languages such as VDM, Z and B. The authors of that paper advocated a combination of algebraic and imperative specifications, of which ASM provided an example. A further example is the "algebraic specification with implicit state" approach of [6].

Modern specification techniques such as Z, TLA and FOCUS follow logic-based guidelines, such as "a specification is a (huge) logical expression", "implementation (refinement) is implication", and "composition is conjunction". The ASM formalism was not designed along these guidelines, but it does not contradict them. It might be useful to critically review those guidelines in the light of ASM.

One may very well expect many related representations of algorithms to arise, in particular further variants of non-deterministic, distributed interactive algorithms and other variants, both small-step and large-step, together with interesting characterizing theorems, in analogy to Gurevich's theorem. In the long term, we may get used to seeing this approach as an adequate starting point for computer science curricula.

13 Acknowledgements

I gratefully acknowledge Yuri Gurevich's patient answers to my many elementary questions on ASM. I owe much to Egon Börger, as he introduced me to ASM. Without Dines Bjørner's invitation to the Stara Lesna school in June 2004 and his friendly, persistent proposals, I would never have written this contribution. Andreas Glausch pointed out weak points in a preliminary version of this paper, thus soliciting a comprehensive update, and – hopefully – a solid simplification. Chris George helped in polishing the English style. Thanks to all of them.

References

1. A. Blass and Y. Gurevich. Ordinary Small-Step Algorithms. *ACM Trans. Comput. Logic*, 7:2, 2006.
2. A. Blass, Y. Gurevich, D. Rosenzweig and B. Rossman. General Interactive Small-Step Algorithms. Technical report, Microsoft Research, August 2005.
3. E. Börger and R. Stärk. *Abstract State Machines - A Method for High-Level System Design and Analysis*. Springer, 2003.
4. G. Cantor. *Gesammelte Abhandlungen Mathematischen und Philosophischen Inhalts*. Berlin: Springer, 1932.
5. A.B. Cremers and T.N. Hibbard. Formal Modeling of Virtual Machines. *IEEE on Software Engineering*, SE-4 No 5:426–436, September 1978.

6. P. Dauchy and M.-C. Gaudel. Implicit state in algebraic specifications. In *ISCORE'93*, volume No 01/93 of *Informatik-Berichte*. Universität Hannover, U.W. Lipeck and G. Koschorreck, eds., 1993.

7. H. Ganzinger. Programs as Transformations of Algebraic Theories. In *11. GI-Jahrestagung*, volume 50 of Informatikfachberichte, W. Brauer, ed., pages 32–41. Springer, 1981.

8. H. Ganzinger. Denotational Semantics for Languages with Modules. In D. Bjørner, editor, *Formal Description of Programming Concepts – II*, pages 3–20. North-Holland, 1983.

9. M.-C. Gaudel and A. Zamulin. Imperative Algebraic Specifications. In *PSI'99, Novosibirsk, June 1999*, volume 1755 of *Lecture Notes in Computer Science*, pages 17–39. Springer, 2000.

10. A. Glausch and W. Reisig. Distributed Abstract State Machines and their Expressive Power. Technical Report 196, Humboldt-Universität zu Berlin, Institut für Informatik, Unter den Linden 6, 10099 Berlin, Germany http://www.informatik.hu-berlin.de/top, January 2006.

11. Y. Gurevich. Evolving Algebras 1993: Lipari Guide. In Egon Börger, editor, *Specification and Validation Methods*, pages 9–36. Oxford University Press, 1995.

12. Y. Gurevich. A new thesis. *American Mathematical Society Abstracts*, page 317, August 1985.

13. Y. Gurevich. Sequential Abstract State Machines Capture Sequential Algorithms. *ACM Transactions on Computational Logic*, 1(1):77–111, Juli 2000.

14. D.E. Knuth. *Art of Computer Programming, Volume 1: Fundamental Algorithms*. Addison-Wesley Professional, 1973.

15. L. Lamport. Time, clocks, and the ordering of events in a distributed system. *Communications of the ACM*, 21(7):558–565, 1978. Reprinted in several collections, including Distributed Computing: Concepts and Implementations, P.L. McEntire, J.G. O'Reilly, R.E .Laison, ed., IEEE Press, 1984.

16. A.R.J. Milner. Software Science: From Virtual to Reality. *Bulletin of the EATCS*, (87):12–16, 2005. EATCS Award Lecture.

17. C.A. Petri. Kommunikation mit Automaten. *Schriften des Institutes für Instrumentelle Mathematik Bonn*, 1962.

18. V.R. Pratt. Modeling concurrency with partial orders. *Intl. Journal of Parallel Programming*, 15(1):33–71, Feb 1986.

19. Wolfgang Reisig. On Gurevich's Theorem on Sequential Algorithms. *Acta Informatica*, 39(5):273–305, 2003.

20. A. Tarski. Contributions to the theory of models I. *Indagationes Mathematicae*, 16:572–581, 1954.

21. E. Zucca. From Static to Dynamic Abstract Data-Types. In A. Szalas and W. Penczek, editors, *MFCS 96*, volume 1113 of *Lecture Notes in Computer Science*, pages pp 579–590, 1996.

ASM Indexes

The event-B Modelling Method: Concepts and Case Studies

Dominique Cansell[1] and Dominique Méry[2]

[1] LORIA, Campus scientifique, BP 239, F-54506 Vandoeuvre-lés-Nancy CEDEX, France (also at: Université de Metz), Dominique.Cansell@loria.fr
[2] LORIA, Campus scientifique, and Université Henri Poincaré Nancy 1, BP 239, F-54506 Vandoeuvre-lés-Nancy, France, Dominique.Mery@loria.fr

1 Introduction

1.1 Overview of B

Classical B is a state-based method developed by Abrial for specifying, designing and coding software systems. It is based on Zermelo–Fraenkel set theory with the axiom of choice. Sets are used for data modelling, *generalised substitutions* are used to describe state modifications, the refinement calculus is used to relate models at varying levels of abstraction, and there are a number of structuring mechanisms (machine, refinement and implementation) which are used in the organisation of a development. The first version of the B method is extensively described in The B Book [2]. It is supported by the Atelier B tool [50] and by the B Toolkit [78].

Central to the classical B approach is the idea of a software operation which will perform according to a given specification if called within a given pre-condition. Subsequent to the formulation of the classical approach, Abrial and others have developed a more general approach in which the notion of *event* is fundamental. An event has a firing condition (a guard) as opposed to a pre-condition. It may fire when its guard is true. Event-based models have proved useful in requirements analysis, in modelling distributed systems and in the discovery/design of both distributed and sequential programming algorithms.

After extensive experience with B, current work by Abrial has proposed a formulation of a second version of the method [4]. This distills experience gained with the event-based approach and provides a general framework for the development of *discrete systems*. Although this widens the scope of the method, the mathematical foundations of both versions of the method are the same.

1.2 Proof-based Development

Proof-based development methods [2, 15, 86] integrate formal proof techniques into the development of software systems. The main idea is to start with a very abstract model of the system under development. Details are gradually added to this first model by building a sequence of more concrete models. The relationship between two successive models in this sequence is that of *refinement* [2, 15, 17, 47]. The essence of the refinement relationship is that it preserves already proved *system properties* including safety properties and termination.

A development process gives rise to a number of *proof obligations*, which guarantee its correctness. Such proof obligations are discharged by the proof tool using automatic and interactive proof procedures supported by a proof engine [50, 51].

At the most abstract level, it is obligatory to describe the static properties of a model's data by means of an *invariant* predicate. This gives rise to proof obligations relating to the consistency of the model. These are required to ensure that data properties which are claimed to be invariant are preserved by the events or operations of the model. Each refinement step is associated with a further invariant which relates the data of the more concrete model to those of the abstract model and states any additional invariant properties of the (possibly richer) concrete data model. These invariants, so-called *gluing invariants* are used in the formulation of the proof obligations of the refinement.

The goal of a B development is to obtain a *proved model*. Since the development process leads to a large number of proof obligations, the mastering of proof complexity is a crucial issue. Even if a proof tool is available, its effective power is limited by classical results over logical theories and we must distribute the complexity of the proofs over the components of the current development process, for example by refinement. Refinement has the potential to decrease the complexity of the proof process whilst allowing for traceability of requirements.

B models rarely need to make assumptions about the *size* of a system being modelled, for example the number of nodes in a network. This is in contrast to model-checking approaches [49]. The price to be paid is that we face possibly complex mathematical theories and difficult proofs. The reuse of developed models and the structuring mechanisms available in B help in decreasing the complexity. Where B has been exercised on known difficult problems, the result has often been a simpler proof development than has been achieved by users of other more monolithic techniques [85].

1.3 Scope of Modelling in B

The scope of the B method concerns the complete process of software and system development. Initially, the B method was restricted mainly to the development of software systems [20, 66, 74] but a wider scope for the method has emerged with the incorporation of the event-based approach [3, 4, 13, 31, 33, 99] and is related to the systematic derivation of reactive distributed systems. Events are expressed simply in the rich syntax of the B language. Abrial and Mussat [13] introduced elements to handle liveness properties. Refinement in the event-based B method does not deal with fairness constraints but introduces explicit counters to ensure the happening of abstract events, while new events are introduced in the refined model. Among several case studies developed in B, we can mention the METEOR project [20] for controlling train traffic, the PCI protocol [36] and the IEEE 1394 Tree Identify Protocol [10]. Finally, B has been combined with CSP for handling communications systems [30, 31], and has also been combined with action systems [33, 99].

The proposed second version of B can be compared to action systems [16], UNITY programs [47] and TLA [71] specifications, but there is no notion of abstract fairness like that in TLA or UNITY.

1.4 Related Techniques

The B method is a state-based method integrating set theory, predicate calculus and generalized substitution language. We now briefly compare with some related notations.

Like Z [100] (see also the chapter by Henson et al. in this book [65]), B is based on the ZF set theory; the two notations share the same roots, but we can point to a number of interesting differences. Z expresses a state change by use of before and after predicates, whereas the predicate transformer semantics of B allows a notation which is closer to programming. Invariants in Z are incorporated into operation descriptions and alter their meaning, whereas an invariant in B is checked against the state changes described by the operations and events to ensure consistency. Finally B makes a careful distinction between the logical properties of pre-conditions and guards, which are not clearly distinguished in Z.

The refinement calculus used in B for defining refinement between models in the event-based B approach is very close to Back's action systems, but tool support for action systems appears to be less mechanized than that for B.

TLA$^+$ [72] (see also the chapter by Merz in this book [83]) can be compared to B, since it includes set theory with the ϵ operator of Hilbert. The semantics of TLA temporal operators is expressed over traces of states whereas the semantics of B actions is expressed in the weakest precondition calculus. Both semantics are equivalent with respect to safety properties, but the trace semantics of TLA$^+$ allows an expression of fairness and eventuality properties that is not directly available in B.

VDM [69] (see also the chapter by Fitzgerald in this book [58]) is a method with similar objectives to classical B. Like B, it uses partial functions to model data, which can lead to meaningless terms and predicates, for example when a function is a applied outside its domain. VDM uses a special three-valued logic to deal with indefiniteness. B retains classical two-valued logic, which simplifies proofs at the expense of requiring more care with indefiniteness. Recent approaches to this problem will be mentioned later.

The ASM method [34, 62] (see also the chapter by Reisig in this book [95]) and B share common objectives related to the design and analysis of (software/hardware) systems. Both methods bridge the gap between human understanding and formulation of real-world problems and the deployment of their computer-based solutions. Each has a simple scientific foundation: B is based on set theory, and the ASM method is based on the algebraic framework with an abstract state change mechanism. An ASM is defined by a signature, an abstract state, a finite collection of rules and a specific rule; rules provide an operational style that is very useful for modelling specification and programming mechanisms. Like B, ASM includes a refinement relation for the incremental design of systems; the tool support of ASM is under development but it allows one to verify and to analyse ASMs. In applications, B seems to be more mature than ASM, even though the latter has several real successes such as the validation [101] of Java and the Java Virtual Machine.

1.5 Summary of Chapter

The following sections provide a short description of event B:

- The B language and elements on the classical B method: syntax and semantics of operations, events, assertions, predicates, machines, models.
- The B modelling language and a simple introductory example: event B, refinement, proof-based development.
- The other sections illustrate the event B modelling method by case studies:
  - sequential algorithms;
  - combining coordination and refinement for sorting;
  - spanning-trees algorithms;
  - a distributed leader election algorithm.
- The final section concludes the chapter with some words on B modelling techniques and ongoing research.

2 The B Language

2.1 The B Language for Sets, Predicates and Logical Structures

The development of a model starts with an analysis of its mathematical structure, i.e., sets, constants and properties over sets and constants, and we produce the mathematical landscape by requirements elicitation. However, the statement of the mathematical properties can be expressed using various assumed properties, for instance, a constant n may be a natural number and may be required to be greater than 3, which is classically and formally written as $n \in \mathbb{N} \wedge n \geq 3$, or a set of *persons* may be required not empty, which is classically and formally written as *persons* $\neq \emptyset$. Abrial et al. [9] have developed a *structure language* which allows one to encode mathematical structures and their accompanying theorems. Structures improve the possibility of mechanized proofs, but they are not yet in the current version of the B tools; there is a close connection with structuring mechanisms and the algebraic structures [57], but the main difference is in the use of sets rather than of abstract data types. The mathematical structures of B are built using the notation of set theory, and we list the main notation used (and its meaning) below; the complete notation is described in The B Book [2].

Sets and Predicates

Constants can be defined using first-order logic and the set-theoretical notation of B. A set can be defined using either the comprehension schema $\{\, x \mid x \in s \wedge P(x)\}$, or the Cartesian product schema $s \times t$ or using operators over sets such power $\mathbb{P}(s)$, intersection $\cap$ and union $\cup$. $y \in s$ is a predicate which can sometimes be simplified either from $y \in \{\, x \mid x \in s \wedge P(x)\}$ into $y \in s \wedge P(y)$, or from $x \mapsto y \in s \times t$ into $x \in s \wedge y \in t$, or from $t \in \mathbb{P}(s)$ into $\forall x . (\, x \in t \Rightarrow x \in s)$, where x is a fresh variable. A pair is denoted by either $(\, x , y\,)$ or $x \mapsto y$.

A relation over two sets s and t is an element of $\mathbb{P}(s \times t)$; a relation r has a domain dom(r) and a co-domain ran(r). A function f from the set s to the set t is a relation such that each element of dom(f) is related to at most one element of the set t.

A function f is either partial $f \in A \nrightarrow B$, or total $f \in A \rightarrow B \rightarrow$. Then, we can define the term $f(x)$ for every element x in dom(f) using the choice function $(f(x) = \text{choice}(f[\{x\}])$ where $f[\{x\}]$ is the subset of t, whose elements are related to x by f. The choice function assumes that there exists at least one element in the set, which is not the case for the ϵ operator which can be applied to an empty set $\emptyset$ and returns some value. If $x \mapsto y \in f$ then $y = f(x)$ and $f(x)$, is well defined, only if f is a function and x is in dom(f).

We summarize in Table 1 the set-theoretical notation that can be used in the writing of formal definitions related to constants. In fact, the modelling of data is oriented towards sets, relations and functions; the task of the specifier is to use the notation effectively.

A Simple Case Study

Since we have only a small amount of space for explaining the concepts of B, we shall use a very simple case study, namely the development of models for computing the *factorial* function; we can illustrate the expressivity of the B language for predicates. Other case studies can be found in earlier publications (see for instance, [2, 3, 8, 10, 11, 36, 40, 41]). When considering the definition of a function, we can use various styles to characterize it. A function is mathematically defined as a (binary) relation over two sets, called the source and

Name	Syntax	Definition
Binary relation	$s \leftrightarrow t$	$\mathcal{P}(s \times t)$
Composition of relations	$r_1; r_2$	$\{x, y \mid x \in a \ \wedge \ y \in b \ \wedge$
		$\exists z.(z \in c \ \wedge \ x, z \in r_1 \ \wedge \ z, y \in r_2)\}$
Inverse relation	r^{-1}	$\{x, y \mid x \in \mathcal{P}(a) \ \wedge \ y \in \mathcal{P}(b) \ \wedge \ y, x \in r\}$
Domain	$\mathrm{dom}(r)$	$\{a \mid a \in s \ \wedge \ \exists b.(b \in t \ \wedge \ a \mapsto b \in r)\}$
Range	$\mathrm{ran}(r)$	$\mathrm{dom}(r^{-1})$
Identity	$\mathrm{id}(s)$	$\{x, y \mid x \in s \ \wedge \ y \in s \ \wedge \ x = y\}$
Restriction	$s \lhd r$	$\mathrm{id}(s); r$
Co-restriction	$r \rhd s$	$r; \ \mathrm{id}(s)$
Anti-restriction	$s \lhd\!\!\!- r$	$(\mathrm{dom}(r) - s) \lhd r$
Anti-co-restriction	$r \rhd\!\!\!- s$	$r \rhd (\mathrm{ran}(r) - s)$
Image	$r[w]$	$\mathrm{ran}(w \lhd r)$
Overriding	$q \lhd\!\!\!- r$	$(\mathrm{dom}(r) \lhd\!\!\!- q) \cup r$
Partial function	$s \nrightarrow t$	$\{r \mid r \in s \leftrightarrow t \ \wedge \ (r^{-1}; r) \subseteq \mathrm{id}(t)\}$

Table 1. Set-theoretical notation

the target and it satisfies the *functionality property*. The set-theoretical framework of B invites us to follow this method for defining functions; however, a recursive definition of a given function is generally used. The recursive definition states that a given mathematical object exists and that it is the least solution of a fixed-point equation. Hence, the first step of a B development proves that the function defined by a relation is the least fixed-point of the given equation. Properties of the function might be assumed, but we prefer to advocate a style of *fully proved development* with respect to a minimal set of assumptions. The first step enumerates a list of basic properties considered as axioms and the final step reaches a point where both definitions are proved to be equivalent.

First, we define the mathematical function *factorial*, in a classical way: the first line states that *factorial* is a total function from $\mathbb{N}$ into $\mathbb{N}$, and the subsequent lines state that *factorial* satisfies a fixed-point equation and, by default, this is assumed to be the least fixed-point:

$$factorial \in \mathbb{N} \longrightarrow \mathbb{N} \wedge$$
$$factorial(0) = 1 \wedge$$
$$\forall n.(n \geq 0 \Rightarrow factorial(n + 1) = (n + 1) \times factorial(n))$$

factorial is a B *constant* and has B *properties*.

In previous work on B [38], we used this definition and wrote it as a B property (a logical assumption or an axiom of the current theory) but nothing tells us that the definition is consistent and that it defines an *existing* function. A solution is to define the *factorial* function using a fixed-point schema such that the *factorial* function is the least fixed-point of the given equation over relations. The *factorial* function is the smallest relation satisfying some conditions and, especially, functionality; the functionality is stated as a *logical consequence* of the B properties. The point is not new, but it allows us to introduce students to some ideas that put together fixed-point theory, set theory, theory of relations and functions, and the process of validation by proof (mechanically done by a prover). The computation of the *factorial* function starts with a definition of the *factorial* function which is carefully and formally justified using the theorem prover. *factorial* is still a B constant but it is defined differently.

The *factorial* function is a relation over natural numbers and it is defined by its graph over pairs of natural numbers:

(AXIOMS OR B PROPERTIES)

$$
\begin{array}{l}
factorial \ \in \ \mathbb{N} \ \leftrightarrow \ \mathbb{N} \ \wedge \\
0 \ \mapsto \ 1 \ \in \ factorial \ \wedge \\
\forall (n, fn) \cdot \left(\begin{array}{l} n \mapsto fn \in factorial \\ \Rightarrow \\ n + 1 \mapsto (n+1) \times fn \in factorial \end{array} \right)
\end{array}
$$

The *factorial* function satisfies the fixed-point equation and is the least fixed-point:

(AXIOMS OR B PROPERTIES)

$$
\forall f \cdot \left(\begin{array}{l} \left(\begin{array}{l} f \in \mathbb{N} \ \leftrightarrow \ \mathbb{N} \ \wedge \\ 0 \ \mapsto \ 1 \ \in \ f \ \wedge \\ \forall (n, fn).(n \mapsto fn \in f \Rightarrow n + 1 \mapsto (n+1) \times fn \in f) \end{array} \right) \\ \Rightarrow \\ factorial \subseteq f \end{array} \right)
$$

The statements above are B properties of the *factorial* function, and from these B properties, we can derive the functionality of the resulting least fixed-point: *factorial is a function* is a logical consequence of the new definition of *factorial*:

(CONSEQUENCES OR B ASSERTIONS)

$$
\begin{array}{l}
factorial \ \in \ \mathbb{N} \ \longrightarrow \ \mathbb{N} \ \wedge \\
factorial(0) = 1 \ \wedge \\
\forall n.(n \ \in \ \mathbb{N} \ \Rightarrow \ factorial(n+1) = (n+1) \times factorial(n))
\end{array}
$$

Now, *factorial* has been proved to be a function and no assumption concerning the functionality has been left unspecified or simply an assumption. Proofs are carried out using first-order predicate calculus together with set theory and arithmetic. When we have proved that *factorial* is a function, this means that every derived property can be effectively obtained by a mechanical process of proof; the proof can be reused in another case study, if necessary. The proof is an application of the induction principle; every inductive property mentions a property over values of the underlying structure, namely $\mathcal{P}(n)$; hence we should quantify over predicates and derive theorems in higher-order logic [9]. Using a quantification over subsets of a set, we can get higher order theorems. For instance, $\mathcal{P}(n)$ is represented by the set $\{n|n \in NATURAL \ \wedge \ \mathcal{P}(n)\}$, and the inductive property can be stated as follows; here, the first expression is given in the B language and the second expression (equivalent to the first is given) in classical mathematical notation (succ denotes the successor function defined over natural numbers):

B statement	**classical logical statement**
$\forall P \cdot \begin{pmatrix} P \subseteq \mathbb{N} \wedge \\ 0 \in P \wedge \\ \text{succ}[P] \subseteq P \\ \Rightarrow \\ \mathbb{N} \subseteq P) \end{pmatrix}$	$\forall \mathcal{P} \cdot \begin{pmatrix} \mathcal{P}(n) \ \text{a property on } \mathbb{N} \wedge \\ \mathcal{P}(0) \wedge \\ \forall n \geq 0 \cdot (\mathcal{P}(n) \ \Rightarrow \ \mathcal{P}(n+1)) \\ \Rightarrow \\ \forall n \geq 0 \cdot \mathcal{P}(n) \end{pmatrix}$

The higher-order aspect is achieved by the use of set theory, which offers the possibility to *quantify over all the subsets of a set*. Such quantification indeed give s the possibility to climb up to higher-order in a way that is always framed.

The structure language introduced by Abrial et al. [9] can be useful for providing the ability to reuse already formally validated properties. It is then clear that the first step of our modelling process is an analysis of the mathematical landscape. An analysis of properties is essential when dealing with the indefiniteness of expressions, and the work of Abrial et al. [9] and the doctoral thesis of Burdy [29] propose different ways to deal with this question. For instance, the existence of a function such as *factorial* may appear obvious, but the technique of modelling might lead to silly models if no proof of definiteness is done. In the proof of the functionality of *factorial*, it is necessary to instantiate the variable P in the inductive property by the following set:

$$\{n|n \in \mathbb{N} \ \wedge \ 0..n \ \lhd \ factorial \ \in \ 0..n \ \longrightarrow \ \mathbb{N}\}$$

Now, we consider the structures in B used for organizing axioms, definitions, theorems and theories.

Logical Structures in B

The B language of predicates, denoted $\mathcal{BP}$, for expressing data and properties combines set theory and first-order predicate calculus with a simple arithmetic theory. The B environment can be used to derive theorems from axioms; B provides a simple way to express axioms and theorems using abstract machines without variables. This is a way to use the underlying B prover and to implement the proof process that we have described.

An abstract machine has a name m; the clause SETS contains definitions of the sets in the problem; and the clause CONSTANTS allows one to introduce information related to the mathematical structure of the problem to be solved.

```
MACHINE
  m
SETS
  s
CONSTANTS
  c
PROPERTIES
  P(s, c)
ASSERTIONS
  A(x)
END
```

The clause PROPERTIES contains the effective definitions of constants: it is very important to list carefully the properties of constants in a way that can be easily used by a tool. The clause ASSERTIONS contains the list of theorems to be discharged by the proof engine. The proof process is based on sequent calculus; the prover provides (semi-)decision procedures [50] for proving the validity of a given logical fact, called a sequent and allows one to build the proof interactively by applying possible rules of sequent calculus.

For instance, the machine FACTORIAL_DEF introduces a new constant called $factorial$ satisfying the properties given above. The functionality of $factorial$ is derived from the assumptions in the clause ASSERTIONS.

MACHINE
  $FACTORIAL\_DEF$
CONSTANTS
  $factorial$
PROPERTIES
  $factorial \in \mathbb{N} \leftrightarrow \mathbb{N} \wedge$
  $0 \mapsto 1 \in factorial \wedge$
  $\forall (n, fn).(n \mapsto fn \in factorial \Rightarrow n + 1 \mapsto (n + 1) \times fn \in factorial) \wedge$
  $$\forall f \cdot \left(\begin{array}{l} f \in \mathbb{N} \leftrightarrow \mathbb{N} \wedge \\ 0 \mapsto 1 \in f \wedge \\ \forall (n, fn).(n \mapsto fn \in f \Rightarrow n + 1 \mapsto (n + 1) \times fn \in f) \\ \Rightarrow \\ factorial \subseteq f \end{array} \right)$$
ASSERTIONS
  $factorial \in \mathbb{N} \longrightarrow \mathbb{N}$;
  $factorial(0) = 1$;
  $\forall n.(n \in \mathbb{N} \Rightarrow factorial(n + 1) = (n + 1) \times factorial(n))$
END

The interactive prover breaks a sequent into simpler-to-prove sequents, but the user must know the global structure of the final proof. $\mathcal{BP}$ allows us to define the underlying mathematical structures required for a given problem;

now we shall describe how to specify states and how to describe *transitions* over *states*.

2.2 The B Language of Transitions

The B language is not restricted to classical set-theoretical notation and sequent calculus; it includes notation for defining *transitions* over *states* of the model, called *generalized substitutions*. In its simple form, $x := E(x)$, a generalized substitution looks like an assignment; the B language of generalized substitutions called GSL (Generalized Substitution Language) (see Fig. 2) contains syntactical structures for expressing different kinds of (state) transitions. The generalized substitutions of GSL allow us to write *operations* in the classical B approach [2]; a restriction of GSL leads to *events* in the *event-based B approach* [4, 13]. In the following subsubsections, we address the semantic issues of generalized substitutions and the differences between *operations* and *events*.

Generalized Substitutions

Generalized substitutions provide a way to express transformations of the state variables of a given model. In the construct $x := E(x)$, x denotes a vector of state variables of the model, and $E(x)$ a vector of expressions of the same size as the vector x. The interpretation we shall give here to this statement is *not* however, that of an assignment statement. The class of generalized substitutions contains the following possible forms of generalized substitution:

- $x := E$ (assignment).
- **skip** (stuttering).
- $P|S$ (precondition) (or **pre** P **then** S **end**).
- $S \square T$ (bounded choice) (or **choice** S_1 **or** S_2 **END**).
- $P \Rightarrow S$ (guard) (or **select** (*or* **when**) P **then** S **end**).
- $@z.S$ (unbounded choice).
- $x :\in S$ (set choice), $x : R(x_0, x)$, $x : |R(x_0, x)$ (generalized assignment).
- $S_1; S_2$ (sequencing).
- **while** B **do** S **invariant** J **variant** V **end**.

The meaning of a generalized substitution S is defined in the weakest-precondition calculus [55, 56] by the predicate transformer $\lambda P \in \mathcal{BP}.[S]P$, where $[S]P$ means that S *establishes* P. Intuitively, this means that every *accepted* execution of S, starting from a state s satisfying $[S]P$, terminates in a state satisfying P; certain substitutions can be *feasibly* executed (or accepted for execution) by any physical computational device; this means also that S terminates for every state of $[S]P$. The weakest-precondition operator has properties related to implication over predicates: $\lambda P \in \mathcal{BP}.[S]P$ is monotonic with respect to implication, and it is distributive with respect to the conjunction of predicates. The properties of the weakest-precondition operator have been known, since the work of Dijkstra [55, 56] on the semantics defined by predicate transformers. The definition of $\lambda P \in \mathcal{BP}.[S]P$ is inductively expressed over the syntax of B predicates and the syntax of generalized substitutions. $[S]P$ can be reduced to a B predicate, which is used by the proof-obligations generator. Table 2 contains the inductive definition of $[S]P$.

Name	Generalized substitution S	$[S]P$
Assignment	$x := E$	$P(E/x)$
Skip	$skip$	P
Parallel composition	$x := E \| y := F$	$[x, y := E, F]P$
Non-deterministic choice	$x :\in S$	$\forall v.(v \in S \Rightarrow P(v/x))$
Relational assignment	$x : R(x_0, x)$	$\forall v.(R(x_0, v) \Rightarrow P(v/x))$
Unbounded choice	$@x.S$	$\forall x.[S]P$
Bounded choice	**choice** S_1 **or** S_2 **end** (*or equivalently* $S_1 \| S_2$)	$[S_1]P \ \wedge \ [S_2]P$
Guard	**select** G **then** T **end** (*or equivalently* $G \Longrightarrow S_2$)	$G \Rightarrow [T]P$
Precondition	**pre** G **then** T **end** (*or equivalently* $G \| T$)	$G \ \wedge \ [T]P$
Generalized guard	**any** t **where** G **then** T **end**	$\forall t \cdot (G \Rightarrow [T]P)$
Sequential composition	$S; T$	$[S][T]P$

Table 2. Definitions of GSL and $[S]P$

We say that two substitutions S_1 and S_2 are equivalent, denoted $S_1 = S_2$, if for any predicate P of the B language, $[S_1]P \equiv [S_2]P$. This relation defines a way to compare substitutions. Abrial [2] proved a theorem for the normalized form related to any substitution; this proves that a substitution is characterized by a precondition and a computation relation over variables.

Theorem 1. *[2]*

For any substitution S, there exist two predicates P and Q where x' is not free in P, such that $S = P | @x'.(Q \Longrightarrow x := x')$.

This theorem tells us the importance of the precondition of a substitution, which should be true when the substitution is applied to the current state, otherwise the resulting state is not consistent with the transformation. Q is a relation between the initial state x and the next state x'. In fact, a substitution should be applied to a state satisfying the invariant and should preserve it. Intuitively, this means that, when one applies the substitution, one has to check that the initial state is correct. The weakest-precondition operator allows us to define specific conditions over substitutions:

- Aborted computations: $\mathsf{abt}(S) \overset{def}{=}$ *for any predicate* $R, \neg[S]R$; *this defines the set of states that cannot establish any predicate* R *and that are the non-terminating states.*
- Terminating computations: $\mathsf{trm}(S) \overset{def}{=} \neg\mathsf{abt}(S)$ *this defines the termination condition for the substitution* S.
- Miraculous computations: $\mathsf{mir}(S) \overset{def}{=}$ *for any predicate* $R, [S]R$; *this means that among the states, some states may establish every predicate* R, *for instance* $FALSE$. *These are called miraculous states, since they establish a miracle.*
- Feasible computations: $\mathsf{fis}(S) \overset{def}{=} \neg\mathsf{mir}(S)$. *Miraculous states correspond to non-feasible computations, and the feasibility condition ensures that the computation is realistic.*

Terminating computations and feasible computations play a central role in the analysis of generalized substitutions. Tables 3 and 4 provide two lists of rules for simplifying $\mathsf{trm}(S)$ and $\mathsf{fis}(S)$ into the B predicate language; the two lists are not complete (see [2] for complete lists).

Generalized substitution S	$\mathsf{trm}(S)$
$x := E$	$TRUE$
$skip$	$TRUE$
$x :\in S$	$TRUE$
$x : R(x_0, x)$	$TRUE$
$@x.S$	$\forall x.\mathsf{trm}(S)$
choice S_1 **or** S_2 **end** (*or equivalently* $S_1 \| S_2$)	$\mathsf{trm}(S_1) \ \wedge \ \mathsf{trm}(S_2)$
select G **then** T **end** (*or equivalently* $G \Longrightarrow S_2$)	$G \ \Rightarrow \ \mathsf{trm}(T)$
pre G **then** T **end** (*or equivalently* $G\|T$)	$G \ \wedge \ \mathsf{trm}(T)$
any t **where** G **then** T **end**	$\forall t \cdot (G \ \Rightarrow \ \mathsf{trm}(T))$

Table 3. Examples of definitions for $\mathsf{trm}(S)$

For instance, $\mathsf{fis}(\textbf{select}\ FALSE\ \textbf{then}\ x := 0\ \textbf{end})$ is $FALSE$ and $\mathsf{mir}(\textbf{select}\ FALSE\ \textbf{then}\ x := 0\ \textbf{end})$ is $TRUE$. The substitution $\textbf{select}\ FALSE\ \textbf{then}\ x := 0\ \textbf{end}$ establishes any predicate and is not feasible. We cannot implement such a substitution in a programming language.

A relational predicate can be defined using the weakest-precondition semantics, namely $\mathsf{prd}_x(S)$, by the expression $\neg[S](x \neq x')$ which is the relation characterizing the computations of S. Table 5 contains a list of definitions of the predicate with respect to the syntax.

The next property is proved by Abrial and shows the relationship between weakest-precondition and relational semantics. Predicates $\mathsf{trm}(S)$ and $\mathsf{prd}_x(S)$ are respectively defined in Tables 3 and 5, respectively.

Generalized substitution S	fis(S)
$x := E$	$TRUE$
$skip$	$TRUE$
$x :\in S$	$S \neq \emptyset$
$x : R(x_0, x)$	$\exists v.(R(x_0, v)$
$@x.S$	$\exists x.\text{fis}(S)$
choice S_1 **or** S_2 **end** (*or equivalently* $S_1 \| S_2$)	fis(S_1) $\vee$ fis(S_2)
select G **then** T **end** (*or equivalently* $G \Longrightarrow S_2$)	$G \wedge$ fis(T)
pre G **then** T **end** (*or equivalently* $G|T$)	$G \Rightarrow$ fis(T)
any t **where** G **then** T **end**	$\exists t \cdot (G \wedge$ fis(T))

Table 4. Examples of definitions for fis(S)

Generalized substitution S	$\text{prd}_x(S)$
$x := E$	$x' = E$
$skip$	$x' = x$
$x :\in S$	$x' \in S$
$x : R(x_0, x)$	$R(x, x')$
$@z.S$	$\exists z.\text{prd}_x(S)$ *if* $z \neq x'$
choice S_1 **or** S_2 **end** (*or equivalently* $S_1 \| S_2$)	$\text{prd}_x(S_1)$ $\vee$ $\text{prd}_x(S_2)$
select G **then** T **end** (*or equivalently* $G \Longrightarrow S_2$)	$G \wedge \text{prd}_x(T)$
pre G **then** T **end** (*or equivalently* $G|T$)	$G \Rightarrow \text{prd}_x(T)$
any t **where** G **then** T **end**	$\exists t \cdot (G \wedge \text{prd}_x(T))$

Table 5. Examples of definitions for $\text{prd}_x(S)$

Theorem 2. *[2]*
   For any substitution S, we have: $S = trm(S)|@x'.(prd_x(S) \Longrightarrow x := x')$

Both of the theorems above emphasize the roles of the precondition and the relation in the semantic definition of a substitution. The refinement of two substitutions can be defined simply using the weakest-precondition calculus as follows: S is refined by T (written $S \sqsubseteq T$), if for any predicate P, $[S]P \Rightarrow [T]P$. We can give an equivalent version of this refinement that shows that it decreases the non-determinism. Let us define the following sets: $\text{pre}(S) = \{x|x \in s \wedge \text{trm}(S)\}$, $\text{rel}(S) = \{x, x'|x \in s \wedge x' \in s \wedge \text{prd}_x(S)\}$ and $\text{dom}(S) = \{x|x \in s \wedge \text{fis}(S)\}$, where s is assumed to be the global set of states.

   The refinement can be defined equivalently using the set-theoretical version: S is refined by T if, and only if, $\text{pre}(S) \subseteq \text{pre}(T)$ and $\text{rel}(T) \subseteq \text{rel}(S)$.

We can also use the previous notation and define equivalently the refinement of two substitutions by the expression $\mathsf{trm}(S) \Rightarrow \mathsf{trm}(T)$ and $\mathsf{prd}_x(T) \Rightarrow \mathsf{prd}_x(S)$. The predicate $\mathsf{prd}_x(S)$ relates S to a relation over x and x'; this means that a substitution can be seen as something like a relation over pairs of states.

The weakest-precondition semantics over generalized substitutions provides the semantic foundation for the generator of proof obligations; in the following subsubsections we introduce operations and events, which are two ways to use the B method.

Operations and Events

Generalized substitutions are used to construct *operations* of *abstract machines* or *events* of *abstract models*. Both of these notions will be detailed in Sect. 3.1. However, we should explain the difference between them here. An (abstract) machine is a structure with a part defining data (SETS, CONSTANTS, and PROPERTIES), a part defining state (VARIABLES and INVARIANT) and a part defining operations (OPERATIONS and INITIALISATION); it gives its potential user the ability to only activate the operations, not to access its state directly, and this aspect is very important for refining the machine by making changes of variables and of operations, while keeping their names. An operation has a precondition, and the precondition should be true when one calls the operation. Operations are characterized by generalized substitutions, and their semantics is based on the semantics of generalized substitutions (either in the weakest-precondition-based style or in the relational style). This means that the condition of preservation of the invariant (or proof obligation) is written simply as follows:

$$I \wedge \mathsf{trm}(O) \Rightarrow [O]I \qquad (1)$$

If one calls the operation when the precondition is false, any state can be reached, and the invariant is not ensured. The style of programming is called *generous*, but it assumes that an operation is always called when the precondition is true. An operation can have input and output parameters and it is called in a state satisfying the invariant, it is a passive object, since it requires to be called to have an effect.

On the other hand, an event has a guard and is triggered in a state that validates the guard. Both the operation and the event have a name, but an event has no input and output parameters. An event may be observed or not observed, and possible changes of variables should maintain the invariant of the current model: this style is called *defensive*. Like an operation, an event is characterized by a generalized substitution and can be defined by a relation over variables and primed variables: a before–after predicate, denoted $BA(e)(x, x')$. An event is essentially a reactive object and reacts with respect to its guard $\mathsf{grd}(e)(x)$. However, there is a restriction over the language GSL used for defining events and we authorize only three kinds of generalized substitution (see Table 6). In the definition of an event, three basic substitutions are used to write an event $(x := E(x), x : \in S(x), x : P(x_0, x))$, and the last substitution is the normal form of the three. An event should be *feasible*, and the feasibility is related to the feasibility of the generalized substitution of the event: some next state must be reachable from the given state. Since events are reactive objects, the related proof obligations should guarantee that the current state satisfying the invariant will be feasible. Table 7 contains the definitions of the guards of events. We have left the classical abstract machines of the B classical approach and are illustrating the modelling of systems through events and models.

When using the relational style for defining the semantics of events, we use the style advocated by Lamport [71] in TLA; an event is seen as a transformation between states before the transformation and states after the transformation. Lamport used the priming of variables to separate "before" values from "after" values. Using this notation and supposing that x_0 denotes the value of x before the transition of an event, events can obtain a semantics defined over the primed and unprimed variables in Table 6. The before-after predicate is already defined in The B Book as the predicate $\mathsf{prd}_x(S)$ defined for every substitution S [2, Sect. 2.2]. Merz introduces the TLA/TLA$^+$ modelling language in Chap. 8 of this volume ([83]).

Event : E	Before-After Predicate
begin $x : P(x_0, x)$ **end**	$P(x, x')$
when $G(x)$ **then** $x : P(x_0, x)$ **end**	$G(x) \ \wedge \ P(x, x')$
any t **where** $G(t, x)$ **then** $x : P(x_0, x, t)$ **end**	$\exists t \cdot (G(t, x) \ \wedge \ P(x, x', t))$

Table 6. Definitions of events and before–after predicates of events

Event : E	Guard: grd(E)
begin S **end**	$TRUE$
when $G(x)$ **then** T **end**	$G(x)$
any t **where** $G(t, x)$ **then** T **end**	$\exists t \cdot G(t, x)$

Table 7. Definition of events and guards of events

Any event e has a guard defining the enabledness condition over the current state, and this guard expresses the existence of a next state. For instance, the disjunction of all guards is used for strengthening the invariant of a B system of events to include the freedom of the current model from deadlock. Before we introduce B models, we give the expression stating the preservation of a property (or proof obligation) by a given event e:

$$I(x) \ \Rightarrow \ [e] \ I(x) \tag{2}$$

or, equivalently, in a relational style,

$$I(x) \quad \wedge \quad BA(e)(x, x') \;\Rightarrow\; I(x') \tag{3}$$

$BA(e)(x, x')$ is the before–after relation of the event e, and $I(x)$ is a state predicate over variables x. Equation (1) states the proof obligation of the operation O using the weakest-precondition operator, and equation (3) defines the proof obligation for the preservation of $I(x)$, while e is observed. Since the two approaches are semantically equivalent, the proof-obligations generator of Atelier B can be reused for generating those assertions in the B environment.

The SELECT event is expressed by the previous notation for the WHEN event; both are equivalent. However, the WHEN notation captures the idea of reactivity of guarded events; $B^\sharp$ [4, 67] provides other notation for combining events. The event-B notation is enriched by the notation **begin** x : $|\ P(x_0, x)$ **end**, which means that the value of the variable x is set to any value such that $P(x_0, x)$ where x_0 is the value of x before the event. In the next subsection, we give details of abstract machines and abstract models, which use operations and events.

3 B Models

3.1 Modelling Systems

The systems under consideration are software systems, control systems, protocols, sequential and distributed algorithms, operating systems and circuits; they are generally very complex and have parts interacting with an environment. A discrete abstraction of such a system constitutes an adequate framework: such an abstraction is called a *discrete model*. A discrete model is more generally known as a *discrete transition system* and provides a view of the current system; the development of a model in B follows an incremental process validated by the refinement. A system is modelled by a sequence of models related by the refinement and managed in a project.

A project [2, 4] in B contains information for editing, proving, analysing, mapping and exporting models or components. A B component has two separate forms: the first form concerns the development of software models, and these B components are *abstract machines, refinements and implementations*; the second form is related to modelling reactive systems using the event-based B approach, and the B components are simply called *models*. Each form corresponds to a specific approach to developing B components; the first form is fully supported by the B tools [50, 78], and the second is partly supported [50]. In the following subsubsections, we overview each approach based on the same logical and mathematical concepts.

Modelling Systems in the Classical B Approach

The B method [2] has historically been applied to software systems and has helped in developing safe software for controlling trains [20]. The scope of the method is not restricted to the specification step but includes facilities for designing larger models or machines gathered together in a project. The basic model is called an *abstract machine* and is defined in the A(bstract) M(achine) N(otation) language. We describe an abstract machine in Table. 8. An abstract machine encapsulates variables defining the state of the system; the state should conform to the invariant and each operation should be called when the current state satisfies the invariant. Each operation should preserve the invariant when it is called.

An operation may have input/output parameters and only operations can change state variables. An abstract machine looks like a desk calculator and each time a user presses the button for an operation, it should be checked that the precondition of the operation is true, otherwise no preservation of the invariant can be ensured (for instance, division by zero). Structuring mechanisms will be reviewed in Sect. 3.1. An abstract machine has a name m, the clause SETS contains definitions of sets, the clause **constants** allows one to introduce information related to the mathematical structure of the problem to be solved, and the clause PROPERTIES contains the effective definitions of constants: it is very important to list carefully the properties of constants in a way that can be easily used by the tool. We have not mentioned structuring mechanisms such as *sees, includes, extends, promotes, uses* and *imports*, but these can help in the management of proof obligations.

```
MACHINE
    m
SETS
    s
CONSTANTS
    c
PROPERTIES
    P(s, c)
VARIABLES
    x
INVARIANT
    I(x)
ASSERTIONS
    A(x)
INITIALISATION
    <substitution>
OPERATIONS
    <list of operations>
END
```

The second part of the abstract machine defines the dynamic aspects of state variables and properties over variables using what is generally called an *inductive invariant*, and using *assertions* generally called *safety properties*. The invariant $I(x)$ types the variable x, which is assumed to be initialized with respect to the initial conditions and to be preserved by the operations (or transitions) of the list of operations. Conditions of verification called *proof obligations* are generated from the text of the model using the first part for defining the mathematical theory and the second part is used to generate proof obligations for the preservation (when the operation is called) of the invariant and proof obligations stating the correctness of the safety properties with respect to the invariant. Figure 8 contains an example of an abstract machine with only one operation, setting the variable *result* to the value of $factorial(m)$, where m is a constant.

```
MACHINE
    FACTORIAL_MAC
CONSTANTS
    factorial, m
CONSTANTS
    factorial
PROPERTIES
    m ∈ ℕ ∧
    factorial ∈ ℕ ⇸ ℕ ∧
```

$$\forall f \cdot \left(\begin{array}{l} f \in \mathbb{N} \leftrightarrow \mathbb{N} \wedge \\ 0 \mapsto 1 \in f \wedge \\ \forall(n, fn).(n \mapsto fn \in f \Rightarrow n+1 \mapsto (n+1) \times fn \in f) \\ \Rightarrow \\ factorial \subseteq f \end{array} \right)$$

```
VARIABLES
    result
INVARIANT
    result ∈ ℕ
ASSERTIONS
    factorial ∈ ℕ ⟶ ℕ ;
    factorial(0) = 1 ;
    ∀n.(n ∈ ℕ ⇒ factorial(n+1) = (n+1) × factorial(n))
INITIALISATION
    result :∈ ℕ
OPERATIONS
    computation = begin result := factorial(m) end
END
```

Table 8. An abstract machine for the computation of the factorial function

Modelling Systems in the Event-based B Approach

Abstract machines are based on classical mechanisms such as calls of operations or input/output mechanisms. On the other hand, reactive systems react to the environment with respect to external stimuli; the abstract models of the event-based B approach are intended to integrate the reactivity to stimuli by promoting events rather than operations. In contrast to operations, events have no parameters, and there is no access to state variables. At most one event is observed at any time in the system.

An (abstract) model is made up of a part defining mathematical structures related to the problem to be solved and a part containing elements about state variables, transitions and (safety and invariance) properties of the model. Proof obligations are generated from the model to ensure that the properties hold effectively; this is called *internal consistency* of the model. A model is assumed to be closed, which means that every possible change over the state variables is defined by transitions; transitions correspond to events observed by the specifier. A model m is defined by the following structure. A model has a name m, the clause SETS contains definitions of sets for the problem, the clause CONSTANTS allows one to introduce information related to the mathematical structure of the problem to be solved and the clause PROPERTIES contains the effective definitions of constants: it is very important to list carefully the properties of constants in a way that can be easily used by the tool. Another point is the fact that sets and constants can be considered like parameters, and some extensions of the B method exploit this aspect to introduce parametrization techniques into the development process of B models. The second part of the model defines the dynamic aspects of state variables and properties over variables using an invariant, called generally the inductive invariant, and using assertions called generally safety properties. The invariant $I(x)$ types the variable x, which is assumed to be initialized with respect to the initial conditions and is preserved by events (or transitions) in the list of events.

Conditions of verification called proof obligations are generated from the text of the model, using the first part for defining the mathematical theory and the second part is used to generate proof obligations for the preservation of the invariant and proof obligations stating the correctness of the safety properties with respect to the invariant. The predicate $A(x)$ states properties derivable from the model invariant. A model states that the state variables are always in a given set of possible values defined by the invariant, and it contains the only possible transitions operating over the state variables.

A model is not a program, and no control flow is related to it; however, it requires validation. First, we we define the mathematics for stating sets, properties over sets, invariants and safety properties. The conditions of consistency of the model are called *proof obligations*, and they express the preservation of invariant properties and avoidance of deadlock.

MODEL m
SETS s
CONSTANTS c
PROPERTIES $P(s,c)$
VARIABLES x
INVARIANT $I(x)$
ASSERTIONS $A(x)$
INITIALISATION
  <substitution>
EVENTS
  <list of events>
END

	Proof obligation
(INV1)	$Init(x) \Rightarrow I(x)$
(INV2)	$I(x) \land BA(e)(x,x') \Rightarrow I(x')$
(DEAD)	$I(x) \Rightarrow (\text{grd}(e_1) \lor \ldots \text{grd}(e_n))$

$e_1, \ldots, e_n$ is the list of events of the model m. (INV1) states the initial condition which should establish the invariant. (INV2) should be checked for every event e of the model, where $BA(e)(x,x')$ is the before–after predicate of e. (DEAD) is the condition of freedom from deadlock: at least one event is enabled.

The predicates in the clause ASSERTIONS should be implied by the predicates of the clause INVARIANT. This condition is formalized simply as follows:

$$P(s,c) \land I(x) \Rightarrow A(x)$$

Finally, the substitution of an event must be feasible; an event is feasible with respect to its guard and the invariant $I(x)$ if there is always a possible transition for this event or, equivalently, there exists a next value x' satisfying the before-after predicate of the event. The feasibility of the initialisation event requires that at least one value exists for the predicate defining the initial conditions. The feasibility of an event leads to readability of the form of the event; recognition of the guard in the text of the event simplifies the semantic reading of the event and the translation process of the tool: no guard is hidden inside the event. We summarize the feasibility conditions in the following table.

Event : E	Feasibility : $fis(E)$
$x : Init(x)$	$\exists x \cdot Init(x)$
begin $x : P(x_0,x)$ **end**	$I(x) \Rightarrow \exists x' \cdot P(x,x')$
when $G(x)$ **then** $x : P(x_0,x)$ **end**	$I(x) \land G(x) \Rightarrow \exists x' \cdot P(x,x')$
any l **where** $G(l,x)$ **then** $x : P(x_0,x,l)$ **end**	$I(x) \land G(l,x) \Rightarrow \exists x' \cdot P(x,x',l)$

The proof obligations for a model are generated by the proof-obligations generator of the B environment; sequent calculus is used to state the validity of the proof obligations in the current mathematical environment defined by the constants and properties. Several proof techniques are available, but the proof tool is not able to prove every proof obligation automatically, however, interaction with the prover should allow one to prove every generated proof obligation. We say that a model is *internally consistent* when every proof obligation has been proved. A model uses only three kinds of events, whereas the generalized substitutions are richer; but the objective is to provide a simple and powerful framework for modelling reactive systems. Since the consistency of a model is defined, we should introduce a refinement of models using the refinement of events defined like the refinement of substitution. We now reconsider the example of the *factorial* function and its computation, and propose the model shown in Table 9. As you may notice, the abstract machine *fac* and the abstract model *fac* are very close and the main difference is in the use of events rather than operations: the event *computation* eventually appears or is executed, because of the properties of the mathematical function called *factorial*. The operation *computation* of the machine in Table 8 is passive, but the event *computation* of the model in the Table 9 is reactive when it is possible. Moreover, events may hide other ones and the refinement of models will play a central role in the development process. We present in the next subsubsection some classical mechanisms for structuring developed components of a specification.

Structuring Mechanisms of the B Method

In the last two subsubsections, we introduced B models following the classification into the two main categories *abstract machines* and *models*; both abstract machines and components are called *components* but they do not deal with the same approach. We now give details of the structuring mechanisms of both approaches in order to achieve correctness with respect to references to work on B.

Sharing B Components

The AMN notation provides clauses related to structuring mechanisms in components such as *abstract machines* but also components such as *refinements* or *implementations*. The B development process starts from basic components, mainly *abstract machines*, and is a layered development; the goal is to obtain implementation components through structuring mechanisms such as INCLUDES, SEES, USES, EXTENDS, PROMOTES, IMPORTS and REFINES. The clauses INCLUDES, SEES, USES, EXTENDS, PROMOTES, IMPORTS and REFINES allow one to compose B components in the classical B approach, and every clause leads to specific conditions for use. Several authors [28, 91] have analysed the limits of existing B primitives for sharing data while refining and composing B components; it is clear that the B primitives for structuring B components can be used following strong conditions on the sharing of data and operations. The limits are mainly due to the reuse of already proved B components; reuse of variables, invariants, constants, properties and operations. In fact, the problem to be solved is the management of *interferences* between components, and the seminal solution of Owicki and Gries [89] face a combinatorial explosion of the number of proof obligations. The problem is to compose components according to given constraints of correctness. The new

MODEL
  FACTORIAL_EVENTS
CONSTANTS
  factorial, m
CONSTANTS
  factorial
PROPERTIES
  $m \in \mathbb{N} \wedge$
  $factorial \in \mathbb{N} \leftrightarrow \mathbb{N} \wedge$
  $0 \mapsto 1 \in factorial \wedge$
  $\forall(n, fn).(n \mapsto fn \in factorial \Rightarrow n + 1 \mapsto (n + 1) \times fn \in factorial) \wedge$

$$\forall f \cdot \left(\begin{array}{l} f \in \mathbb{N} \leftrightarrow \mathbb{N} \wedge \\ 0 \mapsto 1 \in f \wedge \\ \forall(n, fn).(n \mapsto fn \in f \Rightarrow n + 1 \mapsto (n + 1) \times fn \in f) \\ \Rightarrow \\ factorial \subseteq f \end{array} \right)$$

VARIABLES
  result
INVARIANT
  $result \in \mathbb{N}$
ASSERTIONS
  $factorial \in \mathbb{N} \longrightarrow \mathbb{N}$;
  $factorial(0) = 1$;
  $\forall n.(n \in \mathbb{N} \Rightarrow factorial(n + 1) = (n + 1) \times factorial(n))$
INITIALISATION
  $result :\in \mathbb{N}$
EVENTS
  $computation =$ **begin** $result := factorial(m)$ **end**
END

Table 9. Abstract model for the computation of the factorial function

event-based B approach considers a different way to cope with structuring mechanisms and considers only two primitives: the REFINES primitive and the DECOMPOSITION primitive.

B Classical Primitives for Combining Components

We focus on the meaning and use of five primitives for sharing data and operations among B components, namely INCLUDES,SEES, USES, EXTENDS and PROMOTES. Each primitive is related to a clause of the AMN notation and allows access to data or operations of already developed components; specific proof obligations state conditions for ensuring sound composition. A structuring primitive makes accessed components visible to various degrees from the accessing component.

The INCLUDES primitive can be used in an abstract machine or in a refinement; the included component allows the including component to modify included variables by included operations; the included invariant is preserved by the including component and is in fact used by the tool for deriving proofs of proof obligations of the including component. The including component cannot modify included variables, but it can use them with read access. No interference is possible under those constraints. The USES primitives can only appear in abstract machines, and the using machines have read-only access to the used machine, which can be shared by other machines. Using machines can refer to shared variables in their invariants, and the data of the used machine are shared among using machines. When a machine uses another machine, the current project must contain another machine including the using and the used machines. The refinement is related to the including machine and the using machine cannot be refined. The SEES primitive refers to an abstract machine imported in another branch of the tree structure of the project and sets, constants and variables can be consulted without change. Several machines can see the same machine. Finally, the EXTENDS primitive can only be applied to abstract machines, and only one machine can extend a given machine; the EXTENDS primitive is equivalent to the INCLUDES primitive followed by the PROMOTES primitive for every operation of the included machine. We can illustrate an implementation, and we can show, for instance, that the implementation in Table 10 implements (refines) the machine in Table 8. The operation *computation* is refined or implemented by a "while" statement. The proof obligations should take into account the termination of the operation in the implementation: the variant establishes the termination. Specific proof obligations are produced to check the absence of overflow of variables.

Organizing Components in a Project

The B development process is based on a structure defined by a collection of components which are either abstract machines, refinements or implementations. An implementation corresponds to a stage of development leading to the production of codes, when the language of substitutions is restricted to the B0 language. The B0 language is a subset of the language of substitutions and translation to C, C++ or ADA is possible with the help of tools. The links between components are defined by the B primitives previously mentioned and by the refinement.

When one is building a software system, the development starts from a document which may be written in a semi-formal specification language; the system is decomposed into subsystems and a model is progressively built using B primitives for composing B components. We emphasize the role of the structuring primitives, since they allow one to distribute the global complexity of the proofs. The B development process covers the classical life cycle: requirements analysis, specification development, (formal) design and validation through the proof process, and implementation. Lano [73] has illustrated

```
IMPLEMENTATION
    FACTORIAL_IMP
REFINES
    FACTORIAL_MAC
VALUES
    m = 5
CONCRETE_VARIABLES
    result, x
INVARIANT
    x ∈ 0..n ∧
    result = factorial(x)
ASSERTIONS
    factorial(5) = 120 ∧
    result ≤ 120
INITIALISATION
    result := 1; x := 0
OPERATIONS
    computation =
        while  x  <  m  do
                    x := x + 1; fn := x × fn
        invariant
                    x ∈ 0..m
                    result = factorial(x)
                    result ≤ factorial(m)
        variant
                    m − x
        end
END
```

Table 10. An implementation of the computation of the factorial function

an object-oriented approach to development, using B, and this identifies the layered development paradigm using B primitives that we have already mentioned. Finally, implementations are B components that are close to real code; in an implementation component, an operation can be refined by a while loop and the checking should prove that the while loop terminates.

Structures for the Event-based B Approach

While the classical B approach is based on the component and structuring primitives of B, the event-based B approach promotes two concepts: the refinement of models and the decomposition of models [4]. As we have already mentioned, the classical B primitives have limits on the scope of their use; we need, mainly, to manage the sharing data but without generating too many proof obligations. So, the main idea of Abrial was not to compose, but to decompose an initial model, and to refine the models obtained after the decomposition step. The new proposed approach simplifies the B method and focuses on the refinement. This means that a previous development in the classical B approach can be replayed in the event-based B approach. Moreover, the foundations of B remain useful and usable in the current environment of Atelier B. In the next subsection, we describe the mathematical foundations of B, and we illustrate the concepts of B in the event-based B approach.

Summary on Structuring Structuring Mechanisms

We have reviewed the structuring mechanisms of the classical B approach and the new mechanisms proposed for the event-based B approach. While the classical approach provides several mechanisms for structuring machines, only two mechanisms support the event-based approach. In fact, the crucial point is to compose abstract models or abstract machines; the limit of composition is related to the production of a too high number of proof obligations. The specifier wants to share state variables in read and write modes; the structuring mechanisms of classical B do not allow the sharing of variables except in read mode. Our work on the feature interaction problem [37] illustrates the use of refinement for composing features; other approaches, based on the detection of interaction by using a model checker on finite models, do not cope with the global problem because of finite models. Finally, we think that the choice of events with refinement provides a simple way to integrate proof into the development of complex systems and conforms to the idea of viewing systems through different abstractions, thanks to the presence of stuttering [71]. We have not mentioned the clause DEFINITIONS, which provides a way to introduce new definitions into a model and is a macro-expansion mechanism.

3.2 Proof-based Development in B

Refinement of B Models

The refinement of a formal model allows one to enrich a model by a *step-by-step* approach. Refinement provides a way to construct stronger invariants and also to add details in a model. It is also used to transform an abstract model into a more concrete version by modifying the description of the states. This is essentially done by extending the list of state variables (possibly suppressing some of them), by refining each abstract event into a corresponding concrete version and by adding new events. The abstract state variables x and the concrete ones y are linked together by means of a *gluing invariant* $J(x,y)$. A number of proof obligations ensure that (1) each abstract event is correctly refined by its corresponding concrete version, (2) each new event refines skip, (3) no new event take control for ever and (4) relative freedom from deadlock is preserved. We now give details of proof obligations of a refinement and introduce the syntax of a refinement in Table 11.

A *refinement* has a name r; it is a model refining a model m in the clause REFINES, and m can itself be a refinement. New sets, new constants and new

REFINEMENT
  r
REFINES
  m
SETS
  t
CONSTANTS
  d
PROPERTIES
  $Q(t,d)$
VARIABLES
  y
INVARIANT
  $J(x,y)$
VARIANT
  $V(y)$
ASSERTIONS
  $B(y)$
INITIALISATION
  $y : INIT(y)$
EVENTS
  <list of events>
END

Table 11. Syntax of a refinement model

properties can be declared in the clauses SETS, CONSTANTS and PROPER-
TIES. New variables y are declared in the clause **variables** and are the concrete variables; the variables x of the refined model m are called the abstract
variables. The gluing invariant defines a mapping between the abstract and
concrete variables; when a concrete event occurs, there must be a corresponding event in the abstract model: the concrete model *simulates* the abstract
model. The clause VARIANT *controls* new events, which cannot take control
over other events of the system. In a refinement, new events may appear, and
they refine an event SKIP; events of the refined model can be strengthened,
and one needs to prove that the refined model does not contain more deadlock
configurations than does the refined one: if a guard is strengthened too much,
it can lead to a dead refined event.

The refinement r of a model m is a system; its trace semantics is based on
traces of states over variables x and y, and the projection of concrete traces
on abstract traces is a stuttering-free trace semantics of the abstract model.
The mapping between abstract and concrete traces was called a refinement
mapping by Lamport [71], and stuttering is the key concept for refining event
systems. When an event e of m is triggered, it modifies some variables y, and
the abstract event refining e modifies x. Proof obligations make precise the
relationship between the abstract model and the concrete model.

In what follows, the abstract system is m and the concrete system is r; $INIT(y)$ denotes the initial condition of the concrete model; $I(x)$ is the invariant of the refined model m; $BAC(y, y')$ is the concrete before–after relation of an event of the concrete system r, and $BAA(x, x')$ is the abstract before–after relation of the corresponding event of the abstract system m; $G_1(x)$, $\ldots$, $G_n(x)$ are the guards of the n abstract events of m; $H_1(y)$, $\ldots$, $H_k(y)$ are the guards of k concrete events of r. Formally, the refinement of a model is defined as follows:

- (REF1) $INIT(y) \Rightarrow \exists x.(Init(x) \wedge J(x, y))$.

The initial conditions of the refinement model imply that there exists an abstract value in the abstract model such that that value satisfies the initial conditions of the abstract model and implies the new invariant of the refinement model.

- (REF2) $I(x) \wedge J(x, y) \wedge BAC(y, y') \Rightarrow \exists x'.(BAA(x, x') \wedge J(x', y'))$.

The invariant in the refinement model is preserved by the refined event, and the activation of the refined event triggers the corresponding abstract event.

- (REF3) $I(x) \wedge J(x, y) \wedge BAC(y, y') \Rightarrow J(x, y')$.

The invariant in the refinement model is preserved by the refined event but the event of the refinement model is a new event which was not visible in the abstract model; the new event refines *skip*.

- (REF4) $I(x) \wedge J(x, y) \wedge (G_1(x) \vee \ldots \vee G_n(x)) \Rightarrow H_1(y) \vee \ldots \vee H_k(y)$.

The guards of events in the refinement model are strengthened, and we have to prove that the refinement model is not more blocked than the abstract model.

- (REF5) $I(x) \wedge J(x, y)) \Rightarrow V(y) \in \mathbb{N}$

and

- (REF6) $I(x) \wedge J(x, y) \wedge BAC(y, y') \Rightarrow V(y') < V(y)$.

New events should not forever block abstract ones.

The refinement of models by refining events is close to the refinement of action systems [15], in UNITY and in TLA, even if there is no explicit semantics based on traces; one can consider the refinement of events to be like a relation between abstract and concrete traces. Stuttering plays a central role in the global process of development where new events can be added into the refinement model. When one is refining a model, one can either refine an existing event by strengthening the guard and/or the before–after predicate (removing non-determinism), or add a new event which is intended to refine the skip event. When one is refining a model by another one, this means that the set of traces of the refined model contains the traces of the resulting model with respect to the stuttering relationship. Models and corresponding refined models are defined and can be validated through the proofs of proof obligations; the refinement supports proof-based development, and we shall illustrate this by a case study on the development of a program for computing the *factorial* function.

Proof-based Development in Action

The B language of predicates, the B language of events, the B language of models and B refinement constitute the B method; however, the objectives of the B method are to provide a framework for developing models and, finally programs. The development process is based on proofs and should be validated by a tool. The current version of Atelier B groups B models into projects; a project is a set of B models related to a given problem. The statement of the problem is expressed in a mathematical framework defined by constants, properties and structures, and the development of a problem starts from a very high-level model which simply states the problem in an event-based style. The proof tool is central in the B method, since it allows us to write models and to validate step-by-step each decision of the development process; it is an assistant used by the user to integrate decisions into models, particularly by refining them. The proof process is fundamental and the interaction of the user in the proof process is a very critical point. We shall examine the various aspects of the development with an example. The problem is to compute the value of the *factorial* function for a given item of data n. We have already proved that the (mathematical) *factorial* function exists, and we can reuse its definition and its properties. Three successive models are provided by a development, namely $Fac1$ (the initial model stating in one shot the computation of $factorial(n)$), $Fac2$ (a refinement of the model $Fac1$, computing $factorial(n)$) step by step and $Fac3$ (completing the development of an algorithm for $factorial(n)$).

We begin by writing a first model which rephrases the problem, and we simply state that an event calculates the value $factorial(n)$ where n is a natural number. The model has only one event, and is a one shot model:

$$\text{computation} =$$
$$\textbf{begin } fn := factorial(n) \textbf{ end}$$

Here, fn is the variable containing the value computed by the program; the expression *"one-shot"* means that we show a solution just by assigning the value of a mathematical function to fn. It is clear that this one shot event is not satisfactory, since it does not describe the algorithmic process for computing the result. Proofs are not difficult, since they are based on the properties stated in the preliminary part of the ASM definition. Our next model will be a refinement of $Fac1$. It will introduce an iterative process of computation based on the mathematical definition of $factorial$. We therefore add a new event $prog$, which extends the partial function under construction called fac that contains a partial definition of the $factorial$ function:

> progress =
>   **when** $n \notin dom(fac)$ **then**
>   **any** x **where**
> $x \in \mathbb{N} \wedge x \in dom(fac) \wedge x+1 \in dom(fac)$
>   **then**
> $fac(x+1) := (x+1) * fac(x)$
>   **end**
>   **end**

The initialisation is simply to set fac to the value for 0: $fac := \{0 \mapsto 1\}$ and there is a new event progress which simulates the progress by adding the next pair in the function fac. Secondly, the event computation is refined by the following event stating that the process stops when the fac variable is defined for n.

> computation =
>   **when** $n \in dom(fac)$ **then**
> $fn := fac(n)$
>   **end**

The computation is based on a calculation of the fixed point of the equation defining $factorial$ and the ordering is the set inclusion over domains of functions; fac is a variable satisfying the following invariant property:

> $fac \in \mathbb{N} \nrightarrow \mathbb{N} \wedge fac \subseteq factorial \wedge$
> $dom(fac) \subseteq 0..n \wedge dom(fac) \neq \emptyset$

fac is a relation over natural numbers and it contains a partial definition of the $factorial$ function; as long as n is not defined for fac, the computing process adds a new pair in fac. The system is deadlock-free, since the disjunction of the guards $n \in dom(fac)$, or $n \notin dom(fac)$, is trivially true. The event progress increases the domain of fac: $dom(fac) \subseteq 0..n$. The proof obligations for the refinement are effectively proved by the proof tool:

> $n \in dom(fac) \vee$
> $(\quad n \notin dom(fac) \wedge$
> $\qquad \exists x.(x \in \mathbb{N} \wedge x \in dom(fac) \wedge x+1 \notin dom(fac)))$

This model is more algorithmic than the first model and it can be refined into a third model, called $Fac3$, closer to the classical algorithmic solution. Two new variables are introduced: a variable i plays the role of an index, and a variable fq is an accumulator. A gluing invariant defines relations between old and new variables:

$$i \in \mathbb{N} \wedge 0..i = \mathsf{dom}(fac) \wedge fq = fac(i)$$

The two events of the second model are refined into the next two events.

```
computation =
    when i = n then
        fn := fq
    end
```

```
progress =
    when i ≠ n then
        i := i + 1 ‖ fq := (i + 1) * fq
    end
```

The proof obligations are completely discharged by the proof tool, and we easily derive the algorithm by analysing the guards of the last model:

```
begin
    i := 0 ‖ fq := 1
    while i ≠ n do
        i := i + 1 ‖ fq := (i + 1) * fq
    end ;
end
```

We can simplify the algorithm by removing the parallel operator and we transform it as follows:

```
begin
    i := 0;
    fq := 1;
    while i ≠ n do
        i := i + 1;
        fq := i * fq;
    end ;
end
```

Case studies can provide information about the development process. Various domains have been used for illustrating the event-based B approach: sequential programs [11, 41], distributed systems [8, 10, 36, 40], circuits [82, 93] and information systems [44]. In the following sections, we illustrate the event-B modelling method by means of case studies:

- sequential algorithms;
- combining coordination and refinement for sorting;

- spanning-tree algorithms;
- a distributed leader election algorithm.

4 Sequential Algorithms

4.1 Primitive Recursive Functions

The Class of Primitive Recursive Functions

In computability theory [96], the primitive recursive functions constitute a strict subclass of the general recursive functions, also called the class of computable functions. Many computable functions are primitive recursive functions such as addition, multiplication, exponentiation and the sign functions; in fact, a primitive function corresponds to a bounded (for) loop, and we shall show how to derive the (for) algorithm from the definition of the primitive recursive function.

The primitive recursive functions are defined by initial functions (the 0-place zero function ζ, the k-place projection function $\pi_i{}^k$ and the successor function σ) and by two combining rules, namely the composition rule and the primitive recursive rule. More precisely, we give the definitions of the functions and rules as follows:

- $\zeta() = 0$
- $\forall i \in \{1, \ldots, k\} : \forall x_1, \ldots, x_k \in \mathbb{N} : \pi_i{}^k(x_1, \ldots, x_k) = x_i$
- $\forall x \in \mathbb{N} : \sigma(n) = n + 1$
- If g is an l-place function, if $h_1, \ldots, h_l$ are n-place functions and if the function f is defined by:

$$\forall x_1, \ldots, x_n \in \mathbb{N} : f(x_1, \ldots, x_n) = g(h_1(x_1, \ldots, x_n), \ldots, h_l(x_l, \ldots, x_n)),$$

  then f is obtained from g and $h_1, \ldots, h_l$ by composition.
- If g is an l-place function, if h is an $(l+2)$-place function and if the function f is defined by

$$\forall x_1, \ldots, x_l, x \in \mathbb{N} \begin{cases} f(x_1, \ldots, x_l, 0) & = g(x_1, \ldots, x_l) \\ f(x_1, \ldots, x_l, x + 1) & = h(x_1, \ldots, x_l, x, f(x_1, \ldots, x_l, x)) \end{cases}$$

  then f is obtained from g and h by primitive recursion.

A function f is primitive recursive, if it is an initial function or can be generated from initial functions by some finite sequence of the operations of composition and primitive recursion. A primitive recursive function is computed by an iteration, and we shall now define a general framework for stating the development of functions defined by primitive recursion using predicate diagrams.

Modelling the Computation of a Primitive Recursive Function

The first step is to define the mathematical function for computing the value of $f(u, v)$, where u and v are two natural numbers; the primitive recursive rule is stated as follows:

- u, v, g, h, f are constants corresponding to values and functions.

CONSTANTS
u, v, g, h, f

- u, v, g, h are supposed to be given;
- g, h are total and are two primitive recursive functions; and
- f is defined by a fixed-point-based rule.

PROPERTIES
$u \in \mathbb{N} \wedge v \in \mathbb{N} \wedge$
$g \in \mathbb{N} \longrightarrow \mathbb{N} \wedge h \in \mathbb{N} \times \mathbb{N} \times \mathbb{N} \longrightarrow \mathbb{N} \wedge$
$f \in \mathbb{N} \times \mathbb{N} \longrightarrow \mathbb{N} \wedge$
$\forall (a, b).\, (\, (a \in \mathbb{N} \wedge b \in \mathbb{N}) \Rightarrow (f(a, 0) = g(a))) \wedge$
$\forall (a, b).\, (\, (a \in \mathbb{N} \wedge b \in \mathbb{N}) \Rightarrow (f(a, b+1) = h(a, b, f(a, b))))$

From the characterization of the constants, the totality of f can be derived, since both g and h are total. The reader should be very careful about the functional notation $f(a, 0)$, which is intended to mean a functional application, but also the membership $(a, 0) \in f$ when f has not yet been proved to be functional. The system uses three variables: two variables are the input values and the third one is the output value VARIABLES *result*.

The required properties are the invariance of the INVARIANT clause and the partial correctness of the system with respect to the pre-conditions and post-conditions of the computation of the function defined by the primitive recursion rule. The invariant property is very simple to establish.

The INVARIANT clause is very simple for the first model and is in fact a typing invariant. The first model has only one visible event, and other events are hidden by the stuttering step; the computation event models or simulates the computation of the resulting value, and simulates the end of a hidden loop:

INVARIANT
    $result \in \mathbb{N}$
INITIALIZATION
    $result :\in \mathbb{N}$

computation =
begin
    $result := f(u, v)$
end

The loop appears in the following model, which is a refinement of *primrec0*:

```
MODEL primrec0
CONSTANTS    u, v, g, h, f
PROPERTIES
   u ∈ N ∧ v ∈ N ∧
   g ∈ N ⟶ N ∧ h ∈ N × N × N ⟶ N ∧
   f ∈ N × N ⟶ N ∧
   ∀ (a, b). ( (a ∈ N ∧ b ∈ N) ⇒ (f(a, 0) = g(a))) ∧
   ∀ (a, b). ( (a ∈ N ∧ b ∈ N) ⇒ (f(a, b + 1) = h(a, b, f(a, b))))
VARIABLES
   result
INVARIANT
   result ∈ N
INITIALIZATION
   result :∈ N
EVENTS
computation =
   begin
      result := f(u, v)
   end
END
```

Iterative Computations from Primitive Recursion

The next model, *primrec1* (see Table 12) is a refinement of *primrec0*; it introduces a new event called *step* and *step* is simulating the progression of an iterative process satisfying a loop invariant.
The new system has two visible events:

1. The first event, computation, is intended to model the end of the iteration, and it concretizes the event computation.
2. The second event, step, is the visible underlying step of the previous stuttering step.

The computation process is organized by the two guards of the two events; it leads us to the following algorithm, which captures the essence of the preceding B models. The final development includes two B models related by the refinement relationship, and provides an algorithm for computing the specified function. The resulting algorithm is called F (Algorithm 1) and uses the algorithms of g and h. The invariant is derived from the B model and does not need further proofs. The development can be instantiated with respect to functions g and h, which are assumed to be primitive recursive.

REFINEMENT *primrec1*
REFINES *primrec0*
VARIABLES $cx, cy, cresult, result$
INVARIANT
$\quad cx \in \mathbb{N} \wedge cy \in \mathbb{N} \wedge cresult \in \mathbb{N} \wedge$
$\quad cx = u \wedge 0 \leq cy \wedge cy \leq v \wedge cresult = f(cx, cy)$
INITIALISATION
$\quad cx := u \parallel cy := 0 \parallel cresult := g(u) \parallel result :\in \mathbb{N}$
EVENTS
computation $=$
  when
$\quad\quad v - cy = 0$
  then
$\quad\quad result := cresult$
  end ;
step $=$
  when
$\quad\quad v - cy \neq 0$
  then
$\quad\quad cy := cy + 1 \parallel$
$\quad\quad cresult := h(cx, cy, cresult)$
  end
END

Table 12. The model *primrec1*

Algorithm F

  precondition   : $u, v \in \mathbb{N}$
  postcondition : $result = f(u, v)$
  local variables : $cx, cy, cresult \in \mathbb{N}$

$cx := u;$
$cy := 0;$
$cresult := G(u);$
while $cy \leq v$ **do**
    invariant   : $0 \leq cy \wedge cy \leq v \wedge cx = u \wedge cresult = f[cx, cy]$
    $cresult := H[cx, cy, cresult];$
    $cy := cy + 1;$
;
$result := cresult;$

        Algorithm 1: F computes the primitive recursive function f

Applying the Above Development
— Addition, Multiplication and Exponentiation

Addition

The mathematical function *addition* is defined by the following rules:

$$\forall x, y \in \mathbb{N} : \begin{cases} addition(x, 0) & = \pi_1{}^1(x) \\ addition(x, y + 1) & = \sigma(addition(x, y)). \end{cases}$$

We assign to g the primitive recursive function ζ and to h the primitive recursive function σ; the development of *primrec* can be replayed. The resulting algorithm is given by substituting g and h by ζ and σ respectively. The algorithm is denoted $ADDITION$ (Algorithm 2).

Algorithm $ADDITION$

> **precondition** : $x, y \in \mathbb{N}$
> **postcondition** : $result = ADDITION(x, y)$
> **local variables**: $cx, cy, cresult \in \mathbb{N}$
>
> $cx := x;$
> $cy := 0;$
> $cresult := \pi_1{}^1(x);$
> **while** $cy \leq y$ **do**
> > **invariant**   : $0 \leq cy \wedge cy \leq y \wedge cx = x \wedge$
> > $\qquad\qquad cresult = addition[cx, cy]$
> > $cresult := \sigma[cresult];$
> > $cy := cy + 1;$
> ;
> $result := cresult;$

Algorithm 2: $ADDITION$ computes the primitive recursive function *addition*

Multiplication

The mathematical function *multiplication* is defined by the following rules:

$$\forall x, y \in \mathbb{N} : \begin{cases} multiplication(x, 0) & = \zeta() \\ multiplication(x, y + 1) & = addition(x, multiplication(x, y)). \end{cases}$$

We assign to g the primitive recursive function $\zeta()$ and to h the primitive recursive function *addition*; the development of *primrec* can be replayed. The resulting algorithm is given by substituting g and h by $\pi_1{}^1$ and *addition* respectively. The algorithm is denoted $MULTIPLICATION$ (Algorithm 3).

Algorithm *MULTIPLICATION*

> **precondition**   : $x, y \in \mathbb{N}$
> **postcondition** : $result = multiplication(x, y)$
> **local variables:** $cx, cy, cresult \in \mathbb{N}$
>
> $cx := x;$
> $cy := 0;$
> $cresult := \zeta();$
> **while** $cy \leq y$ **do**
> > **Invariant**   : $0 \leq cy \wedge cy \leq y \wedge cx = x \wedge$
> > $\qquad\qquad\qquad cresult = multiplication[cx, cy]$
> > $cresult := addition[cx, cresult];$
> > $cy := cy + 1;$
>
> $;$
> $result := cresult;$

Algorithm 3: MULTIPLICATION computes function multiplication

Exponentiation

The mathematical function exp is defined by the following rules:

$$\forall x, y \in \mathbb{N} : \begin{cases} exp(x, 0) & = \sigma(\zeta()) \\ exp(x, y + 1) = multiplication(x, exp(x, y)). \end{cases}$$

We assign to g the primitive recursive function $\sigma(\zeta())$ (since the composition of two primitive recursive functions is still primitive recursive) and to h the primitive recursive function *multiplication*; the primrec development can be replayed. The resulting algorithm is given by substituting g and h respectively by $\sigma(\zeta())$ and *multiplication*. The algorithm is denoted EXP (Algorithm 4).

Algorithm *EXP*

> **precondition**   : $x, y \in \mathbb{N}$
> **postcondition** : $result = exp(x, y)$
> **local variables:** $cx, cy, cresult \in \mathbb{N}$
>
> $cx := x;$
> $cy := 0;$
> $cresult := \sigma(\zeta());$
> **while** $cy \leq y$ **do**
> > **Invariant**   : $0 \leq cy \wedge cy \leq y \wedge cx = x \wedge$
> > $\qquad\qquad\qquad cresult = exp[cx, cy]$
> > $cresult := MULTIPLICATION[cx, cresult];$
> > $cy := cy + 1;$
>
> $;$
> $result := cresult;$

Algorithm 4: EXP computes the primitive recursive function exp

4.2 Other Ways to Compute Addition and Multiplication

If we consider the development for the functions *addition* and *multiplication*, we can reuse the first model in each case and improve the final resulting algorithms. We assume that the mathematical functions are supported by the B prover and that we do not need to define them. The proved models can be reused in other developments and we are now going to refine both functions in a different way.

Developing a New Multiplication Algorithm

The first model states the problem to be solved namely the multiplication of two natural numbers; the second model provides the essence of the algorithmic solution; and the last one implements naturals by sequences of digits. Let a and b be two naturals. The problem is to compute the value of the expression $a*$, where $*$ is the mathematical function standing for natural multiplication. The function *multiplication* is defined by an infix operator $*$. The first model (see Table 13) is a *one-shot* model, computing the result in one step.

```
MODEL multiplication0
CONSTANTS
    a, b
PROPERTIES
    a ∈ N ∧ b ∈ N ∧
VARIABLES
    x, y, m
INVARIANT
    x ∈ N ∧ y ∈ N ∧
    x = a ∧ y = b ∧ m ∈ N
INITIALISATION
    x := a ∥ y := b ∥ m :∈ N
EVENTS
computation =
    begin
        m := a * b
    end
END
```

Table 13. The model *multiplication0*

Now, we need to take an idea and apply it to the model *multiplication0*. There are several ways to define multiplication, for example either $(a-1)*b$ (a primitive recursive function) or $a*b = (2*a)*(b/2)$. We have chosen the second of these ways, since it is the faster one and is simple to implement. We define two new variables, namely cx and cy, to take care of the initial values of a and b (a value-passing mechanism). The induction step will be driven by B, which is strictly decreasing. The new variable M stores any value of cx when cy is odd.

> VARIABLES
> cx, cy, x, y, M, m
> INVARIANT
> $cx \in \mathbb{N} \wedge cy \in \mathbb{N} \wedge M \in \mathbb{N} \wedge$
> $cx * cy + M = x * y$
> INITIALISATION
> $cx, cy, x, y, m :\in (x = a \wedge y = b \wedge cx = a \wedge cy = b \wedge m \in \mathbb{N})\ \|$
> $M := 0$

The event *computation* occurs, when cy is equal to 0. The gluing invariant allows us to conclude that M contains the value of $a * b$.

> computation $=$
>   **when**
> $(cy = 0)$
>   **then**
> $m := M$
>   **end**

Two new events, *prog1* and *prog2*, help in the progression of cy towards 0:

> prog1 $=$
>   **when**
> $(cy \neq 0) \wedge even(cy)$
>   **then**
> $cx := cx * 2 \ \| \ cy := cy/2$
>   **end**
> prog2 $=$
>   **when**
> $(cy \neq 0) \wedge odd(cy)$
>   **then**
> $cx := cx * 2 \ \|$
> $cy := cy/2 \ \|$
> $M := M + cx$
>   **end**

Where $even(cy) = \exists x \cdot (x \in \mathbb{N} \wedge cy = 2 * x)$ and $odd(cy) = \exists x \cdot (x \in \mathbb{N} \wedge cy = 2 * x + 1)$. The proofs are not hard; Atelier B generated 18 proof obligations, only 3 of which were discharged interactively. Finally, we obtain the model *multiplication1* in Table 14.

REFINEMENT *multiplication*1
REFINES *multiplication*0
VARIABLES
  cx, cy, x, y, M, m
INVARIANT
  $cx \in \mathbb{N} \wedge$
  $cy \in \mathbb{N} \wedge$
  $M \in \mathbb{N} \wedge$
  $cx * cy + M = x * y$
INITIALISATION
  $cx, cy, x, y, m :\in (x = a \wedge y = b \wedge cx = a \wedge cy = b \wedge m \in \mathbb{N}) \parallel$
  $M := 0$
EVENTS
computation $=$
  when $(cy = 0)$
  then $m := M$
  end
prog1 $=$
  when $(cy \neq 0) \wedge even(cy)$
  then $cx := cx * 2 \parallel cy := cy/2$
  end
prog2 $=$
  when $(cy \neq 0) \wedge odd(cy)$
  then
    $cx := cx * 2 \parallel$
    $cy := cy/2 \parallel$
    $M := M + cx$
  end
END

Table 14. Refinement model *multiplication*1

A further refinement may lead to the implementation of natural numbers by sequences of binary digits. Division and multiplication by two are implemented by shifting binary digits. Also, one can derive the well-known Algorithm 5 on the following page for computing the multiplication function.

Addition of Two Natural Numbers

The *addition* function can also be redeveloped. The development is decomposed into three steps. The first step writes a *one-shot* model (see Table 15 on the next page) that computes the required result in one step, namely the addition of two natural numbers. Let a and b be two naturals. The problem is to compute the value of the expression $a + b$, where $+$ is the mathematical function standing for the addition of naturals.

The definition of $a + b$ using $a/2$ (and $b/2$) is based on the following properties:

New Algorithm *MULTIPLICATION*

> **precondition** : $a, b \in \mathbb{N}$
> **postcondition** : $m = multiplication(x, y)$
> **local variables:** $cx, cy, x, y, m, M \in \mathbb{N}$

> $x := a;$
> $y := b;$
> $cx := x;$
> $cy := y;$
> $M := 0;$
> **while** $cy \neq 0$ **do**
> > **Invariant** $: 0 \leq M \wedge 0 \leq cy \wedge cy \leq y \wedge cx * cy + M = x * y \wedge x = a \wedge y = b$
> > **if** $(cy \neq 0) \wedge even(cy)$ **then**
> > > $cx := cx * 2 \| cy := cy/2$
> >
> > ;
> > **if** $(cy \neq 0) \wedge odd(cy)$ **then**
> > > $cx := cx * 2 \| cy := cy/2 \| M := M + cx$
> >
> > ;
>
> ;
> $m := M;$

Algorithm 5: New *MULTIPLICATION* computes the function *multiplication*

MODEL *addition0*
CONSTANTS
   a, b
PROPERTIES
   $a \in \mathbb{N} \wedge$
   $b \in \mathbb{N} \wedge$
VARIABLES
   $x, y, result$
INVARIANT
   $x \in \mathbb{N} \wedge y \in \mathbb{N} \wedge result \in \mathbb{N}$
   $x = a \wedge y = b$
INITIALISATION
   $x := a \| y := b \| result :\in \mathbb{N}$
EVENTS
computation $=$
   begin
      $result := a + b$
   end
END

Table 15. The model *addition0* for addition

a	b	$a+b$
$2*n$	$2*m$	$2*(n+m)$
$2*n$	$2*m+1$	$2*(n+m)+1$
$2*n+1$	$2*m$	$2*(n+m)+1$
$2*n+1$	$2*m+1$	$2*(n+m)+2$

Table 16. Four properties of of multiplication

Using these four properties, we try to obtain a general induction schema verified by variables; the four properties lead to the general form $(a+b)*C+P$. The discovery of this relation is based on an analysis of possible transformations over variables; Manna [79] has given hints for stating an inductive assertion starting from properties over values of variables. The associativity and commutativity of mathematical addition justify the form. Moreover, the form can also be justified by the binary coding of A and B as follows:

$$\left(\sum_{i=0}^{n} A_i 2^i\right) + \left(\sum_{i=0}^{n} B_i 2^i\right) = \sum_{i=0}^{n} (A_i + B_i) 2^i, \tag{4}$$

$$\sum_{i=0}^{n} (A_i + B_i) 2^i = \left(\left(\sum_{i=1}^{n} A_i 2^{i-1}\right) + \left(\sum_{i=1}^{n} B_i 2^{i-1}\right)\right) * 2 + (A_0 + B_0), \tag{5}$$

$$\left(\sum_{i=0}^{n} A_i 2^i\right) + \left(\sum_{i=0}^{n} B_i 2^i\right) = \left(\left(\sum_{i=1}^{n} A_i 2^{i-1}\right) + \left(\sum_{i=1}^{n} B_i 2^{i-1}\right)\right) * 2 + (A_0 + B_0). \tag{6}$$

Equation (6) tells us that we obtain a binary addition of the last digits of the two numbers and that we have to store powers of 2 while computing. Two new variables are introduced: C for storing the powers of 2, and P for storing the partial result. We can derive the following invariant and initial conditions:

```
VARIABLES
  A, B, P, a, b, p, C
INVARIANT
  A ∈ N ∧ B ∈ N ∧ P ∈ N ∧ C ∈ N ∧
  (A + B) * C + P = a + b
INITIALISATION
  a, b, A, B, p : (a ∈ N ∧ b ∈ N
    ∧ p ∈ N ∧ P ∈ N ∧ C ∈ N ∧ A = a ∧ B = b) ||
  P, C := 0, 1
```

```
add =
   when
      (B = 0) ∧ (A = 0)
   then
      p := P
   end;
```

The one-shot event of the previous model is then refined by the next event; the result is contained in variable P when A and B are two variables containing 0. Four new events are added to the current model; each event corresponds to a case of the properties given in Table 16 on the preceding page.

Four new events are introduced in this model:

```
prog1 =
   when
      even(A) ∧ even(B)
   then
      A := A/2 || B := B/2 ||
      C := 2 * C
   end;
```

```
prog2 =
   when
      odd(A) ∧ even(B)
   then
      A := A/2 || B := B/2 ||
      C := 2 * C || P := C + P
   end;
```

```
prog3 =
   when
      even(A) ∧ odd(B)
   then
      A := A/2 || B := B/2 ||
      C := 2 * C || P := C + P
   end;
```

```
prog4 =
   when
      odd(A) ∧ odd(B)
   then
      A := A/2 || B := B/2 ||
      C := 2 * C || P := 2 * C + P
   end
```

We also have to code the basic operations for computing $C + P$, $2 * C$ and $2 * C + P$. $C + P$ is solved by storing a binary digit 1 in the corresponding location. $2 * C$ is a shifting operation. $2 * C + P$ is solved by managing a carry. Now, we can refine the current model.

Managing the Carry

The goal of the carry is to implement the basic operation $2 * C + P$; P is concretized by the store Q and the carry R.

```
VARIABLES
   A, B, Q, R, a, b, p, C
INVARIANT
   Q ∈ ℕ ∧ R ∈ ℕ ∧ (R = 0 ∨ R = 1) ∧ P = C * R + Q
INITIALISATION
   a, b, A, B, p : (a ∈ ℕ ∧ b ∈ ℕ ∧ C ∈ ℕ ∧ A = a ∧ B = b) ||
   p :∈ ℕ
   Q, R, C := 0, 0, 1
```

The refined event *add* uses the new variables Q and C. The gluing invariant maintains the relationship over P and the new variables:

$$add = \quad \textbf{when} \ (B = 0) \ \wedge \ (A = 0) \ \textbf{then} \ p := C * R + Q \ \textbf{end} \, ;$$

Events *prog1*, *prog2*, *prog3* and *prog4* are refined and modified by introducing the two new variables. The new variables are modified according to P:

```
prog1 =
    when even(A) ∧ even(B)
    then
        A := A/2||B := B/2||R := 0
        Q := C * R + Q||C := 2 * C
    end ;
```

```
prog4 =
    when odd(A) ∧ odd(B)
    then
        A := A/2||B := B/2||R := 1
        Q := C * R + Q||C := 2 * C
    end
```

```
prog2 =
    when odd(A) ∧ even(B)
    then
        A := A/2 || B := B/2 ||
        if R = 0 then Q := C + Q
        end || C := 2 * C
    end ;
```

```
prog3 =
    when even(A) ∧ odd(B)
    then   A := A/2 || B := B/2 ||
        C := 2 * C ||
        if R = 0 then Q := C + Q
        end
    end ;
```

This model was validated by the tool Atelier B [50], which generated 56 proof obligations; 15 were discharged interactively. Details are incrementally added here; each model provides a view of the computing function. The models are related by the refinement relationship, and the last model can now be refined to produce code.

Production of Code

The refinement process leads to basic operations over natural numbers that can be implemented by operations over bits. The B language provides sequences but experience shows that proofs are harder when sequences are used in a given model. We have used the following definitions of sequences:

SETS $bit = \{ZERO, ONE\}$
CONSTANTS $code$
PROPERTIES
  $code \in \mathbb{N} \times \mathbb{Z} \longrightarrow (\mathbb{Z} \nrightarrow bit)$ $\wedge$
  $\forall k \cdot (k \in \mathbb{Z} \Rightarrow code(0, k) = \emptyset)$ $\wedge$
  $\forall(n, k) \cdot (n \in \mathbb{N} \wedge n \neq 0 \wedge k \in \mathbb{Z} \Rightarrow$
       $code(2 * n, k) = \{k \mapsto ZERO\} \cup code(n, k + 1))$ $\wedge$
  $\forall(n, k) \cdot (n \in \mathbb{N} \wedge k \in \mathbb{Z} \Rightarrow$
       $code(2 * n + 1, k) = \{k \mapsto ONE\} \cup code(n, k + 1)))$ $\wedge$
  $\forall(n, k, x) \cdot (n \in \mathbb{N} \wedge k \in \mathbb{Z} \wedge x \in \mathbf{dom}(code(n, k)) \Rightarrow x \geq k)$

The recursive definition was validated in our previous work [38] on the development of recursive functions using the event-B method. We have defined schemes that allow us to evaluate those functions. A sequence is coded by an integer interval. For instance, consider our second model of multiplication: here shifting of digits is implemented by an insertion of 0 at the head of the sequence, and removing a bit at the head corresponds to multiplication by 2. Questions about the re-usability and decomposition of systems remain to be solved, and will be part of further work aimed at making the method more practical.

VARIABLES
  $A, B, P, a, b, p, cA, cB, kA, kB$
INVARIANT
  $kA \in \mathbb{Z}$ $\wedge$
  $kB \in \mathbb{Z}$ $\wedge$
  $cA \in \mathbb{Z} \nrightarrow bit$ $\wedge$
  $cA = code(A, kA)$ $\wedge$
  $cB \in \mathbb{Z} \nrightarrow bit$ $\wedge$
  $cB = code(B, kB)$

$prog1 =$
  when $(cB \neq \emptyset) \wedge cB(kB) = ZERO$ **then**
    if $cA \neq \emptyset$ **then** $cA := \{kA - 1 \mapsto ZERO\} \cup cA \parallel kA := kA - 1$ **end**
    $\parallel cB := \{kB\} \mathbin{\lhd\mkern-9mu-} cB \parallel kB := kB + 1 \parallel A := 2 * A \parallel B := B/2$
  end

```
prog2 =
    when  (cB ≠ ∅) ∧ cB(kB) = ONE  then
        if cA ≠ ∅ then
            cA := {kA − 1 ↦ ZERO} ∪ cA || kA := kA − 1
        end ||
        cB := {kB} ⩤ cB || kB := kB + 1 ||
        A := 2 ∗ A || B := B/2 || M := M + A
    end
```

The coding allows us to implement the addition $C + Q$, since C is a power of two and C is greater than Q:

$$code(C + Q, 0) = code(C, 0) \;\; \text{⩤} \; code(Q, 0).$$

These properties (and others) were in fact proved in another B machine using only PROPERTIES and ASSERTIONS clauses as in the work on structure [9]. Atelier B generated 10 proof obligations, which were discharged interactively.

We can give a refinement of addition, but only two events are really given. Here cp is the code of p, cQ the code of Q and cC the code of C:

```
add =
    when  cB = ∅ ∧ cA = ∅  then
        if R = 1 then  cp := cC  ⩤ cQ
        else  cp := cQ
        end
    end
```

```
prog1 =
    when cB(kB) ≠ ONE ∧ cA(kA) ≠ ONE  then
        cB := {kB} ⩤ cB || kB := kB + 1 ||
        cA := {kA} ⩤ cA || kA := kA + 1||
        cC := {0 ↦ ZERO} ∪ shift(cC) || R := 0 ||
        if R = 1 then cQ := cC ⩤ cQ end
    end
```

The function $shift$ shifts any value of a sequence (to begin always with 0). Atelier B generated 95 proof obligations, and 53 were discharged interactively, but we can do better using assertion clauses.

A stronger refinement can now be obtained from the current developed model. A coding on a finite sequence of bits $(bs + 1)$ constrains the abstract code to contain a bounded number of bits. We assume that the natural numbers a and b are codable, and we obtain a concrete code for the variables A and B, namely CA and CB:

$$
\begin{aligned}
&CA, CB : (\\
&\quad CA \in 0..bs \rightarrow bit \ \wedge\\
&\quad CA = code(a,0) \ \cup \ ((0..bs) - \mathbf{dom}\,(code(a,0))) \times \{ZERO\} \ \wedge\\
&\quad CB \in 0..bs \rightarrow bit \ \wedge\\
&\quad CB = code(b,0) \ \cup \ ((0..bs) - \mathbf{dom}\,(code(b,0))) \times \{ZERO\})
\end{aligned}
$$

A variable K plays the role of kA and kB and the process halts, when k is $bs + 1$. The gluing invariant for the variables A, B, p and Q (Cp and CQ are the concrete code) is the following:

$$
\begin{aligned}
&K \in 0..bs+1 \ \wedge \ K = kA \ \wedge \ K = kB \ \wedge \ LO \in -1..K-1 \ \wedge\\
&CA \in 0..bs \rightarrow bit \ \wedge\\
&((K..bs) \vartriangleleft CA) = cA \ \cup \ ((K..bs) - \mathbf{dom}\,(cA)) \times \{ZERO\} \ \wedge\\
&CB \in 0..bs \rightarrow bit \ \wedge\\
&((K..bs) \vartriangleleft CB) = cB \ \cup \ ((K..bs) - \mathbf{dom}\,(cB)) \times \{ZERO\} \ \wedge\\
&Cp \in 0..bs+1 \rightarrow bit \ \wedge \ CQ \in 0..bs \rightarrow bit \ \wedge\\
&(0..LO \vartriangleleft CQ = cQ) \ \wedge \ (LO \geq 0 \Rightarrow CQ(LO) = ONE) \ \wedge\\
&\forall i \cdot (i \in (LO+1)..bs \Rightarrow CQ(i) = ZERO)
\end{aligned}
$$

where LO is a new variable; it is the position of the last ONE in CQ. Events add and $prog1$ are refined in the following concrete events:

$$
\begin{aligned}
&add =\\
&\quad \mathbf{when} \ K = bs+1 \ \mathbf{then}\\
&\quad\quad \mathbf{if} \ R = 1 \ \mathbf{then} \ Cp := CQ \ \vartriangleleft\!\!- \{bs+1 \mapsto ONE\}\\
&\quad\quad \mathbf{else} \ Cp := CQ \ \vartriangleleft\!\!- \{bs+1 \mapsto ZERO\}\\
&\quad\quad \mathbf{end}\\
&\quad \mathbf{end}\,;
\end{aligned}
$$

$$
\begin{aligned}
&prog1 =\\
&\quad \mathbf{when} \ K \leq bs \ \wedge \ CB(K) \neq ONE \ \wedge \ CA(K) \neq ONE \ \mathbf{then}\\
&\quad\quad K := K+1 \ \| \ R := 0 \ \|\\
&\quad\quad \mathbf{if} \ R = 1 \ \mathbf{then} \ CQ(K) := ONE \ \| \ LO := K \ \mathbf{end}\\
&\quad \mathbf{end}\,;
\end{aligned}
$$

We also have to express the fact that the coding of the result is in $0..bs+1 \rightarrow bit$ and that it might have an overflow. Multiplication by 2 ($K := K+1$), division by 2 ($K := K+1$) and addition ($CQ(K) := ONE$) are implemented using this coding. Atelier B generated 81 proof obligations, and 25 were discharged interactively.

Properties of Models

In the model in Table 17 on the next page, we have proved all properties used here on the abstract coding. Two induction theorems have also been proved in this machine (the second and third assertions).

4.3 Design of Sequential Algorithms

The design of a sequential algorithm starts with a statement of the specification of the algorithm; the specification of the algorithm is expressed by a precondition over the input data, a postcondition over the output data and a relation between the input and output data. An extension of the guarded command language by Morgan [86] allows one to initiate a development by refinement according to a set of rules. However, no mechanical tool allows one to check the refinement; the notation $x : [pre, post]$ is intended to mean a statement which is correct with respect to the pre-condition and post-condition. This is exactly the case, when one starts an event-B development, since one should then state a *magical* event which is correct with respect to the pre and post conditions. If we consider $x : [pre, post]$ and assume that x is free in pre and $post$, $x : [pre, post]$ is a statement which may modify x but only x, and which satisfies the Hoare triple $\{pre\}\ x : [pre, post]\ \{post\}$.

An equivalent event is defined as follows:

$$
\begin{aligned}
&\text{event } = \\
&\quad \textbf{any } z \\
&\quad \textbf{where} \\
&\qquad pre(x) \ \wedge \ post(x, z) \\
&\quad \textbf{then} \\
&\qquad x := z \\
&\quad \textbf{end}
\end{aligned}
$$

In the above we have illustrated the event-B method by simple sequential algorithms and have emphasized the possibility of reusing a previous development. In the next section, we develop a sorting algorithm.

5 Combining Coordination and Refinement for Sorting

The coordination paradigm improves the development of concurrent/distributed solutions because it provides a simple way to communicate between processes via a data structure called a tuple space. The principles of coordination and of event-driven system development can be fruitfully combined to develop systems and to analyse the development of different solutions of

MODEL   *Code*
SETS $bit = \{ZERO, ONE\}$
CONSTANTS $divtwo, code, power2, suc, shift, pred1$
PROPERTIES
Definition of *divtwo*
$\quad divtwo \in \mathbb{N} \rightarrow \mathbb{N} \wedge \forall x \cdot (x \in \mathbb{N} \Rightarrow divtwo(x) = x/2) \wedge$
Definition of *suc* (successor)
$\quad suc \in \mathbb{N} \rightarrow \mathbb{N} \wedge \forall x \cdot (x \in \mathbb{N} \Rightarrow suc(x) = x + 1) \wedge$
Definition of *code*
$\quad code \in \mathbb{N} \times \mathbb{Z} \rightarrow (\mathbb{Z} \leftrightarrow bit) \wedge$
$\quad \forall k \cdot (k \in \mathbb{Z} \Rightarrow code(0, k) = \emptyset) \wedge$
$\quad \forall (n, k) \cdot (n \in \mathbb{N} \wedge n \neq 0 \wedge k \in \mathbb{Z} \Rightarrow$
$\qquad code(2 * n, k) = \{k \mapsto ZERO\} \cup code(n, k + 1)) \wedge$
$\quad \forall (n, k) \cdot (n \in \mathbb{N} \wedge k \in \mathbb{Z} \Rightarrow$
$\qquad code(2 * n + 1, k) = \{k \mapsto ONE\} \cup code(n, k + 1)) \wedge$
Definition of *power2* (2^n), *pred1* (predecessor) and *shift* (shift code)
$\quad power2 \in \mathbb{N} \rightarrow \mathbb{N} \wedge power2(0) = 1 \wedge$
$\quad \forall k \cdot (k \in \mathbb{N} \Rightarrow power2(k + 1) = 2 * power2(k)) \wedge$
$\quad pred1 \in \mathbb{Z} \rightarrow \mathbb{Z} \wedge \forall x \cdot (x \in \mathbb{Z} \Rightarrow pred1(x) = x - 1) \wedge$
$\quad shift \in (\mathbb{Z} \nrightarrow bit) \rightarrow (\mathbb{Z} \nrightarrow bit) \wedge \forall y \cdot (y \in \mathbb{Z} \nrightarrow bit \Rightarrow shift(y) = (pred1; y))$
ASSERTIONS
$\quad \forall c \cdot (c \in \mathbb{N} \Rightarrow \exists y \cdot (y \in \mathbb{N} \wedge (c = 2 * y \vee c = 2 * y + 1)));$
A number c is odd or even
$\quad \forall P \cdot (P \subseteq \mathbb{N} \wedge 0 \in P \wedge suc[P] \subseteq P \Rightarrow \mathbb{N} \subseteq P);$
This is the recurrence theorem. P is the set of all value which satisfy a property
$\quad \forall K \cdot (K \subseteq \mathbb{N} \wedge 0 \in K \wedge divtwo^{-1}[K] \subseteq K \Rightarrow \mathbb{N} \subseteq K);$
This is another recurrence theorem, like $P(n/2) \Rightarrow P(n)$ ..
$\quad \forall (n, k, x) \cdot (n \in \mathbb{N} \wedge k \in \mathbb{Z} \wedge x \in \mathbf{dom}(code(n, k)) \Rightarrow x \geq k);$
All value in $\mathbf{dom}(code(n, k))$ are greater than or equals to k
$\quad code \in \mathbb{N} \times \mathbb{Z} \rightarrow (\mathbb{Z} \nrightarrow bit);$
Now a code is a partial function
$\quad \forall n \cdot (n \in \mathbb{N} \Rightarrow power2(n) > 0);$
2^n is always greater than 0
$\quad \forall (n, c, k) \cdot (n \in \mathbb{N} \wedge c \in \mathbb{N} \wedge power2(n) > c \wedge k \in \mathbb{Z} \Rightarrow$
$\qquad code(power2(n) + c, k) = code(power2(n), k) \Leftarrow code(c, k));$
This is our property for implementing addition
$\quad \forall (n, k, x) \cdot (n \in \mathbb{N} \wedge k \in \mathbb{Z} \wedge x \in \mathbf{dom}(shift(code(n, k))) \Rightarrow x > k);$
$\quad \forall (n, k) \cdot (n \in \mathbb{N} \wedge k \in \mathbb{Z} \Rightarrow shift(code(n, k)) = code(n, k + 1))$
A useful property of *shift* (which is now a shift)
$\quad \forall n \cdot (n \in \mathbb{N} \Rightarrow code(power2(n), 0) = (0..n - 1) \times ZERO \cup \{n \mapsto ONE\})$
A property which evaluates the code of 2^n
end

Table 17. Model for deriving proofs on the abstract coding

a given problem. Benefits are inherited from both frameworks: the B event-driven approach provides a refinement and the coordination framework provides a simple computation model. In this section, the sorting problem is redeveloped in the B event-driven method using coordination principles for the algorithms, and two programming paradigms are applied, i.e. merging and splitting lists to be sorted.

5.1 Introduction

Overview

The coordination paradigm [45, 98] improves the development of concurrent/distributed solutions because it provides simple way to communicate between processes via a data structure called a tuple space. Coordination and event-driven system development can be fruitfully combined to construct sequential recursive programs and to analyse the development of different solutions of a given problem, in the present case the sorting problem. This combination exploits the fundamental refinement relationship defined in the B event-driven approach [10, 11, 36] and leads to a practical framework for addressing the analysis of program development.

Coordination

The coordination paradigm appears in various programming environments, such as LINDA [45, 98]. The main idea is simple: a collection of processes or agents can cooperate, communicate and exchange data through a unique structure called a tuple space. A tuple space is a heap that can contain items, and processes are authorised to perform several operations, namely to put an item in the tuple space, to withdraw an item and to consult the tuple space. Implementation details are hidden. Any programming language can be extended by specific operations related to the tuple space, as for instance in the C LINDA environment, which extends the C programming language. The coordination paradigm focuses on the development of activities that are inherently concurrent and are simply made coherent through the coordination primitives. As soon as a coordination program is written, tools such as compilers provide a translation to a lower level which manages communications; this means that communications can be used without toil, since we do not have to take care how communications are really implemented. The coordination computation model has been developed in the GAMMA [18] model, and a kernel of a methodology related to proof has been given; Chaudron [48] has defined a refinement in a language of coordination for GAMMA close to the techniques of bi-simulation. We do not define new refinements here. The CHAM (Chemical Abstract Machine) is a chemical view of the coordination computation model. However, even if GAMMA is intended to promote the methodological aspects of program development, nothing has been clearly studied about its relationship to the refinement of event systems.

Integration of Coordination and Event-driven Systems

Event-driven systems are incrementally derived from a very abstract model into a final concrete model through refinement steps. The B event-driven technique is based on the validation by proof of each refinement step, and it starts with a system analysis where mathematical details are carefully analysed and proved or disproved by the proof tool. The idea is to add the coordination primitives as events which modify the tuple space and to get for free a refinement in the coordination framework. A consequence is that it provides a way to execute event-driven systems as a coordinated set of events and allows the refinement of general coordinator structures. The present exercise focuses on the use of both techniques for analysing the sorting problem; we apply two main sorting paradigms namely splitting (Quick-sort) and merging. Finally, we obtain a concrete model which is a sequential algorithm using a stack and which gives a non-recursive algorithm in the Quick-sort family.

The coordination paradigm was introduced and implemented in LINDA [45, 98], and a C LINDA compiler was effectively developed. The original idea was to synchronise processes or agents through a shared data space called a tuple space, using specific primitives extending the programming language. The programming language could be C, SML or a Prolog-like one; coordination primitives manage communication among processes or agents. Coordination is information-driven and makes interaction protocols simple and expressive. For instance, the implementation of Galibert [60] provides a simple way to program in C++ and to use a powerful, high-performance computer, namely the Origin 2000 SGI. Here, we use coordination as a simple way to state actions on data; it is a less structured approach, in contrast to classical programming languages. Every abstract model (in the B event-based approach) can be transformed into a coordinated program; however, we refine as much as possible to obtain a sequential algorithm.

When one writes a coordinated program, one has to identify processes or agents of the system; processes are expressed in a programming notation and the coordination framework allows one to state communications between processes through the tuple space. The coordination primitives include the reading of a value in the tuple space, the writing of a value in the tuple space and waiting for a value in the tuple space. Events play the role of actions of agents or processes and cooperate in the global computation, if any.

5.2 A Well-known Case Study: the Sorting Problem

Sorting a list of values means that one aims to find a permutation of the values such that the resulting list is sorted. We define two constants, f and m, with the following properties:

$$m \in \mathbb{N} \ \wedge$$
$$f \in 1..m \ \rightarrowtail \ \mathbb{N}$$

Here f stands for an abstract array which contains m natural numbers. All elements of the list are different. The variable g, initially set to the initial value f of the list, contains the sorted list in ascending order. The invariant must state that values are preserved between g and f. The invariant holds at the beginning, since $g = f$; the unique event of the system is a sorting, and it sorts in one step g:

INVARIANT
$$g \in 1..m \ \longrightarrow \ \mathbb{N} \ \wedge$$
$$\mathsf{ran}(g) = \mathsf{ran}(f)$$

sorting $=$
begin
$\quad g : \mathbb{N} \wedge$
$\quad \mathsf{ran}(g) = \mathsf{ran}(f) \wedge$
$\quad \forall x.(x \in 1..m - 1 \Rightarrow g(x) \leq g(x + 1))$
end

We know that there is one (and only one) permutation into which the list can be sorted. The sorting event is then enabled. The simplicity of the sorting event allows us to derive the correctness of the abstract system. The sorting is done in one step, which may seem to be magical. The abstract system is refined into another event system which implements a sorting technique, such as the Quick-sort or the merge sort technique. The main idea is to use the coordination paradigm to remove the recursiveness of the solution. The first abstract model is called BASIC-SORTING.

5.3 Applying Two Sorting Paradigms

The previous system is an abstract view of the sorting process. Sorting algorithms are based on specific paradigms, leading to well-known solutions. In our case, we consider two paradigms:

- MERGING TWO SORTED LISTS TO PRODUCE A SORTED LIST. Merge sort and insertion sort use the basic technique of merging two sorted lists; the way in which sorted lists are combined may be different, and the sizes of the two lists may be also different. The insertion sort combines a list containing only one element with any other sorted list. The von Neumann sort combines two lists that have the same size. Nevertheless, the basic technique is the merging of two sorted lists, and the global process increments the size of the intermediate lists, which is a termination condition.
- SPLITTING A LIST INTO TWO LISTS TO OBTAIN TWO PARTITIONED LISTS. In contrast, a list can be split into two lists such that the elements of the first list are smaller than the elements of the second list; the famous Quicksort soring technique is an application of this paradigm. The introduction

of the pivot is very important for the complexity of the sort. The selection sort is another example of a sorting technique and is an extreme case of the Quick-sort – i.e., the pivot is at the extreme "left" or "right"[3] position in the split list. The process converges to a list of one-element sorted lists, which are correctly located.

The coordination paradigm provides us with a computation model, and we use the event-driven paradigm for defining operations on the tuple space. The data structures are supported by the tuple space. A list is defined as an interval over the set of discrete values $1..m$, where m is a constant of the problem. An interval contains successive values, when non-empty. An interval is a subset of $1..m$ with consecutive values, and the intervals are a partition of $1..m$. The invariant will be strengthened to take into account the properties of intervals later.

For the moment, the following invariant says that the tuple space TS is a partition of $1..m$; operations on the tuple space are expressed by events modifying the variable TS:

$$TS \subseteq \mathcal{P}(\,1..m\,) \wedge$$
$$\forall I.(I \in TS \Rightarrow I \neq \emptyset) \wedge$$

$$\forall (I, J).(\\ \quad I \in TS \wedge J \in TS \wedge I \neq J\\ \quad \Rightarrow\\ \quad I \cap J = \emptyset\\ \quad) \wedge\\ \forall i.(i \in 1..m \Rightarrow \exists I.(I \in TS \wedge i \in I))$$

The refinement of the current model BASIC_MODEL leads us either to split intervals, or to combine intervals; we obtain two possible refined models:

- MERGE-SORT *merges two intervals to produce an interval*: the sorting process will stop when only one interval remains in the tuple space.
- SPLIT-SORT *splits an interval into two intervals*: the splitting will stop when no more splitting is possible.

We give no more details about the way the intervals are chosen, since these details may appear later in the refinement process. Both models have to be refined to detail the operations of merging and splitting. No implementation detail addresses the problem of parallel execution, since the model is an abstract model.

The Bottom-up Process MERGE-SORT

This bottom-up process combines intervals by maintaining the invariant of the sorting problem. The merging of two intervals assumes that the restriction of g on each interval is sorted. This property is added to the previous invariant,

---

[3] For understanding the notions of "left" and "tight", kindly visualise the list as a left-to-right sequence of elements.

$$\forall(i,j).(i \in I \ \land j \in I \ \land i \le j \Rightarrow g(i) \le g(j)))$$

The initial conditions state that the tuple space contains only intervals with one element; there is an interval for every possible value of $1..m$; and g is set to the initial value of the list to be sorted.

Init =
  begin
    $g := f \parallel TS := \{x|x \subseteq 1..m \land \exists i.(i \in 1..m \land x = i..i)\}$
  end

We recall that the merge process stops when only one interval is in the tuple space and it contains only $1..m$. Using the invariant, we can prove that g is sorted. The refined *sorting* event is

sorting =
  when $1..m \in TS$ then
    skip
  end ;

The sorting process is specified in detail in a way that identifies intermediate states of the variable g; these intermediate states state that the set of intervals converges towards a unique interval modelling the sorted list. A progress event is defined to model the computation of a merging step. The new event *merge_progress* withdraws two intervals from TS and deposits a new interval which is the merging of the two withdrawn intervals in TS. The merging of two intervals decrements the number of intervals and helps in the convergence of the process:

```
merge_ progress  =
   any  I, J , gp where
      I  ∈  TS ∧
      J  ∈  TS ∧
      I  ≠  J ∧
      gp ∈ I ∪ J  ⟶  ℕ ∧
      ran(gp) = ran((I ∪ J) ◁ g)
      ∀(i1, i2).(
            i1 ∈ I ∪ J  ∧
            i2 ∈ I ∪ J ∧
            i1 ≤ i2
               ⇒
            gp(i1) ≤ gp(i2))
   then
      g := g  ◁- gp ∥
      TS := TS − {I, J} ∪ {I ∪ J}
   end
```

This model is not yet the merging sort, since it is not efficiently implemented. However, the essence of the merging sort is expressed in the current model.

Further refinements introduce details so as to obtain different sorting algorithms based on the merging paradigm, such as the merging sort, the insertion sort and the von Neumann sort. At this point, we are not really using an interval, since $I \cup J$ is not necessarily an interval, but a further refinement will be able to choose intervals adequately to satisfy that constraint.

The Top-down SPLIT-SORT

Quick-sort is based on a strategy of decomposition called splitting the list and, the refinement of the model BASIC_SORTING adds a new invariant expressing the states of intervals resulting from splitting them. The final goal is to obtain a tuple space containing only intervals with one element. Remember that the Quick-sort splits an interval into two intervals in such a way that the elements of the first interval are smaller than the elements of the second one. The invariant is strengthened by the property that intervals can be sorted with respect to their values:

$$
\begin{aligned}
&\forall (I,J).(\\
&\quad I \in TS \ \wedge \ J \in TS \ \wedge \ I \neq J\\
&\quad \Rightarrow\\
&\quad (\forall (i,j).(\\
&\qquad i \in I \ \wedge \ j \in J \ \wedge \ i < j\\
&\qquad \Rightarrow\\
&\qquad g(i) \leq g(j))))
\end{aligned}
$$

When two numbers are in an interval, the values between those two values are also in that interval:

$$
\begin{aligned}
&\forall I.(\\
&\quad I \in TS\\
&\quad \Rightarrow\\
&\quad (\forall (i,j).(\\
&\qquad i \in I \ \wedge \ j \in I\\
&\qquad \Rightarrow\\
&\qquad i..j \ \subseteq \ I)))
\end{aligned}
$$

The initial conditions satisfy the invariant by setting a unique interval in the tuple space: only $1..m$ is in the tuple space.

The split process starts in a tuple space with only one interval, and halts when every interval $i..i$ (for every value i in $1..m$) is in the tuple space. In fact, no more splitting events are possible.

Init $=$ **begin** $\quad g := f \ \|$ $\quad TS := \{1..m\}$ **end**

sorting $=$ **when** $\forall i.(i \in 1..m \Rightarrow i..i \in TS)$ **then** $\quad$ skip   **end** ;

The progress of the global process is achieved by splitting intervals of the tuple space for as long as possible; only intervals with at least two elements can be split. The new event chooses a value called a pivot: it splits an interval into two smaller ones and it updates g. Obviously, the way to update g is very crucial for the implementation, as is the choice of the pivot. Selection sorting is one possible refined model that can be derived, if the pivot is specially chosen: here the pivot is the greatest or the smallest value of the interval:

split_progress =
    any I, k, gp, x **where**
      $I \in TS \land k \in I \land \exists j.(j \in I \land j > k) \land gp \in I \longrightarrow \mathbb{N} \land$
      $x \in \text{ran}(gp) \land \text{ran}(gp) = \text{ran}(I \lhd g) \land$
      $\forall z.(z \in I \land z \leq k \Rightarrow gp(z) \leq x) \land$
      $\forall z.(z \in I \land z > k \Rightarrow gp(z) \geq x)$
    then
      $g := g \lhd\!\!- gp \parallel$
      $TS := TS - \{I\} \cup \{\{y | y \in I \land y \leq k\}, \{y | y \in I \land y > k\}\}$
    end

This model has two main events; one event splits the intervals for as long as there is at least one interval with two values, and there is also an event for completing the process.

Duality of Sorting Models

The two models refine the basic model of the sorting problem; the tuple space frees the designer from implementation details, and structures the computation process. In Fig 1, we summarize the refinement relationship between the three models developed in the previous subsections.

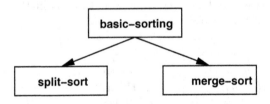

Fig. 1. Development of sorting techniques

Two families of sorting techniques can be redeveloped, and we shall develop the family of sorting techniques based on the split paradigm here. We do not develop sorting algorithms of the merge family in this chapter.

5.4 Introducing a Pivot and an Index

Quick-sort splits arrays by choosing a pivot variable, and it then reorganizes both intervals such that any value in the first interval is smaller than any value in the second interval. The refinement described below defines a pivot (piv) and a concrete index (k), which allows to split the current interval (I). Two index variables, namely $binf$ and $bsup$, define the middle part of an interval. The middle part is not processed by the partitioning process. The partitioning algorithm is not used in our current process, since it can split the current interval into three parts. The control of $binf$ and $bsup$ is fundamental: we must have an increase of $binf$ and e decrease of bsup. The new invariant is enriched by statements about properties satisfied by the new variables, namely piv, k, $binf$ and $bsup$. The variable $ToSplit$ detects the phase of the partitioning process. It can contain three values: No, when no split phase is running; Yes, if the partitioning process is progressing and End, when the partitioning process for a given interval is completed.

The resulting invariant expresses intuitive properties over variables; the proof assistant generates proof obligations for validating the refinement and helps us to add details over variables that were missing. When one is developing abstract models, a proof assistant such as Atelier B is crucial, and avoids the errors that may occur in brain-aided proofs. A proof helps us to choose the correct index (k) to partition the resulting interval when the splitting process stops $(ToSplit = End)$. Explanations are necessary in order to read and understand the invariant.

The first part of the model expresses typing information. I is the current interval, which satisfies properties resulting from the guard of the *choice_interval* event:

$$ToSplit \in \{No, Yes, End\} \ \wedge \ I \subseteq 1..m \ \wedge \ piv \in \mathbb{N} \ \wedge \ binf \in 1..m \ \wedge$$
$$bsup \in 1..m \ \wedge \ k \in \mathbb{N} \ \wedge$$
$$(ToSplit \neq No \ \Rightarrow \ piv \in ran(I \vartriangleleft g)) \ \wedge$$
$$(ToSplit \neq No \ \Rightarrow \ I \in TS) \ \wedge$$
$$(ToSplit \neq No \ \Rightarrow \ I - max(I) \neq \emptyset) \ \wedge$$
$$(ToSplit = Yes \ \Rightarrow \ binf \in I) \ \wedge$$
$$(ToSplit = Yes \ \Rightarrow \ bsup \in I)$$

The splitting of the current interval into two intervals is made possible by controlling the two variables $binf$ and $bsup$. $binf$ may increase and $bsup$ may decrease: *left_partition* can increase $binf$ and *right_partition* can decrease $binf$. Both events may possibly occur when $binf < bsup$ and are complementary with respect to guards. A *swap* event is enabled when both *left_partition* and *right_partition* are no longer enabled and when the two bounds are still satisfy the relationship $binf < bsup$. In this case, we must decide the new bound k, which must split the interval into two non-empty intervals:

$$(ToSplit = End \ \Rightarrow \ k \in I - \{max(I)\}).$$

If we choose $binf - 1$ or $bsup$, this values must be different from the initial value of the greater bound. So, if this greater bound does not change, the other bound must be less and the pivot is still in the first part:

$$
\begin{aligned}
&(ToSplit = Yes \land binf = min(I) \Rightarrow \\
&\qquad piv \notin ran(bsup + 1..max(I) \lhd g)) \land \\
&(ToSplit = Yes \land bsup = max(I) \Rightarrow binf < bsup) \land \\
&(ToSplit = Yes \land bsup = max(I) \Rightarrow \\
&\qquad piv \notin ran(min(I)..binf - 1 \lhd g)) \land \\
&(ToSplit = Yes \land bsup = max(I) \Rightarrow piv \in \mathsf{ran}(I - \{max(I)\} \lhd g)) \land \\
&(ToSplit = Yes \Rightarrow \forall z \cdot (z \in min(I)..binf - 1 \Rightarrow g(z) \le piv)) \land \\
&(ToSplit = Yes \Rightarrow \forall z \cdot (z \in (bsup + 1)..max(I) \Rightarrow g(z) \ge piv)) \land \\
&(ToSplit = Yes \land bsup < binf \Rightarrow binf \le max(I)) \land \\
&(ToSplit = Yes \land bsup \le binf \Rightarrow (binf = bsup \lor binf = bsup + 1)) \land \\
&(binf = bsup \Rightarrow bsup < max(I)) \land \\
&(ToSplit = End \Rightarrow k \in I - \{max(I)\}) \land \\
&(ToSplit = End \Rightarrow \forall z \cdot (z \in min(I)..k \Rightarrow g(z) \le piv)) \land \\
&(ToSplit = End \Rightarrow \forall z \cdot (z \in k + 1..max(I) \Rightarrow g(z) \ge piv))
\end{aligned}
$$

Safety properties can be proved from the invariant and are stated in the clause ASSERTIONS of the B machine. These properties are useful for validating the system itself:

$$
\begin{aligned}
&(ToSplit = Yes \Rightarrow I - max(I) = min(I)..max(I) - 1) \land \\
&(ToSplit = Yes \Rightarrow min(I)..max(I) \subseteq I) \land \\
&(ToSplit = Yes \Rightarrow binf..bsup \subseteq I))
\end{aligned}
$$

The invariant can be proved to be satisfied by the refined events and we list the refined events; the first one is the initialisation event, called Init. The tuple space contains only one interval, namely $1..m$, and the splitting process is not running in the initialisation state:

$$
\begin{aligned}
&\mathsf{Init} \; = \\
&\quad \textbf{begin} \\
&\qquad g := f \parallel TS := \{1..m\} \parallel I := \emptyset \parallel ToSplit := No \parallel \\
&\qquad piv :\in \mathbb{N} \parallel binf :\in 1..m \parallel bsup :\in 1..m \parallel k :\in 1..m \\
&\quad \textbf{end}
\end{aligned}
$$

The event *sorting* does not change; the guard of *split_progress* is very simple. When the partition process is finished ($ToSplit = End$), k is the index result for the partition (see the description of the event *partition*):

```
split_progress =
  when
    ToSplit = End
  then
    ToSplit := Yes ||
    TS := TS − {I} ∪ {{y|y ∈ I ∧ y ≤ k}, {y|y ∈ I ∧ y > k}}
  end;
```

We now introduce five new events. The first one, namely *tchoice_interval*, chooses an interval (not a singleton) in the tuple space and initializes both index and the pivot. After the activation of this event, we can cut the current interval ($ToSplit = Yes$):

```
choice_interval =
  any J, PIV where
    ToSplit = No ∧ J ∈ TS ∧
    PIV ∈ ran((J − max(J)) ◁ g) ∧ min(J) < max(J)
  then
    ToSplit := Yes || I := J ||
    piv := PIV || binf := min(J) || bsup := max(J)
  end;
```

The three next events move the index so as to leave an element less than the pivot before $binf$ and greater than the pivot after $bsup$:

```
left_partition =
  when
    ToSplit = Yes ∧
    binf < bsup ∧
    g(binf) < piv
  then
    binf := binf + 1
  end;
```

```
right_partition =
  when
    ToSplit = Yes ∧
    binf < bsup ∧
    g(binf) ≥ piv ∧
    g(bsup) > piv
  then
    bsup := bsup − 1
  end;
```

```
swap =
  when
    ToSplit = Yes ∧ binf < bsup ∧
    g(binf) ≥ piv ∧ g(bsup) ≤ piv
  then
    binf, bsup := binf + 1, bsup − 1 ||
    g := g  ◁−  {binf ↦ g(bsup)}  ◁−  {bsup ↦ g(binf)}
  end;
```

The last one stops the partitioning process and defines the index k, which makes progress possible (see event *split_progress*).

$$
\begin{array}{l}
\text{partition} = \\
\quad \textbf{when} \\
\qquad ToSplit = Yes \wedge binf \geq bsup \\
\quad \textbf{then} \\
\qquad ToSplit := End \ \| \\
\qquad \textbf{if } binf = bsup \textbf{ then} \\
\qquad\quad \textbf{if } g(binf) \leq piv \textbf{ then} \\
\qquad\qquad k := binf \\
\qquad\quad \textbf{else} \\
\qquad\qquad k := binf - 1 \\
\qquad\quad \textbf{end} \\
\qquad \textbf{else} \\
\qquad\quad k := bsup \\
\qquad \textbf{end} \\
\quad \textbf{end}\,;
\end{array}
$$

5.5 A Set of Bounds and a Concrete Pivot

The goal of the refinement described next is to implement the tuple space by use of a set of initial bounds from every interval in the abstract tuple space. Initially, we tried to introduce this implementation in the first refinement but it led us to a unique proof obligation, whose proof was very long. Hence, we have found another abstraction, which produces more proof obligations than does the initial choice, but they were easier to prove.

The implementation of the pivot is the middle of the chosen interval and now, the choice is deterministic. The relationship between pairs of bounds of the new tuple space TB and the tuple space TS is stated by a gluing invariant and the relationship is a one-to-one relation:

$$
\begin{array}{l}
TB \subseteq 1..m+1 \ \wedge \\
\forall (a,b) \cdot \left(\left(\begin{array}{l} a \in TB \wedge b \in TB \wedge \\ a < b \wedge a+1..b-1 \cap TB = \emptyset \\ \Rightarrow a..b-1 \in TS \end{array} \right) \right)
\end{array}
$$

We add two new variables, namely A and B, which are the bounds of the current abstract interval I, and they satisfy the following gluing invariant:

$$ToSplit = Yes \implies \begin{pmatrix} A \in TB \wedge B \in TB \wedge \\ A < B \wedge A+1..B-1 \cap TB = \emptyset \wedge \\ A..B-1 = I \end{pmatrix} \wedge$$

$$ToSplit = End \implies \begin{pmatrix} A \in TB \wedge B \in TB \wedge \\ A < B \wedge A+1..B-1 \cap TB = \emptyset \wedge \\ A..B-1 = I \end{pmatrix}$$

Two new safety properties can be derived from the current invariant:

$$\forall I \cdot (I \in TS \implies min(I) \in TB \wedge max(I)+1 \in TB);$$

$$\forall (a,b,c) \cdot \begin{pmatrix} a \in TB \wedge b \in TB \wedge c \in TB \wedge \\ a < b \wedge b < c \wedge \\ a+1..b-1 \cap TB = \emptyset \wedge \\ b+1..c-1 \cap TB = \emptyset \\ \implies \\ \forall (x,y) \cdot (x \in a..b-1 \wedge y \in b..c-1 \implies g(x) \le g(y)) \end{pmatrix}$$

We refine only two events. The event *split_progress* adds the unique value $k+1$ in the concrete tuple space (TB):

```
split_progress =
    when ToSplit = End then
        ToSplit := No ||
        TB := TB ∪ {k + 1}
    end ;
```

The event *choice_interval* initializes the concrete bounds A and B of the abstract interval I. It chooses the pivot as the value $g((a+b-1)/2)$ at the middle of the chosen interval:

```
choice_interval =
    any a, b, p where
        ToSplit = No ∧ a ∈ TB ∧ b ∈ TB ∧
        a < b − 1 ∧
        a + 1..b − 1 ∩ TB = ∅ ∧
        p = g((a + b − 1)/2)
    then
        ToSplit := Yes || A := a || B := b ||
        piv := p || binf := a || bsup := b − 1
    end ;
```

5.6 Implementation of the Tuple Space by a Stack

In the next step, we use a stack for implementing the tuple space; it is clear that the current abstract model might be implemented directly in a coordination language such as C LINDA, for instance. However, we recall that the coordination paradigm is a methodological support for development.

In this refinement, we implement the tuple space by a stack. We use three new variables TA, top, and S, which stand for the old variable TB. S (single) contains all bounds intervals which are singletons and which were on the top of the stack TA. All bounds in TB are single ($\in S$) or in the co-domain of TA and vice versa, according to our gluing invariant. Two consecutive bounds in TB are given by two consecutive indices of the stack (an array). The concrete tuple space TA is sorted; top is the dimension of TA. Notice that top is always between 1 and $m + 1$. No stack overflow can occur:

$$
\begin{array}{l}
top \in 1..m + 1 \ \wedge \\
TA \in 1..top \rightarrow 1..m + 1 \ \wedge \\
S \subseteq TB \ \wedge \\
TB = \mathsf{ran}(TA) \cup S \ \wedge \\
\forall (i, j) \cdot \left(
\begin{array}{l}
i \in \mathsf{dom}(TA) \ \wedge \\
j \in \mathsf{dom}(TA) \ \wedge \\
i < j \ \wedge \\
\Rightarrow \\
TA(i) < TA(j))
\end{array}
\right)
\end{array}
$$

When S is empty, the greater bound in the co-domain of TA is $m+1$ and, when S is not empty, it contains consecutive indices from $m + 1$, and the greater bound in the co-domain of TA and the minimum of S are consecutive. Using this technical invariant, it is easier to prove the previous gluing invariant:

$$
\begin{array}{l}
(S = \emptyset \ \Rightarrow \ max(ran(TA)) = m + 1) \ \wedge \\
(S \neq \emptyset \ \Rightarrow \ S = min(S)..m + 1) \ \wedge \\
(S \neq \emptyset \ \Rightarrow \ max(ran(TA)) + 1 = min(S)) \ \wedge
\end{array}
$$

The following properties can be proved from the invariant:

$$
\begin{array}{l}
(ToSplit \neq No \ \Rightarrow \ (top \mapsto B) \in TA) \ \wedge \\
(ToSplit \neq No \ \Rightarrow \ (top - 1 \mapsto A) \in TA) \ \wedge \\
(ToSplit \neq No \ \Rightarrow \ top > 1) \ \wedge \\
(ToSplit \neq No \ \Rightarrow \ top \leq m) \\
TA : 1..top \rightarrowtail 1..m + 1 \ \wedge \\
max(ran(TA)) = TA(top) \ \wedge \\
ran(TA) \cap S = \emptyset \ \wedge
\end{array}
$$

$$\forall(h,n) \cdot \left(\begin{array}{l} n : 1..m+1 \ \wedge \\ h : 1..n \ \rightarrowtail \ 1..n \ \wedge \\ \left(\begin{array}{l} x \in 1..n \ \wedge \\ y \in 1..n \ \wedge \\ x < y \ \wedge \\ \Rightarrow \\ h(x) < h(y)) \end{array} \right) \\ \Rightarrow \\ h = \mathsf{id}(1..n) \end{array} \right)$$

The last property is very important for proving that there is no run stack overflow on our stack. It expresses the fact that the unique increasing into function between $1..m+1$ and $1..m+1$ is the identity. We have proved this in another B machine with other preliminary lemmas such as previous assertions. The initial event is written starting from the previous one:

```
Init =
  begin
    g := f ‖TA := {1 ↦ 1, 2 ↦ m + 1} ‖S := ∅ ‖top := 2 ‖
    ToSplit := No ‖A, B := m + 1, 1 ‖piv :∈ ℕ ‖
    binf :∈ 1..m ‖bsup :∈ 1..m ‖k :∈ 1..m
  end
```

Only three old events change. Now, the guard of *sorting* is $top = 1$: remember that the proof of the refinement assumes that in this case all intervals are singletons. The implementation is very close:

```
sorting =
  when top = 1 then
    skip
  end ;
```

```
split_progress =
  when ToSplit = End then
    ToSplit := No ‖
    top := top + 1 ‖
    TA := (TA ⊲- {top ↦ k + 1}) ⊲- {top + 1 ↦ B}
  end ;
```

The event which chooses the interval is now deterministic. The bounds of the chosen interval are on the top of the stack TA. Notice that the chosen interval is not a singleton ($TA(top - 1) + 1 \neq TA(top)$). The singleton on the top of the stack is removed by a new event as follows:

choice_interval =
  when
    $top > 1$ $\wedge$
    $(TA(top - 1) + 1/ = TA(top))$ $\wedge$
    $ToSplit = No$
  then
    $ToSplit := Yes$ $\|$

$$A, B, piv, binf, bsup : | \left(\begin{array}{l} A = TA(top - 1) \wedge \\ B = TA(top) \wedge \\ piv = g((A + B - 1)/2) \wedge \\ binf = A \wedge \\ bsup = B - 1 \end{array} \right)$$

  end ;

The new event, called elim_single, eliminates every singleton on the top of the stack:

elim_single =
  when
    $top > 1$ $\wedge$
    $TA(top - 1) + 1 = TA(top)$ $\wedge$
    $ToSplit = No$
  then
    $S := S \cup \{TA(top)\}$ $\|$
    $top := top - 1$ $\|$
    $TA := 1..top - 1 \lhd TA$
  end ;

All guards of the above system are very simple to implement and all events are deterministic. We can easily derive from this system an iterative program using array and loops. The set of singletons S is not important in this implementation. If anyone should wish to use it, it can be stored in TA from index m in decreasing order. The iterative version of the algorithm is given in Table 18.

5.7 Conclusion

The iterative algorithm is three times faster than Quick-sort; it was obtained by combining the coordination paradigm and the event-driven paradigm. Every abstract model can be implemented by a coordination program, but we have used the coordination paradigm as a computation model, and refinement allows us to transit from the coordination model to the classical sequential model. Moreover, it provides us with a way to develop a splitting algorithm without any use of recursion. Our experience shows that coordination gives

```
begin
  g := f; TA[1] := 1; TA[2] := m + 1; top := 2;
  / ⋆ ToSplit = No ⋆ /
  while  top ≠ 1 do
    while  top > 1  ∧  TA[top − 1] + 1 = TA[top]  do
      top := top − 1
    od ;
    if top > 1 then
      A := TA[top − 1];
      B := TA[top];
      binf := A;
      bsup := B − 1;
      piv := g[(binf + bsup)div2];
      / ⋆ ToSplit = Yes ⋆ /
      while (binf < bsup) do
        while binf < bsup  ∧  g[binf] < piv do
          binf := binf + 1
        od ;
        while binf < bsup  ∧  g[bsup] > piv do
          bsup := bsup − 1
        od ;
        if binf < bsup then
          temp := g[binf];
          g[binf] := g[bsup];
          g[bsup] := temp;
          binf := binf + 1;
          bsup := bsup − 1
        end
      od ;
      if binf = bsup then
        if g[binf] ≤ piv then
          k := binf
        else
          k := binf − 1
        end
      else
        k := bsup
      end ;
      / ⋆ ToSplit = End ⋆ /
      TA[top] := k + 1; top := top + 1; TA[top] := B
      / ⋆ ToSplit = No ⋆ /
    end
  od
end
```

Table 18. A correct iterative program

us a simple way to think about the activity of events, and it helps in explaining what is really happening when, for instance, a paradigm is applied for sorting. We have not, however, completely explored the "promised land" of coordination, and we have not compared our work with the use of refinement for coordination.

6 Spanning-tree Algorithms

6.1 Introduction

Graph algorithms and graph-theoretical problems provide a challenging battlefield for the incremental development of proved models. The B event-based approach implements an incremental and proved development of abstract models, which are translated into algorithms; we focus our methodology here on the minimum-spanning-tree problem and on Prim's algorithm. The correctness of the resulting solution is based on properties over trees, and we show how the greedy strategy is efficient in this case. We compare some properties proven mechanically with the properties found in a classical textbook on algorithms. This section analyses the proof-based development of minimal-panning-tree algorithms, and Prim's algorithm in particular [92] is produced at the end.

6.2 The Minimum-panning-tree Problem

The minimum-spanning-tree problem or minimal-spanning-tree problem, is the problem of finding a minimum spanning tree with respect to a connected graph. The literature contains several algorithmic solutions such as Prim's algorithm [92] and Kruskal's algorithm [70]. Both of these algorithms implement the greedy method. Typically, we assume that a cost function is related to every edge, and the problem is to infer a globally minimum spanning tree which covers the initial graph. The cost function returns integer values. The minimal-spanning-tree problem is strongly related to practical problems such as the optimisation of circuitry, and the greedy strategy advocates making the choice that is the best one at that moment; it does not always guarantee optimality, but certain greedy strategies do indeed yield a minimal-spanning-tree.

Prim's algorithm is easy to explain, and it underlies mathematical properties related to graph theory and, especially, the general theory of trees. We consider two kinds of solution; the first kind is called a *generic algorithm* because it does not use a cost function. This first, generic solution allows us to develop a second solution: the minimal-spanning-tree.

Let us summarize how Prim's algorithm works. The state of the algorithm during execution contains two sets of nodes of the current graph. The first set of nodes, equipped with a restriction of a relation over the global set of nodes, defines the current spanning tree, starting from a special node called the root of the spanning tree. The second set of nodes is the complement of the first set. The acyclicity of the spanning tree must be preserved when a new edge is added to the current spanning tree, and the basic computation step consists of taking an edge between a node in the current spanning tree and a node in the other set. This choice leads to maintaining the acyclicity of the current spanning tree with the new node added, since the two sets of nodes are disjoint. The process is repeated until the set of remaining, unchosen nodes is empty. The final computed tree is a spanning-tree computed by the generic algorithm. Now, if one adds the cost function, one obtains Prim's algorithm by modifying the choice of the new node and edge to be added to the current spanning tree. In fact, the minimum edge is chosen and the final spanning tree is then the minimum spanning tree. However, the addition of the cost function is a refinement of the generic solution.

The generic minimal-spanning-tree algorithm without a cost function is sketched as follows:

- Precondition. *An undirected connected graph, g, over a set of nodes ND and a node r.*
- Initial step. *tr_nodes (the current set of nodes) contains only r and is included in ND, and tr (the current set of edges) is empty.*
- Computation step. *If $ND - tr\_nodes$ is not empty, then choose a node x in tr_nodes and a node y in $ND - tr\_nodes$ such that the link (x, y) is in g with the minimum cost and add it to tr; then add y to tr_nodes and (x, y) to tr*
- Termination step. *If $ND - tr\_nodes$ is empty ($ND = tr\_nodes$), then tr is a minimum spanning tree on ND.*
- Postcondition (ND, tr) *is a minimum spanning tree.*

Termination of the algorithm is ensured by decreasing the set $ND - tr\_nodes$. The genericity of the solution leads us to the refinement by introducing the cost function in the computation step. We have a clear, simple, abstract view of the problem and of the solution. We can, in fact, state the problem in the B event-based framework. It remains to prove the optimality of the resulting spanning tree; this can be derived using tools and models. Before starting the modelling, we recall the B-event-based modelling technique.

6.3 Development of a Spanning-tree Algorithm

Formal Specification of the Spanning-tree Problem

First we define the elements of the current graph, namely g over the set of nodes ND. The graph is assumed to be undirected, which is modelled by the symmetry of the relation of the graph. Node r is the root of the resulting tree, and we obtain the following B definitions:

$$
\boxed{
\begin{array}{l}
g \subseteq ND \times ND \ \wedge \\
g = g^{-1} \ \wedge \\
r \in ND
\end{array}
}
$$

Termination of the algorithm is clearly related to the properties of the current graph; the existence of the spanning tree is based on the connectivity of the graph. The modelling of a tree uses the acyclicity of the graph. A tree is defined by a root r, a node $r \in ND$ and a parent function t (each node has an unique parent node, except for the root): $t \in ND - \{r\} \longrightarrow ND$. A tree is an acyclic graph. A cycle c in a finite graph t built on a set ND is a subset of ND whose elements are members of the inverse image of c under t, formally, $c \subseteq t^{-1}[c]$. To fulfil the requirement of acyclicity, the only set c that enjoys this property is necessarily the empty set. We formalize this by the left predicate that follows, which can be proved to be *equivalent* to the one on the right, which can be used as an induction rule:

$$
\boxed{
\begin{array}{l}
\forall c \cdot (\\
\quad c \subseteq ND \ \wedge \\
\quad c \subseteq t^{-1}[c] \\
\Rightarrow \\
\quad c = \emptyset \,)
\end{array}
}
\quad \Leftrightarrow \quad
\boxed{
\begin{array}{l}
\forall q \cdot (\\
\quad q \subseteq ND \ \wedge \\
\quad r \in q \ \wedge \\
\quad t^{-1}[q] \subseteq q \\
\Rightarrow \\
\quad ND = q \,)
\end{array}
}
$$

We have proved the equivalence using Atelier B. We can now define a spanning tree (rooted at r and with the parent function t) of a graph g as one whose parent function is included in g, formally

$$
\boxed{
\begin{array}{l}
\mathsf{spanning}\,(t, g) = \\
\left(
\begin{array}{l}
t \in ND - \{r\} \longrightarrow ND \quad \wedge \\
\forall q \cdot (q \subseteq ND \ \wedge \ r \in q \ \wedge \ t^{-1}[q] \subseteq q \ \Rightarrow \ ND = q) \ \wedge \\
t \subseteq g
\end{array}
\right)
\end{array}
}
$$

Now we can define the set $\mathsf{tree}\,(g)$ of all spanning trees (with root r) of the graph g, formally

$$
\boxed{
\mathsf{tree}\,(g) \ = \ \{t \,|\, \mathsf{spanning}\,(t, g)\}
}
$$

We define the property of *being a connected graph* by $\mathsf{connected}(g)$:

$$
\boxed{
\begin{array}{l}
\mathsf{connected}\,(g) = \\
\left(
\begin{array}{l}
g \in ND \leftrightarrow ND \quad \wedge \\
\forall S \cdot (S \subseteq ND \ \wedge \ r \in S \ \wedge \ g[S] \subseteq S \ \Rightarrow \ ND = S)
\end{array}
\right)
\end{array}
}
$$

The graph g and the node r are two global constants of our problem and must satisfy the properties stated above. Moreover, we assert that there is at least one solution to our problem. The optimality of the solution will be analysed later, when we introduce the cost function. Now, we build the first model, which computes the solution in one shot. The event span corresponds to producing a spanning tree among the non-empty set of possible spanning trees for g. The variable st contains the resulting spanning tree:

$$
\begin{array}{l}
\textsf{span } = \\
\quad \textbf{begin} \\
\qquad st :\in \textsf{tree}(g) \\
\quad \textbf{end}
\end{array}
\qquad
st \in ND \leftrightarrow ND
$$

The invariant is very simple and is only a type invariant; the initialization establishes the invariant.

The current model is in fact the specification of the simple spanning-tree problem; we have not yet mentioned the cost function. The next step is to refine the current model into a simple spanning-tree algorithm.

Development of a Simple Spanning-tree Algorithm

The second model introduces a new event, which gradually computes the spanning tree by constructing it in a progressive way. The new event adds a new edge to the current tree tr which partly spans g. The chosen edge is such that the first component of the pair of nodes is in tr_nodes and the second is in $remaining\_nodes$. These two new variables partition the set of nodes, and we obtain the following new properties to add to the invariant of the current model:

$$
\begin{array}{l}
tr\_nodes \subseteq ND \quad \wedge \\
remaining\_nodes \subseteq ND \quad \wedge \\
tr\_nodes \cup remaining\_nodes = ND \quad \wedge \\
tr\_nodes \cap remaining\_nodes = \emptyset
\end{array}
$$

A new event, progress, simulates the computation step of the current solution by choosing a pair maintaining the updated invariant:

```
progress =
  select
    remaining_nodes ≠ ∅
  then
    any x, y where
      x, y ∈ g  ∧  x, y ∈ tr_nodes × remaining_nodes
    then
      tr := tr ∪ {y ↦ x} ||
      tr_nodes := tr_nodes ∪ {y} ||
      remaining_nodes := remaining_nodes − {y}
    end
  end
```

The event span is refined simply by modifying the guard of the previous instance of the event in the abstract model. The event is triggered when the set of remaining nodes is empty: the variable st contains a spanning tree for the graph g:

```
span =
  select
    remaining_nodes = ∅
  then
    st := tr
  end
```

The invariant of the new model states the properties of the two new variables and relates them to previous ones:

$$tr\_nodes \subseteq ND \wedge$$
$$remaining\_nodes \subseteq ND \wedge$$
$$tr\_nodes \cup remaining\_nodes = ND \wedge$$
$$tr\_nodes \cap remaining\_nodes = \emptyset \wedge$$
$$tr \in tr\_nodes − \{r\} \longrightarrow tr\_nodes \wedge$$
$$\forall q \cdot (q \subseteq tr\_nodes \wedge r \in q \wedge tr^{-1}[q] \subseteq q \Rightarrow tr\_nodes = q)$$

The following initialization establishes the invariant:

$$tr := \emptyset ||$$
$$tr\_nodes := \{r\} ||$$
$$remaining\_nodes := ND − \{r\}$$

The absence of deadlock is expressed simply as follows:

$$\begin{array}{l} remaining\_nodes = \emptyset \ \vee \\ remaining\_nodes \neq \emptyset \ \wedge \\ \exists(x,y). \left(\begin{array}{l} x,y \in g \ \wedge \\ x,y \in tr\_nodes \times remaining\_nodes \end{array} \right) \end{array}$$

We have obtained a simple iterative solution to the simple minimal-spanning-tree problem; the solution follows the sketch of the algorithm given in [53] in the subsection describing the generic algorithm. We can derive the algorithm in Table 19 from the current model.

```
algorithm generic_MST
begin   tr := ∅;
  tr_nodes = {r};
  while remaining_nodes ≠ ∅ do
    let x, y where
       x, y ∈ g  ∧  x, y ∈ tr_nodes × remaining_nodes
    then
       tr := tr ∪ {y ↦ x};
       tr_nodes := tr_nodes ∪ {y};
       remaining_nodes := remaining_nodes − {y}
    end
  end_while
  st := tr end
```

Table 19. Derived MST algorithm

The next step refines the current model into a model where the cost function is effectively used.

A Proof View of the Spanning-tree Algorithm

The model above computes a spanning tree when the graph is connected. This algorithm looks like a proof of existence of a spanning tree; the following lemma allows us to prove that the set of spanning trees is not empty, and hence a minimum spanning tree exists.

Theorem 3. *(Existence of a spanning tree.)*
  $\mathsf{connected}\,(g) \Rightarrow \mathsf{tree}\,(g) \neq \emptyset$

However, this lemma requires us to construct a tree from a hypothesis related to the connectivity of the graph. Hence, we must prove an initial inductive theorem on finite sets, which will include the existence of a tree. We suppose that the set ND is finite and there exists a function from ND to $1..n$, where n is the cardinality of ND.

Theorem 4. *(An inductive theorem on finite sets.)*

$$\forall P \cdot ($$
$$P \subseteq \mathbb{P}(ND) \wedge$$
$$\emptyset \in P \wedge$$
$$\forall A \cdot (A \in P \wedge A \neq ND \Rightarrow \exists a \cdot (a \in ND - A \wedge A \cup \{a\} \in P))$$
$$\Rightarrow$$
$$ND \in P)$$

We can use the previous theorem with the set

$$\{A | A \subseteq ND \wedge \exists f \cdot \left(\begin{array}{l} f \in A - \{r\} \longrightarrow A \wedge \\ f \subseteq g \wedge \\ \forall S \cdot \left(\begin{array}{l} S \subseteq ND \wedge r \in S \wedge f^{-1}[S] \subseteq S \\ \Rightarrow \\ A \subseteq S \end{array} \right) \end{array} \right) \}$$

to prove that the set of spanning trees of g is not empty.

6.4 Development of Prim's Algorithm

The cost function is defined on the set of edges and is extended over the global set of possible pairs of nodes:

$$cost : g \longrightarrow \mathbb{Z} \wedge$$
$$\forall (x, y) \cdot (x, y \in g \Rightarrow cost(x \mapsto y) = cost(y \mapsto x)) \wedge$$
$$Cost : \mathbb{P}(g) \longrightarrow \mathbb{Z} \wedge$$
$$Cost(\{\}) = 0 \wedge$$
$$\forall (s, x, y) \cdot \left(\begin{array}{l} s \in \mathbb{P}(g) \wedge x, y \in g - s \\ \Rightarrow \\ Cost(s \cup \{x \mapsto y\}) = Cost(s) + cost(x \mapsto y) \end{array} \right)$$

We have proved that tree(g) is not empty, since the graph g is connected; $mst\_set(g)$, containing every minimum spanning tree of the graph g, is defined as follows:

$$mst\_set(g) =$$
$$\{mst | mst \in \text{tree}(g) \wedge \forall tr \cdot (tr \in \text{tree}(g) \Rightarrow Cost(mst) \leq Cost(tr))\}$$

The set $mst\_set(g)$ is clearly not empty. The first "one-shot" model is refined into the new model, which contains only one event span. We strengthen the definition of the choice of the resulting tree by strengthening the condition over the set and by choosing a candidate in the set of possible minimal-spanning-tree trees:

$$span =$$
$$\textbf{begin}$$
$$st :\in mst\_set(g)$$
$$\textbf{end}$$

The second model gradually computes the spanning tree by adding a new edge to the current tree "under construction" tr spanning a part of g. The tree tr is defined over the set of nodes already treated, called tr_nodes. The event progress is modified to handle the minimality criterion: the guard is modified to integrate the choice of the minimum edge from the remaining possible edges.

$$progress =$$
$$\textbf{select}$$
$$remaining\_nodes \neq \emptyset$$
$$\textbf{then}$$
$$\textbf{any } x, y \textbf{ where}$$
$$x, y \in g \;\land\; x, y \in tr\_nodes \times remaining\_nodes \;\land$$
$$\forall (a, b) \cdot (a \in tr\_nodes \;\land$$
$$b \in remaining\_nodes \;\land$$
$$a, b \in g$$
$$\Rightarrow$$
$$cost(y \mapsto x) \leq cost(b \mapsto a))$$
$$\textbf{then}$$
$$tr := tr \cup \{y \mapsto x\} \;||$$
$$tr\_nodes := tr\_nodes \cup \{y\} \;||$$
$$remaining\_nodes := remaining\_nodes - \{y\}$$
$$\textbf{end}$$
$$\textbf{end}$$

The event span remains unchanged:

$$span =$$
$$\textbf{select}$$
$$remaining\_nodes = \emptyset$$
$$\textbf{then}$$
$$st := tr$$
$$\textbf{end}$$

The invariant includes the invariant of the refined model of the generic refinement, and we add that the current spanning tree tr is a part of a minimum spanning tree of the graph g:

$$\exists T \cdot (T \in mst\_set(g) \;\land\; tr \subseteq T)$$

This invariant implies that after completion, when the event span occurs, the current spanning tree tr is finally a minimal one. Since tree(g) is not empty, then $mst\_set(g)$ is not empty and a tree can be chosen in this non-empty set to prove that a minimal-spanning-tree exists (this minimal-spanning-tree contains $\emptyset$). So the invariant holds for the initialization, using Theorem 3. The difficult task is to prove that the event progress maintains the invariant. We can take the minimum spanning tree given by the invariant if $y \mapsto x$ is in this tree. Otherwise we must provide another minimum tree which includes the current one and the new edge $y \mapsto x$.

In fact, textbooks provide algorithms implementing greedy strategy; we refer our explanations to the book by Cormen et al. [53] for our explanation. These authors proved a theorem that asserts that the choice of the two edges is made following a given requirement, namely a safe edge (a safe edge is an edge that allows the progress of the algorithm). We recall the theorem:

Theorem 5. *(Theorem 24.1 of [53, p. 501])*
Let g be a connected, undirected graph on ND (the set of nodes) with a real-valued weight function cost defined on g (the edges). Let tr be a subset of g that is included in some minimum spanning tree for g, let $(tr\_nodes, ND - tr\_nodes)$ be any cut of g that respects tr_nodes, and let (x, y) be a light edge crossing $(tr\_nodes, ND - tr\_nodes)$. Then edge (x, y) is safe for tr_nodes.

Let us explain the notions of a cut, crossing and a light edge. A cut $(tr\_nodes, ND - tr\_nodes))$ of an undirected graph g is a partition of ND. An edge (x, y) crosses the cut $(tr\_nodes, ND - tr\_nodes)$ if one of its endpoints is in tr_nodes and the other is in $ND - tr\_nodes$. An edge is a light edge crossing a cut if its weight is the minimum of any edge crossing the cut. A light edge is not unique.

Proof. *Let T be a minimum spanning tree that includes tr, and assume that T does not contain the light edge (x, y), since if it does, we have finished. We shall construct another minimum spanning tree T' that includes $tr \cup \{(x, y)\}$ by using a cut-and-paste technique, thereby showing that (x, y) is a safe edge for tr. The edge (x, y) forms a cycle with the edges on the path p from x to y in T. Since x and y are on opposite sides of the cut $(tr\_nodes, ND - tr\_nodes)$, there is at least one edge in T on the path p that also crosses the cut. Let (a, b) be any such edge. The edge (a, b) is not in tr, because the cut respects tr. Since (a, b) is on the unique path from x to y in T, removing (a, b) breaks T into two components. Adding (x, y) reconnects them to form a new spanning tree $T' = T - \{(a, b)\} \cup \{(x, y)\}$. We next show that T' is a minimum spanning tree. Since (x, y) is a light edge crossing $(tr\_nodes, ND - tr\_nodes)$ and (a, b) also crosses this cut, $cost(x, y) \leq cost(a, b)$. Therefore,*

$$Cost(T') = Cost(T) - cost(a, b) + cost(x, y)$$
$$\leq Cost(T)$$

But T is a minimum spanning tree, so that $Cost(T) \leq Cost(T')$; thus, T' must be a minimum spanning tree also. It remains to show that (x, y) is actually a safe edge for tr. We have $tr \subseteq T'$, since $tr \subseteq T$ and $(a, b) \notin tr$; thus, $tr \cup \{(x, y)\} \subseteq T'$. Consequently, since T' is a minimum spanning tree, (x, y) is safe for tr. □

We have to prove that the property above has in fact been incorporated into the B proof engine. However, this is not a simple exercise of translation but a complete formulation of some aspects of graph theory; moreover, the proof has been completely mechanized, as we shall show in the next subsection. Let us compare the theorem and our formulation. The pair $(tr\_nodes, ND - tr\_nodes)$ is a cut in the left part of the implication; the restriction of the tree f to the set of nodes tr_nodes is a tree rooted at r; and (x, y) crosses the cut. Those assumptions imply that there exists a spanning tree sp rooted at r that is minimum on tr_nodes and such that there exists a light cut (a, b) preserving the minimality property. Hence, we express this property formally and it will be proved separately:

$$
\begin{aligned}
&\forall(T, tr\_nodes, x, y) \cdot (\\
&\quad tr\_nodes \subseteq ND \wedge y \in ND \wedge \mathsf{atree}(r, ND, T) \\
&\quad r \in tr\_nodes \wedge x \in tr\_nodes \wedge (y \notin tr\_nodes) \wedge \\
&\quad \mathsf{atree}(r, tr\_nodes, (tr\_nodes - \{r\} \lhd T \rhd tr\_nodes)) \wedge \\
&\quad \forall S \cdot (S \subseteq ND \wedge y \in S \wedge T[S] \subseteq S \Rightarrow S \cap tr\_nodes \neq \emptyset) \\
&\Rightarrow \\
&\quad \exists(a, b, T') \cdot (\\
&\quad\quad a, b \in T \wedge a \notin tr\_nodes \wedge b \in tr\_nodes \wedge \\
&\quad\quad \mathsf{atree}(r, ND, T') \wedge \\
&\quad\quad T' \subseteq (T \cup T^{-1} - \{b \mapsto a, a \mapsto b\}) \cup \{y \mapsto x\} \wedge \\
&\quad\quad Cost(T') = Cost(T) - cost(b \mapsto a) + cost(y \mapsto x) \wedge \\
&\quad\quad y \mapsto x \in T' \wedge \\
&\quad\quad (tr\_nodes - \{r\} \lhd T \rhd tr\_nodes) \subseteq T'))
\end{aligned}
$$

Here we have introduced a predicate $\mathsf{atree}(root, nodes, tree)$ stating that a structure $tree$ is a tree on the set $nodes$ and whose root is $root$:

$$
\begin{aligned}
&\mathsf{atree}(root, nodes, tree) = \\
&\begin{pmatrix} root \in nodes \quad \wedge \\ tree \in nodes - \{root\} \longrightarrow nodes \quad \wedge \\ \forall q \cdot (q \subseteq nodes \wedge root \in q \wedge tree^{-1}[q] \subseteq q \Rightarrow nodes = q) \end{pmatrix}
\end{aligned}
$$

The above property is the key result for ensuring the optimality of the greedy strategy in this process. In the next subsection, we give details of the proof of our theorem.

6.5 On A Theory of Trees

As we have mentioned previously, trees play a central role in the justification of the algorithm; the optimality of the greedy strategy is based mainly on the proof of the theorem used by Cormen et al. [53]. We now need to give details of a theory of trees and the intermediate lemmas required for deriving the theorem. Both the development of the tree identification protocol IEEE 1394 [10] and the development of recursive functions [38] require proofs related to the closure of relations; we apply the same technique for the closure of a function defining a tree.

Let (T, r) be a tree defined by a tree function T and a root r; they satisfy the following axioms $\mathsf{atree}(r, ND, T)$. The closure cl of T^{-1} is the smallest relation that contains $\mathsf{id}(ND)$ and is stable by application of T^{-1}, that is,

$$
\begin{aligned}
&cl \in ND \;\leftrightarrow\; ND \;\wedge \\
&\mathsf{id}(ND) \;\subseteq\; cl \;\wedge \\
&(cl; T^{-1}) \;\subseteq\; cl \;\wedge \\
&\forall r \cdot (\\
&\qquad r \in ND \;\leftrightarrow\; ND \;\wedge \\
&\qquad \mathsf{id}(ND) \;\subseteq\; r \;\wedge \\
&\qquad (r; T^{-1}) \;\subseteq\; r \;\wedge \\
&\Rightarrow \\
&\qquad cl \;\subseteq\; r)
\end{aligned}
$$

Useful properties of this closure can be derived from those definitions; for instance, the closure is a fixed-point; the root r is connected to every node of the connected component; and the closure is transitive. We summarize these properties using our notation:

$$
\begin{aligned}
cl &= \mathsf{id}(ND) \;\cup\; (cl; T^{-1}); \\
r &\times ND \subseteq cl; \\
(T^{-1}&; cl) \subseteq cl; \\
(cl&; cl) \subseteq cl; \\
T &\cap cl = \emptyset; \\
cl &\cap cl^{-1} \subseteq \mathsf{id}(ND);
\end{aligned}
$$

Theorem 6. *(Concatenation of two separate trees.)*

Let $T_1, r_1, N_1, T_2, r_2, N_2, x$ be such that
$$
\begin{cases}
\mathsf{atree}(r_1, N_1, T_1), \\
\mathsf{atree}(r_2, N_2, T_2), \\
N_1 \cap N_2 = \emptyset, \\
N_1 \cup N_2 = ND, \\
x \in N_1.
\end{cases}
$$
Then $\mathsf{atree}(r_1, ND, T_1 \cup T_2 \cup \{r_2 \mapsto x\})$.

Proof Sketch. The proof is made up of several steps. The first step proves that the concatenation is a total function over the set $N_1 \cup N_2$. The second step leads to a more technical task, where we have to prove the inductive property over trees using a splitting of the inductive variable S ($S \cap N_1$ and $S \cap N_2$). □

Theorem 7. *(Subtree property.)*
Let (T, r) be a tree on ND (atree(r, ND, T)) and let b be a node in ND. Then atree$(b, cl[\{b\}], (cl[\{b\}] - \{b\} \lhd T))$.

Proof Sketch: The main difficulty is related to the inductive part. We must prove that, if $S \subseteq cl[\{b\}]$, $b \in S$ and $(cl[\{b\}] - \{b\} \lhd T)^{-1}[S] \subseteq S$, then $cl[\{b\}] \subseteq S$. We use the inductive property on T with the set $S \cup ND - cl[\{b\}]$. □

Theorem 8. *(Complement of a subtree.)*
Let (T, r) be a tree on ND and let b be a node in ND. Then atree$(r, ND - cl[\{b\}], (cl[\{b\}] \lhd\!\!\!- T))$.

Proof Sketch: We have to prove that if $S \subseteq ND - cl[\{b\}]$, $b \in S$ and $(cl[\{b\}] \lhd\!\!\!- T)^{-1}[S] \subseteq S$, then $ND - cl[\{b\}] \subseteq S$. A hint is to use the inductive property on T with the set $S \cup cl[\{b\}]$. □

Now, we must characterize the subtree, where we have reversed the edge between y to the root b. Let $subtree(T, b)$ be the subtree of T with b as root (this is $cl[\{b\}] - \{b\} \lhd T$). This following function seems to be a good choice:

$$ (cl^{-1}[\{y\}] \lhd\!\!\!- subtree(T, b)) \cup (cl^{-1}[\{y\}] \lhd subtree(T, b))^{-1} $$

$(cl^{-1}[\{y\}] \lhd subtree(T, b))^{-1}$ is exactly all reverse edges. $cl^{-1}[\{y\}]$ is the set of all parents of y.

Theorem 9. *(The reverse edge from y to b produces a tree.)*
Let b, y be such that: $\begin{cases} b \in ND \\ y \in cl[\{b\}] \end{cases}$ *, then*

atree$(y, cl[\{b\}], (cl^{-1}[\{y\}] \lhd\!\!\!- subtree(T, b)) \cup (cl^{-1}[\{y\}] \lhd subtree(T, b))^{-1})$.

Proof Sketch. In this case we must use an induction on the tree $cl[\{b\}]$, and sometimes use a second induction with the inductive property in the hypothesis.□

Theorem 10. *(Existence of a spanning tree.)*
Let a, b, x, y be such that $\begin{cases} b, a \in T, \\ y \in cl[\{b\}], \\ x : ND - cl[\{b\}]. \end{cases}$

Then there exists a tree T' such that

$$\begin{cases} T' \subseteq (T \ \cup \ T^{-1} - \{a \mapsto b, b \mapsto a\}) \ \cup \ \{y \mapsto x\}, \\ \mathsf{atree}(r, ND, T'), \\ Cost(T') = Cost(T) - cost(b \mapsto a) + cost(y \mapsto x), \\ y \mapsto x \ \in T', \\ cl[\{b\}] \ \triangleleft T \subseteq T'. \end{cases}$$

Proof Sketch: T' is obtained by concatenation of the two trees identified in the two previous theorems. The two trees are linked by the edge $y \mapsto x$. $\square$.

Finally, we have to prove the existence of an edge $b \mapsto a$ which is safe in the sense of the greedy strategy.

Theorem 11. *(Existence of $b \mapsto a$.)*

$$\text{Let } tr\_nodes, y \text{ by such that } \begin{cases} tr\_nodes \subseteq ND, \\ y \in ND - tr\_nodes, \\ r \in tr\_nodes, \\ \forall S \cdot \begin{pmatrix} S \subseteq ND \ \wedge \ y \in S \ \wedge \ T[S] \subseteq S \\ \Rightarrow \\ S \cap tr\_nodes \ \neq \ \emptyset \end{pmatrix} \end{cases}.$$

$$\text{Then there exist } a \text{ and } b \text{ such that } \begin{cases} a \in tr\_nodes, \\ b \mapsto a \in T, \\ b \notin tr\_nodes, \\ b \in cl^{-1}[\{y\}]. \end{cases}$$

The property of the existence of a minimum spanning tree can now be derived using theorems, and the proof of the property has then been completely mechanized. The development of Prim's algorithm leads us to state and to prove properties over trees. The inductive definition of trees helps in deriving intermediate lemmas asserting that the growing tree converges to the minimal-spanning-tree, according to the greedy strategy. The resulting algorithm has been completely proved and we can partially reuse currently developed models to obtain Dijkstra's or Kruskal's algorithm. The greedy strategy is not always efficient, however, and the optimality of the resulting algorithm is proved in [53, Theorem 24.1]. The greedy method is based on optimisation criteria, and we have developed a collection of models [42] which can be instantiated when the greedy strategy is applicable and when some optimisation criterion is satisfied.

7 Design of Distributed Algorithms by Refinement

Developing distributed algorithms can be made simpler and safer by the use of refinement techniques. Refinement allows one to gradually develop a distributed algorithm step by step, and to tackle complex problems such as the PCI transaction ordering problem [36] or the IEEE 1394 [10]. The B event-based method [4] provides a framework that integrates refinement for deriving models solving distributed problems.

The systems under consideration with our technique are general software systems, control systems, protocols, sequential and distributed algorithms, operating systems and circuits; these are generally very complex and have parts interacting with an environment. A discrete abstraction of such a system constitutes an adequate framework: such an abstraction is called a *discrete model*. A discrete model is more generally known as a *discrete transition system* and provides a view of the current system; the development of a model in B follows an incremental process validated by refinement. A system is modelled by a sequence of models related by refinement and managed in a project. We limit the scope of our work here to distributed algorithms modelled under the *local computation rule* [46] for graphs, and we specialize the proof obligations with respect to the target of the development process which is a distributed algorithm fitting safety and liveness requirements.

The goal of the IEEE 1394 protocol is to elect *in a finite time* a specific node, called the *leader*, in a network made of various nodes linked by communication channels. Once the leader has been elected, each non-leader node in the network should have a well-defined way to communicate with it. This election of the leader has to be done in a distributed and non-deterministic way. The development presented below partially replays the development of the IEEE 1394 protocol, but the resulting algorithm is not the IEEE 1394 protocol. In fact, we present the development of a distributed leader election, and we partially reuse the models of the development of the IEEE 1394 protocol: the first, second and third models are reused from our paper [10], and the problem of contention is solved by assigning a static priority to each site. The resulting algorithm is derived from the last B model in the sequence.

7.1 The Basic Mathematical Structure

Before considering details of the protocol, we shall give a very solid definition of the main topology of the network. It is essentially formalized by means of a set ND of nodes subject to the following assumptions:

1. The network is represented by a graph g built on ND.
2. The links between the nodes are *bidirectional*.
3. A node is *not directly connected to itself*:

$$
\begin{array}{ll}
1. & g \subseteq ND \times ND \\
2. & g = g^{-1} \\
3. & \mathsf{id}(ND) \cap g = \emptyset
\end{array}
$$

Item 2 above is formally represented by a *symmetric graph* whose domain (and thus co-domain too) corresponds to the entire *finite set* of nodes. The symmetry of the graph is due to the representation of the non-oriented graph by pairs of nodes and the link x-y is represented by the two pairs $x \mapsto y$ and $y \mapsto x$. Item 3 is rendered by saying that the graph is *not reflexive*.

There are two other very important properties of the graph: it is *connected and acyclic*. Both of these properties are formalized by claiming that the relation between each node and the spanning trees of the graph having that node as a root is *total* and *functional*. In other words, each node in the graph can be associated with one and exactly one tree rooted at that node and spanning the graph. We can model a tree by a root r, which is a node, i.e., $r \in ND$, and a parent function t (each node has a unique parent node, except for the root): $t \in ND - \{r\} \longrightarrow ND$. The tree is an acyclic graph. A cycle c in a finite graph t built on a set $N < D$ is a subset of ND whose elements are members of the inverse image of c under t; formally, $c \subseteq t^{-1}[c]$. To fulfil the requirement of acyclicity, the only set c that enjoys this property is thus the empty set. This can be formalized by the left predicate that follows, which can be proved to be *equivalent* to the one on the right, and which can be used as an induction rule:

$$\forall c \cdot (c \subseteq ND \wedge c \subseteq t^{-1}[c] \Rightarrow c = \emptyset)$$

$$\Updownarrow \text{ i.e., } \Leftrightarrow$$

$$\forall q \cdot (q \subseteq ND \wedge r \in q \wedge t^{-1}[q] \subseteq q \Rightarrow ND = q)$$

We have proved the equivalence using the tools B4free-with-Click'n'Prove [51] and Atelier B [50]. We can now define a spanning tree (with root r and parent function t) of a graph g as one whose parent function is included in g; formally,

$$\text{spanning}(r,t,g) = \begin{pmatrix} r \in ND \quad \wedge \\ t \in ND - \{r\} \longrightarrow ND \quad \wedge \\ \forall q \cdot (q \subseteq ND \wedge r \in q \wedge t^{-1}[q] \subseteq q \Rightarrow ND = q) \quad \wedge \\ t \subseteq g \end{pmatrix}$$

As mentioned above, each node in the graph can be associated with exactly one tree that is rooted at that node and spans the graph. For this purpose, we define the following total function f connecting each node r of the graph with its spanning tree $f(r)$:

$$f \in ND \rightarrow (ND \twoheadrightarrow ND)$$

$$\forall(r,t) \cdot \begin{pmatrix} r \in ND \wedge \\ t \in ND \twoheadrightarrow ND \\ \Rightarrow \\ t = f(r) \Leftrightarrow \text{spanning}(r,t,g) \end{pmatrix}$$

The graph g and the function f are thus *two global constants of the problem*. Since g and f are not instantiated, we do not have to deal with the size of the network, and automatic techniques based on model checking are not helpful for understanding how the algorithm workings. The special issue [52] presented a collection of verification techniques using model checking and the size of the network is clearly a practical bound. In contrast verification using PVS [54] and I/O automata is more adequate than model checking, but the invariants and proofs remain very difficult to understand. This is why we advocate the use of refinement, which provides an incremental way to derive both the algorithm and the proof. Moreover, refinement allows us to derive a election distributed algorithm for new leader, which is not possible in the verification-oriented approach.

7.2 The First Model, *leaderelection0*: the One-shot Election

Given the basic mathematical structure developed in the previous section, the essence of the abstract algorithm implemented by the protocol is very simple: it consists in building gradually (and non-deterministically) *one of the spanning trees* of the graph. Once this has been done, the *root* of that tree is *the elected leader,* and the communication structure between the other nodes and the leader is obviously the *spanning tree itself*. The protocol, considered globally, thus has *two variables*: (1) the future spanning tree, sp, and (2) the future leader ld. The gradual construction of the spanning tree simulates induction steps.

The first formal model of the development contains the definitions and properties of the two global constants (the above graph g and function f, together with their properties), and the definitions of two global variables sp and ld, typed in a very loose way: sp is a binary relation built on ND and ld is a node. The dynamic aspect of the protocol consists essentially made of one *event*, called elect, which claims *what the result of the protocol is, when it is completed*. In other words, at this level, there is no protocol, just the formal definition of its intended result, namely a spanning tree sp and its root ld:

```
elect =
   begin
      ld, sp : spanning (ld, sp, g)
   end
```

As can be seen, the election is done in one step. In other words, the spanning tree appears at once. The analogy of someone closing and opening their eyes can be used here to *explain* the process of election at this very abstract level.

7.3 Refining the First Model *leaderelection0*

In this section, we present two successive refinements of the previous initial model. In the first refinement, we obtain the essence of a *distributed* algorithm.

MODEL
   leaderelection0
SETS
   ND
CONSTANTS
   g, f
DEFINITIONS
   spanning$(r, t, g) =$

$$\left(\begin{array}{l} r \in ND \quad \wedge \\ t \in ND - \{r\} \longrightarrow ND \quad \wedge \\ \forall q \cdot (q \subseteq ND \ \wedge \ r \in q \ \wedge \ t^{-1}[q] \subseteq q \ \Rightarrow \ ND = q) \quad \wedge \\ t \subseteq g \end{array} \right)$$

PROPERTIES
   $g \subseteq ND \times ND \ \wedge \ g = g^{-1} \ \wedge \ \text{id}(ND) \cap g = \emptyset \ \wedge \ f \in ND \rightarrow (ND \twoheadrightarrow ND)$

$$\forall (r,t) \cdot \left(\begin{array}{l} r \in ND \ \wedge \\ t \in ND \twoheadrightarrow ND \\ \Rightarrow \\ t = f(r) \ \Leftrightarrow \ \text{spanning}\,(r, t, g) \end{array} \right)$$

VARIABLES
   ld, ts
INVARIANT
   $ld \in ND \ \wedge \ sp \in ND \twoheadrightarrow ND$
ASSERTIONS
   $\forall x \cdot (x \in ND \ \Rightarrow \ f(x) \cap f(x)^{-1} = \emptyset)$
INITIALISATION
   $ld :\in ND \parallel sp :\in ND \twoheadrightarrow ND$
EVENTS
elect $=$
  begin
    $ld, sp : \text{spanning}\,(ld, sp, g)$
  end
END

Table 20. 1st model, *leaderelection0*, of the distributed leader election algorithm

In the second refinement, we introduce some *communication mechanisms* between the nodes.

First Refinement *leaderelection1*
— Gradual Construction of a Spanning Tree

In the first model *leaderelection0* (Table 20) the construction of the spanning tree was performed in one shot. Of course, in a more realistic (concrete) formalization, this is not the case any more. In fact, the tree is constructed on a step-by-step basis. For this purpose, a new variable, called tr, and a new event, called progress, are introduced. The variable tr represents a sub-graph of g, it is made of several trees (it is thus a *forest*) which will *gradually converge* to the final tree, which we intend to build eventually. This convergence is performed by the event progress. This event involves two nodes x and y, which are neighbours in the graph g. Moreover, x and y are assume to be both outside the domain of tr. In other words, neither of them has a *parent* in tr. However, the node x is the parent of all its *other neighbours* (if any) in g. This last condition can be formalized by means of the predicate $g[\{x\}] = tr^{-1}[\{x\}] \cup \{y\}$ since the set of neighbours of x in g is $g[\{x\}]$ while the set of sons of x in tr is $tr^{-1}[\{x\}]$. When these conditions are fulfilled, then the event progress can be enabled and its action has the effect of making the node y the parent of x in tr. The abstract event elect is now refined. Its new version is concerned with a node x which happens to be the parent of all its neighbours in g. This condition is formalized by the predicate $g[\{x\}] = tr^{-1}[\{x\}]$. When this condition is fulfilled, the action of elect makes x the leader ld and tr the spanning tree sp. The following are the formal representations of these events:

progress $=$
    any x,y **where**
        $x,y \in g \wedge x \notin \mathrm{dom}(tr) \wedge y \notin \mathrm{dom}(tr)$
        $\wedge\ g[\{x\}] = tr^{-1}[\{x\}] \cup \{y\}$
    then
        $tr := tr \cup \{x \mapsto y\}$
    end
	elect $=$
	    any x **where**
	        $x \in ND\ \wedge$
	        $g[\{x\}] = tr^{-1}[\{x\}]$
	    then
	        $ld, sp := x, tr$
	    end

The new event progress clearly refines *skip*, since it only updates the variable tr, which is a *new variable* in this refinement with no existence in the abstraction. Notice also that progress clearly decreases the quantity $\mathsf{card}(g) - \mathsf{card}(tr)$. The situation is far less clear concerning the refinement of the event elect. We have to prove that when its guard is true, then tr is indeed a spanning tree of the graph g, whose root is precisely x. Formally, this leads to proving the following:

$$\forall x \cdot (\, x \in ND\ \wedge\ g[\{x\}] = tr^{-1}[\{x\}]\ \Rightarrow\ \mathsf{spanning}\,(x, tr, g)\,)$$

According to the definition of the constant function f, the above property is clearly equivalent to

$$\forall x \cdot (\, x \in ND\ \wedge\ g[\{x\}] = tr^{-1}[\{x\}]\ \Rightarrow\ tr = f(x)\,)$$

This means that tr and $f(x)$ should have the same domain, namely $ND - \{x\}$, and that for all n in $ND - \{x\}$, $tr(n)$ is equal to $f(x)(n)$. This amounts to proving the following:

$$ND = \{x\} \cup \{n \mid n \in ND - \{x\} \wedge f(x)(n) = tr(n)\}$$

This is done using the *inductive property* associated with each spanning tree $f(x)$. Notice that we also need the following invariants:

$$tr \in ND \twoheadrightarrow ND$$
$$\mathsf{dom}\,(tr) \lhd (tr \cup tr^{-1}) = \mathsf{dom}\,(tr) \lhd g$$
$$tr \cap tr^{-1} = \emptyset$$

This new model (Table 21) although more concrete than the previous one, is nevertheless still an abstraction of the *real* protocol: it just explains how the leader can be eventually elected by the gradual transformation of the forest tr into a unique tree spanning the graph g.

Second Refinement, *leaderelection2*
— Introducing Communication Channels

In the previous refinement, the event progress was still very abstract: as soon as two nodes x and y with the required properties were detected, the corresponding action took place immediately. In other words, y became the parent of x *in one shot*. In the *real* protocol, things are not so "magic": once a node x has detected that it is the parent of all its neighbours except one, y, it sends a *request* to y in order to ask it to become its parent. Node y then *acknowledges* this request and, finally, node x establishes a *parent* connection with node y. This connection, which is thus established in *three distributed steps*, is clearly closer to what happens in the real protocol. We shall see, however, in the next refinement that what we have just described is not yet the final word. But let us formalize this for the moment. In order to do so, we need to define at least two new variables: *req*, to handle the requests, and *ack*, to handle the acknowledgements. *req* is a partial function from ND to itself. When a pair $x \mapsto y$ belongs to *req*, this means that node x has send a request to node y asking it to become its parent: the functionality of *req* is due to the fact that x has only one parent. Clearly, *req* is also included in the graph g. When node y sends an acknowledgement to x this is because y has *already* received a request from x: *ack* is thus a partial function included in *req*:

$$req \in ND \twoheadrightarrow ND$$
$$req \subseteq g$$
$$ack \subseteq req$$
$$tr \subseteq ack$$
$$ack \cap ack^{-1} = \emptyset$$

Notice that when a pair $x \mapsto y$ belongs to *ack*, it means that y has sent an acknowledgment to x (clearly y can send several acknowledgements since it

REFINEMENT
  leaderelection1
REFINES
  leaderelection0
VARIABLES
  ld, ts, tr
INVARIANT
  $tr \in ND \twoheadrightarrow ND$
  $\mathsf{dom}\,(tr) \vartriangleleft (tr \cup tr^{-1}) = \mathsf{dom}\,(tr) \vartriangleleft g$
  $tr \cap tr^{-1} = \emptyset$
ASSERTIONS
  $\forall x \cdot (\, x \in ND \land g[\{x\}] = tr^{-1}[\{x\}] \;\Rightarrow\; tr = f(x)\,)$
INITIALISATION
  $ld :\in ND \parallel sp :\in ND \twoheadrightarrow ND \parallel tr := \emptyset$
EVENTS
progress $=$
  any x, y **where**
    $x, y \in g \land x \notin \mathsf{dom}(tr) \land y \notin \mathsf{dom}(tr)$
    $\land \; g[\{x\}] = tr^{-1}[\{x\}] \cup \{y\}$
  then
    $tr := tr \cup \{x \mapsto y\}$
  end ;
elect $=$
  any x **where**
    $x \in ND \land$
    $g[\{x\}] = tr^{-1}[\{x\}]$
  then
    $ld, sp := x, tr$
  end
END

Table 21. 2nd model, *leaderelection1*, of the distributed leader election algorithm

might be the parent of several nodes). It is also clear that it is not possible in this case for the pair $y \mapsto x$ to belong to *ack*.

The final connection between x and y is still represented by the function tr. Thus tr is included in *ack*. All this can be formalized as shown. Two new events are defined in order to manage requests and acknowledgements: send_req, and send_ack. As we shall see, the event progress is modified, whereas the event elect is left unchanged. Here are the new events and the refined version of progress:

send_req =
  any x, y **where**
    $x, y \in g \ \wedge \ y, x \notin ack \ \wedge$
    $x \notin \text{dom}\,(req) \ \wedge$
    $g[\{x\}] = tr^{-1}[\{x\}] \ \cup \ \{y\}$
  then
    $req := req \ \cup \ \{x \mapsto y\}$
  end

send_ack =
  any x, y **where**
    $x, y \in req \ \wedge$
    $x, y \notin ack \ \wedge$
    $y \notin \text{dom}\,(req)$
  then
    $ack := ack \ \cup \ \{x \mapsto y\}$
  end

progress =
  any x, y **where**
    $x, y \in ack \ \wedge$
    $x \notin \text{dom}\,(tr)$
  then
    $tr := tr \ \cup \ \{x \mapsto y\}$
  end

The event send_req is enabled when a node x discovers that it is the parent of all its neighbours except one y: $g[\{x\}] = tr^{-1}[\{x\}] \ \cup \ \{y\}$. Notice that, as expected, this condition is exactly the one that allowed the event progress in the previous model to be enabled. Moreover, x must not have already sent a request to any node: $x \notin \text{dom}\,(req)$. Finally, x must not have already sent an acknowledgement to node y: $y, x \notin ack$. When these conditions are fulfilled, then the pair $x \mapsto y$ is added to req. The event send_ack is enabled when a node y receives a request from node x; moreover y must not have already sent an acknowledgement to node x: $x, y \in req$ and $x, y \notin ack$. Finally, node y must not have sent a request to any node: $y \notin \text{dom}\,(req)$ (we shall see very soon what happens when this condition does not hold). When these conditions are fulfilled, node y sends an acknowledgement to node x: the pair $x \mapsto y$ is thus added to ack. The event progress is enabled when a node x receives an acknowledgement from node y: $x, y \in ack$. Moreover node x has not yet established any parent connection: $x \notin \text{dom}\,(tr)$. When these conditions are fulfilled, the connection is established: the pair $x \mapsto y$ is added to tr.

The events send_req and send_ack clearly refine *skip*. Moreover their actions increment the cardinals of req and ack, respectively (these cardinals are bounded by that d g). It remains for us to prove that the new version of the event progress is a correct refinement of its abstraction. The actions being the same, it just remains for us to prove that the concrete guard implies the abstract one. This amounts to proving the following left predicate, which is added as an invariant:

$$\forall (x, y) \cdot \begin{pmatrix} x, y \in ack \quad \wedge \\ x \notin \operatorname{dom}(tr) \\ \Rightarrow \\ x, y \in g \quad \wedge \\ x \notin \operatorname{dom}(tr) \quad \wedge \\ y \notin \operatorname{dom}(tr) \quad \wedge \\ g[\{x\}] = tr^{-1}[\{x\}] \cup \{y\} \end{pmatrix}$$

$$\forall (x, y) \cdot \begin{pmatrix} x, y \in req \quad \wedge \\ x, y \notin ack \\ \Rightarrow \\ x, y \in g \quad \wedge \\ x \notin \operatorname{dom}(tr) \quad \wedge \\ y \notin \operatorname{dom}(tr) \quad \wedge \\ g[\{x\}] = tr^{-1}[\{x\}] \cup \{y\} \end{pmatrix}$$

When we try to prove that the left predicate is maintained by the event send_ack, we find that the right predicate above must also be proved. It is thus added as a new invariant, which, this time, can easily be proved to be maintained by all events.

The problem of contention.

The guard of the event send_ack above contains the condition $y \notin \operatorname{dom}(req)$. If this condition does not hold when the other two guarding conditions hold, that is $x, y \in req$ and $x, y \notin ack$ hold, then clearly x has sent a request to y and y has sent a request to x: each one of them wants the other to be its parent! This problem is called the *contention* problem. In this case, no acknowledgements should be sent, since then each node x and y would be the parent of the other. In the *real* protocol the problem is solved by means of timers. As soon as a node y discovers a contention with node x, it waits for a very short delay in order to be certain that the other node x has also discovered the problem. The very short delay in question is at least equal to the message transfer time between nodes (such a time is supposed to be *bounded*). After this, each node randomly chooses (with probability $1/2$) to wait for either a *short* or a *long* delay (the difference between the two is at least twice the message transfer time). After the chosen delay has passed, each node sends a new request to the other *if it is in a situation to do so*. Clearly, if both nodes choose the same delay, the contention situation will reappear. However, if they do not choose the same delay, then the one with the larger delay becomes the parent of the other: when it wakes up, it discovers the request from the other but it has not itself already sent its own request, it can therefore send an acknowledgement and thus become the parent. According to the law of large numbers, the probability for both nodes to choose the same delay indefinitely is null. Thus, at some point, they will (in probability) choose different delays and one of them will thus become the parent of the other. Rather than to reuse the complete IEEE 1394 development [10], we have reused a part of the development and developed a new solution for solving the contention problem; the new algorithm was discovered after a misunderstanding of the initial IEEE 1394 solution.

When two nodes are in contention (and at most two nodes can be in contention, it has been proved mechanically and formally), both nodes cannot send an acknowledgement to the other node; one of them should not be able to send this acknowledgement and the other one must do it. The main idea is to introduce a *unique counter* called ctr, and this means that each node is uniquely identified and must be identifiable. In a real network, one can assume that pieces of equipment might be uniquely identified by a unique address, for instance, but it not the general rule. The IEEE 1394 protocol does not make any assumption about the identification of nodes.

$$ctr \in ND \rightarrowtail \mathbb{N}$$

The corresponding new event is called solve_cnt. As in the case of send_ack, the action of this event adds the pair $x \mapsto y$ to ack:

$$
\begin{aligned}
&\textsf{solve\_cnt} = \\
&\quad \textbf{any } x, y \textbf{ where} \\
&\qquad x, y \in req - ack \quad \wedge \ y \in \mathrm{dom}\,(req) \wedge \ ctr(x) < ctr(y) \\
&\quad \textbf{then} \\
&\qquad ack := ack \ \cup \ \{x \mapsto y\} \\
&\quad \textbf{end}
\end{aligned}
$$

The two differences with respect to the guard of the event send_ack concern the condition $y \in \mathrm{dom}\,(req)$, which is true in solve_cnt and false in send_ack, and the guard $ctr(x) < ctr(y)$ is added to the event solve_cnt. Since ctr is an injection, the two nodes x and y cannot both trigger this event. The proof of the invariant requires the following extra invariants:

$$
\forall\,(x,y) \cdot \left(
\begin{array}{l}
x, y \in req - ack \ \wedge \\
y \in \mathrm{dom}\,(req) \\
\Rightarrow \\
y, x \in req
\end{array}
\right)
$$

$$
\forall\,(x,y) \cdot \left(
\begin{array}{l}
x, y \in req - ack \ \wedge \\
y \in \mathrm{dom}\,(req) \ \wedge \\
ctr(x) < ctr(y) \\
\Rightarrow \\
x, y \notin ack
\end{array}
\right)
$$

$$\forall\,(x,y,z)\cdot \left(\begin{array}{l} x,y \in req \,\wedge \\ z \in g[\{x\}] \,\wedge \\ z \neq y \\ \Rightarrow \\ z,x \in tr \end{array} \right)$$

The complete formalization of the solution of the real IEEE 1394 protocol (involving the timers and the random choices) has not been addressed, neither in the current development nor in [10]. Further work on the integration of timers needs to be done.

7.4 Final Refinements: Localization

In the previous refinement (Table 22) the guards of the various events were defined in terms of *global* constants or variables such as g, tr, req and ack. A closer look at this refinement shows that these constants or variables are used in expressions of the following form: $g^{-1}[\{x\}]$, $tr^{-1}[\{x\}]$, $ack^{-1}[\{x\}]$, dom(req) and dom(tr). These forms dictate the kind of *data refinement* that we now undertake.

The fourth, fifth and sixth models progressively introduce local information, which is related to abstract global values. These models are shown in Tables 23–25; the model *leaderelection5* introduces message communications (TR, REQ, ACK).

We declare five new variables nb (for "neighbours"), ch (for "children"), ac (for "acknowledged"), dr (for "domain of req"), and dt (for "domain of tr"). The following are the declarations of these variables, together with simple definitions of them in terms of the global variables:

$nb \in ND \rightarrow \mathbb{P}(ND)$	$\forall x \cdot (\, x \in ND \;\Rightarrow\; nb(x) \;=\; g^{-1}[\{x\}]\,)$
$ch \in ND \rightarrow \mathbb{P}(ND)$	$\forall x \cdot (\, x \in ND \;\Rightarrow\; ch(x) \;\subseteq\; tr^{-1}[\{x\}]\,)$
$ac \in ND \rightarrow \mathbb{P}(ND)$	$\forall x \cdot (\, x \in ND \;\Rightarrow\; ac(x) \;=\; ack^{-1}[\{x\}]\,)$
$dr \subseteq ND$	$dr = $ dom(req)
$dt \subseteq ND$	$dt = $ dom(tr)

Given a node x, the sets $nb(x)$, $ch(x)$ and $ac(x)$ are assumed to be *stored* locally within the node. As the varying sets $ch(x)$ and $ac(x)$ are subsets of the constant set $nb(x)$, it is certainly possible to refine their encoding further. Likewise, the two sets dr and dt still appear to be global, but they can clearly be encoded locally in each node by means of local Boolean variables.

It is worth noticing that the definition of the variable ch above is not given in terms of an equality, rather in terms of an inclusion (and thus it is not really a definition). This is due to the fact that the set $ch(y)$ cannot be updated while the event progress is taking place: this is because this event can act only on its *local* data. A new event in *leaderelection3*, receive_cnf (for

REFINEMENT *leaderelection2*
REFINES *leaderelection1*
CONSTANTS
  ctr
PROPERTIES
ctr $\in ND \rightarrowtail \mathbb{N}$
VARIABLES
  ld, ts, tr, req, ack
INVARIANT
  $req \in ND \nrightarrow ND$
  $req \subseteq g$
  $ack \subseteq req$
  $tr \subseteq ack$
  $ack \cap ack^{-1} = \emptyset$
  $\forall (x, y)\cdot$
  $$\begin{pmatrix} x, y \in ack & \wedge \\ x \notin \mathsf{dom}(tr) \\ \Rightarrow \\ x, y \in g & \wedge \\ x \notin \mathsf{dom}(tr) & \wedge \\ y \notin \mathsf{dom}(tr) & \wedge \\ g[\{x\}] = tr^{-1}[\{x\}] \cup \{y\} \end{pmatrix}$$
  $\forall (x, y)\cdot$
  $$\begin{pmatrix} x, y \in req & \wedge \\ x, y \notin ack \\ \Rightarrow \\ x, y \in g & \wedge \\ x \notin \mathsf{dom}(tr) & \wedge \\ y \notin \mathsf{dom}(tr) & \wedge \\ g[\{x\}] = tr^{-1}[\{x\}] \cup \{y\} \end{pmatrix}$$
  $\forall (x, y) \cdot$
  $$\begin{pmatrix} x, y \in req - ack & \wedge \\ y \in \mathsf{dom}(req) \\ \Rightarrow \\ y, x \in req \end{pmatrix}$$
  $\forall (x, y) \cdot$
  $$\begin{pmatrix} x, y \in req - ack & \wedge \\ y \in \mathsf{dom}(req) & \wedge \\ ctr(x) < ctr(y) \\ \Rightarrow \\ x, y \notin ack \end{pmatrix}$$
  $\forall (x, y, z) \cdot$
  $$\begin{pmatrix} x, y \in req & \wedge \\ z \in g[\{x\}] & \wedge \\ z \neq y \\ \Rightarrow \\ z, x \in tr \end{pmatrix}$$

ASSERTIONS
  $\mathsf{id}(ND) \cap ack = \emptyset$
  $\mathsf{id}(ND) \cap req = \emptyset$
  $\mathsf{id}(ND) \cap tr = \emptyset$
INITIALISATION
  $ld :\in ND \parallel tr := \emptyset \parallel ack := \emptyset \parallel$
  $sp :\in ND \nrightarrow ND \parallel req := \emptyset$
EVENTS
send_req =
  any x, y **where**
    $x, y \in g \wedge y, x \notin ack \wedge$
    $x \notin \mathsf{dom}(req) \wedge$
    $g[\{x\}] = tr^{-1}[\{x\}] \cup \{y\}$
  then
    $req := req \cup \{x \mapsto y\}$
  end ;
send_ack =
  any x, y **where**
    $x, y \in req \wedge$
    $x, y \notin ack \wedge$
    $y \notin \mathsf{dom}(req)$
  then
    $ack := ack \cup \{x \mapsto y\}$
  end ;
solve_cnt =
  any x, y **where**
    $x, y \in req - ack \wedge$
    $y \in \mathsf{dom}(req) \wedge$
    $ctr(x) < ctr(y)$
  then
    $ack := ack \cup \{x \mapsto y\}$
  end ;
progress =
  any x, y **where**
    $x, y \in ack \wedge x \notin \mathsf{dom}(tr)$
  then
    $tr := tr \cup \{x \mapsto y\}$
  end ;
elect =
  any x **where**
    $x \in ND \wedge$
    $g[\{x\}] = tr^{-1}[\{x\}]$
  then
    $ld, sp := x, tr$
  end
END

Table 22. 3rd model, *leaderelection2* of the distributed leader election algorithm

REFINEMENT
  leaderelection3
REFINES
  leaderelection2
CONSTANTS
  nb
PROPERTIES
  $nb \in ND \rightarrow \mathbb{P}(ND)$
  $\forall x \cdot (x \in ND \Rightarrow nb(x) = g^{-1}[\{x\}])$
VARIABLES
  ld, ts, tr, req, ack, ch
INVARIANT
  $ch \in ND \rightarrow \mathbb{P}(ND)$
  $\forall x \cdot (x \in ND \Rightarrow ch(x) \subseteq tr^{-1}[\{x\}])$
INITIALISATION
  $ld :\in ND \;\| ch = ND \times \{\emptyset\}$
  $tr := \emptyset \;\| req := \emptyset \;\| ack := \emptyset$
EVENTS
elect $=$
  any x **where**
    $x \in ND \;\wedge$
    $nb(x) = ch(x)$
  then
    $ld := x$
  end
send_req $=$
  any x, y **where**
    $x, y \in g \;\wedge\; y, x \notin ack \;\wedge$
    $x \notin \mathrm{dom}\,(req) \;\wedge$
    $nb(x) = ch(x) \;\cup\; \{y\}$
  then
    $req := req \;\cup\; \{x \mapsto y\}$
  end ;
receive_cnf $=$
  any x, y **where**
    $x, y \in tr \;\wedge$
    $x \notin ch(y)$
  then
    $ch(y) := ch(y) \;\cup\; \{x\}$
  end
END

Table 23. 4th model, *leaderelection3*, of the distributed leader election algorithm

REFINEMENT
  leaderelection4
REFINES
  leaderelection3
VARIABLES
  $ld, ts, tr, req, ack, ch, dr, ac, dt$
INVARIANT
  $ac \in ND \rightarrow \mathbb{P}(ND)$
  $dr \subseteq ND$
  $dt \subseteq ND$
  $\forall x \cdot (\, x \in ND \;\Rightarrow\; ac(x) \;=\; ack^{-1}[\{x\}] \,)$
  $dr = \mathsf{dom}\,(req)$
  $dt = \mathsf{dom}\,(tr)$
INITIALISATION
  $ld \; :\in \; ND \; \| ch = ND \times \{\emptyset\}$
  $tr := \emptyset \; \| req := \emptyset \; \| ack := \emptyset \; \|$
  $ac = ND \times \{\emptyset\} \; \| dr := \emptyset \; \| dt := \emptyset \; \|$
EVENTS
send_req $=$
  any x, y **where**
    $x \in ND - dr \;\wedge\; y \in ND - ac(x) \;\wedge\; nb(x) = ch(x) \;\cup\; \{y\}$
  then
    $req := req \;\cup\; \{x \mapsto y\} \;\|\; dr := dr \;\cup\; \{x\}$
  end
send_ack $=$
  any x, y **where**
    $x, y \in req \quad \wedge\; x \notin ac(y) \quad \wedge\; y \notin dr$
  then
    $ack := ack \;\cup\; \{x \mapsto y\} \;\|\; ac(y) := ac(y) \;\cup\; \{x\}$
  end
solve_cnt $=$
  any x, y **where**
    $x, y \in req \quad \wedge$
    $x \notin ac(y) \quad \wedge\; y \in dr \quad \wedge\; ctr(x) < ctr(y)$
  then
    $ack := ack \;\cup\; \{x \mapsto y\} \;\|\; ac(y) := ac(y) \;\cup\; \{x\}$
  end
progress $=$
  any x, y **where**
    $x, y \in ack \quad \wedge\; x \notin dt$
  then
    $tr := tr \;\cup\; \{x \mapsto y\} \;\|\; dt := dt \;\cup\; \{x\}$
  end
END

Table 24. 5th model, *leaderelection4*, of the distributed leader election algorithm

REFINEMENT   *leaderelection5*
REFINES   *leaderelection4*
VARIABLES
   $ld, ts, TR, REQ, ACK, ch, dr, ac, dt$
INVARIANT
   $REQ \in ND \times ND \;\; \wedge \;\; req = REQ \cup ack \;\; \wedge \;\; REQ \cap ack = \emptyset$
   $ACK \in ND \times ND \;\; \wedge \;\; ack = ACK \cup tr \;\; \wedge \;\; ACK \cap tr = \emptyset$
   $TR \in ND \times ND \;\; \wedge \;\; TR \subseteq tr \;\; \wedge \;\; \forall(x, y) \cdot (\, x, y \in TR \;\Rightarrow\; x \notin ch(y))$
INITIALISATION
   $ld :\in ND \;\|ch = ND \times \{\emptyset\} \;\|ac = ND \times \{\emptyset\} \;\|dr := \emptyset \;\|dt := \emptyset \;\|$
   $TR := \emptyset \;\| \quad REQ := \emptyset \;\|ACK := \emptyset$
EVENTS
send_req = *Local node x*
   any x, y **where**
      $x \in ND - dr \;\wedge\; y \in ND - ac(x) \;\wedge\; nb(x) = ch(x) \;\cup\; \{y\}$
   then
      $REQ := REQ \;\cup\; \{x \mapsto y\} \;\|\; dr := dr \;\cup\; \{x\}$
   end
send_ack = *Local node y*
   any x, y **where**
      $x, y \in REQ \quad \wedge \; y \notin dr$
   then
      $REQ := REQ -; \{x \mapsto y\} \;\|\; ACK := ACK \;\cup\; \{x \mapsto y\} \;\|$
      $ac(y) := ac(y) \;\cup\; \{x\}$
   end
solve_cnt = *Local node y*
   any x, y **where**
      $x, y \in REQ \;\wedge\; y \in dr \quad \wedge \; ctr(x) < ctr(y)$
   then
      $REQ := REQ -; \{x \mapsto y\} \;\|\; ACK := ACK \;\cup\; \{x \mapsto y\} \;\|$
      $ac(y) := ac(y) \;\cup\; \{x\}$
   end
progress = *Local node x*
   any x, y **where**
      $x, y \in ACK$
   then
      $ACK := ACK - \{x \mapsto y\} \;\|\; TR := TR \;\cup\; \{x \mapsto y\} \;\|\; dt := dt \;\cup\; \{x\}$
   end
receive_cnf = *Local node y*
   any x, y **where**
      $x, y \in TR$
   then
      $TR := TR -; \{x \mapsto y\} \;\|\; ch(y) := ch(y) \;\cup\; \{x\}$
   end
END

Table 25. 6th model, *leaderelection5*, of the distributed leader election algorithm

receive confirmation) is thus necessary to update the set $ch(y)$. The following are the refinement of the various events:

elect $=$
  any x **where**
    $x \in ND \wedge$
    $nb(x) = ch(x)$
  then
    $ld := x$
  end

send_req $=$
  any x, y **where**
    $x \in ND - dr \wedge$
    $y \in ND - ac(x) \wedge$
    $nb(x) = ch(x) \cup \{y\}$
  then
    $req := req \cup \{x \mapsto y\} \parallel$
    $dr := dr \cup \{x\}$
  end

send_ack $=$
  any x, y **where**
    $x, y \in req \quad \wedge$
    $x \notin ac(y) \quad \wedge$
    $y \notin dr$
  then
    $ack := ack \cup \{x \mapsto y\} \parallel$
    $ac(y) := ac(y) \cup \{x\}$
  end

solve_cnt $=$
  any x, y **where**
    $x, y \in req \quad \wedge$
    $x \notin ac(y) \quad \wedge$
    $y \in dr \quad \wedge$
    $ctr(x) < ctr(y)$
  then
    $ack := ack \cup \{x \mapsto y\} \parallel$
    $ac(y) := ac(y) \cup \{x\}$
  end

progress $=$
  any x, y **where**
    $x, y \in ack \quad \wedge$
    $x \notin dt$
  then
    $tr := tr \cup \{x \mapsto y\} \parallel$
    $dt := dt \cup \{x\}$
  end

receive_cnf $=$
  any x, y **where**
    $x, y \in tr \wedge$
    $x \notin ch(y)$
  then
    $ch(y) := ch(y) \cup \{x\}$
  end

The Proofs that these events correctly refine their respective abstractions are technically trivial. We now give, in the following table, the local node *in charge* of each event as encoded above:

event	node
elect	x
send_req	x
send_ack	y
solve_cnt	y
progress	x
receive_cnf	y

The reader may be surprised to see formulas such as $req := req \cup \{x \mapsto y\}$ and $x, y \in req$. They correspond in fact to writing and reading operations done by corresponding local nodes, as explained in the following table:

formula	explanation
$req := req \cup \{x \mapsto y\}$	x sends a request to y
$x, y \in req$	y reads a request from x
$ack := ack \cup \{x \mapsto y\}$	y sends an acknowledgement to x
%hline $x, y \in ack$	x reads an acknowledgement from y
$tr := tr \cup \{x \mapsto y\}$	x sends a confirmation to y
$x, y \in tr$	y reads a confirmation from y

The total number of proofs (all done mechanically with Atelier B [50] and B4free with Click'n'Prove [51]) was to 106, where 24 required an easy interaction. The proofs help us to understand the contention problem and the role of graph properties in the correctness of the solution. The refinements gradually introduce the various invariants of the system. No assumption is made about the size of the network. The proofs led us to the discovery of the confirmation event in order to obtain the complete correctness, and we chose to introduce a priority mechanism to solve the contention problem, which was not the solution for the IEEE 1394 protocol: a new distributed algorithm for leader election is proposed. ACK, REQ and TR model communication channels; they contain messages that currently have been sent but not yet received. We give the algorithm for the local node x below; x sends messages to another node y. We assume that each site has a unique number and that ctr is defined by this assignment:

Leader Election Algorithm
Local Node $x \in ND$
Local variables $nb, ch, ac \subseteq ND, ld \in ND, dr, dt \in Bool$

> **if** $nb = ch$ **then** $ld := x$ **fi**
> **if** $mes(y, ack) \in ACK$
> **then**
> $send(mes(x, tr), y) \parallel dt := dt \cup \{y\} \parallel$
> $ACK := ACK - \{mes(y, ack)\}$ **fi**
> **if** $\neg dr \wedge y \notin ac \wedge nb = ch \cup \{y\}$
> **then**
> $send(mes(x, req), y) \parallel dr := TRUE$ **fi**
> **if** $mes(y, req) \in REQ \wedge \neg dr$
> **then**
> $send(mes(x, ack), y) \parallel ac := ac \cup \{y\} \parallel$
> $REQ := REQ - \{mes(y, req)\}$ **fi**
> **if** $mes(y, req) \in REQ \wedge dr \wedge ctr(y) < ctr(x)$
> **then**
> $send(mes(x, ack), y) \parallel ac := ac \cup \{y\} \parallel$
> $REQ := REQ - \{mes(y, req)\}$ **fi**
> **if** $mes(y, tr) \in TR$
> **then**
> $ch := ch \cup \{y\} \parallel TR := TR - \{mes(y, tr)\}$ **fi**

We have used programming-like notation for modelling message communications (see model *leaderelection*5 in Table 25). The meaning of each communication primitive is, in detail,

- $send(mes(x, req), y)$ adds the message $mes(x, req)$ to REQ;
- $send(mes(x, ack), y)$ adds the message $mes(x, req)$ to ACK;
- $send(mes(x, tr), y)$ adds the message $mes(x, req)$ to TR.

Our algorithm is correct with respect to the invariant of the development; we have not mentioned the question of termination. Termination can be derived if one assumes a minimal fairness for each site: if a site can trigger an event, it will eventually trigger it, as long as it remains enabled.

8 Conclusion

B has a large community of users whose contributions go beyond the scope of this document; we have focused on the event-B approach to illustrate the foundations of B. Before we conclude our text, we must complete the B landscape with an outline of work on B and with B.

8.1 Work on B and with B

The series of conferences [22–24, 26, 63, 102] on B (in association with the Z community) and books [2, 59, 64, 73, 99] on B demonstrate the strong activity in this field. The expressivity of the B language has led to three kinds of work using the concepts of B: extension of the B method, combination of B with other approaches and applications of B. We have already mentioned applications of the B method in the introduction and, now, we sketch the extensions of B and proposals to integrate B with other methods.

Extending the B Method

The concept of ab event as introduced into B by Abrial [3], acts on the global state space of the system and has no parameters; Papatsaras and Stoddart [90], have contrasted this global style of development with one based on interacting components which communicate by means of shared events; parameters in events are permitted. The parametrisation of events was also considered by Butler and Walden [33], who were implementing action systems in B AMN.

Events may or may not happen, and new modalities are required to manage them; the language of assertions of B is becoming too poor to express temporal properties such as liveness, for instance. Abrial and Mussat [13] introduced modalities into abstract systems and developed proof obligations related to liveness properties; Méry [81] showed how the concepts of B could easily be used to deal with liveness and fairness properties. Bellegarde et al. [21] analysed extension of B using the LTL logic, and its impact on the refinement of event systems. There are problems related to the refinement of systems while maintaining liveness and even fairness properties; this is difficult and in many cases not possible, because the refinement maintains previously validated properties of the abstract model and it cannot maintain every liveness property.

Recently, McIver et al. [80] and Morgan et al. [87] have extended the generalized substitution language to handle probability in B; an abstract probabilistic choice is added to B operators. A methodology for using this extension has been proposed.

Combining B with Other Formalisms

The limited expressivity of the B language has inspired work on several proposals. Butler [31] investigated a mixed language including B AMN and CSP, where CSP is used to structure abstract machines; this idea was exploited by Schneider and Treharne [97, 103], who used it to control B machines.

Since diagrammatic formalisms offer a visual representation of models, an integration of B with UML was performed by Butler and Snook [32] and by Le Dang and Souquières [75–77]; B provides a semantic framework for UML components and allows one to analyse UML models. An interesting problem would be to study the impact of B refinement on UML models.

Mikhailov and Butler [84] combined the theorem proving and model checking; they focused on the B method, a theorem-proving tool associated with it, and the Alloy specification notation and its model checker *Alloy Constraint Analyser*. Software development in B can be assisted using Alloy, and Alloy can be used for verifying the refinement of abstract specifications.

8.2 On the Proof Process

The proof process is supported by a proof assistant which is either a part of an environment called Atelier B [50], or an environment called Click'n'Prove [7]. A free version is available [51]. Work on theories and reusing theories has been addressed by Abrial et al. in [9].

8.3 Final Remarks

The design of (software) systems is an activity based on logico-mathematical concepts such as set-theoretical definitions; it gives rise to proof obligations that capture the essence of its correctness. The use of theoretical concepts is due mainly to the requirements for safety and quality in the developed systems; it appears that mathematics can help in improving the quality of software systems. B is a method that can help designers to construct safer systems and it provides a realistic framework for developing pragmatic engineering. Mathematical theories [9] can be derived from scratch or reused; in forthcoming work, mechanisms for re-usability of developments will demonstrate the increasing power of the application of B in realistic case studies [8, 10, 40]. The available tools are already very helpful and will evolve towards a tool set for developing systems. The proof tool is probably a crucial element in the B approach, and recent developments of the prover, combined with refinement, validate the applicability of the B method for deriving correct reactive systems from abstract specifications. Another promising point is the introduction of patterns into the event-B methodology. In [4], Abrial described new B method related to B events. The European Union project RODIN [67, 94] is aimed at creating a methodology and supporting open tool platform for the cost-effective rigorous development of dependable complex software systems and services, using especially the event-B method; it will provide a suitable framework for further work on event-B.

Acknowledgements

We thank J.-R. Abrial for his continued help, support and comments; Dines Bjørner and Martin Henson accepted a long delays in obtaining the LaTeX files, and we thank them for their support. It was a pleasure to spend two weeks with Dines and Martin in Slovakia, and we especially enjoyed the daily pedagogical meetings. Thanks!

References

1. D. Abraham, D. Cansell, P. Ditsch, D. Méry and C. Proch. Synthesis of the QoS for digital TV services. In *First International Workshop on Incentive Based Computing - IBC'05*, Amsterdam, 2005.
2. J.-R. Abrial. *The B Book - Assigning Programs to Meanings*. Cambridge University Press, 1996.
3. J.-R. Abrial. Extending B without changing it (for developing distributed systems). In [63], pages 169–190.
4. J.-R. Abrial. B$^{\#}$: Toward a synthesis between Z and B. In *ZB [24]*, pages 168–177, 2003.
5. J.-R. Abrial. Event based sequential program development: Application to constructing a pointer program. In *[14]*, pages 51–74.
6. J.-R. Abrial. Formal methods in industry: Achievements, problems, future. In [88], pages 761–768.
7. J.-R. Abrial and D. Cansell. Click'n'Prove: Interactive proofs within set theory. In *[19]*, pages 1–24.
8. J.-R. Abrial and D. Cansell. Formal construction of a non-blocking concurrent queue algorithm (a case study in atomicity). *Journal of Electronic Comp.Sci.*, 11(5):744–770, 2005.
9. J.-R. Abrial, D. Cansell and G. Laffitte. "Higher-order" mathematics in B. In [23], pages 370–393.
10. J.-R. Abrial, D. Cansell and D. Méry. A Mechanically Proved and Incremental Development of IEEE 1394 Tree Identify Protocol. *Formal Aspects of Computing*, 14(3):215–227, 2003.
11. J.-R. Abrial, D. Cansell and D. Méry. Formal derivation of spanning trees algorithms. In [24], pages 457–476.
12. J.-R. Abrial, D. Cansell and D. Méry. Refinement and reachability in event$_b$. In Treharne et al. [102], pages 222–241.
13. J.-R. Abrial and L. Mussat. Introducing Dynamic Constraints in B. In *[22]*, pages 83–128.
14. K. Araki, S. Gnesi, and D. Mandrioli, editors. *FME 2003: Formal Methods, International Symposium of Formal Methods Europe*, Pisa, Italy, September 8–14, 2003, Proceedings, volume 2805 of *Lecture Notes in Computer Science. Springer, 2003*.
15. R. Back. *On correct refinement of programs.* Journal of Computer and System Sciences, *23(1):49–68, 1979.*
16. R. Back. *A calculus of refinements for program derivations.* Acta Informatica, *25:593–624, 1998.*
17. R. Back and J. von Wright. Refinement Calculus: A Systematic Introduction. *Graduate Texts in Computer Science. Springer, 1998.*
18. J.P. Banâtre, A. Coutant and D. Le Métayer. *The γ-model and its discipline of programming.* Science of Computer Programming, *15:55–77, 1990.*

19. D.A. Basin and B. Wolff, editors. *Theorem Proving in Higher Order Logics, 16th International Conference, TPHOLs 2003, Rom, September 8–12, 2003, Proceedings*, volume 2758 of *Lecture Notes in Computer Science*. Springer, 2003.

20. P. Behm, P. Benoit, A. Faivre and J.-M. Meynadier. METEOR: A successful application of B in a large project. In *Proceedings of FM'99: World Congress on Formal Methods*, Lecture Notes in Computer Science, pages 369–387, 1999.

21. F. Bellegarde, C. Darlot, J. Julliand and O. Kouchnarenko. Reformulate dynamic properties during b refinement and forget variants and loop invariants. In *ZB [26]*, pages 230–249, 2000.

22. D. Bert, editor. *B'98: Recent Advances in the Development and Use of the B Method, Second International B Conference*, Montpellier, France, April 22–24, 1998, Proceedings, volume 1393 of *Lecture Notes in Computer Science*. Springer, 1998.

23. D. Bert, J. P. Bowen, M. C. Henson, and K. Robinson, editors. *ZB 2002: Formal Specification and Development in Z and B, 2nd International Conference of B and Z Users*, Grenoble, France, January 23-25, 2002, Proceedings, volume 2272 of *Lecture Notes in Computer Science*. Springer, 2002.

24. D. Bert, J. P. Bowen, S. King, and M. A. Waldén, editors. *ZB 2003: Formal Specification and Development in Z and B, Third International Conference of B and Z Users, Turku, Finland, June 4-6, 2003, Proceedings*, volume 2651 of *Lecture Notes in Computer Science*. Springer, 2003.

25. Dines Bjørner and Martin C. Henson, editors. *Logics of Specification Languages*. EATCS Monograph in Computer Science. Springer, 2007.

26. J. P. Bowen, S. Dunne, A. Galloway, and S. King, editors. *ZB 2000: Formal Specification and Development in Z and B*, First International Conference of B and Z Users, York, UK, August 29 – September 2, 2000, Proceedings, volume 1878 of *Lecture Notes in Computer Science*. Springer, 2000.

27. M. Bubak, J. Dongarra, and J. Wasniewski, editors. *Recent Advances in Parallel Virtual Machine and Message Passing Interface, 4th European PVM/MPI Users' Group Meeting*, Krakow, Poland, November 3–5, 1997, Proceedings, volume 1332 of *Lecture Notes in Computer Science*. Springer, 1997.

28. M. Büchi and R. Back. Compositional symmetric sharing in B. In *World Congress on Formal Methods [104]*, pages 431–451, 1999.

29. L. Burdy. *Traitement des expressions dépourvues de sens de la théorie des ensembles – Application à la méthode B*. PhD thesis, CNAM, 2000.

30. M. Butler. Stepwise Refinement of Communicating Systems. *Science of Computer Programming*, 27:139–173, 1996.

31. M. Butler. CSP2B: A Practical Approach to Combining CSP and B. *Formal Aspects of Computing*, 12:182–196, 200.

32. M. Butler and C. Snook. Verifying dynamic properties of UML models by translation to the B language and toolkit. In *UML 2000 WORKSHOP Dynamic Behaviour in UML Models: Semantic Questions*, York, October 2000.

33. M. Butler and M. Walden. Parallel Programming with the B Method. In [99], pages 183–195.

34. E. Börger and R. Stärk. *Abstract State Machines: A Method for High-Level System Design and Analysis*. Springer, 2003.

35. D. Cansell. *The Seventeen Provers of the World*, volume 3600 of *Lecture Notes in Artificial Intelligence*, pages 142–150.

36. D. Cansell, G. Gopalakrishnan, M.D. Jones, D. Méry and Airy Weinzoepflen. Incremental proof of the producer/consumer property for the PCI protocol. In ZB [23], pages 22–41.

37. D. Cansell and D. Méry. Abstraction and refinement of features. In S. Gilmore and M. Ryan, editors, *Language Constructs for Designing Features*. Springer, 2000.

38. D. Cansell and D. Méry. Développement de fonctions définies récursivement en B : Application du B événementiel. Rapport de recherche, Laboratoire Lorrain de Recherche en Informatique et ses Applications, January 2002.

39. D. Cansell and D. Méry. Logical foundations of the B method. *Computers and Informatics*, Vol. 22, 2003.

40. D. Cansell and D. Méry. Formal and incremental construction of distributed algorithms: On the distributed reference counting algorithm. *Theoretical Computer Science*, 2006.

41. D. Cansell and D. Méry. Incremental parametric development of greedy algorithms. In *Automatic Verification of Critical Systems, AVoCS 2006, 2006-09*, pages 48–62, Nancy, France, 2006.

42. D. Cansell and D. Méry. Incremental parametric development of greedy algorithms. In S, Merz and T. Nipkow, editors, *Automatic Verification of Critical Systems - AVoCS 2006, 2006-09*, pages 48–62, Nancy, France, 2006.

43. D. Cansell, D. Méry, and C. Proch. Modelling system scheduler by refinement. In *IEEE ISoLA Workshop on Leveraging Applications of Formal Methods, Verification, and Validation, ISOLA'05*, Columbia, USA, 2005.

44. D. Cansell and D. Méry. Event B, in [59].

45. N. Cariero and D. Gelernter. *How to write parallel programs: A first course.* MIT Press, 1990.

46. J. Chalopin and Y. Métivier. A bridge between the asynchronous message passing model and local computations in graphs. In [68], pages 212–223.

47. K. M. Chandy and J. Misra. *Parallel Program Design: A Foundation.* Addison-Wesley, 1988.

48. M. Chaudron. Notions of Refinement for a Coordination Language for GAMMA. Technical report, Leiden University, The Netherlands, 1997.

49. E. M. Clarke, O. Grumberg, and D. A. Peled. *Model Checking.* MIT Press, 2000.

50. ClearSy, Aix-en-Provence. *Atelier B*, 2002. Version 3.6.

51. ClearSy, Aix-en-Provence. *B4free*, 2004. http://www.b4free.com.

52. J. Cooke, S. Maharaj, J. Romijn, and C. Shankland. Editorial. *Formal Aspects of Computing*, 14(3):199, 2003.

53. T. H. Cormen, C. E. Leiserson, R. L. Rivest, and C. Stein. *Introduction to Algorithms.* MIT Press and McGraw-Hill, 2001.

54. M. Devillers, D. Griffioen, J. Romin, and F. Vaandrager. Verification of a Leader Election Protocol: Formal Methods Applied to IEEE 1394. *Formal Methods in System Design*, 16:307–320, 2000.

55. E. W. Dijkstra. *A Discipline of Programming.* Prentice-Hall, 1976.

56. E. W. Dijkstra and C. S. Scholten. *Predicate Calculus and Program Semantics.* Texts and Monographs in Computer Science. Springer, 1990.

57. H. Ehrig and B. Mahr. *Fundamentals of Algebraic Specification 1, Equations and Initial Semantics.* EATCS Monographs on Theoretical Computer Science. Springer, 1985.

58. John Fitzgerald. *The Typed Logic of Partial Functions and the Vienna Development Method*. Springer, 2007. See [25].
59. M. Frappier and H. Habrias, editors. *Software Specification Methods An Overview Using a Case Study*. Hermes Science Publishing, London, April 2006.
60. O. Galibert. YLC, A C++ Linda System on Top of PVM. In *PVM/MPI [27]*, pages 99–106, 1997.
61. M.-C. Gaudel and J. Woodcock, editors. *FME '96: Industrial Benefit and Advances in Formal Methods, Third International Symposium of Formal Methods Europe, Co-Sponsored by IFIP WG 14.3, Oxford, UK, March 18-22, 1996, Proceedings*, volume 1051 of *Lecture Notes in Computer Science*. Springer, 1996.
62. Y. Gurevitch. *Evolving Algebras 1993: Lipari Guide*, in *Specification and Validation Methods*, pages 9–36. Oxford University Press, 1995.
63. H. Habrias, editor. *First Conference on the B Method*, Nantes, France, April 22-24 1996. IRIN-IUT de Nantes, ISBN 2-906082-25-2.
64. H. Habrias. *Spécification formelle avec B*. Hermès, 2001.
65. Martin C. Henson, Moshe Deutsch, and Steve Reeves. *Z Logic and its Applications*. Springer, 2007. See [25].
66. J. Hoare, J. Dick, D. Neilson, and I. Holm Sørensen. Applying the B technologies on CICS. In [61], pages 74–84.
67. S. Hallerstede, J.-R. Abrial and M. Butler. An open extensible tool environment for event-B. In *ICFEM 2006, Eighth International Conference on Formal Engineering Methods*, November 2006.
68. J. Jedrzejowicz and A. Szepietowski, editors. *Mathematical Foundations of Computer Science 2005, 30th International Symposium, MFCS 2005, Gdansk, Poland, August 29 - September 2, 2005, Proceedings*, volume 3618 of Lecture Notes in Computer Science. Springer, 2005.
69. C. B. Jones. *Systematic Software Development Using VDM*. Prentice-Hall International, 1986.
70. J. B. Kruskal. On the shortest spanning subtree and the traveling salesman problem. *Proceedings of the American Mathematical Society*, 7:48–50, 1956.
71. L. Lamport. A temporal logic of actions. *ACM Transactions on Programming Languages and Systems*, 16(3):872–923, May 1994.
72. L. Lamport. *Specifying Systems: The TLA$^+$+ Language and Tools for Hardware and Software Engineers*. Addison-Wesley, 2002.
73. K. Lano. *The B Language and Method: A Guide to Practical Formal Development*, FACIT. Springer, 1996.
74. K. Lano, J. Bicarregui, and A. Sanchez. Invariant-based synthesis and composition of control algorithms using B. In *FM'99, B Users Group Meeting, Applying B in an Industrial Context: Tools, Lessons and Techniques*, pages 69–86, 1999.
75. H. Ledang and J. Souquières. Formalizing UML behavioral diagrams with B. In *Tenth OOPSLA Workshop on Behavioral Semantics: Back to Basics*, Tampa Bay, Florida, Oct 2001.
76. H. Ledang and J. Souquières. Modeling class operations in B: application to UML behavioral diagrams. In *16th IEEE International Conference on Automated Software Engineering, ASE'2001*, Loews Coronado Bay, San Diego, USA, Nov 2001.
77. H. Ledang and J. Souquières. Contributions for modelling UML state-charts in B. In *Third International Conference on Integrated Formal Methods - IFM'2002*, Turku, Finland, Springer, May 2002.

78. B-Core (UK) Ltd. *B-Toolkit User's Manual*, release 3.2 edition, 1996.

79. Z. Manna. *Mathematical Theory of Computation*. McGraw-Hill, 1974.

80. A. McIver, C. Morgan, and T. S. Hoang. Probabilistic termination in B. In [24], pages 216–239.

81. D. Méry. Requirements for a temporal B: Assigning Temporal Meaning to Abstract Machines ... and to Abstract Systems. In A. Galloway and K. Taguchi, editors, *IFM'99 Integrated Formal Methods 1999*, Workshop on Computing Science, York, June 1999.

82. D. Méry, D. Cansell, C. Proch, D. Abraham, and P. Ditsch. The challenge of QoS for digital television services. *EBU Technical Review*, April 2005.

83. S. Merz. *The Specification Language TLA$^+$*. Springer, 2007. See [25].

84. L. Mikhailov and M. J. Butler. An approach to combining B and Alloy. In [23], pages 140–161, 2002.

85. L. Moreau and J. Duprat. A Construction of Distributed Reference Counting. *Acta Informatica*, 37:563–595, 2001.

86. C. Morgan. *Programming from Specifications*, Prentice Hall, 1990.

87. C. Morgan, T. S. Hoang, and J.-R. Abrial. The challenge of probabilistic event B: extended abstract. In [102], pages 162–171.

88. Leon J. Osterweil, H. Dieter Rombach, and Mary Lou Soffa, editors. *28th International Conference on Software Engineering (ICSE 2006)*, Shanghai, China, May 20–28, 2006. ACM, 2006.

89. S. Owicki and D. Gries. An axiomatic proof technique for parallel programs I. *Acta Informatica*, 6:319–340, 1976.

90. A. Papatsaras and B. Stoddart. Global and communicating state machine models in event driven B: A simple railway case study. In [23], pages 458–476.

91. M.-L. Potet and Y. Rouzaud. Composition and refinement in the B-method. In [22], pages 46–65.

92. R. C. Prim. Shortest connection and some generalizations. *Bell Systems Technical Journal*, Vol. 36, 1957.

93. C. Proch. *Assistance au développement incrémental et prouvé de systèmes enfouis*. PhD thesis, Université Henri Poincaré Nancy 1, 2006.

94. Project RODIN. Rigorous open development environment for complex systems. http://rodin-b-sharp.sourceforge.net/, 2004. 2004–2007.

95. Wolfgang Reisig. *Abstract State Machines for the Classroom*. Springer, 2007. See [25].

96. H. Rogers Jr. *Theory of Recursive Functions and Effective Computability*. MIT Press, 1967.

97. S. Schneider and H. Treharne. Communicating B machines. In [23], pages 416–435.

98. Scientific Computing Associates Inc., 246 Church Street, Suite 307 New Haven, CT 06510, USA. *Original LINDA C-Linda Reference Manual*, 1990.

99. E. Sekerinski and K. Sere, editors. *Program Development by Refinement: Case Studies Using the B Method*. FACIT. Springer, 1998.

100. J. M. Spivey. *Understanding Z: A specification language and its formal semantics*. Cambridge University Press, 1987.

101. R. Stärk, J. Schmid, and E. Börger. *Java and the Java Virtual Machine*. Springer, 1998.

102. H. Treharne, S. King, M. C. Henson, and S. A. Schneider, editors. *ZB 2005: Formal Specification and Development in Z and B, 4th International Conference of B and Z Users*, Guildford, UK, April 13-15, 2005, Proceedings, volume 3455 of Lecture Notes in Computer Science. Springer, 2005.

103. H. Treharne and S. Schneider. How to drive a B machine. In [26], pages 188–208.

104. J. M. Wing, J. Woodcock, and J. Davies, editors. *FM'99, Formal Methods, World Congress on Formal Methods in the Development of Computing Systems,* Toulouse, France, September 20–24, 1999, Proceedings, Volume I, volume 1708 of *Lecture Notes in Computer Science.* Springer, 1999.

Event B Indexes

A Methodological Guide to the CafeOBJ Logic

Răzvan Diaconescu

Institute of Mathematics "Simion Stoilow", PO Box 1-764, Bucharest 014700, Romania, Razvan.Diaconescu@imar.ro

1 The CafeOBJ Specification Language

CafeOBJ is an *executable* industrial-strength algebraic specification language; it is a modern successor of OBJ and incorporates several new algebraic specification paradigms. It was developed in Japan with large-scale support from the Japanese government. Its definition is given in [12], a presentation of its logical foundations can be found in [14], and a presentation of some methodologies developed around CafeOBJ can be found in [15, 16]. CafeOBJ is intended to be used mainly for system specification, formal verification of specifications, rapid prototyping, and even programming.

In this chapter we present the logic underlying CafeOBJ and illustrate its intimate relationship to the specification and verification methodologies.

First, let us briefly overview some of CafeOBJ most important features.

1.1 Equational Specification and Programming

Equational specification and programming is inherited from OBJ [18, 26] and constitutes the basis of the language, the other features being somehow built on top of it. As with OBJ, CafeOBJ is *executable* (by term rewriting), which gives an elegant declarative method of functional programming, often referred as *algebraic programming*.[1] As with OBJ, CafeOBJ also permits equational specification modulo several equational theories such as associativity, commutativity, identity, idempotency, and combinations of all these. This feature is reflected at the execution level by term rewriting modulo such equational theories.

---

[1] Although this paradigm may be used for programming, from the applications point of view, this aspect is secondary to its specification side.

1.2 Behavioural Specification

Behavioural specification [13, 21, 22, 29, 39, 40] provides a generalisation of ordinary algebraic specification. Behavioural specification characterises how objects (and systems) *behave*, not how they are implemented. This new form of abstraction can be very powerful in the specification and verification of software systems, since it naturally embeds other useful paradigms such as concurrency, object orientation, constraints, and non-determinism (see [22] for details). Behavioural abstraction is achieved by using specification with hidden sorts and a behavioural concept of satisfaction based on the idea of indistinguishability of states that are observationally the same, which also generalises process algebra and transition systems (see [22]). The CafeOBJ behavioural specification paradigm is based on the *coherent hidden algebra* (CHA) of [13], which is both a simplification and an extension of the classical hidden algebra of [22] in several directions, most notably by allowing operations with multiple hidden sorts in the arity. Coherent hidden algebra comes very close to the "observational logic" of Hennicker and Bidoit [29].

CafeOBJ directly supports behavioural specification and its proof theory through special language constructs, such as

- hidden sorts (for states of systems),
- behavioural operations (for direct "actions" and "observations" on states of systems),
- behavioural coherence declarations for non-behavioural operations (which may be either derived (indirect) "observations" or "constructors" on states of systems), and
- behavioural axioms (stating behavioural satisfaction).

The main behavioural proof method is based on *coinduction*. In CafeOBJ, coinduction can be used either in the classical hidden-algebra sense [22] for proving the behavioural equivalence of states of objects, or for proving behavioural transitions (which appear when behavioural abstraction is applied to preorder algebra).

Besides language constructs, CafeOBJ supports behavioural specification and verification by several methodologies. CafeOBJ currently highlights a methodology for concurrent hierarchical object composition which features high reusability, not only of specification code but also of verifications [11, 12, 30]. Behavioural specification in CafeOBJ may also be effectively used as an object-oriented (state-oriented) alternative to classical data-oriented specifications. Experiments seem to indicate that an object-oriented style of specification, even of basic data types (such as sets and lists) may lead to higher simplicity of code and drastic simplification of the verification process [12].

Behavioural specification is reflected at the execution level by the concept of *behavioural rewriting* [12, 13], which refines ordinary rewriting with a condition ensuring the correctness of the use of behavioural equations in proving strict equalities.

1.3 Preorder Algebra Specification

Preorder algebra (POA) specification in CafeOBJ is based on a simplified *unlabelled* version of Meseguer's *rewriting logic* [32] specification framework for concurrent systems, which gives a non-trivial extension of traditional algebraic specification towards concurrency. POA incorporates many different models of concurrency in a natural, simple, and elegant way, thus giving CafeOBJ a wide range of applications. Unlike Maude [4], the current CafeOBJ design does not fully support *labelled* rewriting logic, which permits full reasoning about multiple transitions between states (or system configurations), but it provides proof support for reasoning about the *existence* of transitions between states (or configurations) of concurrent systems via a built-in predicate with dynamic definition encoding into equational logic of both the proof theory of POA and the user-defined transitions (rules). At the level of the semantics, this amounts to the fact that CafeOBJ POA models are preorders rather than categories. This avoids many of the semantic complications resulting from the labelled version of rewriting logic.

From a methodological perspective, CafeOBJ develops the use of POA transitions for specifying and verifying the properties of *declarative encoding of algorithms* (see [12]), as well as for specifying and verifying transition systems. The restriction of rewriting logic to its unlabelled version (POA) is also motivated by the fact that this paradigm plays only a secondary role in the CafeOBJ methodologies.

1.4 Module System

The principles of the CafeOBJ module system are inherited from OBJ, which builds on ideas first realised in the language Clear [3], most notably the concept of an institution [17, 19]. The CafeOBJ module system features

- several kinds of imports;
- sharing for multiple imports;
- parametrised programming allowing multiple parameters, views for parameter instantiation, and integration of CafeOBJ specifications with executable code in a lower-level language; and
- module expressions.

However, the concrete design of the language revises the OBJ view of importation modes and parameters [12].

1.5 Type System and Partiality

CafeOBJ has a type system that allows subtypes based on *order-sorted algebra* (OSA) [20, 24]. This provides a mathematically rigorous form of run-time type checking and error handling, giving CafeOBJ a syntactic flexibility comparable to that of untyped languages, while preserving all the advantages of strong typing. CafeOBJ does not do partial operations directly, but rather handles them by using error sorts and a sort membership predicate in the style of *membership equational logic* (MEL) [33].

1.6 Notations and Terminology

We assume some familiarity with basic (naive) set theory and a rather mild familiarity with category theory (except in Sect. 5, which uses a little more category theory). For categories, we generally use the same notation and terminology as MacLane [31], except that composition is denoted by ";" and written in the diagrammatic order. The application of functions (functors) to arguments may be written either normally using parentheses, or else in diagrammatic order without parentheses, or, more rarely, by using subscripts or superscripts. The category of sets is denoted by $\mathbb{S}et$, and the category of categories[2] by $\mathbb{C}at$. The opposite of a category $\mathbb{C}$ is denoted by $\mathbb{C}^{\mathrm{op}}$. The class of objects of a category $\mathbb{C}$ is denoted by $|\mathbb{C}|$ and the set of arrows in $\mathbb{C}$ having the object a as source and the object b as target is denoted as $\mathbb{C}(a, b)$.

2 Data Type Specification

2.1 Basic Data Type Specification

Basic Specification

Consider a simple specification of natural numbers with addition:

```
mod!SIMPLE-NAT {
  [ Nat ]
  op 0 : -> Nat
  op s_ : Nat -> Nat
  op _+_ : Nat Nat -> Nat
  vars M N : Nat
  eq N + (s M) = s(N + M) .
  eq N + 0 = N .
}
```

This specification consists of:

- A header (i.e., the part before {...}) giving the name of the specification (SIMPLE-NAT) and the kind of denotation (mod!).
- The sort (type) declaration ([Nat]), representing the set of elements of the sort (or "type"); the name "sort" is common in algebraic specification, the name "type" is common in programming.

---

[2] We steer clear of any foundational problems related to the "category of all categories". Several solutions can be found in the literature; see, for example, [31].

- The operation declarations, starting with op (for 0, s_, and _+_), representing functions on the set(s) of elements.
- The variable declarations, starting with vars (such as M and N). In CafeOBJ, the variables can also be declared on the spot (such as M:Nat).
- Axioms (the statements starting with "eq)" defining the equality between elements.

Signatures

The *operation declarations* consist of:

- The **name** of the operation, which can be in *mix-fix* syntax, showing the position of the arguments by "_ " when an application of the operation is written.
- The **arity** of the operation, which is a string of (declared) sorts. The arity of an operation may consist of
  - an empty string (as in the case of 0); such operations are called *constants*,
  - only one sort (such as "Nat" in the case of s_),
  - several sorts (such as "Nat Nat" in the case of _+_); these sorts may also be different.
- The **sort** of the operation, which is a declared sort.

The sort and the operation declaration form the **signature** of the specification.

Definition 1. *Let S^* denote the set of all finite sequences of elements from S, where $[]$ is the empty sequence.*

An S-sorted signature (S, F) is an $S^* \times S$-indexed set $F = \{F_{w \to s} \mid w \in S^*,\ s \in S\}$ of operation symbols.

Note that this definition permits overloading, *in that the sets $F_{w \to s}$ need not be disjoint. We call $\sigma \in F_{[] \to s}$ (sometimes denoted simply $F_{\to s}$) a constant symbol of sort s.*

A signature morphism φ from a signature (S, F) to a signature (S', F') is a pair $(\varphi^{\mathrm{sort}}, \varphi^{\mathrm{op}})$ consisting of

- *a map $\varphi^{\mathrm{sort}} : S \to S'$ of sorts, and*
- *maps $\varphi^{\mathrm{op}}_{w \to s} : F_{w \to s} \to F'_{(\varphi^{\mathrm{sort}})^*(w) \to \varphi^{\mathrm{sort}}(s)}$ for all $w \in S^*$ and $s \in S$.*

A graphical representation of the signature can be very useful. This graphical notation for algebraic specification was first introduced by the ADJ group by extending the classical set-theory graphical representation of sets and functions. We represent

- sorts (types) by discs, and
- operations by multi-source arrows.

The signature SIMPLE-NAT can be represented graphically as follows:

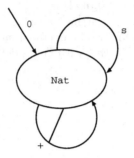

Terms and Axioms

A *variable declaration* introduces a new variable of a declared sort. The *axioms* consist of formal equalities between terms. The terms denote elements of the corresponding sort; they are basically operations applied to arguments, which are either (complex) terms, constants, or variables. An application of an operation to arguments has to respect the arity of the operation, i.e. the argument must have the sort indicated by the arity.

Definition 2. *An (S, F)-term t of sort $s \in S$ is a structure of the form $\sigma(t_1, \ldots, t_n)$, where $\sigma \in F_{w \to s}$ and $t_1, \ldots, t_n$ are (S, F)-terms of sorts $s_1 \ldots s_n$, and where $w = s_1 \ldots s_n$.*

In CafeOBJ, we can check the well-formedness of a term by means of the command **parse**:

```
SIMPLE-NAT> parse s 0 0 .
[Error] no successful parse
```

or

```
SIMPLE-NAT> parse s 0 + 0 .
((s 0) + 0) : Nat
```

(Notice that SIMPLE-NAT> is a CafeOBJ prompt.) The first term is not well-formed, hence the parsing error. The second term is wellformed, and the CafeOBJ system parses the term as

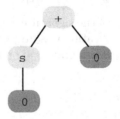

and tells the user that the sort of the term is Nat.

Notice that another possible parsing for s 0 + 0 is s(0 + 0):

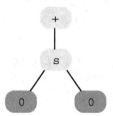

However, the system does not choose this possibility, because the operation s_ has higher precedence than the operation _+_.

Denotations

Specifications are formal descriptions of a certain class of (possible) implementations. In algebraic-specification terminology, "implementation" is explained by the concept of a **model** and "possible implementations" are explained by the concept of **denotation**.

The models of CafeOBJ data type specifications are called *algebras*. Algebras are ideal mathematical entities that interpret the syntactic constituents of the signatures of the specifications as ideal semantic entities. Algebras interpret:

- sorts as sets, and
- operations as functions on these sets,

such that the interpretation of the operations is compatible with the interpretation of the sorts. Software (or system) implementations of specifications can be regarded as algebras.

Definition 3. *Given a sort set S, an S-indexed (or sorted) set A is a family $\{A_s\}_{s \in S}$ of sets indexed by the elements of S; in this context, $a \in A$ means that $a \in A_s$ for some $s \in S$. Given an S-indexed set A and $w = s_1 \ldots s_n \in S^*$, let $A_w = A_{s_1} \times \cdots \times A_{s_n}$; in particular, let $A_{[]} = \{\star\}$ (some one point set).*

A (S, F)-algebra A consists of

- *an S-indexed set A (the set A_s is called the carrier of A of sort s), and*
- *a function $A_\sigma : A_w \to A_s$ for each $\sigma \in F_{w \to s}$.*

If $\sigma \in F_{\to s}$, then A_σ determines a point in A_s which may also be denoted A_σ.

Definition 4. *Given a signature morphism $\varphi : (S, F) \to (S', F')$ and an (S', F')-algebra A', we can define the φ-reduct of A' to (S, F), denoted $A' \restriction_\varphi$ (or simply $A' \restriction_{(S,F)}$ when φ is an inclusion of signatures),*

- *to have carriers $A'_{\varphi(s)}$ for $s \in S$, and*
- *to have operations $(A' \restriction_\varphi)_\sigma = A'_{\varphi(\sigma)}$ for $\sigma \in F$.*

Then A' is called a φ-expansion of A along φ.

Equations

These are the axioms of CafeOBJ specifications. They are formal equalities between (well-formed) terms denoting equalities between actual elements (in algebras).

Definition 5. *Any F-term $t = \sigma(t_1 \ldots t_n)$, where $\sigma \in F_{w \to s}$ is an operation symbol and $t_1, \ldots, t_n$ are F-(sub)terms corresponding to the arity w, is interpreted as an element $A_t \in A_s$ in a (S, F)-algebra A by $A_t = A_\sigma(A_{t_1} \ldots A_{t_n})$.*

Definition 6. *An* equation *is an equality $t = t'$ between F-terms t and t'.*

Let ρ_1 and ρ_2 be any (S, F)-sentences, then $\rho_1 \wedge \rho_2$ (their conjunction) is also a (S, F)-sentence. Sentences can also be formed with other Boolean operators: disjunction, implication, and negation.

Let X be a set of variables for a signature (S, F), then $(\forall X)\rho$ is a (S, F)-sentence for each $(S, F \cup X)$-sentence ρ (and similarly for existential quantification).

A universal Horn sentence *for an algebraic signature (S, F) is a sentence of the form $(\forall X)C$ if H, where H is a finite conjunction of equational atoms and C is an equational atom, and C if H is the implication of C by H. Universal Horn sentences are also called* conditional equations. *An* unconditional equation *is just a conditional equation for which the hypothesis H is true.*

CafeOBJ restricts the sentences to Horn ones, and hence the equational part of CafeOBJ has conditional equations as sentences.

Definition 7. *Given an algebraic signature morphism $\varphi \colon (S, F) \to (S', F')$, every (S, F)-sentence ρ can be translated to an (S', F')-sentence ρ', denoted $\varphi(\rho)$, by replacing any symbol of (S, F) from ρ by its corresponding symbol from (S', F') given by φ.*[3]

Definition 8. *The* satisfaction *between algebras and sentences is the Tarskian satisfaction defined inductively on the structure of sentences. Given a fixed arbitrary signature (S, F) and an (S, F)-algebra A,*

- *$A \models t = t'$ if $A_t = A_{t'}$ for equations;*
- *$A \models \rho_1 \wedge \rho_2$ if $A \models \rho_1$ and $A \models \rho_2$, and similarly for the other Boolean operators; and*
- *for every $(S, F \cup X)$-sentence $A \models (\forall X)\rho$ if $A' \models \rho$ for each expansion A' of A along the signature inclusion, $(S, F) \hookrightarrow (S, F \cup X)$.*

---

[3] In the particular case of quantification, notice that this changes the sorts of the variables.

Operation Attributes

Some equations, such as the *commutativity* and *associativity* of operations, can be specified as operation attributes. For example:

```
op _+_ : Nat Nat -> Nat { comm }
```

has the same meaning as

```
eq M + N = N + M .
```

and

```
op _+_ : Nat Nat -> Nat { assoc }
```

has the same meaning as

```
eq (M + N) + P = M + (N + P) .
```

However, the specification of such equations as operation attributes has the advantage of avoiding non-terminating computations. (In computations, they are not used directly as rewrite rules. Instead, computations are performed as *rewriting modulo the operation attributes*.)

Booleans and Predicates

CafeOBJ has a built-in (predefined) data type of **Boolean values**, called BOOL. The essential part of its signature can be represented as

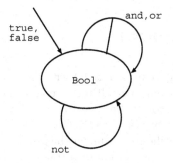

We can use the Boolean data type for defining the "strictly less than" relation between the natural numbers as follows:

```
op _<_ : Nat Nat -> Bool
eq 0 < (s M) = true .
eq (s M) < (s N) = M < N .
eq M < M = false .
eq (s M) < 0 = false .
```

Predicates in CafeOBJ are the same as Boolean-valued operations, so we may use the short-hand notation

```
pred _<_ : Nat Nat
```

Conditional Equations

The built-in sort Boolean data type BOOL supports the use of conditional equations which are equations valid under a condition represented as a Boolean term. For example, conditional equations can be used to define a maximum function on pairs of naturals:

```
op max : Nat Nat -> Nat { comm }
ceq max(M:Nat, N:Nat) = M if (N > M) or (M == N).
```

Initial models

The header of a specification may start with either mod! or mod*. mod! means that the denotation of the specification is *initial*, which means that it essentially consists of only one model (modulo isomorphism). Informally, the initial model of a specification is obtained by the following two steps:

1. We construct all well-formed terms from the signature of the specification.
2. We identify the terms which are equal under the equations of the specification.

For example, the model giving the denotation of the following CafeOBJ specification

```
mod!STRG {
  [ S ]
  ops a b : -> S
  op __ : S S -> S { assoc }
}
```

consists of all strings that can be formed with the characters a and b.

The first step is to construct all terms of the form a, b, ab, ba, aa, bb, a(ab), a(ba), b(ab), b(ba), (ab)a, (ab)b, (ba)a, (ba)b, (ab)(ab), (ab)(ba), (ba)(ab), (ba)(ba), etc.

The second step identifies terms under the associativity equation (specified as an attribute of the concatenation operation __). For example (a(ab))b, (aa)(bb), a(a(bb)), a((ab)b), ((aa)b)b are all identified in one element, denoted as (aabb).

In the following, we develop formally the concept of an initial algebra for a CafeOBJ equational specification.

Definition 9. *An S-indexed (or sorted) function $f: A \to B$ is a family $\{f_s: A_s \to B_s\}_{s \in S}$.*

Also, for an S-sorted function $f: A \to B$, let $f_w: A_w \to B_w$ denote the function product mapping a tuple of elements $(a_1, \ldots, a_n)$ to the tuple $(f_{s_1}(a_1), \ldots, f_{s_n}(a_n))$.

An (S, F)-homomorphism from one (S, F)-algebra A to another B is an S-indexed function $h: A \to B$ such that

$$h_s(A_\sigma(a)) = B_\sigma(h_w(a))$$

for every $\sigma \in F_{w \to s}$ and $a \in A_w$.

A (S, F)-*homomorphism* $h\colon A \to B$ *is an* (S, F)-*isomorphism if and only if each function* $h_s\colon A_s \to B_s$ *is bijective (i.e. one-to-one and onto, in an older terminology).*

The category (class) of algebras of a signature (S, F) *is denoted* $\mathsf{Alg}(S, F)$.

Definition 10. *An algebra A is* initial *for a class* $\mathbb{C}$ *of algebras when, for each algebra $B \in \mathbb{C}$, there exists an unique homomorphism $A \to B$.*

Notice that initial algebras are unique up to isomorphisms.

The Existence of Initial Algebras for Specifications

Definition 11. *An F-congruence on an (S, F)-algebra A is an S-sorted family of relations, $\equiv_s$ on A_s, each of which is an equivalence relation, and which also satisfy the* congruence property *that, given any $\sigma \in F_{w \to s}$ and any $a \in A_w$, then $A_\sigma(a) \equiv_s A_\sigma(a')$ whenever $a \equiv_w a'$.[4]*

Definition 12. *Each congruence on an (S, F)-algebra A determines a* quotient *algebra $A/\!\equiv$ such that*

- $(A/\!\equiv)_s = (A_s)/\!\equiv_s$ *for each sort $s \in S$, i.e. the equivalence classes of $\equiv_s$, and*
- $(A/\!\equiv)_\sigma(a/\!\equiv) = A_\sigma(a)/\!\equiv$ *for each operation symbol $\sigma \in F_{w \to s}$ and each $a \in A_w$.*

For an algebra homomorphism $h\colon A \to B$, let its kernel $=_h$ *be defined by $a =_h b$ iff $h(a) = h(b)$.*

Proposition 1. *For any algebra homomorphism h, its kernel $=_h$ is a congruence.*

Proposition 2. *For any surjective algebra homomorphism $q\colon A \to A'$ and any algebra homomorphism $h'\colon A \to B$, there exists a unique algebra homomorphism $h'\colon A' \to B$ such that $q; h' = h$ if and only if $=_q\, \subseteq\, =_h$:*

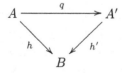

Definition 13. *Given a set of universal Horn sentences Γ, a congruence $\equiv$ on an algebra A is* closed under Γ-substitutivity *if for each $(\forall X)C$ if $H \in \Gamma$, for any expansion A' of A to $(S, F \cup X)$, $A'_H \subseteq \equiv$ implies $A'_C \subseteq \equiv$.*

---

[4] This means that $a_i \equiv_{s_i} a'_i$ for $i = 1, \ldots, n$, where $w = s_1 \ldots s_n$ and $a = (a_1, \ldots, a_n)$.

Proposition 3. *For any algebra A, $A/{\equiv} \models \Gamma$ if and only if $\equiv$ is closed under Γ-substitutivity.*

Proposition 4. *The least congruence that is closed under Γ-substitutivity, denoted $=_\Gamma$, exists as the intersection of all congruences that are closed under Γ-substitutivity.*

Corollary 1. *For any algebra A, $A/{=_\Gamma}$ is the free algebra over A satisfying Γ:*

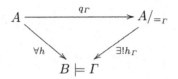

By taking A as $0_{(S,F)}$, the *initial term algebra* (i.e. initial in $\mathsf{Alg}(S, F)$), defined by

- $(0_{(S,F)})_s$ is the set T_F of all F-terms of sort s, and
- $(0_{(S,F)})_\sigma(t_1, \ldots, t_n) = \sigma(t_1, \ldots, t_n)$ for each operation symbol $\sigma \in F_{w \to s}$ and each list of terms $t_1 \ldots t_n$ corresponding to w,

we obtain the following:

Corollary 2. *Each set Γ of conditional equations admits an initial algebra, which is $0_{(S,F)}/{=_\Gamma}$.*

Loose Denotations

On the other hand, `mod*` means that the denotation of the specification is *loose*, which means that we consider all possible interpretations of the specification which satisfy the equations.

For example, (almost) the same specification as above, but specified with loose denotation,

```
mod* SEMI-GROUP {
  [ S ]
  ops a b : -> S
  op __ : S S -> S { assoc }
}
```

has as its models *all* semigroups with *all* interpretations of the two constants a and b.

2.2 Specifying Partial Functions

Subsorts

A specification of natural numbers with subtypes distinguishes two subsorts of Nat:

```
mod!BARE-NAT {
    [ NzNat Zero < Nat ]
    op 0 : -> Zero
    op s_ : Nat -> NzNat
}
```

The subsorts (of a sort) represent subsets of the elements of the sort.

In CafeOBJ, a subsort relationship is specified by using the "less than" symbol < inside a sort declaration. In this example, Zero is the sort of zero (0), and NzNat is the sort of the non-zero natural numbers.

The use of subsorts allows a more precise definition of operations. In the case of BARE-NAT, the constant 0 is declared to be of (sub)sort Zero rather than Nat, and the sort of the successor function s_ is declared as the sort NzNat of non-zero naturals rather than Nat. The latter declaration embeds a very basic piece of information about the successor function: zero can never be the result of applying a successor function to an element.

The graphical representation of signatures uses disc inclusion for subsorts:

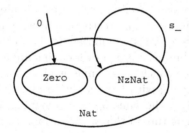

Operation Overloading

Consider the example of the specification SIMPLE-NAT of natural numbers with addition, and enriched with subsorts. The signature of this specification can be represented graphically by

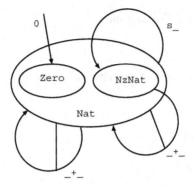

In this specification, the operation _+_ is *overloaded*, in the sense that the same operation symbol is used twice with different ranks or arities:

```
op _+_ : Nat Nat -> Nat
op _+_ : NzNat Nat -> NzNat
```

Notice that the sorts in the arity of the second operation are subsorts of the corresponding sorts in the arity of the first operation. The same applies to the sorts of the operations.

The second _+_ is in fact a restriction of the first, but it helps with the precision of evaluations at the most primitive syntactic level.

If a non-zero natural takes part in the addition, then the result should always be a non-zero natural number.

Another kind of operation overloading occurs when overloaded operations act on sorts which are not related directly or indirectly by a subsort relationship. In such a situation, there is no interference between the meanings of the overloaded operations, but such use of overloading might increase the expressivity of the specification. Such an example is given by a specification of the length of a list of elements, with both addition of natural numbers and list concatenation specified by the same operation symbol. Here is the graphical representation of the signature of this specification:

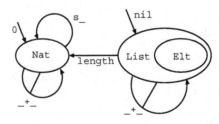

Partial Functions Via Subsorts

Subsorts also constitute the simplest (and most limited) form of partiality for functions. **Partial functions** are those functions which do not evaluate for all values of the arguments, but only for a subset of those values. In some cases, this subset of values (called the *domain*) of the partial function can be handled by using subsorts.

For example, the division of rational numbers can be defined only when the second argument is non-zero:

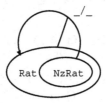

In this example, the sort of rational numbers is `Rat`, the sort of non-zero rational numbers is `NzRat`, and the division operation is `_/_`.

Error handling

An accurate specification style based on subsorts permits precise information about the types of the elements. The CafeOBJ command `parse` shows us whether a term is well formed, and what is its smallest sort. For example

```
BARE-NAT> parse s s 0 .
```

gives the answer

```
(s (s 0)) : NzNat
```

During the computation process, the information about the sort of an element becomes more accurate. For example, in the case of rational numbers,

```
RAT> parse 2 / 2 .
(2 / 2) : NzRat
```

but when this expression is evaluated (by using the CafeOBJ command `red`),

```
RAT> red 2 / 2 .
-- reduce in RAT : 2 / 2
1 : NzNat
```

the CafeOBJ system gives us the smallest sort of the element, which is the non-zero naturals. In the case of an attempt to evaluate a partial function for values of the arguments which do not belong to its domain, the system indicates an error to us:

```
RAT> parse 2 / 0 .
(2 / 0) : ?Rat
```

This is achieved by using an **error supersort** (`?Rat`) that stores all ill-formed expressions, which are considered as error values.

In CafeOBJ, the error supersorts are built into the system, so although they are in general hidden from the user, they are used for signalling parsing errors.

Dynamic Type Checking

As we saw above, more accurate information about the sort of an element may appear during the computation process. the error-handling system is flexible enough to take advantage of this situation. This is called *dynamic type checking*. For example:

```
RAT> parse 2 / ((3 / 2) + (1 / 2)) .
(2 / ((3 / 2) + (1 / 2))) : ?Rat
```

gives an error because the sort of (3 / 2) + (1 / 2) is computed as Rat rather than as NzRat. However, the CafeOBJ system still attempts to evaluate this expression, and during the computation the system "discovers" that (3 / 2) + (1 / 2) is indeed a non-zero rational:

```
RAT> red 2 / ((3 / 2) + (1 / 2)) .
-- reduce in RAT : 2 / (3 / 2 + 1 / 2)
1 : NzNat
```

Sort Constraints

A more complex case of partiality of functions occurs when the domain of the function can be specified in the language. For example, the following specification of a minus function on naturals as a partial function uses the "less than" predicate for naturals:

```
op _-_ : ?Nat ?Nat -> ?Nat
vars M N : Nat
ceq (M - N) :is Nat = true if not(M < N) .
eq (s M) - (s N) = M - N .
eq M - 0 = M .
```

We use the built-in error supersort ?Nat and the built-in **sort membership predicate**

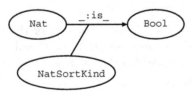

Here, NatSortKind is the (predefined) sort/set of the sort names (directly or indirectly) related to Nat by the subsorting relation. The first equation gives the sort constraint defining the domain of the partial function _-_, while the last two equations define the function.

Kinds and Sorts

The semantics of the sort membership predicate is given by "membership algebra".

Definition 14. *A* membership algebraic signature *is a triple* (K, F, kind) *where K is a set of* kinds, (K, F) *is an algebraic signature, and* kind: $S \to K$ *is a function that assigns to each element in its domain, called "sort", a kind. Given a membership algebraic signature (K, F, kind), a (K, F, kind)-algebra A is a (K, F)-algebra together with sets $A_s \subseteq A_{\text{kind}(s)}$ for each "sort" s.*

Sentences in membership algebra have two types of atom, namely atomic equations $t = t'$, where t, t' are any F-terms of the same "kind", and atomic memberships $t: s$, where s is a "sort" and t is an F-term of "kind" kind(s).

A membership algebra A satisfies an equation $t = t'$ when $A_t = A_{t'}$ and satisfies an atomic membership $t: s$ when $A_t \in A_s$.

The *subsort* relationship $s < s'$ is modelled in membership algebra by the Horn sentence $(\forall x)x: s'$ **if** $x: s$. Hence a signature with subsorts corresponds to a Horn presentation in membership algebra. This leads to the conclusion that the existence of initial algebras for equational specifications (Corollary 2) can be extended to order-sorted equational specifications.

2.3 Inference and Reduction

Group Theory

Consider the following specification of the group theory:

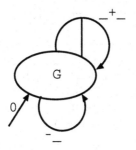

```
mod* GROUP {
  [ G ]
  op 0 : -> G
  op _+_ : G G -> G {assoc}
  op -_ : G -> G
  var X : G
  eq 0 + X = X .
  eq (- X) + X = 0 .
}
```

The denotation of this specification consists of all groups. However, this fact is not obvious with the current specification, since the standard specification of group theory contains two more equations:

```
eq X + 0 = X .
eq X + (- X) = 0 .
```

These two equations can be deduced from the three axioms of the specification (two explicit equations plus the associativity attribute for _+_).

Proving X + 0 = X

The first equation can be deduced from the second equation (which we prove later) and the axioms of GROUP by the following inference chain:

$\vdash 0 + a = a$ by the first axiom,

$0 + a = a \vdash (a + (-a)) + a = a$ by the second equation,

$(a + (-a)) + a = a \vdash a + ((-a) + a) = a$ by the associativity of $\_ + \_$,

$a + ((-a) + a) = a \vdash a + 0 = a$ by the second axiom.

Proving X + (- X) = 0:

The second equation can be deduced from the axioms of GROUP by the following inference chain:

$\vdash (-(-a)) + (-a) = 0$

(by the second axiom for $x \leftarrow (-a)$),

$(-(-a)) + (-a) = 0 \vdash (-(-a)) + (0 + (-a)) = 0$

(by the first axiom for $x \leftarrow (-a)$),

$(-(-a)) + (0 + (-a)) = 0 \vdash (-(-a)) + (((-a) + a) + (-a)) = 0$

(by the second axiom),

$(-(-a)) + (((-a) + a) + (-a)) = 0 \vdash ((-(-a)) + (-a)) + (a + (-a)) = 0$

(by the associativity of $\_ + \_$),

$((-(-a)) + (-a)) + (a + (-a)) = 0 \vdash 0 + (a + (-a)) = 0$

(by the second axiom for $x \leftarrow (-a)$),

$0 + (a + (-a)) = 0 \vdash a + (-a) = 0$

(by the first axiom for $x \leftarrow a + (-a)$).

Equational Inference.

The inference steps in equational logic obey the principle of *replacing equals by equals*, which means that, in a term, we replace an *instance* of a side of an equation by the *corresponding instance of the other side of the equation.*

- An **instance** of a term is obtained by substituting the variables of the term by (well-formed) terms of the same sort as the variable to be substituted.
- By the "corresponding instance of the other side of the equation" we mean that, for both instances, we use the same substitutions for the variables.

Definition 15. *Given an algebraic signature* (S, F) *and sets* X *and* Y *of variables (i.e. new constant symbols), an* (S, F)-*substitution* $\theta \colon X \to Y$ *is a function* $X \to T_{F \cup Y}$.

For any $(S, F \cup X)$-*sentence* ρ, *we denote by* $\rho\theta$ *the* $(S, F \cup Y)$-*sentence determined by replacing each symbol* $x \in X$ *in* ρ *by the term* $\theta(x)$.

Definition 16. *The* equational proof system *is generated by the following rules:*

$$\frac{}{\{(\forall X)t = t\}} \; R. \qquad \frac{\{(\forall X)t = t'\}}{\{(\forall X)t' = t\}} \; S. \qquad \frac{\{(\forall X)t = t', (\forall X)t' = t''\}}{\{(\forall X)t = t''\}} \; T.$$

For each operation symbol $\sigma \in F$:

$$\frac{\{(\forall X)t_i = t'_i | 1 \le i \le n\}}{\{(\forall X)\sigma(t_1, \ldots, t_n) = \sigma(t'_1, \ldots, t'_n)\}} \; OC.$$

For all $(\forall Y)C$ **if** $H \in \Gamma$, *subst* $\theta \colon Y \to X$

$$\frac{\{\Gamma \cup \{(\forall X)H\theta\}}{\{(\forall X)C\theta\}} \; \Gamma.$$

The completeness of equational deduction can be obtained from Corollary 1 by noticing that $=_\Gamma$ on $T_F(X)$ (the free (S, F)-algebra over X) is

$$\{(t, t') \mid \Gamma \vdash^e (\forall X)t = t'\},$$

where $\vdash^e$ is the equational provability relation.

Corollary 3. *The equational proof system is sound and complete., i.e.* $E \models \rho$ *if and only if* $E \vdash^e \rho$.

The completeness of equational logic is due to a well-known result by Birkhoff [2], and it has been extended to the many-sorted case in [23].

Rewriting.

Equational deduction can be regarded as a computation process by starting with a term and applying the principle of replacing equals by equals, with the (instances of the) left-hand side of equations replaced by (the corresponding instances of) the right-hand side of equations until this is not possible any more. This is called **rewriting**.

For example, the CafeOBJ "reduce" (which rewrites using equations from left to right),

```
GROUP> reduce (- - a) + (- a) + a + (- a) .
```

gives the result $0 : G$ after three rewriting steps modulo the associativity attribute of $\_+\_$. This reduction process can be visualised as follows:

$$(-\, -\, a) + (-a) + a + (-a) \vdash (-\, -\, a) + 0 + (-a) \quad \text{first rewrite,}$$
$$(-\, -\, a) + 0 + (-a) \vdash (-\, -\, a) + (-a) \qquad\qquad \text{second rewrite,}$$
$$(-\, -\, a) + (-a) \vdash 0 \qquad\qquad\qquad\qquad\qquad \text{third rewrite.}$$

Proof by Rewriting

Rewriting of terms can be used for mechanising equational inference. For example, the proof of

    eq X + (- X) = 0 .

can be done as follows by rewriting:

$$a + (-a) \vdash 0 + a + (-a) \qquad\qquad\qquad \text{first rewrite,}$$
$$0 + a + (-a) \vdash (-(-a)) + (-a) + a + (-a) \qquad \text{second rewrite,}$$
$$(-(-a)) + (-a) + a + (-a) \vdash (-(-a)) + 0 + (-a) \ \text{third rewrite,}$$
$$(-(-a)) + 0 + (-a) \vdash (-(-a)) + (-a) \qquad\qquad \text{fourth rewrite,}$$
$$(-(-a)) + (-a) \vdash 0 \qquad\qquad\qquad\qquad\quad\ \text{fifth rewrite.}$$

Notice that the first two rewrites are actually *backward rewrites*, in the sense that the rewritings are performed by replacing an instance of the right-hand side of a equation with the corresponding instance of the left-hand side of the equation. The last three rewrites are *ordinary rewrites*, and therefore they can be performed automatically. Ordinary rewriting is called **reduction**.

The CafeOBJ **proof score** for this proof by rewriting is as follows:

```
open GROUP .
  op a : -> G .
start a + (- a) .
apply -.1 at (1) .                    -- 1st backward rewrite
apply -.2 with X = (- a) at [1] . -- 2nd backward rewrite
apply reduce at term .            -- reduce the whole term
close
```

where the backward rewritings are done by using the command **apply** and the last three automatically by **reduce**.

Deduction by Rewriting

Definition 17. *The* rewriting proof system *is generated by* $R.$, $T.$, $OC.$, *and* $\Gamma.$ *Let* $\vdash^r$ *denote its entailment relation.*

As a consequence of Corollary. 3, we obtain the following proposition.

Proposition 5. *The rewriting proof system is sound.*

Definition 18. *An F-context $c[z]$ is any F-term c with a marked variable z occurring only once in c.*

Proposition 6. *The rewriting proof system can be generated by $R.$, $T.$, and the following rule:*

$$RW.\ (\forall X)H\theta \vdash^r (\forall X)c[t\theta] = c[t'\theta] \text{ for any substitution } \theta\colon Y \to X, \text{ each}$$
$$\text{sentence } (\forall Y)t = t' \text{ if } H, \text{ and each context } c.$$

Normal Forms

When a term cannot be rewritten any more, we say that it is a **normal form**. For example, 0, 0+a, a+b, etc. are normal forms in GROUP.

When there are no infinite rewrite chains, we say that rewriting **terminates**. In this situation, in principle, each input term may be rewritten to several normal forms. For example, (-(-a))+(-a)+a+(-a) has both a+(-a) and 0 as normal forms when we consider the equations of GROUP as rewrite rules (from left to right).

However, when the rewriting is in addition **confluent**, the normal form of a term is unique. Confluence is a basic property which says that whenever there are several choices for rewriting, it does not matter which one we chose in the sense that from each choice there would be a continuation of the rewriting to the same result. This can be visualised by the following picture:

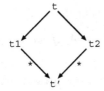

This picture can be interpreted as follows: if t can be rewritten to both t1 and t2 (in one step), then t1 and t2 can be rewritten (possibly in several steps) to the same term t'.

For the rest of this section, A should typically be taken as the set/algebra of terms, or of terms modulo some equational theory in the case of rewriting modulo operation attributes (such as associativity and/or commutativity).

Definition 19. *A binary reflexive relation R on a set A is* confluent *when, for each element $a, b, c \in A$, if aRb and aRc then there exists an element $d \in A$ such that bRd and cRd.*

Proposition 7. *If $>$ is a confluent preorder relation on a set A, then the relation $\downarrow$ defined by*

$$b \downarrow c \quad \text{if and only if there exists } d \in A \quad \text{with} \quad b > d \quad \text{and} \quad c > d$$

is the equivalence generated by $>$ (i.e. the least equivalence containing $>$).

Proposition 8. *Given an algebra A, if $>$ is a confluent preorder preserving the operations, then $\downarrow$ is a congruence.*

Rewriting as a Decision Procedure

Termination and confluence together ensure the completeness of rewriting as a decision procedure for equality, since given two terms we can decide whether they are equal for a certain specification just by comparing their unique normal forms.

The completeness of rewriting as a decision procedure is justified by Theorem 1 below.

Let us assume that all our signatures contain a distinguished sort b with a constant $\mathbf{t}$ and that each hypothesis H of a conditional equation $(\forall X)t = t'$ **if** H can be regarded as a term $\overline{H}$ of sort b such that, for each expansion A' of an algebra A to $(S, F \cup X)$, we have that

$$A' \models H \text{ if and only if } A'_{\overline{H}} = A'_{\mathbf{t}}.$$

Let $\overline{\Gamma} = \{(\forall X)t = t' \text{ if } \overline{H} \mid (\forall X)t = t' \text{ if } H \in \Gamma\}.$

This determines a relation $>_{\overline{\Gamma}}$ on any $(S, F \cup X)$-algebra A by $A_t >_{\overline{\Gamma}} A_{t'}$ if and only if $\overline{\Gamma} \vdash^r (\forall X)t = t'\}$.

Let $\downarrow_\Gamma$ be the equivalence generated by $>_\Gamma$.

Proposition 9. *If $>_\Gamma$ is confluent, then $\downarrow_\Gamma$ is a congruence.*

Proposition 10. *For any algebra A, if $>_\Gamma$ is confluent then a $\downarrow_\Gamma a'$ implies $a =_\Gamma a'$.*

An element $n \in A$ is a *normal form* for a relation $>$ on A when, for each element $a \in A$, $n > a$ implies $n = a$.

Proposition 11. *On any algebra A, if $>_{\overline{\Gamma}}$ is confluent and $A_{\mathbf{t}}$ is a normal form then $A/\downarrow_{\overline{\Gamma}} \models \overline{\Gamma}$.*

Theorem 1. *On any algebra A, if $>_{\overline{\Gamma}}$ is confluent and $A_{\mathbf{t}}$ is a normal form then $\downarrow_{\overline{\Gamma}} == _{\overline{\Gamma}}$.*

CafeOBJ implements rewriting as a decision procedure by the built-in semantic equality predicate ==. For example in SIMPLE-NAT,

```
SIMPLE-NAT> reduce (s s 0) + (s 0) == (s 0) + (s s 0) .
```

gives the result true : Bool, since the equations of SIMPLE-NAT are taken as rewrite rules from left to right and both sides of == are reduced to the same normal form (s s s 0).

2.4 Induction

Inductive Properties

Consider a specification of natural numbers with successor and addition given by SIMPLE-NAT. The denotation of SIMPLE-NAT consists of the initial model, whose main carrier (i.e., underlying set) consists of all terms formed only by 0 and s_, i.e., 0, (s 0), (s s 0), (s s s 0), ...

The operations 0 and s_ are called the **constructors** of the specification SIMPLE-NAT. The commutativity of the addition is an **inductive property** in the sense that it holds for the (initial) denotation of SIMPLE-NAT, but it is *not* an equational consequence of the axioms of the specification. In order to see this, it is enough to consider the loose denotation version of SIMPLE-NAT a model of lists interpreting _+_ as concatenation, and to notice that list concatenation is not commutative.

The Inductive Proof of the Commutativity of Addition

The proof of the commutativity of _+_ in SIMPLE-NAT involves a structural induction, which is an induction on the structure of the terms of the carrier of the denotation of SIMPLE-NAT.

    open SIMPLE-NAT

We declare temporary working variables as arbitrary constants

    ops i j : -> Nat .

We need the following two lemmas.

Lemma 1. $(s\ i) + j = s(i + j)$

Proof. We prove this lemma by induction on j.
The base case:

    red (s i) + 0 == s(i + 0) .

gives true.
The induction step uses the following hypothesis.

    eq (s i) + j = s(i + j) .

The proof of the induction step,

    red (s i) + (s j) == s(i + (s j)) .

gives true.

Lemma 2. $0 + j = j$

Proof. We prove this lemma by induction on j.
The base case:

    red 0 + 0 == 0 .

gives true.
The induction step uses the following hypothesis.

    eq 0 + j = j .

The proof of the induction step,

    red 0 + (s j) == s j .

gives `true`.

We now declare the proven equations (i.e., the two lemmas above),

```
eq (s I:Nat) + J:Nat = s (I + J) .
eq 0 + J:Nat = J:Nat .
```

and then proceed with the main proof. We show that,

```
i + j =  j + i
```

by induction on j.
The base case:

```
reduce i + 0 == 0 + i .
```

gives `true`. For the induction step we use the following hypothesis.

```
eq i + j = j + i .
```

The proof of the induction step,

```
red i + (s j) == (s j) + i .
```

gives `true`.

3 Transitions

3.1 Specifying Transitions

Algorithm Specification

Rewriting rules can be used to specify algorithms by showing transitions between various states of the algorithm. For example a crude version of the bubble sort algorithm may be specified as follows in CafeOBJ:

```
mod!SORTING-NAT {
  protecting(STRG-NAT)
  vars N N' : Nat
  ctrans (N . N') => (N' . N) if N' < N .
}
```

Notice this very compact encoding of the bubble sort algorithm by only one conditional transition.

The Logic of Transitions

The logic of CafeOBJ transitions is called *preorder algebra*.

Definition 20. *POA signatures are just ordinary algebraic signatures.*

POA models are preorder algebras, *which are interpretations of the signatures in the category of preorders* Pre *rather than the category of sets* Set. *This means that each sort is interpreted as a preorder, and each operation as a preorder functor.*

The atomic sentences of POA are either equations or transitions $t => t'$, *with t and t' being terms of the same sort. POA sentences are formed from (atomic) equations and transitions by iterations of the usual logical connectives and quantification.*[5]

A transition $t => t'$ is satisfied by a preorder algebra M when the interpretations of the terms are in the preorder relation of the carrier, i.e. $M_t \leq M_{t'}$.

The Initial Denotation of an Algorithm Specification

SORTING-NAT is an initial (or tight) denotation specification in the sense that it specifies a standard initial model. This model is a model of the data type of strings of natural numbers (in which the strings are thought as *possible states* of the algorithm), enriched with transitions between the states of the algorithm by applying the bubble sort rule (as specified by the conditional transition of SORTING-NAT) in all possible ways.

In the model, there exists at most one transition between two states, which means that our models capture the existence of the possibility of a transition between two states of the algorithm rather than all possible transitions between the states.

A fragment of this model corresponding to the sorting of 3 . 2 . 1 can be visualised as follows:

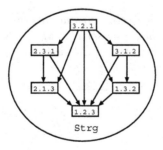

Operations on Transitions

SORTING-NAT is a typical example of POA specification.

---

[5] However, CafeOBJ restricts the POA sentences to Horn ones.

In the initial model of this specification, the operation interpretations extend from the elements of the underlying data type (i.e. the states of the algorithm) to the transitions. For example, in the case of SORTING-NAT, not only do the strings "concatenate", but also the transitions can "concatenate", as depicted in the following picture.

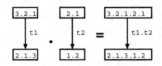

Definition 21. *A* **POA**-*congruence (preorder algebra congruence) on a preorder algebra for a signature* (S, F) *is a pair* $(\sim, \sqsubseteq)$ *such that*

- $\sim$ *is an F-congruence on M;*
- $\sqsubseteq$ *is an (S-sorted) preorder on M compatible with the operations and which contains* $M_\le$, *i.e.* $M_\le \,\subseteq\, \sqsubseteq$; *and*
- $a' \sim a, a \sqsubseteq b, b \sim b'$ *implies* $a' \sim b'$ *for all elements* a, a', b, b' *of M.*

Congruences form a partial order under inclusion, i.e. $(\sim, \sqsubseteq) \subseteq (\sim', \sqsubseteq')$ *if and only if* $\sim\,\subseteq\,\sim'$ *and* $\sqsubseteq\,\subseteq\,\sqsubseteq'$.

Proposition 12. *Each* **POA**-*congruence on a preorder algebra M determines a quotient preorder algebra homomorphism* $M \to M/_{(\sim, \sqsubseteq)}$ *such that*

- *the algebra underlying* $M/_{(\sim, \sqsubseteq)}$ *is the quotient algebra* $M/_\sim$; *and*
- $m/_\sim \,\le\, m'/_\sim$ *if and only if* $m \sqsubseteq m'$.

Definition 22. *For a preorder algebra homomorphism* $h\colon M \to N$, *let its kernel* $ker(h) = (=_h, \le_h)$ *where* $a =_h b$ *iff* $h(a) = h(b)$ *and* $a \le_h b$ *iff* $h(a) \le h(b)$.

Proposition 13. $ker(h)$ *is a* **POA**-*congruence.*

Proposition 14. *For any surjective preorder algebra homomorphism* $q\colon M \to M'$ *and any preorder homomorphism* $h'\colon M \to N$, *there exists a unique preorder homomorphism* $h'\colon M' \to N$ *such that* $q; h' = h$ *if and only if* $ker(q) \subseteq ker(h)$.

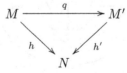

Definition 23. *Given a set* Γ *of universal Horn sentences in POA, a* **POA**-*congruence* $(\sim, \sqsubseteq)$ *on a preorder algebra M is closed under* Γ-*substitutivity if for each* $(\forall X)C$ *if* $H \in \Gamma$, *and for any expansion M' of M to* $(S, F \cup X)$, $M'_H \subseteq (\sim, \sqsubseteq)$ *implies* $M'_C \subseteq (\sim, \sqsubseteq)$.

Proposition 15. *For any preorder algebra M, $M/_{(\sim,\sqsubseteq)} \models \Gamma$ if and only if $(\sim,\sqsubseteq)$ is closed under Γ-substitutivity.*

Proposition 16. *The least **POA**-congruence closed under Γ-substitutivity, denoted $(=_\Gamma, \leq_\Gamma)$, exists as the infimum of all **POA**-congruences that are closed under Γ-substitutivity.*

Corollary 4. *For any preorder algebra M, $M/_{(=_\Gamma, \leq_\Gamma)}$ is the free preorder algebra over M satisfying Γ.*

By considering the initial term algebra $0_{(S,F)}$ for the preorder algebra M in Corollary 4, we obtain the existence of initial preorder algebras of Horn POA theories.

Corollary 5. *Each set Γ of universal Horn sentences in POA admits an initial model.*

Completeness of POA Deduction

Definition 24. *The POA proof system is generated by the following rules (for a given signature (S,F)):*

$$\frac{}{\{(\forall X)t = t\}} \ R. \qquad \frac{}{\{(\forall X)t => t\}} \ R. \qquad \frac{\{(\forall X)t = t'\}}{\{(\forall X)t' = t\}} \ S.$$

$$\frac{\{(\forall X)t = t', (\forall X)t' = t''\}}{\{(\forall X)t = t''\}} \ T. \qquad \frac{\{(\forall X)t => t', (\forall X)t' => t''\}}{\{(\forall X)t => t''\}} \ T.$$

For each operation symbol $\sigma \in F$:

$$\frac{\{(\forall X)t_i = t_i' | 1 \leq i \leq n\}}{\{(\forall X)\sigma(t_1, \ldots, t_n) = \sigma(t_1', \ldots, t_n')\}} \ OC.$$

and

$$\frac{\{(\forall X)t_i => t_i' | 1 \leq i \leq n\}}{\{(\forall X)\sigma(t_1, \ldots, t_n) => \sigma(t_1', \ldots, t_n')\}} \ OC.$$

For all $(\forall Y)C$ if $H \in \Gamma$, subst $\theta : Y \to X$

$$\frac{\{\Gamma \cup \{(\forall X)H\theta\}}{\{(\forall X)C\theta\}} \ \Gamma.$$

By noticing that $(=_\Gamma, \leq_\Gamma)$ in the term algebra $T_F(X)$ is given by

$$=_\Gamma = \{(t,t') \mid \Gamma \vdash^{POA} (\forall X)t = t'\}$$

and

$$\leq_\Gamma = \{(t,t') \mid \Gamma \vdash^{POA} (\forall X)t \to t'\}$$

where $\vdash^{POA}$ is the provability relation of the preorder-algebra proof system, we obtain the following corollary.

Corollary 6. *The POA proof system is sound and complete.*

Specification of Generic Algorithms

Many algorithms have a certain degree of independence of the actual data type, in the sense that they do not depend on all details of the data type, but rather on some of its properties.

This is the case for sorting too, since the bubble sort algorithm also works for integers, reals, etc. In fact, this sorting algorithm can be specified for strings over any data type which has a partial order. We can therefore use the CafeOBJ generic (or parametrised) specification paradigm and specify a generic sorting algorithm over any partial order by reusing the specification STRG(Y :: POSET) of generic strings over a partial order:

```
mod! SORTING(Y :: POSET) {
  protecting(STRG(Y))
  vars N N' : Elt
  ctrans N . N' => N' . N if (N' <= N) and (N =/= N') .
}
```

The sorting of strings of natural numbers can be obtained by instantiating the abstract partial order of SORTING to the natural numbers with the usual ordering:

```
mod!SORTING-NAT {
  protecting(SORTING(NAT))
}
```

Execution of Algorithms

Algorithms specified with POA in CafeOBJ can also be executed, and results can thus be obtained.

For example, we can execute SORTING-NAT and actually sort strings of naturals by using the CafeOBJ command "exec":

```
select SORTING-NAT
SORTING-NAT> exec (3 . 2 . 1) .
-- execute in SORTING-STRG-NAT: (3 . 2 . 1)
1 . 2 . 3 : Strg
```

Some algorithm properties

Notice that an algorithm is not necessarily **confluent**, meaning that in a certain state of the algorithm there may be several transitions to different states from which the algorithm can never reach a common state. SORTING-NAT is an example of a confluent algorithm since, from any state s, the algorithm finally reaches the state of the sorted string corresponding to s.

Also, an algorithm is not necessarily **terminating**, meaning that there may be infinite chains of transitions. SORTING-NAT is an example of a terminating algorithm, since bubble sort always terminates.

3.2 Algorithm verification

Transition Predicates

In CafeOBJ, verification of POA algorithms is realised at a data type level. That is, all reasoning about algorithm properties is done as the usual data-type reasoning. This is essentially based on an encoding of transitions as data, which is achieved via the built-in (many-sorted) transition predicate _==>_ .

The meaning of the transition predicate _==>_ is that of *existence of transitions*:

> s ==> s' **if and only if there exists at least one transition between the state** s **and the state** s'

For example, in the case of the algorithm SORTING-NAT for sorting strings of naturals, we can do the following testing:

```
SORTING-NAT> red (2 . 3 . 1) ==> (1 . 2 . 3) .
```

gives **true**, while,

```
SORTING-NAT> red (2 . 2 . 1) ==> (1 . 2 . 3) .
```

gives **false**.
Unlike the language Maude, the CafeOBJ methodology for algorithm verification is limited to reasoning about the *existence* of transitions between states of the algorithm, and does not discriminate between different (parallel) transitions between two given states.

Algorithm Verification

The possibility of reasoning about the existence of transitions between the states of an algorithm permits a wide range of verifications of algorithm properties.

For example, we can prove generic termination for the bubble sort algorithm. By a *generic property* we mean a property proved at the level of a generic algorithm, which then holds for all instances of the algorithm.

We consider the generic sorting algorithm SORTING(Y :: POSET) and use a classical technique for proving algorithm termination. We define a *weight function* on the states of the algorithm, with natural numbers as values, which becomes strictly lower along any transition. Because the natural numbers are well founded with respect to this "smaller-than" ordering, the existence of such a weight function means that there are no infinite chains of transitions between the states of the sorting algorithm.

The Weight Function.

We define the weight function `disorder`, which intuitively measures a kind of "distance" from the current state of the algorithm to the sorted state:

```
mod!SORTING-PROOF {
  protecting(SORTING + NAT)
  op disorder : Strg -> Nat
  op _>>_ : Elt Strg -> Nat
  vars E E' : Elt
  var S : Strg
  eq disorder(nil) = 0 .
  eq disorder(E) = 0 .
  eq disorder(E . S) = disorder(S) + (E >> S) .
  eq E >> nil = 0 .
  cq E >> E' = 0 if E <= E' .
  cq E >> E' = 1 if (E' <= E) and (E =/= E') .
  eq E >> (E' . S) = (E >> E') + (E >> S) .
}
```

Visualisation of Sorting

Let us visualise how `disorder` (represented by the balls below) becomes lower along transitions between some of the states of the instance of `SORTING` for the natural numbers:

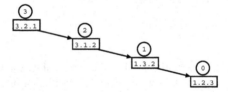

Termination Proof

So, we have to prove that,

$$s ==> s' \text{ implies disorder } (s') < \text{disorder}(s)$$

for any (different) states s and s'. We prove this theorem by using two lemmas.

Lemma 3. *disorder (e' . e . s) < disorder (e . e' . s) if e' < e for a string s and elements e and e'.*

Proof. The CafeOBJ proof score of this lemma is as follows:

```
open SORTING-PROOF .
ops e e' : -> Elt .
op s : -> Strg .
```

where the hypothesis is eq e' <= e = true . and the conclusion is,

```
red disorder(e' . e . s) < disorder(e . e' . s) .
close
```

Lemma 4. *disorder (e . s) < disorder (e . s')*
if (e >> s) == (e >> s') and disorder (s) < disorder (s'), for an el-
ement e, and strings s and s'.

Proof. The CafeOBJ proof score of this lemma is as follows:

```
open SORTING-PROOF .
op e : -> Elt .
ops s s' : -> Strg .
```

where the hypothesis is

```
eq (e >> s) = (e >> s') .
eq disorder(s) < disorder(s') = true .
```

and the conclusion is:

```
red disorder(e . s) < disorder(e . s') .
close
```

Now we return to the main part of the termination proof. If we have a one-step transition s ==> s', we can represent it as

```
(s . e . e' . s') ==> (s . e' . e . s')
```

where s and s' are strings, and e'and e are elements. Then we apply Lemma 3:

```
(e . e' . s') ==> (e' . e . s')
```

and then Lemma 4 iteratively, by induction on the length of s.

3.3 Non-determinism

Non-deterministic Naturals

Non-confluent algorithms correspond to non-deterministic computations. Non-determinism in POA is achieved by the use of "choice" transitions.

The following is an example of a non-deterministic choice of natural numbers:

```
mod!NNAT {
  extending(NAT)
  op _|_ : Nat Nat -> Nat { assoc comm }
}
```

The specification NNAT introduces new elements into the sort Nat of natural numbers: the "non-deterministic" natural is a multi-set of ordinary natural numbers expressing all possible choices of one natural number from the multi-set.

The Denotation of Specification of the Non-deterministic Natural Numbers

In the denotation of NNAT, (a fragment of) the sort Nat can be visualised as follows:

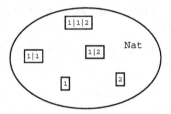

Non-deterministic Choice

The non-deterministic choice is specified by two transitions, as the following specification in CafeOBJ shows:

```
mod!NNAT-CHOICE {
  protecting(NNAT)
  vars M N : Nat
  trans N | M => N .
  trans N | M => M .
}
```

The denotation of NNAT-CHOICE adds to the denotation of NNAT transitions between the multi-sets of naturals as given by the two rules of the denotations. This can be visualised as follows:

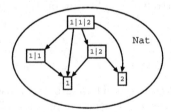

Testing for the Existence of Transitions

We can check the existence of transitions by using the built-in transition predicate _==>_.

    NNAT-CHOICE> red (1 | 1 | 2) ==> (1 | 2) .

gives true, and

    NNAT-CHOICE> red (1 | 1 | 2) ==> (2 | 2) .

gives false.

Proving Properties of Non-deterministic Naturals

The operations on naturals extend automatically on to the new entities of sort Nat, which may be either non-deterministic naturals or transitions (choices). In this way, they are available for reasoning about non-deterministic naturals.

For example, let us consider the problem of proving that 3 is less than any choice of (4 | 4 | 5). We can formulate this by using the "less than" predicate _<_:

   3 < (4 | 4 | 5)

In the absence of any axioms describing the relationship between _<_ and _|_, we have to force all the applications of the transition axioms on to the non-deterministic natural (4 | 4 | 5). Therefore, if there exists no transition from 3 < (4 | 4 | 5) to false, this means that 3 is less than any choice from (4 | 4 | 5). This is validated by the CafeOBJ system, since if we try the evaluation

   NNAT-CHOICE> red ((3 < (4 | 4 | 5)) ==> false) == true .

then we obtain false.

3.4 Linear Generation of Case Analyses

This POA methodology is useful for building proof scores involving complex case analysis.

Orthogonal Case Analysis

Consider the following two functions on the natural numbers:

```
mod!FG-fun {
  protecting(NAT)
  ops F G : NzNat -> Nat
  var X : NzNat
  eq F(1) = 10 .
  cq F(X) = 5 if (2 <= X) and (X <= 4) .
  cq F(X) = 2 if (5 <= X) and (X <= 9) .
  cq F(X) = 1 if (10 <= X) .
  cq G(X) = 8 if (1 <= X) and (X <= 7) .
  cq G(X) = 9 if (8 <= X) and (X <= 9) .
  cq G(X) = 10 if (10 <= X) .
}
```

Let us consider the problem of proving that for all positive natural numbers X and Y, F(X) + G(Y) is greater than 9.

Notice that there are four cases for the argument X, and three cases for the argument Y. The cases for X and the cases for Y are **orthogonal**, in the sense that they are completely independent of each other, so that they can be combined freely. This means that the total number of cases for this problem is twelve.

The total proof term for this problem is the conjunction of the twelve instances of the formula 9 <= F(X) + G(Y) for all combinations of the atomic cases. In general, the complexity of the total proof term is exponential with respect to the number of arguments (parameters), and so in principle will be the complexity of its execution by the system, i.e. the actual proof.

This cannot be avoided, and since the effort of executing the proof term is supported entirely by the system, this exponential complexity is not so severe. Much more severe would be an exponential complexity at the level of the specification effort for generating the total proof term. Fortunately, the orthogonality of the arguments permits a linear generation of the total proof term with respect to the number of arguments of the problem.

The generation of the total proof term is encoded in POA. This encoding is **meta-level** with respect to the specification level of the actual problem, since the meaning of the entities introduced by the encoding is different from the meanings of the entities of the specification FG-fun.

The POA specification of the generation algorithm for the total proof term involves the following steps.

Preliminaries

This includes the opening of the FG-fun module, and the introduction of auxiliary variables:

```
open FG-fun
var A : NzNat .
```

Specification of the Cases for the Parameters

We introduce one temporary variable (specified as an arbitrary constant) for each case, and we specify the conditions of each case.

The following is the specification of the cases for the parameter X:

```
ops x1 x2 x3 x4 : -> NzNat .
```

the condition for the first case is:

```
eq x1 = 1 .
```

the conditions for the second case are:

```
cq (A <= x2) = true if (A <= 2) .
cq (x2 <= A) = true if (4 <= A) .
```

the conditions for the third case are:

```
cq (A <= x3) = true if (A <= 5) .
cq (x3 <= A) = true if (9 <= A) .
```

the condition for the fourth case is:

```
cq (A <= x4) = true if (10 <= A) .
```

The following is the specification of the cases for the parameter Y:

```
ops y1 y2 y3 : -> NzNat .
```

the conditions for the first case are:

```
cq (A <= y1) = true if (A <= 1) .
cq (y1 <= A) = true if (7 <= A) .
```

the conditions for the second case are:

```
cq (A <= y2) = true if (A <= 8) .
cq (y2 <= A) = true if (9 <= A) .
```

the condition for the third case is:

```
cq (A <= y3) = true if (10 <= A) .
```

Generation of the Total Proof Term

The generation of the parametrised initial proof term is represented by:

```
vars X Y : NzNat .
var Z : Nat .
pred Term : NzNat NzNat Nat .
trans Term(X,Y,Z) => (Z <= F(X) + G(Y)) .
```

The partial proof term is obtained by instantiation of the first parameter with the cases for X:

```
pred Term1 : NzNat Nat .
trans Term1(Y,Z) => Term(x1,Y,Z) and
Term(x2,Y,Z) and
Term(x3,Y,Z) and
Term(x4,Y,Z) .
```

The total proof term is obtained by instantiation of the second parameter with the cases for Y:

```
pred Term2 : Nat .
trans Term2(Z) => Term1(y1,Z) and Term1(y2,Z) and
                  Term1(y3,Z) .
```

The generation of the total proof term can be represented graphically by the following tree:

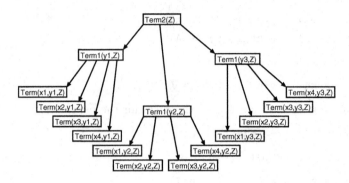

Execution of the Proof Term.

The actual proof of `9 <= F(X) + G(Y)` can now be performed automatically
by

```
exec Term2(9) .
```

and we obtain **true**.

The above **exec** command performs a two-level computation. First, it generates the total proof term containing the conjunction of the twelve instances
of the initial proof term. This is a meta-level computation by using the transitions. Second, it evaluates the final proof term in accordance with the data
of the specification **FG-fun**.

Case Debugging

This methodology for linear generation of case analyses via meta-level encoding in POA permits fast isolation of failure cases. For example,

```
exec Term2(10) .
```

gives **false**.

In order to find the cases for which this proof fails, we try the proof terms
at the level below the top level. We obtain the result

```
exec Term1(y1,10) .
```

gives **false**.

From the proof terms below **Term1(y1,10)**, only

```
exec Term(x4,y1,10) .
```

gives **false**. We then conclude that the failure can be localised to the case
`(x4,y1)`.

```
close
```

Case Intersection

Consider a more complicated proof goal, that $F(X) * G(Y) + F(Y) * G(X)$ is greater than 18 for all positive naturals X and Y. In this situation, both parameters X and Y range over the cases for both F and G. For this problem, we have to "intersect" the cases determined by F with the cases determined by G, and obtain five atomic cases for both X and Y:

$$\{1\}, \{2,3,4\}, \{5,6,7\}, \{8,9\}, \{10,11,\ldots\} \ .$$

In these five cases the parameters X and Y are orthogonal.

The CafeOBJ Code for the Generation of the Total Proof Term for Case Intersection

```
open FG-fun
  var A : NzNat .
  ops x1 x2 x3 x4 : -> NzNat .
-- the condition for the 1st case
  eq x1 = 1 .
-- the conditions for the 2nd case:
  cq (A <= x2) = true if (A <= 2) .
  cq (x2 <= A) = true if (4 <= A) .
-- the conditions for the 3rd case:
  cq (A <= x3) = true if (A <= 5) .
  cq (x3 <= A) = true if (9 <= A) .
-- the condition for the 4th case:
  cq (A <= x4) = true if (10 <= A) .
-- the specification of the cases for the parameter Y:
  ops y1 y2 y3 : -> NzNat .
-- the conditions for the 1st case:
  cq (A <= y1) = true if (A <= 1) .
  cq (y1 <= A) = true if (7 <= A) .
-- the conditions for the 2nd case:
  cq (A <= y2) = true if (A <= 8) .
  cq (y2 <= A) = true if (9 <= A) .
-- the condition for the 3rd case:
  cq (A <= y3) = true if (10 <= A) .
  vars X Y : NzNat .
  var Z : Nat .
  pred Term : NzNat NzNat Nat .
  trans Term(X,Y,Z) => (Z <= F(X) + G(Y)) .
-- partial proof term by instantiation of
-- the 1st parameter with the cases for X
  pred Term1 : NzNat Nat .
  trans Term1(Y,Z) => Term(x1,Y,Z) and
```

```
                    Term(x2,Y,Z) and
                    Term(x3,Y,Z) and
                    Term(x4,Y,Z) .
-- total proof term by instantiation of
-- the 2nd parameter with the cases for Y
  pred Term2 : Nat .
  trans Term2(Z) =>  Term1(y1,Z) and Term1(y2,Z) and
                    Term1(y3,Z) .
```

The proof of the problem is undertaken by the automatic execution:

```
  exec Term2(18) .
```

which gives true.

```
  close
```

4 Behavioural Specification

4.1 Basic Behavioural Specification

Behavioural specification distinguishes two kinds of sorts (types):

- *hidden*, for the states of abstract machines (or objects), and
- *visible*, for (ordinary) data types.

While the equality relation between "visible" (data type) elements is strict equality, the equality between "hidden" elements is the (loose) *behavioural (observational)* equality. Informally, two states are behaviourally equal when they cannot be distinguished by "observing" them over the data types. "Observations" are made via successive applications of *behavioural* operations ending with a visible sort. The set of behavioural operations is a precisely specified subset of the operations of the specification.

It is the looseness of behavioural equality that is the key to the benefits of behavioural-specification methodologies.

Specification of Bank Account Abstract Machine

```
mod* ACCOUNT {
  protecting(INT)
  *[ Account ]*
  op init : -> Account
  bop balance : Account -> Nat
  bop _deposit_ : Account Nat -> Account
  bop _withdraw_ : Account Nat -> Account
  var N : Nat
  var A : Account
```

```
  eq balance(init) = 0 .
  eq balance(A deposit N) = balance(A) + N .
  cq balance(A withdraw N) = balance(A) - N if N <= balance(A) .
  cq balance(A withdraw N) = balance(A) if balance(A) < N .
}
```

The CafeOBJ notation uses *[...]* for declaring hidden sorts and bop for declaring that an operation is behavioural. The space of the states of the ACCOUNT abstract machine is denoted by the hidden sort Account, and the abstract machine uses the (predefined) data type INT of integers. Behavioural specification signatures are called "hidden algebra(ic) signatures".

Definition 25. *A hidden algebraic signature* (H, V, F, F^b) *consists of*

- *disjoint sets H of* hidden sorts *and V of (ordinary)* visible sorts,
- *a set F of $(H \cup V)$-sorted operation symbols, and*
- *a distinguished subset $F^b \subseteq F$ of* behavioural operations.

Behavioural operations are required to have at least one hidden sort in their arity.

The graphical representation of the signatures of behavioural modules uses the following conventions:

- hidden sorts are represented as grey ellipsoidal discs; and
- behavioural operations are represented by thick arrows.

The following is the graphical representation of the signature of the abstract machine for a bank account:

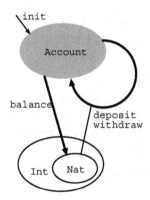

Behavioural Denotations

Definition 26. *Given a hidden algebraic signature* (H, V, F, F^b), *an* (H, V, F, F^b)*-algebra is just an* $(H \cup V, F)$*-algebra.*

Unlike data modules, which usually have initial denotations, behavioural modules usually have loose denotations (specified by mod*). This means that several denotations of the abstract machine for the bank account may interpret the hidden sort Account and the operations related to Account in different ways, while the type INT of integers has the standard interpretation.

ACCOUNT: a Model

For example, one model of ACCOUNT can be visualised as

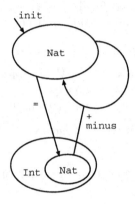

where

    eq init = 0

and where the function minus is specified as

    op minus : Nat Nat -> Nat
    cq minus(M:Nat,N:Nat) = M - N if N <= M .
    cq minus(M:Nat,N:Nat) = M if M < N .

ACCOUNT: Another Model

A second model of ACCOUNT keeps trace of the number of banking operations (deposits and withdrawals) and interprets Account as a set of pairs of natural numbers, with the first component holding the balance of the account and the second component holding the number of banking operations:

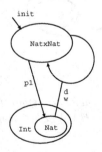

Here, p_1 is the projection on the first component,

```
eq init = < 0, 0 >
```

and the specification of d and w are as follows:

```
op d : NatxNat Nat -> NatxNat .
eq d(< N1:Nat, N2:Nat >, M:Nat) = < M + N1, N2 +  1 > .
op w : NatxNat Nat -> NatxNat .
cq w(< N1:Nat, N2:Nat >, M:Nat) = < N1 - M, N2 + 1 >
   if M <= N1 .
cq w(< N1:Nat, N2:Nat >, M:Nat) = < N1, N2 + 1 > if N1 < M .
```

Behavioural Equivalence

Ordinary (strict) equality is the appropriate equality relationship between data elements. In the case of the states of an abstract machine, the meaningful equality is **behavioural equality**, denoted $\sim$.

Two states s and s' (of the same hidden sort) are *behaviourally equal* (*equivalent*) if and only if

$$c(s) = c(s')$$

for all visible sorted *behavioural contexts* c. A *behavioural context* $c[z]$ is a term with a marked variable z with only one occurrence and such that all operations above z are behavioural.

The meaning of behavioural equivalence is that two states are behaviourally equal if they appear to be the same under all possible observations corresponding to all appropriate applications of behavioural operations.

Consider the states (a deposit 10 withdraw 5) and (a deposit 5) for an arbitrary state a of ACCOUNT. In the first model of ACCOUNT, these two states are equal in the strict ordinary sense, while in the second model they are equal *only* behaviourally. In fact, we have that in all models of ACCOUNT

$$(a \text{ deposit } 10 \text{ withdraw } 5) \sim (a \text{ deposit } 5)$$

for all states a.

The behavioural-equivalence relation is characterised by the following mathematical property.

Definition 27. *Given a* (H, V, F, F^b)-*algebra* A, *a hidden congruence* $\sim$ *on* A *is just an* F^b-*congruence which is the identity on the visible sorts.*

The largest hidden F-*congruence* $\sim_A$ *on* A *is called* behavioural equivalence.

Theorem 2. *Behavioural equivalence always exists.*

Behavioural Equations

Behavioural-equivalence properties can be specified in CafeOBJ by *behavioural equations* (by using the keyword beq).

As example, consider the following specification of *behavioural lists*, in which the lists are specified as a behavioural type rather than a data type:

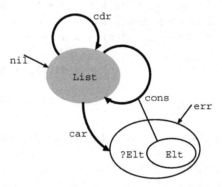

```
mod* BLIST {
  [ Elt ]
  op err : -> ?Elt

  *[ List ]*
  op nil : -> List
  bop cons : Elt List -> List
  bop car : List -> ?Elt
  bop cdr : List -> List
  var E : Elt
  var L : List
  eq car(nil) = err .
  eq car(cons(E, L)) = E .
  beq cdr(nil) = nil .
  beq cdr(cons(E, L)) = L .
}
```

The elements of the lists are specified by the (loose) sort Elt, which has an error constant err. The usual operations on lists (cons, car, and cdr) are behavioural.

Notice that while the first two equations are strict (since they are equations between data elements), the last two equations, between states of the (hidden) sort List, are behavioural. This means that in the implementation of this specification the elements denoted by the sides of these equations need not necessarily be strictly equal, but only *behaviourally* equal.

Definition 28. *Given a hidden algebraic signature (H, V, F, F^b), a* behavioural equation $t \sim t'$ *consists of a pair of F-terms of the same sort.*

An (H, V, F, F^b)-algebra A satisfies such an equation, i.e. $A \models t \sim t'$, when $A_t \sim_A A_{t'}$.

Array with Pointer Implementation

In order to illustrate this situation, consider the implementation of a list by a one-dimensional arrays of number with a pointer. In this model,

- cons(E, L) moves the pointer forward by one position and assigns the value E to the topmost cell of the array;
- cdr(L) moves the pointer backwards if possible, otherwise it leaves it in the same position; and
- car(L) gives the value of the topmost cell.

Behavioural equivalence between two states of the array-with-pointer model is given by the identity of the two arrays on the parts *before the pointer* only. For example the following arrays are behaviourally equivalent:

however, they are not strictly equal. Hence the array-with-pointer model of behavioural lists satisfies the behavioural equation above, but does not satisfy its strict version.

The array-with-pointer model satisfies strictly the equation

```
beq cdr(nil) = nil .
```

However, with a small modification such that cdr(L) moves the pointer backwards if possible, otherwise it leaves it in the same position and marks the first cell of the array by 0, we have the result that this equation is not satisfied strictly any more, but is satisfied only behaviourally.

Behavioural Objects

A concept of a *behavioural object* can be defined by interpreting classical object-oriented concepts within behavioural specification.

A behavioural object B is a behavioural specification which

- has a distinguished hidden sort $h(B)$ for the space of the states of B , and
- is such that all behavioural operations are *monadic,* i.e. they have only one hidden sort in the arity.

A behavioural operation is called an

- **action** when it changes the states of B, i.e. is defined on $h(B)$ (possibly parametrised by several data arguments) and evaluates to $h(B)$, and an

- **observation** when it evaluates the states of B to data values, i.e. is defined on $h(B)$ (possibly parametrised by several data arguments) and evaluates to a visible (data) sort.

Below is the formal definition of the concept of a behavioural object.

Definition 29. *[11] A behavioural object B is a pair consisting of a behavioural presentation $((H_B, V_B, F_B^b, F_B), E_B)$ and a hidden sort $h_B \in H_B$ such that each behavioural operation in F_B^b is monadic, i.e. it has only one hidden sort in its arity.*

The hidden sort h_B denotes the (space of the) states of B.

The visible sorted behavioural operations on h_B are called B-observations.

The h_B-sorted behavioural operations on h_B are called B-actions.

The h_B-sorted operations with a visible sorted arity are called constant states.[6]

For any behavioural object B, a B-algebra is just an algebra for the signature of B satisfying the sentences E_B of the presentation of the object B. The class of B-algebras is denoted by $\mathsf{Alg}(B)$.

In classical object-oriented jargon, "action" = "method", and "observation" = "attribute". In the object ACCOUNT, the actions are deposit and withdraw and the observation is balance. In the object BLIST, the actions are cons and cdr, and the observation is car.

4.2 Behavioural Proofs

Coinduction Principle

Theorem 2 provides the foundation for the following coinduction proof method:

1. Define an equivalence relation R (called a **coinduction relation**) for each hidden sort.
2. Prove that R is a hidden congruence.
3. Prove that sRs' for the states s and s' which have to be proved behaviourally equivalent.

An example of coinduction

For the bank account object ACCOUNT, we want to prove that

$$(\text{a deposit 10 withdraw 5}) \sim (\text{a deposit 5})$$

We follow the coinduction proof method:

---

[6] They should be considered as parametrised by the data arguments of the arity.

Definition of an equivalence relation _R_

```
open ACCOUNT .
pred _R_ : Account Account .
eq (A1:Account R A2:Account) = (balance(A1) == balance(A2)) .
```

Proof that _R_ is a hidden congruence

```
ops a a' : -> Account .
ops n n' : -> Nat .
```

We introduce the hypothesis

```
eq balance(a) = balance(a') .
```

The preservation of _R_ by deposit,

```
red (a deposit n) R (a' deposit n) .
```

gives true.
The preservation of _R_ by withdraw involves a simple case analysis:
case n <= balance(a):

```
eq n <= balance(a) = true .
eq n <= balance(a') = true .
red (a withdraw n) R (a' withdraw n) .
```

gives true.
case balance(a) < n':

```
eq balance(a) < n' = true .
eq balance(a') < n' = true .
red (a withdraw n') R (a' withdraw n') .
```

also gives true.

Proof of s R s'

```
red (a deposit 10 withdraw 5)  R   (a deposit 5)  .
```

which gives true.

Parametrised Coinduction Relations

For the behavioural list object BLIST, the coinduction relation R is defined by

$(1$ R $1')$ if and only if $car(cdr^n(1)) = car(cdr^n(1'))$

for all natural numbers n.

The universal quantification "for all natural numbers n" can be specified
in CafeOBJ by making cdr second-order and by parametrisation of R:

```
mod* BLIST-PROOF {
  protecting(BLIST + NAT)
  var N : Nat
  vars L L' : List
  bop cdr : Nat List -> List
  eq [cdr1] : cdr(0, L) = L .
  eq [cdr2] : cdr(s N, L) = cdr(N, cdr(L)) .
  pred _R[_]_ : List Nat List
  eq [r-def] : (L R[N] L') =
    (car(cdr(N, L)) == car(cdr(N, L'))) .
}
```

Proof of Hidden Congruence for the Parametrised Coinduction Relation

The following is the proof score that R is a hidden congruence:

```
open BLIST-PROOF
op e : -> Elt .
op n : -> Nat .
ops l1 l2 : -> List .
```

hypothesis:

```
eq [hyp] : car(cdr(N:Nat, l1)) = car(cdr(N:Nat, l2)) .
```

preservation of R by car:

```
start car(l1) == car(l2) .
apply -.cdr1 within term .
apply .hyp within term .
apply reduce within term .
```

preservation of R by cdr:

```
start cdr(l1) R[n] cdr(l2) .
apply .r-def within term .
apply -.cdr2 within term .
apply .hyp within term .
apply reduce within term .
```

preservation of R by cons. Case analysis:

```
red cons(e, l1) R[0] cons(e, l2) .
red cons(e, l1) R[s n] cons(e, l2) .
close
```

4.3 Behavioural Coherence

Example

For the bank account object ACCOUNT, we can prove by induction on the structure of the behavioural contexts that

$$a \sim a' \text{ if and only if } \mathtt{balance}(a) = \mathtt{balance}(a')$$

for all states a and a' of the object.

This means a significant simplification of the definition of behavioural equivalence for the ACCOUNT abstract machine, and is due essentially to the fact that

$$(a \mathtt{\ deposit\ } n) \sim (a' \mathtt{\ deposit\ } n) \text{ if } a \sim a'$$

and

$$(a \mathtt{\ withdraw\ } n) \sim (a' \mathtt{\ withdraw\ } n) \text{ if } a \sim a'$$

for all states a and a' of the object and each natural number n, where the behavioural equivalence is defined by equality under balance.

In such a situation, the actions deposit and withdraw may be specified not as behavioural operations, but as ordinary operations. This property of the actions deposit and withdraw of preserving behavioural equivalence (defined as equality under balance) is called *behavioural coherence*.

Definition 30. *An operation symbol σ is* coherent *for an algebra A when it preserves the behavioural equivalence, i.e.*

$$A_\sigma(a) \sim_A A_\sigma(a') \text{ whenever } a \sim_A a' \text{ (possibly componentwise).}$$

An operation symbol σ is coherent *with respect to a presentation (Σ, E) when it is coherent in each algebra of the presentation.*

Behavioural Coherence as an Attribute

At the level of the language, the behavioural-coherence property is considered as an axiom and is specified as an operation attribute. Therefore the signature of the bank account object specification can be changed to

```
*[ Account ]*
op init : -> Account
bop balance : Account -> Nat
op _deposit_  : Account Nat -> Account  { coherent }
op _withdraw_ : Account Nat -> Account  { coherent }
```

and its signature can be represented graphically by

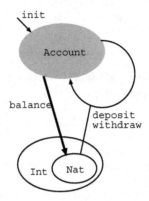

Notice that the difference between this representation of the signature of the account object and the previous representation consists only in the arrow representing the monadic part of the actions `deposit` and `withdraw`, which is now drawn as a thin arc. This is due to the fact that these two operations are now specified as ordinary operations rather than actions (behavioural operations).

Hidden Constructors

In the behavioural object `BLIST` of lists, the behavioural-equivalence relation between the states of `List` can be proved to be

$$l \sim l' \text{ if and only if } \mathtt{car}(\mathtt{cdr}^n(l)) = \mathtt{car}(\mathtt{cdr}^n(l'))$$

for all list states l and l' and all natural numbers n.

This shows a fundamental methodological difference between `car` and `cdr` on the one hand, and `cons` on the other, since `cons` does not play any role in the definition of behavioural equivalence. This also corresponds to the situation in the case of the specification of lists as a data type, in which `cons` is methodologically regarded as a *constructor*, and therefore has a methodological meaning different from `car` and `cdr`.

The absence of `cons` from the simplified definition of the behavioural-equivalence relation between lists is technically due to the fact that `cons` is behaviourally coherent. Such "constructors" on the hidden sorts are called **hidden constructors**, and they are required to be behaviourally coherent.

The CafeOBJ specification of the signature of `BLIST` with `cons` specified as a coherent operation is therefore as follows:

```
op cons : Elt List -> List  { coherent }
bop car : List -> ?Elt
bop cdr : List -> List
```

4.4 Behavioural non-determinism

Non-deterministic Choice

We can specify a non-deterministic choice of natural numbers by means of an abstract machine. The non-deterministic naturals are represented as a behavioural type by using

- the hidden sort NNat, and
- a "choice" observation _->_, indicating whether a certain natural number can be chosen from a certain state of the abstract machine for non-deterministic natural numbers.

The hidden constructor _|_ builds the non-deterministic naturals:

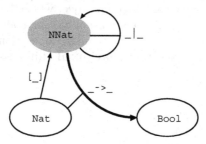

```
mod* NNAT-HSA {
  protecting(NAT)
  *[ NNat ]*
  op [_] : Nat -> NNat
  op _|_ : NNat NNat -> NNat { coherent }
  bop _->_ : NNat Nat -> Bool
  vars S1 S2 : NNat
  vars M N : Nat
  eq [M] -> N = (M == N) .
  eq S1 | S2 -> N = (S1 -> N) or (S2 -> N) .
}
```

Behavioural Coherence for Non-determinism

Notice that the non-deterministic constructor _|_ is automatically coherent. The behavioural equivalence between the states of the non-deterministic-naturals abstract machine is given only by the choice observation $s \sim s'$ if and only if $(s \rightarrow n) = (s' \rightarrow n)$ for all naturals n.

Proofs about Non-deterministic Choice

This very simple definition of the behavioural equivalence of the abstract machine for non-deterministic-naturals permits simple proofs for some behavioural properties of the non-deterministic hidden constructor.

Proof of Commutativity.

    red (s1 | s2) -> n == (s2 | s1) -> n .

Proof of Associativity.

    red ((s1 | s2) | s3) -> n == (s1 | (s2 | s3)) -> n .

4.5 Behavioural Inheritance

Inheritance of Behavioural Objects

Suppose we wish to have a bank account object which, besides actions such as
deposit and withdraw and the observation balance, also has another observation history, giving the number of banking operations (deposits or withdrawals). This can be solved by **behavioural inheritance** of the ACCOUNT
object as follows:

```
mod* HACCOUNT {
  protecting(ACCOUNT)
  *[ HAccount < Account ]*
  op init : -> HAccount
  bop _deposit_  : HAccount Nat -> HAccount
  bop _withdraw_ : HAccount Nat -> HAccount
  bop history : HAccount -> Nat
  eq history(init) = 0 .
  eq history(A:HAccount withdraw N:Nat) = history(A) + 1 .
  eq history(A:HAccount deposit  N:Nat) = history(A) + 1 .
}
```

The signature of this specification can be represented graphically as follows:

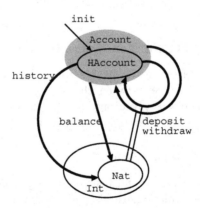

Behavioural-Inheritance Specification Methodology

The object inheritance specification process involves the following steps:

1. We import the module defining the inherited object.
2. We define a new hidden sort for the states of the new (inheriting) object as a subsort of the hidden sort of the states of the inherited object.
3. We overload all actions of the inherited object in the inheriting object.
4. We add new actions and/or observations and behavioural operations for the inheriting object on its hidden (sub)sort.
5. Finally, we add new axioms for the newly introduced operations on the inheriting object.

Preservation of Behavioural Equivalence

One important aspect of object inheritance is that the inherited object is protected. In the case of behavioural objects, this is expressed by the fact that its behavioural equivalence is preserved, in the sense that any two states are behaviourally equivalent for the inherited object whenever they are behaviourally equivalent for the inheriting object.

For example, in the case of the bank account object HACCOUNT, the behavioural equivalence of the inherited abstract machine is given by

$$a1 \sim_{\text{Account}} a2 \text{ if and only if } \texttt{balance}(a1) = \texttt{balance}(a2)$$

while the behavioural equivalence of the inheriting abstract machine is

$$a1 \sim_{\text{HAccount}} a2 \text{ if and only if } \begin{aligned} \texttt{balance}(a1) &= \texttt{balance}(a2) \text{ and} \\ \texttt{history}(a1) &= \texttt{history}(a2) \end{aligned}$$

This means that $a1 \sim_{HAccount} a2$ implies $a1 \sim_{Account} a2$.

The mechanism responsible for the preservation of behavioural equivalence during the inheriting process is a *new* hidden sort for the states of the inheriting object, specified as a subsort of the hidden sort of the inherited object. This matches the intuition that each state of the inheriting object should also be regarded as a state of the inherited object.

4.6 Behavioural Refinement

Behavioural Sets

Consider the following simple specification of a behavioural object of sets:

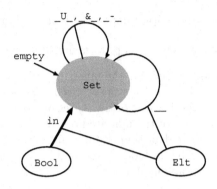

```
mod* BSET (X :: TRIV) {
  *[ Set ]*
  op empty : -> Set
  op __ : Elt Set -> Set { coherent }
  op _U_ : Set Set -> Set { coherent }
  op _&_ : Set Set -> Set { coherent }
  op _-_ : Set Set -> Set { coherent }
  bop _in_ : Elt Set -> Bool
  vars E E' : Elt
  vars S S1 S2 : Set
  eq E in empty = false .
  eq E in (E' S) = (E == E') or (E in S) .
  eq E in (S1 U S2) = (E in S1) or (E in S2) .
  eq E in (S1 & S2) = (E in S1) and (E in S2) .
  eq E in (S1 - S2) = (E in S1) and not (E in S2) .
}
```

Notice that this specification has only one behavioural operation, namely the membership observation in.

Behavioural Refinement

We want to show that the behavioural sets defined above can be *refined* to behavioural lists.

Behavioural-object refinement consists of the following:

1. A mapping between the hidden sorts of the "abstract" object and the "refined" object, preserving the state space of the objects.
2. A mapping from the behavioural operations of the "abstract" object to the (possibly derived) behavioural or (behaviourally) coherent operations of the "refined" object which is consistent with the mapping of sorts.

These mapping are such that the axioms of the "abstract" object are satisfied by the "refined" object via this mapping between the signatures. Such mappings between the signatures are a relaxed form of (hidden-algebra) *signature morphisms*.

Definition 31. *A* hidden-algebra signature morphism $\varphi \colon (H, V, F, F^b) \to (H', V', F', F'^b)$ *is a signature morphism* $(H \cup V, F) \to (H' \cup V', F')$ *such that*

- $\varphi(V) \subseteq V'$ *and* $\varphi(H) \subseteq H'$,
- $\varphi(F^b) = F'^b$ *and* $\varphi^{-1}(F'^b) \subseteq F^b$,

These conditions say that hidden-sorted signature morphisms preserve visibility and invisibility for both sorts and operations, and the object-oriented intuition behind the inclusion $F'^b \subseteq \varphi(F^b)$ is the encapsulation of classes (in the sense that no new "methods" or "attributes" can be defined on an imported class).

However, this last inclusion condition applies only to the case when signature morphisms are used as module imports (in this case they are called *horizontal* signature morphisms); when they model specification refinement, this condition might be dropped (in this case they are called *vertical* signature morphisms).

Behavioural Lists Refine Behavioural Sets

In our example, the behavioural sets are the "abstract" object and the behavioural lists are the "refined" object. This corresponds to the intuition that sets can be implemented as lists.

Since not all operations of BSET (such as $\cup$ and $\cap$) can be refined to operations of BLIST, we have two choices:

- extend BLIST with refinements of all operations of BSET, or
- consider the following simpler version BASIC-BSET of behavioural sets illustrated by the signature below:

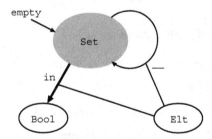

Then, the refinement of behavioural sets to behavioural lists refines:

- the hidden sort Set to the hidden sort List (this means that each state of a set object can be implemented as a state of the list object),
- the hidden constructor __ to the hidden constructor cons, and
- the membership observation (E in L) to the *derived* observation (E == car(L)) or-else (car(L) =/= err) and-also (E in cdr(L)) .

Notice that the "refined" list object has the observation `car` and the action `cdr` as new behavioural operations and also adds error handling.

Notice also that the derived observation which refines in uses some operational versions of the usual Boolean connectives, which evaluate as follows:

- if the left-hand-side argument of `or-else` evaluates to `true`, then the result is `true` and the evaluation of the right-hand-side argument is omitted, and
- if the left-hand-side argument of `and-also` evaluates to `false`, then the result is `false` and the evaluation of the right-hand-side argument is again omitted.

This refinement can be represented graphically as follows:

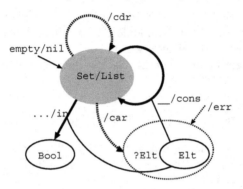

where the convention for the graphical notation for the signatures has been extended as follows:

- refinement of sorts and operations is represented by _/_ and sharing of the same figure (disc or arrow) in the diagram, and
- newly introduced sorts and operations are represented by dotted lines.

CafeOBJ Coding of Refinement

We encode this refinement in CafeOBJ by using an import as follows:

```
protecting(BLIST)
```

We introduce a notation for the derived observation:

```
op _in_ : Elt List -> Bool { coherent }
```

Note that the coherence of this derived observation is provable from the rest of the specification; we omit this proof.

```
eq E:Elt in L:List = (E == car(L)) or-else (car(L) =/= err
                                 and-also E in cdr(L)) .
```

Proof of Refinement

In order to prove that BLIST (or BLIST') refines BASIC-BSET, we have only to show that the equations

```
eq E in empty = false .
eq E in (E' S) = (E == E') or (E in S) .
```

are actually consequences of BLIST':

```
open LIST' .
ops e e1 e2 : -> Elt .
op l : -> List .
```

For the first equation, we have the following proof score:

```
red (e in nil) == false .
```

which gives true. For the second equation, the basic cases are as follows:

```
eq e1 in l = true .
eq e2 in l = false .
```

The proof score by case analysis is as follows:

```
red e1 in cons(e,l) == true .
red e2 in cons(e,l) == false .
red e in cons(e,l) == true .
```

All these proof scores evaluate to true.

```
close
```

Extension of Refinement

The refinement of the behavioural basic sets to behavioural lists can be extended to the behavioural sets of BSET by adding some derived operations to BLIST as follows:

```
op append : List List -> List
beq append(nil, L:List) = L .
beq append (cons(E:Elt, L1:List), L2) =
              cons(E, append(L1, L2)) .
```

The operation append refines the union ∪ (the proof would be similar to the above one). Similarly, we can define an intersection of lists, and even a list difference.

4.7 Hierarchical Object Composition

Compound Systems

Composing already existing **component** systems in order to define a new **compound** system is the most fundamental and important method of system construction. In this methodology, both component and compound systems are considered as behavioural **objects**.

We illustrate the basic methodology of parallel object composition (without synchronisation) by use of the parallel composition of two ACCOUNTs by composing two bank account objects.

I. Specification of the Projections

We create two different account objects by renaming the hidden sort of the already defined specification ACCOUNT of the bank account object:

```
mod* ACCOUNT-SYS {
  protecting(ACCOUNT * hsort Account -> Account1)
  protecting(ACCOUNT * hsort Account -> Account2)
```

The composition of the two account objects is regarded as a new object with a new hidden sort (AccountSys) for its states and two **projection operations** (account1 and account2) to the two hidden sorts of the component account objects. The projection operations are defined as behavioural:

```
*[ AccountSys ]*
bop account1 : AccountSys -> Account1
bop account2 : AccountSys -> Account2
```

II. Specification of Actions at the Level of the Compound Object

All the actions of the components are lifted to actions of the compound object. Notice that each action name is renamed after the component of origin:

```
bop deposit1 : AccountSys Nat -> AccountSys
bop deposit2 : AccountSys Nat -> AccountSys
bop withdraw1 : AccountSys Nat -> AccountSys
bop withdraw2 : AccountSys Nat -> AccountSys
```

III. Specification of the Observations at the Level of the Compound Object

The observations of the compound object are defined just as abbreviations of the observations of the components:

```
bop balance1 : AccountSys -> Nat
bop balance2 : AccountSys -> Nat
```

The Signature of the Composition

The signature of this composition can be visualised as follows:

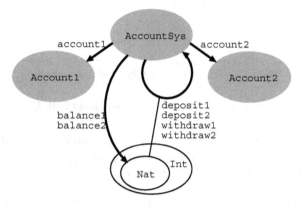

IV. Relating the Actions at the Compound Level to Those at the Components Level.

We relate the actions at the level of the compound object to the actions of the component objects via the projection operations:

```
var AS : AccountSys
var N : Nat
eq account1(deposit1(AS, N)) = deposit(account1(AS), N) .
eq account2(deposit2(AS, N)) = deposit(account2(AS), N) .
eq account1(withdraw1(AS, N)) = withdraw(account1(AS), N) .
eq account2(withdraw2(AS, N)) = withdraw(account2(AS), N) .
```

The actions originating from one component do not change the state of the other component. This basically means that each component can operate independently. This kind of composition is called **parallel composition**:

```
eq account1(deposit2(AS, N)) = account1(AS) .
eq account1(withdraw2(AS, N)) = account1(AS) .
eq account2(deposit1(AS, N)) = account2(AS) .
eq account2(withdraw1(AS, N)) = account2(AS) .
```

V. Relating the Observations at the Compound Level to Those at the Component Level.

The observations of the compound object are just abbreviations of the observations of the components:

```
eq balance1(AS) = balance(account1(AS)) .
eq balance2(AS) = balance(account2(AS)) .
}
```

The formal definition of parallel object composition is as follows:

Definition 32. *[11] A behavioural object B is a parallel composition of behavioural objects B_1 and B_2 when*

- $H_B = H_{B_1} \uplus H_{B_2} \uplus \{h_B\}$;[7]
- $V_B = V_{B_1} \cup V_{B_2}$;
- $(F_B)_{w \to s} = (F_{B_1})_{w \to s} \cup (F_{B_2})_{w \to s}$ *when all sorts in ws are visible;*
- $(F_B)_{w \to s} = (F_{B_i})_{w \to s}$ *when ws contains hidden sorts from H_{B_i} only, for $i \in \{1, 2\}$;*
- $(F_B)_{w \to s} = \emptyset$ *when ws contains hidden sorts from both H_{B_1} and H_{B_2} only;*
- $(F_B)_{h_B \to h_{B_i}} = \{\pi_i\}$ *for $i \in \{1, 2\}$;*
- $(F_B)_{h_B w \to h_B} = \{\sigma_i \mid \sigma \in (F_{B_i})_{h_{B_i} w \to h_{B_i}} \quad B_i\text{-action}, \ i \in \{1, 2\}\}$;[8]
- *the behavioural operations F_B^b are those from $F_{B_1}^b$, $F_{B_2}^b$, π_1, π_2, and the actions and the observations on h_B; and*
- $E_B = E_{B_1} \cup E_{B_2} \cup$
  $\{(\forall\{x\} \cup W)\pi_i(\sigma_i(x, W)) = \sigma(\pi_i(x), W) \mid \sigma \quad B_i\text{-action}, i \in \{1, 2\}\}$
  $\cup \{(\forall\{x\} \cup W)\pi_j(\sigma_i(x, W)) = \pi_j(x) \mid \sigma \quad B_i\text{-action} \ \{i, j\} = \{1, 2\}\}$
  $\cup \{e(\sigma) \mid \sigma \quad B\text{-observation}\} \cup \bigcup_c a \ B\text{-state constant} \ E(c)$,

where $e(\sigma)$ is a derived observational definition of σ and $E(c)$ is a derived constant set of definitions for c.

For each B-observation σ, we say that an equation $(\forall\{x\} \cup W)\sigma(x, W) = \tau_\sigma[\pi_i(x), W]$, where τ_σ is a visible sorted derived behavioural B_i-operation, is a derived observational definition of σ when $i \in \{1, 2\}$.

For each B-state constant c we say that $E(c) = \{\pi_i(c) = c_i \mid c_i \ a \ B_i\text{-state constant } i \in \{1, 2\}\}$ is a derived constant set of definitions for c.

We denote by $B_1 \| B_2$ the class of behavioural objects B which are parallel compositions of behavioural objects B_1 and B_2.

UML Representation of Parallel Composition

We can represent the parallel composition of the two bank account objects in UML notation as follows:

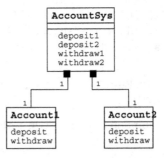

---

[7] By $\uplus$ we denote the disjoint union.

[8] In order to simplify the notation, the arity of actions and observations is always denoted with the hidden sort in the head position, e.g. $h_B w$.

In this representation, the connectors correspond to the projection operations.

Hierarchical Object Composition

The object composition methodology permits iteration of levels of composition, whereby compound objects may become component objects for a higher level of composition:

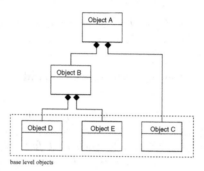

Equivalent Objects.

Definition 33. *[11] Given an object B, two B-algebras A and A' are equivalent, denoted $A \equiv A'$, when*

- $A_{h_B} = A'_{h_B}$ *and* $\sim_A = \sim_{A'}$ *on the sort h_B, and*
- $A_\sigma = A'_\sigma$ *for each B-action σ.*

Notice that the equality between behavioural equivalences $\sim_A$ on A and $\sim_{A'}$ on A' contains the equality of the interpretations of the observations too. However, this formulation avoids the potential troubles caused by a possible lack of direct observations, i.e. cases when the behavioural equivalence with help of derived behavioural operations to the visible (data) sorts.

Definition 34. *Two behavioural objects B and B' are equivalent, denoted $B \equiv B'$, when there exists a pair of mappings[9] Φ: $\mathsf{Alg}(B) \rightarrow \mathsf{Alg}(B')$ and Ψ: $\mathsf{Alg}(B') \rightarrow \mathsf{Alg}(B)$ which are inverse to each other modulo algebra equivalence, i.e. $A \equiv \Psi(\Phi(A))$ for each B-algebra A and $A' \equiv \Phi(\Psi(A'))$ for each B'-algebra A'.*

Note that isomorphic objects are equivalent.

The following gives the compositionality property of behavioural equivalence.

---

[9] The mappings may be considered as functions when one is working with *classes* of algebras, and functors when working with *categories* of algebras.

Proposition 17. *[11] For any behavioural objects B_1 and B_2, for each parallel composition $B \in B_1 \| B_2$, we have that*

$$a \sim_A a' \text{ if and only if } A_{\pi_1}(a) \sim_{A_1} A_{\pi_1}(a') \text{ and } A_{\pi_2}(a) \sim_{A_2} A_{\pi_2}(a')$$

for each B-algebra A, with elements $a, a' \in A_{h_B}$, and where $A_i = A{\restriction}_{B_i}$ for each $i \in \{1, 2\}$.

The following shows that parallel composition without synchronisation is unique modulo equivalence of objects.

Proposition 18. *[11] Let B_1 and B_2 be behavioural objects. Then all $B, B' \in B_1 \| B_2$ have isomorphic classes of algebras. Consequently, B and B' are equivalent objects, i.e. $B \equiv B'$.*

The following gives the final semantics of parallel composition without synchronisation.

Theorem 3. *[11] Let $B \in B_1 \| B_2$ and let A_i be algebras of B_i for $i \in \{1, 2\}$ such that they are consistent on the common data part. Then there exists a B-algebra A expanding A_1 and A_2 such that for any other B-algebra A' expanding A_1 and A_2 there exists a unique B-algebra homomorphism $A' \to A$ expanding A_1 and A_2.*

The following shows that parallel composition without synchronisation is commutative and associative modulo equivalence of objects.

Theorem 4. *[11] For all behavioural objects B_1, B_2, and B_3*

1. $B_1 \| B_2 = B_2 \| B_1$, *and*
2. $B_{(12)3} \equiv B_{1(23)}$ *for all $B_{(12)3} \in B_{12} \| B_3$ and all $B_{1(23)} \in B_1 \| B_{23}$, where B_{ij} is any composition in $B_i \| B_j$:*

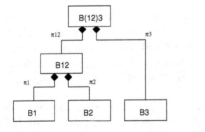 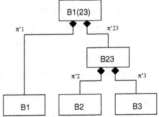

4.8 Composition with Synchronisation

Synchronisation

Synchronisation among components can occur when communications between them exist. In general, the analysis of situations where synchronisation can occur is not simple. However, the following two cases can be identified.

Broadcasting: some action of the compound object is projected to at least two components, affecting changes of their states simultaneously.

Client-server: the projected state of the compound object (via a projection) depends on the state of a different component.

Example: Transfer between Accounts

As an example, we add a transfer action to the bank account system obtained by parallel composition of two accounts:

```
mod* ACCOUNT-SYS-TRANSF {
  protecting(ACCOUNT-SYS)
```

The transfer action is specified as an action at the level of the compound object, and models a transfer action from the first account to the second one:

```
  bop transfer : AccountSys Nat -> AccountSys
```

Here is the signature of the system of two bank accounts with transfer:

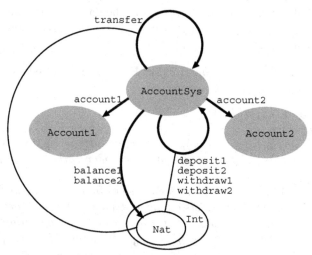

The Equations for the Transfer

These are

```
  eq account1(transfer(AS, N)) = withdraw(account1(AS), N) .
  ceq account2(transfer(AS, N)) = account2(AS)
      if N > balance1(AS) .
  ceq account2(transfer(AS, N)) = deposit(account2(AS), N)
      if N <= balance1(AS) .
}
```

Broadcasting and Client-Server Computing

Although very simple, this example contains both of the above synchronisation cases:

- *broadcasting* appears because `transfer` changes the states of both account components, and
- *client-server computing* appears because `transfer` is related to a deposit in `ACCOUNT2` by using information about `ACCOUNT1`.

Compound Object Action Specification

The specification of the projections of the compound object actions is done by conditional equations subject to the following conditions:

- each condition is a quantifier-free formula formed from equations by iteration of logical connectives, the terms of the equations being compositions between a projection and a composition chain of actions/observations (at the level of the components) or terms in the data signature; and
- the conditions corresponding to a projected action are disjoint and their disjunction is true.

Definition 35. *[11] A behavioural object B is a synchronised composition of behavioural objects B_1 and B_2 when*

- $H_B = H_{B_1} \uplus H_{B_2} \uplus \{h_B\}$;
- $V_B \supseteq V_{B_1} \cup V_{B_2}$;
- $(F_B)_{w \to s} \supseteq (F_{B_1})_{w \to s} \cup (F_{B_2})_{w \to s}$ *when all sorts in ws are visible*;
- $(F_B)_{w \to s} = (F_{B_i})_{w \to s}$ *when ws contains hidden sorts from H_{B_i} only, for $i \in \{1, 2\}$;*
- $(F_B)_{w \to s} = \emptyset$ *when ws contains hidden sorts from both H_{B_1} and H_{B_2} only;*
- *for each $i \in \{1, 2\}$, there exists a unique string w_i of visible sorts, such that $(F_B)_{h_B w_i \to h_{B_i}}$ is not empty, and it contains only one operation symbol π_i;*
- $(F_B)_{h_B w \to h_B} \supseteq \{\sigma_i \mid \sigma \in (F_{B_i})_{h_{B_i} w \to h_{B_i}} \quad B_i\text{-action}, \ i \in \{1, 2\}\};$
- *the behavioural operations F_B^b of F_B are those from $F_{B_1}^b$, $F_{B_2}^b$, π_1, π_2, and the actions and observations on h_B; and*
- $E_B = E_{B_1} \cup E_{B_2} \cup \bigcup_{\sigma \ B\text{-action}} E_\sigma \cup \{e(\sigma) \mid \sigma \ a \ B\text{-observation}\}$
  $\cup \bigcup_{c \ a \ B\text{-state constant}} E(c),$

where E_σ is a complete set of derived action definitions for σ, $e(\sigma)$ is a derived observational definition for σ, and $E(c)$ is a derived constant set of definitions for c.

For any B-action σ,

$$\{(\forall\{x\} \cup W \cup W_i) \ \pi_i(\sigma(x, W), W_i) = \\ \tau^i_{\sigma,k}[x, W, W_i] \ \text{if} \ C^i_{\sigma,k}[x, W, W_i] \mid \tau^i_{\sigma,k} \ a \ term, i \in \{1, 2\}, k \in \{1, \ldots, n_i\}\}$$

is a complete set of derived action definitions for σ when the following conditions apply.

1. *Each $\tau^i_{\sigma,k}[x, W, W_i]$ is an h_{B_i}-sorted term of behavioural or coherent B_i-operations applied either to $\pi_i(x, W_i)$ or to a B_i-state constant.*

2. Each $C^i_{\sigma,k}[x, W, W_i]$ is a quantifier-free formula formed by iterations of negations, conjunctions, and disjunctions from equations formed by terms which are either data signature terms or visible sorted terms of the form $c[\pi_j(x, W_j)]$ where c is some derived behavioural B_j-operation with $W_j \subseteq W \cup W_j$ and such that

- the disjunction $(\forall\{x\} \cup W \cup W_i) \vee \{C^i_{\sigma,k} \mid k \in \{1, \ldots, n_i\}\}$ is true for each $i \in \{1, 2\}$,
- for a given i, the conditions $C^i_{\sigma,k}$ are disjoint, i.e. $(\forall\{x\} \cup W \cup W_i)$ $C^i_{\sigma,k} \wedge C^i_{\sigma,k'}$ is false whenever $k \neq k'$.

We write $B_1 \otimes B_2$ for the class of behavioural objects B which are synchronised compositions of behavioural objects B_1 and B_2.

4.9 Verification of Compound Objects

Compositionality of Verification

In object-oriented programming, reusability of source code is important, but in object-oriented specification, reusability of proofs is also very important because of the complexity of the verification process. We call this **compositionality of verification** of components.

The following result provides the foundations of the CafeOBJ verification methodologies in the case of compositions with synchronisation.

Theorem 5. [11] For any behavioural objects B_1 and B_2, for each composition with synchronisation $B \in B_1 \otimes B_2$, we have that

$$a \sim_A a' \text{ if and only if } (\forall W_i)A_{\pi_i}(a, W_i) \sim_{A_i} A_{\pi_i}(a', W_i) \text{ for } i \in \{1, 2\}$$

for each B-algebra A, with elements $a, a' \in A_{h_B}$, and where $A_i = A{\upharpoonright}_{B_i}$ for each $i \in \{1, 2\}$.

An important consequence of Theorem 5 is the final semantics for synchronised parallel composition.

Theorem 6. Let $B \in B_1 \otimes B_2$, let A_i be algebras of B_i for $i \in \{1, 2\}$, and let A_V be an algebra for the data part of B such that they are consistent on the common data part. Then there exists a B-algebra A expanding A_1, A_2, and A_V such that for any other B-algebra A' expanding A_1, A_2, and A_V there exists an unique B-algebra homomorphism $A' \to A$ expanding A_1, A_2, and A_V.

Example: Dynamic System of Accounts with User Database Management.

Here, we specify a dynamic bank account system with a user management mechanism provided by a user database (USER-DB) that enables us to query whether a user already has an account in the system. The dynamic aspect of this composition is that the number of components (accounts in this case) is changed dynamically while the compound system is working. This is technically reflected by the fact that the projection account is parametrised by the data of user identifiers. The user database is obtained by reusing the behavioural-set object BSET and by renaming two of its sorts:

```
mod* USER-DB protecting(BSET *
     { hsort Set -> UserDB, sort Elt -> UId })
```

The signature of this specification can be visualised as follows:

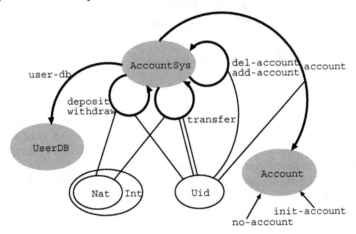

The Equations for the Projection on UserDB

```
eq   user-db(add-account(AS, U)) = (U empty) U user-db(AS) .
eq   user-db(del-account(AS, U)) = user-db(AS) - (U empty) .
eq   user-db(transfer(AS, U, U', N)) = user-db(AS) .
eq   user-db(deposit(AS, U, N)) = user-db(AS) .
eq   user-db(withdraw(AS, U, N)) = user-db(AS) .
```

The Equations for the Projection on Account

The equations for add-account and del-account are:

```
ceq account(add-account(AS, U'), U) = init-account
    if (U == U') and not(U in user-db(AS)) .
ceq account(add-account(AS, U'), U) = account(AS, U)
    if (U =/= U') or (U in user-db(AS)) .
ceq account(del-account(AS, U'), U) = no-account
    if (U == U') .
ceq account(del-account(AS, U'), U) = account(AS, U)
    if (U =/= U') .
```

The equations for `transfer` are:

```
ops cond1 cond2 cond3 : AccountSys UId UId UId Nat -> Bool
ceq account(transfer(AS, U', U'', N), U) =
    withdraw(account(AS, U'), N)
    if cond1(AS, U, U', U'', N) .
eq  cond1(AS, U, U', U'', N) =
    (U == U') and (U' in user-db(AS))and
    (U'' in user-db(AS)) and (U' =/= U'') .
ceq account(transfer(AS, U', U'', N), U) =
    deposit(account(AS, U''), N)
    if cond2(AS, U, U', U'', N) .
eq  cond2(AS, U, U', U'', N) =
    (U == U'') and (U' in user-db(AS)) and
    (U'' in user-db(AS)) and (U' =/= U'') and
    N <= balance(account(AS, U')) .
ceq account(transfer(AS, U', U'', N), U) =
    account(AS, U)
    if cond3(AS, U, U', U'', N) .
eq  cond3(AS, U, U', U'', N) =
    not(cond1(AS, U, U', U'', N) or
    cond2(AS, U, U', U'', N)) .
```

The equations for `deposit` and `withdraw` are:

```
ceq account(deposit(AS, U', N), U) =
    account(AS, U)
    if  not(U' in user-db(AS)) or (U =/= U') .
ceq account(deposit(AS, U', N), U) =
    deposit(account(AS, U), N)
    if  (U == U') and (U' in user-db(AS)) .
ceq account(withdraw(AS, U', N), U) =
    account(AS, U)
    if  not(U' in user-db(AS)) or (U =/= U') .
ceq account(withdraw(AS, U', N), U) =
    withdraw(account(AS, U), N)
if  (U == U') and (U' in user-db(AS)) .
```

Encoding Behavioural Equivalence of Compound Objects

We use Theorem 5 for encoding the behavioural equivalence of the compound object for the bank account:

```
mod BEQ-ACCOUNT-SYS {
  protecting(ACCOUNT-D-SYS-TRANSF)
  pred _R[_]_ : AccountSys UId AccountSys
```

```
pred _=b=_    : UserDB UserDB
vars AS1 AS2 : AccountSys
var U : UId
eq AS1 R[U] AS2 = (account(AS1, U) =b= account(AS2, U))
                  and (user-db(AS1) =b= user-db(AS2)) .
op id : -> UId
eq (a1:Account =b= a2:Account) =
   (balance(a1) == balance(a2)) .
eq (Udb1:UserDB =b= Udb2:UserDB) =
   (id in Udb1 == id in Udb2) .
}
```

The constant id stands for an arbitrary user identifier, and can be regarded as a Skolem constant. Notice also the use of the parametrised relation for handling the conjunction indexed by the user identifiers.

Concurrency Proofs in the Compound Object

We now analyse the true concurrency of deposits of the two (possibly) different users. This is a safety property for the system of bank accounts and is formulated by the following behavioural commutativity property:

$$\texttt{deposit}(\texttt{deposit}(as, u2, n2), u1, n1) \sim \texttt{deposit}(\texttt{deposit}(as, u1, n1), u2, n2)$$

This involves a case analysis which is an orthogonal combination of atomic cases for the users with respect to their membership of the user accounts data base.

Generation of Case Analysis

We apply the methodology for the linear generation of case analyses (see Sect. 3.4):

```
mod PROOF-TREE {
  protecting(BEQ-ACCOUNT-SYS)
--> Arbitrary amounts for withdrawal:
  ops n1 n2 : -> Nat
--> Arbitrary user identifiers:
  ops u u1 u1' u2 u2' : -> UId
--> Arbitrary state of the account system:
  op as : -> AccountSys
--> 1st user is in the data base:
  eq u1 in user-db(as) = true .
--> 2nd user is in the data base:
  eq u2 in user-db(as) = true .
--> 1st user is not in the data base:
```

```
  eq u1' in user-db(as) = false .
--> 2nd user is not in the data base:
  eq u2' in user-db(as) = false .
--> Basic proof term:
  vars U U1 U2 : UId
  op TERM : UId UId UId -> Bool
--> Liner cases analysis generation encoding:
  op TERM1 : UId UId -> Bool
  trans TERM1(U, U1) => TERM(U, U1, u2) and TERM(U, U1, u2') and
                        TERM(U, U1, u1) and TERM(U, U1, u1') .
  op TERM2 : UId -> Bool
  trans TERM2(U) => TERM1(U, u1) and TERM1(U, u1') .
--> Final proof term:
  op RESULT : -> Bool
  trans RESULT => TERM2(u1) and TERM2(u1') and
                  TERM2(u2) and TERM2(u2') and TERM2(u) .
}
```

The Execution of the Proof Term

We now instantiate the generic proof term to our specific problem (of true concurrency of withdrawals):

```
open PROOF-TREE
  trans TERM(U, U1, U2) =>
  deposit(deposit(as, U2, n2), U1, n1) R[U]
  deposit(deposit(as, U1, n1), U2, n2) .
exec RESULT .
close
```

The execution of the proof term returns **true**.

If we consider the **withdraw** operation rather than **deposit**, the execution of the proof term returns **false**. In order to isolate the failure case(s), we can use the debugging method associated with the orthogonal linear generation of case analyses (see Sect. 3.4). We find first get TERM2(u1) gives **false**, then that TERM1(u1,u1) gives **false**, and finally only that TERM(u1,u1,u1) gives **false**.

This corresponds to the case when there are two withdrawals corresponding to the same user. The true concurrency of two withdrawal actions for the same user depends on the relationship between the balance of the user and the amounts required; in some cases one action can be performed while the other cannot.

5 Institutional Semantics

One of the fundamental principles of research and development in algebraic specification today is that each algebraic specification and programming language or system has an underlying logic in which all language constructs can be rigorously defined as mathematical entities, and such that the semantics of specifications or programs is given by the model theory of this underlying logic. All modern algebraic specification languages, including CafeOBJ, follow this principle strictly. Another example is CASL [35].

On the other hand, there are numerous algebraic specification languages in use, some of them tailored to specific classes of applications, and hence a large class of logics underlying algebraic specification languages. However, many of the phenomena in algebraic specification are independent of the actual language and its underlying logic (see [17, 19, 41], etc.). This potential to perform algebraic specification at a general level is realized by the theory of institutions [19], which is a categorical, abstract, model-theoretic meta-theory of logics originally intended for specification and programming, but also very suitable for model theory [8, 9, 10, 27, 28, 38, 42, 43].

The use of the concept of an institution in algebraic specification is manifold:

- It provides a rigorous concept of the logic underlying algebraic specification languages, a logic thus being a mathematical entity.
- It provides a framework for developing basic algebraic-specification concepts and results independently of the actual underlying logic. This leads to greater conceptual clarity, and appropriate uniformity and unity, with the benefit of a simpler and more efficient top-down approach to algebraic-specification theory that contrasts with the conventional bottom-up approach.
- It provides a framework for rigorous translations, encoding, and representations between algebraic specification systems via various morphism concepts between institutions.

5.1 Institutions

Definition 36. *An* institution $(\mathbb{S}ig, Sen, \mathrm{MOD}, \models)$ *consists of:*

1. *A category $\mathbb{S}ig$, whose objects are called* signatures.
2. *A functor $Sen: \mathbb{S}ig \to \mathbb{S}et$, giving for each signature a set whose elements are called* sentences *over that signature.*
3. *A functor $\mathrm{MOD}: \mathbb{S}ig^{\mathrm{op}} \to \mathbb{C}at$ giving for each signature Σ a category whose objects are called Σ-models, and whose arrows are called Σ-(model) homomorphisms.*
4. *A relation $\models_\Sigma \subseteq |\mathrm{MOD}(\Sigma)| \times Sen(\Sigma)$ for each $\Sigma \in |\mathbb{S}ig|$, called Σ-satisfaction.*

These are such that for each morphism $\varphi\colon \Sigma \to \Sigma'$ *in* $\mathbb{S}ig$, *the* satisfaction condition

$$M' \models_{\Sigma'} Sen(\varphi)(e) \quad \textit{iff} \quad \mathrm{MOD}(\varphi)(M') \models_{\Sigma} e \ \textit{holds for each } M' \in$$

$|\mathrm{MOD}(\Sigma')|$ *and* $e \in Sen(\Sigma)$. *We may denote the reduct functor* $\mathrm{MOD}(\varphi)$ *by* $\_\!\upharpoonright_\varphi$ *and the sentence translation* $Sen(\varphi)$ *simply by* $\varphi(\_)$. *When* $M = M'\!\upharpoonright_\varphi$, *we say that* M' *is an* expansion *of* M *along* φ.

The formal-specification interpretation of institution concepts is as follows. The signatures of the institution provide the syntactic entities for the specification language, the models provide possible implementations, the sentences are formal statements encoding the properties of the implementations, and the satisfaction relation tells us when a certain implementation satisfies a certain property.

5.2 The CafeOBJ institution

CafeOBJ is a multi-logic language. This means that different features of CafeOBJ require different underlying institutions. For example, behavioural specification has coherent hidden algebra [13] as its underlying institution, while preorder algebra specification has POA as its underlying institution. Both institutions are in fact extensions of the more conventional equational-logic institution. On the other hand, they can be combined into "coherent hidden preorder algebra" which extends both of them. Other features of CafeOBJ require other institutions. Therefore, as a consequence of its multi-logic aspect, CafeOBJ involves a system of institutions and extension relationships between them rather than a single institution.

The solution to the multi-logic aspect of CafeOBJ is given by the concept of a *Grothendieck institution*, which flattens the underlying system of institutions to a single institution in which the flattened components still retain their identity. Grothendieck institutions were invented in [7], but their spirit had already appeared in [5], and although initially motivated by CafeOBJ semantics, they provide a solution for the semantics of any multi-logic language. For example, CASL, when used together with its extensions, has also adopted Grothendieck institutions as its semantics [36].

Institution Morphisms

Institution morphisms [19] provide the necessary concept for relating different institutions.

Definition 37. *An* institution morphism
$(\Phi, \alpha, \beta)\colon (\mathbb{S}ig', Sen', \mathrm{MOD}', \models') \to (\mathbb{S}ig, Sen, \mathrm{MOD}, \models)$ *consists of:*

1. A functor $\Phi\colon \mathbb{S}ig' \to \mathbb{S}ig$.

2. *A natural transformation* $\alpha\colon \Phi; \mathrm{Sen} \Rightarrow \mathrm{Sen}'$.

3. *A natural transformation* $\beta\colon \mathrm{Mod}' \Rightarrow \Phi^{\mathrm{op}}; \mathrm{Mod}$.

These are such that for any signature Σ', *the following* satisfaction condition *holds:*

$$M' \models'_{\Sigma'} \alpha_{\Sigma'}(e) \quad \textit{iff} \quad \beta_{\Sigma'}(M') \models_{\Sigma'\Phi} e$$

for any model $M' \in \mathrm{Mod}'(\Sigma')$ *and any sentence* $e \in \mathrm{Sen}(\Sigma'\Phi)$.

An adjoint *institution morphism is an institution morphism such that the functor* $\Phi\colon \mathbb{S}\mathrm{ig}' \to \mathbb{S}\mathrm{ig}$ *has a left adjoint.*[10]

Institutions and their morphisms, with the obvious composition, form a category denoted $\mathbb{I}ns$.

This type of structure-preserving institution mapping, introduced in the seminal paper [19], has a forgetful flavour in that it maps from a "richer" institution to a "poorer" institution. The dual concept of institution mapping, called *comorphism*, [25] in which the mapping between the categories of signatures is reversed, can be interpreted in actual examples as embedding a "poorer" institution into a "richer" one. Any adjunction between the categories of signatures determines a "duality" pair consisting of an institution morphism and an institution comorphism; this was observed for the first time in [1, 45]. Below, we may notice that all institution morphisms involved in the semantics of CafeOBJ are adjoint.

Indexed Institutions

We now recall the concept of an "indexed category" [37]. A good reference for indexed categories, which also discusses applications to algebraic specification theory, is [44].

Definition 38. *An* indexed category *[44] is a functor* $B\colon I^{\mathrm{op}} \to \mathbb{C}\mathrm{at}$; *sometimes we denote* $B(i)$ *as* B_i *(or* B^i) *for an index* $i \in |I|$, *and* $B(u)$ *as* B^u *for an index morphism* $u \in I$.

The following "flattening" construction, which provides the canonical fibration associated with an indexed category, is known as the *Grothendieck construction*, and plays an important role in mathematics.

Definition 39. *Given an indexed category* $B\colon I^{\mathrm{op}} \to \mathbb{C}\mathrm{at}$, *let* $B^\sharp$ *be the* Grothendieck category *having* $\langle i, \Sigma \rangle$, *with* $i \in |I|$ *and* $\Sigma \in |B_i|$, *as objects, and* $\langle u, \varphi \rangle\colon \langle i, \Sigma \rangle \to \langle i', \Sigma' \rangle$, *with* $u \in I(i, i')$ *and* $\varphi\colon \Sigma \to \Sigma' B^u$, *as arrows. The composition of arrows in* $B^\sharp$ *is defined by* $\langle u, \varphi \rangle; \langle u', \varphi' \rangle = \langle u; u', \varphi; (\varphi' B^u) \rangle$.

Indexed institutions [7] extend indexed categories to institutions.

---

[10] Adjoint institution morphisms were previously called "embedding" institution morphisms in [7, 5].

Definition 40. *[7] Given a category I of indices, an* indexed institution $\mathcal{J}$ *is a functor* $\mathcal{J}: I^{\mathrm{op}} \to \mathbb{I}\mathrm{ns}$. *For each index* $i \in |I|$ *we denote the institution* $\mathcal{J}^i$ *by* $(\mathbb{S}ig^i, \mathrm{Mod}^i, \mathrm{Sen}^i, \models^i)$ *and for each index morphism* $u \in I$, *we denote the institution morphism* $\mathcal{J}^u$ *by* $(\Phi^u, \alpha^u, \beta^u)$.

Grothendieck Institutions

Grothendieck institutions [7] extend the flattening Grothendieck construction from indexed categories to indexed institutions.

Definition 41. *The* Grothendieck institution $\mathcal{J}^\sharp$ *of an indexed institution* $\mathcal{J}: I^{\mathrm{op}} \to \mathbb{I}\mathrm{ns}$ *is defined as follows:*

1. *its category of signatures* $\mathbb{S}ig^\sharp$ *is the Grothendieck category of the* indexed *category of signatures* $\mathbb{S}ig: I^{\mathrm{op}} \to \mathbb{C}at$ *of the indexed institution* $\mathcal{J}$.
2. *its model functor* $\mathrm{Mod}^\sharp: (\mathbb{S}ig^\sharp)^{\mathrm{op}} \to \mathbb{C}at$ *is given by*
   - $\mathrm{Mod}^\sharp(\langle i, \Sigma \rangle) = \mathrm{Mod}^i(\Sigma)$ *for each index* $i \in |I|$ *and signature* $\Sigma \in |\mathbb{S}ig^i|$, *and*
   - $\mathrm{Mod}^\sharp(\langle u, \varphi \rangle) = \beta^u_{\Sigma'}; \mathrm{Mod}^i(\varphi)$ *for each* $\langle u, \varphi \rangle: \langle i, \Sigma \rangle \to \langle i', \Sigma' \rangle$.
3. *its sentence functor* $\mathrm{Sen}^\sharp: \mathbb{S}ig^\sharp \to \mathbb{S}et$ *is given by*
   - $\mathrm{Sen}^\sharp(\langle i, \Sigma \rangle) = \mathrm{Sen}^i(\Sigma)$ *for each index* $i \in |I|$ *and signature* $\Sigma \in |\mathbb{S}ig^i|$, *and*
   - $\mathrm{Sen}^\sharp(\langle u, \varphi \rangle) = \mathrm{Sen}^i(\varphi); \alpha^u_{\Sigma'}$ *for each* $\langle u, \varphi \rangle: \langle i, \Sigma \rangle \to \langle i', \Sigma' \rangle$.
4. $M \models^\sharp_{\langle i, \Sigma \rangle} e$ *iff* $M \models^i_\Sigma e$ *for each index* $i \in |I|$, *signature* $\Sigma \in |\mathbb{S}ig^i|$, *model* $M \in |\mathrm{Mod}^\sharp(\langle i, \Sigma \rangle)|$, *and sentence* $e \in \mathrm{Sen}^\sharp(\langle i, \Sigma \rangle)$.

By the satisfaction condition of the institution $\mathcal{J}^i$ *for each index* $i \in |I|$ *and the satisfaction condition of the institution morphism* $\mathcal{J}^u$ *for each index morphism* $u \in I$, *we obtain the following proposition.*

Proposition 19. *[7]* $\mathcal{J}^\sharp$ *is an institution and for each index* $i \in |I|$, *there exists a canonical institution morphism* $(\Phi^i, \alpha^i, \beta^i): \mathcal{J}^i \to \mathcal{J}^\sharp$ *mapping any signature* $\Sigma \in |\mathbb{S}ig^i|$ *to* $\langle i, \Sigma \rangle \in |\mathbb{S}ig^\sharp|$ *and such that the components of* α^i *and* β^i *are identities.*

By [5, 7], under suitable conditions, the important properties of institutions (including theory colimits, free construction (called liberality), model amalgamation (called exactness), and inclusion systems) can be "globalised" from the components of the indexed institution to the Grothendieck institution.

If we replace institution morphisms by institution comorphisms, we can define "comorphism-based" Grothendieck institutions [34]. When the institution morphisms of the indexed institution are adjoint, the Grothendieck institution and the corresponding comorphism-based Grothendieck institution are isomorphic [34]. It is easy to notice that this actually happens in the case of CafeOBJ.

The CafeOBJ Cube

Now we are ready to define the actual CafeOBJ institution as the Grothendieck institution of the indexed institution below, called the CafeOBJ cube. (The actual CafeOBJ cube consists of the full arrows; the dotted arrows denote the morphisms from components of the indexed institution to the Grothendieck institution.)

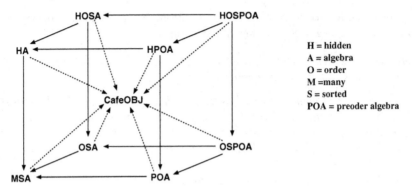

H = hidden
A = algebra
O = order
M = many
S = sorted
POA = preoder algebra

The details of the institutions of the CafeOBJ cube can be found in [14]. We present them briefly below.

As presented above, the institution MSA of many-sorted algebra has "algebraic signatures" (consisting of sets of sort symbols and sorted function symbols) as signatures, algebras interpreting the sort symbols as sets and the function symbols as functions, and (possibly conditional) universally quantified equations as sentences.

As in other algebraic specification languages, the conditions of equations are encoded as Boolean-valued terms, and hence in reality MSA should be thought of as a *constraint equational logic* in the sense of [6]. Alternatively, one may adopt membership equational logic [33] as the base equational-logic institution.

OSA extends the MSA institution with order sortedness such that the set of sorts of a signature is a partially ordered set rather than a discrete set, and algebras interpret the subsort relationship as set inclusion. The forgetful institution morphism from OSA to MSA just forgets the order sortedness.

As we have already seen above, the institution POA has the same signatures as MSA, but the models interpret the sort symbols as preorders and the function symbols as preorder functors (i.e. functors between preorders). In CafeOBJ, POA sentences are Horn sentences formed from equations and transitions. Their satisfaction by models is determined by the preorder relation between the interpretations of the terms of the transition. The forgetful institution morphism from POA to MSA essentially forgets the preorder relationship between the elements of models.

The institution HA of "coherent hidden algebra" is the institution underlying behavioural specification, and has hidden algebraic signatures, algebras as models, and (possibly conditional) strict and behavioural equations as sentences. Note that coherence declarations need not be registered as sentences of HA, because they are just abbreviations of conditional behavioural equations. There is a forgetful institution morphism from HA to MSA that forgets the distinction between visible and hidden.

These extensions of MSA towards three different paradigms can all be combined into HOSPOA (see [14] for details). All institutions in the CafeOBJ cube can be seen as subinstitutions of HOSPOA by means of the adjoint comorphisms corresponding to the forgetful institution morphisms.

Various extensions of CafeOBJ can be considered by transforming the CafeOBJ cube into a "hyper-cube" and by flattening it to a Grothendieck institution.

6 Structured Specifications

6.1 Imports

Basic imports

Consider the problem of specifying the data type of strings of natural numbers. We can *reuse* the data type of natural numbers (NAT) (predefined in CafeOBJ, but it can also be user-defined), and focus on the specification of strings.

```
mod!STRG-NAT {
  protecting(NAT)
  [ Nat < Strg ]
  op nil : -> Strg
  op _._ : Strg Strg -> Strg { assoc }
  eq nil . S:Strg = S .
  eq S:Strg . nil = S .
}
```

The most basic reuse of specifications is called an **import**. Imports are the most important module-structuring construct. The declaration responsible for the import of the natural-numbers specification is "protecting(NAT)". The most important effect of an import declaration is that, although hidden, all ingredients of the imported specification (such as the sorts, operations, and axioms) are available at the level of the importing specification.

The part of a module besides the import (or parameter) declarations is called the **body of the module**.

In the case of STRG-NAT, the body consists of

- the introduction of a new sort Strg, which is also declared as a super-sort of the imported sort Nat (meaning that each natural number is already a string of length 1);

- the introduction of the string operations `nil` for the empty string and `_._` for the string concatenation; and
- The string axioms (including the associativity of concatenation, specified as an operation attribute).

The availability of the ingredients of the imported module `NAT` at the level of `STRG-NAT` can easily be checked as follows:

```
STRG-NAT> red 2 + 1 .
-- reduce in STRG-NAT : 2 + 1
3 : NzNat
```

Multiple Imports

Suppose we enhance the above `STRG-NAT` specification of strings of naturals with an integer-valued length function. Then we import both `STRG-NAT` and an integer-number module `INT` as follows:

```
mod!LENGTH-STRG-NAT {
  protecting(STRG-NAT + INT)
  op #_ : Strg -> Int
  eq # nil = 0 .
  eq # N:Nat = 1 .
  eq #(S:Strg . S':Strg) = (# S) + (# S') .
}
```

Notice that the module `NAT` of the natural numbers is a submodule (i.e. it is imported by) of both `STRG-NAT` and `INT`. In such a case, `NAT` contributes *only once* to `LENGTH-STRG-NAT`, i.e. only one copy of `NAT` is imported by `LENGTH-STRG-NAT`. In other words, in `LENGTH-STRG-NAT`, `NAT` is **shared** (between `STRG-NAT` and `INT`).

The situation for the module imports in this example can be represented graphically as

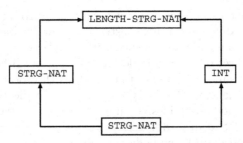

If we read such a graphical representations of a module structure as a partial order, the sharing of imported modules corresponds to the greatest lower bound in this partial order given by the module imports.

Module Sums

An alternative way to import both of the modules STRG-NAT and INT into LENGTH-STRG-NAT is to use only one compact import declaration rather than two import declarations, one for each imported module:

```
protecting(STRG-NAT + INT)
```

This is a module-structuring mechanism which builds the **sum** of the two modules and corresponds to the *lowest upper bound* of the two modules in the absolute *partial order of the module imports*. The sum of the modules is a module itself, which of course respects the sharing principle for the common submodules.

The graphical representation of the module structure for LENGTH-STRG-NAT can be updated as follows:

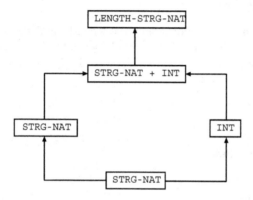

Importation Modes

CafeOBJ admits three kinds of importation style, which are called **importation modes**:

- protecting,
- extending, and
- using.

Methodologically, the most important importation mode (and also the most frequently used and the most recommended) is the *protecting* one. This means that the declarations in the importing specification do not alter anything in the imported data type. From a denotational point of view, the importation mode plays a crucial role in *establishing the denotation* of the importing module from the denotations of the imported modules.

Protecting Imports

In the case of STRG-NAT, the import of NAT in protecting mode means that at the level of STRG-NAT the data type of natural numbers is unchanged, which basically means that

- there is no new element of sort Nat, and
- there is no collapse of elements of sort Nat.

The protecting property of the imported data type is *semantic*, in the sense that this property is not guaranteed and even its violation cannot be signalled by the system. The correctness of the importation declarations is the responsibility of the specifier.

Extending Imports

In the case of extending imports, only the second condition is required, which means that we are allowed to add new elements to the imported types, but not to collapse elements of the imported type. Below, we present an example of an extending importation:

```
mod!BARE-NAT {
  [ Nat ]
  op 0 : -> Nat
  op s_ : Nat -> Nat
}
mod!NAT-INFINITY {
  extending(BARE-NAT)
  op omega : -> Nat
  eq s omega = omega .
}
```

Here the constant omega stands for "infinity" and is added as new element of the sort Nat. The denotation of NAT-INFINITY is *initial* and consists of the model of natural numbers enriched with an "infinity" element.

6.2 Parameters

Parametrised Specification

In the case of STRG-NAT the choice of the natural numbers as the underlying data type for strings is rather arbitrary, in the sense that the data type of strings does not really depend in any way on the natural numbers. This means that strings can be specified as a **generic data type** in which the underlying data type is left as a parameter:

```
mod!STRG (T :: TRIV){
  [ Elt < Strg ]
  op nil : -> Strg
  op _._ : Strg Strg -> Strg { assoc }
  eq nil . S:Strg = S .
  eq S:Strg . nil = S .
}
```

where TRIV is just the very simple specification of bare sets of elements:

```
mod* TRIV [ Elt ]
```

The parameter TRIV of STRG has loose denotation, which means that one can obtain the strings STRG(A) over any particular set A of elements by interpreting the sort Elt of elements as A.

Parameters vs. Imports

The relationship between a parameter and a parametrised module is similar to that of an import, but strictly speaking it is not an import, since the parameter should be regarded as *injected* rather than included in the parametrised module.

This is the same as saying that the parametrised module imports a copy of the parameter, rather than the parameter itself. This copy is labelled by the label of the parameter, which is T in the example above. This situation can be represented graphically by

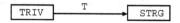

Parameter Instantiation

One can obtain the strings of naturals from the generic strings of STRG by instantiating the parameter T to the data type of natural numbers:

```
STRG(T <= view to NAT sort Elt -> Nat)
```

This instantiation maps the sort Elt of TRIV to Nat.

In general, parameter instantiation interprets the parameter data as a concrete data type. This means that

- each sort of the parameter is mapped to a sort of the data type, and
- each operation of the parameter is mapped to an operation of the data type such that the sort mapping is respected, and such that
- the axioms of the parameter are satisfied by the data type via the mapping of sorts and operations.

Views

The mappings from the parameter specification to the concrete data type are called "views".

In the example above, we had a rather simple view. Now, let us consider generic strings over a partially ordered data type:

```
mod!STRG (P :: POSET){
  [ Elt < Strg ]
  op nil : -> Strg
  op _._ : Strg Strg -> Strg { assoc }
  eq nil . S:Strg = S .
  eq S:Strg . nil = S .
}
```

where the parameter POSET is the specification of partial orders:

```
mod* POSET {
  [ Elt ]
  pred _<=_ : Elt Elt
  vars E1 E2 E3 : Elt
  eq E1 <= E1 = true .
  cq E1 = E2 if (E1 <= E2) and (E2 <= E1) .
  cq (E1 <= E3) = true if (E1 <= E2) and (E2 <= E3) .
}
```

The instantiation of the parameter P of STRG to the natural numbers with the usual "less than or equal" order between naturals maps

- the sort Elt to the sort Nat, and
- the predicate (Boolean-valued operation) _<=_ on Elt to the (derived) operation (E1 < E2) or (E1 == E2) on Nat .

Notice that this mapping is correct because the axioms of POSET are satisfied by NAT via the mapping. Such verification requires a proof score.

Verification of View Definition

We first build the following working environment for the proof:

```
mod!NAT-POSET {
  protecting(NAT)
  op _leq_ : Nat Nat -> Bool
  eq E1:Nat leq E2:Nat = (E1 < E2) or (E1 == E2) .
}
```

We then we open the environment and introduce some working variables as temporary constants:

```
open NAT-POSET .
ops e e' e'' : -> Nat .
ops e1 e1' e1'' : -> Nat .
ops e2 e2' e2'' : -> Nat .
ops e3 e3' e3'' : -> Nat .
ops e4 e4' e4'' : -> Nat .
```

The proof score for the **reflexivity** axiom is very simple:

```
red e leq e .
```

This gives

```
true : Bool
```

The proof score for the **anti-symmetry** axiom is obtained by using the following lemma about naturals,

```
eq (E:Nat < E':Nat) and (E' < E) = false .
```

and by making explicit the implication connective in terms of _and_ and _or_ connectives:

```
red not((e leq e') and (e' leq e)) or (e == e') .
```

The result is

```
true : Bool
```

Finally, the proof score for the **transitivity** axiom requires a case analysis.
Case 1:

```
eq e1 = e1' .
eq e1' = e1'' .
red e1 leq e1'' .
```

gives **true.**
Case 2:

```
eq e2 = e2' .
eq e2' < e2'' = true .
red e2 leq e2'' .
```

gives **true.**
Case 3:

```
eq e3 < e3' = true .
eq e3'' = e3' .
red e3 leq e3'' .
```

gives **true.**
Case 4:

```
eq e4 < e4' = true .
eq e4' < e4'' = true .
```

also gives **true,** but only after an induction proof.

View Specification

The view defined above can be specified in CafeOBJ as follows:

```
view nat-poset from POSET to NAT {
  sort Elt -> Nat,
  op (E1:Elt <= E2:Elt) -> ((E1:Nat < E2:Nat) or (E1 == E2))
}
```

The strings over ordered naturals are then obtained by the instantiation `STRG(P <= nat-poset)`

Default Conventions

From the syntactic point of view this is the most complete specification of a parameter instantiation. CafeOBJ has some default conventions for shorthand notation for views and parameter instantiations. For example, one can specify an "instant" instantiation:

```
STRG(P <= view to NAT { sort Elt -> Nat,
           op (E1:Elt <= E2:Elt) -> (E1:Nat < E2:Nat) or
                                    (E1 == E2) })
```

In the case of simpler instantiations, such as the strings of natural numbers (discarding the partial order), we can use

```
STRG(T <= NAT)
```

or even

```
STRG(NAT)
```

which means that the sort `Elt` of the parameter is mapped to the *principal* sort (which can be declared or determined by implementation-dependent conventions) `Nat` of `NAT`.

Notice that this level of default cannot be used for instantiating `STRG(P :: POSET)` because of the need to specify the mapping of `_<=_`.

The mechanism of parameter instantiation is based on the *presentation pushout* technique. In the case of the instantiation of strings of naturals, the module structure involved in the process of parameter instantiation can be represented graphically as

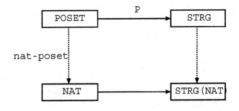

by using the following convention:

- *dotted arrows* for views,
- *unlabelled arrows* for imports, and
- *labelled arrows* for parameters.

Multiple Parameters

Consider the parametrised specification of the mathematical concept of a homomorphism between two semigroups. The parameter semigroup is specified as follows:

```
mod* SEMIGROUP {
  protecting(TRIV)
  op _+_ : Elt Elt -> Elt { assoc }
}
```

The specification of the homomorphism uses two semigroup parameters, one as the source, and the other as the target of the homomorphism:

```
mod* SG-HOM (S1 :: SEMIGROUP, S2 :: SEMIGROUP) {
  op h : Elt.S1 -> Elt.S2
  vars X Y : Elt.S1
  eq h(X + Y) = h(X) + h(Y) .
}
```

In this example, we have used two parametrisations with the same parameter module. In general, in the case of multiple parametrisation, the parameter modules are different.

Graphical Representation of Multiple Parameters

The module structure of this example can be represented by the following diagram:

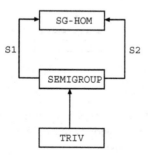

Instantiating Multiple Parameters

Now we can obtain the powers of 2 by instantiating the semigroup homomorphism to the following one:

```
mod! POWER-OF-2 {
  protecting(SG-HOM(S1 <= view to NAT  sort Elt -> Nat, op _+_ -> _+_,
                    S2 <= view to NAT  sort Elt -> Nat, op _+_ -> _*_))
  eq h(1) = 2 .
}
```

This instantiation uses several default (notations for) views. In the case of S1, we have a complete default view and hence the most compact notation possible. The sort Elt is mapped to the principal sort Nat of NAT, while the operation _+_ is mapped to the operation with the same name. The latter mapping uses the convention that in the absence of an explicit declaration, the sort or operations are mapped to entities with the same name and, in the case of operations, the rank is matched. In the case of S2, we have only a partial default view. The sort Elt is also mapped to Nat, as in the case of S1, and hence this is skipped. However the operation _+_ is mapped to the multiplication of naturals.

The module structure of POWER-OF-2 can be represented by the following diagram:

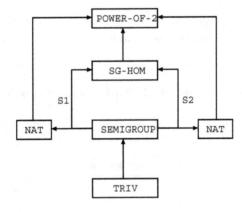

Module Expressions

Module expressions build new complex modules on the spot by combining existing modules. Module expressions are terms over modules formed by using the following module operations:

- imports,
- sums,
- parametrised modules,
- views and parameter instantiations, and

- renaming of sorts and operations.

Module expressions can be given names by using the CafeOBJ command `make` and then used and, especially, reused later in the specification as a module.

The command `make` evaluates the module expressions to a module.

6.3 Institution Independence

The concept of specification in CafeOBJ is a special case of structured specification in an arbitrary institution instantiated to the CafeOBJ institution. Our institution-independent structured specifications follows [41]; however CafeOBJ specifications can be constructed by employing only a subset of the specification building operations defined in [41].[11]

Definition 42. *Given an institution* $(\mathbb{S}ig, Sen, \text{MOD}, \models)$, *its structured specifications (or specifications for short) are defined from the finite presentations by iteration of the specification-building operators presented below. The semantics of each specification* SP *is given by its signature* $Sig[\text{SP}]$ *and its category of models* $Mod[\text{SP}]$, *where* $Mod[\text{SP}]$ *is a full subcategory of* $\text{MOD}(Sig[\text{SP}])$.

> PRES. *Each finite* presentation (Σ, E) *(i.e.* Σ *is a signature and* E *is a finite set of* Σ-sentences) *is a specification such that*
> - $Sig[(\Sigma, E)] = \Sigma$ *and*
> - $Mod[(\Sigma, E)] = \text{MOD}(\Sigma, E)$.[12]
>
> UNION. *For any specifications* SP_1 *and* SP_2 *such that* $Sig[\text{SP}_1] = Sig[\text{SP}_2]$ *we can take their* union $\text{SP}_1 \cup \text{SP}_2$ *with*
> - $Sig[\text{SP}_1 \cup \text{SP}_2] = Sig[\text{SP}_1] = Sig[\text{SP}_2]$ *and*
> - $Mod[\text{SP}_1 \cup \text{SP}_2] = Mod[\text{SP}_1] \cap Mod[\text{SP}_2]$.
>
> TRANS. *For any specification* SP *and signature morphism* $\varphi \colon Sig(\text{SP}) \to \Sigma'$, *we can take its* translation *along* φ, *denoted by* $\text{SP} \star \varphi$, *such that*
> - $Sig[\text{SP} \star \varphi] = \Sigma'$ *and*
> - $Mod[\text{SP} \star \varphi] = \{M' \in \text{MOD}(\Sigma') \mid M'\!\restriction_\varphi \in Mod[\text{SP}]\}$.
>
> FREE. *For any specification* SP' *and signature morphism* $\varphi \colon \Sigma \to Sig[\text{SP}']$ *we can take the* persistently free specification of SP' *along* φ, *denoted* SP'^φ, *such that*
> - $Sig[\text{SP}'^\varphi] = Sig[\text{SP}']$, *and*
> - $Mod[\text{SP}'^\varphi] = \{M' \in Mod[\text{SP}'] \mid M' \text{ strongly persistently } \beta_{\text{SP}'};$
> $\text{MOD}(\varphi)\text{-free }\}$, *where* $\beta_{\text{SP}'}$ *is the subcategory inclusion* $Mod[\text{SP}'] \to \text{MOD}(Sig[\text{SP}'])$.
>
> *The strongly persistent freeness property says that for each* $N' \in Mod[\text{SP}']$ *and for each model homomorphism* $h \colon M'\!\restriction_\varphi \to N'\!\restriction_\varphi$ *there exists a unique model homomorphism* $h' \colon M' \to N'$ *such that* $h'\!\restriction_\varphi = h$.

---

[11] CafeOBJ specifications do not involve the "derivation"-building operation.

[12] $\text{MOD}(\Sigma, E)$ is the subcategory of all Σ-models satisfying all sentences in E.

Definition 43. *A* specification morphism $\varphi\colon \mathrm{SP}_1 \to \mathrm{SP}_2$ *between specifications* SP_1 *and* SP_2 *is a signature morphism* $\varphi\colon Sig[\mathrm{SP}_1] \to Sig[\mathrm{SP}_2]$ *such that* $M\!\restriction_\varphi \in Mod[\mathrm{SP}_1]$ *for each* $M \in Mod[\mathrm{SP}_2]$.

With the exception of "including" or "using" imports (see [12]), any CafeOBJ specification construct can be reduced to the kernel specification-building language of Definition 42. In the case of initial denotations, "including" and "using" imports can be included by adding corresponding variants of the building operation FREE.

For example, CafeOBJ imports correspond to specification inclusions (a simple import can be obtained as a union (UNION) between a structured specification and a presentation (PRES)), module parameters correspond to specification injections, "views" to arbitrary specification morphisms, parameter instantiations to specification pushouts (obtained by translations (TRANS) and union (UNION)), and modules with initial denotation are obtained as free specifications (FREE).

Acknowledgements

The author is deeply grateful to the CafeOBJ team at the Japan Advanced Institute of Science and Technology from 1996 to 2000, especially to its leader Professor Kokichi Futatsugi and to Shusaku Iida, for their wonderful collaboration on the development of CafeOBJ and for their friendship.

References

1. M. Arrais and J.L. Fiadeiro. Unifying theories in different institutions. In M. Haveraaen, O. Owe, and O.-J. Dahl, editors, *Recent Trends in Data Type Specification, Proceedings of 11th Workshop on Specification of Abstract Data Types*, Volume 1130 of Lecture Notes in Computer Science, pages 81–101. Springer, 1996.
2. G. Birkhoff. On the structure of abstract algebras. *Proceedings of the Cambridge Philosophical Society*, 31:433–454, 1935.
3. R. Burstall and J. Goguen. The semantics of Clear, a specification language. In D. Bjørner, editor, *Proceedings, 1979 Copenhagen Winter School on Abstract Software Specification*, Volume 86 of Lecture Notes in Computer Science, pages 292–332, Springer, 1980.
4. M. Clavel, S. Eker, P. Lincoln and J. Meseguer. Principles of Maude. *Electronic Notes in Theoretical Computer Science*, 4, 1996. Proceedings, First International Workshop on Rewriting Logic and its Applications, Asilomar, California, September 1996.
5. R. Diaconescu. Extra theory morphisms for institutions: logical semantics for multi-paradigm languages. *Applied Categorical Structures*, 6(4):427–453, 1998. A preliminary version appeared as JAIST Technical Report IS-RR-97-0032F in 1997.

6. R. Diaconescu. Category-based constraint logic. *Mathematical Structures in Computer Science*, 10(3):373–407, 2000.
7. R. Diaconescu. Grothendieck institutions. *Applied Categorical Structures*, 10(4):383–402, 2002. A Preliminary version appeared as IMAR Preprint 2-2000, ISSN 250-3638, February 2000.
8. R. Diaconescu. Institution-independent ultraproducts. *Fundamenta Informaticæ*, 55(3–4):321–348, 2003.
9. R. Diaconescu. Elementary diagrams in institutions. *Journal of Logic and Computation*, 14(5):651–674, 2004.
10. R. Diaconescu. An institution-independent proof of Craig Interpolation Theorem. *Studia Logica*, 77(1):59–79, 2004.
11. R. Diaconescu. Behavioural specification of hierarchical object composition. *Theoretical Computer Science*, 343(3):305–331, 2005.
12. R. Diaconescu and K. Futatsugi. *CafeOBJ Report: The Language, Proof Techniques, and Methodologies for Object-Oriented Algebraic Specification*, volume 6 of AMAST Series in Computing. World Scientific, 1998.
13. R. Diaconescu and K. Futatsugi. Behavioural coherence in object-oriented algebraic specification. *Universal Computer Science*, 6(1):74–96, 2000. The first version appeared as JAIST Technical Report IS-RR-98-0017F, June 1998.
14. R. Diaconescu and K. Futatsugi. Logical foundations of CafeOBJ. *Theoretical Computer Science*, 285:289–318, 2002.
15. R. Diaconescu, K. Futatsugi and Shusaku Iida. Component-based algebraic specification and verification in CafeOBJ. In J. M. Wing, J.C.P. Woodcock and J. Davies, editors, *FM'99 – Formal Methods*, volume 1709 of Lecture Notes in Computer Science, pages 1644–1663. Springer, 1999.
16. R. Diaconescu, K. Futatsugi and S. Iida. CafeOBJ Jewels. In K. Futatsugi, A. Nakagawa and T. Tamai, editors, *Cafe: An Industrial-Strength Algebraic Formal Method*. Elsevier, 2000.
17. R. Diaconescu, J. Goguen, and P. Stefaneas. Logical support for modularisation. In G. Huet and G. Plotkin, editors, *Logical Environments, Proceedings of a Workshop held in Edinburgh, Scotland, May 1991*, pages 83–130, Cambridge University Press, 1993.
18. K. Futatsugi, J. Goguen, J.-P. Jouannaud and J. Meseguer. Principles of OBJ2. In B. K. Reid, editor, *Proceedings of the 12th ACM Symposium on Principles of Programming Languages*, pages 52–66. ACM, 1985.
19. J. Goguen and R. Burstall. Institutions: Abstract model theory for specification and programming. *Journal of the Association for Computing Machinery*, 39(1):95–146, January 1992.
20. J. Goguen and R. Diaconescu. An Oxford survey of order sorted algebra. *Mathematical Structures in Computer Science*, 4(4):363–392, 1994.
21. J. Goguen and R. Diaconescu. Towards an algebraic semantics for the object paradigm. In Hartmut Ehrig and Fernando Orejas, editors, *Recent Trends in Data Type Specification*, volume 785 of Lecture Notes in Computer Science, pages 1–34. Springer, 1994.
22. J. Goguen and G. Malcolm. A hidden agenda. Technical Report CS97-538, University of California at San Diego, 1997.
23. J. Goguen and J. Meseguer. Completeness of many-sorted equational logic. *Houston Journal of Mathematics*, 11(3):307–334, 1985.

24. J. Goguen and J. Meseguer. Order-sorted algebra I: Equational deduction for multiple inheritance, overloading, exceptions and partial operations. *Theoretical Computer Science*, 105(2):217–273, 1992. Also, Programming Research Group Technical Monograph PRG–80, Oxford University, December 1989.

25. J. Goguen and G. Roşu. Institution morphisms. *Formal Aspects of Computing*, 13:274–307, 2002.

26. J. Goguen, T. Winkler, J. Meseguer, K. Futatsugi and Jean-Pierre Jouannaud. Introducing OBJ. In Joseph Goguen and Grant Malcolm, editors, *Software Engineering with OBJ: Algebraic Specification in Action*. Kluwer, 2000.

27. D. Găină and A. Popescu. An institution-independent generalization of Tarski's Elementary Chain Theorem. *Journal of Logic and Computation*, 16(6):713–735, 2006.

28. D. Găină and A. Popescu. An institution-independent proof of Robinson consistency theorem. *Studia Logica*, 85(1):41–73, 2007.

29. R. Hennicker and M. Bidoit. Observational logic. In A. M. Haeberer, editor, *Algebraic Methodology and Software Technology, Proceedings of AMAST'99*, Volume 1584 of Lecture Notes in Computer Science, pages 263–277. Springer, 1999.

30. S. Iida, K. Futatsugi, and R. Diaconescu. Component-based algebraic specification: behavioural specification for component-based software engineering. In *Behavioral Specifications of Businesses and Systems*, pages 103–119. Kluwer, 1999.

31. S. Mac Lane. *Categories for the Working Mathematician*. Springer, second edition, 1998.

32. J. Meseguer. Conditional rewriting logic as a unified model of concurrency. *Theoretical Computer Science*, 96(1):73–155, 1992.

33. J. Meseguer. Membership algebra as a logical framework for equational specification. In F. Parisi-Pressice, editor, *Proceedings of WADT'97*, Volume 1376 of Lecture Notes in Computer Science, pages 18–61. Springer, 1998.

34. T. Mossakowski. Comorphism-based Grothendieck logics. In K. Diks and W. Rytter, editors, *Mathematical Foundations of Computer Science*, volume 2420 of Lecture Notes in Computer Science, pages 593–604. Springer, 2002.

35. T. Mossakowski. Relating CASL with other specification languages: the institution level. *Theoretical Computer Science*, 286:367–475, 2002.

36. T. Mossakowski. Heterogeneous specification and the heterogeneous tool set. Habilitation thesis, University of Bremen, 2005.

37. R. Paré and D. Schumacher. Abstract families and the adjoint functor theorems. In P.T. Johnstone and R. Paré, editors, *Indexed Categories and Their Applications*. Springer, 1978.

38. M. Petria and R. Diaconescu. Abstract Beth definability in institutions. *Journal of Symbolic Logic*, 71(3):1002–1028, 2006.

39. H. Reichel. Behavioural equivalence – a unifying concept for initial and final specifications. In *Proceedings, Third Hungarian Computer Science Conference*. Akademiai Kiado, 1981. Budapest.

40. H. Reichel. *Initial Computability, Algebraic Specifications, and Partial Algebras*. Clarendon, 1987.

41. D. Sannella and A. Tarlecki. Specifications in an arbitrary institution. *Information and Control*, 76:165–210, 1988. An earlier version appeared in *Proceedings, International Symposium on the Semantics of Data Types*, Volume 173 of Lecture Notes in Computer Science, Springer, 1985.

42. A. Tarlecki. Free constructions in algebraic institutions. In M.P. Chytil and V. Koubek, editors, *Proceedings, International Symposium on Mathematical Foundations of Computer Science*, Volume 176 of Lecture Notes in Computer Science, pages 526–534. Springer, 1984. Extended version: Report CSR-149-83, Computer Science Department, University of Edinburgh.

43. A. Tarlecki. Quasi-varieties in abstract algebraic institutions. *Journal of Computer and System Sciences*, 33(3):333–360, 1986. Original version, Report CSR-173-84, Computer Science Department, University of Edinburgh.

44. A. Tarlecki, R. Burstall and J. Goguen. Some fundamental algebraic tools for the semantics of computation, part 3: Indexed categories. *Theoretical Computer Science*, 91:239–264, 1991. Also, Monograph PRG-77, August 1989, Programming Research Group, Oxford University.

45. U. Wolter. Institutional frames. In *Recent Trends in Data Type Specification. Proceedings of the 10th Workshop on Algebrauic Data Type Specification, Santa Margherita, Italy, 1994.*, Volume 906 of Lecture Notes in Computer Science, pages 469–482. Springer, Berlin, 1995.

CafeOBJ Indexes

CASL – the Common Algebraic Specification Language

Till Mossakowski[1], Anne E. Haxthausen[2], Donald Sannella[3], and Andrezj Tarlecki[4]

[1] DFKI Lab Bremen and University of Bremen, DE-28334 Bremen (P.O. Box 330 440) Germany, till@tzi.de
[2] Department of Informatics and Mathematical Modelling, Technical University of Denmark, DK-2800 Kgs. Lyngby, Denmark, ah@imm.dtu.dk
[3] LFCS, School of Informatics, University of Edinburgh, Edinburgh, UK, dts@inf.ed.ac.uk
[4] Institute of Informatics, Warsaw University and Institute of Computer Science, Polish Academy of Science, Warsaw, Poland, tarlecki@mimuw.edu.pl

Summary. CASL is an expressive specification language that has been designed to supersede many existing algebraic specification languages and provide a standard. CASL consists of several layers, including basic (unstructured) specifications, structured specifications and architectural specifications; the latter are used to prescribe the modular structure of implementations.

We describe a simplified version of the CASL syntax, semantics and proof calculus for each of these three layers and state the corresponding soundness and completeness theorems. The layers are orthogonal in the sense that the semantics of a given layer uses that of the previous layer as a "black box", and similarly for the proof calculi. In particular, this means that CASL can easily be adapted to other logical systems.

We conclude with a detailed example specification of a warehouse, which serves to illustrate the application of both CASL and the proof calculi for the various layers.

Key words: Algebraic specification, formal software development, logic, calculus, institution

1 Introduction

Algebraic specification is one of the most extensively developed approaches in the formal-methods area. The most fundamental assumption underlying algebraic specification is that programs are modelled as algebraic structures that include a collection of sets of data values together with functions over those sets. This level of abstraction is commensurate with the view that the correctness of the input/output behaviour of a program takes precedence over all its other properties. Another common element is that specifications of programs consist mainly of logical *axioms*, usually in a logical system in which equality has a prominent role, describing the properties that the functions are required to satisfy – often just by their interrelationship. This *property-oriented* approach is in contrast to *model-oriented* specifications in frameworks such as VDM [28] which consist of a simple realization of the required behaviour. However, the theoretical basis of algebraic specification is largely in terms of constructions on algebraic models, so it is at the same time much more model-oriented than approaches such as those based on type theory (see e.g. [52]), where the emphasis is almost entirely on syntax and formal systems of rules, and semantic models are absent or regarded as of secondary importance.

CASL [4] is an expressive specification language that was designed by CoFI, the international Common Framework Initiative for algebraic specification and development [18, 48], with the goal of subsuming many previous algebraic specification languages and of providing a standard language for the specification and development of modular software systems.

This chapter gives an overview of the semantic concepts and proof calculi underlying CASL. Section 2 starts with *institutions* and *logics*, abstract formalizations of the notion of a logical system. The remaining sections follow the layers of the CASL language:

1. *Basic specifications* provide the means to write specifications in a particular institution, and provide a proof calculus for reasoning within such unstructured specifications. The institution underlying CASL, together with its proof calculus, is presented in Sects. 3 (for *many-sorted basic specifications*) and 4 (the extension to *subsorting*). Section 5 explains some of the language constructs that allow one to write down theories in this institution rather concisely.

2. *Structured specifications* express how more complex specifications are built from simpler ones (Sect. 6). The semantics and proof calculus are given in a way that is parametrized over the particular institution and proof calculus for basic specifications. Hence, the institution and proof calculus for basic specifications can be changed without the need to change anything for structured specifications.

3. *Architectural specifications*, in contrast to structured specifications, prescribe the modular structure of the *implementation*, with the possibility of enforcing separate development of composable, reusable implementation units (Sect. 7). Again, the semantics and proof calculus in this layer are formulated in terms of the semantics and proof calculus given in the previous layers.

4. Finally, *libraries of specifications* allow the (distributed) storage and retrieval of named specifications. Since this is rather straightforward, space considerations led to the omission of this layer of CASL in the present work.

For the sake of simplicity, this chapter covers only a simplified version of CASL, and mainly introduces semantic concepts; language constructs are treated only briefly in Sect. 5. A full account of CASL, also covering libraries of specifications, is given in [50] (see also [4, 18, 37]), while a gentle introduction is provided in [49].

2 Institutions and Logics

First, before considering the particular concepts underlying CASL, we recall how specification frameworks in general may be formalized in terms of institutions [22].

An *institution* $I = (\mathbf{Sign}, \mathbf{Sen}, \mathbf{Mod}, \models)$ consists of

- a category **Sign** of *signatures*;
- a functor $\mathbf{Sen}\colon \mathbf{Sign} \to \mathbf{Set}$ giving, for each signature Σ, a set of *sentences* $\mathbf{Sen}(\Sigma)$, and for each signature morphism $\sigma\colon \Sigma \to \Sigma'$, a *sentence translation map* $\mathbf{Sen}(\sigma)\colon \mathbf{Sen}(\Sigma) \to \mathbf{Sen}(\Sigma')$, where $\mathbf{Sen}(\sigma)(\varphi)$ is often written $\sigma(\varphi)$;
- a functor $\mathbf{Mod}\colon \mathbf{Sign}^{op} \to \mathcal{CAT}$ [5] giving, for each signature Σ, a category of *models* $\mathbf{Mod}(\Sigma)$, and for each signature morphism $\sigma\colon \Sigma \to \Sigma'$, a *reduct functor* $\mathbf{Mod}(\sigma)\colon \mathbf{Mod}(\Sigma') \to \mathbf{Mod}(\Sigma)$, where $\mathbf{Mod}(\sigma)(M')$ is often written $M'|_\sigma$; and
- a satisfaction relation $\models_\Sigma \subseteq |\mathbf{Mod}(\Sigma)| \times \mathbf{Sen}(\Sigma)$ for each $\Sigma \in \mathbf{Sign}$,

such that for each $\sigma\colon \Sigma \to \Sigma'$ in **Sign**, the following *satisfaction condition* holds:

$$M' \models_{\Sigma'} \sigma(\varphi) \qquad \Longleftrightarrow \qquad M'|_\sigma \models_\Sigma \varphi$$

for each $M' \in \mathbf{Mod}(\Sigma')$ and $\varphi \in \mathbf{Sen}(\Sigma)$.

An *institution with unions* is an institution equipped with a partial binary operation $\cup$ on signatures, such that there are two "inclusions" $\iota_1\colon \Sigma_1 \to \Sigma_1 \cup \Sigma_2$ and $\iota_2\colon \Sigma_2 \to \Sigma_1 \cup \Sigma_2$. We write $M|_{\Sigma_i}$ for $M|_{\iota_i}\colon \Sigma_i \to \Sigma_1 \cup \Sigma_2$ $(i = 1, 2)$ whenever ι_i is clear from the context. Typically (e.g. in the CASL institution), $\cup$ is a total operation. However, in institutions without overloading, two signatures giving the same name to different things cannot generally be united.

When $\Sigma_1 \cup \Sigma_2 = \Sigma_2$, where $\iota_2\colon \Sigma_2 \to (\Sigma_1 \cup \Sigma_2 = \Sigma_2)$ is the identity, we say that Σ_1 is a *subsignature* of Σ_2, written $\Sigma_1 \subseteq \Sigma_2$.

Further properties of signature unions, as well as other requirements on institutions, are needed only in Sect. 7 on architectural specifications and will be introduced there.

---

[5] Here, $\mathcal{CAT}$ is the quasi-category of all categories. As the meta-theory, we use $ZFCU$, i.e. ZF with the axiom of choice and a set-theoretic universe U. This allows the construction of quasi-categories, i.e. categories with more than one class of objects. See [25].

Within an arbitrary but fixed institution, we can easily define the usual notion of *logical consequence* or *semantic entailment*. Given a set of Σ-sentences Γ and a Σ-sentence φ, we say that φ *follows from* Γ, written $\Gamma \models_\Sigma \varphi$, iff for all Σ-models M, we have $M \models_\Sigma \Gamma$ implies $M \models_\Sigma \varphi$. (Here, $M \models_\Sigma \Gamma$ means that $M \models_\Sigma \psi$ for each $\psi \in \Gamma$.)

Coming to proofs, a logic [33] extends an institution with proof-theoretic entailment relations that are compatible with semantic entailment.

A *logic $\mathcal{LOG}$* = $(\mathbf{Sign}, \mathbf{Sen}, \mathbf{Mod}, \models, \vdash)$ is an institution $(\mathbf{Sign}, \mathbf{Sen}, \mathbf{Mod}, \models)$ equipped with an *entailment system* $\vdash$, that is, a relation $\vdash_\Sigma \subseteq \mathcal{P}(\mathbf{Sen}(\Sigma)) \times \mathbf{Sen}(\Sigma)$ for each $\Sigma \in |\mathbf{Sign}|$, such that the following properties are satisfied for any $\varphi \in \mathbf{Sen}(\Sigma)$ and $\Gamma, \Gamma' \subseteq \mathbf{Sen}(\Sigma)$:

1. *Reflexivity:* $\{\varphi\} \vdash_\Sigma \varphi$,
2. *Monotonicity:* if $\Gamma \vdash_\Sigma \varphi$ and $\Gamma' \supseteq \Gamma$ then $\Gamma' \vdash_\Sigma \varphi$,
3. *Transitivity:* if $\Gamma \vdash_\Sigma \varphi_i$ for $i \in I$ and $\Gamma \cup \{\varphi_i \mid i \in I\} \vdash_\Sigma \psi$, then $\Gamma \vdash_\Sigma \psi$,
4. $\vdash$-*translation:* if $\Gamma \vdash_\Sigma \varphi$, then for any $\sigma \colon \Sigma \to \Sigma'$ in $\mathbf{Sign}$, $\sigma(\Gamma) \vdash_{\Sigma'} \sigma(\varphi)$,
5. *Soundness:* if $\Gamma \vdash_\Sigma \varphi$ then $\Gamma \models_\Sigma \varphi$.

A logic is *complete* if, in addition, $\Gamma \models_\Sigma \varphi$ implies $\Gamma \vdash_\Sigma \varphi$.

It is easy to obtain a complete logic from an institution by simply defining $\vdash$ as $\models$. Hence, $\vdash$ might appear to be redundant. However, the point is that $\vdash$ will typically be defined via a system of finitary *derivation rules*. This gives rise to a notion of *proof* that is absent when the institution is considered on its own, even if the relation that results coincides with semantic entailment, which is defined in terms of the satisfaction relation.

3 Many-Sorted Basic Specifications

CASL's basic specification layer is an expressive language that integrates subsorts, partiality, first-order logic and induction (the latter expressed using *sort generation constraints*).

3.1 The Many-Sorted Institution

The institution underlying CASL is introduced in two steps [9, 16]. In this section, we introduce the institution of many-sorted partial first-order logic with sort generation constraints and equality, $PCFOL^=$. In Sect. 4, subsorting is added.

Signatures

A *many-sorted signature* $\Sigma = (S, TF, PF, P)$ consists of a set S of *sorts*, $S^* \times S$-indexed families TF and PF of *total-* and *partial-function symbols*, with $TF_{w,s} \cap PF_{w,s} = \emptyset$ for each $(w, s) \in S^* \times S$, and where constants are treated as functions with no arguments; and an S^*-indexed family P of *predicate symbols*. We write $f : w \to s \in TF$ for $f \in TF_{w,s}$ (with $f : s$ for empty w), $f : w \to? \ s \in PF$ for $f \in PF_{w,s}$ (with $f :\to? \ s$ for empty w) and $p : w \in P$ for $p \in P_w$.

Although $TF_{w,s}$ and $PF_{w,s}$ are required to be disjoint, so that a function symbol with a given profile cannot be both partial and total, function and predicate symbols may be overloaded: we do not require, for example, $TF_{w,s}$ and $TF_{w',s'}$ (or $TF_{w,s}$ and $PF_{w',s'}$) to be disjoint for $(w, s) \neq (w', s')$. To ensure that there is no ambiguity in sentences, however, symbols are always qualified by profiles when used. In the CASL language constructs (see Sect. 5), such qualifications may be omitted when they are unambiguously determined by the context.

Given signatures Σ and Σ', a *signature morphism* $\sigma : \Sigma \to \Sigma'$ maps sorts, function symbols and predicate symbols in Σ to symbols of the same kind in Σ'. A partial-function symbol may be mapped to a total-function symbol, but not vice versa, and profiles must be preserved, so for instance $f : w \to s$ in Σ maps to a function symbol in Σ' with a profile $\sigma^*(w) \to \sigma(s)$, where σ^* is the extension of σ to finite strings of symbols. Identities and composition are defined in the obvious way, giving a category **Sign** of $PCFOL^=$-signatures.

Models

Given a finite string $w = s_1 \ldots s_n$ and sets $M_{s_1}, \ldots, M_{s_n}$, we write M_w for the Cartesian product $M_{s_1} \times \cdots \times M_{s_n}$. Let $\Sigma = (S, TF, PF, P)$.

A *many-sorted Σ-model* M consists of a non-empty *carrier set* M_s for each sort $s \in S$, a total function $(f_{w,s})_M : M_w \to M_s$ for each total-function symbol $f : w \to s \in TF$, a partial function $(f_{w,s})_M : M_w \rightharpoonup M_s$ for each partial-function symbol $f : w \to? \ s \in PF$, and a predicate $(p_w)_M \subseteq M_w$ for each predicate symbol $p : w \in P$. Requiring carriers to be non-empty simplifies deduction and makes it unproblematic to regard axioms (see Sect. 3.1) as implicitly universally quantified. A slight drawback is that the existence of initial models is lost in some cases, even if only equational axioms are used, namely if the signature is such that there are no ground terms of some sort. However, from a methodological point of view, specifications with such signatures are typically used in a context where a loose rather than an initial semantics is appropriate.

A *many-sorted Σ-homomorphism* $h : M \to N$ maps the values in the carriers of M to values in the corresponding carriers of N in such a way that the values of functions and their definedness are preserved, as well as the truth of predicates. Identities and composition are defined in the obvious way. This gives a category **Mod**(Σ).

Concerning *reducts*, if $\sigma : \Sigma \to \Sigma'$ is a signature morphism and M' is a Σ'-model, then $M'|_\sigma$ is a Σ-model with $(M'|_\sigma)_s := M'_{\sigma(s)}$ for $s \in S$ and analogously for $(f_{w,s})_{M'|_\sigma}$ and $(p_w)_{M'|_\sigma}$. The same applies to any Σ'-homomorphism $h' : M' \to N'$: its reduct $h'|_\sigma : M'|_\sigma \to N'|_\sigma$ is the Σ-

homomorphism defined by $(h'|_\sigma)_s := h'_{\sigma(s)}$ for $s \in S$. It is easy to see that a reduct preserves identities and composition, so we obtain a functor $\mathbf{Mod}(\sigma)\colon \mathbf{Mod}(\Sigma') \to \mathbf{Mod}(\Sigma)$. Moreover, it is easy to see that reducts are compositional, i.e., we have, for example, $(M''|_\theta)|_\sigma = M''|_{\sigma;\,\theta}$ for all signature morphisms $\sigma\colon \Sigma \to \Sigma'$, $\theta\colon \Sigma' \to \Sigma''$ and Σ''-models M''. This means that we have indeed defined a functor $\mathbf{Mod}\colon \mathbf{Sign}^{op} \to \mathcal{CAT}$.

Sentences

Let $\Sigma = (S, TF, PF, P)$. A *variable system over* Σ is an S-sorted, pairwise disjoint family of variables $X = (X_s)_{s \in S}$. Let such a variable system be given.

As usual, the *many-sorted Σ-terms* over X are defined inductively as comprising the variables in X, which have uniquely determined sorts, together with applications of function symbols to argument terms of appropriate sorts, where the sort is determined by the profile of its outermost function symbol. This gives an S-indexed family of sets $T_\Sigma(X)$ which can be made into a (total) many-sorted Σ-model by defining $(f_{w,s})_{T_\Sigma(X)}$ to be the term-formation operations for $f : w \to s \in TF$ and $f : w \to? \ s \in PF$, and $(p_w)_{T_\Sigma(X)} = \emptyset$ for $p : w \in P$.

An atomic Σ-formula is either an application $p_w(t_1, \ldots, t_n)$ of a predicate symbol to terms of appropriate sorts, an *existential equation* $t \overset{e}{=} t'$ or *strong equation* $t \overset{s}{=} t'$ between two terms of the same sort, or an assertion *def t* that the value of a term is defined. This defines the set $AF_\Sigma(X)$ of *many-sorted atomic Σ-formulas* with variables in X. The set $FO_\Sigma(X)$ of *many-sorted first-order Σ-formulas* with variables in X is then defined by adding a formula *false* and closing under implication $\varphi \Rightarrow \psi$ and universal quantification $\forall x : s \bullet \varphi$. We use the usual abbreviations $\neg\varphi$ for $\varphi \Rightarrow false$, $\varphi \wedge \psi$ for $\neg(\varphi \Rightarrow \neg\psi)$, $\varphi \vee \psi$ for $\neg(\neg\varphi \wedge \neg\psi)$, *true* for $\neg false$ and $\exists x : s \bullet \varphi$ for $\neg\forall x : s \bullet \neg\varphi$.

A *sort generation constraint* states that a given set of sorts is generated by a given set of functions. Technically, sort generation constraints also contain a signature morphism component; this allows them to be translated along signature morphisms without sacrificing the satisfaction condition. Formally, a sort generation constraint over a signature Σ is a triple $(\widetilde{S}, \widetilde{F}, \theta)$, where $\theta\colon \overline{\Sigma} \to \Sigma$, $\overline{\Sigma} = (\overline{S}, \overline{TF}, \overline{PF}, \overline{P})$, $\widetilde{S} \subseteq \overline{S}$ and $\widetilde{F} \subseteq \overline{TF} \cup \overline{PF}$.

Now a Σ-*sentence* is either a closed many-sorted first-order Σ-formula (i.e. a many-sorted first-order Σ-formula over the empty set of variables), or a sort generation constraint over Σ.

Given a signature morphism $\sigma\colon \Sigma \to \Sigma'$ and a variable system X over Σ, we can obtain a variable system $\sigma(X)$ over Σ' by taking

$$\sigma(X)_{s'} := \bigcup_{\sigma(s)=s'} X_s$$

Since $T_\Sigma(X)$ is total, the inclusion $\zeta_{\sigma,X}\colon X \to T_{\Sigma'}(\sigma(X))|_\sigma$ (regarded as a variable valuation) leads to a term evaluation function

$$\zeta_{\sigma,X}^{\#} : T_\Sigma(X) \to T_{\Sigma'}(\sigma(X))|_\sigma$$

that is total as well. This can be inductively extended to a translation along σ of Σ-first order formulas with variables in X by taking $\sigma(t) := \zeta_{\sigma,X}^{\#}(t)$, $\sigma(p_w(t_1,\ldots,t_n)) := \sigma_w(p)_{\sigma^*(w)}(\sigma(t_1),\ldots,\sigma(t_n))$, $\sigma(t \overset{e}{=} t') := \sigma(t) \overset{e}{=} \sigma(t')$, $\sigma(\forall x : s \bullet \varphi) = \forall x : \sigma(s) \bullet \sigma(\varphi)$, and so on. The translation of a Σ-constraint $(\widetilde{S}, \widetilde{F}, \theta)$ along σ is the Σ'-constraint $(\widetilde{S}, \widetilde{F}, \theta; \sigma)$. It is easy to see that sentence translation preserves identities and composition, so sentence translation is functorial.

Satisfaction

Variable valuations are total, but the value of a term with respect to a variable valuation may be undefined, owing to the application of a partial function during the evaluation of the term. Given a variable valuation $\nu : X \to M$ for X in M, *term evaluation* $\nu^{\#} : T_\Sigma(X) \rightharpoonup M$ is defined in the obvious way, with $t \in dom(\nu^{\#})$ iff all partial functions in t are applied to values in their domains.

Even though the evaluation of a term with respect to a variable valuation may be undefined, the satisfaction of a formula φ in a model M is always defined, and it is either true or false: that is, we have a two-valued logic. The application $p_w(t_1,\ldots,t_n)$ of a predicate symbol to a sequence of argument terms is satisfied with respect to a valuation $\nu : X \to M$ iff the values of all of $t_1,\ldots,t_n$ are defined under $\nu^{\#}$ and give a tuple belonging to p_M. A definedness assertion *def* t is satisfied iff the value of t is defined. An existential equation $t_1 \overset{e}{=} t_2$ is satisfied iff the values of t_1 and t_2 are defined and equal, whereas a strong equation $t_1 \overset{s}{=} t_2$ is also satisfied when the values of both t_1 and t_2 are undefined; thus the two kinds of equation coincide for defined terms. Satisfaction of other formulae is defined in the obvious way. A formula φ is satisfied in a model M, written $M \models \varphi$, iff it is satisfied with respect to all variable valuations into M.

A Σ-constraint $(\widetilde{S}, \widetilde{F}, \theta)$ is satisfied in a Σ-model M iff the carriers of $M|_\theta$ of sorts in $\widetilde{S}$ are generated by the function symbols in $\widetilde{F}$, i.e. for every sort $s \in \widetilde{S}$ and every value $a \in (M|_\theta)_s$, there is a $\overline{\Sigma}$-term t containing only function symbols from $\widetilde{F}$ and variables of sorts not in $\widetilde{S}$ such that $\nu^{\#}(t) = a$ for some valuation ν into $M|_\theta$.

For a sort generation constraint $(\widetilde{S}, \widetilde{F}, \theta)$, we can assume without loss of generality that all the result sorts of function symbols in $\widetilde{F}$ occur in $\widetilde{S}$. If not, we can just omit from $\widetilde{F}$ those function symbols not satisfying this requirement, without affecting the satisfaction of the sort generation constraint: in the $\overline{\Sigma}$-term t witnessing the satisfaction of the constraint, any application of a function symbol with a result sort outside $\widetilde{S}$ can be replaced by a variable of that sort, which obtains as its assigned value the evaluation of the function application.

For a proof of the satisfaction condition, see [37].

3.2 Proof Calculus

We now come to the proof calculus for CASL many-sorted basic specifications. The rules of derivation are given in Figs. 1 and 2.

$$
\begin{array}{cc}
 & [\varphi] \quad [\varphi \Rightarrow false] \\
 & \vdots \qquad \vdots \\
\textbf{(Absurdity)}\ \dfrac{false}{\varphi} \qquad \textbf{(Tertium non datur)}\ \dfrac{\psi \qquad \psi}{\psi}
\end{array}
$$

$$
\begin{array}{cccc}
& [\varphi] \\
& \vdots \\
\textbf{($\Rightarrow$-intro)}\ \dfrac{\psi}{\varphi \Rightarrow \psi} & \textbf{($\Rightarrow$-elim)}\ \dfrac{\varphi \quad \varphi \Rightarrow \psi}{\psi} & \textbf{($\forall$-elim)}\ \dfrac{\forall x : s.\varphi}{\varphi}
\end{array}
$$

$\textbf{($\forall$-intro)}\ \dfrac{\varphi}{\forall x : s.\varphi}$ where x_s occurs freely only in local assumptions

$\textbf{(Reflexivity)}\ \dfrac{}{x_s \stackrel{e}{=} x_s}$ if x_s is a variable

$\textbf{(Congruence)}\ \dfrac{\varphi}{(\bigwedge_{x_s \in FV(\varphi)} x_s \stackrel{e}{=} \nu(x_s)) \Rightarrow \varphi[\nu]}$ if $\varphi[\nu]$ defined

$\textbf{(Substitution)}\ \dfrac{\varphi}{(\bigwedge_{x_s \in FV(\varphi)} D(\nu(x_s))) \Rightarrow \varphi[\nu]}$
if $\varphi[\nu]$ defined and $FV(\varphi)$ occur freely only in local assumptions

$\textbf{(Totality)}\ \dfrac{}{D(f_{w,s}(x_{s_1}, \ldots, x_{s_n}))}$ if $w = s_1 \ldots s_n, f \in TF_{w,s}$

$\textbf{(Function Strictness)}\ \dfrac{t_1 \stackrel{e}{=} t_2}{D(t)}$ t some subterm of t_1 or t_2

$\textbf{(Predicate Strictness)}\ \dfrac{p_w(t_1, \ldots, t_n)}{D(t_i)}$ $i \in \{1, \ldots, n\}$

Fig. 1. First-order deduction rules for CASL basic specifications

The first rules (up to $\forall$-Intro) are standard rules of first-order logic [6]. The rules Reflexivity, Congruence and Substitution differ from the standard rules since they have to take into account the potential undefinedness of terms. Hence, Reflexivity holds only for variables (which by definition are always defined), and Substitution needs the assumption that the terms being substituted are defined. (Note that definedness, $D(t)$, is just an abbreviation for the existential equality $t \stackrel{e}{=} t$.) Totality, Function Strictness and Predicate Strictness have self-explanatory names; they allow definedness statements to

$$(S, F, \theta : \bar{\Sigma} \to \Sigma)$$

(Induction) $\dfrac{\varphi_1 \wedge \cdots \wedge \varphi_k}{\bigwedge_{s \in S} \forall x : \theta(s) \bullet \Psi_s(x)}$

$F = \{f_1 : s_1^1 \ldots s_{m_1}^1 \to s^1; \ \ldots; \ f_k : s_1^k \ldots s_{m_k}^k \to s^k\},$

Ψ_{s_j} is a formula with one free variable x of sort $\theta(s_j), j = 1, \ldots, k,$

$\varphi_j = \forall x_1 : \theta(s_1^j), \ldots, x_{m_j} : \theta(s_{m_j}^j) \bullet$
$$\left(D(\theta(f_j)(x_1, \ldots, x_{m_j})) \wedge \bigwedge_{i=1,\ldots,m_j; \ s_i^j \in S} \Psi_{s_i^j}(x_i) \right)$$
$$\Rightarrow \Psi_{s_j} \left(\theta(f_j)(x_1, \ldots, x_{m_j}) \right)$$

(Sortgen-intro) $\dfrac{\varphi_1 \wedge \cdots \wedge \varphi_k \Rightarrow \bigwedge_{s \in S} \forall x : \theta(s) \bullet p_s(x)}{(S, F, \theta : \bar{\Sigma} \to \Sigma)}$

$F = \{f_1 : s_1^1 \ldots s_{m_1}^1 \to s^1; \ \ldots; \ f_k : s_1^k \ldots s_{m_k}^k \to s^k\},$
for $s \in S$, the predicates $p_s : \theta(s)$ occur only in local assumptions,
and for $j = 1, \ldots, k,$
$\varphi_j = \forall x_1 : \theta(s_1^j), \ldots, x_{m_j} : \theta(s_{m_j}^j) \bullet$
$$\left(D(\theta(f_j)(x_1, \ldots, x_{m_j})) \wedge \bigwedge_{i=1,\ldots,m_j; \ s_i^j \in S} p_{s_i^j}(x_i) \right)$$
$$\Rightarrow p_{s_j} \left(\theta(f_j)(x_1, \ldots, x_{m_j}) \right)$$

Fig. 2. Induction rules for CASL basic specifications

be inferred. Finally, the two rules in Fig. 2 deal with sort generation constraints. If these are seen as second-order universally quantified formulas, Induction corresponds to second-order ∀-Elim, and Sortgen-Intro corresponds to second-order ∀-Intro. The φ_j correspond to the inductive bases and inductive steps that have to be shown, while the formula $\bigwedge_{s \in S} \forall x : \theta(s) \bullet \Psi_s(x)$ is the statement that is shown by induction. Note that if S consists of more than one sort, we have a simultaneous induction over several sorts.

A *derivation* of $\Phi \vdash \varphi$ is a tree (called a *derivation tree*) such that

- the root of the tree is φ;
- all the leaves of the tree are either in Φ or marked as local assumptions;
- each non-leaf node is an instance of the conclusion of some rule, with its children being the correspondingly instantiated premises; and
- any assumptions marked by [...] in the proof rules are marked as local assumptions.

If Φ and φ consist of Σ-formulas, we also write $\Phi \vdash_\Sigma \varphi$. In practice, one works with acyclic graphs instead of trees, since this allows the reuse of lemmas.

Some rules contain a condition that some variables occur freely only in local assumptions. These conditions are the usual eigenvariable conditions of natural-deduction-style calculi. They mean, more precisely, that if the specified variables occur freely in an assumption in a proof tree, the assumption must be marked as local and have been used in the proof of the premise of the respective rule.

In order to carry out a proof in the calculus, it is convenient to prove some derived rules. We list only a few here:

$$(\wedge\text{-}\mathbf{Intro})\ \frac{\varphi \qquad \psi}{\varphi \wedge \psi}$$

$$(\wedge\text{-}\mathbf{Elim1})\ \frac{\varphi \wedge \psi}{\varphi}$$

$$(\wedge\text{-}\mathbf{Elim2})\ \frac{\varphi \wedge \psi}{\psi}$$

Recall that $\varphi \wedge \psi$ is defined[6] to be $(\varphi \Rightarrow \psi \Rightarrow \text{false}) \Rightarrow \text{false}$.[7]

Proof of $\wedge$-Intro. Assume φ and ψ. Assume further (aiming at a proof using $\Rightarrow$-Intro) that $\varphi \Rightarrow \psi \Rightarrow \text{false}$. By $\Rightarrow$-Elim twice, we obtain *false*. Hence, $(\varphi \Rightarrow \psi \Rightarrow \text{false}) \Rightarrow \text{false}$ by $\Rightarrow$-Intro.   □

Proof of $\wedge$-Elim1. Assume $(\varphi \Rightarrow \psi \Rightarrow \text{false}) \Rightarrow \text{false}$. We want to prove φ using Tertium non datur. Obviously, φ can be proved from itself. It remains to prove it from $\varphi \Rightarrow \text{false}$. Now from $\varphi \Rightarrow \text{false}$, using $\Rightarrow$-Intro twice and $\Rightarrow$-Elim once, we obtain $\varphi \Rightarrow \psi \Rightarrow \text{false}$. Hence, by $\Rightarrow$-Elim with our main assumption, we obtain *false*. Absurdity, we get φ. The proof of $\wedge$-Elim2 is similar.   □

The following theorem is proved in [44]:

Theorem *The above proof calculus yields an entailment system. Equipped with this entailment system, the* CASL *institution* $PCFOL^=$ *becomes a sound logic. Moreover, it is complete if sort generation constraints are not used.*

With sort generation constraints, inductive data types such as the natural numbers can be specified monomorphically (i.e., up to isomorphism). By Gödel's incompleteness theorem, there cannot be a recursively axiomatized complete calculus for such systems.

Theorem *If sort generation constraints are used, the* CASL *logic is not complete. Moreover, there cannot be a recursively axiomatized sound and complete entailment system for many-sorted* CASL *basic specifications.*

Instead of using the above calculus, it is also possible to use an encoding of the CASL logic into second-order logic; see [37].

---

[6] This is not the same definition as in [50], but it allows us to keep things simple. The proofs would also go succeed with the definitions of [50], but would be a little more complex.

[7] Note that $\Rightarrow$ associates to the right.

4 Subsorted Basic Specifications

CASL allows the user to declare a sort as a subsort of another. In contrast to most other subsorted languages, CASL interprets subsorts as injective embeddings between carriers – not necessarily as inclusions. This allows for more general models in which values of a subsort are represented differently from values of the supersort, an example being integers (represented as 32-bit words) as a subsort of reals (represented using floating-point representation). Furthermore, to avoid problems with modularity (as described in [24, 34]), there are no requirements like monotonicity, regularity or local filtration imposed on signatures. Instead, the use of overloaded functions and predicates in formulae of the CASL language is required to be sufficiently disambiguated, such that all parses have the same semantics.

4.1 The Subsorted Institution

In order to cope with subsorting, the institution for basic specifications presented in Sect. 3 has to be modified slightly. First a category of subsorted signatures is defined (each signature is extended with a pre-order $\leq$ on its set of sorts), and a functor from this category into the category of many-sorted signatures is defined. Then the notions of models, sentences and satisfaction can be borrowed from the many-sorted institution via this functor. Technical details follow below, leading to the institution of subsorted partial first-order logic with sort generation constraints and equality ($SubPCFOL^=$).

Signatures

A *subsorted signature* $\Sigma = (S, TF, PF, P, \leq)$ consists of a many-sorted signature (S, TF, PF, P) together with a reflexive, transitive *subsort relation* $\leq$ on the set S of sorts.

For a subsorted signature, we define *overloading relations* for function and predicate symbols: two function symbols $f : w_1 \to s_1$ (or $f : w_1 \to? s_1$) and $f : w_2 \to s_2$ (or $f : w_2 \to? s_2$) are in an *overloading relation* iff there exists a $w \in S^*$ and $s \in S$ such that $w \leq w_1, w_2$ and $s_1, s_2 \leq s$. Similarly, two qualified predicate symbols $p : w_1$ and $p : w_2$ are in an overloading relation iff there exists a $w \in S^*$ such that $w \leq w_1, w_2$.

Let $\Sigma = (S, TF, PF, P, \leq)$ and $\Sigma' = (S', TF', PF', P', \leq')$ be subsorted signatures. A *subsorted signature morphism* $\sigma : \Sigma \to \Sigma'$ is a many-sorted signature morphism from (S, TF, PF, P) into (S', TF', PF', P') preserving the subsort relation and the overloading relations.

With each subsorted signature $\Sigma = (S, TF, PF, P, \leq)$ we associate a many-sorted signature $\widehat{\Sigma}$, which is the extension of the underlying many-sorted signature (S, TF, PF, P) with

- a total *embedding* function symbol $em : s \to s'$ for each pair of sorts $s \leq s'$;

- a partial *projection* function symbol $pr : s' \to? \ s$ for each pair of sorts $s \leq s'$; and
- a unary *membership* predicate symbol $in(s) : s'$ for each pair of sorts $s \leq s'$.

It is assumed that the symbols used for injection, projection and membership are distinct and are not used otherwise in Σ.

In a similar way, any subsorted signature morphism σ from Σ into Σ' extends to a many-sorted signature morphism $\widehat{\sigma}$ from $\widehat{\Sigma}$ into $\widehat{\Sigma'}$.

The construction $\widehat{}$ is a functor from the category of subsorted signatures **SubSig** into the category of many-sorted signatures **Sign**.

Models

For a subsorted signature $\Sigma = (S, TF, PF, P, \leq)$, with embedding symbols *em*, projection symbols *pr* and membership symbols *in*, the *subsorted models* for Σ are ordinary many-sorted models for $\widehat{\Sigma}$ satisfying a set $Ax(\Sigma)$ of sentences (formalized in [50], section III.3.1.2) that ensuring the following.

- Embedding functions are injective.
- The embedding of a sort into itself is the identity function.
- All compositions of embedding functions between the same two sorts are equal functions.
- Projection functions are injective when defined.
- Embedding followed by projection is identity.
- Membership in a subsort holds just when the projection to the subsort is defined.
- Embedding is compatible with those functions and predicates that are in the overloading relations.

Subsorted Σ-homomorphisms are ordinary many-sorted $\widehat{\Sigma}$-homomorphisms. Hence, the category of subsorted Σ-models **SubMod**(Σ) is a full subcategory of **Mod**$(\widehat{\Sigma})$, i.e. **SubMod**$(\Sigma) = $ **Mod**$(\widehat{\Sigma}, Ax(\Sigma))$.

The *reduct* of Σ'-models and Σ'-homomorphisms along a subsorted signature morphism σ from Σ into Σ' is the many-sorted reduct along the signature morphism $\widehat{\sigma}$. Since subsorted signature morphisms preserve the overloading relations, this is well defined and leads to a functor **Mod**$(\widehat{\sigma})$: **SubMod**$(\Sigma') \to$ **SubMod**(Σ).

Sentences

For a subsorted signature Σ, the *subsorted sentences* are the ordinary many-sorted sentences for the associated many-sorted signature $\widehat{\Sigma}$. Moreover, the *subsorted translation of sentences* along a subsorted signature morphism σ is the ordinary many-sorted translation along $\widehat{\sigma}$.

The syntax of the CASL language (see Sect. 5) allows the user to omit subsort injections, thus permitting the axioms to be written in a simpler and more intuitive way. Static analysis then determines the corresponding sentences of the underlying institution by inserting the appropriate injections.

Satisfaction

Since subsorted Σ-models and Σ-sentences are just certain many-sorted $\widehat{\Sigma}$-models and $\widehat{\Sigma}$-sentences, the notion of *satisfaction* for the subsorted case follows directly from the notion of satisfaction for the many-sorted case. Since reducts and sentence translation in the subsorted case are ordinary many-sorted reducts and sentence translation, the satisfaction condition is satisfied for the subsorted case as well.

4.2 Borrowing of Proofs

The proof calculus can borrowed from the many-sorted case. To prove that a Σ-sentence φ is a Σ-consequence of a set of assumptions Φ, one just has to prove that φ is a $\widehat{\Sigma}$-consequence of Φ and $Ax(\Sigma)$, i.e.

$$\Phi \vdash_\Sigma \varphi$$

if and only if

$$\Phi \cup Ax(\Sigma) \vdash_{\widehat{\Sigma}} \varphi$$

Soundness and (for the sublogic without sort generation constraints) completeness follow from the many-sorted case.

5 CASL Language Constructs

Since the level of syntactic constructs will be treated only informally in this chapter, we shall just give a brief overview of the constructs for writing basic specifications (i.e. specifications in-the-small) in CASL. A detailed description can be found in the CASL language summary [30] and the CASL semantics [9].

The CASL language provides constructs for declaring sorts, subsorts, operations[8] and predicates that contribute to the signature in the obvious way. Operations, predicates and subsorts can also be defined in terms of others; this leads to a corresponding declaration plus a defining axiom.

Operation and predicate symbols may be overloaded; this can lead to ambiguities in formulas. A formula is well formed only if there is a unique way of consistently adding profile qualifications, up to equivalence with respect to the overloading relations.

---

[8] At the level of syntactic constructs, functions are called operations.

```
%list [_], nil, _ :: _
%prec { _ :: _ } < { _ ++ _ }

spec LIST [sort Elem] =
    free type List[Elem] ::= nil | _ :: _(head :? Elem; tail :? List[Elem]);
    sort NEList[Elem] = {L : List[Elem] • ¬L = nil};
    op _++_ : List[Elem] × List[Elem] → List[Elem];
    forall e : Elem; K, L : List[Elem]
        • nil ++ L = L                          %(concat_nil)%
        • (e :: K) ++ L = e :: K ++ L           %(concat_cons)%
end
```

Fig. 3. Specification of lists over an arbitrary element sort in CASL

Binary operations can be declared to be associative, or commutative, idempotent, or to have a unit. This leads to a corresponding axiom, and, in the case of associativity, to an associativity annotation.

For operations and predicates, mix-fix syntax is provided. Precedence and associativity annotations may help to disambiguate terms containing mix-fix symbols. There is also a syntax for literals such as numbers and strings, which allows the usual data types to be specified purely in CASL, without the need for magic built-in modules.

The **type**, **free type** and **generated type** constructs allow the concise description of data types. These are expanded into a declaration of the corresponding constructor and selector operations and axioms relating the selectors and constructors. In the case of generated and free data types, a sort generation constraint is also produced. Free data types additionally lead to axioms that assert the injectivity of the constructors and the disjointness of their images.

A typical CASL specification is shown in Fig. 3. The translation of CASL constructs into the underlying mathematical concepts is formally defined in the CASL semantics [9], which gives the semantics of the language constructs in two parts. The *static semantics* checks the well-formedness of a specification and produces a signature as result; it fails to produce any result for ill-formed phrases. The *model semantics* provides the corresponding model-theoretic part of the semantics and produces a class of models as a result, and is intended to be applied only to phrases that are well formed according to the static semantics. A statically well-formed phrase may still be ill-formed according to the model semantics, and then no result is produced.

6 Structured Specifications

The CASL structuring concepts and constructs and their semantics do not depend on a specific framework of basic specifications. This means that the design of many-sorted and subsorted CASL specifications, as explained in the previous sections, is orthogonal to the design of structured specifications that we are now going to describe (this also holds for the remaining parts of CASL, i.e. architectural specifications and libraries). In this way, we achieve the result that the CASL basic specifications as given above can be restricted to sublanguages or extended in various ways (or even replaced completely) without the need to reconsider or change the syntax and semantics of structured specifications. The central idea for achieving this form of genericity is the notion of an institution introduced in Sect. 2. Indeed, many different logics, including first-order [22], higher-order [14], polymorphic [51], modal [17, 66], temporal [21], process [21], behavioural [11, 54], coalgebraic [47] and object-oriented [2, 23, 31, 64, 65] logics have been shown to be institutions.

```
SPEC ::= BASIC-SPEC
       | SPEC₁ and SPEC₂
       | SPEC with σ
       | SPEC hide σ
       | SPEC₁ then free { SPEC₂ }
```

Fig. 4. Simplified syntax of CASL structured specifications

6.1 Syntax and Semantics of Structured Specifications

Given an arbitrary but fixed institution with unions, it is now possible to define *structured specifications*. Their syntax is given in Fig. 4. The syntax of the basic specifications BASIC-SPEC (as well as that of signature morphisms σ) is left unexplained, since it is provided together with the institution.

Figure 5 shows the semantics of structured specifications [9, 60]. The static semantics is shown on the left of the figure, using judgements of the form $\vdash$ *phrase* $\triangleright$ *result* (read: *phrase* statically elaborates to *result*). The model semantics is shown on the right, using judgements of the form $\vdash$ *phrase* $\Rightarrow$ *result* (read: *phrase* evaluates to *result*).

As might be expected, we assume that every basic specification (statically) determines a signature and a (finite) set of axioms, which in turn determine the class of models of this specification.

Using the model semantics, we can define semantic entailment as follows: a well-formed Σ-specification SP entails a Σ-sentence φ, written $SP \models_\Sigma \varphi$, if φ is satisfied in all SP-models. A specification is consistent if its model class

$$\frac{\vdash \text{BASIC-SPEC} \triangleright \langle \Sigma, \Gamma \rangle}{\vdash \text{BASIC-SPEC} \triangleright \Sigma}$$

$$\frac{\vdash \text{BASIC-SPEC} \triangleright \langle \Sigma, \Gamma \rangle \quad \mathcal{M} = \{M \in \mathbf{Mod}(\Sigma) \mid M \models \Gamma\}}{\vdash \text{BASIC-SPEC} \Rightarrow \mathcal{M}}$$

$$\frac{\vdash SP_1 \triangleright \Sigma_1 \quad \vdash SP_2 \triangleright \Sigma_2 \quad \Sigma_1 \cup \Sigma_2 \text{ is defined}}{\vdash SP_1 \textbf{ and } SP_2 \triangleright \Sigma_1 \cup \Sigma_2}$$

$$\frac{\vdash SP_1 \triangleright \Sigma_1 \quad \vdash SP_2 \triangleright \Sigma_2 \quad \Sigma' = \Sigma_1 \cup \Sigma_2 \text{ is defined} \quad \vdash SP_1 \Rightarrow \mathcal{M}_1 \quad \vdash SP_2 \Rightarrow \mathcal{M}_2 \quad \mathcal{M} = \{M \in \mathbf{Mod}(\Sigma') \mid M|_{\Sigma_i} \in \mathcal{M}_i, \ i = 1,2\}}{\vdash SP_1 \textbf{ and } SP_2 \Rightarrow \mathcal{M}}$$

$$\frac{\vdash SP \triangleright \Sigma}{\vdash SP \textbf{ with } \sigma \colon \Sigma \to \Sigma' \triangleright \Sigma'}$$

$$\frac{\vdash SP \triangleright \Sigma \quad \vdash SP \Rightarrow \mathcal{M} \quad \mathcal{M}' = \{M \in \mathbf{Mod}(\Sigma') \mid M|_\sigma \in \mathcal{M}\}}{\vdash SP \textbf{ with } \sigma \colon \Sigma \to \Sigma' \Rightarrow \mathcal{M}'}$$

$$\frac{\vdash SP \triangleright \Sigma'}{\vdash SP \textbf{ hide } \sigma \colon \Sigma \to \Sigma' \triangleright \Sigma}$$

$$\frac{\vdash SP \triangleright \Sigma' \quad \vdash SP \Rightarrow \mathcal{M} \quad \mathcal{M}' = \{M|_\sigma \mid M \in \mathcal{M}\}}{\vdash SP \textbf{ hide } \sigma \colon \Sigma \to \Sigma' \Rightarrow \mathcal{M}'}$$

$$\frac{\vdash SP_1 \triangleright \Sigma_1 \quad \vdash SP_2 \triangleright \Sigma_2 \quad \Sigma_1 \subseteq \Sigma_2}{\vdash SP_1 \textbf{ then free } \{ SP_2 \} \triangleright \Sigma_2}$$

$$\frac{\vdash SP_1 \triangleright \Sigma_1 \quad \vdash SP_2 \triangleright \Sigma_2 \quad \iota \colon \Sigma_1 \to \Sigma_2 \text{ is the inclusion} \quad \vdash SP_1 \Rightarrow \mathcal{M}_1 \quad \vdash SP_2 \Rightarrow \mathcal{M}_2 \quad \mathcal{M}' = \{M \mid M \text{ is } \mathbf{Mod}(\iota)\text{-free over } M|_\iota \text{ in } \mathcal{M}_2\}}{\vdash SP_1 \textbf{ then free } \{ SP_2 \} \Rightarrow \mathcal{M}'}$$

M being $\mathbf{Mod}(\iota)$-free over $M|_\iota$ in $\mathcal{M}_2$ means that for each model $M' \in \mathcal{M}_2$ and model morphism $h \colon M|_\iota \to M'|_\iota$, there exists a unique model morphism $h^\# \colon M \to M'$ with $h^\#|_\iota = h$.

Fig. 5. Semantics of structured specifications

is non-empty. We also have a simple notion of refinement between specifications: SP_1 refines to SP_2, written $SP_1 \rightsquigarrow SP_2$, if every SP_2-model is also an SP_1-model. Given a Σ_1-specification SP_1 and a Σ_2-specification SP_2, a *specification morphism* $\sigma \colon SP_1 \to SP_2$ is a signature morphism $\sigma \colon \Sigma_1 \to \Sigma_2$ such that for each SP_2-model M, $M|_\sigma$ is an SP_1-model. Note that $\sigma \colon SP_1 \to SP_2$ is a specification morphism iff $SP_1 \rightsquigarrow SP_2 \textbf{ hide } \sigma$.

The above description is a somewhat simplified version of the CASL structured specifications. The first simplification concerns the way signature morphisms are given. It is quite inconvenient to be forced to always write down a complete signature morphism, listing explicitly how each fully qualified symbol is mapped. As a solution to this problem, CASL provides a notion of *symbol maps*, based on an appropriate notion of an *institution with symbols*. Symbol maps are a very concise notation for signature morphisms. Qualifications with profiles, symbols that are mapped identically and even those whose mapping is determined uniquely may be omitted.

The second simplification concerns the fact that it is often very convenient to define specifications as extensions of existing specifications. For example, in SPEC **then free** { SPEC′ }, typically SPEC′ is an extension of SPEC, and one does not really want to repeat all the declarations in SPEC again in SPEC′ just for the sake of turning SPEC′ into a self-contained specification. Therefore, CASL has a construct SP **then** SP', where SP' can be a *specification fragment* that is interpreted in the context (referred to as the *local environment*) coming from SP. This extension construct can be simulated using a translation along a signature inclusion and a union.

Details of these features can be found in [9, 35, 49].

6.2 A Proof Calculus for Structured Specifications

As explained above, the semantics of CASL structured specifications is parametrized over an institution that provides the semantics of the basic specifications. The situation for the proof calculus is similar: here, we need a logic, i.e. an institution equipped with an entailment system. Based on this, it is possible to design a logic-independent proof calculus [15] for proving entailments of the form $SP \vdash \varphi$, where SP is a structured specification and φ is a formula; see Fig. 6. Figure 7 shows an extension of the structured proof calculus to refinements between specifications. Note that for the latter calculus, an *oracle for conservative extensions* is needed. A specification morphism $\sigma \colon SP_1 \to SP_2$ is conservative iff each SP_1-model is the σ-reduct of some SP_2-model.[9]

$$(CR) \; \frac{\{SP \vdash \varphi_i\}_{i \in I} \quad \{\varphi_i\}_{i \in I} \vdash \varphi}{SP \vdash \varphi} \qquad (basic) \; \frac{\varphi \in \Gamma}{\langle \Sigma, \Gamma \rangle \vdash \varphi}$$

$$(sum1) \; \frac{SP_1 \vdash \varphi}{SP_1 \textbf{ and } SP_2 \vdash \iota_1(\varphi)} \qquad (sum2) \; \frac{SP_2 \vdash \varphi}{SP_1 \textbf{ and } SP_2 \vdash \iota_2(\varphi)}$$

$$(trans) \; \frac{SP \vdash \varphi}{SP \textbf{ with } \sigma \vdash \sigma(\varphi)} \qquad (derive) \; \frac{SP \vdash \sigma(\varphi)}{SP \textbf{ hide } \sigma \vdash \varphi}$$

Fig. 6. Proof calculus for entailment in structured specifications

---

[9] Besides this model-theoretic notion of conservativeness, there also is a weaker consequence-theoretic notion: $SP_2 \models \sigma(\varphi)$ implies $SP_1 \models \varphi$. There is a proof-theoretic notion coinciding with the consequence-theoretic one for complete logics: $SP_2 \vdash \sigma(\varphi)$ implies $SP_1 \vdash \varphi$. For the calculus of refinement, we need the model-theoretic notion.

$$(Basic) \ \frac{SP \vdash \Gamma}{\langle \Sigma, \Gamma \rangle \rightsquigarrow SP} \qquad (Sum) \ \frac{SP_1 \ \textbf{with} \ \iota_1 \rightsquigarrow SP \quad SP_2 \ \textbf{with} \ \iota_2 \rightsquigarrow SP}{SP_1 \ \textbf{and} \ SP_2 \rightsquigarrow SP}$$

$$(Trans_1) \ \frac{SP \rightsquigarrow SP' \ \textbf{with} \ \theta \quad \theta = \sigma^{-1}}{SP \ \textbf{with} \ \sigma \rightsquigarrow SP'} \qquad (Trans_2) \ \frac{SP \rightsquigarrow SP' \ \textbf{hide} \ \sigma}{SP \ \textbf{with} \ \sigma \rightsquigarrow SP'}$$

$$(Derive) \ \frac{SP \rightsquigarrow SP''}{SP \ \textbf{hide} \ \sigma \rightsquigarrow SP'} \quad \begin{array}{l} \text{if } \sigma : SP' \to SP'' \\ \text{is conservative} \end{array}$$

$$(Trans\text{-}equiv) \ \frac{(SP \ \textbf{with} \ \sigma) \ \textbf{with} \ \theta \rightsquigarrow SP'}{SP \ \textbf{with} \ \sigma; \theta \rightsquigarrow SP'}$$

Fig. 7. Proof calculus for refinement of structured specifications

Theorem (Soundness [15]) The calculus for structured entailment is sound, i.e. $SP \vdash \varphi$ implies $SP \models \varphi$. Also, the calculus for refinement between finite structured specifications is sound, i.e. $SP_1 \rightsquigarrow SP_2$ implies $SP_1 \approx\!\!\!\!> SP_2$.

Before we can state a completeness theorem, we need to formulate some technical assumptions about the underlying institution I.

An institution has the *Craig interpolation property* if for any pushout

$$
\begin{array}{ccc}
\Sigma & \xrightarrow{\ \sigma_1\ } & \Sigma_1 \\
\ \ \downarrow{\scriptstyle \sigma_2} & & \ \ \downarrow{\scriptstyle \theta_2} \\
\Sigma_2 & \xrightarrow{\ \theta_1\ } & \Sigma'
\end{array}
$$

and any Σ_1-sentence φ_1 and any Σ_2-sentence φ_2, with

$$\theta_2(\varphi_1) \models \theta_1(\varphi_2),$$

there exists a Σ-sentence φ (called the *interpolant*) such that

$$\varphi_1 \models \sigma_1(\varphi) \text{ and } \sigma_2(\varphi) \models \varphi_2.$$

A cocone for a diagram in **Sign** is called *(weakly) amalgamable* if it is mapped to a (weak) limit under **Mod**. $\mathcal{I}$ (or **Mod**) admits *(finite) (weak) amalgamation* if the (finite) colimit cocones are (weakly) amalgamable, i.e. if **Mod** maps (finite) colimits to (weak) limits. An important special case is that of pushouts in the signature category, which are prominently used, for instance, in instantiations of parametrized specifications; see Sect. 6.3. (Recall also that finite limits can be constructed from pullbacks and terminal objects, so that finite amalgamation reduces to preservation of pullbacks and terminal objects, and, dually, pushouts and initial objects). Here, the (weak) amalgamation property requires that a pushout

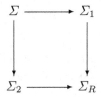

in **Sign** is mapped by **Mod** to a (weak) pullback

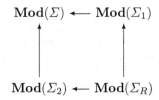

of categories. Explicitly, this means that any pair $(M_1, M_2) \in \mathbf{Mod}(\Sigma_1) \times \mathbf{Mod}(\Sigma_2)$ that is *compatible* in the sense that M_1 and M_2 reduce to the same Σ-model can be *amalgamated* to a unique Σ_R-model M, (or weakly amalgamated to a not necessarily unique model; i.e. there exists a (unique) $M \in \mathbf{Mod}(\Sigma_R)$ that reduces to M_1 and M_2, respectively), and similarly for model morphisms.

An institution *has conjunction* if for any Σ-sentences φ_1 and φ_2, there is a Σ-sentence φ that holds in a model iff φ_1 and φ_2 hold. The notion of an institution *having implication* is defined similarly.

Theorem (Completeness [15]) Under the assumptions that

- the institution has the *Craig interpolation property*,
- the institution admits *weak amalgamation*,
- the institution *has conjunction* and *implication*, and
- the logic is *complete*,

the calculi for structured entailment and refinement between finite structured specifications are complete.

In fact, the assumption of Craig interpolation and weak amalgamation can be restricted to those diagrams for which it is really needed. Details can be found in [15]. Notice, though, that even a stronger version of the interpolation property, namely Craig-Robinson interpolation as in [20], still needs closure of the set of sentences under implication in order to ensure the completeness of the above compositional proof system.

A problem with the above result is that Craig interpolation often fails, for example, it does not hold for the Casl institution *SubPCFOL$^=$* (although it does hold for the sublanguage with sort-injective signature morphisms and without subsorts and sort generation constraints; see [13]). This problem may be overcome by adding a "global" rule to the calculus, which does a kind of normal-form computation, while maintaining the structure of specifications to guide proof search as much as possible; see [41, 42].

Checking Conservativity in the CASL *Institution*

The proof rules for refinement are based on an oracle that checks the conservativeness of extensions. Hence, logic-specific rules for checking conservativeness are needed. For CASL, conservativeness can be checked by syntactic criteria, for example, free types and recursive definitions over them are always conservative. But more sophisticated rules are also available; see [44]. Note that checking conservativeness is at least as complicated as checking non-provability: for a Σ-specification SP, $SP \not\models \varphi$ iff SP **and** $\langle \Sigma, \{\neg\varphi\} \rangle$ is consistent iff SP **and** $\langle \Sigma, \{\neg\varphi\} \rangle$ is conservative over the empty specification. Hence, even checking conservativeness in first-order logic is not recursively enumerable, and thus there is no recursively axiomatized complete calculus for this task.[10]

Proof Rules for Free Specifications

An institution-independent proof theory for free specifications has not been developed yet (and it is not known whehter this is feasible at all). Hence, for free specifications, one needs to develop proof support for each institution separately. For the CASL institution, this has been sketched in [40]. The main idea is just to mimic the construction of a quotient term algebra, and to restrict proof support to those cases (e.g. Horn clause theories) where the free model is given by such a construction. Details can be found in [40].

6.3 Named and Parametrized Specifications and Views

Structured specifications may be *named*, so that a reuse of a specification may be replaced by a *reference* to it through its name. A named specification may declare some *parameters*, the union of which is extended by a *body*; it is then called *generic*. This is written as

$$\textbf{spec } SpName[ParSp] = BodySp,$$

where $BodySp$ is an extension of $ParSp$. See Fig. 3 for an example of a generic specification of lists.

A reference to a generic specification should *instantiate* it by providing, for each parameter, an *argument specification* together with a *fitting morphism* from the parameter to the argument specification. Fitting may also be

---

[10] The situation is in fact even more subtle. The model-theoretic notion of conservative extension (or, equivalently, of refinement between specifications involving hiding) corresponds to second-order existential quantification. It is well known that the semantics of second-order logic depends on the background set theory [32]. For example, one can build a specification and an extension of it that is conservative (or, equivalently, provide another specification to which it refines) iff the continuum hypothesis holds—a question that is independent of our background metatheory $ZFCU$.

achieved by (explicit) use of named *views* between the parameter and argument specifications. The union of the arguments, together with the translation of the generic specification by an expansion of the fitting morphism, corresponds to a pushout construction–taking into account any explicit *imports* of the generic specification, which allow symbols used in the body to be declared also by arguments.

Since parametrization may be expressed in terms of union and translation, we omit its semantics and proof rules here.

Semantically, a view $v\colon SP_1 \to SP_2$ from a Σ_1-specification SP_1 to a Σ_2-specification SP_2 is basically a *specification morphism* $\sigma\colon SP_1 \to SP_2$, leading to a proof obligation $SP_1 \rightsquigarrow SP_2$ **hide** σ. A similar proof obligation is generated for anonymous instantiations of parametrized specifications (i.e. instantiations not given by a named view).

Naming specifications and referencing them by name leads to *graphs* of specifications. This is formalized as a *development graph* [41, 42, 44], which expresses *sharing* between specifications, thereby leading to a more efficient proof calculus, and providing management of proof obligations and proofs for structured specification, as well as management of change.

7 Architectural Specifications

Architectural specifications in CASL provide a means for stating how implementation units are used as building blocks for larger components. (Dynamic interaction between modules and dynamic changes of software structure are currently beyond the scope of this approach.)

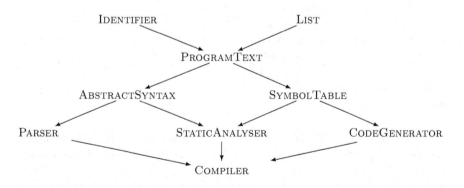

Fig. 8. Structure of the specification of a compiler. The arrows indicate the extension relations between specifications

Units are represented as names with which a specification is associated. Such a named unit is to be thought of as an arbitrarily selected model of the specification. Units may be parametrized, whereby specifications are associated with both the parameters and the result. The result specification is required to extend the parameter specifications. A parametrized unit is to be understood as a function which, given models of the parameter specifications, outputs a model of the result specification; this function is required to be *persistent* in the sense that reducing the result to the parameter signatures reproduces the parameters.

Units can be assembled via unit expressions, which may contain operations such as renaming or hiding of symbols, amalgamation of units, and application of a parametrized unit. Terms containing such operations will only be defined if symbols that are identified, for example, by renaming them to the same symbol or by amalgamating units that have symbols in common, are also interpreted in the same way in all "collective" models of the units defined so far.

An architectural specification consists of declarations and/or definitions of a number of units, together with a way of assembling them to yield a result unit.

Example 1 A (fictitious) specification structure for a compiler might look roughly as depicted in Fig. 8. The corresponding architectural specification in CASL might have the following form:

arch spec BUILDCOMPILER =
units I :   IDENTIFIER **with sorts** *Identifier, Keyword*;
          L :   ELEM $\rightarrow$ LIST[ELEM];
          $IL =$ $L[I$ **fit sort** *Elem* $\mapsto$ *Identifier*]
          $KL =$ $L[I$ **fit sort** *Elem* $\mapsto$ *Keyword*]
          PT : PROGRAMTEXT **given** IL, KL;
          AS : ABSTRACTSYNTAX **given** PT;
          ST : SYMBOLTABLE **given** PT;
          P :   PARSER **given** AS;
          SA : STATICANALYSER **given** AS, ST;
          CG : CODEGENERATOR **given** ST
result P **and** SA **and** CG
end

(Here, the keyword **with** is used just to list some of the defined symbols. The keyword **given** indicates imports.) According to the above specification, the parser, the static analyser and the code generator would be constructed building upon a given abstract syntax and a given mechanism for symbol tables, and the compiler would be obtained by just putting together the former three units. Roughly speaking, this is only possible (in a manner that can be statically checked) if all symbols that are shared between the parser, the static analyser and the code generator already appear in the units for the abstract syntax or the symbol tables—otherwise, incompatibilities might occur that make it impossible to put the separately developed components together.

For instance, if both STATICANALYSER and CODEGENERATOR declare an operation *lookup* that serves to retrieve symbols from the symbol table, then the corresponding implementations might turn out to be substantially different, so that the two components fail to be compatible. Of course, this points to an obvious flaw in the architecture: *lookup* should have been declared in SYMBOLTABLE.

Consider an institution with unions $I = (\mathbf{Sign}, \mathbf{Sen}, \mathbf{Mod}, \models)$. We assume that the signature category is finitely cocomplete and that the institution admits amalgamation. We also assume that signature unions are exhaustive in the sense that, given two signatures Σ_1 and Σ_2 and their union $\Sigma_1 \xrightarrow{\iota_1} (\Sigma_1 \cup \Sigma_2) \xleftarrow{\iota_2} \Sigma_2$, for any models $M_1 \in \mathbf{Mod}(\Sigma_1)$ and $M_2 \in \mathbf{Mod}(\Sigma_2)$, there is at most one model $M \in \mathbf{Mod}(\Sigma_1 \cup \Sigma_2)$ such that $M|_{\iota_1} = M_1$ and $M|_{\iota_2} = M_2$. We formally present a small but representative subset of the CASL architectural specifications in such a framework. This fragment–or, rather, its syntax–is given in Fig. 9.

Architectural specifications: $ASP ::= \mathbf{arch\ spec}\ Dcl^*\ \mathbf{result}\ T$
Unit declarations: $Dcl ::= U : SP \mid U : SP_1 \xrightarrow{\tau} SP_2$
Unit terms: $T ::= U \mid U[T\ \mathbf{fit}\ \sigma] \mid T_1\ \mathbf{and}\ T_2$

Fig. 9. A fragment of the architectural specification formalism

Example 1 additionally uses unit definitions and imports. Unit definitions $U = T$ introduce a (non-parametrized) unit and give its value by means of a unit term. Imports can be regarded as syntactical sugar for a parametrized unit which is instantiated only once: if $U_1 : \text{SPEC}_1$, then

$$U_2 : \text{SPEC}_2\ \mathbf{given}\ U_1$$

abbreviates

$$U_2' : \text{SPEC}_1 \to \text{SPEC}_2;$$
$$U_2 = U_2'[U_1].$$

We now sketch the formal semantics of our language fragment and show how the correctness of such specifications may be established.

7.1 Semantics of Architectural Specifications

The semantics of architectural specifications introduced above is split into static and model semantics, in very much the same way as was done for structured specifications in Sect. 6.

Unit terms are statically elaborated in a *static context* $C_{st} = (P_{st}, B_{st})$, where P_{st} maps parametrized unit names to signature morphisms and B_{st} maps non-parametrized unit names to their signatures. We require the domains of P_{st} and B_{st} to be disjoint. The empty static context that consists of two empty maps will be written as $C_{st}^{\emptyset}$. Given an initial static context, the static semantics for unit declarations produces a static context by adding the signature for a newly introduced unit, and the static semantics for unit terms determines the signature for the resulting unit.

$$\frac{\vdash UDD^* \rhd C_{st} \qquad C_{st} \vdash T \rhd \Sigma}{\vdash \mathbf{arch\ spec}\ UDD^*\ \mathbf{result}\ T \rhd (C_{st}, \Sigma)}$$

$$\frac{C_{st}^{\emptyset} \vdash UDD_1 \rhd (C_{st})_1 \qquad \cdots \qquad (C_{st})_{n-1} \vdash UDD_n \rhd (C_{st})_n}{\vdash UDD_1 \ldots UDD_n \rhd (C_{st})_n}$$

$$\frac{\vdash SP \rhd \Sigma \qquad U \notin (Dom(P_{st}) \cup Dom(B_{st}))}{(P_{st}, B_{st}) \vdash U : SP \rhd (P_{st}, B_{st} + \{U \mapsto \Sigma\})}$$

$$\frac{\vdash SP_1 \rhd \Sigma_1 \qquad \vdash SP_2 \rhd \Sigma_2 \qquad \tau : \Sigma_1 \to \Sigma_2}{(P_{st}, B_{st}) \vdash U : SP_1 \xrightarrow{\tau} SP_2 \rhd (P_{st} + \{U \mapsto \tau\}, B_{st})}$$

$$\frac{U \in Dom(B_{st})}{(P_{st}, B_{st}) \vdash U \rhd B_{st}(U)}$$

$$\frac{P_{st}(U) = \tau : \Sigma \to \Sigma' \qquad C_{st} \vdash T \rhd \Sigma_T \qquad \sigma : \Sigma \to \Sigma_T}{(\tau' : \Sigma_T \to \Sigma_T', \sigma' : \Sigma' \to \Sigma_T')\ \text{is the pushout of}\ (\sigma, \tau)}{(P_{st}, B_{st}) \vdash U[T\ \mathbf{fit}\ \sigma] \rhd \Sigma_T'}$$

$$\frac{C_{st} \vdash T_1 \rhd \Sigma_1 \qquad C_{st} \vdash T_2 \rhd \Sigma_2}{\Sigma = \Sigma_1 \cup \Sigma_2\ \text{with inclusions}\ \iota_1 : \Sigma_1 \to \Sigma, \iota_2 : \Sigma_2 \to \Sigma}{(P_{st}, B_{st}) \vdash T_1\ \mathbf{and}\ T_2 \rhd \Sigma}$$

Fig. 10. Static semantics of architectural specifications

In terms of the model semantics, a (non-parametrized) unit M over a signature Σ is just a model $M \in \mathbf{Mod}(\Sigma)$. A parametrized unit F over a parametrized unit signature $\tau : \Sigma_1 \to \Sigma_2$ is a persistent partial function $F : \mathbf{Mod}(\Sigma_1) \rightharpoonup \mathbf{Mod}(\Sigma_2)$ (i.e. $F(M)|_\tau = M$ for each $M \in Dom(F)$).

The model semantics for architectural specifications involves interpretations of unit names. These are given by *unit environments* E, i.e. finite maps from unit names to units as introduced above. On the model-semantics side, the analogue of a static context is a *unit context* C, which is just a class of unit environments, and can be thought of as a constraint on the interpretation of unit names. The unconstrained unit context, which consists of all environments, will be written as $C^{\emptyset}$. The model semantics for unit declarations modifies unit contexts by constraining the environments to interpret newly introduced unit names as determined by their specification or definition.

A unit term is interpreted by a *unit evaluator UEv*, a function that yields a unit when given a unit environment in the unit context (the unit environment serves to interpret the unit names occurring in the unit term). Hence, the model semantics for a unit term yields a unit evaluator, given a unit context.

$$\frac{\vdash UDD^* \Rightarrow \mathcal{C} \qquad \mathcal{C} \vdash T \Rightarrow UEv}{\vdash \textbf{arch spec } UDD^* \textbf{ result } T \Rightarrow (\mathcal{C}, UEv)}$$

$$\frac{\mathcal{C}^{\emptyset} \vdash UDD_1 \Rightarrow \mathcal{C}_1 \qquad \cdots \qquad \mathcal{C}_{n-1} \vdash UDD_n \Rightarrow \mathcal{C}_n}{\vdash UDD_1 \ldots UDD_n \Rightarrow \mathcal{C}_n}$$

$$\frac{\vdash SP \Rightarrow \mathcal{M}}{\mathcal{C} \vdash U : SP \Rightarrow \mathcal{C} \times \{U \mapsto \mathcal{M}\}}$$

$$\frac{\vdash SP_1 \Rightarrow \mathcal{M}_1 \qquad \vdash SP_2 \Rightarrow \mathcal{M}_2}{\mathcal{F} = \{F : \mathcal{M}_1 \to \mathcal{M}_2 \mid \text{for } M \in \mathcal{M}_1, F(M)|_\tau = M\}} \\ \overline{\mathcal{C} \vdash U : SP_1 \xrightarrow{\tau} SP_2 \Rightarrow \mathcal{C} \times \{U \mapsto \mathcal{F}\}}$$

$$\frac{}{\mathcal{C} \vdash U \Rightarrow \{E \mapsto E(U) \mid E \in \mathcal{C}\}}$$

$$\frac{\begin{array}{c} \mathcal{C} \vdash T \Rightarrow UEv \\ \left.\text{for each } E \in \mathcal{C}, \; UEv(E)|_\sigma \in Dom(E(U))\right\} (*) \\ \left.\begin{array}{c}\text{for each } E \in \mathcal{C}, \text{ there is a unique } M \in \textbf{Mod}(\Sigma'_T) \text{ such that} \\ M|_{\tau'} = UEv(E) \text{ and } M|_{\sigma'} = E(U)(UEv(E)|_\sigma)\end{array}\right\} (**) \\ UEv' = \{E \mapsto M \mid E \in \mathcal{C}, M|_{\tau'} = UEv(E), M|_{\sigma'} = E(U)(UEv(E)|_\sigma)\}\end{array}}{\mathcal{C} \vdash U[T \textbf{ fit } \sigma] \Rightarrow UEv'}$$

$$\frac{\begin{array}{c} \mathcal{C} \vdash T_1 \Rightarrow UEv_1 \qquad \mathcal{C} \vdash T_2 \Rightarrow UEv_2 \\ \left.\begin{array}{c}\text{for each } E \in \mathcal{C}, \text{ there is a unique } M \in \textbf{Mod}(\Sigma) \text{ such that} \\ M|_{\iota_1} = UEv_1(E) \text{ and } M|_{\iota_2} = UEv_2(E)\end{array}\right\} (***) \\ UEv = \{E \mapsto M \mid E \in \mathcal{C} \text{ and } M|_{\iota_1} = UEv_1(E), M|_{\iota_2} = UEv_2(E)\}\end{array}}{\mathcal{C} \vdash T_1 \textbf{ and } T_2 \Rightarrow UEv}$$

Fig. 11. Model semantics of architectural specifications

The complete semantics is given in Figs. 10 (static semantics) and 11 (model semantics), where we use some auxiliary notation: given a unit context $\mathcal{C}$, a unit name U and a class $\mathcal{V}$,

$$\mathcal{C} \times \{U \mapsto \mathcal{V}\} := \{E + \{U \mapsto V\} \mid E \in \mathcal{C}, V \in \mathcal{V}\},$$

where $E + \{U \mapsto V\}$ maps U to V and otherwise behaves like E. The model semantics assumes that the static semantics has been successful on the constructs considered; we use the notation introduced by this derivation of the static semantics in the model-semantics rules whenever convenient.

The model semantics is easily seen to be compatible with the static semantics in the following sense: we say that $\mathcal{C}$ *fits* $C_{st} = (P_{st}, B_{st})$ if, whenever $B_{st}(U) = \Sigma$ and $E \in \mathcal{C}$, then $E(U)$ is a Σ-model, and a corresponding condition holds for P_{st}. Obviously, $\mathcal{C}^\emptyset$ fits $C_{st}^\emptyset$. Now, if $\mathcal{C}$ fits C_{st}, then $C_{st} \vdash T \triangleright \Sigma$ and $\mathcal{C} \vdash T \Rightarrow UEv$ imply that $UEv(E)$ is a Σ-model for each $E \in \mathcal{C}$. Corresponding statements hold for the other syntactic categories (unit declarations and architectural specifications).

We say that an architectural specification is internally correct (or simply *correct*) if it has both a static and a model semantics. Informally, this means that the architectural design the specification captures is correct in the sense that any realization of the units according to their specifications allows us to construct an overall result by performing the construction prescribed by the resulting unit term.

Checking the correctness of an architectural specification requires checking that all the rules necessary for derivation of its semantics may indeed be applied, that is, all their premises can be derived and the conditions that they capture hold. Perhaps the only steps which require further discussion are the rules of the model semantics for unit application and amalgamation in Fig. 11. Only there do some difficult premises occur, marked by $(*)$, $(**)$ and $(***)$. All the other premises of the semantic rules are "easy" in the sense that they largely just pass on the information collected about various parts of the given phrase, or perform a very simple check that names are introduced before being used, signatures fit as expected, etc.

First we consider the premises $(**)$ and $(***)$ in the rules for unit application and amalgamation, respectively. They impose "amalgamability requirements", which are necessary to actually build the expected models by combining simpler models, as indicated. Such requirements are typically expected to be at least partially discharged by static analysis–similarly to the sharing requirements present in some programming languages (cf. e.g. Standard ML [53]). Under our assumptions, the premise $(**)$ may simply be skipped, as it always holds (since all parametrized units are persistent functions, $E(U)(UEv(E)|_\sigma)|_\tau = UEv(E)|_\sigma$, and so the required unique model $M \in \mathbf{Mod}(\Sigma'_T)$ exists by the amalgamation property of the institution). The premise $(***)$ may fail, though, and a more subtle static analysis of the dependencies between units may be needed to check that it holds for a given construct.

The premise $(*)$ in the rule for application of a parametrized unit requires that the fitting morphism correctly "fits" the actual parameter as an argument for the parametrized unit. To verify this, one typically has to prove that the fitting morphism is a specification morphism from the argument specification to the specification of the actual parameter. Similarly to the case of the proof obligations arising with instantiations of parametrized specifications discussed in Sect. 6.3, this in general requires some semantic or proof-theoretic reasoning. Moreover, a suitable calculus is needed to determine a specification for the actual parameter. One possible naive attempt to provide it might be to build such a specification inductively for each unit term using specifications of its components directly. Let SP_T be such a specification for a term T. In other words, verification conditions aside,

- SP_U is SP, where $U : SP$ is the declaration of U;
- $SP_{T_1 \text{ and } T_2}$ is $(SP_{T_1} \text{ and } SP_{T_2})$;
- $SP_{U[T \text{ fit } \sigma]}$ is $((SP_T \text{ with } \tau') \text{ and } (SP' \text{ with } \sigma'))$, where $U : SP \xrightarrow{\tau} SP'$ is the declaration of U and (τ', σ') is the pushout of (σ, τ), as in the corresponding rule of the static semantics.

It can easily be seen that the SP_T so determined is indeed a correct specification for T, in the sense that if $C_{st} \vdash T \rhd \Sigma$ and $C \vdash T \Rightarrow UEv$ then $\vdash SP_T \rhd \Sigma$ and $\vdash SP_T \Rightarrow \mathcal{M}$, with $UEv(E) \in \mathcal{M}$ for each $E \in \mathcal{C}$. Therefore, we could replace the requirement $(*)$ by $SP \rightsquigarrow SP_T \text{ hide } \sigma$.

However, this would be highly incomplete. Consider a trivial example:

units $U :$ {**sort** s; **op** $a : s$}
$\quad\quad\quad ID :$ {**sort** s; **op** $b : s$} $\rightarrow$ {**sort** s; **op** $b : s$}
$\quad\quad\quad F :$ {**sort** s; **op** $a, b : s$; **axiom** $a = b$} $\rightarrow \ldots$
result $F[\ U \text{ and } ID[U \text{ fit } b \mapsto a]\ ]$

The specification we obtain for the argument unit term of F does not capture that fact that $a = b$ holds in all units that may actually arise as the argument for F here. The problem is that the specification for a unit term built as above disregards entirely any dependencies and sharing that may occur between units denoted by unit terms, and so is often insufficient to verify the correctness of unit applications. Hence, this first try to calculate specifications for architectural unit terms turns out to be inadequate, and a more complex form of architectural verification is needed.

7.2 Verification

The basic idea behind verification for architectural specifications is that we want to extend the static information about units to capture their properties by an additional specification. However, as discussed at the end of the previous section, we must also take into account sharing between various unit components, resulting from inheritance of some parts of units via, for instance, parametrized unit applications. To capture this, we accumulate information about non-parametrized units into a single *global signature* Σ_G, and represent non-parametrized unit signatures as morphisms into this global signature, assigning them to unit names by a map B_v. The additional information resulting from the unit specifications is then accumulated into a single *global specification* SP_G over this signature (i.e. we always have $\vdash SP_G \rhd \Sigma_G$). Finally, of

$$\frac{\vdash Dcl^* :: C_v \qquad C_v \vdash T :: \Sigma \xrightarrow{i} SP'_G \xleftarrow{\theta} SP_G}{\vdash \textbf{arch spec } Dcl^* \textbf{ result } T :: SP'_G \textbf{ hide } i}$$

$$\frac{C_v^\emptyset \vdash Dcl_1 :: (C_v)_1 \qquad \cdots \qquad (C_v)_{n-1} \vdash Dcl_n :: (C_v)_n}{\vdash Dcl_1 \ldots Dcl_n :: (C_v)_n}$$

$$\frac{\begin{array}{c} U \notin (Dom(P_v) \cup Dom(B_v)) \qquad \vdash SP \triangleright \Sigma \\ (\Sigma_G \xrightarrow{\theta} \Sigma'_G \xleftarrow{i} \Sigma) \text{ is the coproduct of } \Sigma_G \text{ and } \Sigma \end{array}}{\begin{array}{c} (P_v, B_v, SP_G) \vdash U : SP :: \\ (P_v, (B_v; \theta) + \{U \mapsto i\}, (SP_G \textbf{ with } \theta) \textbf{ and } (SP \textbf{ with } i)) \end{array}}$$

$$\frac{U \notin (Dom(P_v) \cup Dom(B_v))}{(P_v, B_v, SP_G) \vdash U : SP_1 \xrightarrow{\tau} SP_2 :: (P_v + \{U \mapsto SP_1 \xrightarrow{\tau} SP_2\}, B_v, SP_G)}$$

$$\frac{B_v(U) = \Sigma \xrightarrow{i} SP_G}{(P_v, B_v, SP_G) \vdash U :: \Sigma \xrightarrow{i} SP_G \xleftarrow{id} SP_G}$$

$$\frac{\begin{array}{c} (P_v, B_v, SP_G) \vdash T :: \Sigma_T \xrightarrow{i} SP'_G \xleftarrow{\theta} SP_G \\ P_v(U) = SP \xrightarrow{\tau} SP' \quad \vdash SP \triangleright \Sigma \quad \vdash SP' \triangleright \Sigma' \quad \sigma : \Sigma \to \Sigma_T \\ (\tau' : \Sigma_T \to \Sigma'_T, \sigma' : \Sigma' \to \Sigma'_T) \text{ is the pushout of } (\sigma, \tau) \\ (\tau'' : \Sigma'_G \to \Sigma''_G, i' : \Sigma'_T \to \Sigma''_G) \text{ is the pushout of } (i, \tau') \\ SP \textbf{ with } \sigma; i \rightsquigarrow SP'_G \end{array}}{\begin{array}{c} (P_v, B_v, SP_G) \vdash U[T \textbf{ fit } \sigma] :: \\ \Sigma'_T \xrightarrow{i'} (SP'_G \textbf{ with } \tau'') \textbf{ and } (SP' \textbf{ with } \sigma'; i') \xleftarrow{\theta; \tau''} SP_G \end{array}}$$

$$\frac{\begin{array}{c} (P_v, B_v, SP_G) \vdash T_1 :: \Sigma_1 \xrightarrow{i_1} SP_G^1 \xleftarrow{\theta_1} SP_G \\ (P_v, B_v, SP_G) \vdash T_2 :: \Sigma_2 \xrightarrow{i_2} SP_G^2 \xleftarrow{\theta_2} SP_G \\ \Sigma = \Sigma_1 \cup \Sigma_2 \text{ with inclusions } \iota_1 : \Sigma_1 \to \Sigma, \iota_2 : \Sigma_2 \to \Sigma \\ (\theta'_2 : \Sigma_G^1 \to \Sigma'_G, \theta'_1 : \Sigma_G^2 \to \Sigma'_G) \text{ is the pushout of } (\theta_1, \theta_2) \\ j : \Sigma \to \Sigma'_G \text{ satisfies } \iota_1; j = i_1; \theta'_2 \text{ and } \iota_2; j = i_2; \theta'_1 \end{array}}{\begin{array}{c} (P_v, B_v, SP_G) \vdash T_1 \textbf{ and } T_2 :: \\ \Sigma_1 \cup \Sigma_2 \xrightarrow{j} (SP_G^1 \textbf{ with } \theta'_2) \textbf{ and } (SP_G^2 \textbf{ with } \theta'_1) \xleftarrow{\theta_1; \theta'_2} SP_G \end{array}}$$

Fig. 12. Verification rules

course, we store the entire specification for each parametrized unit, assigning these specifications to parametrized unit names by a map P_v. This results in the concept of a *verification context* $C_v = (P_v, B_v, SP_G)$. A static unit context $ctx(C_v) = (P_{st}, B_{st})$ may easily be extracted from such an extended context: for each $U \in Dom(B_v)$, $B_{st}(U) = \Sigma$, where $B_v(U) = i : \Sigma \to \Sigma_G$, and for each $U \in Dom(P_v)$, $P_{st}(U) = \tau$, where $P_v(U) = SP_1 \xrightarrow{\tau} SP_2$.

Given a morphism $\theta\colon \Sigma_G \to \Sigma'_G$ that extends the global signature (or a global specification morphism $\theta\colon SP_G \to SP'_G$) we write $B_v;\theta$ for the corresponding extension of B_v (mapping each $U \in Dom(B_v)$ to $B_v(U);\theta$). $C_v^\emptyset$ is the "empty" verification context (with the initial global specification[11]).

The intuition described above is reflected in the form of verification judgements, and captured formally by verification rules,

$$\boxed{\ \vdash ASP :: SP\ }$$

Architectural specifications yield a specification of the result,

$$\boxed{\ C_v \vdash Dcl :: C'_v\ }$$

In a verification context, unit declarations yield a new verification context,

$$\boxed{\ (P_v, B_v, SP_G) \vdash T :: \Sigma \xrightarrow{\ i\ } SP'_G \xleftarrow{\ \theta\ } SP_G\ }$$

In a verification context, unit terms yield their signature embedded into a new global specification, obtained as an extension of the kind indicated of the old global specification.

The verification rules used to derive these judgements are shown in Fig. 12, with diagrams to help one read the more complicated rules for unit application and amalgamation given in Fig. 13.

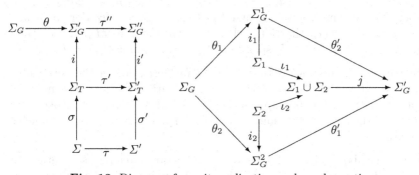

Fig. 13. Diagrams for unit application and amalgamation

---

[11] More precisely, this is the basic specification consisting of the initial signature with no axioms.

It should be easy to see that the verification semantics subsumes (in the obvious sense) the static semantics: a successful derivation of the verification semantics ensures a successful derivation of the static semantics with results that may be extracted from the results of the verification semantics in the obvious way.

More crucially, a successful derivation of the verification semantics of an architectural specification ensures a successful derivation of the model semantics, and hence the correctness of the architectural specification.

To state this more precisely, we need an extension to verification contexts of the notion that a unit context fits a static context: a unit context C_v *fits* a verification context $C_v = (P_v, B_v, SP_G)$, where $\vdash SP_G \Rightarrow \mathcal{M}_G$, if

- for each $E \in \mathcal{C}$ and $U \in Dom(P_v)$ with $P_v(U) = SP \xrightarrow{\tau} SP'$, where $\vdash SP \Rightarrow \mathcal{M}$ and $\vdash SP' \Rightarrow \mathcal{M}'$, we have $E(U)(M) \in \mathcal{M}'$ for all $M \in \mathcal{M}$, and
- for each $E \in \mathcal{C}$, there exists $M_G \in \mathcal{M}_G$ such that for all $U \in Dom(B_v)$, $E(U) = M_G|_{B_v(U)}$; we say then that E is *witnessed by* M_G.

Now, the following claims follow by induction:

- For every architectural specification ASP, if $\vdash ASP :: SP$ with $\vdash SP \Rightarrow \mathcal{M}$, then $\vdash ASP \Rightarrow (\mathcal{C}, UEv)$ for some unit context $\mathcal{C}$ and unit evaluator UEv such that $UEv(E) \in \mathcal{M}$ for all $E \in \mathcal{C}$.
- For any unit declaration Dcl and verification context C_v, if $C_v \vdash Dcl :: C'_v$, then for any unit context $\mathcal{C}$ that fits C_v, $\mathcal{C} \vdash Dcl \Rightarrow \mathcal{C}'$ for some unit context $\mathcal{C}'$ that fits C'_v; this generalizes to sequences of unit declarations in the obvious way.
- For any unit term T and verification context $C_v = (P_v, B_v, SP_G)$, where $\vdash SP_G \Rightarrow \mathcal{M}_G$, if $C_v \vdash T :: \Sigma \xrightarrow{i} SP'_G \xleftarrow{\theta} SP_G$, where $\vdash SP'_G \Rightarrow \mathcal{M}'_G$, then for any unit context $\mathcal{C}$ that fits C_v, $\mathcal{C} \vdash T \Rightarrow UEv$ for some unit evaluator UEv such that for each $E \in \mathcal{C}$ witnessed by $M_G \in \mathcal{M}_G$, there exists a model $M'_G \in \mathcal{M}'_G$ such that $M'_G|_\theta = M_G$ and $M'_G|_i = UEv(E)$.

In particular, this means that a successful derivation of the verification semantics ensures that in the corresponding derivation of the model semantics, whenever the rules for unit application and amalgamation are invoked, the premises marked by $(*)$, $(**)$ and $(***)$ hold. This may also be seen somewhat more directly:

$(*)$ Given the above relationship between verification and model semantics, the requirement $(*)$ in the model-semantics rule for unit application follows from the requirement that SP **with** $\sigma; i \rightsquigarrow SP'_G$ in the corresponding verification rule.

$(**)$ As pointed out already, the premises marked by $(**)$ may be removed by the assumption that the institution that we are working with admits amalgamation.

(∗∗∗) Given the above relationship between verification and model semantics, the existence of the models required by (∗∗∗) in the model-semantics rule for unit amalgamation can be shown by gradually constructing a compatible family of models over the signatures in the corresponding diagram in Fig. 13 (this requires amalgamation again); the uniqueness of the model so constructed follows from our assumption about signature union.

Note that only the checking of the requirement (∗) relies on the information contained in the specifications built for the unit terms by the verification semantics. The other requirements are entirely "static", in the sense that they may still be checked if we replace the specifications by their signatures. This may be used to split the verification semantics into two parts: an extended static analysis, performed without taking specifications into account, but considering in detail all the mutual dependencies between units involved to check properties such as those labelled by (∗∗) and (∗∗∗); and a proper verification semantics, aimed at considering unit specifications and deriving specifications for unit terms from them. See [67] for details.

7.3 Enriched CASL, Diagram Semantics and the Cell Calculus

The verification semantics of architectural specifications presented in the Sect. 7.2 depends crucially on amalgamation in the underlying institution. However, the CASL institution fails to have this property.

Example 2 The simplest case where amalgamation fails is the following: let Σ be the signature with sorts s and t and no operations, and let Σ_1 be the extension of Σ by the subsort relation $s \leq t$. Then the pushout

in **SubSig** fails to be amalgamable (since two models of Σ_1 that are compatible with respect to the inclusion of Σ may interpret the subsort injection differently).

The solution is to embed the CASL institution into an institution that possesses the amalgamation property. The main idea in the definition of the required extended institution is to generalize pre-orders of sorts to *categories* of sorts, i.e. to admit several different subsort embeddings between two given sorts; this gives rise to the notion of an *enriched* CASL *signature*. Details can be found in [63]. This means that before a CASL architectural specification can be statically checked and verification conditions can be proved, it has to be translated to enriched CASL, using such an embedding.

One might wonder why the mapping from subsorted to many-sorted specifications introduced in Sect. 4 is not used instead of introducing enriched CASL. Indeed, this is possible. However, enriched CASL has the advantage of keeping the subsorting information entirely static, avoiding the need for any axioms to capture the built-in structural properties, as would be the case with the mapping described in Sect. 4.

This advantage plays a role in the *diagram semantics* of architectural specifications. This replaces the global signatures that are used in the static semantics by diagrams of signatures and signature morphisms; see [9]. In the "extended static part" of the verification semantics, the commutativity conditions concerning signature morphisms into the global signature have then to be replaced by model-theoretic amalgamation conditions. Given an embedding into an institution with amalgamation such as that discussed above, the latter conditions are equivalent to factorization conditions on the colimit of the embedded diagram. For (enriched) CASL, these factorization conditions can be dealt with using a calculus called the *cell calculus*) for proving equality of morphisms and symbols in the colimit; see [29]. A verification semantics without reference to overall global specifications (and which relies on the amalgamation property) and consequently with more "local" verification conditions is yet to be worked out.

8 Refinement

The standard development paradigm of algebraic specification [5] postulates that formal software development begins with a formal *requirement specification* (extracted from a software project's informal requirements) that fixes only some expected properties but, ideally, says nothing about implementation issues; this is to be followed by a number of *refinement* steps that fix more and more details of the design, so that one finally arrives at what is often termed the *design specification*. The last refinement step then results in an actual *implementation* in a programming language.

One aspect of refinement concerns the way that the specified model class becomes smaller and smaller as more and more design decisions are made during the refinement process, until a monomorphic design specification or program is reached. This is reflected by CASL's concepts of *views* and the corresponding refinement relation $\approx\!\!\!\!>$ between specifications as introduced in Sect. 6. However, views are not expressive enough for refinement, being primarily a means for naming fitting morphisms for parametrized specifications. This is because there are more aspects of refinement than just model class inclusion.

One central issue here is *constructor refinement* [61]. This includes the basic constructions for writing implementation units that can be found in programming languages, for example, enumeration types, algebraic data types (that is, free types) and recursive definitions of operations. Also, unit terms in architectural specifications can be thought of as (logic-independent) constructors: they construct larger units out of smaller ones. Refinements may use these constructors, and hence the task of implementing a specification may be entirely discharged (by supplying appropriate constructs in some programming language), or it may be reduced (via an architectural specification) to the implementation of smaller specifications. A first refinement language following these lines is described in [46]. On the one hand, in this language, one can express chains of model class inclusions, such as

refinement R1 =
    SP1 **refined to**
        SP2 **refined to** SP3
end

which expresses that the model class of SP3 is included in that of SP2, which is in turn included in the model class of SP1. On the other hand, it is possible to refine structured specifications into architectural specifications, introducing a branching into the development:

refinement R2 =
    SP1 **refined to arch spec** ASP
end

Architectural specifications can be further refined by refining their components, as in:

refinement R3 =
    SP **refined to arch spec units**
$$K : SP' \to SP$$
$$A' : SP'$$
           result $K(A')$
    then $\{K$ **to** USP,
        A' **to arch spec units**
$$K' : SP'' \to SP'$$
$$A'' : SP''$$
           result $K'(A'')\}$
    then $\{A'$ **to** $\{K'$ **to** $USP'\}\}$

Here, "**then**" denotes composition of refinements. Details and the formal semantics can be found in [46].

A second central issue concerns *behavioural refinement*. Often, a refined specification does not satisfy the initial requirements literally, but only up to some sort of behavioural equivalence. For example, if stacks are implemented as arrays-with-pointer, then two arrays-with-pointer differing only in their "junk" entries (that is, those beyond the pointer) exhibit the same behaviour in terms of stack operations. Hence, they correspond to the same abstract stack and should be treated as being the same for the purpose of refinement. This can be achieved by using, for example, observational equivalences between models, which are usually induced by sets of observable sorts [12, 59].

9 Tools

A language will be used only if good tool support is available. The Heterogeneous Tool Set (HETS) [45] collects several tools around CASL. It provides tool support for all layers of CASL, as well as for CASL sublanguages and extensions.

HETS consists of parsing, static-analysis and proof management tools, combining various such tools for individual specification languages, thus providing a tool for heterogeneous multi-logic specification. HETS is based on a graph of logics and languages (formalized as institutions). The input language of HETS is Heterogeneous CASL (HETCASL; see [38]). HETCASL includes the structuring constructs of CASL as introduced in Sect. 6. HETCASL extends these with constructs for the translation of specifications along logic translations. The semantics of HETCASL specifications is given in terms of the *Grothendieck institution* [19, 36]. This institution is basically a flattening, or disjoint union, of the logic graph.

The central device for structured theorem proving and proof management in HETS is the formalism of *development graphs*. Development graphs have been used in large industrial-scale applications [27]. The graph structure provides a direct visualization of the structure of specifications, and it also allows one to manage large specifications with hundreds of subspecifications.

A development graph (see Fig. 14 for an example graph generated by the specifications given in Sect. 10) consists of a set of nodes (corresponding to whole structured specifications or parts thereof), and a set of arrows called *definition links*, indicating the dependency of each structured specification involved on its subparts. Each node is associated with a signature and some set of local axioms. The axioms of other nodes are inherited via definition links. Definition links are usually drawn as black solid arrows, denoting an import of another specification that is homogeneous (i.e. stays within the same logic). Double arrows indicate imports that are heterogeneous, i.e. the logic changes along the arrow.

Complementary to definition links, which *define* the theories of related nodes, *theorem links* serve for *postulating* relations between different theories. Theorem links are the central data structure for representing proof obligations that arise in formal developments. Theorem links can be *global* (drawn as solid arrows) or *local* (drawn as dashed arrows): a global theorem link postulates that all axioms of the source node (including the inherited ones) hold in the target node, while a local theorem link postulates only that the local axioms of the source node hold in the target node.

The *proof calculus* for development graphs [40, 42, 44] is given by rules that allow one to prove global theorem links by decomposing them into simpler (local and global) ones. Local theorem links can be proved by turning them into *local proof goals* (associated with a particular node). The latter, in turn, can be proved using a logic-specific calculus as given by an entailment system (see Sect. 2). Currently, the theorem provers Isabelle and SPASS have been

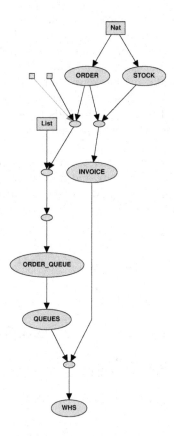

Fig. 14. Development graph for the warehouse example

linked to HETS, allowing one to perform far more efficient reasoning compared with working directly with a calculus for basic specifications.

10 Case Study

This section is intended to illustrate how a system can be specified in CASL and validated/verified using CASL tools. As example we use a specification of a warehouse system by Baumeister and Bert [7]. This system is an information system that keeps track of the stock of products and of orders from customers, and provides operations for adding, cancelling and invoicing orders, and adding products to the stock.

We both present the original specification and analyse its formal properties, which in some places leads to a need to redesign the specification. It is quite common that not only programs but also specification have errors and are subject to correction. A specification may be erroneous because it is ill-formed (either syntactically, or because it does not have a well-defined semantics according to the rules in Sects. 6 and 7). However, even a well-formed specification may be invalid in the sense that it does not meet the original informal specification. We shall see that the calculi developed in Sects. 3.2, 6 and 7 are helpful for detecting both kinds of error. Baumeister and Bert have revised their specifications in response to the problems reported in this chapter, see [8].

First we give an overview of the specifications constituting the overall specification of the warehouse system, and then we present these specifications in more detail, one by one. Finally, we present an architectural specification that describes the modular structure of an implementation of the system.

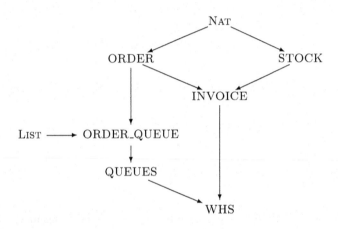

Fig. 15. Structure of the warehouse specification

Figure 15 gives an overview of the specifications and their extension relations. The objects of the system are products, orders, stocks, and queues of pending and invoiced orders. The specifications ORDER and STOCK specify sorts, operations and predicates for orders and stocks, respectively. There is no separate specification for products, but a sort for products is declared in ORDER as well as in STOCK. The main purpose of the INVOICE specification is to specify an operation for invoicing an order for a product in stock. The ORDER_QUEUE and QUEUES specifications specify various kinds of queues of orders. The WHS specification is the top-level specification, in which the main operations of the system are specified.

10.1 Specification of Some Preliminaries

spec NAT = %**mono**
    free type $Nat ::= 0 \mid suc(Nat)$
    preds $\_\_<=\_\_, \_\_>=\_\_ : Nat \times Nat$
    ops $\_\_+\_\_ : Nat \times Nat \to Nat;$
            $\_\_-?\_\_ : Nat \times Nat \to? Nat$
    $\forall\ m,\ n,\ r,\ s,\ t\colon Nat$

    %% axioms concerning predicates
    • $0 <= n$ %(leq_def1_Nat)%
    • $\neg\ suc(n) <= 0$ %(leq_def2_Nat)%
    • $suc(m) <= suc(n) \Leftrightarrow m <= n$ %(leq_def3_Nat)%
    • $m >= n \Leftrightarrow n <= m$ %(geq_def_Nat)%

    %% axioms concerning operations
    • $0 + m = m$ %(add_0_Nat)%
    • $suc(n) + m = suc(n + m)$ %(add_suc_Nat)%
    • $def\ m -?\ n \Leftrightarrow m >= n$ %(sub_dom_Nat)% %**implied**
    • $m -?\ n = r \Leftrightarrow m = r + n$ %(sub_def_Nat)%
then %**mono**
    sort $Pos = \{p\colon Nat \bullet p = 0\}$
    op $suc : Nat \to Pos$
end

NAT and LIST (the latter is shown in Fig. 3) are the usual specifications of natural numbers and lists, taken from the library of CASL basic data types [50]. The **free type** declarations are abbreviations for operation declarations and Peano-like axioms. For example, the **free type** declaration in the specification NAT expands to

spec NAT =
    sort Nat
    ops $0 : Nat;$
            $suc : Nat \to Nat$
    $\forall\ X1\colon Nat;\ Y1\colon Nat$
    • $suc(X1) = suc(Y1) \Leftrightarrow X1 = Y1$ %(ga_injective_suc)%
    • $\neg\ 0 = suc(Y1)$ %(ga_disjoint_0_suc)%
    generated {**sort** Nat
                ops $0 : Nat$
                      $suc : Nat \to Nat$ %(ga_generated_Nat)%}
end

where the **generated** construct leads, in turn, to a sort generation constraint $(\{nat\}, \{0;\ suc\}, id)$.

spec ORDER =
    NAT
then
    sorts *Order, Product*
    ops *reference* : *Order* → *Product*;
           ordered_qty : *Order* → *Pos*
preds *is_pending, is_invoiced* : *Order*
var *o*: *Order*
- ¬ *is_pending*(*o*) ⇔ *is_invoiced*(*o*)
end

The ORDER specification declares a sort *Order* for orders, and "observer" operations *reference* and *ordered_qty* that, for a given order, give the ordered product and the ordered quantity (a positive natural number in the sort *Pos*, which is a subsort of *Nat*) of this, respectively. The predicates *is_pending* and *invoiced* test whether an order is pending or invoiced, respectively. According to the axiom, an order is either pending or invoiced.

spec STOCK =
    NAT
then
    sorts *Stock, Product*
    ops *qty* : *Product* × *Stock* →? *Nat*;
           add : *Product* × *Pos* × *Stock* →? *Stock*;
           remove : *Product* × *Pos* × *Stock* →? *Stock*
    pred __∈__ : *Product* × *Stock*
    vars *p, p'*: *Product*; *n*: *Pos*; *s*: *Stock*
- *def qty*(*p, s*) ⇔ *p* ∈ *s*
- *def add*(*p, n, s*) ⇔ *p* ∈ *s*
- *def remove*(*p, n, s*) ⇔ *p* ∈ *s* ∧ *qty*(*p, s*) ≥ *n*
- *qty*(*p, add*(*p, n, s*)) = *qty*(*p, s*) + *n* if *p* ∈ *s*
- *qty*(*p', add*(*p, n, s*)) = *qty*(*p', s*) if *p* ∈ *s* ∧ *p'* ∈ *s* ∧ ¬ *p'* = *p*
- *qty*(*p, remove*(*p, n, s*)) = *qty*(*p, s*) −? *n* if *p* ∈ *s* ∧ *qty*(*p, s*) ≥ *n*
- *qty*(*p', remove*(*p, n, s*)) = *qty*(*p', s*) if *p* ∈ *s* ∧ *p'* ∈ *s* ∧ ¬ *p'* = *p*
end

The STOCK specification declares a sort *Stock* for stocks and (partial) operations *qty, add* and *remove* for providing information about the number of items of a certain product in stock, and for adding and removing a quantity of items of a product in stock, respectively. The predicate *is_in* (displayed as ∈) tests whether a product is in stock. The first three axioms specify when the partial operations are defined. The remaining axioms specify how the quantity of a product is changed by the *add* and *remove* operations.

An Unintended Consequence

The STOCK specification has some logical consequences that are clearly revealed as not being intended when we look at the process that is being modelled.

The source of the problem is the last axiom. There, $remove(p,n,s)$ may be undefined as its precondition $qty(p,s) \geq n$ is not required to hold. As a consequence, we can prove that each stock contains at most one product:

$$\forall p, p' : Product; \ s : Stock . \ p \in s \wedge p' \in s \Rightarrow p = p'.$$

It is certainly intended to have stocks with more than one product; hence, this consequence of the specification is not intended, showing that the specification is not in accordance with our informal understanding of the problem. This unintended consequence can be proved using the basic-specification proof calculus of Sect. 3.2; however, the recognition that this reveals a discrepancy between the specification and the informal understanding of the problem is necessarily outside the scope of formal calculi.

We first prove a lemma in the specification NAT, using induction. Recall that NAT contains the sort generation constraint $(\{nat\}, \{0; \ suc\}, id)$. We apply the rule Induction with

$$\Psi_{nat}(n) \equiv suc(n) \leq n \Rightarrow false.$$

This means that

$$\varphi_1 \equiv D(0) \Rightarrow \Psi_{nat}(0)$$
$$\varphi_2 \equiv D(suc(n)) \wedge \Psi_{nat}(n) \Rightarrow \Psi_{nat}(suc(n))$$

We now prove φ_2. Assume $D(suc(n)) \wedge \Psi_{nat}(n)$. By $\wedge$-Elim2, $\Psi_{nat}(n) \equiv suc(n) \leq n \Rightarrow false$. Assume that $suc(suc(n)) \leq suc(n)$. By leq_def3_Nat, $\wedge$-Elim1 and $\Rightarrow$-Elim, $suc(n) \leq n$. With Ψ_{nat} and $\Rightarrow$-Elim, we arrive at $false$. By $\Rightarrow$-Intro, we obtain $suc(suc(n)) \leq suc(n) \Rightarrow false$, which is $\Psi_{nat}(suc(n))$. Again by $\Rightarrow$-Intro, we obtain $D(suc(n)) \wedge \Psi_{nat}(n) \Rightarrow \Psi_{nat}(suc(n))$, which is just φ_2.

φ_1 is easy: it follows from leq_def2_Nat by Substitution. By $\wedge$-Intro, we then have $\varphi_1 \wedge \varphi_2$. Hence, by Induction, we arrive at $\forall n : Nat . \Psi_{nat}(n)$, which is

$$\forall n : Nat . \ suc(n) \leq n \Rightarrow false. \tag{1}$$

Let us now come to the proof of the unintended consequence of STOCK:

$$\forall p, p' : Product; \ s : Stock . \ p \in s \wedge p' \in s \Rightarrow p = p'.$$

Using $\forall$-Intro and $\Rightarrow$-Intro, we can reduce this to proving that $p = p'$ follows from

$$p \in s \wedge p' \in s. \tag{2}$$

We do this with the rule Tertium non datur. With the assumption $p = p'$, we immediately have $p = p'$. It remains to show $p = p'$ under the assumption

$$p = p' \Rightarrow false. \tag{3}$$

From (2) and (3) by $\wedge$-Intro, $p \in s \wedge p' \in s \wedge p = p' \Rightarrow false$. With $\Rightarrow$-Elim and the last axiom of STOCK,[12] $qty(p', remove(p, n, s)) = qty(p', c)$. By Function strictness, $D(remove(p, n, s))$. With the third axiom of STOCK, $\wedge$-Elim1, $\Rightarrow$-Elim and $\wedge$-Elim2, we arrive at

$$qty(p, s) \geq n, \tag{4}$$

and by Predicate strictness,

$$D(qty(p, s)). \tag{5}$$

From geq_defNat in the specification NAT, by $\wedge$-Elim1, $m \geq n \Rightarrow n \leq m$. Rules sum1 and trans of the calculus for structured specifications allow us to use this consequence also in STOCK. By Substitution, we obtain $D(qty(p, s)) \Rightarrow qty(p, s) \geq n \Rightarrow n \leq qty(p, s)$. By (5) and (4) using $\Rightarrow$-Elim twice, $n \leq qty(p, s)$. By Substitution,

$$D(suc(qty(p, s))) \Rightarrow suc(qty(p, s)) \leq qty(p, s). \tag{6}$$

From Totality, we have $D(suc(x))$, and with Substitution, we obtain $D(qty(p, s)) \Rightarrow D(suc(qty(p, s)))$. $\Rightarrow$-Elim with (5) gives us

$$D(suc(qty(p, s))).$$

With $\Rightarrow$-Elim and (6), we obtain

$$suc(qty(p, s)) \leq qty(p, s). \tag{7}$$

Equation (1), using again the rules of the calculus for structured specifications, is also derivable in STOCK. With $\forall$-Elim and Substitution, we obtain

$$D(qty(p, s)) \Rightarrow suc(qty(p, s)) \leq qty(p, s) \Rightarrow false$$

With (5) and (7), using $\Rightarrow$-Elim twice, we arrive at $false$. By Absurdity, $p = p'$, which is what we needed to prove.   □

Of course, this proof is rather detailed and tedious. It shows only how proofs could be carried out in principle. In practice, one would use an automated or interactive theorem prover. The Heterogeneous Tool Set (Hets) provides an interface between CASL and the theorem prover Isabelle, which can be used to carry out the proof much more succinctly.

The unintended consequence can be avoided by adding the following missing condition:

- $qty(p', remove(p, n, s)) = qty(p', s)$ if
  $p\ is\_in\ s \wedge p'\ is\_in\ s \wedge \neg\ p' = p \wedge qty(p, s) \geq n.$

---

[12] Note that ψ *if* φ is syntactical sugar for $\varphi \Rightarrow \psi$, and that *not* φ is syntactical sugar for $\varphi \Rightarrow false$.

10.2 Specification of the Warehouse System

spec INVOICE =
    ORDER
and
    STOCK
then
    free type
       Msg ::= *success* | *not_pending* | *not_referenced* | *not_enough_qty*
    free type *OSM* ::= *mk*(*order_of*:*Order*; *stock_of*:*Stock*; *msg_of*:*Msg*)
    pred *referenced*(*o*: *Order*; *s*: *Stock*) $\Leftrightarrow$ *reference*(*o*) $\in$ *s*
    pred *enough_qty*(*o*: *Order*; *s*: *Stock*) $\Leftrightarrow$
        ordered_qty(*o*) $\leq$ *qty*(*reference*(*o*), *s*)
    pred *invoice_ok*(*o*: *Order*; *s*: *Stock*) $\Leftrightarrow$
        is_pending(*o*) $\wedge$ *referenced*(*o*, *s*) $\wedge$ *enough_qty*(*o*, *s*)
    op   *invoice_order* : *Order* $\times$ *Stock* $\rightarrow$ *OSM*
    vars *o*: *Order*; *s*: *Stock*
    • *is_invoiced*(*order_of*(*invoice_order*(*o*, *s*))) *if invoice_ok*(*o*, *s*)
    • *stock_of*(*invoice_order*(*o*, *s*)) =
    remove(*reference*(*o*), *ordered_qty*(*o*), *s*) *if*
    invoice_ok(*o*, *s*)
    • *order_of*(*invoice_order*(*o*, *s*)) = *o if* $\neg$ *invoice_ok*(*o*, *s*)
    • *stock_of*(*invoice_order*(*o*, *s*)) = *s if* $\neg$ *invoice_ok*(*o*, *s*)
    • *reference*(*order_of*(*invoice_order*(*o*, *s*))) = *reference*(*o*)
    • *ordered_qty*(*order_of*(*invoice_order*(*o*, *s*))) = *ordered_qty*(*o*)
    • *msg_of*(*invoice_order*(*o*, *s*)) = *success if invoice_ok*(*o*, *s*)
    • *msg_of*(*invoice_order*(*o*, *s*)) = *not_pending if* $\neg$ *is_pending*(*o*)
    • *msg_of*(*invoice_order*(*o*, *s*)) = *not_referenced if*
    is_pending(*o*) $\wedge$ $\neg$ *referenced*(*o*, *s*)
    • *msg_of*(*invoice_order*(*o*, *s*)) = *not_enough_qty if*
    is_pending(*o*) $\wedge$ *referenced*(*o*, *s*) $\wedge$ $\neg$ *enough_qty*(*o*, *s*)
end

The INVOICE specification defines a predicate *invoice_ok* for testing the conditions for invoicing an order with respect to a stock: the order must be pending, the ordered product must be in stock and the ordered quantity must be less than or equal to the quantity which is in stock. The definition of the predicate uses two auxiliary predicates *referenced* and *enough_qty*, also defined by this specification. (Note that the definition of predicates is written in an abbreviated syntax that expands to a predicate declaration contributing to the signature and an axiom.) The main operation of the specification is the *invoice_order* operation for invoicing an order with respect to a stock. It takes an order and a stock as arguments and returns updated versions of these: the state of the order is changed to "invoiced" and the quantity of the ordered product in stock is reduced by the ordered quantity, but only if the order is invoiceable. Furthermore, the operation returns a message providing information about whether the operation has succeeded or has failed because one of the conditions for invoicing failed. The effect of the operation is specified in an observational style.

spec ORDER_QUEUE =
    LIST [ORDER **fit** $Elem \mapsto Order$] **with** $List[Order] \mapsto OQueue$
then
    pred $\_\in\_ : Order \times OQueue$
    vars $o, o2: Order;\ oq: OQueue$
    • $\neg\ o \in [\ ]$
    • $o2 \in (o :: oq) \Leftrightarrow o2 = o \lor o2 \in oq$
    %% Auxiliary definitions
    ops $\_\leftarrow\_ : OQueue \times Order \to OQueue;$
          $remove : Order \times OQueue \to OQueue$
    vars $o, o2: Order;\ oq: OQueue$
    • $oq \leftarrow o = oq ++ [\ o\ ]$
    • $remove(o, [\ ]) = [\ ]$
    • $remove(o, o2 :: oq) =$
      $o2 :: remove(o, oq)$ **when** $\neg\ o = o2$ **else** $remove(o, oq)$
end

The specification ORDER_QUEUE defines a sort $OQueue$ of queues of orders to be a list in which the elements are orders. This is done by instantiating the generic $List$ specification shown in Fig. 3 and renaming the resulting sort $List[Order]$ to $OQueue$. The predicate is_in tests whether an order is in a given queue. Some auxiliary operations for appending and removing an order to/from a queue are specified as well.

spec QUEUES =
    ORDER_QUEUE
then
    preds $unicity, pqueue, iqueue : OQueue$
    vars $o: Order;\ oq: OQueue$
    • $unicity([\ ])$
    • $unicity(o :: oq) \Leftrightarrow \neg\ o \in oq \land unicity(oq)$
    • $pqueue(oq) \Leftrightarrow (\forall x: Order \bullet x \in oq \Rightarrow is\_pending(x))$
    • $iqueue(oq) \Leftrightarrow (\forall x: Order \bullet x \in oq \Rightarrow is\_invoiced(x))$
    sorts $UQueue = \{oq: OQueue \bullet unicity(oq)\};$
          $PQueue = \{uq: UQueue \bullet pqueue(uq)\};$
          $IQueue = \{uq: UQueue \bullet iqueue(uq)\}$
end

The QUEUES specification defines three subsorts of $OQueue$: $UQueue$ for queues with no repetitions of orders, $PQueue$ for queues containing only pending orders and $IQueue$ for queues containing only invoiced orders.

spec WHS =

QUEUES
and
INVOICE
then
free type
    $GState ::= mk\_gs(porders{:}PQueue;\ iorders{:}IQueue;\ the\_stock{:}Stock)$
op $the\_orders(gs{:}\ GState){:}\ OQueue = porders(gs) \mathbin{+\!\!+} iorders(gs)$
preds $referenced(oq{:}\ OQueue;\ s{:}\ Stock) \Leftrightarrow$
        $\forall\ x{:}\ Order \bullet x \in oq \Rightarrow referenced(x,\ s);$
        $consistent(gs{:}\ GState) \Leftrightarrow$
            $unicity(the\_orders(gs))$
                $\wedge\ referenced(the\_orders(gs),\ the\_stock(gs))$
sort $VGS = \{gs{:}\ GState \bullet consistent(gs)\}$
pred $invoiceable(pq{:}\ PQueue;\ s{:}\ Stock) \Leftrightarrow$
        $\exists\ o{:}\ Order \bullet o \in pq \wedge enough\_qty(o,\ s)$
op $first\_invoiceable : PQueue \times Stock \rightarrow?\ Order$
%% axioms for *first_invoiceable*
vars $o{:}\ Order;\ pq{:}\ PQueue;\ s{:}\ Stock$
• $def\ first\_invoiceable(pq,\ s) \Leftrightarrow invoiceable(pq,\ s)$
• $first\_invoiceable(o :: pq\ as\ PQueue,\ s) =$
  $o\ when\ enough\_qty(o,\ s)\ else\ first\_invoiceable(pq,\ s)$
ops $new\_order : Product \times Pos \times VGS \rightarrow VGS;$
        $cancel\_order : Order \times VGS \rightarrow VGS;$
        $add\_qty : Product \times Pos \times VGS \rightarrow VGS;$
        $deal\_with\_order : VGS \rightarrow VGS;$
        $mk\_order : Product \times Pos \times VGS \rightarrow Order$
%% axioms for *mk_order*
vars $o,\ o1,\ o2{:}\ Order;\ p{:}\ Product;\ n{:}\ Pos;$
        $vgs{:}\ VGS;\ osm{:}\ OSM;\ s2{:}\ Stock$
• $is\_pending(mk\_order(p,\ n,\ vgs))$
• $\neg\ mk\_order(p,\ n,\ vgs) \in the\_orders(vgs)$
• $reference(mk\_order(p,\ n,\ vgs)) = p$
• $ordered\_qty(mk\_order(p,\ n,\ vgs)) = n$

%% axioms for the warehouse operation level
• $new\_order(p,\ n,\ vgs) = vgs\ if\ \neg\ p \in the\_stock(vgs)$
• $new\_order(p,\ n,\ vgs) =$
  $mk\_gs(porders(vgs) \leftarrow mk\_order(p,\ n,\ vgs)\ as\ PQueue,\ iorders(vgs),$
      $the\_stock(vgs))\ if$
  $p \in the\_stock(vgs)$
• $cancel\_order(o,\ vgs) =$
  $mk\_gs(remove(o,\ porders(vgs))\ as\ PQueue,\ iorders(vgs),$
      $the\_stock(vgs))$
  $when\ o \in porders(vgs)$
  $else\ mk\_gs(porders(vgs),\ remove(o,\ iorders(vgs))\ as\ IQueue,$

$$add(reference(o), ordered\_qty(o), the\_stock(vgs)))$$
$$when\ o \in iorders(vgs)\ else\ vgs$$

- $add\_qty(p, n, vgs) = vgs\ if\ \neg\ p \in the\_stock(vgs)$
- $add\_qty(p, n, vgs) =$
  $mk\_gs(porders(vgs), iorders(vgs), add(p, n, the\_stock(vgs)))\ if$
  $p \in the\_stock(vgs)$
- $deal\_with\_order(vgs) = vgs\ if$
  $\neg\ invoiceable(porders(vgs), the\_stock(vgs))$
- $(o1 = first\_invoiceable(porders(vgs), the\_stock(vgs))\ \wedge$
  $osm = invoice\_order(o1, the\_stock(vgs))\ \wedge$
  $o2 = order\_of(osm)\ \wedge$
  $s2 = stock\_of(osm)\ \Rightarrow$
  $deal\_with\_order(vgs) =$
  $mk\_gs(remove(o1, porders(vgs))\ as\ PQueue,$
  $\qquad iorders(vgs) \leftarrow o2\ as\ IQueue, s2))\ if$
  $invoiceable(porders(vgs), the\_stock(vgs))$

end

The WHS specification defines a free type of global states. The components of a global state are a queue of pending orders, a queue of invoiced orders and a stock. A predicate *consistent* defines a desired invariant property for states, and a subtype *VGS* of consistent states is defined. A state is consistent if all orders in the queues are distinct and the products referenced in the orders are products in the stock. A number of state-changing operations are declared and defined in a constructive style by the last seven axioms of the specification: *new_order* for making a new order (i.e. adding it to the queue of pending orders if the ordered product is in stock), *cancel_order* for cancelling an order (i.e. removing it from the queues of orders, and, if the order was invoiced, also "backdating" the stock), *add_qty* for adding a quantity of a product to the stock if the product is in stock and *deal_with_order* for dealing with an order (i.e. invoicing the first invoiceable order, if any, in the queue of pending orders and moving it to the queue of invoiced orders). In order to make the specification of *new_order* constructive, an *Order* constructor *mk_order* is needed, so this is specified as well (since ORDER does not provide this). In addition a number of auxiliary functions and predicates are defined.

We suggest that the *the_orders* operation in WHS should return a *UQueue* instead of an *OQueue*, since this is more precise. Then the clause

$$unicity(the\_orders(gs))$$

in the definition of *consistent* could be omitted.

10.3 The Architectural Decomposition

Before we write an architectural specification that describes a modular structure for the implementation of WHS, let us point out that the simplified

fragment of the CASL architectural specifications studied in Sect. 7 forces the
user to combine all the units involved in the final result expression. This often leads to quite complicated unit expressions, which can be considerably
simplified by "storing" the results of subexpressions as named units within
the list of unit declarations. Indeed, CASL provides *unit definitions*, with a
self-evident syntax and rather obvious semantics, to allow this. We use this
feature in the final architectural specification below:[13]

arch spec WAREHOUSE =
  units
    NATALG: NAT;
    ORDERFUN: NAT → ORDER;
    ORDERALG = ORDERFUN [NATALG];
    STOCKFUN: NAT → STOCK;
    STOCKALG = STOCKFUN [NATALG];
    INVOICEFUN: { ORDER **and** STOCK } → INVOICE;
    QUEUESFUN: ORDER → QUEUES;
    WHSFUN : { QUEUES **and** INVOICE } → WHS;
  result WHSFUN[QUEUESFUN[ORDERALG]
            and INVOICEFUN[ORDERALG **and** STOCKALG]]
end

The architectural specification requires a number of units that should
be combined in the way explained in the "result" part. The unit NATALG
should implement NAT. The generic units ORDERFUN should expand units
implementing NAT into implementations of ORDER. Similar remarks hold
for the generic units STOCKFUN and QUEUESFUN. ORDERALG and STOCK-
ALG should be instantiations of ORDERFUN and STOCKFUN with NATALG.
The generic unit INVOICEFUN should expand implementations of ORDER
and STOCK into implementations of INVOICE. A similar remark holds for
WHSFUN.

A Sharing Problem

The verification semantics of architectural specifications that we presented in
Sect. 7.2 cannot be implemented in full, as it involves some true verification

---

[13] In the original specification, parametrized units with two arguments were also
used. Since, for simplicity, we covered only one-argument units in Sect. 7, in some
places here we combine two units (as well as their specifications) into one. We
have also omitted, in this chapter, and hence in this architectural specification
as well, imports for unit specifications, used in the original specification to require the generic units INVOICEFUN and WHSFUN to work only for arguments
that extend NATALG and, correspondingly, ORDERALG and STOCKALG. Since
the specifications of these omitted imports are included in the specifications of
unit parameters, leaving them out has no effect on the way the units can be
implemented.

conditions (captured notably by the last premise in the rule for unit instantiation in Fig. 12). However, a good part of it can be implemented and provides
useful support for the user. An *extended static analysis* of CASL architectural
specifications can be defined along the same lines as for the verification semantics, but replacing the specifications involved with their signatures. Such
an extended static analysis is implemented within the Heterogeneous Tool Set
[45]. Checking the above architectural specification with this tool leads to the
following error message:

```
Analyzing arch spec Warehouse
*** Error Invoice.casl:208.36-208.50, Amalgamability is not ensured:
sorts Product in OrderFun [NatAlg] and Product in StockFun [NatAlg]
might be different
```

The problem arises because *Product* is declared independently in OR-
DER and in STOCK. Consequently, its realizations in ORDERALG = OR-
DERFUN[NATALG] and STOCKALG = STOCKFUN[NATALG] may be different
and therefore not amalgamable in the arguments for INVOICEFUN and WHS-
FUN.

Technically, this can be seen by studying the rule for unit amalgamation
in Fig. 12; see also the corresponding (second) diagram in Fig. 13. Namely,
elaboration of the two unit terms defining ORDERALG and STOCKALG leads
to a new sort name for *Product* in each case, and therefore two copies of
it will occur in the "global signature" Σ'_G, one linked to the occurrence of
Product in Σ_1 via i_1; θ'_2, and the other to its occurrence in Σ_2 via i_2; θ'_1 (where
Σ_1 and Σ_2 are the signatures of ORDERALG and STOCKALG, respectively).
However, the union signature $\Sigma_1 \cup \Sigma_2$ contains only one occurrence of *Product*,
and therefore for any morphism $j \colon (\Sigma_1 \cup \Sigma_2) \to \Sigma'_G$, either $\iota_1; j \neq i_1; \theta'_2$ or
$\iota_2; j \neq i_2; \theta'_1$. Consequently, the rule cannot be applied, and the analysis of
the amalgamation expression fails.

This problem can be avoided by declaring the *Product* sort only in a separate specification PRODUCT and letting ORDER and STOCK extend
PRODUCT. Then we can use the extended static semantics to show the
correctness of this corrected architectural decomposition:

arch spec WAREHOUSE =
  units
    NATALG: NAT;
    PRODUCTALG: PRODUCT;
    ORDERFUN: { NAT **and** PRODUCT } → ORDER;
    ORDERALG = ORDERFUN [NATALG **and** PRODUCTALG];
    STOCKFUN: { NAT **and** PRODUCT } → STOCK;
    STOCKALG = STOCKFUN [NATALG **and** PRODUCTALG];
    INVOICEFUN: { ORDER **and** STOCK } → INVOICE;
    QUEUESFUN: ORDER → QUEUES;
    WHSFUN: { QUEUES **and** INVOICE } → WHS

result WhsFun [QueuesFun [OrderAlg] **and**
          InvoiceFun [OrderAlg **and** StockAlg]]
end

Referring again to the rule for amalgamation and the corresponding diagrams in Figs. 12 and 13, respectively, the sort name for *Product* is now introduced to the "global signature" only once (when ProductAlg is declared). It is linked to the corresponding names in both Σ_1 and Σ_2 (as before, Σ_1 and Σ_2 are the signatures of OrderAlg and StockAlg, respectively)– consequently, the appropriate morphism $j\colon (\Sigma_1 \cup \Sigma_2) \to \Sigma'_G$ exists, and the rule can be applied with no trouble.

Inconsistent Unit Specifications

There is also a problem with the parameterized units InvoiceFun and Whs-Fun above: their specifications are inconsistent. This is because both IN-VOICE and WHS further constrain some operation symbols occurring in the argument specification ORDER. Hence, a persistent unit function from the model class of the argument specification to that of the result specification cannot exist: those models that do not meet the further constraint cannot be mapped persistently. In WHS, the problem is the *mk_order* function, and in INVOICE, it is the *invoice_order* function. To show, for example, inconsistency of the specification for InvoiceFun, notice that INVOICE $\models \exists o_1, o_2 : Order \,.\, o_1 \neq o_2$, because INVOICE contains a function *invoice_order* that allows one to change the status of an order from *is_pending* to *is_invoiced*. On the other hand, ORDER $\not\models \exists o1, o2 : Order \,.\, o_1 \neq o_2$, because there is an ORDER-model with a singleton carrier set for the sort *Order*. In particular, this ORDER-model does not have an INVOICE-extension.

The deeper reason for these problems is that the specification ORDER is not detailed enough to ensure that the unit OrderAlg can be used in the way needed by the functions *mk_order* and *invoice_order* as specified in INVOICE and WHS. This means that the architectural specification Warehouse represents an unrealistic design decision that cannot lead to an implementation.

Indeed, very loose specifications are often not sufficient in general as good specifications of the components to appear in an architectural decomposition, since often not enough information is provided to make them really usable– and so, providing an architectural design may require additional details before satisfactory specifications of components are obtained.

A better design can be obtained by first refining ORDER. A way to do this is to introduce a function creating new orders. In order to be able to distinguish different orders that happen to involve the same quantity of the same product, we need to introduce labels for orders. We assume that labels are ordered and come with an order-increasing successor function, such that it is always possible to generate fresh, so far unused labels. In the following, Boolean is a standard specification of the Boolean values (true, false), and

RICHTOTALORDER is a specification of total orders, together with a binary maximum operation.

spec ORDER' =   ORDER
and BOOLEAN **and** RICHTOTALORDER **with** *Elem* $\mapsto$ *Label*
then ops   *init_label* : *Label*;
        suc : *Label* $\rightarrow$ *Label*
   type   *Order* ::= *gen_order*(*reference*:*Product*; *ordered_qty*:*Pos*;
                             gen_pending:*Boolean*; *label*:*Label*)
   $\forall$ *l*: *Label*; *o*: *Order*
   • *l* < *suc*(*l*)
   • *is_pending*(*o*) $\Leftrightarrow$ *gen_pending*(*o*) = *True*
   $\forall$ *p1, p2*: *Product*; *q1, q2*: *Pos*; *b1, b2*: *Boolean*; *l1, l2*: *Label*
   • *gen_order*(*p1, q1, b1, l1*) = *gen_order*(*p2, q2, b2, l2*) $\Rightarrow$
    p1 = *p2* $\wedge$ *q1* = *q2* $\wedge$ *b1* = *b2* $\wedge$ *l1* = *l2*   %(gen_order_injective)%
end

INVOICE and WHS have to be refined correspondingly, such that they make use of the new function *gen_order* generating orders:

spec INVOICE' = ORDER'
and INVOICE
then $\forall$ *o*: *Order*; *s*: *Stock*
   • *order_of*(*invoice_order*(*o*, *s*)) =
   gen_order(*reference*(*o*), *ordered_qty*(*o*), *False*, *label*(*o*)) *if*
   msg_of(*invoice_order*(*o*, *s*)) = *success*
end

spec WHS' = INVOICE'   **and**   WHS
then ops   *max_label* : *OQueue* $\rightarrow$ *Label*;
        fresh_label : *VGS* $\rightarrow$ *Label*
   $\forall$ *p*: *Product*; *n*: *Pos*; *vgs*: *VGS*; *o*: *Order*; *oq*: *OQueue*
   • *max_label*([ ]) = *init_label*
   • *max_label*(*o* :: *oq*) = *max*(*label*(*o*), *max_label*(*oq*))
   • *fresh_label*(*vgs*) = *suc*(*max_label*(*the_orders*(*vgs*)))
   • *mk_order*(*p, n, vgs*) = *gen_order*(*p, n, True, fresh_label*(*vgs*))
end

This results, finally, in a new architectural specification WAREHOUSE':

arch spec WAREHOUSE' =
  units
    NATALG: NAT;
    PRODUCTALG: PRODUCT;
    ORDERFUN: { NAT **and** PRODUCT } $\rightarrow$ ORDER';
    ORDERALG = ORDERFUN [NATALG **and** PRODUCTALG];

STOCKFUN: { NAT and PRODUCT } → STOCK;
STOCKALG = STOCKFUN [NATALG and PRODUCTALG];
INVOICEFUN: { ORDER' and STOCK } → INVOICE';
QUEUESFUN: ORDER → QUEUES;
WHSFUN: { QUEUES and INVOICE' } → WHS'
  result WHSFUN [QUEUESFUN [ORDERALG] **and**
                    INVOICEFUN [ORDERALG **and** STOCKALG]]
end

Obviously, ORDER' and INVOICE' refine their corresponding unprimed variants. Moreover, we have the following refinement sequence:

refinement R =
  WHS **refined to**
    WHS' **refined to arch spec** WAREHOUSE'
  end

However, note that WAREHOUSE' is *not* a refinement of WAREHOUSE: formally, this follows because WAREHOUSE is inconsistent, while WAREHOUSE' is not. Indeed, WAREHOUSE' is simply a new design.

A further refinement of WAREHOUSE' would proceed for each component unit separately. For instance,

- ORDER' refines to ORDER'', where the latter replaces the sort *Label* with *Nat* (from the specification of natural numbers).[14] Note though that this does *not* give extra information for use by other components unless WAREHOUSE' is changed accordingly.

- The specification {QUEUES and INVOICE'}→WHS' of the unit WHS-FUN should refine to

    arch spec
    units
      WHSFUN' : {QUEUES and INVOICE'}→WHS'';
      F : WHS'' → WHS'
    result λQ : {QUEUES and INVOICE'} • F[WHSFUN'[Q]]

  where WHS'' uses a more efficient method of generating fresh labels, namely by storing the maximum label used so far as part of the state. This requires replacing the sort *VGS* with a sort involving an extra state component. The construction F needs to recover *VGS* from this new state sort.

11 Conclusion

CASL is a complex specification language that provides both a complete formal semantics and a proof calculus for all of its constructs. A central property

---

[14] This refinement would involve a signature morphism mapping *Label* to *Nat*.

of the design of CASL is the orthogonality between, on the one hand, basic specifications that provide means to write theories in a specific logic and, on the other hand, structured and architectural specifications, which have a logic-independent semantics. This means that the logic for basic specifications can easily be changed while keeping the rest of CASL unchanged. Indeed, CASL is actually the central language in a whole family of languages. CASL concentrates on the specification of abstract data types and (first-order) functional requirements, whereas some (currently still prototypical) *extensions* of CASL also consider the specification of higher-order functions [43, 62] and of reactive [10, 55, 56, 57] and object-oriented [3, 26] behaviour. *Restrictions* of CASL to sublanguages [37, 39] make it possible to use specialized tool support.

Now that the design of CASL and its semantics have been completed and have been laid out in a two-volume book [49, 50], the next step is to put CASL into practical use. A library of basic data types [58] and several case studies [1] have been developed in CASL; they show how CASL works in practice. The Heterogeneous Tool Set [45] provides tool support for all the layers of CASL, as well as for CASL extensions. Also, programming languages (formalized as particular institutions) are being integrated into CASL, leading to a framework and environment for formal software development.

Acknowledgements

This chapter reports results from the Common Framework Initiative (CoFI); hence we thank all the contributors to CoFI, without whom the chapter simply would not exist. This work was partially supported by KBN grant 7T11C 002 21 and the European AGILE project IST-2001-32747, by the British-Polish Research Partnership Programme, and by the project MULTIPLE of the Deutsche Forschungsgemeinschaft under Grants KR 1191/5-1 and KR 1191/5-2.

References

1. CASL case studies. Available at
   http://www.pst.informatik.uni-muenchen.de/~baumeist/CoFI/case.html.
2. S. Alagic. Institutions: Integrating objects, XML and databases. *Information and Software Technology*, 44:207–216, 2002.
3. D. Ancona, M. Cerioli and E. Zucca. Extending CASL by late binding. In C. Choppy, D. Bert and P. Mosses, editors, *Recent Trends in Algebraic Development Techniques, 14th International Workshop, WADT'99*, volume 1827 of Lecture Notes in Computer Science. Springer, pages 53–72, 2000.
4. E. Astesiano, M. Bidoit, H. Kirchner, B. Krieg-Brückner, P.D. Mosses, D. Sannella and A. Tarlecki. CASL: The common algebraic specification language. *Theoretical Computer Science*, 286:153–196, 2002.
5. E. Astesiano, H.-J. Kreowski and B. Krieg-Brückner. *Algebraic Foundations of Systems Specification*. Springer, 1999.

6. J. Barwise and J. Etchemendy. *Language, Proof and Logic.* CSLI Publications, 2002.
7. H. Baumeister and D. Bert. Algebraic specification in CASL. In M. Frappier and H. Habrias, editors, *Software Specification Methods: An Overview Using a Case Study*, chapter 12, pages 209–224. Springer, 2001.
8. H. Baumeister and D. Bert. Algebraic specification in CASL. In M. Frappier and H. Habrias, editors, *Software Specification Methods: An Overview Using a Case Study*, chapter 15. ISTE, 2006.
9. H. Baumeister, M. Cerioli, A. Haxthausen, T. Mossakowski, P. Mosses, D. Sannella and A. Tarlecki. CASL semantics. In [50], Part III.
10. H. Baumeister and A. Zamulin. State-based extension of CASL. In W. Grieskamp, T. Santen and B.Stoddart, editors, *Proceedings IFM 2000*, volume 1945 of Lecture Notes in Computer Science, pages 3–24, Springer, 2000.
11. M. Bidoit and R. Hennicker. On the integration of observability and reachability concepts. In M. Nielsen and U. Engberg, editors, *Foundations of Software Science and Computation Structures, 5th International Conference, FOSSACS 2002*, volume 2303 of Lecture Notes in Computer Science, pages 21–36. Springer, 2002.
12. M. Bidoit, D. Sannella and A. Tarlecki. Observational interpretation of CASL specifications. Submitted for publication, 2006.
13. T. Borzyszkowski. Generalized interpolation in CASL. *Information Processing Letters*, 76(1–2):19–24, 2000.
14. T. Borzyszkowski. Higher-order logic and theorem proving for structured specifications. In C. Choppy, D. Bert, and P. Mosses, editors, *Workshop on Algebraic Development Techniques 1999*, volume 1827 of Lecture Notes in Computer Science, pages 401–418, 2000.
15. T. Borzyszkowski. Logical systems for structured specifications. *Theoretical Computer Science*, 286:197–245, 2002.
16. M. Cerioli, A. Haxthausen, B. Krieg-Brückner and T. Mossakowski. Permissive subsorted partial logic in CASL. In M. Johnson, editor, *Algebraic Methodology and Software Technology: 6th International Conference, AMAST 97*, volume 1349 of Lecture Notes in Computer Science, pages 91–107. Springer, 1997.
17. C. Cirstea. Institutionalising many-sorted coalgebraic modal logic. In *CMCS 2002*, Electronic Notes in Theoretical Computer Science. Elsevier Science, 2002.
18. CoFI. The Common Framework Initiative for algebraic specification and development, electronic archives. Notes and Documents accessible from: http://www.cofi.info/.
19. R. Diaconescu. Grothendieck institutions. *Applied categorical structures*, 10:383–402, 2002.
20. T. Dimitrakos and T. Maibaum. On a generalised modularisation theorem. *Information Processing Letters*, 74(1–2):65–71, 2000.
21. J.L. Fiadeiro and J.F. Costa. Mirror, mirror in my hand: A duality between specifications and models of process behaviour. *Mathematical Structures in Computer Science*, 6(4):353–373, 1996.
22. J.A. Goguen and R.M. Burstall. Institutions: Abstract model theory for specification and programming. *Journal of the Association for Computing Machinery*, 39:95–146, 1992.
23. J.A. Goguen and R. Diaconescu. Towards an algebraic semantics for the object paradigm, In E. Astesiano, G. Reggio and A. Tarlecki, editors, *Recent Trends*

in Data Type Specification: Workshop on Specification of Abstract Data Types: Selected Papers, volume 785 of Lecture Notres in Computer Science, pages 1–29, Springer, 1994.

24. A. Haxthausen and F. Nickl. Pushouts of order-sorted algebraic specifications. In M. Wirsing and M. Nivat, editors, *Proceedings of AMAST'96*, volume 1101 of Lecture Notes in Computer Science, pages 132–147. Springer, 1996.

25. H. Herrlich and G. Strecker. *Category Theory*. Allyn and Bacon, Boston, 1973.

26. H. Hussmann, M. Cerioli and H. Baumeister. From UML to CASL (static part). Technical report, 2000. Università di Genova, DISI-TR-00-06, Italy.

27. D. Hutter, B. Langenstein, C. Sengler, J.H. Siekmann, W. Stephan and W. Wolpers. Verification support environment (VSE). *High Integrity Systems*, 1(6):523–530, 1996.

28. C. B. Jones. *Systematic Software Development Using VDM*. Prentice Hall, 1990.

29. B. Klin, P. Hoffman, A. Tarlecki, L. Schröder, and T. Mossakowski. Checking amalgamability conditions for CASL architectural specifications. In *Mathematical Foundations of Computer Science*, volume 2136 of Lecture Notes in Computer Science, pages 451–463. Springer, 2001.

30. CoFI Language Design Group, B. Krieg-Brückner and P.D. Mosses (eds.). CASL summary. In [50], Part I.

31. A. Lopes and J.L. Fiadeiro. Preservation and reflection in specification. In *Algebraic Methodology and Software Technology*, pages 380–394, 1997.

32. K. Meinke and J. V. Tucker, editors. *Many-sorted Logic and Its Applications*. Wiley, 1993.

33. J. Meseguer. General logics. In H.-D. Ebbinghaus, editor, *Logic Colloquium 87*, pages 275–329. North Holland, 1989.

34. T. Mossakowski. Colimits of order-sorted specifications. In F. Parisi Presicce, editor, *Recent Trends in Algebraic Development Yechniques. Proc. 12th International Workshop*, volume 1376 of Lecture Notes in Computer Science, pages 316–332. Springer, 1998.

35. T. Mossakowski. Specification in an arbitrary institution with symbols. In C. Choppy, D. Bert, and P. Mosses, editors, *Recent Trends in Algebraic Development Techniques, Proc. 14th International Workshop, WADT'99*, volume 1827 of Lecture Notes in Computer Science, pages 252–270. Springer, 2000.

36. T. Mossakowski. Comorphism-based Grothendieck logics. In K. Diks and W. Rytter, editors, *Mathematical Foundations of Computer Science*, volume 2420 of Lecture Notes in Computer Science, pages 593–604. Springer, 2002.

37. T. Mossakowski. Relating CASL with other Specification Languages: The Institution Level. *Theoretical Computer Science*, 286:367–475, 2002.

38. T. Mossakowski. HETCASL - heterogeneous specification. Language summary, 2004. Unpublished report:
    www.informatik.uni-bremen.de/agbkb/forschung/formal_methods/CoFI/
    HetCASL/HetCASL-Summary.ps

39. T. Mossakowski. CASL sublanguages and extensions. In P. D. Mosses, editor, *CASL Reference Manual*, volume 2960 of Lecture Notes in Computer Science, chapter I:7, pages 61–69. Springer, 2004.

40. T. Mossakowski. Heterogeneous specification and the heterogeneous tool set. Habilitation thesis, University of Bremen, 2005.

41. T. Mossakowski, S. Autexier and D. Hutter. Extending development graphs with hiding. In H. Hußmann, editor, *Fundamental Approaches to Software En-*

gineering, volume 2029 of Lecture Notes in Computer Science, pages 269–283. Springer, 2001.

42. T. Mossakowski, S. Autexier and D. Hutter. Development graphs – proof management for structured specifications. *Journal of Logic and Algebraic Programming*, 67(1–2):114–145, 2006.

43. T. Mossakowski, A. Haxthausen and B. Krieg-Brückner. Subsorted partial higher-order logic as an extension of CASL. In C. Choppy, D. Bert and P. Mosses, editors, *Recent Trends in Algebraic Development Techniques, 14th International Workshop, WADT'99*, volume 1827 of Lecture Notes in Computer Science, pages 126–145. Springer-Verlag, 2000.

44. T. Mossakowski, P. Hoffman, S. Autexier and D. Hutter. CASL proof calculus. In [50], Part IV.

45. T. Mossakowski, C. Maeder, K. Lüttich and S. Wölfl. The heterogeneous tool set. Submitted for publication. Hets is available from http://www.tzi.de/cofi/hets.

46. T. Mossakowski, D. Sannella and A. Tarlecki. A simple refinement language for CASL. In J. L. Fiadeiro, editor, *WADT 2004*, volume 3423 of Lecture Notes in Computer Science, pages 162–185. Springer, 2005.

47. T. Mossakowski, L. Schröder, M. Roggenbach and H. Reichel. Algebraic-co-algebraic specification in CoCASL. *Journal of Logic and Algebraic Programming*, 67(1–2):146–197, 2006.

48. P.D. Mosses. CoFI: The Common Framework Initiative for Algebraic Specification and Development. In *TAPSOFT '97, Proceedings of an International Symposium on Theory and Practice of Software Development*, volume 1214 of Lecture Notes in Computer Science, pages 115–137. Springer, 1997.

49. P.D. Mosses and M. Bidoit. CASL – *The Common Algebraic Specification Language: User Manual*, volume 2900 of Lecture Notes in Computer Science, Springer, 2004.

50. P.D. Mosses (ed.). CASL – *The Common Algebraic Specification Language: Reference Manual*, volume 2960 of Lecture Notes in Computer Science, Springer, 2004.

51. M. Nielsen and U. Pletat. Polymorphism in an institutional framework, Technical Report, Technical University of Denmark, 1986.

52. B. Nordström, K. Petersson and J. Smith. *Programming in Martin-Löf's Type Theory: An Introduction*. Oxford University Press, 1990.

53. L. Paulson. *ML for the Working Programmer*. Cambridge University Press, 1996, 2nd edition.

54. A. Popescu and G. Rosu. Behavioral extensions of institutions. In J.L. Fiadeiro, N. Harman, M. Roggenbach and J.M. Rutten, editors, *Proceeeding of Algebra and Coalgebra in Computer Science: First International Conference, CALCO 2005*, volume 3629 of Lecture Notes in Computer Science, pages 331–347, Springer, 2005.

55. G. Reggio, E. Astesiano and C. Choppy. CASL-LTL – a CASL extension for dynamic reactive systems – summary. Technical Report, DISI, Università di Genova, DISI-TR-99-34, Italy, 2000.

56. G. Reggio and L. Repetto. CASL-CHART: a combination of statecharts and of the algebraic specification language CASL. In *Proceedings of AMAST 2000*, volume 1816 of Lecture Notes in Computer Science, pages 243–257, Springer, 2000.

57. M. Roggenbach. CSP-CASL – a new integration of process algebra and algebraic specification. In F. Spoto, G. Scollo and A. Nijholt, editors, *Third AMAST Workshop on Algebraic Methods in Language Processing (AMiLP-3)*, TWLT vol. 21, pages 229-243, University of Twente, 2003.

58. M. Roggenbach, T. Mossakowski and L. Schröder. Libraries. In [50], Part VI.

59. D. Sannella and A. Tarlecki. On observational equivalence and algebraic specification. *Journal of Computer and System Sciences*, 34:150–178, 1987.

60. D. Sannella and A. Tarlecki. Specifications in an arbitrary institution. *Information and Computation*, 76:165–210, 1988.

61. D. Sannella and A. Tarlecki. Toward formal development of programs from algebraic specifications: Implementations revisited. *Acta Informatica*, 25:233–281, 1988.

62. L. Schröder and T. Mossakowski. HasCASL: Towards integrated specification and development of Haskell programs. In H. Kirchner and C. Reingeissen, editors, *Algebraic Methodology and Software Technology, 2002*, volume 2422 of Lecture Notes in Computer Science, pages 99–116. Springer, 2002.

63. L. Schröder, T. Mossakowski, P. Hoffman, B. Klin, and A. Tarlecki. Amalgamation in the semantics of CASL. *Theoretical Computer Science*, 331(1):215–247, 2005.

64. A. Sernadas, J.F. Costa, and C. Sernadas. An institution of object behaviour. In H. Ehrig and F. Orejas, editors, *Recent Trends in Data Type Specification*, volume 785 of Lecture Notes in Computer Science, pages 337–350. Springer, 1994.

65. A. Sernadas and C. Sernadas. Denotational semantics of object specification within an arbitrary temporal logic institution. Research report, Section of Computer Science, Department of Mathematics, Instituto Superior Técnico, 1049-001 Lisboa, Portugal, 1993. Presented at IS-CORE Workshop 93.

66. A. Sernadas, C. Sernadas, C. Caleiro, and T. Mossakowski. Categorical fibring of logics with terms and binding operators. In D. Gabbay and M. de Rijke, editors, *Frontiers of Combining Systems 2*, Studies in Logic and Computation, pages 295–316. Research Studies Press, 2000.

67. A. Tarlecki. Abstract Specification Theory: An Overview. In M. Broy and M. Pizka, editors, *Models, Algebras, and Logics of Engineering Software*, volume 191 of *NATO Science Series: Computer and System Sciences*, pages 43–79. IOS Press, 2003.

CASL Indexes

Concept Index

Duration Calculus

Michael R. Hansen*

Department of Informatics and Mathematical Modelling, Technical University of
Denmark, DK-2800 Kgs. Lyngby, Denmark. mrh@imm.dtu.dk

Duration Calculus (DC) is an interval logic which was introduced to express
and reason about models of real-time systems. DC was introduced by Zhou
Chaochen, Tony Hoare and A.P. Ravn during the ProCoS I Project (ESPRIT
BRA 3104, 1989–1991) [6]. Formal techniques for the construction of safety-
critical systems were investigated in this project, and in an early case study of
gas burner systems, conducted by E.V. Sørensen, A.P. Ravn and H. Rischel,
it turned out that certain requirements for such systems were not expressible
in the real-time formalisms which were available at that time.

A key issue in the design of gas burners is the need to restrict the *duration* of the undesired state where gas is leaking. This state of the system is
unavoidable, as gas must flow for a little while before it can be ignited. But
the accumulated time periods in which gas is leaking over a time *interval* of
given size.

DC was introduced as a logical approach that supported modelling and
reasoning about durational constraints on the states of safety-critical real-time
systems [147]. DC was developed as an extension of Interval Temporal Logic
(ITL) [32, 85] because many timing properties occurring in the case studies
considered were, in fact, interval properties, and if one had a modal logic
for intervals as a basis, these requirements could be formalized in a succinct
manner.

We shall present the basic concepts of DC in this chapter, with an eye
to new applications within the area of security protocols. We shall give some
background on the introduction of DC and a brief survey of some work done
on DC. In [140], there is an overview of early research on DC, in [38], there is a
detailed account of the logical foundations of DC, and in the monograph [145],
there is a detailed account of DC. A comprehensive survey of interval logics can
be found in [27]. A comprehensive introduction to modal logics is presented
in [7].

---

* This work is partially funded by The Danish Council for Strategic Research under
  project **MoDES**.

Furthermore, in the monograph [90], there is a account of temporal logics from a historical perspective, where logics based on notions of intervals are traced back to studies of the meaning of natural language by medieval logicians.

John Buridan[2], for example, regarded the present as a duration and not as a point in time, and he considered the truth of propositions relative to the choice of the present. A proposition *p is true during the present* if and only if (iff) there is a part of the present during which *the truth of p is given*. As an example (from [90]), the proposition "Socrates is alive" is true in the entire present (now) if there is a subinterval where it is given that "Socrates is alive".

Two notions of truth are in play here: a weak notion defining the truth of propositions relative to the choice of the present, and a strong notion of truth given for a certain interval, where the intuition behind the latter notion is that the proposition is true throughout this specific interval, as illustrated in Fig. 1.

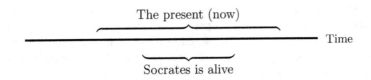

Fig. 1. The duration of the present.

Buridan's logic is formalized in [90] using the notation:

$T(I, p)$: p is true wrt. the interval I.
$given(I, p)$: The truth of p is given for the interval I.
$included(I', I)$: The interval I' is included in I.

The formula $given(I, p)$ must, for example, satisfy

$$given(I, p) \Rightarrow \forall I'.(included(I', I) \Rightarrow given(I', p)) .$$

Furthermore, the truth of a proposition p wrt. an interval I is defined as follows:

$$T(I, p) \triangleq \exists I'.(included(I', I) \land given(I', p)) .$$

In Buridan's system, the conjunction $T(I, p) \land T(I, \neg p)$ may be true in some cases, as illustrated in Fig. 2.

It should be noticed that two kinds of negations occur in this system:

- negation of predicates, for example "alive" and "dead" are negations of each other, and

---

[2] French philosopher, approx. 1300–1360

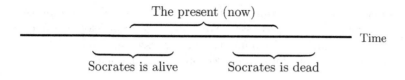

Fig. 2. A Buridan interpretation of "Socrates is alive"

- negation of propositions, for example "Socrates is alive" and "Socrates is not alive" are each other's negations.

We shall later show how this 'durational semantics' of these simple natural language sentences can be expressed in DC; but otherwise, this topic will not be covered any further here. We recommend [90] for a comprehensive treatment, which also includes more recent work in the area of artificial intelligence.

1 Introduction

The basic concepts of DC will be introduced in this section on the basis of a simple example. A formal development is given in Sect. 2. In these two sections, we shall focus on the original *Boolean state model* of DC, and an interval logic having *contracting modalities*, by which only subintervals can be reached. We shall look at a few extensions in later sections.

The example used in this section is that of a shared processor. Applications of DC in the context of shared processors and scheduling have been studied, for example, in [13, 144]. The presentation here is based on [144, 145].

1.1 Boolean State Model

A *real-time system* is a computing system with real-time requirements. We shall model a real-time systems by a set $P_1, P_2, \ldots$ of Boolean-valued functions over time, i.e.

$$P_i : \text{Time} \rightarrow \{0, 1\} \, ,$$

where time is continuous and modelled by the real numbers

$$\text{Time} \mathrel{\widehat{=}} \mathbb{R} \, .$$

Each function P_i is called a *state variable*, and it is a characteristic function for a certain aspect of a system's behaviour. The collection of functions $P_1, P_2, \ldots$ constitutes the *Boolean state model* (or *state model* or just *model*) of the system.

Consider, as a simple example, a shared processor, where n processes $\{p_1, \ldots, p_n\}$ share a single processor. We would like to develop a framework where different scheduling disciplines can be expressed and analyzed.

To formalize the behavior of a shared processor, the model must capture, at least

- which processes are ready to run on the shared processor, and
- which process (if any) is currently running.

There are many ways in which to choose the state variables. Our choice is based on [144]. Let $\Pi = \{1, \ldots, n\}$. For each process $p_i, i \in \Pi$, two state variables are used:

$$\text{Rdy}_i : \text{Time} \to \{0, 1\}$$
$$\text{Run}_i : \text{Time} \to \{0, 1\} \,.$$

The intuition is that

- $\text{Rdy}_i(t) = 1$ iff process p_i is ready at time t, and
- $\text{Run}_i(t) = 1$ iff process p_i is running at time t.

Since only ready processes may run and at most one process may run at a given time, the state variables must satisfy the well-formedness constraints

$$\begin{aligned}\text{Run}_i(t) &\Rightarrow \text{Rdy}_i(t) \\ \text{Run}_i(t) &\Rightarrow \bigwedge_{j \neq i} \neg\text{Run}_j(t) \,,\end{aligned} \tag{1}$$

for any $i, j \in \Pi$ and $t \in \text{Time}$.

These two constraints are examples of *state expressions*, which are Boolean combinations of state variables. They are used to model composite states of a system's behaviour.

1.2 The Notion of a Duration

Suppose that each process p_i, on a regular basis or on demand has to complete a task, and to do so it needs a certain amount $k_i \in \mathbb{R}_+$ of the processor's time. If p_i starts on a task at time b and finishes that task at time e, then we have that

$$\int_b^e \text{Run}_i(t)dt = k_i \,,$$

where we assume that the state variables are integrable in any bounded and closed interval. A computing system would change its state at most a finite number of times in any bounded and closed interval, so this assumption is reasonable.

The term $\int_b^e \text{Run}_i(t)dt$ is called the *duration* of the state Run_i in the interval $[b, e]$ – it is the accumulated length of all the time slots throughout which p_i is running. A notion such as that of duration is surely needed to express the condition that p_i finishes its task in a given interval.

Real-time requirements can be expressed in terms of durations. Consider, for example, the requirement that in any time period longer than 1 s there is an interval throughout which p_i is ready to run and in which p_i finishes its task. This requirement is formalized as follows:

$$\forall b, e \in \text{Time}. e - b \geq 1 \Rightarrow$$
$$\exists a, c \in \text{Time}.$$
$$b \leq a \land a \leq c \land c \leq e \tag{2}$$
$$\land \int_a^c \text{Rdy}_i(t) dt = c - a \land \int_a^c \text{Run}_i(t) dt = k_i .$$

The formula $\int_a^c \text{Rdy}_i(t) dt = c - a$ expresses that Rdy_i holds throughout the interval $[a, c]$. We also say that Rdy_i *lasts* throughout this interval. Using the formalization in the introductory part of this chapter, this formula could be expressed as $given([a, c], \text{Rdy}_i)$, i.e. the readiness of process i is given for $[a, c]$ and also for its subintervals.

Suppose that b and e are the beginning and ending points, respectively, of the period under consideration and that this period is longer than 1 second. Then the formula (2) may be paraphrased as follows: a subinterval $[a, c]$ of $[b, e]$ must exist in which Rdy_i lasts and p_i finishes its task.

The fulfilment of this property depends on the *scheduling strategy* of the processor. The important observation at this point is that even for simple requirements such as (2) above, the formalization in first order logic is heavily dominated by explicit time points (b, e, a and c), and it is not hard to imagine that this inadequacy will scale up when one is formalizing scheduling strategies and their correctness.

1.3 Duration Calculus and Interval Temporal Logic

Either a temporal logic or an interval logic could be used in order to avoid explicit mention of time points. The notion of a duration obviously relies on an interval and so do many real-time properties, and, therefore, DC was introduced as an interval logic. More precisely, DC was introduced as an extension of Interval Temporal Logic [32, 85], with the difference that ITL is based on discrete time, while DC is based on a continuous-time domain.

We shall consider bounded and closed intervals of real numbers:

$$\text{Intv} \;\widehat{=}\; \{ [b, e] \mid b, e \in \mathbb{R} \land b \leq e \} .$$

As ITL is a modal logic of time intervals, a formula ϕ is true (or false) for a given interval $[b, e]$:

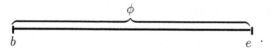

The basic *modality* of ITL is called *chop* (written "$\frown$"), and with chop two consecutive subintervals of a given interval can be reached. The formula $\phi \frown \psi$

(read as "ϕ chop ψ") holds on $[b, e]$ iff there exists an m, where $b \leq m \leq e$, such that ϕ holds on $[b, m]$ and ψ holds on $[m, e]$:

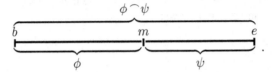

The chop modality is an example of a binary modality. Other modalities can be derived from chop using propositional logic, for example, the unary ("for some subinterval") modality $\Diamond$:

$$\Diamond\phi \;\;\hat{=}\;\; \text{true} \frown (\phi \frown \text{true}) \quad \text{read as "for some subinterval, } \phi\text{"} ,$$

where the formula "true" holds for any interval.

In modal logics, there are standard ways of defining *dual modalities*. The dual of $\Diamond$ is defined by

$$\Box\phi \;\;\hat{=}\;\; \neg\Diamond(\neg\phi) \quad \text{reads: "for all subintervals: } \phi\text{" },\qquad(3)$$

and the dual of chop is defined by:

$$\phi \smile \phi \;\;\hat{=}\;\; \neg((\neg\phi) \frown (\neg\psi)) \quad \text{read as "} \phi \text{ dual-chop } \psi\text{" }.\qquad(4)$$

The reading of $\phi \smile \psi$ is as follows:

$\phi \smile \psi$ holds on $[b, e]$
iff, for all $m \in [b, e]$: ϕ holds on $[b, m]$ or ψ holds on $[m, e]$.

After the next section, this can be calculated on the basis of a formal semantics.

On the basis of the Boolean state model, DC extends ITL with durations, which are terms of the form

$$\int S ,$$

where S is a state expression, i.e., a Boolean combination of state variables. The semantics of S is defined point-wise from the semantics of the state variables. For an interval $[b, e]$, a term $\int S$ denotes a real number

$$\int_b^e S(t)dt .$$

Furthermore, there is a special term ℓ (read as "length") denoting the length of an interval.

Primitive formulas are constructed from terms by use of arithmetic operations and relations. For example, the formula

$$\int(\text{Rdy}_i \wedge \neg\text{Run}_i) < 5$$

holds for intervals where the accumulated time for which process p_i is ready and not running is smaller than 5 (time units). This is an example of a real-time requirement for a composite state.

The following abbreviation,

$$\lceil S \rceil \ \hat{=}\ \int S = \ell \wedge \ell > 0\,, \tag{5}$$

can be used in a DC formulation of the predicate logic formula (2). The formula $\lceil S \rceil$ holds for non-point intervals throughout which S lasts, i.e. throughout which S is 1. We shall use the following abbreviation for point intervals:

$$\lceil \rceil \ \hat{=}\ \ell = 0. \tag{6}$$

The first-order formula (2), expressing a requirement for process p_i, can now be formalized in propositional DC as follows:

$$\square(\ell \geq 1 \Rightarrow \Diamond(\int \mathrm{Run}_i = k_i \wedge \lceil \mathrm{Rdy}_i \rceil))\,. \tag{7}$$

The well-formedness constraints (1), expressing an assumption about p_i, can be formalized as:

$$\begin{aligned} \lceil \mathrm{Run}_i \rceil &\Rightarrow \lceil \mathrm{Rdy}_i \rceil \\ \lceil \mathrm{Run}_i \rceil &\Rightarrow \bigwedge_{j \in \Pi \setminus \{i\}} \lceil \neg \mathrm{Run}_j \rceil. \end{aligned} \tag{8}$$

They must hold for any interval.

Together, the collection of assumptions and requirements describes in a succinct manner the model of a shared processor at a high level of abstraction.

Another goal is that DC can be used to *reason* about intervals. For the example above, we can prove that the constraint

$$k_1 + k_2 + \cdots + k_n \leq 1 \tag{9}$$

must hold, as otherwise the requirements are not feasible for the n processes under the given assumptions. To give a flavour of reasoning about intervals using DC, we now give an informal argument for the case $n = 2$.

Consider an arbitrary interval $[b, e]$ of length 1, where the assumptions and requirements for p_1 and p_2 hold. For this interval, there are two (possibly different) subintervals of $[b, e]$ for which $\int \mathrm{Run}_1 = k_1$ and $\int \mathrm{Run}_2 = k_2$. Hence,

$$\int \mathrm{Run}_1 \geq k_1 \wedge \int \mathrm{Run}_2 \geq k_2 \tag{10}$$

holds for $[b, e]$. Furthermore, we have that

$$\int \mathrm{Run}_1 + \int \mathrm{Run}_2 = \int (\mathrm{Run}_1 \vee \mathrm{Run}_2) \tag{11}$$

as the states Run_1 and Run_2 are mutually exclusive by the assumptions (8), and for any interval, the duration of a state cannot exceed that interval's length, i.e.

$$\int (\mathrm{Run}_1 \vee \mathrm{Run}_2) \leq \ell\,. \tag{12}$$

Therefore, by combination of (10), (11) and (12) and the assumption that the length of $[b, e]$ is 1, we have that

$$k_1 + k_2 \ \leq\ \int \mathrm{Run}_1 + \int \mathrm{Run}_2 \ =\ \int (\mathrm{Run}_1 \vee \mathrm{Run}_2) \ \leq\ \ell \ =\ 1\,.$$

Example: Duration of the Present

Let us reconsider the formalization of the duration of the present which was mentioned in the introductory part of this chapter. It seems reasonable to define $given(I, S)$ in DC by

$$\lceil S \rceil ,$$

assuming S is a state expression and I is the "current" interval. Furthermore, $T(I, \phi)$ can be defined by

$$\Diamond \phi .$$

If we introduce a state variable $A : \text{Time} \to \{0, 1\}$ with the intuition that $A(t) = 1$ iff "Socrates is alive" at time t, then the formula

$$\Diamond \lceil A \rceil \wedge \Diamond \lceil \neg A \rceil \tag{13}$$

corresponds to the situation in Fig. 2, where "Socrates is" both "alive" and "dead" in the present. Furthermore, observe that the negation of the predicate "alive" corresponds to a negation of state expressions, while sentential negations, such as "Socrates is not alive", would correspond to negations of formulas in DC:

$$\neg \Diamond \lceil A \rceil .$$

While (13) is satisfiable in Buridan's theory, the following natural language inference is, as pointed out in [90], invalid in his theory:

"If Socrates is alive, then he is not dead".

Using the DC formalization above, this would correspond to a deduction of $\neg \Diamond \lceil \neg A \rceil$ from $\Diamond \lceil A \rceil$. But this is not possible. One could try to experiment with other definitions of $T(I, \phi)$; but we shall not pursue this topic any further here.

2 Syntax, Semantics and Proof System

In this section, we present the syntax, semantics and proof system of DC. The presentation is based on [38, 145, 147], and DC will be defined as a predicate modal logic, where chop is the basic modality. This, and all derived modalities, are examples of *contracting modalities*, as only subintervals of a given interval can be reached using chop. With contracting modalities, only *safety* properties can be expressed. In Sect. 3.2 we shall see examples of *expanding modalities*, which are used to reach intervals outside a given interval, for example, to express (abstract) liveness properties.

2.1 Syntax

Reasoning about durations involves reasoning about real numbers, and hence DC is introduced as a predicate modal logic, where the first-order part is based on real arithmetic. Concerning the syntactical categories relating to the variables, functions and relations of real arithmetic, the meaning of these categories will be independent of time and time intervals.

The variables used in first-order quantification are called *global variables*, and we assume that an infinite set *GVar* of global variables ranged over by $x, y, z, \ldots$ is given.

Furthermore, we need the function symbols, such as $+$ and $-$, and the relation symbols, such as $=$ and $<$, of real arithmetic in the language of DC. In general we assume that there is an infinite set *FSymb* of *global function symbols* $f^n, g^m, \ldots$ equipped with arities $n, m \geq 0$. If f^n has arity $n = 0$ then f is called a *constant*. The meaning of a global function symbol f^n, $n > 0$, will be an n-ary function $\underline{f}^n : \mathbb{R}^n \to \mathbb{R}$. The meaning of a constant f^0 is a real number $\underline{f}^0 \in \mathbb{R}$.

Similarly, we assume that there is an infinite set *RSymb* of *global relation symbols* $G^n, H^m, \ldots$ equipped with arities $n, m \geq 0$. The meaning of a global relation symbol G^n, $n > 0$, will be an n-ary truth-valued function $\underline{G}^n : \mathbb{R}^n \to \{tt, ff\}$. The constants "true" and "false" are the only two global relation symbols with arity 0, and their meaning are the usual ones: $\underline{\text{"true"}} = tt$ and $\underline{\text{"false"}} = ff$.

When function symbols, for example, $+$ and $-$, and relation symbols, for example, $\geq$ and $=$, occur in formulas they appear in the usual notation and are assumed to have their standard meaning.

Concerning the time-dependent part of the language, we have the following syntactical categories:

- An infinite set *SVar* of *state variables* $P, Q, R, \ldots$ The meaning of a state variable will be a Boolean-valued function of time.
- A special symbol ℓ denoting the length of an interval.
- An infinite set *PLetter* of *temporal propositional letters* $X, Y, \ldots$ The meaning of each temporal propositional letter will be a truth-valued interval function.

The syntactical categories for *state expressions* $S, S_i \in SExp$, *terms* $\theta, \theta_i \in Term$, and *formulas* $\phi, \psi \in Formula$ are defined by the following abstract syntax:

$$S ::= 0 \mid 1 \mid P \mid \neg S_1 \mid S_1 \vee S_2$$

$$\theta ::= x \mid \ell \mid \int S \mid f^n(\theta_1, \ldots, \theta_n)$$

$$\phi ::= X \mid G^n(\theta_1, \ldots, \theta_n) \mid \neg\phi \mid \phi \vee \psi \mid \phi \frown \psi \mid (\exists x)\phi.$$

Abbreviations and Conventions

In state expressions and formulas we shall use the derived propositional con-
nectives for conjunction $\land$, implication $\Rightarrow$, bi-implication $\Leftrightarrow$, and standard
abbreviations concerning quantifiers will be used, for example,

$$\phi \land \psi \;\hat{=}\; \neg((\neg\phi) \lor (\neg\psi)),$$
$$\phi \Rightarrow \psi \;\hat{=}\; ((\neg\phi) \lor \psi),$$
$$\phi \Leftrightarrow \psi \;\hat{=}\; (\phi \Rightarrow \psi) \land (\psi \Rightarrow \phi),$$
$$(\forall x)\phi \;\hat{=}\; \neg((\exists x)\neg\phi).$$

Moreover, whenever $\neg, (\exists x), (\forall x), \Box$ and $\Diamond$ occur in formulas they have higher
precedence than the binary connectives and the binary modalities $\frown$ and $\smile$,
for example

$$(\Box\phi) \Rightarrow (((\forall x)(\neg\psi)) \frown \varphi)$$

can be written as

$$\Box\phi \Rightarrow ((\forall x)\neg\psi \frown \varphi) .$$

Furthermore, the following conventions for quantifiers will be used:

$$\exists x > \theta.\phi \qquad\;\hat{=}\; (\exists x)(x > \theta \land \phi) \quad \text{and similarly for } \geq, \leq, \ldots,$$
$$\forall x > \theta.\phi \qquad\;\hat{=}\; (\forall x)(x > \theta \Rightarrow \phi) \quad \text{and similarly for } \geq, \leq, \ldots,$$
$$\forall x_1, x_2, \ldots, x_n.\phi \;\hat{=}\; (\forall x_1)(\forall x_2) \cdots (\forall x_n)\phi,$$
$$\exists x_1, x_2, \ldots, x_n.\phi \;\hat{=}\; (\exists x_1)(\exists x_2) \cdots (\exists x_n)\phi .$$

The propositional connectives $\neg$ and $\lor$ occur both in state expressions and
in formulas but, as we shall see below, with different semantics. This does not
cause problems, as state expressions always occur in the context of $\int$.

2.2 Semantics

The meanings of state expressions, terms and formulas are, in this section,
explained in terms of the meanings of their constituent parts, i.e. the meaning
of global variables, state variables, and predicate letters. We shall assume
fixed, standard interpretations of the function and relation symbols of real
arithmetic.

The meaning of the global variables is given by a *value assignment* $\mathcal{V}$,
which is a function associating a real number with each global variable:

$$\mathcal{V} : GVar \to \mathbb{R} .$$

Let *Val* stand for the set of all value assignments:

$$Val \;\hat{=}\; GVar \to \mathbb{R} .$$

Two value assignments $\mathcal{V}, \mathcal{V}' \in Val$ are called *x-equivalent* if they agree on
all global variables except x, i.e. if $\mathcal{V}(y) = \mathcal{V}'(y)$ for every global variable y
which is different from x.

An *interpretation* of state variables and propositional letters is a function

$$\mathcal{I} : \begin{pmatrix} SVar \\ \cup \\ PLetters \end{pmatrix} \rightarrow \begin{pmatrix} \text{Time} \rightarrow \{0,1\} \\ \cup \\ \text{Intv} \rightarrow \{\text{tt},\text{ff}\} \end{pmatrix} ,$$

where

- $\mathcal{I}(P) : \text{Time} \rightarrow \{0,1\}$, for every state variable P,
- $\mathcal{I}(P)$ has at most a finite number of discontinuity points in every interval, and
- $\mathcal{I}(X) : \text{Intv} \rightarrow \{\text{tt},\text{ff}\}$, for every propositional letter X.

Thus, each function $\mathcal{I}(P)$ has the property of *finite variability*, and, hence, $\mathcal{I}(P)$ is integrable in every interval.

The semantics of a state expression S, given an interpretation $\mathcal{I}$, is a function

$$\mathcal{I}[\![S]\!] : \text{Time} \rightarrow \{0,1\} ,$$

defined inductively on the structure of state expressions by

$$
\begin{aligned}
\mathcal{I}[\![0]\!](t) &= 0, \\
\mathcal{I}[\![1]\!](t) &= 1, \\
\mathcal{I}[\![P]\!](t) &= \mathcal{I}(P)(t), \\
\mathcal{I}[\![(\neg S)]\!](t) &= \begin{cases} 0 \text{ if } \mathcal{I}[\![S]\!](t) = 1, \\ 1 \text{ if } \mathcal{I}[\![S]\!](t) = 0, \end{cases} \\
\mathcal{I}[\![(S_1 \vee S_2)]\!](t) &= \begin{cases} 1 \text{ if } \mathcal{I}[\![S_1]\!](t) = 1 \text{ or } \mathcal{I}[\![S_2]\!](t) = 1 \\ 0 \text{ otherwise.} \end{cases}
\end{aligned}
$$

Each function $\mathcal{I}[\![S]\!]$ has at most a finite number of discontinuity points in any interval and thus is integrable in every interval.

In the following, we shall use the abbreviations

$$S_\mathcal{I} \mathrel{\hat{=}} \mathcal{I}[\![S]\!] \qquad \text{and} \qquad X_\mathcal{I} \mathrel{\hat{=}} \mathcal{I}(X) .$$

The *semantics of a term* θ in an interpretation $\mathcal{I}$ is a function:

$$\mathcal{I}[\![\theta]\!] : (Val \times \text{Intv}) \rightarrow \mathbb{R} ,$$

defined inductively on the structure of terms by:

$$
\begin{aligned}
\mathcal{I}[\![x]\!](\mathcal{V}, [b,e]) &= \mathcal{V}(x), \\
\mathcal{I}[\![\smallint S]\!][b,e] &= \int_b^e S_\mathcal{I}(t) dt, \\
\mathcal{I}[\![\ell]\!](\mathcal{V}, [b,e]) &= e - b, \\
\mathcal{I}[\![f^n(\theta_1,\ldots,\theta_n)]\!](\mathcal{V}, [b,e]) &= \underline{f}^n(c_1,\ldots,c_n),
\end{aligned}
$$

$$\text{where } c_i = \mathcal{I}[\![\theta_i]\!](\mathcal{V}, [b,e]), \text{ for } 1 \leq i \leq n.$$

The *semantics of a formula* ϕ in an interpretation $\mathcal{I}$ is a function

$$\mathcal{I}[\![\phi]\!] : (Val \times \text{Intv}) \rightarrow \{\text{tt},\text{ff}\} ,$$

defined inductively on the structure of formulas below, where the following abbreviations will be used:

$$\mathcal{I}, \mathcal{V}, [b, e] \models \phi \;\hat{=}\; \mathcal{I}[\![\phi]\!] \, (\mathcal{V}, [b, e]) = \text{tt}$$
$$\mathcal{I}, \mathcal{V}, [b, e] \not\models \phi \;\hat{=}\; \mathcal{I}[\![\phi]\!] \, (\mathcal{V}, [b, e]) = \text{ff} \, .$$

The definition of $\mathcal{I}[\![\phi]\!]$ is

- $\mathcal{I}, \mathcal{V}, [b, e] \models X$ iff $X_{\mathcal{I}}([b, e]) = \text{tt}$.

- $\mathcal{I}, \mathcal{V}, [b, e] \models G^n(\theta_1, \ldots, \theta_n)$ iff $\underline{G}^n(c_1, \ldots, c_n) = \text{tt}$,
  where $c_i = \mathcal{I}[\![\theta_i]\!](\mathcal{V}, [b, e])$ for $1 \le i \le n$.

- $\mathcal{I}, \mathcal{V}, [b, e] \models \neg\phi$ iff $\mathcal{I}, \mathcal{V}, [b, e] \not\models \phi$.

- $\mathcal{I}, \mathcal{V}, [b, e] \models \phi \vee \psi$ iff $\mathcal{I}, \mathcal{V}, [b, e] \models \phi$ or $\mathcal{I}, \mathcal{V}, [b, e] \models \psi$.

- $\mathcal{I}, \mathcal{V}, [b, e] \models \phi^\frown \psi$ iff $\mathcal{I}, \mathcal{V}, [b, m] \models \phi$ and $\mathcal{I}, \mathcal{V}, [m, e] \models \psi$,
  for some $m \in [b, e]$.

- $\mathcal{I}, \mathcal{V}, [b, e] \models (\exists x)\phi$ iff $\mathcal{I}, \mathcal{V}', [b, e] \models \phi$, for some $\mathcal{V}'$ x-equivalent to $\mathcal{V}$.

A formula ϕ is *valid*, written $\models \phi$ iff $\mathcal{I}, \mathcal{V}, [b, e] \models \phi$, for every interpretation $\mathcal{I}$, value assignment $\mathcal{V}$ and interval $[b, e]$. Moreover, a formula ψ is *satisfiable* iff $\mathcal{I}, \mathcal{V}, [b, e] \models \psi$ for some interpretation $\mathcal{I}$, value assignment $\mathcal{V}$ and interval $[b, e]$.

Examples

We now give some examples of valid formulas. First, the validity of the following two formulas,

$$\lceil\rceil \vee (\text{true}^\frown \lceil S \rceil) \vee (\text{true}^\frown \lceil \neg S \rceil) \tag{14}$$

and

$$\lceil\rceil \vee (\lceil S \rceil^\frown \text{true}) \vee (\lceil \neg S \rceil^\frown \text{true}) \, , \tag{15}$$

relies on the finite variability of states, where $\lceil S \rceil$ (see (5)) means that S lasts throughout a non-point interval. Consider, for example, the hypothetical situation shown in Fig. 3, where the length of a "full" section of $\lceil S \rceil$ or $\lceil \neg S \rceil$ is half the length of the preceding section.

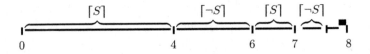

Fig. 3. A Zeno behaviour

Here, in a left neighbourhood of the point 8, S violates the finite-variability assumption and oscillates infinitely often, i.e. exhibits a *Zeno* behaviour. In any non-point interval $[b, 8]$, $0 \leq b < 8$, the formula (14) does not hold, as both $\text{true}^\frown \lceil S \rceil$ and $\text{true}^\frown \lceil \neg S \rceil$ would be false.

The next three formulas express basic properties of durations:

$$\int S + \int \neg S = \ell,$$

$$\int S \leq \ell,$$

$$\int S_1 \geq \int S_2 \text{ if } S_2 \Rightarrow S_1.$$

The following formulas are valid formulas about lasting periods:

$$\lceil S \rceil \Leftrightarrow (\lceil S \rceil ^\frown \lceil S \rceil),$$

$$(\lceil S_1 \rceil \wedge \lceil S_2 \rceil) \Leftrightarrow \lceil S_1 \wedge S_2 \rceil,$$

where the first formula holds because we have a continuous time domain, and the last formula reflects the structure of state expressions.

A 'Possible-World' Semantics

In the presentation above, the semantics of DC was "merged" into the semantics of interval temporal logic. The semantics for Interval Logic (IL) [18] is given in terms of *possible world semantics*, where a *frame* (or a *Kripke frame*) is a pair (W, R), where W is a set, whose elements are called *worlds*, and R is a reachability relation for worlds.

For IL, which has chop as the basic modality, the set of worlds is the set of bounded and closed intervals, and $R \subseteq W \times W \times W$ is a ternary relation on intervals

$$([t_1, t_1'], [t_2, t_2'], [b, e]) \in R \qquad \text{iff} \qquad b = t_1 \wedge t_1' = t_2 \wedge t_2' = e,$$

describing a partitioning of an interval $[b, e]$ into consecutive subintervals, corresponding to the chop modality.

A model consists of a frame and an interpretation function, which defines the truth value of atomic formulas in the possible worlds (intervals).

We can define the truth of atomic formulas for a given interpretation $\mathcal{I}$, value assignment $\mathcal{V}$ and interval $w \in W$, as we have seen earlier in this section. Hence, in a possible-world framework, the semantics for chop is defined as follows:

$(W, R), \mathcal{I}, \mathcal{V}, w \models \phi ^\frown \psi$
iff, for some $w_1, w_2 \in W$, where $(w_1, w_2, w) \in R$:
$(W, R), \mathcal{I}, \mathcal{V}, w_1 \models \phi$ and $(W, R), \mathcal{I}, \mathcal{V}, w_2 \models \psi$.

Possible-world semantics provides a classical way TO GIVE semantics to modal logics; see for example [45, 46]. A excellent, recent account of propositional modal logic is given in [7].

2.3 Proof System

The presentation of the proof system can be divided into one part for predicate interval logic and another part concerning the way DC extends ITL. The first part is based on the proof system S' for IL, which we presented and shown to be complete with respect to *abstract* value and time domains in [18]. In the second step we present the proof system for state durations, which was shown to relative be complete with respect to IL in [37].

Proof System: Interval Logic

The proof system S' is a Hilbert-style proof system.

In the formulation of axioms and rules, the standard notion of a free (global) variable is needed. Furthermore, it is necessary to distinguish terms which are dependent on time intervals from terms which are independent of time intervals, and similarly for formulas.

Terms and formulas which are interval-dependent are called *flexible*; terms and formulas which do not depend on time intervals are called *rigid*. A term is called *flexible* if ℓ or a duration $\int S$ occurs in the term. A formula is called *flexible* if ℓ, a duration $\int S$ or a propositional letter occurs in the formula. A term or formula which is not flexible is called *rigid*.

Note that a rigid formula may contain the chop modality.

The axioms of IL are:

$$\text{A0} \qquad \ell \geq 0 \,.$$

$$\text{A1} \qquad \begin{aligned} ((\phi ^\frown \psi) \wedge (\neg \phi ^\smile \varphi)) &\Rightarrow (\phi ^\frown (\psi \wedge \varphi)) \,. \\ ((\phi ^\frown \psi) \wedge (\varphi ^\smile \neg \psi)) &\Rightarrow ((\phi \wedge \varphi) ^\frown \psi) \,. \end{aligned}$$

$$\text{A2} \qquad ((\phi ^\frown \psi) ^\frown \varphi) \Leftrightarrow (\phi ^\frown (\psi ^\frown \varphi)) \,.$$

$$\text{R} \qquad \begin{aligned} (\phi ^\frown \psi) &\Rightarrow \phi \quad \text{if } \phi \text{ is a rigid formula.} \\ (\phi ^\frown \psi) &\Rightarrow \psi \quad \text{if } \psi \text{ is a rigid formula.} \end{aligned}$$

$$\text{E} \qquad \begin{aligned} (\exists x. \phi ^\frown \psi) &\Rightarrow \exists x. (\phi ^\frown \psi) \quad \text{if } x \text{ is not free in } \psi. \\ (\phi ^\frown \exists x. \psi) &\Rightarrow \exists x. (\phi ^\frown \psi) \quad \text{if } x \text{ is not free in } \phi. \end{aligned}$$

$$\text{L1} \qquad \begin{aligned} ((\ell = x) ^\frown \phi) &\Rightarrow ((\ell \neq x) ^\smile \phi) \,. \\ (\phi ^\frown (\ell = x)) &\Rightarrow (\phi ^\smile (\ell \neq x)) \,. \end{aligned}$$

$$\text{L2} \qquad (x \geq 0 \wedge y \geq 0) \Rightarrow ((\ell = x + y) \Leftrightarrow ((\ell = x) ^\frown (\ell = y))) \,.$$

$$\text{L3} \qquad \begin{aligned} \phi &\Rightarrow (\phi ^\frown (\ell = 0)) \\ \phi &\Rightarrow ((\ell = 0) ^\frown \phi) \,. \end{aligned}$$

These axioms are basically those of [18], except that we use an abbreviation for the dual modality of chop. The first of the axioms for L1, for example, has in [18] the form

$$((\ell = x) \,{}^\frown\, \phi) \Rightarrow \neg((\ell = x) \,{}^\frown\, \neg\phi) \ .$$

Hence, the advantage of using the dual-chop modality is that double negations concerning chop can be avoided. The more direct form obtained by using $\smile$ is also an advantage when conducting proofs.

The inference rules of IL are:

MP	if ϕ and $\phi \Rightarrow \psi$ then ψ.	(Modus ponens)
G	if ϕ then $(\forall x)\phi$.	(Generalisation)
N	if ϕ then $\phi \smile$ false. if ϕ then false $\smile \phi$.	(Necessity)
M	if $\phi \Rightarrow \psi$ then $(\phi \,{}^\frown\, \varphi) \Rightarrow (\psi \,{}^\frown\, \varphi)$. if $\phi \Rightarrow \psi$ then $(\varphi \,{}^\frown\, \phi) \Rightarrow (\varphi \,{}^\frown\, \psi)$.	(Monotonicity)

The first necessity rule reads: if ϕ holds, the ϕ holds for all prefix intervals ($\phi \smile$ false). The second rule has a similar reading for suffix intervals. These rules appear weaker than the necessity rules in [18], where the first rule has the following form: if ϕ then $\neg(\neg\phi \,{}^\frown\, \psi)$. But we shall see later (on p. 315) that the "old" rules can be derived from the new rules.

Predicate Logic

The proof system also contains some axioms of first-order predicate logic with equality. Any axiomatic basis can be chosen. Special care must, however, be taken when universally quantified formulas are instantiated and when an existential quantifier is introduced, as we shall illustrate below.

A term θ is called *free for* x in ϕ if x does not occur freely in ϕ within a scope of $\exists y$ or $\forall y$, where y is any variable occurring in θ. Furthermore, a formula is called *chop free* if $\,{}^\frown\,$ does not occur in the formula.

The axiom schemes concerning quantification are

Q1	$\forall x.\phi(x) \Rightarrow \phi(\theta)$	$\left(\begin{array}{l}\text{if } \theta \text{ is free for } x \text{ in } \phi(x) \text{, and} \\ \text{either } \theta \text{ is rigid or } \phi(x) \text{ is chop-free}\end{array}\right)$.
Q2	$\phi(\theta) \Rightarrow \exists x.\phi(x)$	

The condition that θ is free for x in $\phi(x)$ is standard for predicate logic. The second side-condition is needed, because different occurrences of x in $\phi(x)$ may refer to different intervals owing to occurrences of the chop modality, and a flexible term θ may have different meanings in different intervals.

To illustrate the need for the second part, consider the following formula $\forall x.\phi(x)$:

$$\forall x.(((\ell = x) ^\frown (\ell = x)) \;\Rightarrow\; \ell = 2x)\,,$$

which is valid and not chop-free. If we instantiate $\phi(x)$ with ℓ, which is not rigid, we obtain the following get $\phi(\ell)$:

$$((\ell = \ell) ^\frown (\ell = \ell)) \;\Rightarrow\; \ell = 2\ell\,,$$

which is false on all non-point intervals. The problem in this example is that the flexible term ℓ is substituted into three different parts of a formula, where the parts, owing to the chop modality, will refer to different intervals.

The proof system has to contain some axioms for the first-order logic of real arithmetic. We shall not be explicit about these axioms, but just write "PL" in our proofs when we exploit properties of predicate logic or properties of real numbers.

The system presented so far has neither axioms nor rules concerning durations. It is a system for "pure" interval logic. We introduce the notions of deduction and proof now, so that we can investigate this pure interval logic.

Deduction and Proof

A *deduction of ϕ in IL from a set of formulas Γ* is a sequence of formulas

$$\phi_1$$
$$\vdots$$
$$\phi_n\,,$$

where ϕ_n is ϕ, and each ϕ_i is either a member of Γ, an instance of one of the above axiom schemes or obtained by applying one of the above inference rules to previous members of the sequence. We write $\Gamma \vdash \phi$ to denote that there exists a deduction of ϕ from Γ in IL, and we write $\Gamma, \phi \vdash \psi$ for $(\Gamma \cup \{\phi\}) \vdash \psi$.

In the special case were $\Gamma = \emptyset$, the deduction is called a *proof* of ϕ. In this case we call ϕ a *theorem*, and we write $\vdash \phi$ for $\emptyset \vdash \phi$.

As an illustration of a deduction, we derive the monotonicity rules for the dual of chop:

IL1
$$\phi \Rightarrow \psi \vdash (\phi ^\smile \varphi) \Rightarrow (\psi ^\smile \varphi),$$
$$\phi \Rightarrow \psi \vdash (\varphi ^\smile \phi) \Rightarrow (\varphi ^\smile \psi)\,.$$

Proof. Here is a deduction establishing the first part. (The second part is similar.)

1.	$\phi \Rightarrow \psi$	Assumption
2.	$\neg\psi \Rightarrow \neg\phi$	1, PL
3.	$\neg(\psi ^\smile \varphi) \Rightarrow \neg\psi ^\frown \neg\varphi$	Definition of $^\smile$, PL
4.	$(\neg\psi ^\frown \neg\varphi) \Rightarrow (\neg\phi ^\frown \neg\varphi)$	2, M
5.	$\neg(\psi ^\smile \varphi) \Rightarrow (\neg\phi ^\frown \neg\varphi)$	4, Definition of $^\smile$, PL
6.	$(\phi ^\smile \varphi) \Rightarrow (\psi ^\smile \varphi)$	5, Definition of $^\smile$, PL

The following theorems are not difficult to establish.

IL2 $(\phi \smile (\psi \smile \varphi)) \Leftrightarrow ((\phi \smile \psi) \smile \varphi)$.

IL3 $\Diamond\phi \Leftrightarrow \neg\Box(\neg\phi)$.

IL4 $(\phi \frown \psi) \Leftrightarrow \neg(\neg\phi \smile \neg\psi)$.

IL5 $\Box\phi \Leftrightarrow (\text{false} \smile (\phi \smile \text{false}))$.

The associativity of $\smile$ (IL2) follows from the associativity of chop. The duality properties IL3 and IL4 follow from the definitions of $\Box$ (3) and $\smile$ (4), respectively, by repeated use of the law of double negation $\neg(\neg\phi) \Leftrightarrow \phi$ and the monotonicity rules M. The connection between $\Box$ and $\smile$ (IL5) is easily established by expansion of the definitions.

The necessity rules given in [18], for example "if ϕ then $\neg(\neg\phi \frown \psi)$", are derived from the rules N, using the monotonicity rules (IL1) for $\smile$ and 'false $\Rightarrow \neg\psi$'. Remember that $\neg(\neg\phi \frown \psi)$ is equivalent to $\phi \smile \neg\psi$.

Conventions

Because of the associativity of $\frown$ (A2) and $\smile$ (IL2), we avoid brackets in formulas containing chains of either $\frown$'s (A2) or $\smile$'s. For example, $(\phi_1 \smile \phi_2) \smile \phi_3$ will be written as $\phi_1 \smile \phi_2 \smile \phi_3$. Furthermore, we shall not mention (A2) and (IL2) explicitly when conducting proofs.

Possible-World Semantics and the Proof System: S4

The literature contains an extensive study of propositional modal logics that have a monadic modality, typically named $\Diamond$ (or $\Box$), as the basic modality. In a possible-world semantics (see p. 311), for an interval logic based on a monadic modality, the corresponding frame has a binary reachability relation $R_s \subseteq W \times W$, where

$$([c, d], [b, e]) \in R_s \qquad \text{iff} \qquad [c, d] \subseteq [b, e] .$$

The subset relation is reflexive and transitive, and below we give two axioms formalizing a reflexive and a transitive reachability relation, respectively.

A *normal modal system* [46] comprises axioms and rules for propositional logic together with an axiom, often called K (after S. Kripke),

$$\Box(\phi \Rightarrow \psi) \Rightarrow (\Box\phi \Rightarrow \Box\psi) ,$$

and an inference rule, often called N (the rule of necessitation),

If ϕ then $\Box\phi$.

This weak system (called **K** in [46]) does not place any demand on the reachability relation in a frame, and it is the basis for a class of modal logics. The modal logic S4 (see e.g. [45]), is a logic that extends **K** with an axiom (often called T) formalizing the condition that the accessibility relation is reflexive,

$$\Box\phi \Rightarrow \phi$$

and an axiom (often called 4) formalizing that the accessibility relation is transitive

$$\Box\phi \Rightarrow \Box\Box\phi \,.$$

We can show that IL is an extension of S4, by establishing that the above three axioms (K, T and 4) are theorems of IL and by establishing a deduction in IL for the rule of necessitation:

IL6 $\Box(\phi \Rightarrow \psi) \Rightarrow (\Box\phi \Rightarrow \Box\psi)$.

IL7 $\phi \vdash \Box\phi$.

IL8 $\Box\phi \Rightarrow \phi$.

IL9 $\Box\phi \Rightarrow \Box\Box\phi$.

A proof of K (IL6) can be given as follows:

1. $((\neg\psi \smallfrown \text{true}) \wedge (\phi \smallsmile \text{false})) \Rightarrow ((\neg\psi \wedge \phi) \smallfrown \text{true})$.   A1
2. $(\text{true} \smallfrown \neg\psi \smallfrown \text{true}) \wedge (\text{false} \smallsmile \phi \smallsmile \text{false})$
   $\Rightarrow (\text{true} \smallfrown ((\neg\psi \smallfrown \text{true}) \wedge (\phi \smallsmile \text{false})))$.   A1
3. $(\text{true} \smallfrown \neg\psi \smallfrown \text{true}) \wedge (\text{false} \smallsmile \phi \smallsmile \text{false})$
   $\Rightarrow (\text{true} \smallfrown (\neg\psi \wedge \phi) \smallfrown \text{true})$. $1, 2, M$
4. $(\Diamond\neg\psi \wedge \Box\phi) \Rightarrow \Diamond(\neg\psi \wedge \phi)$. $3, \text{IL5}, \text{Defn. of } \Diamond$
5. $\Box(\phi \Rightarrow \psi) \Rightarrow (\Box\phi \Rightarrow \Box\psi)$. $4, \text{IL3}, \text{PL.}$

A deduction of the rule of necessitation in S4 (IL7) follows by applying N twice and exploiting IL5. A proof of T (IL8) can be established by using L3 and M, exploiting the fact that $\ell = 0 \Rightarrow$ true. We give just the main proof steps for IL9. Observe first that

1. $\vdash (\text{true} \smallfrown \text{true}) \Leftrightarrow \text{true}$.

The direction $\Rightarrow$ follows from R since "true" is a rigid formula, and the other direction follows from L3 and monotonicity using $\ell = 0 \Rightarrow$ true. Using 1. and M twice, we obtain

2. $\vdash (\text{true} \smallfrown \text{true} \smallfrown \neg\phi \smallfrown \text{true} \smallfrown \text{true}) \Rightarrow (\text{true} \smallfrown \neg\phi \smallfrown \text{true})$,

A proof of IL9 follows by using the definition of $\Diamond$ and propositional logic:

3. $\vdash \neg\Diamond(\neg\phi) \Rightarrow \neg\Diamond\Diamond(\neg\phi)$,

Finally the definition of $\Box$.
The converse of IL9, i.e.

IL10 $\Box\Box\phi \Rightarrow \Box\phi$,

is easily established in S4:

1. $\Box\phi \Rightarrow \phi.$ IL8
2. $\Box(\Box\phi \Rightarrow \phi).$ $1, \text{IL7}$
3. $\Box(\Box\phi \Rightarrow \phi) \Rightarrow (\Box\Box\phi \Rightarrow \Box\phi).$ IL6
4. $\Box\Box\phi \Rightarrow \Box\phi.$ $2, 3, \text{MP}$

The theorem IL10 corresponds to a denseness condition on the reachability relation R_s, i.e. if i_1 is a subinterval of i, then there is a subinterval i' of i such that i_1 is a subinterval of i'.

From IL9 and IL10, it is easy to see that a non-empty series of $\Box$'s can be replaced with a single $\Box$:

IL11 $\Box^i\phi \Leftrightarrow \Box\phi$ for $i > 0$,

where $\Box^0\phi \,\hat{=}\, \phi$ and $\Box^{n+1}\phi \,\hat{=}\, \Box(\Box^n\phi)$. A similar result for $\Diamond$ is easily established from IL11 observing that $\Box^i\neg\psi \Leftrightarrow \Box\neg\psi$ for $i > 0$, and exploiting IL3 repeatedly:

IL12 $\Diamond^i\psi \Leftrightarrow \Diamond\psi$ for $i > 0$.

The theorems IL6–IL10 are the basis for establishing a deduction theorem for IL [38, 145]:

Theorem 1 *(Deduction for IL). If a deduction*

$$\Gamma, \phi \vdash \psi$$

involves no application of the generalization rule G in which the quantified variable is free in ϕ, then

$$\Gamma \vdash \Box\phi \Rightarrow \psi \,.$$

Proof System: State Durations

The axioms and rules of DC must reflect the structure of Boolean state expressions and must formalize the finite variability of state variables.

The axioms of DC are:

DCA1 $\int 0 = 0\,.$

DCA2 $\int 1 = \ell\,.$

DCA3 $\int S \geq 0\,.$

DCA4 $\int S_1 + \int S_2 = \int(S_1 \vee S_2) + \int(S_1 \wedge S_2)\,.$

DCA5 $((\int S = x)^\frown(\int S = y)) \Rightarrow (\int S = x + y)\,.$

DCA6 $\int S_1 = \int S_2$, provided $S_1 \Leftrightarrow S_2$ holds in propositional logic.

In order to formalize the finite variability of state expressions, we introduce the notion of *state induction*. Suppose that we want to prove that a formula

ϕ holds for all intervals. Consider an arbitrary state expression S and an arbitrary interval $[t_0, t_n]$. Owing to the finite variability, the interval $[t_0, t_n]$ can be partitioned into a finite number of sections, where either $\lceil S \rceil$ or $\lceil \neg S \rceil$ holds on each section. This situation is illustrated in Fig. 4.

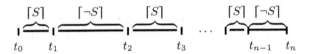

Fig. 4. Finite variability of S

The main idea of state induction is the following.

- Base case: ϕ is established for a point interval.
- Induction step: it is established that ϕ holds for an interval of the form $X \cap (\lceil S \rceil \vee \lceil \neg S \rceil)$, under the assumption that $X \Rightarrow \phi$. Hence, from an arbitrary interval X on which ϕ holds,

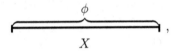

we can conclude that ϕ holds for a larger interval, where X is extended by a section throughout which either S or $\neg S$ holds,

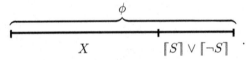

Consider the situation in Fig. 4. The base case guarantees that ϕ holds for the point interval $[t_0, t_0]$. Applying the induction step once (X being $[t_0, t_0]$) we know that ϕ holds on $[t_0, t_1]$. After n repetitions of the inductive step we can conclude that ϕ holds on the full interval $[t_0, t_n]$. Hence, we can conclude that ϕ holds on any interval, under the assumption of finite variability.

Notice that this induction principle would not work for the hypothetical situation shown in Fig. 3, as it would not be possible, for example, to go beyond time point 8 when the above process is started at time 0.

Let $H(X)$ be a formula containing a propositional letter X and let $S_1, S_2, ..., S_n$ be any finite collection of state expressions which are *complete* in the sense that

$$\left(\bigvee_{i=1}^{n} S_i \right) \Leftrightarrow 1 .$$

For a complete collection of state expressions: $S_1, S_2, ..., S_n$, there are two *induction rules*:

IR1   If $H(\lceil\rceil)$ and $H(X) \Rightarrow H(X \vee \bigvee_{i=1}^{n}(X \frown \lceil S_i \rceil))$
then $H(\text{true})$

and

IR2   If $H(\lceil\rceil)$ and $H(X) \Rightarrow H(X \vee \bigvee_{i=1}^{n}(\lceil S_i \rceil \frown X))$
then $H(\text{true})$,

where $H(\phi)$ denotes the formula obtained from $H(X)$ by replacing every occurrence of X in H with ϕ.

In these rules $H(\lceil\rceil)$ is called the *base case*, $H(X)$ is called the *induction hypothesis* and X is called the *induction letter*.

The deduction theorem for IL (Theorem 1) extends to DC [38].

Theorem 2 *(Deduction for DC). If a deduction*

$$\Gamma, \phi \vdash \psi$$

involves

- *no application of the generalization rule G in which the quantified variable is free in ϕ, and*
- *no application of the induction rules IR1 and IR2 in which the induction letter occurs in ϕ,*

then

$$\Gamma \vdash \Box\phi \Rightarrow \psi .$$

The deduction theorems may be used to simplify proofs. In connection with proofs by induction, the following theorem is particularly convenient, as we shall see below. For a proof of the theorem, we refer to [145].

Theorem 3 . *Suppose that $\{S_1, S_2, \ldots, S_n\}$ is a complete set of state expressions. Then*

$$\left.\begin{array}{l} \Gamma \vdash H(\lceil\rceil) \text{ and} \\ \Gamma, H(X) \vdash H(X \vee \bigvee_{i=1}^{n}(X \frown \lceil S_i \rceil)) \end{array}\right\} \text{ implies } \Gamma \vdash H(\text{true}) ,$$

and

$$\left.\begin{array}{l} \Gamma \vdash H(\lceil\rceil) \text{ and} \\ \Gamma, H(X) \vdash H(X \vee \bigvee_{i=1}^{n}(\lceil S_i \rceil \frown X)) \end{array}\right\} \text{ implies } \Gamma \vdash H(\text{true}) ,$$

provided the deductions from $\Gamma, H(X)$ involve no application of the induction rules, where the induction letter occurs in $H(X)$.

The two induction rules can be used to prove properties of the finite variability of states, for example the formulas (14) and (15), which imply the non-existence of infinite oscillation of the state S around a point:

DC1 $\lceil\rceil \vee (\text{true} \frown \lceil S \rceil) \vee (\text{true} \frown \lceil \neg S \rceil)$

and

DC2 $\qquad \lceil \rceil \vee (\lceil S \rceil \frown \text{true}) \vee (\lceil \neg S \rceil \frown \text{true})$.

The proof of DC1, for example, is by induction using $H(X) \;\widehat{=}\; X \Rightarrow DC1$ as the induction hypothesis and $\{S, \neg S\}$ as a complete collection of state expressions. Using Theorem 3 (and propositional logic), the proof is completed by establishing the base case $H(\lceil \rceil)$, i.e. $\lceil \rceil \Rightarrow DC1$, which is trivial, and three easy deductions:

- $(X \Rightarrow DC1) \vdash X \Rightarrow DC1$,
- $(X \Rightarrow DC1) \vdash (X \frown \lceil S \rceil) \Rightarrow DC1$, and
- $(X \Rightarrow DC1) \vdash (X \frown \lceil \neg S \rceil) \Rightarrow DC1$.

An essential property of a proof system is that it is sound, i.e. that every theorem is valid.

Theorem 4 *(Soundness).*

$\vdash \phi$ *implies* $\models \phi$.

The proof of soundness is by induction on the structure of proofs, i.e. the soundness of each axiom and each inference rule of DC must be proved. The axioms and inference rules of IL are treated in [18]. The axioms of DC are simple and are left for the reader. The soundness of IR1 and IR2 relies on the finite variability of states, and we refer to [145] for a proof.

Another important property of a proof system is that it is complete, i.e. every valid formula is provable. As DC extends real-number arithmetic, and, furthermore, natural-number reasoning is used in several case studies, the issue of completeness is a complex matter. The paper introducing DC [147] contains a proof for the design of a simple gas burner system with respect to a specification of requirements. This proof used only induction on states. But a more intuitive proof can be given using induction on natural numbers [145, 151]. Also, in the formalization and proof for a deadline-driven scheduler [74, 139, 145]), properties of natural numbers were used to characterize the deadlines for processes with periodic requests.

We shall not go into details concerning completeness issues for the arithmetical parts, but shall mention a few classical results. In [128] Tarski proved completeness and decidability results for a theory of reals, where atomic formulas involve equality ($=$) and ordering relations ($<, \leq, >, \geq$) and terms are constructed from rational constants and (global) variables using operations for addition, subtraction, negation and multiplication.

For natural-number theory, Presburger gave, in 1930, a decision algorithm for linear arithmetic (excluding multiplication), while Gödel, in 1931, established his famous incompleteness theorem for a theory having addition, subtraction, negation and multiplication as operations.

Concerning theorem proving with real numbers, we refer to [43].

For DC, there is a relative completeness result with respect to ITL [37, 145], which shows that there is a deduction from the collection of valid ITL formulas for every valid formula of DC,. In fact, the proof of relative completeness was based on DC1 and DC2, and not on the induction rules IR1 and IR2. It is not known whether the induction rules can be derived from DC1 and DC2.

The completeness of IL, with abstract value and time domains, was proved in [17], and in [28] there is a completeness result for DC with respect to abstract value and time domains also.

We end this section with proofs of a few theorems about durations to hint at how some of the formulas which have occurred earlier can be proved. In these proofs, we use predicate logic without explicitly mentioning it.

DC3 $\qquad \int S + \int \neg S = \ell$.

The following is a proof of DC3:

1. $\int S + \int \neg S = \int (S \wedge \neg S) + \int (S \vee \neg S)$ DCA4
2. $\int S + \int \neg S = \ell$ $\qquad\qquad\qquad\qquad$ 1, DCA1, DCA2, DCA6

DC4 $\qquad \int S \leq \ell$.

A proof of DC4 can be derived straightforwardly from DC3 by ($\int \neg S \geq 0$) (DCA3).

DC5 $\qquad \int S_1 \geq \int S_2$, if $S_2 \Rightarrow S_1$.

In the following proof of DC5, we exploit the fact that $S_1 \Leftrightarrow (S_2 \vee (\neg S_2 \wedge S_1))$ when $S_2 \Rightarrow S_1$:

1. $\int S_1 = (\int S_2 + \int (\neg S_2 \wedge S_1) - \int (S_2 \wedge (\neg S_2 \wedge S_1)))$ DCA6, DCA4
2. $\int S_1 = (\int S_2 + \int (\neg S_2 \wedge S_1))$ $\qquad\qquad\qquad$ 1, DCA1, DCA6
3. $\int (\neg S_2 \wedge S_1) \geq 0$ $\qquad\qquad\qquad\qquad\qquad\qquad$ DCA3
4. $\int S_1 \geq \int S_2$ $\qquad\qquad\qquad\qquad\qquad\qquad\qquad$ 2, 3

DC6 $\qquad ((\int S \geq x) \frown (\int S \geq y)) \Rightarrow (\int S \geq x + y)$.

In this proof, we use first-order reasoning about reals:

$(\int S \geq x) \frown (\int S \geq y)$
$\Rightarrow \exists z_1 \geq 0.(\int S = x + z_1) \frown \exists z_2 \geq 0.(\int S = y + z_2)$ M
$\Rightarrow \exists z_1, z_2 \geq 0.((\int S = x + z_1) \frown (\int S = y + z_2))$ E
$\Rightarrow \exists z_1, z_2 \geq 0.(\int S = x + z_1 + y + z_2)$ DCA5
$\Rightarrow \int S \geq x + y$.

3 Extensions of Duration Calculus

In this section we shall discuss some limitations of the basic version of DC, and some of the extensions which have been studied and suggested to overcome these limitations.

When one is extending a formalism, there are several issues, for example, the following

1. What can be done in the extension which was not possible before?
2. What is more convenient in the extension?

The focus is often on the first point only. In this section, however, we shall study some extensions to DC with an eye to the second issue.

Some parts of the discussion will be based on the shared-processor model introduced in Sect. 1. Suppose for the moment that we want to specify a Round-Robin scheduling discipline with a time-slice τ_s. So, first p_1 runs on the processor for a time τ_s, then p_2 takes over and runs for a time τ_s, etc. When p_n has finished its time slice on the processor, the whole process repeats. Note, however, that a process is skipped if it is not ready to run, and stops running if it finishes its task before the end of the time slice.

A property of this discipline is:

(TS) *When a process p_i runs on the processor, it will keep running for the whole time slice unless it finishes its task.*

This may be formalized in a propositional fragment of DC by the following two formulas:

$$\Box((\lceil\neg\mathrm{Run}_i\rceil \,^\frown \lceil\mathrm{Run}_i\rceil \,^\frown \lceil\neg\mathrm{Run}_i \land \mathrm{Rdy}_i\rceil) \;\Rightarrow\; \ell > \tau_s) \tag{16}$$

and

$$\Box(\lceil\mathrm{Run}_i\rceil \;\Rightarrow\; \ell \leq \tau_s) . \tag{17}$$

The first formula (16) expresses that p_i keeps running for at least τ_s when it can do so. Notice that in order to capture the two time points where p_i starts running on the processor and stops running again, we have to consider a bigger interval covering both ends, where p_i does not run at either of the ends for some time. This explains the form of the left-hand side of the implication in (16).

The second formula (17) supplements the first by expressing that the process keeps running for at most τ_s, and together these two formulas guarantee the property (TS). This may, however, be an "over-specification" of (TS), as (17) prevents the possibility that p_2 keeps running, which would be meaningful when no other process is ready to run.

Another way to capture the length of the interval throughout which p_i is running is by using first-order quantification:

$$\forall x.\Box((\lceil\neg\mathrm{Run}_i\rceil \,^\frown (\lceil\mathrm{Run}_i\rceil \land \ell = x) \,^\frown \lceil\neg\mathrm{Run}_i \land \mathrm{Rdy}_i\rceil) \;\Rightarrow\; x \geq \tau_s) . \tag{18}$$

But there is a way in which (18) can be expressed in propositional DC. It can be done by a formulation of the form that an interval with a counter-example does not exist:

$$\neg\Diamond(\lceil\neg\mathrm{Run}_i\rceil \,^\frown (\lceil\mathrm{Run}_i\rceil \land \ell < \tau_s) \,^\frown \lceil\neg\mathrm{Run}_i \land \mathrm{Rdy}_i\rceil) . \tag{19}$$

So, even though (TS) can be formalized in propositional DC, the formulas above illustrate an inconvenience in that we need to cover the full interval in which p_i is running.

3.1 Point Properties

When a state expression S occurs in a formula, it occurs in the context of a duration $\int S$ and, therefore, it is not possible to express that S has a specific value at a given time t. To express properties about time points, Mean Value Calculus [152] was introduced. In that calculus, an *event* is a Boolean-valued δ-function, i.e. a Boolean-valued function with value of 1 at *discrete* points. An event takes place at a time point iff the δ-function of the event is 1 at the point.

Integrals of Boolean-valued functions P are replaced by their *mean values* $\overline{P}$:

$$\overline{P} \ : \ \mathbb{Intv} \ \rightarrow \ [0,1] \, ,$$

with the definition:

$$\overline{P}([b,e]) \ = \ \begin{cases} \int_b^e P(t)dt/(e-b) & \text{if } e > b \\ P(e) & \text{if } e = b, \end{cases}$$

for any interval $[b, e]$. Therefore, one can describe point properties of Boolean-valued functions by using their mean values in point intervals, and at the same time, one can also define the integral of a Boolean-valued function P:

$$\int P \ \widehat{=} \ \overline{P} \cdot \ell \, .$$

With respect to our example above, mean values are not particularly useful for expressing (TS) or any other property of the shared processor. However, the events of Mean Value Calculus may be used as follows. Let $\uparrow S$ denote the event where the state expression S goes high, i.e. S changes from 0 to 1. In Mean Value Calculus $\uparrow S$ is a formula, which is true only for point intervals at which S goes high. The property (TS) can then be represented more directly in Mean Value Calculus than in DC, since using events we do not need to cover the interval under consideration:

$$\Box((\uparrow \mathrm{Run}_i \,\widehat{}\, \lceil \mathrm{Run}_i \rceil \,\widehat{}\, \uparrow(\neg \mathrm{Run}_i \wedge \mathrm{Rdy}_i)) \ \Rightarrow \ \ell = \tau_s) \, . \tag{20}$$

A alternative approach was taken in [142], where atomic formulas were used for events, while keeping the basic calculus for the integral of Boolean-valued function.

3.2 Other Interval Modalities

In the area of artificial intelligence, Allen proposed a logic in [1, 2] that had atomic formulas for binary relations on intervals. He showed that there are thirteen binary relations for the relative positions of two intervals, and a binary predicate symbol was introduced for each of them. An example of an atomic formula is $\mathrm{MEETS}(i_1, i_2)$, which holds if the right end point of the interval i_1 equals the left end point of the interval i_2. A system based purely on first-order logic was developed with axioms like the following:

$$\forall i_1, i_2, i_3.(\text{ MEETS}(i_1, i_2) \wedge \text{DURING}(i_2, i_3)$$
$$\Rightarrow (\text{OVERLAPS}(i_1, i_3) \vee \text{DURING}(i_1, i_3) \vee \text{MEETS}(i_1, i_3))) ,$$

where DURING and OVERLAPS are two other predicate symbols in the system.

Furthermore, Halpern and Shoham introduced a modal interval logic in [33, 34] that had six unary modalities in a general setting, where they just assumed that the time domain has a total order. An example is $<B> \phi$, which holds on an interval i if there is an interval i' on which ϕ holds, where i' begins at the same point as i and ends inside i. Each of the thirteen binary relations on intervals corresponds to a unary modality. The logic of Halpern and Shoham was shown to be adequate in the sense that all thirteen relationships of two intervals, established by Allen were expressible. Furthermore, it was described how formulas can express properties of the time domain, such as discreteness and density. Unfortunately, except for the simplest time domains, the validity problem was shown to be undecidable.

With the chop modality, one can only reach subintervals of the interval under consideration, and such modalities are called *contracting*. The modalities, for example, $\square$ and $\lozenge$, derived from chop are also examples of contracting modalities. So it is clear that many of the thirteen binary relations on intervals are not expressible in a modal logic based on chop.

With contracting modalities one can express only *safety properties*, while (unbounded) liveness properties such as "eventually there is an interval where ϕ holds" cannot be expressed. In the following we shall consider *expanding modalities*, with which one can reach intervals outside that under consideration. Using such modalities unbounded liveness properties, as well as properties of the past, can be expressed and reasoned about.

Below, we shall discuss three interval logics with expanding modalities. For a comprehensive survey of interval logics, we refer to [27].

Venema's Propositional Logic

In [129], Venema developed the work of Halpern and Shoham further. An interesting geometrical interpretation was introduced, with the following idea: an interval $[i, j]$ is considered a point (i, j) in the plane. Since $i \leq j$, this point will be to the left of (or above) the line $y = x$, i.e. in the *north-western* half plane.

The unary interval modalities are now interpreted as *compass* modalities. For example, in this interpretation, the formula $<B> \phi$ reads: there is a *southern point* (below the current point) where ϕ holds.

It was shown that two of the six unary modalities of Halpern and Shoham can be expressed by the others and that chop cannot be defined from the unary modalities in a propositional framework. In [130], a propositional interval logic with three binary interval modalities, $\frown$ (denoted by C in [130]), T and D, was presented.

The modalities T and D are expanding and are defined as follows:

- The formula $\phi T\psi$ holds on $[b,e]$ iff there exists $c \geq e$ such that ϕ holds on $[e,c]$ and ψ holds on $[b,c]$:

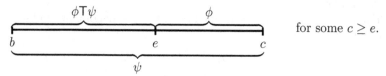

for some $c \geq e$.

- The formula $\phi D\psi$ holds on $[b,e]$ iff there exists $a \leq b$ such that ϕ holds on $[a,b]$ and ψ holds on $[a,e]$:

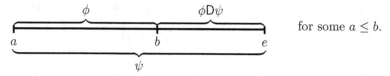

for some $a \leq b$.

In this logic, all thirteen unary interval modalities are definable, and liveness can be specified, as for example shown in [122], where a railway crossing system was considered. Furthermore, there is a complete axiomatisation of a propositional modal logic of the three modalities C, T and D [130]. However, owing to the propositional framework, some of the axioms and rules of this logic are quite complicated.

The formalizations and proofs in connection with case studies using DC often contain a certain amount of real arithmetic in order to reason about durations of states. It would, therefore, be artificial to restrict oneself to a propositional fragment when dealing with such case studies.

Neighbourhood Logic

A first-order logic with expanding modalities, called *neighbourhood logic* (NL), was introduced in [143]. There are two basic modalities in NL, which are both expanding:

- The formula $\diamondsuit_l\phi$, which reads "for some left neighborhood ϕ", is defined as follows: $\diamondsuit_l\phi$ holds on $[b,e]$ iff there exists $a \leq b$ such that ϕ holds on $[a,b]$:

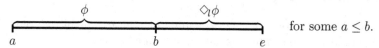

for some $a \leq b$.

- The formula $\diamondsuit_r\phi$, which reads "for some right neighborhood ϕ", is defined as follows: $\diamondsuit_r\phi$ holds on $[b,e]$ iff there exists $c \geq e$ such that ϕ holds on $[e,c]$:

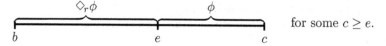

for some $c \geq e$.

NL is an adequate interval logic in the sense that all unary interval modalities [33, 34] are derivable in NL, and is, therefore, a good candidate for use in case studies.

Furthermore, chop can be defined from the two neighbourhood modalities in a first-order framework:

$$\phi^\frown\psi \iff \exists x, y.(\ell = x + y) \land \Diamond_r^c((\ell = x) \land \phi \land \Diamond_r((\ell = y) \land \psi)) \,,$$

where

$$\Diamond_r^c\psi \ \hat{=}\ \Diamond_l\Diamond_r\psi$$

is a derived modality for a right neighbourhood of the start point of the current interval.

The two binary modalities T and D are definable as well.

Later, we shall use the following two modalities of NL:

$$\Diamond_i\phi \ \hat{=}\ \ell > 0 ^\frown (\phi^\frown \ell > 0) \qquad \text{reads "for some inside interval: } \phi\text{".}$$
$$\Diamond_l^c\psi \ \hat{=}\ \Diamond_r\Diamond_l\psi \qquad \text{reads "for some left neighbourhood of the end point: } \phi\text{".}$$

Also the dual modalities $\Box_r$ ("for all right neighbourhoods"), $\Box_i$ ("for all inside intervals"), $\Box_r^c$ ("for all right neighbourhoods of the start point") and $\Box_l^c$ ("for all left neighbourhoods of the end point"), will be used. They are defined in the standard way, e.g.

$$\Box_r\phi \ \hat{=}\ \neg\Diamond_r(\neg\phi) \,.$$

Similarly to the axiomatisation of IL in [17], there is a complete proof system for NL [5]. This proof system is much more intuitive than the propositional calculus for the modalities C, T and D given in [129]. It is, however, not as elegant as that of IL, since axioms and rules come in two versions corresponding to the two basic modalities for left and right neighbourhoods.

It is possible to base DC on NL rather than on ITL. The only problem is that extra care must be taken in connection with the induction rules, as the original induction rules are not sound in an NL-based version. The problem is that intervals of unbounded size can be reached with the expanding modalities. For further details we refer to [114, 145].

Signed Interval Logic

Another approach to achieving expanding modalities was introduced in [21]. The main idea is that intervals have a *direction*.

This logic is based on the chop modality, but the "chop point" is allowed to be outside the interval under consideration. The formula $\phi^\frown\psi$ holds on the interval *from i to j* if there is a point k such that ϕ holds on the interval from i to k and ψ holds on the interval from k to j. The "chop-point" k can be any point, not just one between i and j.

In the figure below, k is chosen to be a future point and the arrows indicate the direction of the interval:

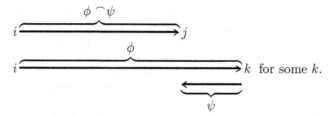

An interval where the start point is before the end point (such as the intervals from i to j and i to k above) is called a *forward interval*; otherwise it is called a *backward interval* (such as that from k to j). A point interval is both a forward and a backward interval. Thus, chop becomes an expanding modality using forward and backward intervals in this framework.

The theory for this logic, called *signed interval logic* (SIL), was first developed in [105], where a complete Hilbert-style proof system, similar to that of IL, was developed. This proof system is much simpler than that of NL. This simplification is, however, not for free, as one has to deal with both forward and backward intervals.

Aiming at theorem proving, in the context of Isabelle and Isabelle/HOL, the theory of SIL was developed further in [106–108]. In particular, a sound and complete labelled natural deduction (LND) system was established for SIL. This labelled natural deduction system was inspired by work on labelled modal logics [10,11,131], in which the possible worlds of the Kripke semantics are made part of the syntax in the form of *labelled formulas*. A labelled formula has, in SIL, the form

$$(i,j) : \phi \,,$$

where i and j denote the interval's end points, and ϕ is an "ordinary" SIL formula, which does not contain any labels.

The benefit of this approach is that it is possible to have a "proper" natural deduction system, with exactly one introduction rule and one elimination rule for each connective and modality.

SIL has the following introduction rule for chop:

$$\frac{(i,k) : \phi \qquad (k,j) : \psi}{(i,j) : \phi^\frown\psi \,.}$$

The elimination rule for chop is:

$$\frac{(i,j) : \phi^\frown\psi \qquad \begin{array}{c} [(i,k):\phi]\ [(k,j):\psi] \\ \vdots \\ (m,n):\varphi \end{array}}{(m,n) : \varphi \,.}$$

This proof system has many advantages to the Hilbert style systems and sequent calculus systems for IL, NL and SIL. We quote p. 11 of [108]:

A number of examples have been conducted in both the sequent calculus and the LND encoding, primarily the latter, though, as it soon became apparent that the LND system was much more convenient. The three main reasons being:

- Reasoning in the LND system is much more intuitive; the intervals, which are part of the logic, can easily be visualized and the connection to the semantics is clearer.
- A higher degree of automation is possible in the LND encoding; this fact owes a lot to the proper natural deduction system defined for SIL.
- Isabelle is inherently a system for doing reasoning in a natural deduction system; the sequent calculus system encoding can seem less natural to use.

The LND system for SIL was encoded in Isabelle and in Isabelle/HOL, thereby providing an excellent platform for encoding other interval logics, for example IL, DC, NL and NL-based DC.

A general approach to the encoding of interval logics in LND SIL was described is [108]. First, one defines the modalities in the logic under consideration in terms of SIL formulas. Then, one derives introduction and elimination rules for each modality. Reasoning in the encoded logic can then be conducted without the need to expand the definitions of the modalities.

The way in which one can deal with interval logics, such as IL and NL, which rely on forward intervals only, is to define (in SIL) the modalities for forward intervals only. For example, the chop modality of IL (denoted $\overset{\text{IL}}{\frown}$ below) is defined by

$$\phi \overset{\text{IL}}{\frown} \psi \,\,\hat{=}\,\, (\mathit{fwd} \wedge \phi) \overset{\text{SIL}}{\frown} (\mathit{fwd} \wedge \psi)\,, \tag{21}$$

where $\overset{\text{SIL}}{\frown}$ is the chop modality for SIL and fwd is a formula ($\ell \geq 0$), which is true for forward intervals only.

Hilbert-style proofs ($\vdash_{\text{IL}} \phi$) in interval logic and deductions in the LND system for SIL ($\Gamma \vdash_{\text{SIL}}^{\text{LND}} (i,j) : \psi$) are related as follows [108]:

Theorem 5 .

$$\vdash_{\text{IL}} \phi \qquad \mathit{iff} \qquad (i,j) : \mathit{fwd} \vdash_{\text{SIL}}^{\text{LND}} (i,j) : \overline{\phi}\,.$$

In this theorem, $\overline{\phi}$ is the SIL formula obtained from the IL formula ϕ by replacing the IL chop modality with its SIL definition according to (21).

The encoding of NL-based DC was developed further in [100, 101] aiming at a formal framework for analyzing temporal properties of security protocols.

Examples

We shall now give some examples using NL. We prefer NL rather than Venema's propositional logic, since reasoning about durations often requires a first-order setting, and we see the main role of SIL as a meta-logic which is used for the encoding of other interval logics.

In an NL-based DC, we can model a variety of abstract liveness properties in a succinct manner. For our shared-processor model of Sect. 1, we can express the fact that all n processes eventually get the same amount of the processor's time:

$$\bigwedge_{i \neq j} \forall \epsilon > 0. \exists T. \square_r (\ell > T \; \Rightarrow \; |\int \mathrm{Run}_i - \int \mathrm{Run}_j| < \epsilon) \,,$$

where $i, j \in \{0, \ldots, n\}$.

We can specify that a state will occur infinitely often in the future by

$$inf(S) \; \hat{=} \; \square_r \Diamond_r \Diamond_r \lceil S \rceil \,,$$

and a strong fairness condition for the shared-processor example can be specified as

$$inf(\mathrm{Rdy}_i) \; \Rightarrow \; inf(\mathrm{Run}_i) \,,$$

expressing that if p_i is ready to run infinitely often, then p_i will actually run on the processor infinitely often.

The operator $\uparrow$ of Mean Value Calculus can be defined as follows:

$$\uparrow S \; \hat{=} \; \ell = 0 \wedge \Diamond_l \lceil \neg S \rceil \wedge \Diamond_r \lceil S \rceil \,.$$

The property (TS) for our shared processor example, can be expressed in the same way as for Mean Value Calculus (20).

3.3 Refined Models for Reactive Real-time Systems

A variety of extensions of the Boolean state model of DC have been developed in order to support specification and verification of reactive real-time computing systems. We refer to [145] for a survey.

The method described below for handling events of a reactive system originates from [112], and was also used in [84, 100, 101], for example, where finite traces (and possibly also readiness and refusal sets) were introduced as functions of time. The reason for choosing this approach is, as we shall later sketch, that there is a clean separation of an untimed description of the events in a reactive system, from the timing properties. The presentation below is based on [101].

Let Event denote the set of all events which may occur. An *untimed trace* is a finite sequence of events

$$e_1 \, e_2 \, \cdots \, e_n \in \mathrm{Event}^* \,,$$

describing the history of the events that have occurred so far, where e_1 is the first event and e_n is the most recent event.

To describe the timed behaviour of the events, a special *trace* variable Tr is introduced:

$$\mathrm{Tr} : \mathbb{Intv} \to \mathrm{Event}^* \,.$$

The intuitive idea here is that for a given interval $[b, e]$, the trace variable gives the trace which is observed at the right end point e of the interval.

Predicates on traces can be used to express timing properties. An example of a predicate is $\text{Tr} = h$, where h is a rigid expression for an untimed trace.

The trace should satisfy a collection of well-formedness properties. Some will be shown below; for the remaining ones, we refer to [101].

First, all intervals with the same end point should have the same trace:

$$\text{Tr} = h \;\Rightarrow\; \Box_l^c(\text{Tr} = h) \,.$$

Note that the two occurrences of the flexible variable Tr appear in different interval contexts.

The trace should exhibit finite variability – only a finite number of events may occur in a bounded and closed interval. In order to express finite variability of traces, the predicate Throughout(h) is introduced:

$$\text{Throughout}(h) \;\widehat{=}\; \ell > 0 \wedge \Box_i(\text{Tr} = h) \,,$$

which is true for non-point intervals inside which the trace is constantly equal to h. The "inside" modality is used so that no constraints on the end points are imposed, and, for example, the formula

$$\text{Throughout}(h)^\frown \text{Throughout}(h \cdot e)$$

is satisfiable, where $h \cdot e$ the list obtained from the list h by adding the event e to the end.

The trace is stable if it is constant throughout a non-point interval, i.e.

$$\text{Stable} \;\widehat{=}\; \exists h.\text{Throughout}(h) \,.$$

The finite variability of traces can be formalized by requiring that for any time point, there is a left and a right neighbourhood where the trace is stable, i.e. by taking the following two formulas,

$$\Diamond_l Stable \qquad \text{and} \qquad \Diamond_r Stable \,, \tag{22}$$

as axioms.

Events can be added to the trace as time progresses. We capture this monotonicity of traces by the two properties (23) and (24) below. In these formulas, the notation $h_1 \preceq h_2$ is used to denote that the sequence h_1 is a prefix of h_2, i.e. h_1 is causally before h_2.

The trace can only grow as time progresses, i.e. the trace of a given interval is a prefix of the trace of any right neighbourhood:

$$\text{Tr} = h \;\Rightarrow\; \Box_r(h \preceq \text{Tr}) \,. \tag{23}$$

Similarly, the trace of any interval in the past is a prefix of the current trace:

$$\text{Tr} = h \;\Rightarrow\; \Box_l^c \Box_l(\text{Tr} \preceq h) \,. \tag{24}$$

These properties are, in fact, sufficient to completely describe the monotonicity and the following, for example, is a theorem:

$$\text{Tr} = h \;\Rightarrow\; \Box_i(\text{Tr} \preceq h)\,,$$

i.e. the trace on any proper inside interval is a prefix of the trace of the current interval.

An advantage of having such traces in the model is that timeless events can be related to states with a duration as described below. An event e *occurs* at a time point (i.e. $\ell = 0$), if the trace is extended by e at that point:

$$\text{Occurs}(e) \;\widehat{=}\; \ell = 0 \land \exists h \in \text{Event}^*. \left(\begin{array}{c} \Diamond_l(\text{Tr} = h) \\ \land \; \Diamond_r(\text{Tr} = h \cdot e) \end{array} \right)\,.$$

To illustrate this framework, suppose that the shared processor is a server in a network, where n agents are sending requests to the server, which then sends an acknowledgement back when the request has been processed. Let req_i denote the event that agent i sends a request to the server, and let ack_i denote the event that the server sends an acknowledgement back to agent i. We assume that it takes k_i time units for the processor to finish its task for agent i.

These network events can be connected with the server's activity as follows. When the event req_i occurs, the process p_i is ready to run on the server immediately afterwards,

$$\text{Occurs}(\text{req}_i) \;\Rightarrow\; \Diamond_r \lceil \text{Rdy}_i \rceil\,,$$

and when the server has finished its task for p_i, i.e. $\int \text{Run}_i = k_i$, then the server sends an acknowledgement back to agent i,

$$\left(\text{Occurs}(\text{req}_i) ^\frown \left(\begin{array}{c} \int \text{Run}_i = k_i \\ \land \; \text{true} ^\frown \lceil \text{Rdy}_i \rceil \end{array} \right) \right) \;\Rightarrow\; (\text{true} ^\frown \text{Occurs}(\text{ack}_i))\,.$$

In [100, 101], a theory of (timed and untimed) traces was developed, aiming at a formal framework for the temporal analysis of security protocols. For example, the theory of traces was extended with alphabets for agents, and standard operations such that parallel activities can be modelled. The theory also supports modelling and analysis of passive attacks (e.g. message interception) and active attacks (e.g. message interruption and message modification) in a network. The theory was formalized using the Isabelle/HOL proof assistant. The formalization is based on an encoding of NL and DC in SIL [106–108]. The separation of the timeless event sequences and the timed traces has the advantage that the inductive proof methods of Paulson [98] can be used to reason about the untimed behaviour, while timing issues are handled in the DC framework.

In [41], models of availability were studied within the framework of this section. The scenario is the following: A collection of clients $C_1, C_2, \ldots$ exchange messages with a server S. Some clients are, however, bad (and are called *attackers*) and want to waste the server's time, thereby degrading the server's availability for the good clients. We want to design the server so that it fulfills some availability requirements. It is not, however, obvious how to formalize such requirements. Another problem is that if there are enough strong attackers, then they alone can keep the server busy, thereby preventing the server from processing the tasks of the good clients. Thus, any reasonable formalization of availability requirements should take some assumptions about the strength of attackers into account.

Work on availability often takes an operational approach, and, for example Meadows [82] has introduced a formal framework for the communication between (possibly hostile) participants, where the concept of the *strength* of the hostile participants is considered. This framework is rather close to a possible implementation, as it essentially describes the sequence of *verification actions* the server should perform in order to detect attackers of given strength, but it is not obvious how to extract information about the availability from the framework.

A more declarative framework for the analysis of security protocols was presented in [41], where availability requirements and various assumptions, for example about the strength of attackers, can be described in an abstract manner. For example, we can express that normal service is available to trusted clients p_i, for $i \in \gamma \subseteq \{1, \ldots n\}$, a fraction x of the time:

$$\Box(\ell > T \implies (\Sigma_{i \notin \gamma} \int \mathrm{Run}_i) \leq (1 - x) \cdot \ell) .$$

The condition $\ell > T$ occurs in this formula because, for small intervals, the property $(\Sigma_{i \notin \gamma} \int \mathrm{Run}_i) \leq (1 - x) \cdot \ell)$ is not feasible.

Assumptions about the strength of attackers are modelled in a similar way. Consider a collection of attackers $p_j, j \in \beta \subseteq \{1, \ldots, n\}$, and assume that they have the ability to waste at most a fraction x_β of the processor's time, before they are detected and interrupted at the server. This assumption is formalized as

$$\ell \geq T \implies (\Sigma_{j \in \beta} \int \mathrm{Run}_j) \leq x_\beta \cdot \ell .$$

On the basis of the cost model of [82], a first attempt was made in [41] to use symbolic reasoning to extract system design parameters from these more abstract specifications of availability requirements and the strength of attackers.

4 Decidability, Undecidability and Model Checking

Interval logics are typically quite expressive logics, which are often undecidable. For example, the propositional interval logic HS with unary modalities *begins*, *ends* and their inverses, devised by Halpern and Shoham [34], has been shown to be highly undecidable for a collection of classes of interval models.

The first results for Duration Calculus [146] showed a decidability result for a simple subset of DC called RDC. The formulas of RDC are given by the following abstract syntax:

$$S ::= 0 \mid 1 \mid P \mid \neg S_1 \mid S_1 \vee S_2$$
$$\phi ::= \lceil S \rceil \mid \neg \phi \mid \phi \vee \psi \mid \phi ^\frown \psi .$$

Decidability results were established for both a discrete-time and a continuous-time interpretation.

In a *discrete-time interpretation* state variables are allowed to change value at natural-number time points only. Furthermore, only intervals that have natural-number end points are considered, and, finally, chop points must be natural numbers.

Theorem 6 *[146]. The satisfiability problem for RDC is decidable for discrete and continuous time.*

The theorem is proved by reducing the satisfiability problem for RDC to the emptiness problem for regular languages, which is decidable. The main idea of this reduction is that a letter in the alphabet describes a section of an interpretation. A letter is a conjunction of state variables or a negation of state variables. $\lceil S \rceil$ is translated as L^+, where L is the set of letters "for which S is true". Disjunction, negation and chop correspond to the union, complement and concatenation, respectively, of regular languages.

Seemingly small extensions to RDC were shown to be undecidable [146] by reducing the halting problem of two-counter machines to the satisfiability problem. The subsets considered were:

- RDC_1, which is defined by

$$\phi ::= \ell = 1 \mid \lceil S \rceil \mid \neg\phi \mid \phi \vee \psi \mid \phi^\frown\psi \, .$$

- RDC_2, which is defined by

$$\phi ::= \int S_1 = \int S_2 \mid \neg\phi \mid \phi \vee \psi \mid \phi^\frown\psi \, .$$

- RDC_3, which is defined by

$$\phi ::= \ell = x \mid \lceil S \rceil \mid \neg\phi \mid \phi \vee \psi \mid \phi^\frown\psi \mid \forall x.\phi \, .$$

The theorems established were:

Theorem 7 *[146]. The satisfiability problem for RDC_1 is undecidable for continuous time.*

Theorem 8 *[146]. The satisfiability problems for RDC_2 and RDC_3 are undecidable for discrete and continuous time.*

The satisfiability problem for RDC_1 is decidable for a discrete-time interpretation as the formula $\ell = 1$ is expressible in RDC as $\lceil 1 \rceil \wedge \neg(\lceil 1 \rceil^\frown \lceil 1 \rceil)$.

The complexity of the satisfiability problem for RDC is non-elementary. Sestoft [125] established this result for discrete time and for continuous time was shown in [103].

In the tool DCVALID [93] RDC, with a discrete-time interpretation is translated into monadic second-order logic over finite strings, which is a slight variant of the weak monadic second-order theory of one successor (WS1S) [12, 19]. The second-order theory is decidable and is used, for instance in the

MONA system [64]. In this translation extensions to RDC are considered, for example quantification over state variables, so that the full power of the chosen second-order logic is exploited.

In [104], it was shown that the language $L_2^\leq$ of the monadic second-order theory of order is decidable for *signal structures*, where signal structures capture the finitely variable interpretations of state variables under a continuous time interpretation. Using this result the decidability of RDC and other specification formalism were established by translations to $L_2^\leq$.

The techniques described in [93,104] were used in [8] to achieve decidability results for a *hybrid* version of RDC where *nominals* are added to the language. Each nominal names a unique interval. In this way more power is added to the logic without sacrificing the complexity of the decision procedure. The new formulas of this logic, called *Hybrid Duration Calculus* or *Hybrid DC*, are:

nominals:	$a,$
satisfaction:	$a : \phi,$
down-arrow binder:	$\downarrow a.\phi,$
existential modality:	$E\phi$.

The formula a holds in the specific interval named by a only, the formula $a : \phi$ holds if ϕ holds in the interval named by a, $\downarrow a.\phi$ holds if ϕ holds under the assumption that a names the current interval, and $E\phi$ holds if there is some interval where ϕ holds. It was shown that propositional neighbourhood logic is expressible in Hybrid DC.

There are certainly more results than those mentioned above. For example, decidable subsets were also considered in [23, 24, 36, 51, 69, 91, 115]. References [94, 125] concern the implementation of tools to check the validity of a subclass of DC and its higher-order version. In [26], there is a bounded model construction for discrete-time DC, which was shown to be NP-complete. Furthermore, in [22], a robust interpretation for a subset of DC was considered, and a semi-decision result was obtained. Model-checking of certain classes of formulas with respect to automata-based implementations was considered in [9, 23, 62, 71, 72, 138, 150]. A proof assistant for DC based on PVS [89] was developed in [80, 123, 126]. A decision procedure [146] for DC was incorporated into this proof assistant.

5 Some Links to Related Work

We end this chapter by giving a brief discussion of and links to some related work on DC which we have not mentioned previously.

5.1 Real State Model

A real state model consists of a set of real-valued functions which describe the behavior of physical components of an embedded software system. In [151], it is investigated how DC can be combined with real analysis, so that real state models can be specified in the framework of DC. See also [143].

In [121], there is another extension of DC, which allows the specification and verification of spatial properties, as well as temporal properties.

5.2 Dependability

The papers [49, 75–78] study the dependability of an implementation, represented as a finite automaton with transition probabilities, with regard to a given requirement formalized in DC.

5.3 Finite-Divergence Model

A model with finite divergence allowing Zeno phenomena with infinitely many state changes in bounded intervals was studied in [40].

5.4 Super-dense Computation

A *super-dense computation* is a sequence of operations which is assumed to be timeless. This is an abstraction used for instance, in the analysis of digital control systems, where the cycle time of an embedded computer may be nanoseconds, while the sampling period of a controller may be seconds. Therefore, the computation time of the embedded software of the digital control system is negligible. In [142] a chop modality called *super-dense chop* was introduced allowing a point to be chopped into multiple points in a finer space. Generalizing the projection operator of interval temporal logic in [86], [31] introduced the *visible* and *invisible* states, and compute non-negligible time through projection onto the visible state. See also [95, 102].

5.5 Infinite Intervals

An alternative to the use of expanding modalities is to introduce infinite intervals into DC. An extension of DC allowing both finite and infinite intervals was established in [148].

5.6 Higher-order and Iteration Operators

When DC applied is to real-time programming, advanced operators are needed to explain the programming notions of local variables and channels and of loops. References [29, 30, 57, 141] investigated the semantics and proof rules of the (higher-order) quantifiers over states and the μ operator.

5.7 Case Studies of Embedded Software Systems

DC has been applied in a number of case studies. Examples are an autopilot [111], a railway crossing [124] and interlock [112], a water level monitor [20,59], a gas burner [112], a steam boiler [21, 70, 119], an aircraft traffic controller [53], a production cell [99], a motor-load control system [137], an inverted pendulum [133], chemical concentration [135], heating control [136], redundant control [61], a hydraulic actuator system [109], and the optimal design of a double-tank control system [58]. Furthermore, [14, 52, 132, 149] discuss design methods for embedded software systems.

5.8 Real-time Semantics, Specification and Verification

DC has been used as a meta-language to define real-time semantics of other languages, for example CSP and OCCAM-like languages [54, 55, 117, 118, 142, 144, 149], SDL [83,84], Esterel [96], Constraint Diagrams [63], Fault Trees [35], the RAISE Specification Language (RSL) [73], B [15], Verilog [47, 120], circuits [39], Fischer's mutual exclusion protocol [113], the biphase mark protocol [48, 50] deadline-driven scheduler [139], and other well-known real-time schedulers [13, 16]. In [44], CSP, Object-Z and DC were combined into a uniform framework for the specification of processes, data and time, based on a smooth integration of the underlying semantic models.

5.9 Refinement of DC Specifications

In [81], there was a first attempt to define refinement laws for a restricted set of formulas towards *implementable* formulas. A full exposition of these ideas was given in [110]. References [88, 117, 118] developed techniques to refine implementable formulas into an executable program. References [52,65,66,116] represent work on refining DC formulas into automata. References [134–136] proposed approaches to refining DC specifications into programs following the paradigms of Hoare logic and assumption–commitment logic.

References

1. J.F. Allen (1983) Maintaining Knowledge about Temporal Intervals. *Communications of the ACM* 26(11):832–843, 1983
2. J.F. Allen(1984) Towards a general theory of action and time. *Artificial Intelligence* 23:123–154
3. R. Alur, C. Courcoubetis, T. Henzinger, P.H. Ho (1993) Hybrid automata: An algorithmic approach to the specification and verification of hybrid systems. In *Hybrid Systems*, LNCS 736, Springer, Berlin Heidelberg New York: 209–229
4. R. Alur, D. Dill (1992) The theory of timed automata. In *Real-Time: Theory in Practice*, LNCS 600, Springer, Berlin Heidelberg New York: 45 – 73

5. R. Barua, S. Roy, and C. Zhou (2000) Completeness of neighbourhood logic. *Journal of Logic and Computation* 10(2): 271–295
6. D. Bjørner (1992) Trusted computing systems: the ProCoS experience. In *Proceedings of the 14th international conference on Software engineering*, Melbourne, Australia, ACM Press: 15–34
7. P. Blackburn, M. de Rijke, Y. Venema (2001) Modal Logic. Cambridge University Press
8. T. Bolander, J.U. Hansen, M.R. Hansen (2006) Decidability of hybrid duration calculus. In *International Workshop on Hybrid Logics*, Seattle 2006. To appear in Electronic Notes in Theoretical Computer Science.
9. V.A. Braberman, D.V. Hung (1998) On checking timed automata for linear duration invariants. In *Proceedings of the 19th IEEE Real-Time Systems Symposium*, IEEE Computer Society Press: 264–273
10. D. Basin, S. Matthews, L. Vigano (1997) Labelled propositional modal logics: theory and practice. *Journal of logic and computation* 7(6):685–717
11. D. Basin, S. Matthews, L. Vigano(1998) Labelled modal logics: quantifiers. *Journal of logic, language and information* 7(3):237–263
12. J.R. Buchi (1960) Weak second-order arithmetic and finite automata. *Zeitschrift für Mathematische Logik und Grundlagen der Mathematik.* 6:66–92
13. P. Chan, D.V. Hung (1995) Duration calculus specification of scheduling for tasks with shared resources. In *Asian Computing Science Conference 1995*, LNCS 1023, Springer, Berlin Heidelberg New York: 365–380
14. Z. Chen, J. Wang, C. Zhou(1995) An abstraction of hybrid control systems. In *IEEE Singapore Intl. Conf. on Intelligent Control and Instrumentation.* IEEE Press:1–6
15. S. Colin, G. Mariano, V. Poirriez (2004) Duration Calculus: A Real-Time Semantics for B. In *Theoretical Aspects of Computing – ICTAC 2004*, LNCS 3407, Springer, Berlin Heidelberg New York: 431–446
16. S. Dong, Q. Xu, N. Zhan(1999) A formal proof of the rate monotonic scheduler. In *Proceedings of the Sixth International Conference on Real-Time Computing Systems and Applications.* IEEE Computer Society Press:500–507
17. B. Dutertre (1995) Complete proof systems for first order interval temporal logic. In *Tenth Annual IEEE Symposium on Logic in Computer Science*, IEEE Press:36–43
18. B. Dutertre (1995) On first order interval temporal logic. Technical report, Report No. CSD-TR-94-3, Department of Computer Science, Royal Holloway, University of London
19. C.C. Elgot (1961) Decision problems of finite automata design and related arithmetics. *Transactions of the American Mathematical Society* 98:21–52
20. M. Engel, M. Kubica, J. Madey, D.L. Parnas, A.P. Ravn, A.J. van Schouwen (1993) A formal approach to computer systems requirements documentation. In *Hybrid Systems*, LNCS 736, Springer, Berlin Heidelberg New York: 452–474
21. M. Engel, H. Rischel (1994) Dagstuhl-seminar specification problem - a duration calculus solution. Technical report, Department of Computer Science, Technical University of Denmark – Personal Communication
22. M. Fränzle, M.R. Hansen (2005) A Robust Interpretation of Duration Calculus. In *Theoretical Aspects of Computing – ICTAC 2005*, LNCS 3722, Springer, Berlin Heidelberg New York: 257–271

23. M. Fränzle, M.R. Hansen (2007) Deciding an Interval Logic with Accumulated Durations. In *Tools and algorithms for the construction and analysis of systems – TACAS 2007*, LNCS 4424, Springer, Berlin Heidelberg New York: 201–215

24. M. Fränzle (1996) Synthesizing controllers from duration calculus. In *Formal Techniques in Real-Time and Fault-Tolerant Systems*, LNCS 1135, Springer, Berlin Heidelberg New York:168–187

25. M. Fränzle(1997) Controller Design from Temporal Logic: Undecidability Need Not Matter. PhD Thesis Institut für Informatik und Praktische Mathematik der Christian-Albrechts-Universität Kiel

26. M. Fränzle(2002) Take it NP-easy: Bounded model construction for duration calculus. In *Formal Techniques in Real-Time and Fault-Tolerant Systems*, LNCS 2469, Springer, Berlin Heidelberg New York:245–264

27. V. Goranko, A. Montanari, G. Sciavicco (2004) A Road Map of Propositional Interval Temporal Logics and Duration Calculi. *Journal of Applied Non-classical Logics*, Special issue on Interval Temporal Logics and Duration Calculi, 14(1-2):11–56

28. D.P. Guelev (1998) A calculus of durations on abstract domains: Completeness and extensions. Technical report 139, UNU/IIST (UN University, Inst. of Software Technologz)

29. D.P. Guelev (2000) Complete fragment of higher-order duration μ-calculus. In *Foundations of Software Technology and Theoretical Computer Science (FST&TCS'2000)*, LNCS 1974, Springer, Berlin Heidelberg New York:264–276

30. D.V. Guelev, D.V. Hung (1999) On the completeness and decidability of duration calculus with iteration. In *Advances in Computing Science*, LNCS 1742, Springer, Berlin Heidelberg New York:139–150

31. D.V. Guelev, D.V. Hung (2002) Prefix and projection onto state in duration calculus. In *Proceedings of Workshop on Theory and Practice of Timed Systems*, Electronic Notes in Theoretical Computer Science

32. J. Halpern, B. Moskowski, Z. Manna (1983) A hardware semantics based on temporal intervals. In *ICALP'83*, LNCS 154, Springer, Berlin Heidelberg New York:278–291

33. J. Halpern, Y. Shoham (1986) A propositional modal logic of time intervals. In *Proceedings of the First IEEE Symposium on Logic in Computer Science*, IEEE Press:279–292

34. J. Halpern, Y. Shoham (1991) A propositional modal logic of time intervals. *Journal of the ACM* 33(4):935–962

35. K.M. Hansen, A.P. Ravn, V. Stavridou (1996) From safety analysis to formal specification. Technical report, Department of Information Technology, Technical University of Denmark

36. M.R. Hansen (1994) Model-checking discrete duration calculus. *Formal Aspects of Computing* 6A:826–845

37. M.R. Hansen, C. Zhou (1992) Semantics and completeness of duration calculus. In *Real-Time: Theory in Practice*, LNCS 600, Springer, Berlin Heidelberg New York:209–225

38. M.R. Hansen, C. Zhou (1997) Duration calculus: Logical foundations. *Formal Aspects of Computing* 9:283–330

39. M.R. Hansen, C. Zhou, J. Staunstrup(1992) A real-time duration semantics for circuits. In *TAU'92: 1992 Workshop on Timing Issues in the Specification and Synthesis of Digital Systems*, Princeton Univ., NJ. ACM/SIGDA

40. M.R. Hansen, P.K. Pandya, C. Zhou(1995) Finite divergence. *Theoretical Computer Science* 138:113–139

41. M.R. Hansen, R. Sharp (2003) Using interval logics for temporal analysis of security protocols. In *First ACM Workshop on Formal Methods in Security Engineering (FMSE'03)*, ACM Press:24–31

42. D. Harel, O. Lichtenstein, A. Pnueli (1990) Explicit clock temporal logic. In *Symposium on Logic in Computer Science*, IEEE Press:402–413

43. J. Harrison (1998) Theorem Proving with the Real Numbers. Springer, Berlin Heidelberg New York

44. J. Hoenicke, E.R. Olderog (2002) CSP-OZ-DC: A combination of specification techniques for processes, data and time. *Nordic Journal of Computing* 9(4):301–334

45. G.E. Hughes, M.J. Crestwell (1968) An Introduction to Modal Logic. Routledge

46. G.E. Hughes, M.J Crestwell (1984) A Companion to Modal Logic. Methuen

47. Z. Huibiao, J.F. He (2000) A DC-based semantics for Verilog. In *Proceedings of International Conference on Software: Theory and Practice*. Publishing House of Electronics Industry:421–432

48. D.V. Hung (1998) Modelling and verification of biphase mark protocols in duration calculus using PVS/DC⁻. In *Application of Concurrency to System Design (CSD'98)*, IEEE Computer Society Press:88–98

49. D.V. Hung, C. Zhou(1999) Probabilistic duration calculus for continuous time. *Formal Aspects of Computing*, 11(1):21–44

50. D.V. Hung, P.H. Giang (1996) A sampling semantics of duration calculus. In *Formal Techniques for Real-Time and Fault Tolerant Systems*, LNCS 1135. Springer, Berlin Heidelberg New York: 188–207

51. D.V. Hung, D.P. Guelev (1999) Completeness and decidability of a fragment of duration calculus with iteration. In *Advances in Computing Science*, LNCS 1742. Springer, Berlin Heidelberg New York:139–150

52. D.V. Hung, J. Wand (1996) On design of hybrid control systems using i/o automata models. In *Foundations of Software Technology and Theoretical Computer Science*, LNCS 1180. Springer, Berlin Heidelberg New York:156–167

53. R. Inal (1994) Modular specification of real-time systems. In *1994 Euromicro Workshop on Real-Time Systems*. IEEE Computer Society Press

54. J.F. He (1994) From CSP to hybrid systems. In *A Classical Mind: Essays in Honour of C.A.R. Hoare*. Prentice Hall International:171–190

55. J.F. He, J. Bowen (1992) Time interval semantics and implementation of a real-time programming language. In *1992 Euromicro Workshop on Real-Time Systems*. IEEE Computer Society Press

56. J.F. He, C.A.R. Hoare, M. Fränzle, M. Müller-Olm, E.R. Olderog, M. Schenke, M.R. Hansen, A.P. Ravn, H. Rischel (1994) Provably correct systems. In *Formal Techniques in Real-Time and Fault-Tolerant Systems*, LNCS 863. Springer, Berlin Heidelberg New York:288–335

57. J.F. He, Q. Xu (2000) Advanced features of the duration calculus. In *Millennial Perspectives in Computer Science*. Palgrave:133–146

58. W. He, C. Zhou (1995) A case study of optimization. *The Computer Journal* 38(9):734–746
59. K.T. Hong, D.V. Hung (2001) Formal design of hybrid control systems: Duration calculus approach. In *Proceedings of the Twenty-Fifth Annual International Computer Software and Applications Conference.* IEEE Computer Society Press:423–428
60. F. Jahanian, A.K.L Mok (1986) Safety analysis of timing properties in real-time systems. *IEEE Transaction on Software Engineering* 12(9)
61. J. Gao, Q. Xu (1997) Rigorous design of a fault diagnosis and isolation algorithm. In *Proceedings of the Fifth International Workshop on Hybrid Systems*
62. Y. Kesten, A. Pnueli, J. Sifakis, S. Yovine (1993) Integration graphs: A class of decidable hybrid systems. In *Hybrid Systems*, LNCS 736. Springer, Berlin Heidelberg New York:179–208
63. C. Kleuker (2000) Constraint Diagrams. PhD Thesis, Oldenburg University, Germany
64. N. Klarlund, A. Moller (2001) *MONA Version 1.4: User Manual.* BRICS, Department of Computer Science, University of Aarhus, Denmark
65. M. Kääramees (1995) Transformation of duration calculus specifications to DISCO language. Master's Thesis, Automation and Systems Engineering, Tallinn Technical University, Estonia
66. M. Kääramees(1995) Transforming designs towards implementations. In *1995 Euromicro Workshop on Real-Time Systems*, IEEE Computer Society Press:197–204
67. R. Koymans (1990) Specifying real-time properties with metric temporal logic. *Real-Time Systems* 2(4):255–299
68. L. Lamport (1993) Hybrid systems in tla$^+$. In *Hybrid Systems*, LNCS 736. Springer p. 77–102
69. X. Li (1993) A Mean Value Calculus. PhD Thesis, Software Institute, Academia Sinica
70. X. Li, J. Wang (1996) Specifying optimal design of a steam-boiler system. In *Formal Methods for Industrial Applications*, LNCS 1165. Springer Berlin Heidelberg New York:359–378
71. X. Li, D.V. Hung (1996) Checking linear duration invariants by linear programming. In *Concurrency and Parallelism*, Programming, Networking, and Security, LNCS 1179. Springer Berlin Heidelberg New York:321–332
72. X. Li, D.V. Hung, T. Zheng T (1997) Checking hybrid automata for linear duration invariants. In *Advances in Computing Science*, LNCS 1997. Springer Berlin Heidelberg New York:166–180
73. L. Li, J.F. He (1999) A denotational semantics of timed rsl using duration calculus. In *Proceedings of the Sixth International Conference on Real-Time Computing Systems and Applications.* IEEE Computer Society Press:492–503
74. C.L. Liu, J.W. Layland (1973) Scheduling algorithm for multiprogramming in a hard real-time environment. *Journal of the ACM* 20(1):46–61
75. Z. Liu, A.P. Ravn, E.V. Sørensen, C. Zhou (1993) A probabilistic duration calculus. In *Dependable Computing and Fault-Tolerant Systems Vol. 7: Responsive Computer Systems*. Springer Berlin Heidelberg New York:30–52
76. Z. Liu, A.P. Ravn, E.V. Sørensen, C. Zhou (1994) Towards a calculus of systems dependability. *High Integrity Systems* 1(1):49–75

77. Z. Liu, J. Nordahl, E.V. Sørensen (1995) Composition and refinement of probabilistic real-time systems. In *Mathematics of Dependable Systems*, Oxford University Press:149–163

78. Z. Liu (1996) Specification and verification in DC. In *Mathematics of Dependable Systems*, International Series in Computer Science, Prentice Hall p.182–228

79. Z. Manna, A. Pnueli (1993) Verifying hybrid systems. In *Hybrid Systems*, LNCS 736. Springer, Berlin Heidelberg New York:4–35

80. X. Mao, Q. Xu, D.V. Hung, J. Wang (1996) Towards a proof assistant for interval logics. Technical report, UNU/IIST Report No. 77, UN University, International Institute for Software Technology, Macau

81. P.C. Masiero, A.P. Ravn, H. Rischel (1993) Refinement of real-time specifications. Technical Report ProCoS, Technical Report ID/DTH PCM 1/1, Department of Computer Science, Technical University of Denmark

82. C. Meadows(2001) A cost-based framework for analysis of denial-of-service in networks. *Journal of Computer Security* 9(1/2):143–164

83. C.A. Middelburg (1998) Truth of duration calculus formulae in timed frames. *Fundamenta Informaticae Journal* 36(2/3):235–263

84. S. Mørk, J.C. Godskesen, M.R. Hansen, R. Sharp (1996) A timed semantics for sdl. In *Formal Description Techniques IX: Theory, application and tools*. Chapman & Hall:295–309

85. B. Moszkowski (1985) A temporal logic for multilevel reasoning about hardware. *IEEE Computer* 18(2):10–19

86. B. Moszkowski (1995) Compositional reasoning about projected and infinite time. In *Engineering of Complex Computer Systems*, IEEE Computer Society Press:238–245

87. X. Nicollin, A. Olivero, J. Sifakis, S. Yovine (1993) An approach to the description and analysis of hybrid systems. In *Hybrid Systems*, LNCS 736. Springer, Berlin Heidelberg New York:149–178

88. E.R. Olderog, A.P. Ravn, J.U. Skakkebæk (1996) Refining system requirements to program specifications. In *Formal Methods in Real-Time Systems*, *Trends in Software-Engineering*, chapter 5. Wiley

89. S. Owre, N. Shankar, J. Rushby (1993) Users guide for the pvs specification and verification system, language, and proof checker (beta release) (three volumes). Technical report, Computer Science Laboratory, SRI International, Menlo Park, CA

90. P. Øhrstrøm, P.F. Hasle (1995) Temporal Logic: From Ancient Ideas to Artificial Intelligence. Kluwer Academic

91. P.K. Pandya (1996) Some extensions to propositional mean value calculus: Expressiveness and decidability. In *Computer Science Logic, CSL'95*, LNCS 1092. Springer, Berlin Heidelberg New York:434–451

92. P.K. Pandya (1996) Weak chop inverses and liveness in duration calculus. In *Formal Techniques in Real-Time and Fault-Tolerant Systems*, LNCS 1135. Springer, Berlin Heidelberg New York:148–167

93. P.K. Pandya (2000) Specifying and deciding quantified discrete-time duration calculus formulae using DCVALID. Technical report TCS00-PKP-1, Tata Institute of Fundamental Research, India.

94. P.K. Pandya (1999) DCVALID 1.3: The user manual. Technical report TCS-99/1, Computer Science Group, TIFR, Bombay

95. P.K. Pandya, D.V. Hung (1998) Duration calculus with weakly monotonic time. In *Formal Techniques in Real-Time and Fault-Tolerant Systems*, LNCS 1486. Springer, Berlin Heidelberg New York:55–64

96. P.K. Pandya, Y.S. Ramakrishna, R.K. Shyamasundar (1995) A compositional semantics of Esterel in duration calculus. Technical report, Computer Science Group, TIFR, Bombay

97. L.C. Paulson (1994) Isabelle, A Generic Theorem Prover, LNCS 828. Springer Berlin Heidelberg New York

98. L.C. Paulson (1997) Proving properties of security protocols by induction. In *Proceedings of the 10th IEEE Computer Security Foundations Workshop*, Rockport, Mass. IEEE Press:70–83

99. J.L. Petersen, H. Rischel (1994) Formalizing requirements and design for a production cell system. In *Symposium ADPM '94: Automatisation des Processus Mixtes: Les Systemes Dynamiques Hybrides*. Belgian Institute of Automatic Control, IBRA:37–46

100. H. Pilegaard (2002) Modelling properties of security protocols. MA Thesis, Informatics and Mathematical Modelling, Technical University of Denmark

101. H. Pilegaard, M.R. Hansen,R. Sharp (2003) An approach to analyzing availability properties of security protocols. *Nordic Journal of Computing* 10:337–373

102. Z. Qiu, C. Zhou (1998) A combination of interval logic and linear temporal logic. In *Programming Concepts and Methods*. Chapman & Hall:444–461

103. A. Rabinovich (1998) Non-elementary lower bound for propositional duration calculus. *Information Processing Letters*: 7–11

104. A. Rabinovich (1998) On the decidability of continuous time specification formalism. *Journal of Logic and Computation* 8(5):669–678.

105. T.M. Rasmussen (1999) Signed interval logic. In *Computer Science Logic, CSL'99*, LNCS 1683. Springer Berlin Heidelberg New York:157–171

106. T.M. Rasmussen (2001) Automated proof support for interval logics. In LPAR 2001, LNAI 2250. Springer Berlin Heidelberg New York:317–326

107. T.M. Rasmussen (2001) Labelled natural deduction for interval logics. In *Computer Science Logic, CSL'01*, LNCS 2142. Springer Berlin Heidelberg New York:308–323

108. T.M. Rasmussen (2002) Interval Logic: Proof Theory and Theorem Proving. PhD Thesis, Informatics and Mathematical Modelling, Technical University of Denmark

109. A.P. Ravn, T.J. Eriksen, M. Holdgaard, H. Rischel (1998) Engineering of real-time systems with an experiment in hybrid control. In *Embedded Systems*, LNCS 1494. Springer Berlin Heidelberg New York:316–352

110. A.P. Ravn (1995) Design of Embedded Real-Time Computing Systems. Doctoral Dissertation, Department of Computer Science, Technical University of Denmark

111. A.P. Ravn, H. Rischel (1991) Requirements capture for embedded real-time systems. In *Proceedings of IMACS-MCTS'91 Symposium on Modelling and Control of Technological Systems*, Villeneuve d'Ascq, France, volume 2. IMACS:147–152

112. A.P. Ravn, H. Rischel, K.M. Hansen (1993) Specifying and verifying requirements of real-time systems. *IEEE Transactions on Software Engineering* 19(1):41–55

113. H. Rischel (1992) A duration calculus proof of fischer's mutual exclusion protocol. ProCoS II, ESPRIT BRA 7071, Report No. DTH HR 4/1, Department of Computer Science, Technical University of Denmark

114. S. Roy, C. Zhou (1997) Notes on neighbourhood logic. UNU/IIST Report No. 97, International Institute for Software Technology, Macau

115. S. Satpathy, D.V. Hung, P.K. Pandya (1998) Some results on the decidability of duration calculus under synchronous interpretation. In *Formal Techniques in Real-Time and Fault-Tolerant Systems*, LNCS 1486. Springer, Berlin Heidelberg New York:186–197

116. M. Schenke (1994) Specification and transformation of reactive systems with time restrictions and concurrency. In *Techniques in Real-Time and Fault-Tolerant Systems*, LNCS 863. Springer, Berlin Heidelberg New York:605–620

117. M. Schenke (1995) Requirements to programs: A development methodology for real time systems, part 2. Technical report, Fachbereich Informatik, Universität Oldenburg, Germany

118. M. Schenke, E.R. Olderog (1995) Requirements to programs: A development methodology for real time systems, part 1. Technical report, Fachbereich Informatik, Universität Oldenburg, Germany

119. M. Schenke, A.P. Ravn (1996) Refinement from a control problem to programs. In *Formal Methods for Industrial Applications*, LNCS 1165. Springer Berlin Heidelberg New York:403–427

120. G. Schneider, Q. Xu (1998) Towards a formal semantics of verilog using duration calculus. In *Formal Techniques in Real-Time and Fault-Tolerant Systems*, LNCS 1486. Springer, Berlin Heidelberg New York:282–293

121. A. Schäfer (2004). A Calculus for Shapes in Time and Space. In *Theoretical Aspects of Computing, ICTAC 2004*, LNCS 3407. Springer Berlin Heidelberg New York:463–477

122. J.U. Skakkebæk (1994) Liveness and fairness in duration calculus. In *CONCUR'94: Concurrency Theory*, LNCS 836. Springer, Berlin Heidelberg New York: 283–298

123. J.U. Skakkebæk (1994) A Verification Assistant for a Real-Time Logic. PhD Thesis, Department of Computer Science, Technical University of Denmark

124. J.U. Skakkebæk, A.P. Ravn, H. Rischel, C. Zhou (1992) Specification of embedded, real-time systems. In *Proceedings of 1992 Euromicro Workshop on Real-Time Systems*. IEEE Computer Society Press

125. J.U. Skakkebæk, P. Sestoft (1994) Checking validity of duration calculus formulas. Technical report, ProCoS II, ESPRIT BRA 7071, report no. ID/DTH JUS 3/1, Department of Computer Science, Technical University of Denmark

126. J.U. Skakkebæk, N. Shankar (1994) Towards a duration calculus proof assistant in pvs. In Techniques in *Real-Time and Fault-Tolerant Systems*, LNCS 863. Springer, Berlin Heidelberg New York:660–679

127. E.V.Sørensen, A.P. Ravn, H. Rischel(1990) Control program for a gas burner: Part 1: Informal requirements, ProCoS case study 1. Technical Report ID/DTH EVS2

128. A. Tarski (1948) A decision method for elementary algebra and geometry. RAND Corporation, Santa Monica, California

129. Y. Venema (1990) Expressiveness and completeness of an interval tense logic. *Notre Dame Journal of Formal Logic*, 31(4):529–547

130. Y. Venema (1991) A modal logic for chopping intervals. *Journal of Logic and Computation* 1(4):453–476

131. L. Vigano (2000) Labelled non-classical logics. Kluwer Academic Punlishers
132. J. Wang, H. Weidong (1996) Formal specification of stability in hybrid control systems. In *Hybrid Systems III*, LNCS 1066. Springer, Berlin Heidelberg New York:294–303
133. B.H. Widjaja, W. He, Z. Chen, C. Zhou (1996) A cooperative design for hybrid control systems. In *Proceedings of Logic and Software Engineering International Workshop in Honor of Chih-Sung Tang*. World Scientific:127–150
134. Q. Xu, M. Swarup (1998) Compositional reasoning using assumption-commitment paradigm. In *Compositionality - The Significant Difference*, LNCS 1536. Springer Berlin Heidelberg New York:565–583
135. Q. Xu, H. Weidong (1996) Hierarchical design of a chemical concentration control system. In *Hybrid Systems III: Verification and Control*, LNCS 1066. Springer Berlin Heidelberg New York:270–281
136. Q. Xu, Z. Yang (1996) Derivation of control programs: a heating system. UNU/IIST Report No. 73, International Institute for Software Technology, Macau
137. X. Yu, J. Wang, C. Zhou, and P.K. Pandya (1994) Formal design of hybrid systems. In *Techniques in Real-Time and Fault-Tolerant Systems*, LNCS 863. Springer, Berlin Heidelberg New York:738–755
138. J. Zhao, D.V. Hung (1998) On checking real-time parallel systems for linear duration properties. In *Formal Techniques in Real-Time and Fault-Tolerant Systems*, LNCS 1486. Springer, Berlin Heidelberg New York:241–250
139. Y. Zheng, C. Zhou (1994) A formal proof of the deadline driven scheduler. In *Techniques in Real-Time and Fault-Tolerant Systems*, LNCS 863. Springer, Berlin Heidelberg New York:756–775
140. C. Zhou (1993) Duration Calculi: An overview. In *Proceedings of Formal Methods in Programming and Their Applications*, LNCS 735. Springer Berlin Heidelberg New York:256–266
141. C. Zhou, D.P. Guelev, N. Zhan (2000) A higher-order duration calculus. In *Millennial Perspectives in Computer Science*. Palgrave:407–416.
142. C. Zhou, M.R. Hansen (1996) Chopping a point. In *BCS-FACS 7th Refinement Workshop*. Electronic Workshops in Computing, Springer Berlin Heidelberg New York
143. C. Zhou, M.R. Hansen (1998) An adequate first order logic of intervals. In *Compositionality: The Significant Difference*, LNCS 1536. Springer Berlin Heidelberg New York:584–608
144. C. Zhou, M.R. Hansen, A.P. Ravn, H. Rischel (1991) Duration specifications for shared processors. In *Symposium on Formal Techniques in Real-Time and Fault Tolerant Systems*, LNCS 571. Springer Berlin Heidelberg New York:21–32
145. C. Zhou, M.R. Hansen (2004) Duration Calculus: A formal approach to real-time systems. Springer
146. C. Zhou, M.R. Hansen, P. Sestoft (1993) Decidability and undecidability results for duration calculus. In *STACS'93*, LNCS 665. Springer Berlin Heidelberg New York:58–68
147. C. Zhou, C.A.R. Hoare, A.P. Ravn (1991) A calculus of durations. *Information Processing Letters* 40(5):269–276
148. C. Zhou, D.V. Hung, X. Li (1995) A duration calculus with infinite intervals. In *Fundamentals of Computation Theory, LNCS*, Springer p. 16–41

149. X. Zhou, J. Wang, A.P. Ravn (1996) A formal description of hybrid systems. In *Hybrid Systems III*, LNCS 1066. Springer Berlin Heidelberg New York:511–530

150. C. Zhou, J. Zhang, L. Yang, X. Li (1994) Linear duration invariants. In *Techniques in Real-Time and Fault-Tolerant Systems*, LNCS 863. Springer, Berlin Heidelberg New York:86–109

151. C. Zhou, A.P. Ravn, M.R. Hansen (1993) An extended duration calculus for hybrid systems. In *Hybrid Systems*, LNCS 736. Springer, Berlin Heidelberg New York:36–59

152. C. Zhou, X. Li (1994) A mean value calculus of durations. In *A Classical Mind: Essays in Honour of C.A.R. Hoare*. Prentice Hall International:431–451

DC Indexes

DC Symbol Index

The Logic of the RAISE Specification Language

Chris George[1] and Anne E. Haxthausen[2]

[1] International Institute for Software Technology, United Nations University, Macao, `cwg@iist.unu.edu`
[2] Department of Informatics and Mathematical Modelling, Technical University of Denmark, Lyngby, Denmark, `ah@imm.dtu.dk`

Summary. This chapter describes the logic of the RAISE Specification Language, RSL. It explains the particular logic chosen for RAISE, and motivates this choice as suitable for a wide-spectrum language to be used for designs as well as initial specifications, and supporting imperative and concurrent specifications as well as applicative sequential ones. It also describes the logical definition of RSL, its axiomatic semantics, as well as the proof system for carrying out proofs. Finally, a case study illustrates specification and verification methods in RAISE.

Key words: formal methods, logic, proof, RAISE, RSL

1 Introduction

An important technique for increasing the reliability of software systems is to use formal development methods. Formal methods provide mathematically based languages for specifying software systems and proof systems for verification purposes. During the last two decades a whole range of formal methods have been developed. One of these is RAISE.

The goal of this chapter is to describe and motivate the logic of the RAISE specification language, RSL. This logic is non trivial and interesting because the language supports many different specification styles.

It should be noted that for a given, formal language the term 'logic' can be used in two different but related senses. It may refer to the meanings of the 'logical' (truth-valued) expressions of a language. Alternatively, 'logic' may refer to the proof system, to the inference rules by which one may reason about terms of the language. In designing a language, choices made in the assignment of meanings to expressions influence the possible design of the proof system. For this reason we have chosen to use the term 'logic' as encompassing both senses.

In the remaining part of this section, we give a short introduction to RAISE including a survey of the major specification styles supported by RSL. Then, in Sect. 2, we describe the rationale behind the design choices made for the meanings of 'logical' (truth-valued) expressions in RSL. Next, in Sect. 3, we outline how RSL is formally given an axiomatic semantics in the form of a collection of inference rules that defines well-formedness and meanings of RSL constructs. In Sect. 4 we describe how a proof system is derived from the axiomatic semantics in such a way that it is suitable for doing proofs in practice using a computer based tool. After that, in Sect. 5, a case study shows how a harbour information system can be specified and verified in various ways. Finally, in Sect. 6, we state our conclusions.

1.1 RAISE Background

RAISE ("Rigorous Approach to Industrial Software") is a product consisting of a formal specification language (RSL) [1], an associated method [2] for software development and a set of supporting tools.

The Method

The RAISE method is based on stepwise refinement using the invent and verify paradigm. Specifications are written in RSL. The notion of refinement will be described in Sect. 2.4.

The Language

RSL is a formal, wide-spectrum specification language that encompasses and integrates different specification styles in a common conceptual framework. Hence, RSL enables the formulation of modular specifications which are algebraic or model-oriented, applicative or imperative, and sequential or concurrent. Below, we outline the major syntactic aspects of the language.

A basic RSL specification is called a class expression and consists of declarations of types, values, variables, channels, and axioms. Specifications may also be built from other specifications by renaming declared entities, hiding declared entities, or adding more declarations. Moreover, specifications may be parametrised.

User-declared types may be introduced as abstract sort types as known from algebraic specification, for example

type Colour

or may be constructed from built-in types and type constructors in a model-oriented way, for example

type
  Database = Key $\overrightarrow{m}$ **Nat-set**,
  Key = **Text**

In addition, RSL provides predicative subtypes, union and short record types as known from VDM, and variant type definitions similar to data type definitions in ML.

Values may be defined in a signature-axiom style as known from algebraic specification, for example

value
    black, white : Colour
axiom
    black $\neq$ white

They may also be defined in a pre–post style, for example

value
    square_root : **Real** $\rightarrow$ **Real**
    square_root(x) **as** r **post** r $\geq$ 0.0 $\wedge$ r $*$ r = x
    pre x $\geq$ 0.0

or in an explicit style as known from model-oriented specification, for example

value
    reverse : **Int*** $\rightarrow$ **Int***
    reverse(l) $\equiv$
        if l = $\langle\rangle$ **then** $\langle\rangle$ **else** reverse(tl l) $^\frown$ $\langle$**hd** l$\rangle$ **end**

Functions may be imperative, reading from and/or writing to declared variables:

variable v : **Int**
value
    add_to_v : **Int** $\rightarrow$ **write** v **Unit**
    add_to_v(x) $\equiv$ v := v + x

where **Unit** is the type containing the single value (). In the function type it is stated which variables the function may access.

Functions may describe processes communicating synchronously with each other via declared channels:

channel i : **Int**, o : **Bool**
value
    test : **Int** $\rightarrow$ **in** i **out** o **Unit**
    test(x) $\equiv$ **let** inval = **in**? **in** o!(inval=x) **end**

In Sect. 2, various kinds of value expressions and their meaning will be described.

RSL has also been extended to support real time [3–6].

Semantic Foundations of RSL

RSL has been given a denotational [7] and an axiomatic semantics [8], and a subset of the language has been given an operational semantics [9]. The construction of the denotational model and a demonstration of its existence were presented in [10].

Tool Support

The RAISE tool provide support for constructing, checking and verifying specifications and development relations, and for translating concrete specifications into several programming languages.

History

RAISE was developed during the years 1985–1995 in the CEC-funded projects ESPRIT RAISE (ESPRIT 315) and LaCoS (ESPRIT 5383). RAISE builds upon ideas reflected in a number of other formal methods and languages. The model-oriented language features were inspired by VDM [11] and Z [12], the algebraic features by algebraic specification languages like OBJ [13], Clear [14], ASL [15], ACT ONE [16] and Larch [17], the concurrency features by CCS [18] and CSP [19], and the modularity features by ML [20], Clear, ASL, ACT ONE and Larch.

Applications

RAISE has been used on many applications. The initial ones were within the LaCoS project [21]. It has been used for many years at UNU-IIST, and a collection of case studies from there, illustrating a wide range of styles of use, has been published recently [22]. Also, at the Technical University of Denmark, it has been used in a range of applications have been done, for example [23–26].

2 The RSL Logic

There are a number of possible choices for the logic of a specification language. In this section we present the rationale behind the design of the RSL logic. Section 2.1 introduces the problem of potentially undefined expressions, Sect. 2.2 presents the logic of the applicative subset of RSL, Sect. 2.3 extends this to imperative and concurrent RSL, Sect. 2.4 presents the RSL definition of refinement and relates it to the logic, and Sect. 2.5 introduces the notion of confidence conditions.

2.1 Definedness

A fundamental question to decide about a logic for a specification language is what to do about problematic expressions like 1/0, or **hd** ⟨⟩, or **while true do skip end**. Such expressions do not have very obvious denotations (meanings).

Expressions like these may seem more likely to arise in early specifications or in implementations, but as RSL is a "wide-spectrum" language, intended to support both initial specification and development to code, any of these kinds of expression may occur.

There are two facts to make clear from the start. First, in a reasonably expressive language, such expressions cannot be avoided by purely mechanical means. The equality of an integer expression with zero, for example, is not decidable. If we wish to ensure that such expressions do not occur, then we need to perform such a proof. We can choose to perform such proof as part of "type checking", as in PVS [27] for example, or at some later time. In contrast, it is possible in a typed language mechanically to either reject an expression as ill-typed (1 + **true**, for example) or assign it a type. So our "problematic" expressions will have types.[1]

The second fact is that there is a variety of schemes available to deal with such expressions in a logic. This is not a question of fundamental research, but of choosing from the options available. The choices made will affect the ease with which people can learn and use a language, and the ease of creating and using proof tools for that language. There are two factors in particular that influenced the choices made in the design of RSL:

1. As mentioned above, RSL is a "wide spectrum" language intended to support development to specifications very close to programming languages. This in turn means that the ability to conveniently translate at least the constructs likely to appear in such detailed specifications into a programming language, is something to consider.
2. The design of RSL is as regular as possible. This means that apart from having type **Bool**, there are as few restrictions as possible placed on what kind of expressions may occur in a predicate. In particular, expressions do not need to be applicative: they may have *effect*s by accessing variables and even channels.

One possible approach to problematic expressions like 1/0 is to say that "every expression denotes a value in its type, but it might not be possible or sensible to say which". In this approach 1/0 could be some unknown integer, but **while true do skip end** would have to be equivalent to **skip**, since **skip** is the only value in the type **Unit**. This (a) seems counter-intuitive and (b) seems to preclude any analysis of termination since the logic would equate a non-terminating expression with a terminating one.

---

[1] In languages like RSL which allow overloading there may be a (finite) collection of possible types, but this does not materially affect the following discussion.

Some languages, Z [12] and B [28] for example, take the approach that all expressions denote. It is argued that this gives a simple and intuitive logic. Examples like those based on non-termination can be considered as less relevant to Z, which aims to define initial specifications rather than implementations, though this seems less justified for B. These languages, unlike VDM [11] and RSL, for example, also distinguish between Boolean expressions, *predicates*, and expressions of other types: they have no Boolean type.

RSL, like VDM, from which much of RSL's inspiration came, has a Boolean type, **Bool**, and allows in its logic for expressions that might not denote values in their types. The *definedness* of expressions then becomes a concept needed in the proof theory. The semantics of such languages may, as in RSL's case, be *loose*: there are some expressions whose definedness is not specified, and 1/0 is an example. A programming language implementation in which it raises an exception is acceptable, as is one where it evaluates to 1, say. Looseness is not a critical issue: much more important is how in writing and developing specifications, we can avoid such expressions occurring. We will return to this issue later, in Sect. 2.5.

2.2 Applicative RSL

The discussion about logic for RSL becomes more complicated when we include expressions that can write to variables, or access channels, i.e. expressions that can have *effects*. We will try to give a simple exposition by dealing with applicative expressions first, and explain the additions we need for imperative expressions later. But we shall also try to avoid misleading readers by indicating in the first part where the explanation refers only to applicative expressions.

Equivalence

A basic issue when expressions might not denote values is the meaning of equality. RSL has two "equality" operators, $\equiv$ and $=$. The first of these, equivalence, is more relevant to the discussion of logic, and we will discuss equality $=$ later in this section.

$\equiv$ is sometimes called a "strong" equality, as it allows undefined expressions to be compared. It has the mathematical properties of a congruence, which means that it is an equivalence relation (it is reflexive, transitive and commutative) and (for applicative expressions) it allows substitution: an expression can be replaced by an equivalent one in any context.

The important properties we shall need for equivalence are the following:

1. A defined expression is never equivalent to an undefined one, for example the equivalence

   while true do skip end $\equiv$ skip

is **false**.
2. Equivalence always returns **true** or **false**, i.e. it is always defined.

Equivalence is in fact the same as semantic equality: two expressions are equivalent if they have the same semantics.

A logic that allows undefined expressions and includes a strong equality is often referred to as "three-valued". We prefer to say that there are just two Boolean values (**true** and **false**), and say that only defined expressions have values. There are three "basic" undefined expressions in RSL: **chaos** (equivalent to **while true do skip end**), **stop** (the external choice over the empty set) and **swap** (the internal choice over the empty set). **stop** represents deadlock and arises in RSL because it includes concurrency. The effect of **swap** is not specified: it may be to terminate, to deadlock, to allow an internal choice or to diverge. In practice, we normally want to avoid the possibility of undefined expressions in specifications, and making the main choice one between definedness and otherwise is mostly sufficient. We shall in our examples for simplicity, usually use **chaos** as the archetypal undefined expression.

Convergence

RSL includes concurrency, and so includes the notion of internal (nondeterministic) choice. This also arises if relations or mappings that are "nonfunctional" are allowed. For example, what happens if the map $[1 \mapsto 2, 1 \mapsto 3]$ is applied to the value 1? In RSL, the result is equivalent to the expression $2 \sqcap 3$. This expression is defined, but will not always evaluate to the same result. We use the term *convergent* to mean "defined and having a unique value".

We shall see that definedness and convergence often arise in the proof theory because we need them as conditions for rules to be sound. For example, we will see that

$A \wedge B \equiv B \wedge A$ when A and B are defined
$A \vee \sim A \equiv \textbf{true}$ when A is convergent

(In the non-applicative case these also need the effects of A and B to be at most "read-only".)

However, the case of "defined but nondeterministic" is (a) rare and (b) dealt with by other rules, so in practice we always use convergence even though definedness is occasionally sufficient.

Connectives

How do we define the logical connectives $\wedge$ (and), $\vee$ (or), $\sim$ (not) and $\Rightarrow$ (implies)? The approach in VDM is to use a logic called LPF [29], the "Logic of Partial Functions". The intuition in LPF's definition of $\wedge$, for example, is that for an expression $A \wedge B$, if either A or B evaluates to **false** the whole expression should be **false**, even if the other is undefined. If either evaluates to **true** then the expression evaluates, if at all, to the value of the other. So it is undefined if one of A and B is **true** and the other undefined, or both are undefined. Note that this explanation is symmetric in A and B, and indeed in LPF, as in classical logic, ∧ is symmetric (commutative).

The main problem with LPF is that ∧ is hard to implement in a programming language, because it requires parallel evaluation of the two component expressions, such that if one of them evaluates to **false** then the whole evaluation immediately terminates and returns **false**. For mainly this reason, the designers of RSL chose instead to define the logical connectives in terms of if-expressions, in a "conditional logic".

A ∧ B ≡ **if** A **then** B **else false end**
A ∨ B ≡ **if** A **then true else** B **end**
A ⇒ B ≡ **if** A **then** B **else true end**
∼A ≡ **if** A **then false else true end**

These are not new inventions. This version of ∧, for example, appears as `cand` in some languages, and as `andalso` in some others.

So if-expressions are fundamental, and we need to explain what they mean. We do this formally in terms of proof rules, but here is the intuitive explanation of the meaning of **if** A **then** B **else** C **end** (in the applicative case):

1. If A is undefined, then the expression is equivalent to A.
2. Otherwise, if A is nondeterministic (so it must be **true** ⌈⌉ **false**) the expression is equivalent to B ⌈⌉ C.
3. Otherwise, if A is true then the expression is equivalent to B, and if A is false then the expression is equivalent to C.

This coincides with the meaning of if-expressions in programming languages, and has the immediate consequence that if-expressions, and hence the logical connectives, are easy to implement. This is the main advantage of RSL's conditional logic. The main disadvantage is that we lose the unconditional commutativity of ∧ and ∨. For example,

chaos ∧ **false** ≡ **chaos**
but
false ∧ **chaos** ≡ **false**

∧ and ∨ are in general commutative only when both the components are defined.

This is by no means the only case where we need to be concerned with definedness, and it was decided that the implementability of the logic was the overriding concern.

Incidentally, many other rules of classical logic hold for conditional logic. For example, ∧ and ∨ are associative, and what is sometimes used as the definition of ⇒ holds:

$A \Rightarrow B \equiv {\sim}A \vee B$

All the laws of classical logic hold when expressions are convergent. The laws needing convergence are commutativity and "excluded middle". LPF also needs definedness for "excluded middle".

Quantifiers

RSL includes the quantifiers $\forall$, $\exists$ and $\exists!$. They all quantify over values in the appropriate type. Hence they say nothing about undefined expressions. For example, we can say, correctly, that

$\forall x : \mathbf{Bool} \bullet x = \mathbf{true} \vee x = \mathbf{false}$

without being able to conclude anything about an undefined expression such as **chaos** being either **true** or **false**.

Functions

λ-expressions admit beta reduction (application) only when applied to values in their domain. For example

$\lambda\ (x : \mathbf{Int},\ y: \mathbf{Int}) \bullet x$

cannot be applied to $(0, \mathbf{chaos})$ to give 0. In fact the semantics of function application is standard call by value: if any argument expression is undefined then so is the application.

Axioms

In RSL axioms may be declared. In addition, all value declarations are short for value signatures plus axioms. For example, suppose we have the value declaration

value
   factorial : $\mathbf{Nat} \overset{\sim}{\to} \mathbf{Nat}$
   factorial(n) $\equiv$
     if n = 1 **then** 1 **else** n $*$ factorial(n−1) **end**
   pre n $\geq$ 1

This is short for

value
   factorial : $\mathbf{Nat} \overset{\sim}{\to} \mathbf{Nat}$
axiom
  $\forall$ n : $\mathbf{Nat}$ $\bullet$
   factorial(n) $\equiv$
     if n = 1 **then** 1 **else** n $*$ factorial(n−1) **end**
    pre n $\geq$ 1

and, in turn "e **pre** p" is short for "(p ≡ **true**) ⇒ e". The inclusion of "≡ **true**" is just a technique to ensure that if p is undefined, the precondition reduces to **false**.

So, when can we use this axiom to "unfold" an application of factorial to replace it with its defining expression? We want to use the equivalence within the axiom, remembering that ≡ is a congruence, i.e. allows substitution. We can see that:

1. The actual parameter must be a value in the type **Nat**, i.e. it must be a non-negative integer, because of the meaning of ∀. We cannot unfold, say, factorial(**chaos**) or factorial(−1).
2. The precondition must then be equivalent to **true**. We cannot unfold, say, factorial(0).

So, the rules of the logic ensure that the apparent aim of the specifier, that factorial should be applied only to strictly positive integers, is respected.

Equality

We need to define the symbol =. In RSL its definition is just like that of any other infix operator, such as +. RSL adopts a general "left-to-right" evaluation rule, so the meaning of

$$A = B$$

is the following:

1. Evaluate A. If it is undefined so is the whole expression.
2. Otherwise, evaluate B. If it is undefined, so is the whole expression.
3. Otherwise, compare the results of evaluating A and B and return "true" if they are the same value, "false" otherwise.

= is therefore given a definition in terms of the underlying = for the carrier set of every type in RSL. If either of A or B is undefined then so is the equality. If either of them is nondeterministic, then so is the equality. Otherwise, in the applicative case, the equality is the same as ≡.

The other important feature of = is that it is implementable. Such an equality is sometimes called "programming language equality", as its evaluation is the same as in programming languages (except that many languages decline to fix the evaluation order, preferring the convenience of compiler writers to the confidence of users).

Is it confusing to have both = and ≡? The advice to users is simple: always use = in your expressions, and take care to avoid undefinedness. Users should only write ≡ in function definitions, where it is part of the syntax, and as the main equality in axioms.

We have seen that (for applicative expressions), when expressions are defined and deterministic, equality and equivalence coincide, and so there should be no problem. What happens if a user accidentally forgets to check for definedness? Take the RSL version of an example quoted by Stoddart et al. [30], for example:

value
  s : **Int-infset**
axiom
  card s = 5

Are there any models (implementations) of this specification in which the set s is infinite? (In languages in which all values denote, there may be such models, which is why the example is quoted.)

If s is infinite, then, in RSL, **card** s is undefined. So the axiom expression is apparently undefined, following our rules for equality. What does it mean to have an undefined axiom? In fact we avoid this question: every axiom implicitly has an "≡ **true**" added (like the precondition we discussed earlier). So if s is infinite the axiom would reduce to **false**, and we conclude that there can be no such model: s must be finite as we presumably expected.

There are a few other places where "≡ **true**" is included to make sure that undefined predicates reduce to **false**. These places occur in postconditions and in restrictions, as well as in axioms and preconditions. Restrictions are the predicates following the "bullet" in quantified expressions, implicit let-expressions, comprehensions, comprehended expressions and for-expressions.

2.3 Imperative and Concurrent RSL

When we consider expressions that can have effects i.e. that can read or write variables, or input from or output to channels, we need to extend the logic a little. In this subsection we the necessary extensions.

First, it is perhaps worth noting another problem with the LPF approach if expressions may be imperative. We noted earlier that LPF has to assume some kind of parallel evaluation rule to allow, for example, for one expression in a conjunction to be undefined when the other is false. But if the expressions may write to variables it is unclear how to deal with such effects with LPF's parallel evaluation. What should be the effect on the variable v, for example, of evaluating the following expression?

(v := v + 1 ; **true**) ∧ (v := v − 1 ; **false**)

Imperative specifications, like imperative programs, depend very heavily on evaluation order.

Equivalence

The general semantics of expressions is that they may have effects as well as returning results. For two expressions to be equivalent we require, that they have equivalent effects as well as equivalent results.

The equivalence expression "e1 ≡ e2" expresses a purely logical equivalence. It evaluates to **true** if the expressions would have the same effects, and would return the same results: there is no actual evaluation. Hence, unlike equality, evaluating an equivalence does not generate any effects.

If v is an integer variable, then, in some context, after assigning a value to v, we may know that "v ≡ 1". But, clearly, we cannot assert this in an arbitrary context, because v may have been assigned some other value there. To obtain a congruence relation, we introduce an extra connective "always", □. The expression "□ p" means "p is true in any state", i.e. regardless of the contents of variables. Thus "□ e1 ≡ e2" is a congruence: it allows e1 to be replaced by e2 in any context.

□ is implicitly included in all axioms. Since constant and function definitions are just shorthands for signatures and axioms, it is therefore implicit in any value definition. In practice, users do not need to write it.

Equality

For expressions with effects the difference between equality and equivalence becomes more marked. As we remarked earlier, an equality is evaluated left-to-right. At the end only the result values are compared. Therefore if the expression on the left has effects, these can affect the result of the expression on the right.

Suppose we have an integer variable v and we declare a function to increment it and return its new value:

variable
  v : **Int**
value
  increment : **Unit** → **write** v **Int**
  increment() ≡ v := v + 1 ; v

Now consider the two expressions

  increment() ≡ increment() and increment() = increment()

The first is equivalent to **true**, and its evaluation does not change v. We say that ≡ has only a "hypothetical" evaluation. Even when expressions have effects, ≡ remains reflexive.

The second has an effect of increasing v twice, as both the increment applications are evaluated. And we see that the result of the equality must be false: whatever the initial value of v, the result on the right will be one greater than the result on the left. We can summarise by concluding

  (increment() ≡ increment()) ≡ **true**

and

$(\text{increment}() = \text{increment}()) \equiv (v := v + 2; \text{false})$

The second result may seem surprising, but it is consistent with most programming languages. This does not mean, of course, that one would encourage anyone to write expressions in such a style!

Evaluation Order

The possibility of effects means that we need to be clear about the evaluation order of all expressions. For example, there is an evaluation rule for if-expressions,

if A **then** B **else** C **end** $\equiv$ **let** x = A **in if** x **then** B **else** C **end end**

where the identifier x is chosen so as not to be free in B or C (or such free occurrences would become bound in the let-expression). Such rules, using let-expressions, are very common in the proof rules of RSL, and we need to be clear what the semantics of let-expressions is. Using the let-expression above as an example, its evaluation is as follows:

1. A is evaluated. If it is undefined, then so is the whole expression. Otherwise, it may have effects, and will return a value. Since A must be a Boolean expression, this value must be either **true** or **false**. (If A is non-deterministic, we shall still get one of these, but we do not know which.)
2. The value returned by A is bound to the identifier x, and then we evaluate the second expression in the let-expression, i.e. the if-expression in this example. So we then evaluate either B or C according to the value returned by A.

For example, using our previous discussion about the increment function, we could conclude that

if increment() = increment() **then** B **else** C **end** $\equiv v := v + 2 ; C$

Reasoning Style

It is common in specification methods to use an axiomatic, "equational" style of reasoning for applicative constructs, as one does in mathematics. In RSL we typically use the same style of reasoning, based on equivalences, for imperative sequential descriptions and concurrent descriptions as well as for applicative descriptions. Other methods typically use reasoning based on Hoare logic or weakest preconditions (wp) for sequential imperative descriptions, and perhaps temporal logic for concurrent descriptions. This is mostly a question of style rather than substance: RSL includes preconditions and postconditions, and reasoning in terms of these is possible, and appropriate in particular for discussing iterative expressions (loops). But we generally find that equational reasoning can be used for all styles of specification.

2.4 Refinement in RSL

Since RSL is a modular language, refinement is aimed in particular at allowing substitution. If a module A, say, depends on another module B, say, then if we have a module B' that refines B, substituting B' for B should produce a module A' that refines A by construction. Refinement is required to be monotonic with respect to module composition. It is then possible to use *separate development* [2] to develop specifications expressed in several modules: modules can be developed independently, and provided each development can be shown to be a refinement, then putting the refined modules together will refine the specification as a whole.

A definition of refinement in RSL is that class expression B' *refines* class expression B provided:

1. The *signature* of B' includes that of B.
2. All the *properties* of B hold in B'.

The *signature* of a class consists of the type identifiers declared in it, together with the types (if any) for which they are abbreviations, the value, variable and channel identifiers, together with their types, and the object identifiers, together with the signatures of their classes. The *properties* of a class are defined in the book on the RAISE method [2].

The first condition for refinement ensures that substituting B' for B in some context will not generate type errors. It leads to a somewhat more restricted notion of refinement than in some languages that do not meet RSL's requirement to support separate development. Identifiers have to remain the same (though this can easily be fixed by RSL's renaming construct). Types that are abbreviations have to maintain the same abbreviation: if we declare in B, say,

type T = **Int-set**

then we cannot refine type T in B' to be, say, the type of lists of integers (**Int***), because in general we would get type errors when substituting B' for B to make A'. There is a standard technique in the RAISE method [2] for overcoming this problem, by first abstracting the original definition. We change the definition of T in B to

type T
value setof : T → **Int-set**

Both the type T and the function setof are left abstract. The abstraction expresses that a set can be extracted from a T value, rather than saying a T value is a set. Other definitions in B will also need changing, of course, using setof. Then we can define, in B',

type T = Int*
value
　setof : T → **Int-set**
　setof(t) ≡ **elems** t

These definitions in B′ refine those in B.

A feature of RSL is that the language can itself express the properties of any class expression. This in turn means that the logical conditions for refinement can be expressed in RSL, and indeed the RAISE Tool [31] can generate these as an RSL theory.

The second condition for refinement effectively says that anything that can be proved about a class can be proved about a class that refines it. So the stronger the properties of a module the less "room" there is to refine it. This is why, in particular, we adopt a particular kind of theory for functions. The definition of factorial given earlier in Sect. 2.2 says nothing about what the factorial function is when the arguments are not in the domain type **Nat** or do not satisfy the precondition: the definition given applies only for strictly positive arguments. It is then possible to refine factorial, if desired, by defining factorial(0) and even factorial for negative arguments. In fact, unless the function is declared with a domain type that is maximal (one that has no subtypes, such as **Int** rather than **Nat**), and without any precondition, it is impossible in RSL to say what its domain is. This is intentional: if we could calculate the domain it would be a property of the definition and allow for no refinement that enlarged the domain.

Another feature of the logic of RSL is that it can distinguish between determinism and nondeterminism. To be more precise, consider

value
　f() : **Unit** $\xrightarrow{\sim}$ **Int**
axiom
　f() = 1 ∨ f() = 2   (1)

We term this a *loose* specification: it has more than one model, and so more than one refinement. In fact, there are three: one where f() always returns 1, another where f() always returns 2, and a third,

f() : **Unit** $\xrightarrow{\sim}$ **Int**
f() ≡ 1 ⌐ 2   (2)

Here f is nondeterministic, and its theory is different from that of either of the others. So the "more deterministic" refinement ordering supported by some specification languages is not supported by RSL (though it is often not clear when people speak of nondeterminism, whether they mean looseness (1) or nondeterminism (2): often they actually mean looseness). Nondeterminism is important in analysing concurrency, so we need to be clear about the distinction between it and looseness.

2.5 Confidence Conditions

We return to the "problematic expressions" that we started discussing at the start of Sect. 2. We have discussed how the logic of RSL can deal with undefined expressions. We can also see how to write expressions that are safe from undefinedness. For example, suppose we have an RSL finite map (many–one relation) m with an **Int** domain type and a **Text** range type. Suppose we want to specify that all the texts in the map are non-empty. If we write

$$\forall\, x : \textbf{Int} \bullet m(x) \neq \text{''''}$$

then m(x) may be undefined for values of x not in the domain of the map. As it happens, in this case, the implicit "$\equiv$ **true**" in the quantified expression takes care of the undefinedness, but (a) we do not encourage users to write specifications based on such details of the logic, and (b) the "$\equiv$ **true**" will not be there when we transform this into an implementation with a loop, say, and we should perhaps help the implementor a little. So, there is a general rule that you never write a map application without making sure that it is guarded by a check that the argument is in the domain. Therefore, there should be an "x $\in$ **dom** m" condition, which may be the left of an implication or conjunction, the condition of an if-expression (with the application in the "then" part), or part of a precondition of the function definition in which the application occurs. Here (remembering the other rule of thumb, that $\forall$ expressions almost always use $\Rightarrow$) we should obviously have written

$$\forall\, x : \textbf{Int} \bullet x \in \textbf{dom}\ m \Rightarrow m(x) \neq \text{''''}$$

and we see that the conditional logic means that the application is only evaluated only when the map argument is in the map's domain.

Guard conditions, like "x $\in$ **dom** m" for the application "m(x)", are called "confidence conditions" in RSL. We use this term because it is not always necessary to include them if our aim is just to avoid undefinedness: the quantified expression above is an example. But if we always include them then we have more confidence that the specification does not include undefined expressions, which means in turn that it is less likely to be inconsistent. The RAISE tools [31] include a "confidence condition generator" that generates the confidence conditions for a range of potentially undefined expressions. Map arguments being in domains, list arguments being in index sets, and partial operator and function arguments being in domain types and satisfying preconditions are in practice the most important of these conditions. Checking that they hold in the contexts that generate them is not in general decidable, and it needs proof tools to discharge them formally.

Confidence conditions are usually best checked by inspection: they act as reminders. Unfortunately, as the specifier's skill increases the "hit rate" of conditions requiring attention becomes low, and so the possibility of missing them during inspection rises. We now have proof tool support for discharging many of them automatically.

3 The Axiomatic Semantics: A Logic for Definition

In this section, we explain how RSL is given a proof theory [8] that provides the axiomatic semantics of RSL.

3.1 Purpose and Role

The purpose of the proof theory is to provide formation rules for determining whether a specification is well-formed (type correct etc.) and proof rules for reasoning about specifications, for example deciding whether two RSL terms are equivalent (they have the same meaning) or deciding whether an RSL specification is a refinement of another RSL specification.

The role of the proof theory is to provide an axiomatic semantics that defines the meaning of RSL whereas the role of the denotational semantics [7] is just to ensure consistency of the proof theory by providing a model. The reason for taking this view of roles is the fact that the proof theory is needed anyway (since we should be able to reason about specifications) and it is much more comprehensible than the denotational semantics (since its metalanguage is much simpler). The RSL type checker implements the formation rules, while the RAISE justification editor implements a proof system (see Sect. 4) that is derived from the axiomatic semantics.

3.2 The Form of the Definition of the Axiomatic Semantics

The axiomatic semantics consists of a collection of *inference rules* of the form

$$\frac{\text{premise}_1 \ \ldots \ \text{premise}_n}{\text{conclusion}}$$

where the upper part consists of a possibly empty list of formulae, called the premises, and the lower part consists of a formula, called the conclusion. The most important kinds of formulae are those for expressing the static semantics of RSL terms, refinement of RSL terms and equivalences between RSL terms. The formulae may contain term variables.

As usual, the inference rules can be instantiated by consistently replacing term variables with actual, variable-free terms of the same syntactic category. A rule represents all its legal instantiations. An instantiated rule expresses that if the (instantiated) premises hold then also the (instantiated) conclusion holds.

3.3 The Collection of Inference Rules

In this section, we give examples of some important classes of inference rules.

Formation Rules

For each RSL term that is not defined to be a context independent short-hand (see below), there is an inference rule defining its static semantics. For instance, the rule

---

context $\vdash$ **true** $:\preceq$ **Bool**

---

states that the RSL term **true** is well-formed and has type **Bool** as its static semantics. This rule is simple, having no premises and not referring to the context,[2] but many rules have static premises expressing that sub-terms are well-formed, have appropriate types, refer only to names declared in the context, etc.

The formation rules provide a decidable test for whether terms are well-formed.

Context-independent Equivalence Rules

There is a class of inference rules that define a context-independent equivalence relation $\cong$. Intuitively, $\vdash$ $term_1$ $\cong$ $term_2$ asserts that the two terms $term_1$ and $term_2$ are equivalent in all respects, i.e. have the same properties (attributes, static semantics and dynamic meaning) and can be substituted for each other anywhere.

The context-independent equivalence rules typically express algebraic laws like commutativity of the concurrency operator:

$\vdash$ value_expr$_1$ $\|$ value_expr$_2$ $\cong$
   value_expr$_2$ $\|$ value_expr$_1$

A subclass of these rules, the context-independent expansion rules, have the role of expressing that certain RSL terms are shorthands for others. For instance, the rule

---

$\vdash$ value_expr$_1$ $\wedge$ value_expr$_2$ $\cong$
   if value_expr$_1$ **then** value_expr$_2$ **else false end**

---

states that a conjunction of the form value_expr$_1$ $\wedge$ value_expr$_2$ is a shorthand for **if** value_expr$_1$ **then** value_expr$_2$ **else false end** (compare the discussion of the meaning of the RSL connectives in Sect. 2.2).

When a term is defined to be a shorthand, there do not need to be any other rules having a conclusion concerning that term – all properties are to

---

[2] A context provides assumptions about identifiers and operators. In its most basic form, a context is an RSL class expression.

be derived from the term that it is a shorthand for. For a term that is not a shorthand, there will typically be several rules having a conclusion concerning that term.

Context-dependent Equivalence Rules

There is another class of inference rules that define a context-dependent equivalence relation, $\simeq$ for stating that in a given context two terms are equivalent in the weaker sense that they have the same meaning (which may depend on the context), but not necessarily the same static properties. For example, their free variables might differ. An example of such a rule is

context $\vdash$ value_expr $:\preceq$ opt_access_desc_string **Bool**
context $\vdash$ **read-only-convergent** value_expr

---

context $\vdash$
   if value_expr **then** value_expr **else true end** $\simeq$
      true

This states that, in a given context, the value expression **if** value_expr **then** value_expr **else true end** is equivalent to **true**, if the constituent value_expr is (1) well-formed with type **Bool**, and (2) read-only and convergent. The first condition in the rule ensures that the equivalence between the two terms can be proved only when these are both well-formed. Otherwise, the rule would not be sound (one could, for example, prove **if** 1 **then** 1 **else true end** $\simeq$ **true**). The second condition in the rule ensures that the if-expression does not have any side effects and is convergent. Otherwise, one could e.g. prove

   if x := 1; **true then** x := 1; **true else true end** $\simeq$ **true**.

As in the context-independent case, there is a subclass of these rules, the role of which is to define shorthands.

Refinement Rules

A collection of inference rules define the refinement relation.

Auxiliary Rules

There are several collections of rules that define auxiliary functions and relations, which are used in the premises of the other rules.

For instance, there is a collection of rules that define *attribute* functions *new* and *free*, which take an RSL term as an argument and return the set of identifiers and operators that are declared and occur free in the term, respectively. These are used in the premises of other rules to express restrictions on identifiers or operators appearing in the conclusion.

3.4 Relation to Denotational Semantics

RSL has been given a denotational semantics in [7]. This denotational semantics can be extended in an obvious way to cover also the formulae of the metalanguage of the axiomatic semantics. For instance, the meaning of a formula of the form *value_expr* can be defined to be the same as the meaning of the value expression $\square(value\_expr \equiv \mathbf{true})$.

There are some questions about how we can achieve completeness and soundness for a language as large as RSL. This is not to claim that RSL is particularly large, merely that any rich language will have similar problems. Soundness and completeness with respect to the denotational semantics are discussed in the following subsections.

3.5 Soundness

The defining proof rules can either be asserted as the true definition, and so declared as sound a priori, or else be proved against the denotational semantics [32]. In the first case, it would still be desirable to check the denotational semantics against the proof rules. But it is difficult to see how this could be done other than in an informal manner. The denotational semantics is some 350 pages of formulae, and there are a number of known errors in it (and an unknown number of others!). It is, however, thought that there are no substantial problems with this document, and that the errors could be "fixed" without radical change. One can therefore take the view that the defining proof rules form an axiomatic semantics, and that the denotational semantics provides evidence of the existence of a model satisfying these properties. This is largely the view taken in the book on the RAISE method [2], where specifications are described in terms of their signatures and logical properties, and refinement between specifications is correspondingly defined in terms of signature inclusion and property entailment. It is a useful feature of RSL that its logic is powerful enough to itself express the properties needed to show refinement.

3.6 Completeness

The completeness of a set of proof rules is rather easier to deal with. First, there are language constructs that are defined in terms of others. So, for example, the five kinds of value definition in the language can all be expressed as one, a signature plus an axiom.

For the constructs that are left, one defines a collection of "normal forms" and adds rules to show how other forms may be made normal. Then the operators are defined in terms of the normal forms. This is the way the defining rules for RSL were written.

Completeness is relative, of course, to the rules for the built-in types, including **Bool**, **Int** and **Real**. The definitional rules ignore the rules for these types completely. In a proof, one would expect to use standard definitions of such types.

4 The RSL Proof System: A Logic for Proof

When we consider a suitable logic for conducting proofs, our concerns become more practical. We have to take care of soundness, of course: we must not enable the proof of invalid theorems. But what the user will, in practice, be most concerned with is the ability to prove valid theorems, and preferably being able to do so automatically.

This raises the question of completeness. It seems obvious at first that the proof system should be complete (all valid theorems should be provable). But in practice it seems worth sacrificing completeness in a few places to obtain more ease of proof in the vast majority of cases. In fact we sacrificed completeness in favour of a simplified language for proof rules. In particular, the language does not include contexts, which are, in general, much more easily handled implicitly by a tool, and as a consequence RSL's 'local-expressions', which allow local definitions, are not catered for with full generality.

So, the proof system is sound but incomplete compared with the axiomatic semantics, though most of the incompleteness is handled by a tool.

4.1 The Justification Editor

The proof rules are intended for application by a tool, the RAISE *justification editor*. We can therefore immediately assume a mechanism for type-checking, and make a general assertion that a proof rule may be applied only to well-formed expressions, and application succeeds only when it gives a result that is also well-formed. The tool also handles the *context*, the bindings of names to their definitions, which further simplifies the rule language.

The general form of a rule is the inference rule introduced in Sect. 3. But most of the proof rules take the form

$$term_1 \simeq term_2 \textbf{ when } term_3$$

where $term_3$ (termed the *side condition*) is the conjunction of the premises. The context is the same for all the terms. Such a rule allows an expression matching $term_1$ to be replaced by the corresponding instantiation of $term_2$ (or vice versa), provided the instantiated $term_3$ can be proved. The important point about the justification editor is that it allows proof rules to be applied to *sub*-expressions of a goal. The basic style of proof is to

- select a sub-expression (a mouse drag)
- show the applicable proof rules (a menu)
- select and apply a rule (mouse clicks)

The applicable rules are selected by syntax, and are generally few in number, so supporting easy selection. This allows a very user-controlled, natural, flexible style of proof.

Side conditions generate separate proof obligations, so that a proof becomes a tree. The branches can be proved in any order, and so one may choose whether to check a side condition first, in order to check that a strategy is applicable, or proceed with the main proof first, in order to check that a strategy is appropriate.

The term *justification* was coined for a proof in which not all steps have to be proved formally. The tool accepts the informal assertion that a goal is true, or that an expression may be replaced by another asserted as equivalent. The tool keeps track of such informal steps. A justification may be stored and then loaded again, for the proof to be reviewed, or pretty-printed or for informal steps to perhaps be made formal.

4.2 Proof Rule Language

The language for expressing proof rules is, in fact, a small extension of RSL. A correspondingly small extension to the type checker allows proof rules to be type-checked. The justification editor supports the input of proof rules: they are mostly not built-in. This allows for greater transparency, and the main document listing the rules [33] was in fact generated from the input given to the justification editor.

The proof rule language has a number of rules for instantiation of term variables that are implicit in their names. For example, names differing only in the number of primes must have the same maximal type, but names may otherwise have different types. Names starting with "p_" may be matched only by pure expressions, those starting with "ro_" may be matched only by read-only expressions, those involving "eb" must be Boolean expressions, etc.

For example, the rule for if-expressions mentioned in Sect. 3 is written

[if_annihilation1]
    if eb **then** eb **else true end** $\simeq$ **true**
      when convergent(eb) $\wedge$ **readonly**(eb)

The first line is the rule name (which appears in selection menus). There are various naming conventions, which together indicate that this rule may be used to "annihilate" or remove an if-expression. (Or, applied right-to-left, to introduce one.) The side condition uses two of the "special functions" that are used in many proof rules. Their (partial) evaluation is built into the justification editor, so that **readonly**, for example, will generally be discharged automatically when it holds. **convergent** can be more difficult to prove, of course.

"**convergent**(eb)" is just an abbreviation for "eb **post true**". Special functions typically express simple concepts but may have more complicated definitions. There are special functions, for example, to express the conditions necessary for a new binding not to capture free names (**no_capture**), for a replacement binding to capture only names that the previous one did (**no_new_capture**), and for an expression to match a pattern (**matches**).

Of particular importance in a language with *effects* (assignments to variables, input and output) are rules showing the order of evaluation. Without these many constructs would be ambiguous. There is a general "rule of thumb" that evaluation is left-to-right. More formally, it is defined by "_evaluation" rules. The evaluation of an if-expression, for example, is given by

[if_evaluation]
> **if** eb **then** e **else** e' **end** $\simeq$
>> **let** id $=$ eb **in if** id **then** e **else** e' **end end**
>>> **when no_capture**(id, e) $\wedge$ **no_capture**(id, e')

This rule is always applicable left-to-right – the side condition requires only the choice of an identifier not free in e or e' – and shows that the guard condition is evaluated before anything else. If eb does not terminate, then neither will the let-expression. Otherwise eb will evaluate to either **true** or **false** and the corresponding if_annihilation rule can be applied. To deal with the case where eb is nondeterministic, we have

[let_int_choice]
> **let** b $=$ e $\lceil\rceil$ e' **in** e1 **end** $\simeq$
>> **let** b $=$ e **in** e1 **end** $\lceil\rceil$ **let** b $=$ e' **in** e1 **end**

To show that the rules are sound, we have divided them into "basic" rules, which are just rewritings of the definitional rules of Sect. 3, and "derived" rules, which should be derivable from the basic ones. There are just over 200 basic rules, and currently well over 2000 derived ones, which shows the importance of convenience in proof.

4.3 Context Rules

No distinction between basic and derived rules is made in the justification editor, as this distinction is generally uninteresting for the user. A distinction that *is* made is between the rules of RSL and the rules that users may apply because they are axioms of their specifications, termed *context rules*. For example, when one is proving something in the context of the axiom

axiom
> [is_in_empty] $\forall$ x : Elem $\bullet$ $\sim$is_in(x, empty)

(where the type Elem, the constant empty and the function is_in are also declared in the context), the *context rule*

[is_in_empty]
  is_in(e, empty) $\simeq$ **false**
    when convergent(e) $\wedge$ **pure**(e) $\wedge$ **isin_subtype**(e, Elem)

is available. Note the way in which the universal quantifier gives rise to a
term variable "e". Value definitions, since they are equivalent to signatures
and axioms, also generate context rules.

Some type definitions also give rise to context rules. Variant types generate
induction rules, and disjointness rules asserting that different constructors
generate different values. Record types are treated as singleton variants, and
so also generate induction rules.

4.4 Definition Versus Proof

We can now summarise the main differences between rules used for definition
and those used for proof:

- The defining rules need to be concerned with well-formedness (scope and
  type) rules, while the rules for proof can assume terms are well-formed.
- If the defining rules were the only definition they would necessarily be
  considered sound and complete, because they would be the only reference.
  But we also have a denotational semantics and can conclude, conventionally, that with respect to that semantics they need to be sound, and it is
  desirable that they also be complete.

  Rules for proof are more concerned with utility. The smaller a set of defining rules we have, the more easily can we show it to be sound. In general,
  as long as the search problem is manageable, the larger the set of rules for
  proof we have the easier proofs will be.
- A simple meta language for proof rules helps users understand, choose and
  apply rules. Context information is best handled by tools rather than by
  direct manipulation. This leads, in the case of RSL, to incompleteness for
  local-expressions, which contain definitions.

There are some questions about how we achieve completeness and soundness for a language as large as RSL. This is not to claim RSL to be particularly
large, merely that any rich language will have similar problems.

5 Case Study

This section is intended to illustrate how a system can be specified in RSL
and verified using various RAISE tools. The example considered is a harbour
information system, with functions for interrogating and changing the data,
and invariant properties that the data must satisfy. First, in Sect. 5.1, a simple version of the system is specified and is proved to preserve the invariant
properties, and in Sect. 5.2 alternative methods of verification are discussed.
Next, in Sect. 5.3, we consider a more complex version of the system.

5.1 A Simple Version

In this section, we give an applicative, explicit (model-oriented) specification of a simple version of the system. In the RAISE method book [2] it has been shown how such an applicative, explicit specification can be developed from a more abstract (algebraic) specification, and how it can be transformed further into an imperative specification.

Requirements

The harbour is illustrated in Fig. 1.

Ships arriving at a harbour have to be allocated berths in the harbour which are vacant and which they will fit, or to wait in a "pool" until a suitable berth is available. We assume that all ships will have to arrive and to wait (perhaps only notionally) in the pool before they can dock.

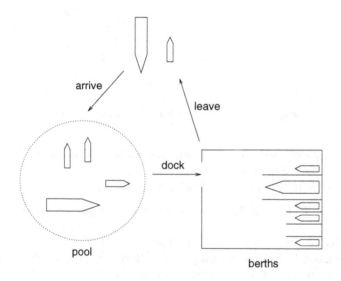

Fig. 1. Harbour

The requirements are to develop a system that provides the following functions to allow the harbour master to control the movement of ships in and out of the harbour:

- **arrive:** to register the arrival of a ship;
- **dock:** to register a ship docking in a berth;
- **leave:** to register a ship leaving a berth.

Specification

We first ask what the objects of a harbour are, and what their static and dynamic relationships are. The objects of a harbour are ships, a fixed collection of berths and a pool. The pool consists of a collection of ships, and a berth is either empty or occupied by a ship. A ship may or may not fit a berth. The entity relationships are shown in Fig. 2. The ships in the pool and the

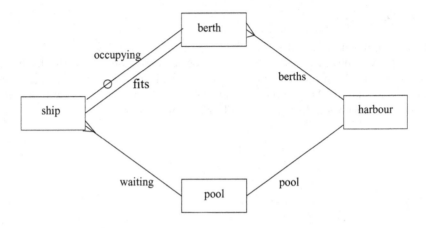

Fig. 2. Entity relationships for harbour system

ship occupancy of berths will change dynamically when ships arrive, dock and leave. All other relations are static.

Our plan is to develop the following modules:

- A scheme TYPES, defining types and static properties for the basic objects.
- A global object T that is an instantiation of TYPES.
- A scheme HARBOUR, defining a type *Harbour* for data about the state of the harbour and the required top-level functions.

So, the structure of the specification should be

> **scheme** TYPES = **class** ... **end**
> **object** T : TYPES
> **scheme** HARBOUR = **class** ... **end**

The HARBOUR module can access types and functions defined in TYPES by qualifying their names with a T.

In the following we will first present the contents of the TYPES module and then the contents of the HARBOUR module.

The TYPES *Module*

In the following, we show the declarations that should constitute the TYPES module.

First, we identify the basic objects of the system: ships and berths. For these, we declare two types, *Ship* and *Berth*:

type Ship, Berth

Then, we look for static properties of the objects. According to the requirements, a ship may or may not *fit* a berth. So, we declare a function that can test this static relationship:

value fits : Ship × Berth → **Bool**.

However, we leave it underspecified.

No other static properties are mentioned in the requirements. However, we decide that it would be convenient to let each berth have a unique index as a static attribute. Therefore, we specify a function that can observe the index of a berth:

value
  indx : Berth → Index
axiom
  [berths_indexable] ∀ b1, b2 : Berth • indx(b1) = indx(b2) ⇒ b1 = b2

We define the type *Index* to be the subtype of all integers in an interval determined by two underspecified integer constants *min* and *max*:

type
  Index = {| i : **Int** • i ≥ min ∧ max ≥ i |}
value
  min, max : **Int**
axiom
  [index_not_empty] max ≥ min

At this point, we leave it open whether ships and berths should have additional attributes. Later we may e.g. decide to let them have an attribute *size* in terms of which the *fits* relation could then be calculated.

The HARBOUR *Module*

The HARBOUR module should contain:

- an explicit definition of the type of interest (the type *Harbour* of harbour states);
- an explicit definition of some useful observer (query) functions;
- an explicit definition of three required generator functions, namely *arrive*, *dock* and *leave*

- an explicit definition of guards for the generators;
- an explicit definition of a function (*consistent*) to express the state invariant.

The state of a harbour is given by the pool of waiting ships and how ships are occupying the berths. Hence, a natural concrete type to use for Harbour is a short record having a component *pool*, which is a set of waiting ships and a component berths, which is a map from the indices of occupied berths to the ships that are docked in those berths:

type /* type of interest */
  Harbour ::
    pool : T.Ship-**set**
    berths : T.Index $\overrightarrow{m}$ T.Ship

It turns out that the following observer (query) functions will be useful:

value /* observer (query) functions */
  waiting : T.Ship × Harbour → **Bool**
  waiting(s, h) ≡ s ∈ pool(h)

  is_docked : T.Ship × Harbour → **Bool**
  is_docked(s, h) ≡ s ∈ **rng** berths(h)

  is_vacant : T.Berth × Harbour → **Bool**
  is_vacant(b, h) ≡ T.indx(b) ∉ **dom** berths(h)

  is_occupied_by : T.Berth × T.Ship × Harbour → **Bool**
  is_occupied_by(b, s, h) ≡
    (T.indx(b) ∈ **dom** berths(h)) ∧ (berths(h)(T.indx(b)) = s)

These are all given explicit definitions utilising the chosen concrete *Harbour* type. Actually, *waiting* and *is_occupied_by* are basic observers, from which we could have derived (i.e. in terms of which we could have given definitions of) *is_docked* and *is_vacant*. However, we gave a shorter, equivalent definition of *is_docked* and *is_vacant*. One could also imagine other useful query functions, e.g. one for giving the location of a ship. These can be added later, if needed.

A constant *empty* representing the state of an empty harbour and the three required generator functions, *arrive*, *dock* and *leave*, can be given explicit definitions utilising the chosen concrete *Harbour* type:

value /* generator functions */
  empty : Harbour = mk_Harbour({}, [ ])

  arrive : T.Ship × Harbour $\overset{\sim}{\to}$ Harbour
  arrive(s, h) ≡ mk_Harbour(pool(h) ∪ {s}, berths(h))
  pre can_arrive(s, h)

dock : T.Ship × T.Berth × Harbour $\xrightarrow{\sim}$ Harbour
dock(s, b, h) ≡ mk_Harbour(pool(h) \ {s}, berths(h) † [T.indx(b) ↦ s])
pre can_dock(s, b, h)

leave : T.Ship × T.Berth × Harbour $\xrightarrow{\sim}$ Harbour
leave(s, b, h) ≡ mk_Harbour(pool(h), berths(h) \ {T.indx(b)})
pre can_leave(s, b, h)

The generator functions are all partial as there are situations where they cannot sensibly be applied. Preconditions define when they may be applied. The preconditions are formulated using auxiliary functions (called "guards") can_arrive, etc. All these guards are derived from (i.e. given explicit definitions in terms of) the observers:

value /∗ guards ∗/
can_arrive : T.Ship × Harbour → **Bool**
can_arrive(s, h) ≡ ∼ waiting(s, h) ∧ ∼ is_docked(s, h)

can_dock : T.Ship × T.Berth × Harbour → **Bool**
can_dock(s, b, h) ≡
    waiting(s, h) ∧ ∼ is_docked(s, h) ∧ is_vacant(b, h) ∧ T.fits(s, b)

can_leave : T.Ship × T.Berth × Harbour → **Bool**
can_leave(s, b, h) ≡ is_occupied_by(b, s, h)

Finally, we consider what the desired *invariants* (properties that should always be true) of the data are. Some possibilities are

- at most one ship can be in any one berth;
- a ship cannot be in two places at once, i.e.
  - it cannot be waiting and docked at once, and
  - it cannot be docked in two distinct berths at once;
- a ship can only be in a berth that it fits.

Sometimes we can express (part of) the invariant in the data structure, and this applies to the first of our invariant items. We have modelled the berths by a finite map from berth index to ship, and since finite maps are deterministic, at most one ship can be associated with any berth index, and hence with any berth (since *indx* is a total function and hence deterministic). If we wish to formalise this argument we would want to prove

∀ ... • is_occupied_by(b,s1,h)∧is_occupied_by(b,s2,h) ⇒ s1=s2

which unfolds to

∀ ...•...∧berths(h)(T.indx(b))=s1∧berths(h)(T.indx(b))=s2 ⇒ s1=s2 which is immediate.

We then introduce a predicate *consistent* that tests whether a harbour state satisfies the remaining invariants. We specify it explicitly in terms of the observer functions:

consistent : Harbour → **Bool**
consistent(h) ≡
  (∀ s : T.Ship •
    ~ (waiting(s, h) ∧ is_docked(s, h)) ∧
    (∀ b1, b2 : T.Berth •
      is_occupied_by(b1, s, h) ∧ is_occupied_by(b2, s, h) ⇒ b1 = b2) ∧
    (∀ b : T.Berth •
      is_occupied_by(b, s, h) ⇒ T.fits(s, b))
)

Proof Obligations

Our goal is to prove that the initial state *empty* satisfies the state invariant

consistent(empty)

and that the state-changing functions preserve the state invariant, e.g.

∀ h : Harbour, s : T.Ship •
  consistent(h) ∧ can_arrive(s, h) ⇒ consistent(arrive(s, h))

Proof Using eden

Below, we show how the second of the proof obligations can be discharged using the RAISE justification editor 'eden'.

The proof is carried out by a series of steps in which proof rules are applied to transform the goal (proof obligation) into a new goal(s), the truth of which ensures the truth of the original goal. In the proof goals are written within "half-brackets" ⌊ and ⌋, and the names of the proof rules applied are written between the goals. We have hidden some of the intermediate goals using comma-separated lists of the names of the proof rules applied.

The proof is performed in the context of the HARBOUR specification, which means that we may use the definitions of that specification in the proof. More precisely, each of the definitions gives rise to context rules. As an example, the record type definition of the *Harbour* type gives rise to the following two rules, among others:

[pool_mk_Harbour] pool(mk_Harbour(p, b)) ≃ p
[berths_mk_Harbour] berths(mk_Harbour(p, b)) ≃ b

First we show the proof, and then we shall explain some of the steps.

⌊∀ h : Harbour, s : T.Ship •

consistent(h) ∧ can_arrive(s, h) ⇒ consistent(arrive(s, h))⌋
all_assumption_inf, imply_deduction_inf1 :
[gen_131] consistent(h) ∧ can_arrive(s, h) ⊢
⌊consistent(arrives(s, h))⌋
/* unfold all function applications */
application_expr_unfold2, application_expr_unfold1, all_name_change,
all_assumption_inf, application_expr_unfold1, application_expr_unfold1,
application_expr_unfold1, application_expr_unfold1,
application_expr_unfold1,

⌊ ~ (s′ ∈ pool(mk_Harbour(pool(h) ∪ {s}, berths(h))) ∧
        s′ ∈ **rng** berths(mk_Harbour(pool(h) ∪ {s}, berths(h))))
    ∧
    (∀ b1, b2 : T.Berth •
      ((T.indx(b1) ∈
        dom berths(mk_Harbour(pool(h) ∪ {s}, berths(h)))) ∧
        (berths(mk_Harbour(pool(h) ∪ {s}, berths(h)))(T.indx(b1)) = s′)
) ∧
      (T.indx(b2) ∈
        dom berths(mk_Harbour(pool(h) ∪ {s}, berths(h)))) ∧
        (berths(mk_Harbour(pool(h) ∪ {s}, berths(h)))(T.indx(b2)) = s′) ⇒
        b1 = b2)
    ∧
    (∀ b : T.Berth •
      (T.indx(b) ∈
        dom berths(mk_Harbour(pool(h) ∪ {s}, berths(h)))) ∧
        (berths(mk_Harbour(pool(h) ∪ {s}, berths(h)))(T.indx(b)) = s′) ⇒
        T.fits(s′, b))⌋
/* simplify */
simplify, application_expansion3,
application_expansion3, application_expansion3, simplify,
and_associativity :
⌊~ ((s′ = s ∨ s′ ∈ pool(h)) ∧ s′ ∈ **rng** berths(h)) ∧
    (∀ b1, b2 : T.Berth •
      (T.indx(b1) ∈ **dom** berths(h) ∧ (berths(h))(T.indx(b1)) = s′) ∧
      T.indx(b2) ∈ **dom** berths(h) ∧ (berths(h))(T.indx(b2)) = s′ ⇒
      b1 = b2) ∧
    (∀ b : T.Berth •
      T.indx(b) ∈ **dom** berths(h) ∧ (berths(h))(T.indx(b)) = s′ ⇒
      T.fits(s′, b))⌋
/* fold in applications of is_occupied_by */
substitution1, substitution1, substitution1 :
⌊~ ((s′ = s ∨ s′ ∈ pool(h)) ∧ s′ ∈ **rng** berths(h)) ∧
    (∀ b1, b2 : T.Berth •

(is_occupied_by(b1, s′, h)) ∧ is_occupied_by(b2, s′, h) ⇒
b1 = b2) ∧

(∀ b : T.Berth • is_occupied_by(b, s′, h) ⇒ T.fits(s′, b))⌟
/* remove the two last conjuncts
  using the consistent(h) assumption of gen_131 */
consistent, consistent, simplify,
/* prove this by case analysis */
two_cases_inf :

- [gen_695] s = s′ ⊢
  ⌞~ ((s′ = s ∨ s′ ∈ pool(h)) ∧ s′ ∈ **rng** berths(h))⌟
  simplify, gen_695,
  imply_modus_ponens_inf :

  - ⌞can_arrive(s, h)⌟
    gen_131, qed

  - ⌞can_arrive(s, h) ⇒ ~ (s ∈ **rng** berths(h))⌟
    application_expr_unfold1, application_expr_unfold1, simplify, qed

- [gen_694] ~ (s = s′) ⊢
  ⌞~ ((s′ = s ∨ s′ ∈ pool(h)) ∧ s′ ∈ **rng** berths(h))⌟
  simplify,
  imply_modus_ponens_inf :

  - ⌞consistent(h)⌟
    gen_131, qed

  - ⌞consistent(h) ⇒ ~ (s′ ∈ pool(h) ∧ s′ ∈ **rng** berths(h))⌟
    application_expr_unfold1, application_expr_unfold1,
    application_expr_unfold1, simplify, qed

In the first step of the proof, we assume that we have a fixed but arbitrary ship s and harbour h.

In the second step, we use the rule

[imply_deduction_inf1]

$$\frac{[id]\ \text{ro\_eb} \vdash \text{ro\_eb}'}{\text{ro\_eb} \Rightarrow \text{ro\_eb}'}$$

when **convergent**(ro_eb) ∧ **pure**(ro_eb)

obtaining a new goal, which must be proved in the context of an assumption named [gen_131].

Then, we perform a number of steps in which we repeatedly use the *application_expr_unfold* rules to unfold function applications according to their definitions in HARBOUR.

Next, we simplify the goal obtained, using, among others the *simplify* rule which automatically applies a number of rules according to some built-in strategy. In this case [*pool_mk_Harbour*] and [*berths_mk_Harbour*] are two of the rules that it applies.

After that, we substitute three of the subterms with applications of the function *is_occupied_by*, using its definition in HARBOUR. By this technique, we reach a goal that we prove by a case analysis with two cases.

Proof via Translation

The original RAISE tools, which are the tools mostly discussed in this chapter, are being superseded by a new tool which is much more portable [31]. This new tool provides support for proof via translation [34] to PVS [27], thus making available the power of the PVS proof engine. This approach, based on a "shallow" embedding of RSL into PVS, can provide only a limited proof system because PVS is applicative – imperative and concurrent RSL is excluded. PVS also has a different logic from RSL that excludes undefinedness and nondeterminism (the "every expression denotes a value" approach described in Sect. 2), and so special care in that the translation, including the generation of extra lemmas based on confidence conditions, is needed to ensure the translation is sound. A "deep" embedding into PVS would entail the modelling of RSL's semantics in the PVS logic. This may be possible, and might be useful for exercises in checking RSL proof rules, but would be unlikely to produce a tool useful in practice for performing proofs about RSL specifications.

The PVS translator does not need many proof rules for RAISE, because the target constructs of the translation are either built into PVS (like arithmetic), defined by built-in expansions (like abstract data types) or defined in the PVS prelude (like sets and lists). A few additional constructs (including maps) are defined in an "RSL prelude". This contains only a few theorems, most of the definitions being constructive.

We have used the new tool to translate the proof obligations of Sect. 5.1 into PVS and proved them using the PVS proof engine. The consistency of the *empty* state was proved automatically. The other three proofs were completed with about half the number of proof steps required with eden. Detailed figures are given later, in Sect. 5.3.

In the remaining of this section we shall compare the styles of proof in PVS and eden.

Consider the point commented "/* prove this by case analysis */" in the eden proof. Here the proof goal is

$$\llcorner {\sim} \left(\left(s' = s \vee s' \in \text{pool}(h)\right) \wedge s' \in \textbf{rng } \text{berths}(h)\right) \lrcorner$$

Note that eden keeps assumptions hidden unless the user asks to see them. The hidden assumptions at this point are *can_arrive(s, h)* and *consistent(h)*.

The state of the PVS proof at about the same point is

```
[-1]   pool(h!1)(s!2) OR s!1 = s!2
[-2]   EXISTS (d: Index):
          nonnil?(berths(h!1)(d)) AND
```

```
              s!2 = rng_part(berths(h!1)(d))
[-3]   FORALL (s: T.Ship):
         NOT (pool(h!1)(s) AND
             (EXISTS (d: Index):
                 nonnil?(berths(h!1)(d)) AND
                     s = rng_part(berths(h!1)(d))))
         AND
         ((FORALL (b1: T.Berth, b2: T.Berth):
             (nonnil?(berths(h!1)(T.indx(b1))) AND
              (rng_part(berths(h!1)(T.indx(b1))) = s))
             AND
             nonnil?(berths(h!1)(T.indx(b2))) AND
              (rng_part(berths(h!1)(T.indx(b2))) = s)
             IMPLIES b1 = b2)
           AND
           (FORALL (b: T.Berth):
             nonnil?(berths(h!1)(T.indx(b))) AND
             (rng_part(berths(h!1)(T.indx(b))) = s)
             IMPLIES T.fits(s, b)))
 |-------
[1]    pool(h!1)(s!1)
[2]    EXISTS (d: Index):
         nonnil?(berths(h!1)(d)) AND
             s!1 = rng_part(berths(h!1)(d))
```

Essentially, this means that we have to prove (using the sequent numbers for the sequents)

$$[-1] \land [-2] \land [-3] \Rightarrow [1] \lor [2]$$

which is logically equivalent to

$$\sim [1] \land \sim [2] \land [-3] \Rightarrow \sim ([-1] \land [-2])$$

We will see below that this second formulation has the same structure as the eden goal.

In PVS, s!1, s!2 and h!1 correspond to s, s' and h, respectively in RSL. Sets are modelled by predicates in PVS, and so s' ∈ pool(h) becomes pool(h!1)(s!2).

RSL maps are like partial functions: they can be applied only to values in their domain. In PVS, where we have only total functions, we model a map as a total function that returns nil when applied to values not in the domain. We use a PVS "datatype" Maprange:

```
Maprange[rng: TYPE]: DATATYPE
BEGIN
```

```
nil: nil?
mk_rng(rng_part: rng): nonnil?
END Maprange
```

This is like a variant type in RSL, with values that are either `nil`, or constructed from a `rng` value by a constructor `mk_rng` and 'destructed' by the accessor `rng_part`. `nil?` and `nonnil?` are recognizers, predicates over the `Maprange` type. So in the assumption `[-2]` above, for example, `nonnil?(berths(h!1)(d))` corresponds to $d \in \textbf{dom }berths(h)$, and `rng_part-(berths(h!1)(d))` corresponds to $berths(h)(d)$

Using these correspondences, we see that the goal in the eden proof corresponds to $\sim$ (`[-1]` $\wedge$ `[-2]`) in PVS. In PVS, such a negated goal becomes a positive assumption. Conjoined assumptions are typically, as here, "flattened" during proof into separate assumptions. The assumption `[-3]` is `consistent(h!1)` (unfolded) and hence corresponds to one of the two eden assumptions. The other eden assumption corresponds to $\sim$ `[1]` $\wedge$ $\sim$ `[2]` which is the result of unfolding the assumption `can_arrive(s!1,h!1)`, which produces the conditions that the ship is not waiting and not in a berth. Negated assumptions become positive, disjoined goals in PVS, and disjoined goals are typically, as here, flattened into separate goals. The transposition of negative assumptions into goals, and vice versa, can make proof in PVS quite confusing, especially when there are many more sequents than in this simple example.

The fact that eden keeps assumptions hidden is the main reason that the eden goal is so much shorter. Added to this is the tendency in PVS to unfold early. One typically sets unfolding of (non-recursive) functions to be automatic so that simplification can take advantage of it. In eden, unfolding is not automated, and so one tends to do it only when necessary.

In this proof, the structure of the assumption `[-1]` suggests, as in the eden proof, splitting on the case where `s!1 = s!2`. The first case, when they are equal, makes the assumption `[-2]` identical to the goal `[2]`, which should be enough to complete the proof of this case, and in fact PVS does this automatically and the case never appears. In eden we still have to identify the relevant assumption ($can\_arrive(s,h)$) and unfold it.

The use of PVS and its proof engine improves the capability for automatic proof, which was a weakness of eden. It may be possible to improve this further with special tactics designed for RSL (especially for proving confidence conditions). PVS also provides the possibility of replaying proofs after changes to the specification, a feature of the justification editor that was never implemented. Inventing proofs initially is often hard, but redoing them by hand after changes is extremely tedious.

An alternative for translating proof obligations into PVS is to translate them into Isabelle/HOL [35]. Such a translation has been defined in another project [36, 37]. That translation is based on an institution representation from an institution of RSL to an institution of higher-order-logic and has been proved sound with respect to the denotational semantics of RSL.

5.2 Other Ways to Verify Specifications

Proof is the ideal method to use to verify properties such as the maintenance of consistency. But, in general, proof is expensive because it is very time-consuming and requires a considerable amount of expertise: we are still, it seems, some way from being able to perform automatically the kinds of proof we need to do. It is also expensive because if we change the specification we will need to redo the proof, and while good proof tools will redo what they can, and allow us to edit the proof script, redoing proofs can still be very time-consuming. So proof is currently used, if at all, only for very critical software or in hardware design, where the costs of making changes are much higher than they are for software.

In doing proof it is often very difficult to distinguish between something for which we have not yet found the right tactic, and something that is not provable: "The hardest proofs are those which aren't true". It is therefore a good idea to use model checking or testing to obtain more assurance that the property to be proved is indeed true before we try to prove it.

There are several alternatives to proof, which we shall introduce in this section. We will see that they are progressively cheaper to use, but also give us progressively less assurance that there are no errors.

Model Checking

Model checking has become an increasingly popular approach in recent years. The basic idea is to exhaustively test a system. That is, a property such as maintenance of consistency is asserted and then checked as being true in every possible state of the system. One can immediately see that the possible states must be (a) finite and (b) not too numerous for such an approach to be feasible, and typically much of the work in model checking is involved in reducing the size of the state space. For a general introduction to model checking, see [38, 39].

Reducing the state space typically involves reducing types to finite ranges, but usually also involves making an abstraction of the system. There is therefore an advantage in performing model checking on specifications as opposed to programs in that specifications are often already abstract. For example, our specification of the harbour contains very limited information about ships and berths.

At the time of writing, we are developing a translator from RSL to the language of the symbolic model checker SAL [40, 41]. We translated the harbour specification by hand. In order to make the system finite, and to define what was currently underspecified, we:

- defined the abstract type *Ship* as the natural numbers from 1 to 4, and also indexed the berths from 1 to 4; and
- defined *fits* as the condition that the ship number is at most the berth index.

We then checked the condition that consistency is maintained in all states, and this returned "true". The model checker created a transition relation with 1015 nodes based on 24 Boolean variables and computed the result in 2 seconds (on a Pentium 4 PC with 512MB of memory).

To obtain some assurance that our model was correct, we then asserted the condition that there is no state with all of the berths full. The model checker generated a (unique) counterexample when ship 1 is in berth 1, ship 2 in berth 2, etc., and a sequence of *arrive* and *dock* invocations to achieve it.

For a reasonably small finite model, model checking is as good as proof because the checking is exhaustive. The problem is that we usually have to reduce the problem to a finite model before we can use model checking, while there is no need to reduce before using proof, and we may make mistakes in the reduction process. There is also the danger that there is an inconsistency possible with five ships, or fewer berths than ships, that our reduced model cannot discover. Model checking is, however, much cheaper than proof, and the generation of traces to show how failure states can be reached is of great assistance in understanding and correcting problems.

Testing

A specification that is completely concrete can often be translated automatically into a programming language and executed. The RAISE tools have translators to SML [42] and to C++. There is also a recent extension to RSL, the **test_case** declaration. A **test_case** declaration consists of a sequence of test cases with a syntax rather like that for axioms, with an optional identifier plus an expression. The expression can be of any type. Test cases do not affect the semantics of specifications, but translators will generate code to evaluate them and print the identifier and result values. Commonly a test case takes the form

[id] expression = expected_result

which means that outputs can easily be checked (being just **true** for each test case) and that the expected results of tests are documented in the specification.

In the case of an imperative specification, a typical test case has the form

[id] method_call ; condition

where *condition* is a predicate over the state variable(s) designed to check that the method has worked correctly (when the condition will return **true**). But the condition can be any type of expression; when debugging, for example, we might use a test case to output the state after a method call: see the test case [t5] below for an example.

To prepare the harbour specification for translation, we did the following:

- We defined the types *Ship* and *Berth* concretely as follows

  type
      Ship == s1 | s2 | s3 | s4 | s5 | s6 | s7 | s8,
      Berth == b1 | b2 | b3 | b4

- We defined the type *Index* for berths as the subtype of **Int** ranging from 1 to 4, *size* for ships in the range 1 to 8 in the obvious manner, *size* for berths in the range 1 to 8 as twice the index, and *fits* by

  value
      fits : Ship × Berth → **Bool**
      fits(s, b) ≡ size(s) ≤ size(b)

- We changed the definition of *consistent* slightly to make it translatable:

  value
      all_ships : Ship-**set** = {s1, s2, s3, s4, s5, s6, s7, s8},

      consistent : Harbour → **Bool**
      consistent(h) ≡
        (∀ s : T.Ship •
          s ∈ all_ships ⇒
            ∼ (waiting(s, h) ∧ is_docked(s, h)) ∧ ...)

  Quantifiers can be translated if they can be seen syntactically to be quantifying over finite sets.
- We extended the applicative specification into an imperative one by adding the definitions for state variables:

  object
      H : HARBOUR

  variable
      pool : T.Ship-**set** := {},
      berths : T.Index $\overrightarrow{m}$ T.Ship := [ ]

- We added two functions for creating a state value from the variables, and for checking consistency using the applicative *consistent* – these are merely convenient shorthands:

  value
      state : **Unit** → **read** pool, berths H.Harbour
      state() ≡ H.mk_Harbour(pool, berths),

      consistent : **Unit** → **read** pool, berths **Bool**
      consistent() ≡ H.consistent(state())

- We defined imperative generators based on the applicative ones, for example

  value
   arrive : T.Ship $\xrightarrow{\sim}$ **write** pool **Unit**
   arrive(s) ≡ pool := pool ∪ {s}
   post consistent()
   pre consistent() ∧ H.can_arrive(s, state()),

  Note that this definition has a postcondition as well as a precondition. The precondition has been strengthened by the conjunct *consistent*, as we want to check that such generators preserve consistency. It is a recent addition to RSL that postconditions may be added to explicit functions like this one. The translation for this function will optionally include checks that at the start of invocation the precondition is satisfied, and at exit the postcondition is satisfied.

- We added some test cases:

  test_case
   [t1] empty() ; arrive(s3) ; pool = {s3} ∧ berths = [ ],
   [t2] arrive(s2) ; pool = {s3, s2} ∧ berths = [ ],
   [t3] dock(s2, b1) ; pool = {s3} ∧ berths = [indx(b1) ↦ s2],
   [t4] leave(s2, b1) ; pool = {s3} ∧ berths = [ ],
   [t5] dock(s3, b1) ; (pool, berths)

  Note that, for an imperative specification each test case after the first inherits the state from the previous one. This makes it easier to write a series of test cases to create a complex state, and was the reason for making an imperative extension of the original specification.

  The last test case contains an intentional error: ship *s3* does not fit berth *b1*. The output of compiling and running the translated C++ code is

  ```
  [t1] true
  [t2] true
  [t3] true
  [t4] true
  I_HARBOUR.rsl:22:7: Precondition of dock(s3, b1) not
      satisfied
  I_HARBOUR.rsl:22:7: Function call dock(s3, b1) does not
      satisfy postcondition
  [t5] ({},[1+>s3])
  ```

  The first part of the warning messages is the file:line:column reference to where in the specification the problem occurred.

  The failure in the precondition of *dock* is the failure of the *fit* check. The failure in the postcondition is because *consistent* includes checking that ships can only be in berths that they fit: the default action of the translated program is to continue after an error, and we can see that the final *dock* operation has been completed, with ship *s3* recorded as being in berth with index 1, which it does not fit.

Testing is a comparatively cheap way to gain assurance of correctness. It has limitations, of course, in particular its incompleteness. But it has one advantage that no amount of theorem proving or model checking can compete with: it can be applied to the final implementation. The problem with only verifying a specification is that we cannot discover errors such as incorrect implementation or wrong assumptions about the environment (hardware, operating system, other software, user behaviour, etc.). Test cases developed for the specification, and which include the expected results, can be applied later to the final implementation.

Inspection

Inspection is commonly used as a quality assurance measure for program code and other documents, and is just as applicable to specifications. Specifications are commonly easier to read than code, because of their use of abstraction and their relative shortness. Inspection techniques range from "peer inspection", where colleagues inspect each others' work, to more formal approaches involving meetings and recorded results.

Inspections are most effective when there are particular things that people are looking for, and the use of checklists like that in the book on the RAISE method [2] is common.

An aid to inspection is the generation of confidence conditions (see Sect. 2.5). The harbour specification only generates two such conditions:

TYPES.rsl:13:32: CC:
−− subtype not empty
$\exists$ i : **Int** • i $\geq$ min $\land$ max $\geq$ i

HARBOUR.rsl:59:16: CC:
−− application arguments and/or precondition
T.indx(b) $\in$ **dom** berths(h)

The first is clearly satisfied because of the *index_not_empty* axiom. The second is the second conjunct of the definition of *is_occupied_by* and is identical to the first conjunct, and so is immediately satisfied.

It is unusual to obtain so few confidence conditions from a specification. Inspecting confidence conditions is useful but not always effective. In practice only a few, perhaps 5%, will not be satisfied and it is hard to spot them unless one is very disciplined. Confidence conditions can be proved: any proof of a property of a specification will also involve proving them. They are also included (optionally) in translated code, and so can be checked in tests. The translator to SAL will also enable them to be checked during model checking.

5.3 A More Complex Version

The harbour example presented so far is rather simple. In this section we show a rather more realistic example and the consequences that arise when we verify it. We start with a class diagram (Fig. 3) showing classes for ships, berths and anchorages. An anchorage is a place where ships can anchor; the collection of these is what we have previously called the pool.

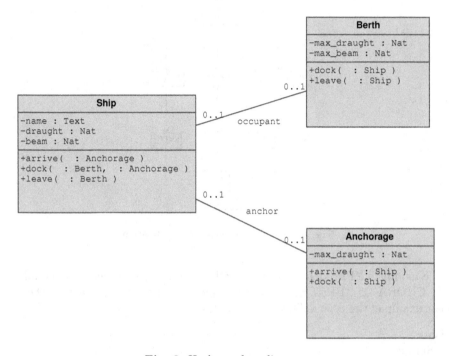

Fig. 3. Harbour class diagram

We have included a few attributes for each class, and intend to model *fits* by the conditions that the berth has sufficient draught (depth of water) and sufficient width for the beam (width) of a ship. We add a condition that different anchorages may have different depths, and so ships will also need to fit their anchorages.

The relations *anchor* and *occupant* are defined to be navigable in both directions. This means that the state of a ship will include a berth (if it is docked) and the state of a berth state will include a ship (if it is occupied). A similar statement can be made about ships and anchorages. We have therefore chosen to maximise the dynamic information (unlike in our earlier harbour design) and will have more complicated consistency requirements.

We have also added the signatures of the methods for each class. The idea is that when a ship arrives it will change the state of the ship (to record the anchorage) and the state of the anchorage (to record the ship). The methods *arrive* in the two classes will each make the changes to their object's state. We will later define a user method *arrive* that will invoke both of these.

This class diagram can be automatically translated into RSL. The resulting module structure is shown in Fig. 4.

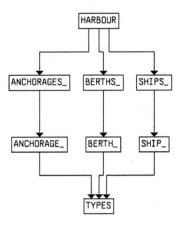

Fig. 4. Modules of harbour specification

The module TYPES defines some globally used non-class types. The modules ANCHORAGE_, BERTH_ and SHIP_ model one instance of each of these. For example, the type definition in SHIP_ is

type
  Ship ::
    name : **Text**
    draught : **Nat**
    beam : **Nat**
    berth : Optional_Berth
    anchorage : Optional_Anchorage

where *Optional_Berth* and *Optional_Anchorage* are defined in TYPES as

type
  Optional_Berth == no_Berth | a_Berth(id:Berth_Id),
  Optional_Anchorage == no_Anchorage | an_Anchorage(id:Anchorage_Id)

We see that (navigable) relations are modelled as attributes. The identifiers like *Anchorage_Id* used to model the relations are used in the next layer of modules, namely ANCHORAGES_, etc. Each of these represents the collection of corresponding objects in the system. The collection is modelled as a map. For example, in SHIPS_ we have

type
  Ships = Ship_Id $\overrightarrow{m}$ SHIP_.Ship

At the top level, the whole harbour is modelled as a record containing the three components:

type
  Harbour ::
    ships : SHIPS_.Ships
    berths : BERTHS_.Berths
    anchorages : ANCHORAGES_.Anchorages

A feature of the architecture of the RSL modules is that it is hierarchical: modules may invoke only methods of those below them in the hierarchy. So, for example, we can construct a method *arrive* in the top level HARBOUR module that invokes the methods *arrive* in ANCHORAGE_ and SHIP_: these last two methods may not invoke each other. Such a hierarchical approach has many advantages over the much looser configurations often adopted in object-oriented designs. For example, a bottom-up verification or testing strategy is possible, and changes in the design of one branch do not affect others.

Consistency

We can split the consistency conditions into two groups:

Structural consistency is generic, and depends only on the relations and their navigability. It has two components:

- Object identifiers used as attributes must exist, i.e. they must be in the domain of the corresponding map. For example, if a ship has a berth attribute a_Berth(bid), the berth identifier *bid* must be in the domain of the *berths* component of the harbour. This condition has to be defined in HARBOUR, the lowest point in the hierarchy where SHIP_ and the type *Harbour* are visible.
- For bi-navigable relations, the reverse navigation must give the correct result. For example, if a ship identified by *sid* has a berth attribute a_Berth(bid), the berth identified by *bid* must have its occupant attribute set to a_Ship(sid). This also has to be defined in HARBOUR.

Structural consistency conditions are defined by the translator, according to the navigability and multiplicities of the relations in the model, in a predicate *consistent* in the top-level module. This function also calls functions *consistent* in its child modules (here ANCHORAGES_, etc). These, in turn, call functions *consistent* in their child modules, for every identifier in their collection. The functions *consistent* in ANCHORAGE_, etc., are left unelaborated.

Application consistency depends on the particular system being modelled. It is specified by adding to the consistency functions created for structural consistency. For example, for a SHIP_, we see that it must not be in a berth and in an anchorage at the same time. We therefore elaborate the definition of *consistent* in SHIP_:

value
    consistent : Ship → **Bool**
    consistent(s) ≡
        berth(s) = no_Berth ∨ anchorage(s) = no_Anchorage

Considering the collection of ships, we see that we must not record the same berth or the same anchorage for different ships. We add to *consistent* in SHIPS_ the necessary conjuncts. For example, for berths, where c is the collection of ships,

    (∀ id1, id2 : Ship_Id, b : Berth_Id •
        id1 ∈ **dom** c ∧ id2 ∈ **dom** c ∧
        SHIP_.berth(c(id1)) = a_Berth(b) ∧
        SHIP_.berth(c(id2)) = a_Berth(b) ⇒ id1 = id2)

There are similar conditions to be added to *consistent* in BERTHS_ and ANCHORAGES_.

Finally, considering the conditions that ships in berths and in anchorages must fit them, we see that this involves comparing attributes of ships with attributes of anchorages or berths, and so must be added to *consistent* in HARBOUR. For example, for anchorages, where s is the harbour state,

    (∀ id1 : Ship_Id •
        id1 ∈ **dom** ships(s) ⇒
            case SHIP_.anchorage(ships(s)(id1)) **of**
                no_Anchorage → **true**,
                an_Anchorage(id2) →
                    SHIP_.draught(ships(s)(id1)) ≤
                        ANCHORAGE_.max_draught(anchorages(s)(id2))
        end)

Verification

As with the simpler version of the harbour system we can use proof, model checking, testing or inspection. For this version, we conducted some proofs using PVS for comparison with the simpler version. We proved the confidence conditions, the consistency of an empty harbour, and the preservation of consistency by the three generators.

The confidence conditions for this example turned out to be extremely easy to check. Generating them into RSL produced 85 of them. After translating into PVS, it was found that they produced 53 type check conditions, and one extra one as a lemma to be proved. There are fewer in PVS than in RSL, because PVS has mechanisms for recognising and subsuming the same condition arising in the same context. 52 of these 53 conditions were proved automatically, the last was proved immediately from the *index_not_empty* lemma, and the extra lemma was proved in one step by the PVS tactic `grind`.

The four consistency conditions (for the empty harbour and the three generators) were proved rather more tediously. We counted the number of proof steps needed for each for the two versions of the harbour system, calling the simpler one version 1 and this version 2: see Table 1. We also include figures in this table for proofs performed with the original RAISE tool eden.

Table 1. Proof steps required to prove consistency

Version	1		2
Tool	eden	PVS	PVS
empty	17	1	1
arrive	51	21	266
dock	204	108	325
leave	114	51	177

The numbers of proof steps are of course subject to the skill of the user, and could certainly be reduced somewhat. But we doubt whether much improvement on these figures could be achieved without the design of special tactics and/or lemmas.

eden seems to need about twice as many steps as PVS. This is mainly because its simplification strategies are weaker than those of PVS; this is most clearly demonstrated by the consistency of *empty*, which PVS can deal with in one step. At the same time, as we discussed earlier in Sect. 5.1, eden is easier to use in the sense that it is possible to preserve the structure of the goals, which makes it much easier to understand where you are in the proof.

Comparing versions 1 and 2 of the specification and the proofs in PVS, the large variation in *arrive* is probably because of the introduction of the notion of fitting an anchorage; otherwise there seems to be a threefold increase in the length of the proofs, and they have become rather tedious: it took some 4 hours to perform the proofs for version 2.

6 Conclusions

6.1 Summary

RSL is a wide-spectrum language, supporting axiomatic as well as model-oriented specifications, the applicative style as well as the imperative one, and the concurrent style as well as the sequential one. The logic needs sufficient power to deal with this wide range, and we have explained the logic and the motivation for the various choices made in designing it. We have also seen how the logic is expressive enough to express the RAISE notion of refinement.

We have also described the logical style in which RSL is defined by its axiomatic semantics, and the related style of providing proof rules for actually performing proofs.

Proofs may be involved in the RAISE method in various ways:

- proofs of confidence conditions: conditions such as that values are in their subtypes, and that the preconditions of functions and operators are satisfied when they are invoked;
- proofs of refinement between modules;
- proofs of particular (user-defined) properties of specifications.

We have seen that an important kind of property is consistency, which can be divided into *structural* and *application* components. Checking that generator functions (methods) preserve consistency is a very useful activity in software development, and often in danger of being overlooked if there is too much concentration on what such methods must change. In a recent project on developing a support environment for mobile devices [43] a count of errors found and corrected showed that 50% of them were in the consistency conditions rather than in the methods.

We have discussed proofs of consistency performed with the original RAISE tool eden and with a more recent tool [31] which uses translation to PVS. We also saw how the size of the proofs, and hence the time taken to complete them, grew substantially as we moved from a simple to a slightly more realistic version of the harbour example. While proof is a powerful technique it is also expensive, and we have looked at other validation and verification techniques that may be used with RAISE, and the tool support available for them: model checking, testing and inspection.

6.2 Future Work

Most of the future work planned is related to the RAISE tools [31]. At present, a model-checking capability is being added, as mentioned in Sect. 5.2, and there are also ideas on adding an aspect-oriented transformation and refactoring mechanism that would support the extension of specifications while maintaining properties already checked. Recently we also made two prototype tools that support development steps from applicative RSL specification towards imperative programs: the first is a translator from RSL to Java (5.0) and the other is a transformer from applicative to imperative specifications. Both were specified in RSL. The first tool was made by a bootstrapping process, and the second used the first tool to translate the specification into an implementation in Java. We plan to extend both prototypes to cover larger subsets than they can handle at present.

References

1. The RAISE Language Group. *The RAISE Specification Language*, BCS Practitioner Series. Prentice Hall, 1992.
2. The RAISE Method Group. *The RAISE Development Method*. BCS Practitioner Series. Prentice Hall, 1995. Available by ftp from `ftp://ftp.iist.unu.edu/pub/RAISE/method_book`.
3. A. Haxthausen and X. Yong. A RAISE Specification Framework and Justification Assistant for the Duration Calculus. In *Proceedings of ESSLLI-98 Workshop on Duration Calculus*, pages 51–58, 1998.
4. L. Li and J. He. A Denotational Semantics of Timed RSL using Duration Calculus. In *RTCSA'99: Proceedings of The Sixth International Conference on Real-Time Computing Systems and Applications*, pages 492–503. IEEE Computer Society Press, December 1999.
5. C.W. George and X. Yong. An Operational Semantics for Timed RAISE. In Jeannette M. Wing, Jim Woodcock, and Jim Davies, editors, *FM'99: Proceedings of the World Congress on Formal Methods in the Development of Computing Systems, Volume 2*, number 1709 in Lecture Notes in Computer Science, pages 1008–1027. Springer, September 1999.
6. A. Haxthausen and X. Yong. Linking DC together with TRSL. In *Proceedings of 2nd International Conference on Integrated Formal Methods (IFM'2000), Schloss Dagstuhl, Germany, November 2000*, number 1945 in Lecture Notes in Computer Science, pages 25–44. Springer, 2000.
7. R.E. Milne. Semantic Foundations of RSL. Technical Report RAISE/CRI/-DOC/4/V1, CRI A/S, 1990.
8. R.E. Milne. The Proof Theory for the RAISE Specification Language. Technical Report RAISE/STC/REM/12/V3, STC Technology Ltd, 1990.
9. D. Bolignano and M. Debabi. RSL: An Integration of Concurrent, Functional and Imperative Paradigms. Technical Report LACOS/BULL/MD/3/V12.48, Bull, 1993.
10. D. Bolignano and M. Debabi. Higher Order Communicating Processes with Value-passing, Assignment and Return of Results. In *Proceedings of ISAAC '92*, number 650 in Lecture Notes in Computer Science. Springer-Verlag, 1992.
11. Cliff B. Jones. *Systematic Software Development Using VDM*. Prentice Hall International, second edition, 1990.
12. J. M. Spivey. *The Z Notation: A Reference Manual*. Prentice Hall International Series in Computer Science, Prentice Hall, 2nd edition, 1992.
13. K. Futatsugi, J.A. Goguen, J.-P. Jouannaud, and J. Meseguer. Principles of OBJ-2. In *12th Annual Symposium on Principles of Programming*, pages 52–66. ACM, 1985.
14. R.M. Burstall and J.A. Goguen. The semantics of CLEAR: a specification language. In *Proceedings of Advanced Course on Abstract Software Specifications*, volume 86 of Lecture Notes in Computer Science, pages 292–332. Springer, 1980.
15. M. Wirsing. *A Specification Language*. PhD thesis, Technical University of Munich, 1983.
16. H. Ehrig and B. Mahr. *Fundamentals of Algebraic Specification 1: Equations and Initial Semantics*, volume 6 of EATCS Monographs on Theoretical Computer Science, Springer, 1985.

17. J. Guttag, J.J. Horning and J.M. Wing. Larch in five easy pieces. Technical Report 5, Digital Equipment Corporation System Research Center, Palo Alto, California, 1985.

18. R. Milner. *Calculus of Communicating Systems*, volume 92 of *Lecture Notes in Computer Science*. Springer, 1980.

19. C.A.R. Hoare. *Communicating Sequential Processes*. Prentice-Hall, 1985.

20. D.B. MacQueen. Modules for Standard ML. *Polymorphism*, II(2), 1985.

21. B. Dandanell, J. Gørtz, J. Storbank Pedersen, and E. Zierau. Experiences from Applications of RAISE. In *Proceedings of FME'93*, number 670 of Lecture Notes in Computer Science. Springer, 1993.

22. Hung Dang Van, Chris George, Tomasz Janowski, and Richard Moore. *Specification Case Studies in RAISE*. FACIT. Springer, 2002. Available from ftp://ftp.iist.unu.edu/pub/RAISE/case_studies.

23. A.E. Haxthausen and J. Peleska. Formal Development and Verification of a Distributed Railway Control System. *IEEE Transactions on Software Engineering*, 26(8):687–701, 2000.

24. M.P. Lindegaard, P. Viuf, and A.E. Haxthausen. Modelling Railway Interlocking Systems. In *Proceedings of the 9th IFAC Symposium on Control in Transportation Systems 2000*, June 13–15, 2000, Braunschweig, Germany, pages 211–217, 2000.

25. A.E. Haxthausen and J. Peleska. A Domain Specific Language for Railway Control Systems. In *Proceedings of the Sixth Biennial World Conference on Integrated Design and Process Technology, (IDPT2002), Pasadena, California*, June 23-28 2002.

26. A.E. Haxthausen and T. Gjaldbæk. Modelling and Verification of Interlocking Systems for Railway Lines. In *Proceedings of 10th IFAC Symposium on Control in Transportation Systems*. Elsevier Science, 2003.

27. S. Owre, J.M. Rushby, and N. Shankar. PVS: A prototype verification system. In Deepak Kapur, editor, *11th International Conference on Automated Deduction (CADE)*, volume 607 of *Lecture Notes in Artificial Intelligence*, pages 748–752, Springer, 1992.

28. J.R. Abrial. *The B Book: Assigning Programs to Meanings*. Cambridge University Press, 1996.

29. H. Barringer, J.H. Cheng, and C.B. Jones. A logic covering undefinedness in program proofs. *Acta Informatica*, 21:251–269, 1984.

30. Bill Stoddart, Steve Dunne, and Andy Galloway. Undefined expressions and logic in Z and B. *Formal Methods in System Design: An International Journal*, 15(3):201–215, November 1999.

31. Chris George. RAISE Tools User Guide. Technical Report 227, UNU-IIST, P.O. Box 3058, Macau, February 2001. The tools are available free from http://www.iist.unu.edu.

32. R. E. Milne. The Formal Basis for the RAISE Specification Language. In D.J. Andrews, J.F. Groote, and C.A. Middelburg, editors, *Semantics of Specification Languages*, Workshops in Computing, Utrecht, 1993. Springer.

33. Chris George and Søren Prehn. The RAISE Justification Handbook. Technical Report LACOS/CRI/DOC/7, Computer Resources International, 1994.

34. Aristides Dasso and Chris W. George. Transforming RSL into PVS. Technical Report 256, UNU/IIST, P.O. Box 3058, Macau, May 2002.

35. Tobias Nipkow, Lawrence C. Paulson, and Markus Wenzel. *Isabelle/HOL —
    A Proof Assistant for Higher-Order Logic*, volume 2283 of Lecture Notes in
    Computer Science. Springer, 2002.
36. M.P. Lindegaard. *Proof Support for RAISE – by a Reuse Approach based on
    Institutions*. PhD thesis, IMM, Technical University of Denmark, 2004.
37. M.P. Lindegaard and A.E. Haxthausen. Proof Support for RAISE – by a Reuse
    Approach based on Institutions. In *Proceedings of AMAST'04*, number 3116 in
    Lecture Notes in Computer Science, pages 319–333. Springer-Verlag, 2004.
38. Edmund M. Clarke, Orna Grumberg, and A. Peled. *Model Checking*. MIT Press,
    1999.
39. Béatrice Bérard, Michel Bidoit, Alain Finkel, François Laroussinie, Antoine Pe-
    tit, Laure Petrucci, and Philippe Schnoebelen. *Systems and Software Verifica-
    tion: Model-Checking Techniques and Tools*. Springer, 2001.
40. Leonardo de Moura, Sam Owre, Harald Rueß, John Rushby, N. Shankar, Maria
    Sorea, and Ashish Tiwari. SAL 2. In R. Alur and D. Peled, editors, *Computer-
    Aided Verification, CAV 2004*, volume 3114 of *Lecture Notes in Computer Sci-
    ence*, pages 496–500, Springer, 2004.
41. L. de Moura, S. Owre, and N. Shankar. The SAL language manual. Technical
    Report SRI-CSL-01-02, SRI International, 2003. Available from http://sal.
    csl.sri.com.
42. Robin Milner, Mads Tofte, Robert Harper, and David MacQueen. *The Defini-
    tion of Standard ML: Revised*. MIT Press, 1997.
43. Satyajit Acharya and Chris George. Specifying a Mobile Computing Application
    Environment Using RSL. Technical Report 300, UNU-IIST, P.O. Box 3058,
    Macau, May 2004.

RAISE Indexes

The Specification Language TLA$^+$

Stephan Merz

INRIA Lorraine, LORIA, 615 rue du Jardin Botanique, F-54602 Villers-lès-Nancy, France, `Stephan.Merz@loria.fr`

1 Introduction

The specification language TLA$^+$ was designed by Lamport for formally describing and reasoning about distributed algorithms. It is described in Lamport's book Specifying Systems [29], which also gives good advice on how to make the best use of TLA$^+$ and its supporting tools. Systems are specified in TLA$^+$ as formulas of the Temporal Logic of Actions, TLA, a variant of linear-time temporal logic also introduced by Lamport [27]. The underlying data structures are specified in (a variant of) Zermelo–Fränkel set theory, the language accepted by most mathematicians as the standard basis for formalizing mathematics. This choice is motivated by a desire for conciseness, clarity, and formality that befits a language of formal specification where executability or efficiency are not of major concern. TLA$^+$ specifications are organized in modules that can be reused independently.

In a quest for minimality and orthogonality of concepts, TLA$^+$ does not formally distinguish between specifications and properties: both are written as logical formulas, and concepts such as refinement, composition of systems, and hiding of the internal state are expressed using logical connectives of implication, conjunction, and quantification. Despite its expressiveness, TLA$^+$ is supported by tools such as model checkers and theorem provers to aid a designer in carrying out formal developments.

This chapter attempts to formally define the core concepts of TLA and TLA$^+$ and to describe the motivation behind some choices, in particular with respect to competing formalisms. Before doing so, an introductory overview of system specification in TLA$^+$ is given using the example of a resource allocator. Lamport's book remains the definitive reference for the language itself and on the methodology for using TLA$^+$. In particular, the module language of TLA$^+$ is only introduced by example, and the rich standard mathematical library is only sketched.

The outline of this chapter is as follows. Sect. 2 introduces TLA$^+$ by means of a first specification of the resource allocator and illustrates the use of the TLC model checker. The logic of TLA is formally defined in Sect. 3, followed by an overview of the TLA$^+$ proof rules for system verification in Sect. 4. Section 5 describes the version of set theory that underlies TLA$^+$, including some of the constructions most frequently used for specifying data. The resource allocator example is taken up again in Sect. 6, where an improved high-level specification is given and a step towards a distributed refinement is taken. Finally, Sect. 7 contains some concluding remarks.

2 Example: A Simple Resource Allocator

We introduce TLA$^+$ informally, by means of an example that will also serve as a running example for this chapter. After stating the requirements informally, we present a first system specification, and describe the use of the TLA$^+$ model checker TLC to analyse its correctness.

2.1 Informal Requirements

The purpose of the resource allocator is to manage a (finite) set of resources that are shared among a number of client processes. The allocation of resources is subject to the following constraints.

1. A client that currently does not hold any resources and that has no pending requests may issue a request for a set of resources.

   Rationale: We require that no client should be allowed to "extend" a pending request, possibly after the allocator has granted some resources. A single client process might concurrently issue two separate requests for resources by appearing under different identities, and therefore the set of "clients" should really be understood as identifiers for requests, but we shall not make this distinction here.

2. The allocator may grant access to a set of available (i.e., not currently allocated) resources to a client.

   Rationale: Resources can be allocated in batches, so an allocation need not satisfy the entire request of the client: the client may be able to begin working with a subset of the resources that it requested.

3. A client may release some resources that it holds.

   Rationale: Similarly to allocation, clients may return just a subset of the resources they currently hold, freeing them for allocation to a different process.

4. Clients are required to eventually free the resources they hold once their entire request has been satisfied.

The system should be designed such that it ensures the following two properties.

- *Safety:* no resource is simultaneously allocated to two different clients.
- *Liveness:* every request issued by some client is eventually satisfied.

2.2 A First TLA$^+$ Specification

A first TLA$^+$ specification of the resource allocator appears in Fig. 1 on the following page. Shortcomings of this model will be discussed in Sect. 6, where a revised specification will appear.

TLA$^+$ specifications are organised in modules that contain declarations (of parameters), definitions (of operators), and assertions (of assumptions and theorems). Horizontal lines separate different sections of the module *SimpleAllocator*; these aid readability, but have no semantic content. TLA$^+$ requires that an identifier must be declared or defined before it is used, and that it cannot be reused, even as a bound variable, in its scope of validity.

The first section declares that thr module *SimpleAllocator* is based on the module *FiniteSet*, which is part of the TLA$^+$ standard library (discussed in Sect. 5). Next, the constant and variable parameters are declared. The constants *Clients* and *Resources* represent the sets of client processes and of resources managed by the resource allocator. Constant parameters represent entities whose values are fixed during system execution, although they are not defined in the module, because they may change from one system instance to the next. Observe that there are no type declarations: TLA$^+$ is based on Zermelo–Fränkel (ZF) set theory — so all values are sets. The set *Resources* is assumed to be finite – the operator *IsFiniteSet* is defined in the module *FiniteSet*. The variable parameters *unsat* and *alloc* represent the current state of the allocator by recording the outstanding requests of the client processes, and the set of resources allocated to the clients. In general, variable parameters represent entities whose values change during system execution; in this sense, they correspond to program variables.

The second section contains the definition of the operators *TypeInvariant* and *available*. In general, definitions in TLA$^+$ take the form

$$Op(arg_1, \ldots, arg_n) \triangleq exp.$$

In TLA$^+$, multiline conjunctions and disjunctions are written as lists "bulleted" with the connective, and indentation indicates the hierarchy of nested conjunctions and disjunctions [26]. The formula *TypeInvariant* states the intended "types" of the state variables *unsat* and *alloc*, which are functions that associate a set of (requested or received) resources with each client.[1] Observe, again, that the variables are not constrained to these types: *TypeInvariant* just declares a formula, and a theorem towards the end of the module asserts that the allocator specification respects the typing invariant. This theorem will have to be proven by considering the possible transitions of the system.

---

[1] In TLA$^+$, the power set of a set S is written as SUBSET S.

─────────── MODULE *SimpleAllocator* ───────────

EXTENDS *FiniteSet*
CONSTANTS *Clients, Resources*
ASSUME *IsFiniteSet(Resources)*
VARIABLES
    unsat,   *unsat[c]* denotes the outstanding requests of client c
    alloc   *alloc[c]* denotes the resources allocated to client c

───────────────────────────

$TypeInvariant \triangleq$
    $\wedge\ unsat \in [Clients \rightarrow \text{SUBSET } Resources]$
    $\wedge\ alloc \in [Clients \rightarrow \text{SUBSET } Resources]$
$available \triangleq$ set of resources free for allocation
    $Resources \setminus (\text{UNION}\{alloc[c] : c \in Clients\})$

───────────────────────────

$Init \triangleq$ initially, no resources have been requested or allocated
    $\wedge\ unsat = [c \in Clients \mapsto \{\}]$
    $\wedge\ alloc = [c \in Clients \mapsto \{\}]$
$Request(c, S) \triangleq$ Client c requests set S of resources
    $\wedge\ S \neq \{\} \wedge unsat[c] = \{\} \wedge alloc[c] = \{\}$
    $\wedge\ unsat' = [unsat\text{EXCEPT}![c] = S]$
    $\wedge$ UNCHANGED*alloc*
$Allocate(c, S) \triangleq$ Set S of available resources are allocated to client c
    $\wedge\ S \neq \{\} \wedge S \subseteq available \cap unsat[c]$
    $\wedge\ alloc' = [alloc\text{EXCEPT}![c] = @ \cup S]$
    $\wedge\ unsat' = [unsat\text{EXCEPT}![c] = @ \setminus S]$
$Return(c, S) \triangleq$ Client c returns a set of resources that it holds.
    $\wedge\ S \neq \{\} \wedge S \subseteq alloc[c]$
    $\wedge\ alloc' = [alloc\text{EXCEPT}![c] = @ \setminus S]$
    $\wedge$ UNCHANGED*unsat*
$Next \triangleq$ The system's next−state relation
    $\exists c \in Clients, S \in \text{SUBSET } Resources :$
        $Request(c, S) \vee Allocate(c, S) \vee Return(c, S)$
$vars \triangleq \langle unsat, alloc \rangle$

───────────────────────────

$SimpleAllocator \triangleq$ The complete high−level specification
    $\wedge\ Init \wedge \square[Next]_{vars}$
    $\wedge\ \forall c \in Clients : \text{WF}_{vars}(Return(c, alloc[c]))$
    $\wedge\ \forall c \in Clients : \text{SF}_{vars}(\exists S \in \text{SUBSET } Resources : Allocate(c, S))$

───────────────────────────

$Safety \triangleq \forall c_1, c_2 \in Clients : c_1 \neq c_2 \Rightarrow alloc[c_1] \cap alloc[c_2] = \{\}$
$Liveness \triangleq \forall c \in Clients, r \in Resources : r \in unsat[c] \rightsquigarrow r \in alloc[c]$

───────────────────────────

THEOREM*SimpleAllocator* $\Rightarrow \square TypeInvariant$
THEOREM*SimpleAllocator* $\Rightarrow \square Safety$
THEOREM*SimpleAllocator* $\Rightarrow Liveness$

─────────────────────

Fig. 1. A simple resource allocator.

The set *available* is defined to contain those resources that are currently not allocated to any client.

The third section contains a list of definitions, which constitute the main body of the allocator specification. The state predicate *Init* represents the initial condition of the specification: no client has requested or received any resources. The action formulas *Request*(c, S), *Allocate*(c, S), and *Return*(c, S) model a client c requesting, receiving, or returning a set S of resources. In these formulas, unprimed occurrences of state variables (e.g., *unsat*) denote their values in the state before the transition, whereas primed occurrences (e.g., *unsat'*) denote their values in the successor state, and UNCHANGEDt is just a shorthand for $t' = t$. Also, function application is written using square brackets, so *unsat*[c] denotes the set of resources requested by client c. The EXCEPT construct models a function update; more precisely, when t denotes a value in the domain of the function f, the expression [f EXCEPT ![t] $= e$] denotes the function g that agrees with f except that $g[t]$ equals e. In the right-hand side e of such an update, @ denotes the previous value $f[t]$ of the function at the argument position being updated. For example, the formule *Allocate*(c, S) requires that S be a nonempty subset of the available resources that are part of the request of client c, allocates those resources to c, and removes them from the set of outstanding requests of c.

The action formula *Next* is defined as the disjunction of the request, allocate, and return actions, for some client and some set of resources; it defines the next-state relation of the resource allocator. Again, there is nothing special about the names *Init* and *Next*, they are just conventional for denoting the initial condition and the next-state relation.

The overall specification of the resource allocator is given by the temporal formula *SimpleAllocator*. This is defined as a conjunction of the form

$$I \wedge \Box[N]_v \wedge L$$

where I is the initial condition (a state predicate), N is the next-state relation, and L is a conjunction of fairness properties, each concerning a disjunct of the next-state relation. While not mandatory, this is the standard form of system specification in TLA$^+$, and it corresponds to the definition of a transition system (or state machine) with fairness constraints. More precisely, the formula $\Box[N]_v$ specifies that every transition either satisfies the action formula N or leaves the expression v unchanged. In particular, this formula admits "stuttering transitions" that do not affect the variables of interest. Stuttering invariance is a key concept of TLA that simplifies the representation of refinement, as well as compositional reasoning; we shall explore temporal formulas and stuttering invariance in more detail in Sect. 3.4.

The initial condition and the next-state relation specify how the system *may* behave. Fairness conditions complement this by asserting what actions *must* occur (eventually). The weak fairness condition for the return action states that clients should eventually return the resources they hold. The strong fairness condition for resource allocation stipulates that for each client c, if it is possible to allocate some resources to c infinitely often, then the allocator should eventually give some resources to c.

The following section of the specification defines the two main correctness properties *Safety* and *Liveness*. The formula *Safety* asserts a safety property [10] of the model by stating that no resource is ever allocated to two distinct clients. Formula *Liveness* represents a liveness property that asserts that whenever some client c requests some resource r, that resource will eventually be allocated to c.[2] Observe that there is no formal distinction in TLA$^+$ between a system specification and a property: both are expressed as formulas of temporal logic. Asserting that a specification S has a property F amounts to claiming validity of the implication $S \Rightarrow F$. Similarly, refinement between specifications is expressed by (validity of) implication, and a single set of proof rules is used to verify properties and refinement; we shall explore deductive verification in Sect. 4.

Finally, the module *SimpleAllocator* asserts three theorems stating that the specification satisfies the typing invariant as well as the safety and liveness properties defined above. A formal proof language for TLA$^+$, based on a hierarchical proof format [28], is currently being designed.

2.3 Model-Checking the Specification

Whereas programs can be compiled and executed, TLA$^+$ models can be validated and verified. In this way, confidence is gained that a model faithfully reflects the intended system, and that it can serve as a basis for more detailed designs and, ultimately, for implementations. Tools can assist the designer in carrying out these analyses. In particular, simulation lets a user explore some traces, possibly leading to the detection of deadlocks or other unanticipated behavior. Deductive tools such as model checkers and theorem provers assist in the formal verification of properties. The TLA$^+$ model checker TLC is a powerful and eminently useful tool for verification and validation, and we shall now illustrate its use for the resource allocator model of Fig. 1.

TLC can compute and explore the state space of finite-state instances of TLA$^+$ models. Besides the model itself, TLC requires a second input file, called the *configuration file*, which defines the finite-state instance of the model to be analysed, and that declares which of the formulas defined in the model represents the system specification and which are the properties to be verified over that finite-state instance.[3] Figure 2 shows a configuration file for analysing the module *SimpleAllocator*. Definitions of the sets *Clients* and *Resources* fix specific instance of the model that TLC should consider. In our case, these sets consist of symbolic constants. The keyword SPECIFICATION indicates which formula represents the main system specification, and the

---

[2] The formula $P \rightsquigarrow Q$ asserts that any state that satisfies P will eventually be followed by a state satisfying Q.

[3] TLC ignores any theorems asserted in the module.

```
CONSTANTS
    Clients = {c1,c2,c3}
    Resources = {r1,r2}
SPECIFICATION
    SimpleAllocator
INVARIANTS
    TypeInvariant Safety
PROPERTIES
    Liveness
```

Fig. 2. Sample configuration file for TLC

keywords INVARIANTS and PROPERTIES define the properties to be verified by TLC. (For a more detailed description of the format and the possible directives that can be used in configuration files, see Lamport's book [29] and the tool documentation [23].)

```
TLC Version 2.0 of January 16, 2006
Model-checking
Parsing file SimpleAllocator.tla
Parsing file /sw/tla/tlasany/StandardModules/FiniteSets.tla
Parsing file /sw/tla/tlasany/StandardModules/Naturals.tla
Parsing file /sw/tla/tlasany/StandardModules/Sequences.tla
Semantic processing of module Naturals
Semantic processing of module Sequences
Semantic processing of module FiniteSets
Semantic processing of module SimpleAllocator
Implied-temporal checking--satisfiability problem has 6 branches.
Finished computing initial states: 1 distinct state generated.
--Checking temporal properties for the complete state space...
Model checking completed. No error has been found.
    Estimates of the probability that TLC did not check
    all reachable states because two distinct states had
    the same fingerprint:
        calculated (optimistic):  2.673642557349254E-14
        based on the actual fingerprints:  6.871173129000332E-15
1633 states generated, 400 distinct states found,
0 states left on queue.
The depth of the complete state graph search is 6.
```

Fig. 3. TLC output

Running TLC on this model produces an output similar to that shown in Fig. 3; some details may vary according to the version and the installation of TLC. First, TLC parses the TLA$^+$ input file and checks it for well-formedness. It then computes the graph of reachable states for the instance of the model defined by the configuration file, verifying the invariants "on the fly" as it computes the state space. Finally, the temporal properties are verified over the state graph. In our case, TLC reports that it has not found any error. In order to improve efficiency, TLC compares states on the basis of a hash code ("fingerprint") during the computation of the state space, rather than comparing them precisely. In the case of a hash collision, TLC will mistakenly identify two distinct states and may therefore miss part of the state space. TLC attempts to estimate the probability that such a collision occurred during the run, on the basis of the distribution of the fingerprints. TLC also reports the number of states that it generated during its analysis, the number of distinct states, and the depth of the state graph, i.e. the length of the longest cycle. These statistics can be valuable information; for example, if the number of generated states is lower than expected, some actions may have preconditions that never evaluate to true. It is a good idea to use TLC to verify many, properties, even trivial ones, as well as some non-properties. For example, one can attempt to assert the negation of each action guard as an invariant in order to let TLC compute a finite execution that ends in a state where the action can actually be activated. For our example, the TLC run is completed in a few seconds; most of the running time is spent on the verification of the property *Liveness*, which is expanded into six properties, for each combination of clients and resources.

After this initial success, we can try to analyse somewhat larger instances, but this quickly leads to the well-known problem of state space explosion. For example, increasing the number of resources from two to three in our model results in a state graph that contains 8000 distinct states (among 45 697 states generated in all), and the analysis will take a few minutes instead of seconds.

One may observe that the specification and the properties to be verified are invariant with respect to permutations of the sets of clients and resources. Such symmetries are frequent, and TLC implements a technique known as symmetry reduction, which can counteract the effect of state-space explosion. In order to enable symmetry reduction, we simply extend the TLA$^+$ module by the definition of the predicate

$$Symmetry \;\triangleq\; Permutations(Clients) \cup Permutations(Resources)$$

(the operator *Permutations* is defined in the standard TLC module, which must therefore be added to the EXTENDS clause) and to indicate

    SYMMETRY Symmetry

in the configuration file. Unfortunately, the implementation of symmetry reduction in TLC is not compatible with checking liveness properties, and in fact, TLC reports a meaningless "counter-example" when symmetry reduction is enabled during the verification of the liveness property for our example. However, when restricted to checking the invariants, symmetry reduction with respect to both parameter sets reduces the number of states explored to

50 (and to 309 for three clients and three resources), and the run times are similarly reduced to fractions of a second for either configuration.

We can use TLC to explore variants of our specification. For example, verification succeeds when the strong fairness condition

$$\forall\, c \in \textit{Clients} \,:\, \text{SF}_{\textit{vars}}(\exists\, S \in \text{SUBSET } \textit{Resources} \,:\, \textit{Allocate}(c, S))$$

is replaced by the following condition about individual resources:

$$\forall\, c \in \textit{Clients}, r \in \textit{Resources} \,:\, \text{SF}_{\textit{vars}}(\textit{Allocate}(c, \{r\})).$$

However, the liveness condition is violated when the strong fairness condition is replaced by either of the two following fairness conditions:

$$\forall\, c \in \textit{Clients} \,:\, \text{WF}_{\textit{vars}}(\exists\, S \in \text{SUBSET } \textit{Resources} \,:\, \textit{Allocate}(c, S))$$
$$\text{SF}_{\textit{vars}}(\exists\, c \in \textit{Clients}, S \in \text{SUBSET } \textit{Resources} \,:\, \textit{Allocate}(c, S)).$$

It is a good exercise to attempt to understand these alternative fairness hypotheses in detail and to explain the verification results. Fairness conditions and their representation in TLA are formally defined in Sect. 3.3.

3 TLA: The Temporal Logic of Actions

TLA$^+$ combines TLA, the Temporal Logic of Actions [27], and mathematical set theory. This section introduces the logic TLA by defining its syntax and semantics. In these definitions, we aim at formality and rigor; we do not attempt to explain how TLA may be used to specify algorithms or systems. Sections 4 and 5 explore the verification of temporal formulas and the specification of data structures in set theory, respectively.

3.1 Rationale

The logic of time has its origins in philosophy and linguistics, where it was intended to formalize temporal references in natural language [22, 38]. Around 1975, Pnueli [37] and others recognized that such logics could be useful as a basis for the semantics of computer programs. In particular, traditional formalisms based on pre-conditions and post-conditions were found to be ill-suited for the description of reactive systems that continuously interact with their environment and are not necessarily intended to terminate. Temporal logic, as it came to be called in computer science, offered an elegant framework for describing safety and liveness properties [10, 25] of reactive systems. Different dialects of temporal logic can be distinguished according to the properties assumed of the underlying model of time (e.g., discrete or dense) and the connectives available to refer to different moments in time (e.g., future vs. past references). For computer science applications, the most controversial distinction has been between linear-time and branching-time logics. In the linear-time view, a system is identified with the set of its executions, modeled as infinite sequences of states, whereas the branching-time view also considers the branching structure of a system. Linear-time temporal logics, including TLA, are appropriate for formulating correctness properties that must hold for all the runs of a system. In contrast, branching-time temporal logics can also express possibility properties, such as the existence of a path from every reachable state, to a "reset" state. The discussion of the relative merits and deficiencies of these two kinds of temporal logic is beyond the scope of this chapter, but see, for example, [42] for a good summary, with many references to earlier papers.

Despite initial enthusiasm about temporal logic as a language to describe system properties, attempts to actually write complete system specifications as lists of properties expressed in temporal logic revealed that not even a component as simple as a FIFO queue could be unambiguously specified [39]. This observation has led many researchers to propose that reactive systems should be modeled as state machines, while temporal logic should be retained as a high-level language to describe the correctness properties. A major break-through came with the insight that temporal logic properties are decidable over finite-state models, and this has led to the development of model-checking techniques [14], which today are routinely applied to the analysis of hardware circuits, communication protocols, and software.

A further weakness of standard temporal logic becomes apparent when one attempts to compare two specifications of the same system written at different levels of abstraction. Specifically, atomic system actions are usually described via a "next-state" operator, but the "grain of atomicity" typically changes during refinement, making comparisons between specifications more difficult. For example, in Sect. 6 we shall develop a specification of the resource allocator of Fig. 1 as a distributed system where the allocator and the clients communicate by asynchronous message passing. Each of the actions will be split into a subaction performed by the allocator, the corresponding subaction performed by the client, and the transmission of a message over the network, and these subactions will be interleaved with other system events. On the face of it, the two specifications are hard to compare because they use different notions of "next state".

TLA has been designed as a formalism where system specifications and their properties are expressed in the same language, and where the refinement relation is reduced to logical implication. The problems mentioned above are addressed in the following ways. TLA is particularly suited to writing state machine specifications, augmented with fairness conditions, as we have seen in the case of the resource allocator. It is often desirable to expose only that part of the state used to specify a state machine which makes up its externally vis-ible interface, and TLA introduces quantification over state variables to hide the internal state, which a refinement is free to implement in a different man-ner. The problem with incompatible notions of "next state" at different levels of abstraction is solved by systematically allowing for stuttering steps that do not change the values of the (high-level) state variables. Low-level steps of an implementation that change only new variables are therefore allowed by the high-level specification. Similar ideas can be found in Back's refinement calculus [11] and in Abrial's Event-B method [9] (see also the chapter by Cansell and Méry in this book). Whereas finite stuttering is desirable for a simple representation of refinement, infinite stuttering is usually undesirable, because it corresponds to livelock, and the above formalisms rule it out via proof obligations that are expressed in terms of well-founded orderings. TLA adopts a more abstract and flexible approach because it associates fairness conditions, stated in temporal logic, with specifications, and these must be shown to be preserved by the refinement, typically using a mix of low-level fairness hypotheses and well-founded ordering arguments.

On the basis of these concepts, TLA provides a unified logical language to express system specifications and their properties. A single set of logical rules is used for system verification and for proving refinement.

3.2 Transition Formulas

The language of TLA distinguishes between transition formulas, which describe states and state transitions, and temporal formulas, which characterize behaviors (infinite sequences of states). Basically, transition formulas are ordinary formulas of untyped first-order logic, but TLA introduces a number of specific conventions and notations.

Assume a signature of first-order predicate logic,[4] consisting of:

- $\mathcal{L}_F$ and $\mathcal{L}_P$, which are at most denumerable, of function and predicate symbols, each symbol being of given arity; and
- a denumerable set $\mathcal{V}$ of variables, partitioned into denumerable sets $\mathcal{V}_F$ and $\mathcal{V}_R$ of flexible and rigid variables.

These sets should be disjoint from one another; moreover, no variable in $\mathcal{V}$ should be of the form v'. By $\mathcal{V}_{F'}$, we denote the set $\{v' \mid v \in \mathcal{V}_F\}$ of primed flexible variables, and by $\mathcal{V}_E$, the union $\mathcal{V} \cup \mathcal{V}_{F'}$ of all variables (rigid and flexible, primed or unprimed).

Transition functions and *transition predicates* (also called *actions*) are first-order terms and formulas built from the symbols in $\mathcal{L}_F$ and $\mathcal{L}_P$, and from the variables in $\mathcal{V}_E$. For example, if f is a ternary function symbol, p is a unary predicate symbol, $x \in \mathcal{V}_R$, and $v \in \mathcal{V}_F$, then $f(v, x, v')$ is a transition function, and the formula

$$C \triangleq \exists v' : p(f(v, x, v')) \wedge \neg(v' = x)$$

is an action. Collectively, transition functions and predicates are called *transition formulas* in the literature on TLA.

---

[4] Recall that TLA can be defined over an arbitrary first-order language. The logic of TLA$^+$ is just TLA over a specific set-theoretical language that will be introduced in Sect. 5.

Transition formulas are interpreted according to ordinary first-order logic semantics: an *interpretation* $\mathcal{I}$ defines a universe $|\mathcal{I}|$ of values and interprets each symbol in $\mathcal{L}_F$ by a function and each symbol in $\mathcal{L}_P$ by a relation of appropriate arities. In preparation for the semantics of temporal formulas, we distinguish between the valuations of flexible and rigid variables. A *state* is a mapping $s : \mathcal{V}_F \to |\mathcal{I}|$ of the flexible variables to values. Given two states s and t and a valuation $\xi : \mathcal{V}_R \to |\mathcal{I}|$ of the rigid variables, we define the combined valuation $\alpha_{s,t,\xi}$ of the variables in $\mathcal{V}_E$ as the mapping such that $\alpha_{s,t,\xi}(x) = \xi(x)$ for $x \in \mathcal{V}_R$, $\alpha_{s,t,\xi}(v) = s(v)$ for $v \in \mathcal{V}_F$, and $\alpha_{s,t,\xi}(v') = t(v)$ for $v' \in \mathcal{V}_{F'}$. The semantics of a transition function or transition formula E, written $[\![E]\!]^{\mathcal{I},\xi}_{s,t}$, is then simply the standard predicate logic semantics of E with respect to the extended valuation $\alpha_{s,t,\xi}$. We may omit any of the superscripts and subscripts if there is no danger of confusion.

We say that a transition predicate A is *valid* for the interpretation $\mathcal{I}$ iff $[\![A]\!]^{\mathcal{I},\xi}_{s,t}$ is true for all states s, t and all valuations ξ. It is *satisfiable* iff $[\![A]\!]^{\mathcal{I},\xi}_{s,t}$ is true for some s, t, and ξ.

The notions of free and bound variables in a transition formula are defined as usual, with respect to the variables in $\mathcal{V}_E$, as is the notion of substitution of a transition function a for a variable $v \in \mathcal{V}_E$ in a transition formula E, written $E[a/v]$. We assume that capture of free variables in a substitution is avoided by an implicit renaming of bound variables. For example, the variables v and x are free in the action C defined above, whereas v' is bound. Observe in particular that at the level of transition formulas, we consider v and v' to be distinct, unrelated variables.

State formulas are transition formulas that do not contain free, primed, flexible variables. For example, the action C above is actually a state predicate. Because the semantics of state formulas depends only on a single state, we simply write $[\![P]\!]^{\xi}_{s}$ when P is a state formula. Transition formulas all of whose free variables are rigid variables are called *constant formulas*; their semantics depends only on the valuation ξ.

Beyond these standard concepts from first-order logic, TLA introduces some specific conventions and notations. If E is a state formula, then E' is the transition formula obtained from E by replacing each free occurrence of a flexible variable v in E with its primed counterpart v' (where bound variables are renamed as necessary). For example, since the action C above is a state formula with v as its single free flexible variable, the formula C' is formed by substituting v' for v. In doing so, the bound variable v' of C has to be renamed, and we obtain the formula $\exists y : p(f(v', x, y)) \wedge \neg(y = x)$.

For an action A, the state formula ENABLED A is obtained by existential quantification over all primed flexible variables that have free occurrences in A. Thus, $[\![\text{ENABLED } A]\!]^{\xi}_{s}$ holds if $[\![A]\!]^{\xi}_{s,t}$ holds for some state t; this is a formal counterpart of the intuition that the action A may occur in the state s. For actions A and B, the composite action $A \cdot B$ is defined as $\exists z : A[z/v'] \wedge B[z/v]$, where v is a list of all flexible variables v_i such that v_i occurs free in B or

v_i' occurs free in A, and z is a corresponding list of fresh variables. It follows that $[\![A \cdot B]\!]^\xi_{s,t}$ holds iff both $[\![A]\!]^\xi_{s,u}$ and $[\![B]\!]^\xi_{u,t}$ hold for some state u.

Because many action-level abbreviations introduced by TLA are defined in terms of implicit quantification and substitution, their interplay can be quite delicate. For example, if P is a state predicate, then ENABLED P is obviously just P, and therefore (ENABLED P)$'$ equals P'. On the other hand, ENABLED (P') is a constant formula – if P does not contain any rigid variables then ENABLED (P') is valid iff P is satisfiable. Similarly, consider the action

$$A \triangleq v \in \mathbb{Z} \wedge v' \in \mathbb{Z} \wedge v' < 0$$

in the standard interpretation where $\mathbb{Z}$ denotes the set of integers, 0 denotes the number zero, and $*$ and $<$ denote multiplication and the "less than" relation, respectively. It is easy to see that ENABLED A is equivalent to the state predicate $v \in \mathbb{Z}$, and hence (ENABLED $A)[(n*n)/v, (n'*n')/v']$ simplifies to $(n * n) \in \mathbb{Z}$. However, substituting in the definition of the action yields

$$A[(n * n)/v, (n' * n')/v'] \equiv (n * n) \in \mathbb{Z} \wedge (n' * n') \in \mathbb{Z} \wedge (n' * n') < 0,$$

which is equivalent to FALSE, and so ENABLED $(A[(n * n)/v, (n' * n')/v'])$ is again equivalent to FALSE: substitution does not commute with the ENABLED operator. Similar pitfalls exist for action composition $A \cdot B$.

For an action A and a state function t, one writes $[A]_t$ (pronounced "square A sub t") for $A \vee t' = t$, and, dually, $\langle A \rangle_t$ ("angle A sub t") for $A \wedge \neg(t' = t)$. Therefore, $[A]_t$ is true of any state transition that satisfies A, but in addition it permits stuttering steps that leave (at least) the value of t unchanged. Similarly, $\langle A \rangle_t$ demands not only that A be true but also that the value of t changes during the transition. As we shall see below, these constructs are used to encapsulate action formulas in temporal formulas.

3.3 Temporal Formulas

Syntax

We now define the temporal layer of TLA, again with the aim of giving precise definitions of syntax and semantics. The inductive definition of temporal formulas (or just "formulas") is given as follows:

- Every state formula is a formula.
- Boolean combinations (the connectives $\neg$, $\wedge$, $\vee$, $\Rightarrow$, and $\equiv$) of formulas are formulas.
- If F is a formula, then so is $\Box F$ ("always F").
- If A is an action and t is a state function, then $\Box[A]_t$ is a formula (pronounced "always square A sub t").
- If F is a formula and $x \in \mathcal{V}_R$ is a rigid variable, then $\exists x : F$ is a formula.
- If F is a formula and $v \in \mathcal{V}_F$ is a flexible variable, then $\boldsymbol{\exists} v : F$ is a formula.

In particular, an action A by itself is not a temporal formula, not even in the form $[A]_t$. Action formulas occur within temporal formulas only in subformulas $\square[A]_t$. We assume quantifiers to have lower syntactic precedence than the other connectives, and so their scope extends as far to the right as possible.

At the level of temporal formulas, if $v \in \mathcal{V}_F$ is a flexible variable, then we consider unprimed occurrences v as well as primed occurrences v' to be occurrences of v, and the quantifier $\exists$ binds both kinds of occurrence. More formally, the set of free variables of a temporal formula is a subset of $\mathcal{V}_F \cup \mathcal{V}_R$. The free occurrencesof (rigid or flexible) variables in a state formula P, considered as a temporal formula, are precisely the free occurrences in P, considered as a transition formula. However, a variable $v \in \mathcal{V}_F$ has a free occurrence in $\square[A]_t$ iff either v or v' has a free occurence in A, or if v occurs in t. Similarly, the substitution $F[e/v]$ of a state function e for a flexible variable v substitutes both e for v and e' for v' in the action subformulas of F, after bound variables have been renamed as necessary. For example, substitution of the state function $h(v)$, where $h \in \mathcal{L}_F$ and $v \in \mathcal{V}_F$, for w in the temporal formula

$$\exists v : p(v, w) \wedge \square[q(v, f(w, v'), w')]_{g(v,w)}$$

results in the formula, up to renaming of the bound variable,

$$\exists u : p(u, h(v)) \wedge \square[q(u, f(h(v), u'), h(v'))]_{g(u,h(v))}.$$

Because state formulas do not contain free occurrences of primed flexible variables, the definitions of free and bound occurrences and of substitutions introduced for transition formulas and for temporal formulas agree on state formulas, and this observation justifies the use of the same notation at both levels of formula. Substitutions of terms for primed variables or of proper transition functions for variables are not defined at the temporal level of TLA.

Semantics

Given an interpretation $\mathcal{I}$, temporal formulas are evaluated with respect to an ω-sequence $\sigma = s_0 s_1 \ldots$ of states $s_i : \mathcal{V}_F \to |\mathcal{I}|$ (in the TLA literature, σ is usually called a *behavior*), and with respect to a valuation $\xi : \mathcal{V}_R \to |\mathcal{I}|$ of the rigid variables. For a behavior $\sigma = s_0 s_1 \ldots$, we write σ_i to refer to state s_i, and we write $\sigma|_i$ to denote the suffix $s_i s_{i+1} \ldots$ of σ. The following inductive definition assigns a truth value $[\![F]\!]_\sigma^{\mathcal{I},\xi} \in \{\mathbf{t}, \mathbf{f}\}$ to temporal formulas; the semantics of the quantifier $\exists$ over flexible variables is deferred to Sect. 3.4.

- $[\![P]\!]_\sigma^{\mathcal{I},\xi} = [\![P]\!]_{\sigma_0}^{\mathcal{I},\xi}$: state formulas are evaluated at the initial state of the behavior.
- The semantics of Boolean operators is the usual one.
- $[\![\square F]\!]_\sigma^{\mathcal{I},\xi} = \mathbf{t}$ iff $[\![F]\!]_{\sigma|_i}^{\mathcal{I},\xi} = \mathbf{t}$ for all $i \in \mathbb{N}$: this is the standard "always" connective of linear-time temporal logic.

- $\llbracket \Box [A]_t \rrbracket_\sigma^{\mathcal{I},\xi} = \mathbf{t}$ iff for all $i \in \mathbb{N}$, either $\llbracket t \rrbracket_{\sigma_i}^{\mathcal{I},\xi} = \llbracket t \rrbracket_{\sigma_{i+1}}^{\mathcal{I},\xi}$ or $\llbracket A \rrbracket_{\sigma_i,\sigma_{i+1}}^{\mathcal{I},\xi} = \mathbf{t}$ holds: the formula $\Box [A]_t$ holds iff every state transition in σ that modifies the value of t satisfies A.

- $\llbracket \exists\, x : F \rrbracket_\sigma^{\mathcal{I},\xi} = \mathbf{t}$ iff $\llbracket F \rrbracket_\sigma^{\mathcal{I},\eta} = \mathbf{t}$ for some valuation $\eta : \mathcal{V}_R \to |\mathcal{I}|$ such that $\eta(y) = \xi(y)$ for all $y \in \mathcal{V}_R \setminus \{x\}$: this is standard first-order quantification over (rigid) variables.

Validity and satisfiability of temporal formulas are defined as expected. We write $\models_{\mathcal{I}} F$ (or simply $\models F$ when $\mathcal{I}$ is understood) to denote that F is valid for (all behaviors based on) the interpretation $\mathcal{I}$.

Derived Temporal Formulas

The abbreviations for temporal formulas include the universal quantifiers $\forall$ and $\boldsymbol{\forall}$ over rigid and flexible variables. The formula $\Diamond F$ ("eventually F"), defined as $\neg\Box\neg F$, asserts that F holds for some suffix of the behavior; similarly, $\Diamond \langle A \rangle_t$ ("eventually angle A sub t") is defined as $\neg\Box[\neg A]_t$ and asserts that some future transition satisfies A and changes the value of t. We write $F \leadsto G$ ("F leads to G") for the formula $\Box(F \Rightarrow \Diamond G)$, which asserts that whenever F is true, G will become true eventually. Combinations of the "always" and "eventually" operators express "infinitely often" ($\Box\Diamond$) and "always from some time onward" ($\Diamond\Box$). Observe that a formula F can be both infinitely often true and infinitely often false, and thus $\Diamond\Box F$ is strictly stronger than $\Box\Diamond F$. These combinations are the basis for expressing fairness conditions. In particular, weak and strong fairness for an action $\langle A \rangle_t$ are defined as

$$\begin{aligned}
\mathrm{WF}_t(A) &\triangleq (\Box\Diamond\neg\mathrm{ENABLED}\,\langle A \rangle_t) \vee \Box\Diamond\langle A \rangle_t \\
&\equiv \Diamond\Box\mathrm{ENABLED}\,\langle A \rangle_t \Rightarrow \Box\Diamond\langle A \rangle_t \\
&\equiv \Box(\Box\mathrm{ENABLED}\,\langle A \rangle_t \Rightarrow \Diamond\langle A \rangle_t) \\
\mathrm{SF}_t(A) &\triangleq (\Diamond\Box\neg\mathrm{ENABLED}\,\langle A \rangle_t) \vee \Box\Diamond\langle A \rangle_t \\
&\equiv \Box\Diamond\mathrm{ENABLED}\,\langle A \rangle_t \Rightarrow \Box\Diamond\langle A \rangle_t \\
&\equiv \Box(\Box\Diamond\mathrm{ENABLED}\,\langle A \rangle_t \Rightarrow \Diamond\langle A \rangle_t)
\end{aligned}$$

Informally, fairness conditions assert that an action should eventually occur if it is "often" enabled; they differ in the precise interpretation of "often". Weak fairness $\mathrm{WF}_t(A)$ asserts that the action $\langle A \rangle_t$ must eventually occur if it remains enabled from some point onwards. In other words, the weak fairness condition is violated if, eventually, $\mathrm{ENABLED}\,\langle A \rangle_t$ remains true without $\langle A \rangle_t$ ever occurring.

The strong fairness condition, expressed by the formula $\mathrm{SF}_t(A)$, requires $\langle A \rangle_t$ to occur infinitely often provided that the action is enabled infinitely often, although it need not remain enabled forever. Therefore, strong fairness is violated if, from some point onward, the action is repeatedly enabled but never occurs. It is a simple exercise in expanding the definitions of temporal formulas to prove that the various formulations of weak and strong fairness given above are actually equivalent, and that $\mathrm{SF}_t(A)$ implies $\mathrm{WF}_t(A)$.

When one is specifying systems, the choice of appropriate fairness conditions for system actions often requires some experience. Considering again the allocator example of Fig. 1, it would not be enough to require weak fairness for the *Allocate* actions, because several clients may compete for the same resource: allocation of the resource to one client disables allocating the resource to any other client until the first client returns the resource.

3.4 Stuttering Invariance and Quantification

The formulas $\square[A]_t$ are characteristic of TLA. As we have seen, they allow for "stuttering" transitions that do not change the value of the state function t. In particular, repetitions of states cannot be observed by formulas of this form. Stuttering invariance is important in connection with refinement and composition [25]; see also Sect. 3.5.

To formalize this notion, for a set V of flexible variables we define two states s and t to be V-equivalent, written $s =_V t$, iff $s(v) = t(v)$ for all $v \in V$. For any behavior σ, we define its V-*unstuttered variant* $\natural_V \sigma$ as the behavior obtained by replacing every maximal finite subsequence of V-equivalent states in σ by the first state of that sequence. (If σ ends in an infinite sequence of states all of which are V-equivalent, that sequence is simply copied at the end of $\natural_V \sigma$.)

Two behaviors σ and τ are V-*stuttering equivalent*, written $\sigma \approx_V \tau$, if $\natural_V \sigma = \natural_V \tau$. Intuitively, two behaviors σ and τ are V-stuttering equivalent if one can be obtained from the other by inserting and/or deleting finite repetitions of V-equivalent states. In particular, the relation $\approx_{\mathcal{V}_F}$, which we also write as $\approx$, identifies two behaviors that agree up to finite repetitions of identical states.

TLA is insensitive to stuttering equivalence: the following theorem states that TLA is not expressive enough to distinguish between stuttering-equivalent behaviors.

Theorem 1 (stuttering invariance). *Assume that F is a TLA formula whose free flexible variables are among V, that $\sigma \approx_V \tau$ are V-stuttering equivalent behaviors, and that ξ is a valuation. Then $\llbracket F \rrbracket_\sigma^{\mathcal{I},\xi} = \llbracket F \rrbracket_\tau^{\mathcal{I},\xi}$.*

For the fragment of TLA formulas without quantification over flexible variables, whose semantics was defined in Sect. 3.3, it is not hard to prove Theorem 1 by induction on the structure of formulas [6, 27]. However, its extension to full TLA requires some care in the definition of quantification over flexible variables: it would be natural to define that $\llbracket \exists v : F \rrbracket_\sigma^{\mathcal{I},\xi} = \mathbf{t}$ iff $\llbracket F \rrbracket_\tau^{\mathcal{I},\xi} = \mathbf{t}$ for some behavior τ whose states τ_i agree with the corresponding states σ_i for all variables except for v. This definition, however, would not preserve stuttering invariance. As an example, consider the formula F defined below:

$$F \triangleq \land v = c \land w = c$$
$$\land \Diamond(w \neq c) \land \Box[v \neq c]_w$$

The formula F asserts that both of the variables v and w initially equal the constant c, that eventually w should be different from c, and that v must be different from c whenever w changes value. In particular, F implies that the value of v must change strictly before any change in the value of w, as illustrated in the picture. Therefore, $\sigma_1(w)$ must equal c.

Now consider the formula $\exists v : F$, and assume that τ is a behavior that satisfies $\exists v : F$, according to the above definition. It follows that $\tau_0(w)$ and $\tau_1(w)$ must both equal c, but that $\tau_i(w)$ is different from c for some (smallest) $i > 1$. The behavior $\tau|_{i-1}$ cannot satisfy $\exists v : F$ because, intuitively, "there is no room" for the internal variable v to change before w changes. However, this is in contradiction to Theorem 1 because τ and $\tau|_{i-1}$ are $\{w\}$-stuttering equivalent, and w is the only free flexible variable of $\exists v : F$.

This problem is solved by defining the semantics of $\exists v : F$ in such a way that stuttering invariance is ensured. Specifically, the behavior τ may contain extra transitions that modify only the bound variable v. Formally, we say that two behaviors σ and τ are *equal up to* v iff σ_i and τ_i agree on all variables in $\mathcal{V}_F \setminus \{v\}$, for all $i \in \mathbb{N}$. We say that σ and τ are *similar up to* v, written $\sigma \simeq_v \tau$ iff there exist behaviors σ' and τ' such that

- σ and σ' are stuttering equivalent ($\sigma \approx \sigma'$),
- σ' and τ' are equal up to v, and
- τ' and τ are again stuttering equivalent ($\tau' \approx \tau$).

Being defined as the composition of equivalence relations, $\simeq_v$ is itself an equivalence relation.

Now, we define $[\![\exists v : F]\!]^{\mathcal{I},\xi}_\sigma = \mathbf{t}$ iff $[\![F]\!]^{\mathcal{I},\xi}_\tau = \mathbf{t}$ holds for some behavior $\tau \simeq_v \sigma$. This definition can be understood as "building stuttering invariance into" the semantics of $\exists v : F$. It therefore ensures that Theorem 1 holds for all TLA formulas.

3.5 Properties, Refinement, and Composition

We have already seen in the example of the resource allocator that TLA makes no formal distinction between system specifications and their properties: both are represented as temporal formulas. It is conventional to write system specifications in the form

$$\exists x : Init \land \Box[Next]_v \land L$$

where v is a tuple of all of the state variables used to express the specification, the variables x are internal (hidden), $Init$ is a state predicate representing the initial condition, $Next$ is an action that describes the next-state relation, usually written as a disjunction of individual system actions, and L is a conjunction of formulas $\mathrm{WF}_v(A)$ or $\mathrm{SF}_v(A)$ asserting fairness assumptions about disjuncts of *Next*. However, other forms of system specifications are possible and can occasionally be useful. Asserting that a system (specified by) S satisfies a property F amounts to requiring that every behavior that satisfies S must also satisfy F; in other words, it asserts the validity of the implication $S \Rightarrow F$. For example, the theorems asserted in module *SimpleAllocator* (Fig. 1) state three properties of the resource allocator.

System Refinement

TLA was designed to support stepwise system development based on a notion of *refinement*. In such an approach, a first, high-level specification formally states the problem at a high level of abstraction. A series of intermediate models then introduce detail, adding algorithmic ideas. The development is finished when a model is obtained that is detailed enough so that an implementation can be read off immediately or even mechanically generated (for example, based on models of shared-variable or message-passing systems). The fundamental requirement for useful notions of refinement is that they must preserve system properties, such that properties established at a higher level of abstraction are guaranteed to hold for later models, including the final implementation. In this way, crucial correctness properties can be proven (or errors can be detected) early on, simplifying their proofs or the correction of the model, and these properties need never be reproven for later refinements.

A lower-level model, expressed by a TLA formula C, preserves all TLA properties of an abstract specification A if and only if for every formula F, if $A \Rightarrow F$ is valid, then so is $C \Rightarrow F$. This condition is in turn equivalent to requiring the validity of $C \Rightarrow A$. Because C is expressed at a lower level of abstraction, it will typically admit transitions that are invisible at the higher level, acting on state variables that do not appear in A. The stuttering invariance of TLA formulas is therefore essential to make validity of implication a reasonable definition of refinement.

Assume that we are given two system specifications *Abs* and *Conc* in the standard form,

$$Abs \;\triangleq\; \exists\, x \,:\, AInit \wedge \Box[ANext]_v \wedge AL \quad \text{and}$$

$$Conc \;\triangleq\; \exists\, y \,:\, CInit \wedge \Box[CNext]_w \wedge CL.$$

Proving that *Conc* refines *Abs* amounts to showing the validity of the implication $Conc \Rightarrow Abs$, and, using standard quantifier reasoning, this reduces to proving

$$(CInit \wedge \Box[CNext]_w \wedge CL) \;\Rightarrow\; (\exists\, x \,:\, AInit \wedge \Box[ANext]_v \wedge AL).$$

The standard approach to proving the latter implication is to define a state function t in terms of the free variables w (including y) of the left-hand side, and to prove

$$(CInit \wedge \Box[CNext]_w \wedge CL) \;\Rightarrow\; (AInit \wedge \Box[ANext]_v \wedge AL)[t/x].$$

In the computer science literature, the state function t is usually called a *refinement mapping*. Proof rules for refinement will be considered in some more detail in Sect. 4.5. A typical example of system refinement in TLA$^+$ will be given in Sect. 6.3, where a "distributed" model of the resource allocator will be developed that distinguishes between the actions of the allocator and those of the clients.

Composition of systems.

Stuttering invariance is also essential for obtaining a simple representation of the (parallel) composition of components, represented by their specifications. Assume that A and B are specifications of two components that we wish to compose in order to form a larger system. Each of these formulas describes the possible behaviors of the "part of the world" relevant to the respective component, represented by the state variables that have free occurrences in the specification of the component. A system that contains both components (possibly among other constituents) must therefore satisfy both A and B: composition is conjunction. Again, state transitions that correspond to a local action of one of the components are allowed because they are stuttering transitions of the other component. Any synchronisation between the two components is reflected in changes of a common state variable (the interfaces of the components), and these changes must be allowed by both components.

As a test of these ideas, consider the specification of a FIFO queue shown in Fig. 4 which is written in the canonical form of a TLA specification. The queue receives inputs via the channel *in* and sends its outputs via the channel *out*; it stores values that have been received but not yet sent in an internal queue q. Initially, we assume that the channels hold some "null" value and that the internal queue is empty. An enqueue action, described by the action *Enq*, is triggered by the reception of a new message (represented as a change of the input channel *in*); it appends the new input value to the internal queue. A dequeue action, specified by the action *Deq*, is possible whenever the internal queue is non-empty: the value at the head of the queue is sent over the channel *out* and removed from the queue.

We expect that two FIFO queues in a row implement another FIFO queue. Formally, let us assume that the two queues are connected by a channel *mid*, the above principles then lead us to expect that the formula[5]

$$Fifo[mid/out] \wedge Fifo[mid/in] \Rightarrow Fifo$$

will be valid. Unfortunately, this is not true, for the following reason: the formula *Fifo* implies that the *in* and *out* channels never change simultaneously,

---

[5] TLA$^+$ introduces concrete syntax, based on module instantiation, for writing substitutions such as *Fifo[mid/out]*.

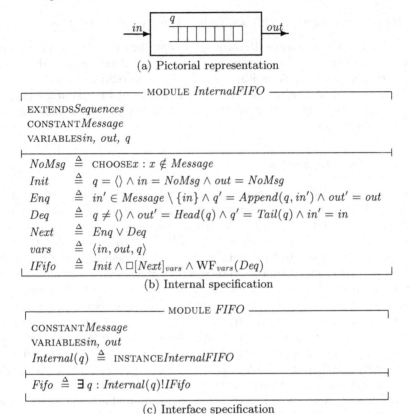

(a) Pictorial representation

———————— MODULE $InternalFIFO$ ————————

EXTENDS $Sequences$
CONSTANT $Message$
VARIABLES $in,\ out,\ q$

$NoMsg \triangleq$ CHOOSE $x : x \notin Message$
$Init \triangleq q = \langle\rangle \wedge in = NoMsg \wedge out = NoMsg$
$Enq \triangleq in' \in Message \setminus \{in\} \wedge q' = Append(q, in') \wedge out' = out$
$Deq \triangleq q \neq \langle\rangle \wedge out' = Head(q) \wedge q' = Tail(q) \wedge in' = in$
$Next \triangleq Enq \vee Deq$
$vars \triangleq \langle in, out, q \rangle$
$IFifo \triangleq Init \wedge \Box[Next]_{vars} \wedge \mathrm{WF}_{vars}(Deq)$

(b) Internal specification

———————— MODULE $FIFO$ ————————

CONSTANT $Message$
VARIABLES $in,\ out$
$Internal(q) \triangleq$ INSTANCE $InternalFIFO$

$Fifo \triangleq \exists\, q : Internal(q)!IFifo$

(c) Interface specification

Fig. 4. Specification of a FIFO queue

whereas the conjunction on the left-hand side allows such changes (if the left-hand queue performs an Enq action while the right-hand queue performs a Deq). This technical problem can be attributed to a design decision taken in the specification of the FIFO queue to disallow simultaneous changes to its input and output interfaces, a specification style known as "interleaving specifications". In fact, the above argument shows that the composition of two queues specified in interleaving style does not implement an interleaving queue. The choice of an interleaving or a non-interleaving specification style is made by the person who writes the specification; interleaving specifications are usually found to be easier to write and to understand. The problem disappears if we explicitly add an "interleaving" assumption to the composition: the implication

$$Fifo[mid/out] \wedge Fifo[mid/in] \wedge \Box[in' = in \vee out' = out]_{in,out} \Rightarrow Fifo \tag{1}$$

is valid, and its proof will be considered in Sect. 4.5. Alternatively, one can write a non-interleaving specificationof a queue that allows input and output actions to occur simultaneously.

3.6 Variations and Extensions

We now discuss some of the choices that we have made in the presentation of TLA, as well as possible extensions.

Transition Formulas and Priming

Our presentation of TLA is based on standard first-order logic, to the extent that this is possible. In particular, we have defined transition formulas as formulas of ordinary predicate logic over a large set $\mathcal{V}_E$ of variables where v and v' are unrelated. An alternative presentation might consider $'$ as an operator, resembling the next-time modality of temporal logic. The two styles of presentation result in the same semantics of temporal formulas. The style adopted in this chapter corresponds well to the verification rules of TLA, explored in Sect. 4, where action-level hypotheses are considered as ordinary first-order formulas over an extended set of variables.

Compositional Verification

We have argued in Sect. 3.5 that composition is represented in TLA as conjunction. Because components can rarely be expected to operate correctly in arbitrary environments, their specifications usually include some assumptions about the environment. An *open system specification* is one that does not constrain its environment; it asserts that the component will function correctly provided that the environment behaves as expected. One way to write such a specification is in the form of implications $E \Rightarrow M$ where E describes the assumptions about the environment and M the specification of the component. However, it turns out that often a stronger form of specification is desirable that requires the component to adhere to its description M for at least as long as the environment has not broken its obligation E. In particular, when systems are built from "open" component specifications, this form, written $E \overset{+}{\Rightarrow} M$, admits a strong composition rule that can discharge mutual assumptions between components [4, 15]. It can be shown that the formula $E \overset{+}{\Rightarrow} M$ is actually definable in TLA, and that the resulting composition rule can be justified in terms of an abstract logic of specifications, supplemented by principles specific to TLA [5, 7].

TLA*

The language of TLA distinguishes between bthe tiers of transition formulas and of temporal formulas; transition formulas must be guarded by "brackets" to ensure stuttering invariance. Although a separation between the two tiers is natural when one is writing system specifications, it is not a prerequisite for obtaining stuttering invariance. The logic TLA* [36] generalizes TLA in that it distinguishes between *pure* and *impure* temporal formulas. Whereas pure formulas of TLA* contain impure formulas in the same way that temporal formulas of TLA contain transition formulas, impure formulas generalize transition formulas in that they admit Boolean combinations of F and $\circ G$, where F and G are pure formulas and $\circ$ is the next-time modality of temporal logic. For example, the TLA* formula

$$\Box\big[A \Rightarrow \circ\Diamond\langle B\rangle_u\big]_t$$

requires that every $\langle A\rangle_t$ action must eventually be followed by $\langle B\rangle_u$. Assuming appropriate syntactic conventions, TLA* is a generalization of TLA because every TLA formula is also a TLA* formula, with the same semantics. On the other hand, it can be shown that every TLA* formula can be expressed in TLA using some additional quantifiers. For example, the TLA* formula above is equivalent to the TLA formula[6]

$$\exists\, v \;:\; \land \Box((v = c) \equiv \Diamond\langle B\rangle_u)$$
$$\land \Box[A \Rightarrow v' = c]_t$$

where c is a constant and v is a fresh flexible variable. TLA* thus offers a richer syntax without increasing the expressiveness, allowing high-level requirement specifications to be expressed more directly. (Kaminski [21] has shown that TLA* without quantification over flexible variables is strictly more expressive than the corresponding fragment of TLA.) Besides offering a more natural way to write temporal properties beyond standard system specifications, the propositional fragment of TLA* admits a straightforward complete axiomatization. (No complete axiomatization is known for propositional TLA, although Abadi [1] axiomatized an early version of TLA that was not invariant under stuttering.) For example,

$$\Box[F \Rightarrow \circ F]_v \Rightarrow (F \Rightarrow \Box F)$$

where F is a temporal formula and v is a tuple containing all flexible variables with free occurrences in F, is a TLA* formulation of the usual induction axiom of temporal logic; this is a TLA formula only if F is in fact a state formula.

Binary Temporal Operators

TLA can be considered as a fragment of the standard linear-time temporal logic (LTL) [34]. In particular, TLA does not include binary operators such as **until**. The main reason for that omission is the orientation of TLA towards

---

[6] Strictly, this equivalence is true only for universes that contain at least two distinct values; one-element universes are not very interesting.

writing specifications of state machines, where such operators are not necessary. Moreover, nested occurrences of binary temporal operators can be hard to interpret. Nevertheless, binary temporal operators are definable in TLA using quantification over flexible variables. For example, suppose that P and Q are state predicates whose free variables are in the tuple w of variables, that v is a flexible variable that does not appear in w, and that c is a constant. Then P **until** Q can be defined as the formula

$$\exists v : \wedge (v = c) \equiv Q$$
$$\wedge \Box[(v \neq c \Rightarrow P) \wedge (v' = c \equiv (v = c \vee Q'))]_{\langle v, w \rangle}$$
$$\wedge \Diamond Q$$

The idea is to use the auxiliary variable v to remember whether Q has already been true. As long as Q has been false, P is required to hold. For arbitrary TLA formulas F and G, the formula F **until** G can be defined along the same lines, using a technique similar to that shown abive for the translation of TLA* formulas.

4 Deductive System Verification in TLA

Because TLA formulas are used to describe systems as well as their properties, the proof rules for system verification are just logical axioms and rules of TLA. More precisely, a system described by a formula *Spec* has a property *Prop* if and only if every behavior that satisfies *Spec* also satisfies *Prop*, that is, iff the implication *Spec* $\Rightarrow$ *Prop* is valid. (To be really precise, the implication should be valid over the class of interpretations where the function and predicate symbols have the intended meaning.) System verification, in principle, therefore requires reasoning about sets of behaviors. The TLA proof rules are designed to reduce this temporal reasoning, whenever possible, to a proof of verification conditions expressed in the underlying predicate logic, a strategy that is commonly referred to as *assertional reasoning*. In this section, we present some typical rules and illustrate their use. We are not trying to be exhaustive, more information can be found in Lamport's original paper on TLA [27].

4.1 Invariants

Invariants characterize the set of states that can be reached during system execution; they are the basic form of safety properties and the starting point for any form of system verification. In TLA, an invariant is expressed by a formula of the form $\Box I$, where I is a state formula.

A basic rule for proving invariants is given by

$$\frac{I \wedge [N]_t \Rightarrow I'}{I \wedge \Box[N]_t \Rightarrow \Box I} \text{(INV1)}.$$

This rule asserts that whenever the hypothesis $I \wedge [N]_t \Rightarrow I'$ is valid as a transition formula, the conclusion $I \wedge \Box[N]_t \Rightarrow \Box I$ is a valid temporal formula. The hypothesis states that every possible transition (stuttering or not) preserves I; thus, if I holds initially, it is guaranteed to hold forever. Formally, the correctness of the rule (INV1) is easily established by induction on behaviors. Because the hypothesis is a transition formula, it can be proven using ordinary first-order reasoning, including "data" axioms that characterize the intended interpretations.

For example, we can use the invariant rule (INV1) to prove the invariant $\Box(q \in Seq(Message))$ of the FIFO queue that was specified in module *InternalFIFO* in Fig. 4(b) on page 420. We have to prove

$$IFifo \Rightarrow \Box(q \in Seq(Message)) \qquad (2)$$

which, by the rule (INV1), the definition of the formula *IFifo*, and propositional logic, can be reduced to proving

$$Init \Rightarrow q \in Seq(Message), \qquad (3)$$

$$q \in Seq(Message) \wedge [Next]_{vars} \Rightarrow q' \in Seq(Message). \qquad (4)$$

Because the empty sequence is certainly a finite sequence of messages, the proof obligation (3) follows from the definition of *Init* and appropriate data axioms. Similarly, the proof of (4) reduces to proving preservation of the invariant by the *Deq* and *Enq* actions, as well as under stuttering, and these proofs are again straightforward.

The proof rule (INV1) requires that the invariant I is *inductive*: it must be preserved by every possible system action. As with ordinary mathematical induction, it is usually necessary to strengthen the assertion and find an "induction hypothesis" that makes the proof go through. This idea is embodied in the following derived invariant rule

$$\frac{Init \Rightarrow I \qquad I \wedge [Next]_t \Rightarrow I' \qquad I \Rightarrow J}{Init \wedge \Box[Next]_t \Rightarrow \Box J} \text{(INV)}.$$

In this rule, I is an inductive invariant that implies J. The creative step consists in finding this inductive invariant. Typically, inductive invariants contain interesting "design" information about the model and represent the overall correctness idea. Some formal design methods, such as the B method [8] (see also the chapter by Cansell and Méry in this book) therefore demand that an inductive invariant be documented with the system model.

For example, suppose we wish to prove that any two consecutive elements of the queue are different. This property can be expressed in TLA$^+$ by the state predicate

$$J \triangleq \forall i \in 1..Len(q) - 1 : q[i] \neq q[i+1]$$

We have used some TLA$^+$ syntax for sequences in writing the formula J; in particular, a sequence s in TLA$^+$ is represented as a function whose values can be accessed as $s[1]$, ..., $s[Len(s)]$. The sequence formed of the values $e_1, \ldots, e_n$ is written as $\langle e_1, \ldots, e_n \rangle$, and the concatenation of two sequences s and t is written $s \circ t$.

The invariant rule (INV1) is not strong enough to prove that J is an invariant, because J is not necessarily preserved by the *Enq* step: there is no information about how the old value *in* of the input channel relates to the values in the queue. (Try this proof yourself to see why it fails.) The proof succeeds using the rule (INV) and the inductive invariant

$$
\begin{aligned}
Inv \;\; &\triangleq \;\; \text{LET} \;\; oq \triangleq \langle out \rangle \circ q \\
&\;\;\;\; \text{IN} \quad \wedge \; in = oq[Len(oq)] \\
&\qquad\qquad \wedge \; \forall \, i \in 1..Len(oq) - 1 \; : \; oq[i] \neq oq[i+1],
\end{aligned}
$$

which asserts that the current value of the input channel can be found either as the last element of the queue or (if the queue is empty) as the current value of the output channel.

4.2 Step Simulation

When one is proving refinement between two TLA specifications, a crucial step is to show that the next-state relation of the lower-level specification, expressed as $\Box[M]_t$, say, simulates the next-state relation $\Box[N]_u$ of the higher-level specification, up to stuttering. The following proof rule is used for this purpose; it relies on a previously proven state invariant I:

$$
\frac{I \wedge I' \wedge [M]_t \Rightarrow [N]_u}{\Box I \wedge \Box[M]_t \Rightarrow \Box[N]_u} \;\; \text{(TLA2)}.
$$

In particular, it follows from (TLA2) that the next-state relation can be strengthened by an invariant:

$$
\Box I \wedge \Box[M]_t \Rightarrow \Box[M \wedge I \wedge I']_t.
$$

Note that the converse of this implication is not valid: the right-hand side holds for any behavior where t never changes, independently of the formula I.

We may use (TLA2) to prove that the FIFO queue never dequeues the same value twice in a row:

$$
IFifo \Rightarrow \Box[Deq \Rightarrow out' \neq out]_{vars}. \tag{5}
$$

For this proof, we make use of the inductive invariant *Inv* introduced in Sect. 4.1 above. By rule (TLA2), we have to prove

$$
Inv \wedge Inv' \wedge [Next]_{vars} \Rightarrow [Deq \Rightarrow out' \neq out]_{vars}. \tag{6}
$$

The proof of (6) reduces to the three cases of a stuttering transition, an *Enq* action, and a *Deq* action. Only the last case is nontrivial. Its proof relies on the definition of *Deq*, which implies that q is non-empty and that $out' = Head(q)$.

In particular, the sequence oq contains at least two elements, and therefore Inv implies that $oq[1]$, which is just out, is different from $oq[2]$, which is $Head(q)$. This suffices to prove $out' \neq out$.

4.3 Liveness Properties

Liveness properties, intuitively, assert that something good must eventually happen [10, 24]. Because formulas $\Box[N]_t$ are satisfied by a system that always stutters, the proof of liveness properties must ultimately rely on fairness properties of the specification that are assumed. TLA provides rules to deduce elementary liveness properties from the fairness properties assumed for a specification. More complex properties can then be inferred with the help of well-founded orderings.

The following rule can be used to prove a leads-to formula from a weak fairness assumption, a similar rule exists for strong fairness:

$$\frac{\begin{array}{c} I \wedge I' \wedge P \wedge [N]_t \Rightarrow P' \vee Q' \\ I \wedge I' \wedge P \wedge \langle N \wedge A \rangle_t \Rightarrow Q' \\ I \wedge P \Rightarrow \text{ENABLED}\,\langle A \rangle_t \end{array}}{\Box I \wedge \Box[N]_t \wedge \text{WF}_t(A) \Rightarrow (P \rightsquigarrow Q)}\,\text{(WF1)}^{\textbf{.}}$$

In this rule, I, P, and Q are state predicates, I is again an invariant, $[N]_t$ represents the next-state relation, and $\langle A \rangle_t$ is a "helpful action" [33] for which weak fairness is assumed. Again, all three premises of (WF1) are transition formulas. To see why the rule is correct, assume that σ is a behavior satisfying $\Box I \wedge \Box[N]_t \wedge \text{WF}_t(A)$, and that P holds for state σ_i. We have to show that Q holds for some σ_j with $j \geq i$. By the first premise, any successor of a state satisfying P has to satisfy P or Q, so P must hold for as long as Q has not been true. The third premise ensures that in all of these states, action $\langle A \rangle_t$ is enabled, and so the assumption of weak fairness ensures that eventually $\langle A \rangle_t$ occurs (unless Q has already become true before that happens). Finally, by the second premise, any $\langle A \rangle_t$-successor (which, by assumption, is in fact an $\langle N \wedge A \rangle_t$-successor) of a state satisfying P must satisfy Q, which proves the claim.

For our running example, we can use the rule (WF1) to prove that every message stored in the queue will eventually move closer to the head of the queue or even to the output channel. Formally, let the state predicate $at(k, x)$ be defined by

$$at(k, x) \;\triangleq\; k \in 1..Len(q) \wedge q[k] = x$$

We shall use (WF1) to prove

$$Fifo I \Rightarrow \big(at(k, x) \rightsquigarrow (out = x \vee at(k - 1, x))\big) \tag{7}$$

where k and x are rigid variables. The following outline of the proof illustrates the application of the rule (WF1); the lower-level steps are all inferred by non-temporal reasoning and are omitted.

1. $at(k,x) \wedge [Next]_{vars} \Rightarrow at(k,x)' \vee out' = x \vee at(k-1,x)'$
   1.1. $at(k,x) \wedge m \in Message \wedge Enq \Rightarrow at(k,x)'$
   1.2. $at(k,x) \wedge Deq \wedge k = 1 \Rightarrow out' = x$
   1.3. $at(k,x) \wedge Deq \wedge k > 1 \Rightarrow at(k-1,x)'$
   1.4. $at(k,x) \wedge vars' = vars \Rightarrow at(k,x)'$
   1.5. Q.E.D.
      follows from steps 1.1–1.4 by the definitions of $Next$ and $at(k,x)$.
2. $at(k,x) \wedge \langle Deq \wedge Next \rangle_{vars} \Rightarrow out' = x \vee at(k-1,x)'$
   follows from steps 1.2 and 1.3 above.
3. $at(k,x) \Rightarrow \text{ENABLED} \langle Deq \rangle_{vars}$
   for any k, $at(k,x)$ implies that $q \neq \langle \rangle$ and thus the enabledness condition.

However, the rule (WF1) cannot be used to prove the stronger property that every input to the queue will eventually be dequeued, expressed by the TLA formula

$$FifoI \Rightarrow \forall m \in Message : in = m \rightsquigarrow out = m, \tag{8}$$

because there is no single "helpful action": the number of Deq actions necessary to produce the input element in the output channel depends on the length of the queue. Intuitively, the argument used to establish property (7) must be iterated. The following rule formalizes this idea as an induction over a well-founded relation $(D, \succ)$, i.e. a binary relation such that there does not exist an infinite descending chain $d_1 \succ d_2 \succ \ldots$ of elements $d_i \in D$:

$$\frac{(D, \succ) \text{ is well−founded} \qquad F \Rightarrow \forall d \in D : \big(G \rightsquigarrow (H \vee \exists e \in D : d \succ e \wedge G[e/d]) \big)}{F \Rightarrow \forall d \in D : (G \rightsquigarrow H)} \text{(LATTICE)}.$$

In this rule, d and e are rigid variables such that d does not occur in H and e does not occur in G. For convenience, we have stated the rule (LATTICE) in a language of set theory. Also, we have taken the liberty of stating the assumption that $(D, \succ)$ is well-founded as if it were a logical hypothesis. As an illustration of the expressiveness of TLA, we observe in passing that, in principle, this hypothesis could be stated by the temporal formula

$$\begin{aligned} &\wedge \forall d \in D : \neg(d \succ d) \\ &\wedge \boldsymbol{\forall} v : \Box(v \in D) \wedge \Box[v \succ v']_v \Rightarrow \Diamond\Box[\text{FALSE}]_v, \end{aligned}$$

whose first conjunct expresses the irreflexivity of $\succ$ and whose second conjunct asserts that any sequence of values in D that can change only by decreasing with respect to $\succ$ must eventually become stationary. In system verification, however, well-foundedness is usually considered as a "data axiom" and is outside the scope of temporal reasoning.

Unlike the premises of the rules considered so far, the second hypothesis of the rule (LATTICE) is itself a temporal formula which requires that every occurrence of G, for any value $d \in D$, must be followed either by an occurrence of H or again by some G, for some smaller value e. Because there cannot be an infinite descending chain of values in D, H must eventually become true. In applications of the rule (LATTICE), this hypothesis must be discharged by another rule for proving liveness, either a fairness rule such as (WF1) or another application of (LATTICE).

If we choose $(\mathbb{N}, >)$, the set of natural numbers with the standard "greater-than" relation, as the well-founded domain, the proof of the liveness property (8) that asserts that the FIFO queue eventually outputs every message it receives can be derived from property (7) and the invariant *Inv* of Sect. 4.1 using the rule (LATTICE).

Lamport [27] lists further (derived) rules for liveness properties, including introduction rules for proving formulas $\mathrm{WF}_t(A)$ and $\mathrm{SF}_t(A)$ that are necessary when proving refinement.

4.4 Simple Temporal Logic

The proof rules considered so far support the derivation of typical correctness properties of systems. In addition, TLA satisfies some standard axioms and rules of linear-time temporal logic that are useful when one is preparing for the application of verification rules. Figure 5 contains the axioms and rules of "simple temporal logic", adapted from [27].

$$(\mathrm{STL1}) \quad \frac{F}{\Box F} \qquad\qquad (\mathrm{STL4}) \quad \Box(F \Rightarrow G) \Rightarrow (\Box F \Rightarrow \Box G)$$

$$(\mathrm{STL2}) \quad \Box F \Rightarrow F \qquad\qquad (\mathrm{STL5}) \quad \Box(F \wedge G) \equiv (\Box F \wedge \Box G)$$

$$(\mathrm{STL3}) \quad \Box\Box F \equiv \Box F \qquad\qquad (\mathrm{STL6}) \quad \Diamond\Box(F \wedge G) \equiv (\Diamond\Box F \wedge \Diamond\Box G)$$

Fig. 5. Rules of simple temporal logic.

It can be shown that this is just a non-standard presentation of the modal logic S4.2 [19], implying that these laws by themselves, characterize a modal accessibility relation for $\Box$ that is reflexive, transitive, and locally convex (confluent). The latter condition asserts that for any state s and states t, u that are both accessible from s, there is a state v that is accessible from t and u.

Many derived laws of temporal logic are useful for system verification. Particularly useful are rules about the "leadsto" operator such as

$$\frac{F \Rightarrow G}{F \rightsquigarrow G}, \qquad \frac{F \rightsquigarrow G \quad G \rightsquigarrow H}{F \rightsquigarrow H},$$

$$\frac{F \rightsquigarrow H \quad G \rightsquigarrow H}{(F \vee G) \rightsquigarrow H}, \qquad \frac{F \Rightarrow \Box G \quad F \rightsquigarrow H}{.F \rightsquigarrow (G \wedge H)}.$$

In principle, such temporal logic rules can be derived from the rules of Fig. 5. In practice, it can be easier to justify them from the semantics of temporal logic. Because the validity of propositional temporal logic is decidable, they can be checked automatically by freely available tools.

4.5 Quantifier Rules

Although we have seen in Sect. 3.4 that the semantics of quantification over flexible variables is non-standard, the familiar proof rules of first-order logic are sound for both types of quantifier:

$$F[c/x] \Rightarrow \exists\, x \,:\, F \,\, (\exists\mathrm{I}), \qquad \frac{F \Rightarrow G}{(\exists\, x \,:\, F) \Rightarrow G}\,(\exists\mathrm{E}),$$

$$F[t/v] \Rightarrow \exists\hspace{-0.6em}\exists\, v \,:\, F \,\, (\exists\hspace{-0.6em}\exists\,\mathrm{I}), \qquad \frac{F \Rightarrow G}{(\exists\hspace{-0.6em}\exists\, v \,:\, F) \Rightarrow G}\,(\exists\hspace{-0.6em}\exists\,\mathrm{E}).$$

In these rules, x is a rigid and v is a flexible variable. The elimination rules $(\exists\mathrm{E})$ and $(\exists\hspace{-0.4em}\exists\,\mathrm{E})$ require the usual proviso that the bound variable should not be free in the formula G. In the introduction rules, t is a state function, while c is a constant function. Observe that if we allowed an arbitrary state function in the rule $(\exists\mathrm{I})$, we could prove

$$\exists\, x \,:\, \Box(v = x) \tag{9}$$

for any state variable v from the premise $\Box(v = v)$, provable by (STL1). However, the formula (9) asserts that v remains constant throughout a behavior, which can obviously not be valid.

Since existential quantification over flexible variables corresponds to hiding of state components, the rules $(\exists\hspace{-0.4em}\exists\,\mathrm{I})$ and $(\exists\hspace{-0.4em}\exists\,\mathrm{E})$ play a fundamental role in proofs of refinement for reactive systems. In this context, the "witness" t is often called a *refinement mapping* [2]. For example, the concatenation of the two low-level queues provides a suitable refinement mapping for proving the validity of the formula (1 on page 420), which claimed that two FIFO queues in a row implement a FIFO queue, assuming interleaving of changes to the input and output channels.

Although the quantifier rules are standard, one should recall from Sect. 3.2 that care has to be taken when substitutions are applied to formulas that contain implicit quantifiers. In particular, the formulas $\mathrm{WF}_t(A)$ and $\mathrm{SF}_t(A)$ contain the subformula ENABLED $\langle A \rangle_t$, and therefore $\mathrm{WF}_t(A)[e/v]$ is not generally equivalent to the formula $\mathrm{WF}_{t[e/v]}(A[e/v, e'/v'])$. The consequences of this inequivalence for system verification are discussed in more detail in Lamport's original paper on TLA [27].

In general, refinement mappings need not always exist. For example, $(\exists\hspace{-0.4em}\exists\,\mathrm{I})$ cannot be used to prove the TLA formula

$$\exists\hspace{-0.6em}\exists\, v \,:\, \Box\Diamond\langle\mathrm{TRUE}\rangle_v, \tag{10}$$

which is valid, except over universes that contain a single element. Formula (10) asserts the existence of a flexible variable whose value changes infinitely often. (Such a variable can be seen as an "oscillator", which would trigger system transitions.) In fact, an attempt to prove (10) by the rule ($\exists$ I) would require one to exhibit a state function t whose value is certain to change infinitely often in any behavior. Such a state function cannot exist: consider a behavior σ that ends in infinite stuttering, then the value of t never changes over the stuttering part of σ.

One approach to solving this problem, introduced in [2], consists of adding *auxiliary variables* such as history and prophecy variables. Formally, this approach consists in adding special introduction rules for auxiliary variables. The proof of $G \Rightarrow \exists v : F$ is then reduced to first proving a formula of the form $G \Rightarrow \exists a : G_{aux}$ using a rule for auxiliary variables, and then using the rules ($\exists$ E) and ($\exists$ I) above to prove $G \wedge G_{aux} \Rightarrow \exists v : F$. The details are beyond the scope of this introductory overview.

5 Formalized Mathematics: The Added Value of TLA$^+$

The definitions of the syntax and semantics of TLA in Sect. 3 were given with respect to an arbitrary language of predicate logic and its interpretation. TLA$^+$ instantiates this generic definition of TLA with a specific first-order language, namely Zermelo–Fränkel set theory with choice. By adopting a standard interpretation, TLA$^+$ specifications are precise and unambiguous about the "data structures" on which specifications are based. We have seen in the example proofs in Sect. 4, that reasoning about data accounts for most of the steps that need to be proven during system verification. Besides fixing the vocabulary of the logical language and the intended interpretation, TLA$^+$ also introduces facilities for structuring a specification as a hierarchy of modules for declaring parameters and, most importantly, for defining operators. These facilities are essential for writing actual specifications and must therefore be mastered by any user of TLA$^+$. However, from the foundational point of view adopted in this chapter, they are just syntactic sugar. We shall therefore concentrate on the set-theoretic foundations, referring the reader to Lamport's book [29] for a detailed presentation of the language of TLA$^+$.

5.1 Elementary Data Structures: Basic Set Theory

Elementary set theory is based on a signature that consists of a single binary predicate symbol $\in$ and no function symbols. TLA$^+$ heavily relies on Hilbert's choice operator. The syntax of transition-level terms and formulas defined in Sect. 3.2 is therefore extended by an additional term formation rule that defines CHOOSEx : A to be a transition function whenever $x \in \mathcal{V}_E$ is a variable and A is an action.[7] The occurrences of x in the term CHOOSEx : A are bound.

---

[7] Temporal formulas are defined as indicated in Sect. 3.3 on page 413; in particular, CHOOSE is never applied to a temporal formula.

To this first-order language there corresponds a set-theoretic interpretation: every TLA$^+$ value is a set. Moreover, $\in$ is interpreted as set membership and the interpretation is equipped with an (unspecified) choice function ε mapping every non-empty collection C of values to some element $\varepsilon(C)$ of C, and mapping the empty collection to an arbitrary value. The interpretation of a term CHOOSE$x : P$ is defined as

$$[\![\text{CHOOSE}x \ : \ P]\!]_{s,t}^{\xi} \ = \ \varepsilon(\{d \ | \ [\![P]\!]_{\alpha_{s,t,\xi}[d/x]} = \mathbf{t}\})$$

This definition employs the choice function to return some value satisfying P provided there is some such value in the universe of set theory. Observe that in this semantic clause, the choice function is applied to a collection that need not be a set (i.e., an element of the universe of the interpretation); in set-theoretic terminology, ε applies to classes and not just to sets. Because ε is a function, it produces the same value when applied to equal arguments. It follows that the choice 'function' satisfies the laws

$$(\exists x \ : \ P) \equiv P[(\text{CHOOSE}x \ : \ P)/x] \tag{11}$$

$$(\forall x \ : \ (P \equiv Q)) \Rightarrow (\text{CHOOSE}x \ : \ P) = (\text{CHOOSE}x \ : \ Q) \tag{12}$$

TLA$^+$ avoids undefinedness by underspecification [18], and so CHOOSE$x : P$ denotes a value even if no value satisfies P. To ensure that a term involving choice actually denotes the expected value, the existence of some suitable value should be proven. If there is more than one such value, the expression is underspecified, and the user should be prepared to accept any of them. In particular, any properties should hold for all possible values. However, observe that for a given interpretation, choice is deterministic, and that it is not "monotone": no relationship can be established between CHOOSE$x : P$ and CHOOSE$x : Q$ even when $P \Rightarrow Q$ is valid (unless P and Q are actually equivalent). Therefore, whenever a specification *Spec* contains an underspecified application of choice, any refinement *Ref* is constrained to make the same choices in order to prove *Ref* $\Rightarrow$ *Spec*; this situation is fundamentally different from non-determinism, where implementations may narrow the set of allowed values.

In the following, we shall freely use many notational abbreviations of TLA$^+$. For example, $\exists x, y \in S : P$ abbreviates $\exists x : \exists y : x \in S \wedge y \in S \wedge P$. Local declarations are written as LET $\_$ IN $\_$, and IF $\_$ THEN $\_$ ELSE $\_$ is used for conditional expressions.

From membership and choice, one can build up the conventional language of mathematics [32], and this is the foundation for the expressiveness of TLA$^+$.

Figure 6 on the following page lists some of the basic set-theoretic constructs of TLA$^+$; we write

$$\{e_1, \ldots, e_n\} \ \triangleq \ \text{CHOOSE}S \ : \ \forall x \ : \ (x \in S \ \equiv \ x = e_1 \vee \ldots \vee x = e_n)$$

to denote set enumeration and assume the additional bound variables in the defining expressions of Fig. 6 to be chosen such that no variable clashes occur. The two comprehension schemes act as binders for the variable x, which must

union	$\text{UNION}\,S \;\triangleq\; \text{CHOOSE}\,M : \forall x : (x \in M \equiv \exists\,T \in S : x \in T)$
binary union	$S \cup T \;\triangleq\; \text{UNION}\{S, T\}$
subset	$S \subseteq T \;\triangleq\; \forall x : (x \in S \Rightarrow x \in T)$
powerset	$\text{SUBSET}\,S \;\triangleq\; \text{CHOOSE}\,M : \forall x : (x \in M \equiv x \subseteq S)$
comprehension 1	$\{x \in S : P\} \;\triangleq\; \text{CHOOSE}\,M : \forall x : (x \in M \equiv x \in S \wedge P)\}$
comprehension 2	$\{t : x \in S\} \;\triangleq\; \text{CHOOSE}\,M : \forall y : (y \in M \equiv \exists x \in S : y = t)$

Fig. 6. Basic set-theoretic operators

not have free occurrences in S. The existence of sets defined in terms of choice can be justified from the axioms of Zermelo–Fränkel set theory [41], which provide the deductive counterpart of the semantics underlying TLA$^+$. However, it is well-known that without proper care, set theory is prone to paradoxes. For example, the expression

$$\text{CHOOSE}\,S : \forall x : (x \in S \equiv x \notin x)$$

is a well-formed constant formula of TLA$^+$, but the existence of a set S containing precisely those sets which do not contain themselves would lead to the contradiction that $S \in S$ iff $S \notin S$; this is of course Russell's paradox. Intuitively, S is "too big" to be a set. More precisely, the universe of set theory does not contain values that are in bijection with the collection of all sets. Therefore, when one is evaluating the above TLA$^+$ expression, the choice function is applied to the empty collection, and the result depends on the underlying interpretation. Perhaps unexpectedly, however, we can infer from (12) that

$$(\text{CHOOSE}\,S : \forall x : (x \in S \equiv x \notin x)) = (\text{CHOOSE}\,x : x \in \{\}).$$

Similarly, a generalized intersection operator dual to the union operator of Fig. 6 does not exist, because generalized intersection over the empty set of sets cannot be sensibly defined.

On the positive side, we have exploited the fact that no set can contain all values in the definition

$$NoMsg \;\triangleq\; \text{CHOOSE}\,x : x \notin Message$$

that appears in Fig. 4(b) on page 420. Whatever set is denoted by $Message$, $NoMsg$ will denote some value that is not contained in $Message$. If a subsequent refinement wanted to fix a specific "null" message value $null \notin Message$, it could do so by restricting the class of admissible interpretations via an assumption of the form

$$\text{ASSUME}(\text{CHOOSE}\,x : x \notin Message) = null$$

Because all properties established for the original specification hold for all possible choices of $NoMsg$, they will continue to hold for this restricted choice.

5.2 More Data Structures

Besides their use in elementary set operations, functions are a convenient way to represent different kinds of data structures. A traditional construction of functions within set theory, followed in Z and B [8,40], is to construct functions as special kinds of relations, which are represented as ordered pairs. TLA$^+$ takes a different approach: it assumes functions to be primitive and assumes tuples to be a particular kind of function. The set of functions whose domain equals S and whose codomain is a subset of T is written as $[S \rightarrow T]$, the domain of a function f is denoted by DOMAIN f, and the application of a function f to an expression e is written as $f[e]$. The expression $[x \in S \mapsto e]$ denotes a function with domain S that maps any $x \in S$ to e; again, the variable x must not occur in S and is bound by the function constructor. (This expression can be understood as the TLA$^+$ syntax for a lambda expression $\lambda x \in S : e$.) Thus, any function f obeys the law

$$f = [x \in \text{DOMAIN} f \mapsto f[x]], \tag{13}$$

and this equation can in fact serve as a characteristic predicate for functional values. TLA$^+$ introduces a notation for overriding a function at a certain argument position (a similar "function update" is central in Gurevich's ASM notation [12]; see also the chapter by Reisig in this book). Formally,

$$[f \text{EXCEPT}![t] = u] \triangleq [x \in \text{DOMAIN} f \mapsto \text{IF } x = t \text{ THEN } u \text{ ELSE } f[x]]$$

where x is a fresh variable. Again, this notation generalises to updates of a function at several argument positions; also, the notation @ can be used within the subexpression u to denote the original value of $f[t]$.

By combining choice, sets, and function notation, one obtains an expressive language for defining mathematical structures. For example, the standard TLA$^+$ module introducing natural numbers defines them as an arbitrary set with a constant zero and a successor function satisfying the usual Peano axioms [29, p. 345], and Lamport goes on to define similarly the integers and the real numbers, ensuring that the integers are a subset of the reals. In particular, the arithmetic operators over these sets are identical rather than just overloaded uses of the same symbols.

Recursive functions can be defined in terms of choice, for example

$$factorial \triangleq$$
$$\text{CHOOSE} f : f = [n \in Nat \mapsto \text{IF } n = 0 \text{ THEN } 1 \text{ ELSE } n * f[n-1]],$$

which TLA$^+$, using some syntactic sugar, offers us to write more concisely as

$$factorial[n \in Nat] \triangleq \text{IF } n = 0 \text{ THEN } 1 \text{ ELSE } n * factorial[n-1].$$

Of course, as with any construction based on choice, such a definition should be justified by proving the existence of a function that satisfies the recursive equation. Unlike the standard semantics of programming languages, TLA$^+$

does not commit to the least fixed point of a recursively defined function in cases where there are several solutions.

Tuples are represented in TLA$^+$ as functions,

$$\langle t_1, \ldots, t_n \rangle \ \triangleq\ [i \in 1..n \mapsto \text{IF } i = 1 \text{ THEN } t_1 \ \ldots \ \text{ELSE } t_n],$$

where $1..n$ denotes the set $\{j \in Nat : 1 \leq j \wedge j \leq n\}$ (and i is a "fresh" variable). Selection of the ith element of a tuple is therefore just a function application. Strings are defined as tuples of characters, and records are represented as functions whose domains are finite sets of strings. The update operation on functions can thus be applied to tuples and records as well. The concrete syntax of TLA$^+$ offers us special support for record operations. For example, one writes $acct.balance$ instead of $acct[\text{"balance"}]$.

$$
\begin{aligned}
Seq(S) &\ \triangleq\ \text{UNION}\{[1..n] \to S : n \in Nat\} \\
Len(s) &\ \triangleq\ \text{CHOOSE} \, n \in Nat : \text{DOMAIN } s = 1..n \\
Head(s) &\ \triangleq\ s[1] \\
Tail(s) &\ \triangleq\ [i \in 1..Len(s) - 1 \mapsto s[i+1]] \\
s \circ t &\ \triangleq\ [i \in 1..Len(s) + Len(t) \mapsto \\
&\qquad \text{IF } i \leq Len(s) \text{ THEN } s[i] \text{ ELSE } t[i - Len(s)]] \\
Append(s, e) &\ \triangleq\ s \circ \langle e \rangle \\
SubSeq(s, m, n) &\ \triangleq\ [i \in 1..(1 + n - m) \mapsto s[i + m - 1]]
\end{aligned}
$$

Fig. 7. Finite sequences.

The standard TLA$^+$ module *Sequences* that has already appeared as a library module used for the specification of the FIFO queue in Fig. 4(b) on page 420, represents finite sequences as tuples. The definitions of the standard operations, some of which are shown in Fig. 7, are therefore quite simple. However, this simplicity can sometimes be deceptive. For example, these definitions do not reveal that the *Head* and *Tail* operations are "partial". They should be validated by proving the expected properties, such as

$$\forall s \in Seq(S) : Len(s) \geq 1 \Rightarrow s = \langle Head(s) \rangle \circ Tail(s).$$

6 The Resource Allocator Revisited

Armed with a better understanding of the language TLA$^+$, let us reconsider the resource allocator specification of Sect. 2. We have already verified several properties of the simple allocator specification of Fig. 1 by model checking, and we could use the deduction rules of Sect. 4 to prove these properties in full generality. Does this mean that the specification is satisfactory?

Consider the following scenario: two clients c_1 and c_2 both request resources r_1 and r_2. The allocator grants r_1 to c_1 and r_2 to c_2. From our informal description in Sect. 2.1, it appears that we have reached a deadlock state: neither client can acquire the missing resource as long as the other one does not give up the resource it holds, which it is not required to do. Why then did TLC not report any deadlock, and how could we prove liveness?

Formally, the model contains no deadlock because, according to requirement (3), each client is allowed to give up resource it is holding. The problem with the model is that it actually *requires* clients to eventually give up the resources, even if they have not yet received the full share of resources that they asked for. This requirement is expressed by the seemingly innocous fairness condition

$$\forall\, c \in Clients\ :\ \mathrm{WF}_{vars}(Return(c, alloc[c])),$$

whereas the informal requirement (4) demands only that clients return their resources once their entire request has been satisfied. We should therefore have written

$$\forall c \in Clients\ :\ \mathrm{WF}_{vars}\big(unsat[c] = \{\} \wedge Return(c, alloc[c])\big).$$

Rerunning TLC on the modified specification produces the expected counter-example.

The bigger lesson of this example is that errors can creep into formal specifications just as easily as into programs, and that a model can be inappropriate even if it satisfies all correctness properties. Validation, for example by simulation runs or a review of the model, is extremely important for avoiding this kind of error. We will now revisit the allocator specification and present a corrected model. We will then present a refinement of that model that prepares an implementation as a distributed system.

6.1 A Scheduling Allocator

The specification *SimpleAllocator* (Fig. 1 on page 404) is too simple because the allocator is free to allocate resources in any order. Therefore, it may "paint itself into a corner", requiring cooperation from the clients to recover. We can prevent this from happening by having the allocator fix a schedule according to which access to resources will be granted. Figures 8 on the next page and 9 on page 437 contain a formal TLA⁺ model based on this idea.

Compared with the specification of the simple allocator in Fig. 1 on page 404, the new specification contains two more state variables, *pool* and *sched*. The variable *sched* contains a sequence of clients, representing the allocation schedule. The variable *pool* contains a set of clients that have requested resources but have not yet been scheduled for allocation. Consequently, the request action merely inserts the client into the pool. The allocation action is restricted to giving out resources to a client only if no client that appears earlier in the schedule is demanding any of them.

―――――――――― MODULE *SchedulingAllocator* ――――――――――

EXTENDS*FiniteSet, Sequences, Naturals*
CONSTANTS*Clients, Resources*
ASSUME*IsFiniteSet(Resources)*
VARIABLES*unsat, alloc, pool, sched*

―――

TypeInvariant $\triangleq$
  $\wedge$ *unsat* $\in$ [*Clients* $\rightarrow$ SUBSET *Resources*]
  $\wedge$ *alloc* $\in$ [*Clients* $\rightarrow$ SUBSET *Resources*]
  $\wedge$ *pool* $\in$ SUBSET *Clients* $\wedge$ *sched* $\in$ *Seq*(*Clients*)
available $\triangleq$ *Resources* \ (UNION{*alloc*[*c*] : *c* $\in$ *Clients*})
PermSeqs(*S*) $\triangleq$ set of permutations of finite set *S*, represented as sequences
  LET *perms*[*ss* $\in$ SUBSET *S*] $\triangleq$
      IF *ss* = {} THEN $\langle \rangle$
      ELSE LET *ps* $\triangleq$ [*x* $\in$ *ss* $\mapsto$ {*Append*(*sq*, *x*) : *sq* $\in$ *perms*[*ss* \ {*x*}]}]
            IN   UNION{*ps*[*x*] : *x* $\in$ *ss*}
  IN   *perms*[*S*]
Drop(*seq*, *i*) $\triangleq$ *SubSeq*(*seq*, 1, *i* − 1) $\circ$ *SubSeq*(*seq*, *i* + 1, *Len*(*seq*))

―――

Init $\triangleq$
  $\wedge$ *unsat* = [*c* $\in$ *Clients* $\mapsto$ {}] $\wedge$ *alloc* = [*c* $\in$ *Clients* $\mapsto$ {}]
  $\wedge$ *pool* = {} $\wedge$ *sched* = $\langle \rangle$
Request(*c*, *S*) $\triangleq$
  $\wedge$ *unsat*[*c*] = {} $\wedge$ *alloc*[*c*] = {} $\wedge$ *S* $\neq$ {}
  $\wedge$ *unsat'* = [*unsat*EXCEPT ![*c*] = *S*] $\wedge$ *pool'* = *pool* $\cup$ {*c*}
  $\wedge$ UNCHANGED$\langle$*alloc*, *sched*$\rangle$
Allocate(*c*, *S*) $\triangleq$
  $\wedge$ *S* $\neq$ {} $\wedge$ *S* $\subseteq$ *available* $\cap$ *unsat*[*c*]
  $\wedge$ $\exists i \in$ DOMAIN *sched* :
      $\wedge$ *sched*[*i*] = *c* $\wedge$ $\forall j \in$ 1..*i* − 1 : *unsat*[*sched*[*j*]] $\cap$ *S* = {}
      $\wedge$ *sched'* = IF *S* = *unsat*[*c*] THEN *Drop*(*sched*, *i*) ELSE *sched*
  $\wedge$ *alloc'* = [*alloc*EXCEPT ![*c*] = @ $\cup$ *S*] $\wedge$ *unsat'* = [*unsat*EXCEPT ![*c*] = @ \ *S*]
  $\wedge$ UNCHANGED*pool*
Return(*c*, *S*) $\triangleq$
  $\wedge$ *S* $\neq$ {} $\wedge$ *S* $\subseteq$ *alloc*[*c*]
  $\wedge$ *alloc'* = [*alloc*EXCEPT ![*c*] = @ \ *S*]
  $\wedge$ UNCHANGED$\langle$*unsat*, *pool*, *sched*$\rangle$
Schedule $\triangleq$
  $\wedge$ *pool* $\neq$ {} $\wedge$ *pool'* = {}
  $\wedge$ $\exists sq \in$ *PermSeqs*(*pool*) : *sched'* = *sched* $\circ$ *sq*
  $\wedge$ UNCHANGED$\langle$*unsat*, *alloc*$\rangle$
Next $\triangleq$
  $\vee$ $\exists c \in$ *Clients*, *S* $\in$ SUBSET *Resources* :
      Request(*c*, *S*) $\vee$ *Allocate*(*c*, *S*) $\vee$ *Return*(*c*, *S*)
  $\vee$ *Schedule*
vars $\triangleq$ $\langle$*unsat*, *alloc*, *pool*, *sched*$\rangle$

―――

Fig. 8. Specification of an allocator with scheduling (part 1 of 2)

$$Allocator \triangleq \land Init \land \Box[Next]_{vars}$$
$$\land \forall c \in Clients \ : \ WF_{vars}(unsat[c] = \{\} \land Return(c, alloc[c]))$$
$$\land \forall c \in Clients \ : \ WF_{vars}(\exists S \in \text{SUBSET } Resources \ : \ Allocate(c, S))$$
$$\land WF_{vars}(Schedule)$$

Fig. 9. Specification of an allocator with scheduling (part 2 of 2)

The specification contains a new action *Schedule*, which establishes the allocation schedule. Because this is a high-level specification, we do not commit to any specific scheduling policy: instead we show the protocol to be correct if the processes in the pool are scheduled in an arbitrary order. The auxiliary operator *PermSeqs(S)* recursively computes the set of permutation sequences of a finite set S. The idea is that $\langle x_1, \ldots, x_n \rangle$ is a permutation of a non-empty finite set S if and only if $\langle x_1, \ldots, x_{n-1} \rangle$ is a permutation of $S \setminus \{x_n\}$. The formal expression in TLA$^+$ makes use of an auxiliary, recursively defined function *perms* that computes the set of permutations *perms[T]* of any subset $T \subseteq S$, in a style that is similar to the recursive definition of functions over inductive data types in a functional programming language. We could have used a simpler, more declarative definition of the action *Schedule*, such as

$$Schedule \triangleq$$
$$\land pool \neq \{\} \land pool' = \{\}$$
$$\land \exists sq \in Seq(Clients) \ : \ \land \{sq[i] \ : \ i \in \text{DOMAIN } sq\} = pool$$
$$\land \forall i, j \in 1..Len(sq) \ : \ sq[i] = sq[j] \Rightarrow i = j$$
$$\land \text{UNCHANGED}\langle unsat, alloc \rangle.$$

In this formulation, the schedule is simply required to be any injective sequence (containing no duplicates) formed from the elements of *pool*. The two definitions are logically equivalent. However, this definition would not be acceptable for TLC, because the set *Seq(Clients)* is infinite, even if *Clients* is finite.

Looking at the fairness conditions, observe that the fairness requirement on the return action has been amended as indicated above, so that it agrees with the informal specification. The fairness condition for the allocation action is similar to the one adopted for the simple allocator specification, but with weak fairness substituted for strong fairness. The idea behind this change is that the non-determinism present in the original specification has been resolved by the introduction of the allocation schedule, so that the simpler condition now suffices. (Of course, this intuition will have to be formally verified!) There is an additional weak fairness requirement for the scheduling action, asserting that the allocator should periodically update its schedule when new clients have issued requests.

6.2 Analysis Using Model Checking

We can again ask TLC to verify the safety and liveness properties described in Sect. 2.3. For an instance consisting of three clients and two resources, TLC computes 1690 distinct states and requires about 30 seconds for verification. What sets TLC apart from more conventional model checkers is its ability to evaluate an input language in which models can be expressed at the high level of abstraction that was used in Figs. 8 on page 436 and 9 on the previous page: neither the definition of the operator *PermSeqs* nor the relatively complicated fairness constraints pose a problem. (For better efficiency, we could override the definition of *PermSeqs* by a method written in Java, but this is not a big concern for a list that contains at most three elements.)

Given our experience with the verification of the simple allocator model, one should be suspicious of the quick success obtained with the new model. As Lamport [29, Sect. 14.5.3] writes, it is a good idea to verify as many properties as possible.

Figure 10 contains a lower-level invariant of the scheduling allocator that can be verified using TLC.

$UnscheduledClients \triangleq$ set of clients that are not in the schedule
$\quad Clients \setminus \{sched[i] \ : \ i \in \text{DOMAIN } sched\}$
$PrioResources(i) \triangleq$ bound on resources requested by i-th client in schedule
$\quad available$
$\quad \cup \ \text{UNION}\{unsat[sched[j]] \cup alloc[sched[j]] \ : \ j \in 1..i - 1\}$
$\quad \cup \ \text{UNION}\{alloc[c] \ : \ c \in UnscheduledClients\}$
$AllocatorInvariant \triangleq$
$\quad \wedge \ \forall c \in pool \ : \ unsat[c] \neq \{\} \ \wedge \ alloc[c] = \{\}$
$\quad \wedge \ \forall i \in \text{DOMAIN } sched \ : \ \wedge \ unsat[sched[i]] \neq \{\}$
$\quad\qquad\qquad\qquad\qquad\qquad\quad \wedge \ \forall j \in 1..i - 1 \ : \ alloc[sched[i]] \cap unsat[sched[j]] = \{\}$
$\quad\qquad\qquad\qquad\qquad\qquad\quad \wedge \ unsat[sched[i]] \subseteq PrioResources(i)$

Fig. 10. Lower-level invariant of the scheduling allocator

The first conjunct of the formula *AllocatorInvariant* says that all clients in the set *pool* have requested resources, but do not hold any. The second conjunct concerns the clients in the schedule, It is split into three subconjuncts: first, each client in the schedule has some outstanding requests, second, no client may hold a resource that is requested by a prioritized client (appearing earlier in the schedule); and, finally, the set of outstanding requests of a client in the schedule is bounded by the union of the set of currently available resources, the resources requested or held by prioritized clients, and the resources held by clients that do not appear in the schedule. The idea behind this last conjunct is to assert that a client's requests can be satisfied using resources that either are already free or are held by prioritized clients. It follows that prioritized clients can obtain their full set of resources, after which they are required to eventually release them again. Therefore, the scheduling allocator works correctly even under the worst-case assumption that clients will give up resources only after their complete request has been satisfied.

Verification by Refinement

Beyond these correctness properties, TLC can also establish a formal refinement relationship between the two allocator specifications. The scheduling allocator operates under some additional constraints. Moreover, it introduces the variable *sched*, which did not appear in the specification of the simple allocator, and which is therefore not constrained by that specification. More interestingly, the scheduling policy and the (weaker) liveness assumptions imply that the (original) fairness constraints are effectively met. The scheduling allocator therefore turns out to be a refinement of the simple allocator, implying the correctness properties by transitivity!

We can use TLC to verify this refinement, for small finite instances, using the module *AllocatorRefinement* that appears in Fig. 11.

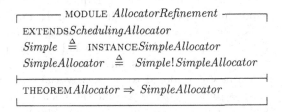

Fig. 11. Asserting a Refinement Relationship.

This module extends the module *SchedulingAllocator*, thus importing all declarations and definitions of that module, and defines an instance *Simple* of the module *SimpleAllocator*, whose parameters are (implicitly) instantiated by the entities of the same name inherited from module *SchedulingAllocator*. All operators *Op* defined in the instance are available as *Simple!Op*. (It would have been illegal to extend both modules *SchedulingAllocator* and *SimpleAllocator* because they declare constants and variables, as well as define operators, with the same names.) The module then asserts that specification *Allocator* implies the specification *SimpleAllocator*. In order to have this implication checked by TLC, we again defined an instance consisting of three clients and two resources and stipulate

```
SPECIFICATION Allocator
PROPERTIES SimpleAllocator
```

in the configuration file. TLC found the implication to be valid, requiring just 6 seconds.

6.3 Towards a Distributed Implementation

The specification *Allocator* defined in the module *SchedulingAllocator* of Figs. 8 on page 436 and 9 on page 437 describes an overall algorithm (or, rather, a class of algorithms) for resource allocation; analysis by TLC has indicated that this algorithm satisfies the desired correctness properties, even under worst-case assumptions about the clients' behavior. However, the model does not indicate the architecture of the system as a set of independent, communicating processes. Our next goal is therefore to refine that specification into one that is implementable as a distributed system. In particular, we shall assume that the allocator and the clients may run on different processors. Therefore, each process should have direct access only to its local memory, and explicit, asynchronous message passing will be used to communicate with other processes. Instead of a centralized representation of the system state based on the variables *unsat* and *alloc*, we will distinguish between the allocator's view and each client's view of its pending requests and allocated resources. Similarly, the basic actions such as the request for resources will be split into two parts, with different processes being responsible for carrying them out: in the first step, the client issues a request, updates its local state, and sends a corresponding message to the allocator. Subsequently, the allocator receives the message and updates its table of pending requests accordingly.

Figures 12 on the next page and 13 on page 442 contain a TLA$^+$ model based on this idea. This model contains variables *unsat*, *alloc*, and *sched* as before, but these are now considered to be local variables of the allocator. New variables *requests* and *holding* represent the clients' views of pending resource requests and of resources currently held; we interpret *requests*[c] and *holding*[c] as being local to the client process c. The communication network is (very abstractly) modeled by the variable *network* which holds the set of messages in transit between the different processes.

Except for the action *Schedule*, which is a private action of the allocator, all of the actions that appeared in the specification *SchedulingAllocator* have been split into two actions as explained above. For example, client c is considered to perform the action *Request*(c, S) because only its local variables and the state of the communication network are modified by the action. The allocator later receives the request message m and performs the action *RReq*(m). The fairness conditions of our previous specification are complemented by weak fairness requirements for the actions *RReq*(m), *RAlloc*(m), and *RRet*(m) which are associated with message reception (for all possible messages m); these requirements express the condition that messages will eventually be received and handled.

The observant reader may be somewhat disappointed with the form of the specification of this "distributed" implementation because the formula *Implementation* is again written in the standard form

$$Init \land \Box[Next]_v \land L$$

─────── MODULE *AllocatorImplementation* ───────

EXTENDS *FiniteSets, Sequences, Naturals*
CONSTANTS *Clients, Resources*
ASSUME *IsFiniteSet(Resources)*
VARIABLES *unsat, alloc, sched, requests, holding, network*
Sched $\triangleq$ INSTANCE *SchedulingAllocator*

───

Messages $\triangleq$
   [*type* : {"request", "allocate", "return"}, *clt* : *Clients, rsrc* : SUBSET *Resources*]
TypeInvariant $\triangleq$
   $\land$ *Sched!TypeInvariant*
   $\land$ *requests* $\in$ [*Clients* $\rightarrow$ SUBSET *Resources*]
   $\land$ *holding* $\in$ [*Clients* $\rightarrow$ SUBSET *Resources*]
   $\land$ *network* $\in$ SUBSET *Messages*

───

Init $\triangleq$
   $\land$ *Sched!Init*
   $\land$ *requests* = [*c* $\in$ *Clients* $\mapsto$ {}] $\land$ *holding* = [*c* $\in$ *Clients* $\mapsto$ {}] $\land$ *network* = {}
Request(c, S) $\triangleq$ client *c* requests set *S* of resources
   $\land$ *requests*[*c*] = {} $\land$ *holding*[*c*] = {} $\land$ *S* $\neq$ {}
   $\land$ *requests′* = [*requests* EXCEPT ![*c*] = *S*]
   $\land$ *network′* = *network* $\cup$ {[*type* $\mapsto$ "request", *clt* $\mapsto$ *c*, *rsrc* $\mapsto$ *S*]}
   $\land$ UNCHANGED⟨*unsat, alloc, sched, holding*⟩
RReq(m) $\triangleq$ allocator handles request message sent by some client
   $\land$ *m* $\in$ *network* $\land$ *m.type* = "request" $\land$ *network′* = *network* \ {*m*}
   $\land$ *unsat′* = [*unsat* EXCEPT ![*m.clt*] = *m.rsrc*]
   $\land$ UNCHANGED⟨*alloc, sched, requests, holding*⟩
Allocate(c, S) $\triangleq$ allocator decides to allocate resources *S* to client *c*
   $\land$ *Sched!Allocate(c, S)*
   $\land$ *network′* = *network* $\cup$ {[*type* $\mapsto$ "allocate", *clt* $\mapsto$ *c*, *rsrc* $\mapsto$ *S*]}
   $\land$ UNCHANGED⟨*requests, holding*⟩
RAlloc(m) $\triangleq$ some client receives resource allocation message
   $\land$ *m* $\in$ *network* $\land$ *m.type* = "allocate" $\land$ *network′* = *network* \ {*m*}
   $\land$ *holding′* = [*holding* EXCEPT ![*m.clt*] = @ $\cup$ *m.rsrc*]
   $\land$ *requests′* = [*requests* EXCEPT ![*m.clt*] = @ \ *m.rsrc*]
   $\land$ UNCHANGED⟨*unsat, alloc, sched*⟩
Return(c, S) $\triangleq$ client *c* returns resources in *S*
   $\land$ *S* $\neq$ {} $\land$ *S* $\subseteq$ *holding*[*c*]
   $\land$ *holding′* = [*holding* EXCEPT ![*c*] = @ \ *S*]
   $\land$ *network′* = *network* $\cup$ {[*type* $\mapsto$ "return", *clt* $\mapsto$ *c*, *rsrc* $\mapsto$ *S*]}
   $\land$ UNCHANGED⟨*unsat, alloc, sched, requests*⟩
RRet(m) $\triangleq$ allocator receives returned resources
   $\land$ *m* $\in$ *network* $\land$ *m.type* = "return" $\land$ *network′* = *network* \ {*m*}
   $\land$ *alloc′* = [*alloc* EXCEPT ![*m.clt*] = @ \ *m.rsrc*]
   $\land$ UNCHANGED⟨*unsat, sched, requests, holding*⟩
Schedule $\triangleq$ *Sched!Schedule* $\land$ UNCHANGED⟨*requests, holding, network*⟩

───

Fig. 12. An implementation of the allocator (part 1 of 2)

$Next \triangleq$
  $\lor \exists\, c \in Clients, S \in$ SUBSET $Resources$:
       $Request(c, S) \lor Allocate(c, S) \lor Return(c, S)$
  $\lor \exists\, m \in network$: $RReq(m) \lor RAlloc(m) \lor RRet(m)$
  $\lor Schedule$
$vars \triangleq \langle unsat, alloc, sched, requests, holding, network \rangle$

$Liveness \triangleq$
  $\land\ \forall\, c \in Clients$: $\mathrm{WF}_{vars}(requests[c] = \{\} \land Return(c, holding[c]))$
  $\land\ \forall\, c \in Clients$: $\mathrm{WF}_{vars}(\exists\, S \in$ SUBSET $Resources$: $Allocate(c, S))$
  $\land\ \mathrm{WF}_{vars}(Schedule)$
  $\land\ \forall\, m \in Messages$:
       $\mathrm{WF}_{vars}(RReq(m)) \land \mathrm{WF}_{vars}(RAlloc(m)) \land \mathrm{WF}_{vars}(RRet(m))$
$Implementation \triangleq Init \land \Box[Next]_{vars} \land Liveness$

THEOREM $Implementation \Rightarrow Sched\,!\,Allocator$

Fig. 13. An implementation of the allocator (part 2 of 2)

that we have seen so often in this chapter. From the discussion of system composition as conjunction in Sect. 3.5, one might have expected to see a conjunction of specifications, one for each process. There are two technical problems with doing so. First, the clients' variables *requests* and *holding* are represented as arrays such that each client accesses only the corresponding array field. The specification of client c should really only specify *requests*[c] and *holding*[c], but the composition should ensure type correctness and ensure that the remaining array fields remain unchanged. This is possible, but cumbersome to write down. (Lamport discusses this issue in more detail in [29, Chap. 10].) Second, the current implementation of TLC expects specifications in the standard form and does not handle conjunctions of process specifications.

The module *AllocatorImplementation* claims that the model obtained in this way is a refinement of the scheduling allocator specification, and we can again use TLC to verify this theorem for finite instances. However, TLC quickly produces a counterexample that ends in the states shown in Fig. 14.

In state 7, client c1 has returned resource r1 to the allocator. In the transition to state 8, it issues a new request for the same resource, which is handled by the allocator (according to the action *RReq*) in the transition to state 9. This action modifies the variable *unsat* at position c1 although the value of *alloc*[c1], is not the empty set – a transition that is not allowed by the scheduling allocator.

Intuitively, the problem is due to the asynchronous communication network underlying our model, which makes the allocator receive and handle the request message before it receives the earlier return message. Indeed, it is easy to see that if one allowed the allocator to handle the new request before releasing the old one, it might become confused and deregister r1 for client c1 even though the client still held the resource (granted in response to the second

```
STATE 7:
/\ holding = (c1 :> {} @@ c2 :> {} @@ c3 :> {})
/\ alloc = (c1 :> {r1} @@ c2 :> {} @@ c3 :> {})
/\ requests = (c1 :> {} @@ c2 :> {} @@ c3 :> {})
/\ sched = << >>
/\ network = {[type |-> "return", clt |-> c1, rsrc |-> {r1}]}
/\ unsat = (c1 :> {} @@ c2 :> {} @@ c3 :> {})

STATE 8:
/\ holding = (c1 :> {} @@ c2 :> {} @@ c3 :> {})
/\ alloc = (c1 :> {r1} @@ c2 :> {} @@ c3 :> {})
/\ requests = (c1 :> {r1} @@ c2 :> {} @@ c3 :> {})
/\ sched = << >>
/\ network = { [type |-> "request", clt |-> c1, rsrc |-> {r1}],
   [type |-> "return", clt |-> c1, rsrc |-> {r1}] }
/\ unsat = (c1 :> {} @@ c2 :> {} @@ c3 :> {})

STATE 9:
/\ holding = (c1 :> {} @@ c2 :> {} @@ c3 :> {})
/\ alloc = (c1 :> {r1} @@ c2 :> {} @@ c3 :> {})
/\ requests = (c1 :> {r1} @@ c2 :> {} @@ c3 :> {})
/\ sched = << >>
/\ network = {[type |-> "return", clt |-> c1, rsrc |-> {r1}]}
/\ unsat = (c1 :> {r1} @@ c2 :> {} @@ c3 :> {})
```

Fig. 14. Model checking the correctness of the implementation.

request). It depends on the underlying communication network whether such a race condition can occur or not. If messages between any pair of processes are delivered in order, the TLA+ model could represent the communication network as a set of message queues. If communication is truly asynchronous and message order is not guaranteed, one should add the precondition

$$alloc[m.clt] = \{\}$$

to the definition of the action $RReq(m)$ so that a new request will be processed only after the return message corresponding to the previous grant has been received. With this correction, TLC confirms the refinement theorem for our small instance in about 2 minutes.

Finally, we can assert the invariant shown in Fig. 15 to confirm our intuition about how the variables associated with the clients and the allocator relate to each other. The verification of this invariant for the usual small instance of the model with three clients and two resources generates 64 414 states (17 701 of which are distinct) and takes about 12 seconds.

$RequestsInTransit(c) \quad \triangleq \qquad$ requests sent by c but not yet received
$\quad \{msg.rsrc : msg \in \{m \in network : m.type = \text{``request''} \wedge m.clt = c\}\}$
$AllocsInTransit(c) \quad \triangleq \qquad$ allocations sent to c but not yet received
$\quad \{msg.rsrc : msg \in \{m \in network : m.type = \text{``allocate''} \wedge m.clt = c\}\}$
$ReturnsInTransit(c) \quad \triangleq \qquad$ return messages sent by c but not yet received
$\quad \{msg.rsrc : msg \in \{m \in network : m.type = \text{``return''} \wedge m.clt = c\}\}$
$Invariant \quad \triangleq \quad \forall c \in Clients :$
$\quad \wedge \; Cardinality(RequestsInTransit(c)) \leq 1$
$\quad \wedge \; requests[c] = \quad unsat[c]$
$\qquad\qquad\qquad \cup \; \text{UNION}\, RequestsInTransit(c)$
$\qquad\qquad\qquad \cup \; \text{UNION}\, AllocsInTransit(c)$
$\quad \wedge \; alloc[c] = \quad holding[c]$
$\qquad\qquad\qquad \cup \; \text{UNION}\, AllocsInTransit(c)$
$\qquad\qquad\qquad \cup \; \text{UNION}\, ReturnsInTransit(c)$

Fig. 15. Relating the allocator and client variables by an invariant

6.4 Some Lessons Learnt

Starting from the informal requirements for the allocator problem presented in Sect. 2.1, it would have been tempting to come up directly with a model similar to the "implementation" presented in Sect. 6.3, or even a more detailed one. However, a low-level specification is at least as likely to contain errors as a program, and the whole purpose of modeling is to clarify and analyse a system at an adequate level of abstraction. The seemingly trivial *SimpleAllocator* specification in Fig. 1 on page 404 helped us discover the need to fix a schedule for resource allocation. It also illustrated the need to validate models: success in model checking (or proving) correctness properties by itself does not guarantee that the model is meaningful. A similar problem would have been more difficult to detect at the level of detail of the final specification, where there are additional problems of synchronisation and message passing to worry about. The specification *SchedulingAllocator* introduced the idea of determining a schedule and thereby fixed the problem in the original specification while remaining at the same high level of abstraction. Finally, the module *AllocatorImplementation* introduced a step towards a possible implementation by attributing the state variables and the actions to separate processes, and by introducing explicit communication.

For each model, TLC was of great help in analysing various properties. Although only small instances can be handled by model checking before running into the state explosion problem, doing so greatly increases one's confidence in the models. Variants of the specifications can be checked without great effort, and various properties (invariants and more general temporal properties) can be verified in a single run. Deductive verification, based on the proof rules of Sect. 4, can then establish system properties in a fully rigorous way. In our own work, we have defined a format of "predicate diagrams" for TLA$^+$ specifications [13]. We have found these diagrams to be helpful in determining appropriate fairness hypotheses. The format is supported by a tool [17] that uses model checking to identify abstract counter-examples, indicating either too weak an abstraction or missing fairness or ordering annotations.

7 Conclusions

The design of software systems requires a combination of ingenuity and careful engineering. While there is no substitute for intuition, the correctness of a proposed solution can be checked by precise reasoning over a suitable model, and this is in the realm of logics and (formalized) mathematics. The rôle of a formalism is to *help* the user in the difficult and important activity of writing and analysing formal models. TLA$^+$ builds on the experience of classical mathematics and adds a thin layer of temporal logic in order to describe system executions, in particular to express fairness properties. A distinctive feature of TLA is its attention to refinement and composition, reflected in the concept of stuttering invariance. Unlike property-oriented specification languages based on temporal logic, TLA favors the specification of systems as state machines, augmented by fairness conditions and by hiding.

Whereas the expressiveness of TLA$^+$ undoubtedly helps in writing concise, high-level models of systems, it is not so clear a priori that it lends itself as well to the analysis of these models. For example, we have pointed out several times the need to prove conditions of "well-definedness" related to the use of the choice operator. These problems can, to some extent, be mastered by adhering to standard idioms, such as primitive-recursive definitions, that ensure well-definedness. For the specification of reactive systems, TLA adds some proper idioms that control the delicate interplay between temporal operators. For example, restricting fairness conditions to subactions of the next-state relation ensures that a specification is machine closed [3], i.e., that its allowed behavior is entirely described by the initial condition and its next-state relation. Having an expressive specification language is also helpful when new classes of systems arise. For example, Abadi and Lamport [3] have described a format for specifying real-time systems in TLA$^+$, and Lamport [30] describes how discrete real-time systems can be verified using TLC.

The main tool supporting TLA$^+$ is the model checker TLC [43]. It can analyse system specifications in standard form, written in a sublanguage of TLA$^+$ that ensures that the next-state relation can be effectively computed. All the TLA$^+$ specifications that appeared in this chapter fall into this fragment, and indeed the input language of TLC is more expressive than that of most other model checkers. Deductive verification of TLA$^+$ specifications can be supported by proof assistants, and in fact several encodings of TLA in the logical frameworks of different theorem provers have been proposed [16,20,35], although no prover is yet available that fully supports TLA$^+$.

Lamport has recently defined the language $^+$CAL, a high-level algorithmic language for describing concurrent and distributed algorithms. The expressions of $^+$CAL are those of TLA$^+$, but $^+$CAL provides standard programming constructs such as assignment, sequencing, conditionals, loops, non-deterministic choice, and procedures. The $^+$CAL compiler generates a TLA$^+$ specification from a $^+$CAL program which can then be verified using TLC [31]. A useful complement could be the generation of executable code from a fragment of $^+$CAL for specific execution platforms.

Acknowledgements.

I am indebted to Leslie Lamport for providing the subject of this article, for his encouragement of this work, and for his detailed comments on earlier versions. Parts of this chapter have their roots in an earlier paper on TLA, written with Martín Abadi [6]. I have had the opportunity on several occasions to teach about TLA$^+$, and fruitful discussions with students helped me prepare this chapter.

References

1. M. Abadi. An axiomatization of Lamport's Temporal Logic of Actions. In J.C.M. Baeten and J.W. Klop, editors, *CONCUR '90, Theories of Concurrency: Unification and Extension*, volume 458 of Lecture Notes in Computer Science, pages 57–69. Springer, 1990.
2. M. Abadi and L. Lamport. The existence of refinement mappings. *Theoretical Computer Science*, 81(2):253–284, May 1991.
3. M. Abadi and L. Lamport. An old-fashioned recipe for real time. *ACM Transactions on Programming Languages and Systems*, 16(5):1543–1571, Sept. 1994.
4. M. Abadi and L. Lamport. Conjoining specifications. *ACM Transactions on Programming Languages and Systems*, 17(3):507–534, May 1995.
5. M. Abadi and S. Merz. An abstract account of composition. In J. Wiedermann and P. Hajek, editors, *Mathematical Foundations of Computer Science*, volume 969 of Lecture Notes in Computer Science, pages 499–508. Springer, 1995.
6. M. Abadi and S. Merz. On TLA as a logic. In M. Broy, editor, *Deductive Program Design*, NATO ASI Series F, pages 235–272. Springer, 1996.
7. M. Abadi and G. Plotkin. A logical view of composition. *Theoretical Computer Science*, 114(1):3–30, June 1993.
8. J.-R. Abrial. *The B-Book: Assigning Programs to Meanings*. Cambridge University Press, 1996.
9. J.-R. Abrial. Extending B without changing it (for developing distributed systems). In H. Habrias, editor, *1st Conference on the B Method*, pages 169–190. IRIN Institut de recherche en informatique de Nantes, 1996.
10. B. Alpern and F.B. Schneider. Defining liveness. *Information Processing Letters*, 21(4):181–185, Oct. 1985.
11. R. Back and J. von Wright. *Refinement calculus—A systematic introduction*. Springer, 1998.
12. E.Börger and R. Stärk. *Abstract State Machines: A Method for High-Level System Design and Analysis*. Springer, 2003.

13. D. Cansell, D. Méry and S. Merz. Diagram refinements for the design of reactive systems. *Journal of Universal Computer Science*, 7(2):159–174, 2001.
14. E.M. Clarke, O. Grumberg and D. Peled. *Model Checking*. MIT Press, Cambridge, Mass., 1999.
15. W.-P. de Roever, H. Langmaack, and A. Pnueli, editors. *Compositionality: The Significant Difference*, volume 1536 of *Lecture Notes in Computer Science*. Springer, 1998.
16. U. Engberg, P. Gronning and L. Lamport. Mechanical verification of concurrent systems with TLA. In *Fourth International Conference on Computer-Aided Verification (CAV '92)*, volume 663 of Lecture Notes in Computer Science, pages 44–55. Springer, 1992.
17. L. Fejoz, D. Méry and S. Merz. DIXIT: Visualizing predicate abstractions. In R. Bharadwaj and S. Mukhopadhyay, editors, *Automatic Verification of Infinite-State Systems (AVIS 2005)*, Edinburgh, UK, Apr. 2005, pages 39–48. To appear in ENTCS.
18. D. Gries and F. B. Schneider. Avoiding the undefined by underspecification. In J. van Leeuwen, editor, *Computer Science Today: Recent Trends and Developments*, volume 1000 of Lecture Notes in Computer Science, pages 366–373. Springer., 1995.
19. G. E. Hughes and M. J. Cresswell. *A New Introduction to Modal Logic*. Routledge, 1996.
20. S. Kalvala. A formulation of TLA in Isabelle. Available at ftp://ftp.dcs.warwick.ac.uk/people/Sara.Kalvala/tla.dvi, Mar. 1995.
21. M. Kaminski. Invariance under stuttering in a temporal logic of actions. *Theoretical Computer Science*, 2006. To appear.
22. H. W. Kamp. *Tense Logic and the Theory of Linear Order*. PhD thesis, University of California at Los Angeles, 1968.
23. L. Lamport. The TLA home page. http://www.research.microsoft.com/users/lamport/tla/tla.html.
24. L. Lamport. Proving the correctness of multiprocess programs. *IEEE Transactions on Software Engineering*, SE-3(2):125–143, Mar. 1977.
25. L. Lamport. What good is temporal logic? In R. E. A. Mason, editor, *Information Processing 83: Proceedings of the IFIP 9th World Congress*, Paris, Sept. 1983, pages 657–668, 1983. North-Holland, 1983.
26. L. Lamport. How to write a long formula. *Formal Aspects of Computing*, 6(5):580–584, 1994.
27. L. Lamport. The Temporal Logic of Actions. *ACM Transactions on Programming Languages and Systems*, 16(3):872–923, May 1994.
28. L. Lamport. How to write a proof. *American Mathematical Monthly*, 102(7):600–608, 1995.
29. L. Lamport. *Specifying Systems*. Addison-Wesley., 2002.
30. L. Lamport. Real-time model checking is really simple. In D. Borrione and W. J. Paul, editors, *Correct Hardware Design and Verification Methods (CHARME 2005)*, volume 3725 of *Lecture Notes in Computer Science*, pages 162–175. Springer, 2005.
31. L. Lamport. Checking a multithreaded algorithm with =+CAL. In S. Dolev, editor, *20th International Symposium on Distributed Computing (DISC 2006)*, Stockholm, 2006. To appear.
32. A. C. Leisenring. *Mathematical Logic and Hilbert's ε-Symbol*, University Mathematical Series. Macdonald, 1969.

33. Z. Manna and A. Pnueli. Verification of concurrent programs: The temporal framework. In R. Boyer and J. Moore, editors, *The Correctness Problem in Computer Science*, pages 215–273. Academic Press, London, 1982.

34. Z. Manna and A. Pnueli. *The Temporal Logic of Reactive and Concurrent Systems: Specification*. Springer, New York, 1992.

35. S. Merz. Isabelle/TLA. Available at `http://isabelle.in.tum.de/library/HOL/TLA`, 1997. Revised 1999.

36. S. Merz. A more complete TLA. In J. Wing, J. Woodcock, and J. Davies, editors, *FM'99: World Congress on Formal Methods*, volume 1709 of Lecture Notes in Computer Science, pages 1226–1244. Springer, 1999.

37. A. Pnueli. The temporal logic of programs. In *Proceedings of the 18th Annual Symposium on the Foundations of Computer Science*, pages 46–57. IEEE, 1977.

38. A. N. Prior. *Past, Present and Future*. Clarendon Press, 1967.

39. A. P. Sistla, E. M. Clarke, N. Francez, and Y. Gurevich. Can message buffers be characterized in linear temporal logic? *Information and Control*, 63:88–112, 1984.

40. M. Spivey. *The Z Notation: A Reference Manual*. Prentice Hall, 1992.

41. P. Suppes. *Axiomatic Set Theory*. Dover, 1972.

42. M. Vardi. Branching vs. linear time: Final showdown. In T. Margaria and W. Yi, editors, *Tools and Algorithms for the Construction and Analysis of Systems (TACAS 2001)*, volume 2031 of *Lecture Notes in Computer Science*, pages 1–22. Springer, 2001. See `http://www.cs.rice.edu/~vardi/papers/` for more recent versions of this paper.

43. Y. Yu, P. Manolios, and L. Lamport. Model checking TLA+ specifications. In L. Pierre and T. Kropf, editors, *Correct Hardware Design and Verification Methods (CHARME'99)*, volume 1703 of *Lecture Notes in Computer Science*, pages 54–66. Springer, 1999.

TLA$^+$ Indexes

The Typed Logic of Partial Functions and the Vienna Development Method

John S. Fitzgerald

Centre for Software Reliability, Newcastle University, Newcastle upon Tyne, NE1 7RU, United Kingdom, John.Fitzgerald@ncl.ac.uk

For Harry Fitzgerald, Engineer (1928–2004)

Summary. Decisions about the logic underpinning a formal specification language have important consequences for the utility of the formalism. This chapter describes the major features of the typed Logic of Partial Functions (LPF) as it has been implemented in support of the Vienna Development Method's Specification Language, VDM-SL. It compares attempts to realise the logic in different environments: a user-centred proof support tool, a specification interpreter and an automated proof tool. Future directions in integrated proof support for the language are suggested.

1 Introduction

The logic that underpins a specification language has great practical significance, directly affecting the capabilities of the tools that are so necessary to the successful application of the language in professional practice. Decisions regarding logic are therefore influenced by methodological and pragmatic concerns, as well as by the desire to provide an intuitive and elegant theory. The Vienna Development Method's Specification Language (VDM-SL) has a long history of use, both as a vehicle for research and as a tool in the development of computer-based systems. Machine support for the coding and analysis for VDM specifications has been available for VDM-SL for well over a decade, and there is considerable experience at proving properties of specifications and refinements in the formalism. Nevertheless, the logic underpinning VDM, and its susceptibility to machine support, remain the subject of debate and research.

The Logic of Partial Functions (LPF) is closely associated with VDM, although its potential for application goes well beyond that particular formalism. The aims of this chapter are to give an account of LPF and attempts to realise it in various support environments for VDM, ranging from an interpreter to automated provers, and to identify the next steps in the provision of integrated support for reasoning about VDM specifications.

In order to understand the requirements for a logic supporting VDM-SL, it is worth reviewing the distinguishing characteristics of the specification language and a little of its history (Sect. 2). The key features of Typed LPF, notably the handling of undefined terms, are introduced in Sects. 3 and 4. Using LPF to reason about models expressed in VDM-SL entails the addition of types and other relevant features, discussed in Sect. 5. Contrasting approaches to tool support for LPF-based reasoning in VDM-SL are discussed in Sect. 6, leading to a discussion of future directions and concluding remarks (Sect. 7).

2 The Vienna Development Method

The Vienna Development Method (VDM), is a collection of techniques for the modelling, specification and design of computer-based systems. A comprehensive introduction to VDM, including notions of both specification and refinement, is to be found in the 1990 edition of Jones's text [31]. The common formal language on which the techniques are based is the VDM Specification Language (VDM-SL), standardised by the ISO in 1996 [7]. Although the specification language VDM-SL has been standardised, its community has generally stopped short of imposing a methodology around its use. Indeed, it has been closely associated with many of the concepts of "lightweight" formal methods [28]. The IFAD VDMTools encouraged experimentation with formal techniques in a variety of application domains [5, 27], leading to the development of guidelines for system modelling and analysis that subsequently formed part of the approach advocated in the most recent work on VDM [22] and VDM^{++} [23]. This chapter concentrates on the logic supporting the forms of VDM described above, and in particular the support tools. However, it is important to note the work of the Irish School of VDM [6], which has stressed the development of operator calculi underpinning modelling in a VDM setting.

2.1 Historical Context

Jones [33] gave an account of the development of the specification language and the refinement methodology. In examining the logic underpinning VDM, it is useful to identify three (very loosely defined) phases in its history.

The 1970s saw the origin of VDM in programming language description and compiler design, and a subsequent widening of the method to encompass the development of sequential and concurrent systems more generally. The stress was on the fundamental features of the language, its formal semantics and the development of a basis for reasoning about models in terms of proving properties of programming language concepts.

In the 1980s and 1990s, the ambition of the technology widened to encompass computing systems in general and to go beyond specification to refinement as well. LPF was proposed as a response to the challenge of proving properties of systems incorporating partial functions. Proofs at this stage were largely rigorous rather than formal.

As the specification language became more stable, an analytic strand of work emerged with the development of experimental support systems for specification and analysis, including formal reasoning. Some of the support technology became strong enough to withstand industrial application and, over this period, practical experience with the modelling technology grew significantly. Recently the tools development effort has opened up, following changes in the ownership of commercial VDM technology. There has been a renewal of interest in interoperability between tools supporting different aspects of the systems development process, and less in "self-contained" formal reasoning.

Each of these three periods is considered in more detail in Sects. 2.2- 2.4 below, stressing the role of proof and the logic underpinning the specification language.

2.2 The Origins of VDM: Programming Language Definition

VDM's roots lie in work on programming language definition, notably the attempt to give a formal definition of the semantics of the PL/I language using a notation that came to be known as the *Vienna Definition Language* (VDL) [45]. It is apparent that proof was an issue in the Vienna group from an early stage. In 1968, Peter Lucas was concerned with proving the equivalence of programming language concepts [43] as parts of compiler correctness arguments. There was extensive exploration of alternative forms of argument. For example, Lucas's paper uses a "twin machine" notion later described with Jones [35]. In 1970, Henhapl and Jones addressed implementations of the block concept with the use of a homomorphic retrieve function [26]. There were implicit concerns about the style or quality of proof at this stage, but concern with full formalisation only came later when tool support for formal analysis became feasible. The handling of undefined terms had surfaced as an issue by 1969. Lucas [44] refers to McCarthy's approach to handling undefinedness by means of conditional interpretations of propositional connectives [46, 47], an approach subsequently rejected in LPF. The dispersal of the group in 1975 led to different emphases in the subsequent development of the modelling languages, the methodology and the associated proof techniques.

2.3 Rigorous Specification and Rigorous Proof

The 1980s saw a shift in research emphasis from the definition language towards a development 'method' [12, 29], although the term 'method' has always been used loosely in VDM to refer to a set of development techniques rather than a prescriptive approach. The process of standardisation gathered momentum, and work in a wide range of application areas was catalysed by the VDM Symposia.[1], which subsequently developed into the FME and FM Symposia[2]

Jones's 1986 book [30] contains many of the elements of VDM-SL as it is known now, albeit with a strong emphasis on an implicit style of operation specification. As an example of the content of a VDM model at this stage, consider the example in Fig. 1, an extract from a larger model used in Jones's 1986 text.

$Queueb$ :: s : Qel^*
$\quad\quad\quad i$: $\mathbb{N}$

where

$inv\text{-}Queueb(mk\text{-}Queueb(s, i))$ $\quad\triangleq\quad$ $i \leq \textbf{len}\ s$

$ENQUEUE\ (e\colon Qel)$
ext wr s : Qel^*
post $s = \overleftarrow{s} \frown [e]$

$DEQUEUE\ ()\ e\colon Qel$
ext rd s : Qel^*
$\quad\quad\textbf{wr}\ i$: $\mathbb{N}$
pre $i < \textbf{len}\ s$
post $i = \overleftarrow{i} + 1 \wedge e = \overleftarrow{s}\,(i)$

Fig. 1. Specification of a "biased queue", after Jones [30]

The specification in Fig. 1 describes a *biased queue*, and has been selected because it is slightly more interesting than the usual stack or queue example. The specification describes a queue as a sequence of values s plus a separate pointer i containing the index number of the value in the sequence currently at the head of the queue. New arrivals are added at the end of the queue with high index numbers, and removals from the queue just involve copying the ith item out as a result and incrementing the pointer.

VDM-SL is a *model-oriented language*. A model of a system state is constructed from basic types, such as that of natural numbers ($\mathbb{N}$) and type

---

[1] The first symposium was held in 1987 in Brussels. Among the contributions were papers from Blikle and Monahan on denotational semantics of VDM, and Jones reported work on discharging proof obligations. The proceedings report little work on tool support, except for LaTeX macros. A report by the standardisation team appeared to suggest, rather optimistically, that its work would be done by 1988 – the standard was actually approved by ISO in 1996!

[2] See http://www.fmeurope.org

constructors such as X^*, which represents the type of all finite sequences of elements drawn from the type X. In Fig. 1, the state contains two variables: s representing the sequence of elements in a queue, and i representing the pointer to the last element taken off the queue. Permitted assignments of values to these variables are constrained by a data type invariant. In VDM-SL, invariants are arbitrary predicates; membership of a type entails satisfaction of the invariant. Thus, in the example, a pair containing the values

$$s = [5, 7, 7, 4, 2]$$
$$i = 9$$

would not be a valid member of the type $Queueb$, because 9 is greater than the length of s, violating the invariant.

Operations are units of functionality capable of modifying the content of the state. In the example above, they are specified *implicitly*, by means of a post-condition that characterises the permissible states resulting from the operation. This admits *loose specification*: the possibility of multiple implementations satisfying the postcondition. In the *ENQUEUE* operation above, the resulting state is defined uniquely. Note the use of read (**rd**) and read/write (**wr**) keywords acting as framing constraints to indicate the access rights that an operation has to the state variables.

Operation specifications are further restricted by preconditions which characterise the domain of the inputs and "before" states to which they are applicable. The model does not define the effect of applying an implementation of an operation to values that do not satisfy the precondition.

This example nicely illustrates some key features of VDM. It is not the most abstract specification that could be written. In fact, it is termed *biased* because of the unnecessary history stored at the low index end of the sequence. When data are dequeued, they remain in situ in the sequence. For example, the state

$$s = [5, 7, 7, 4, 2]$$
$$i = 3$$

is, in terms of the effects of future *ENQUEUE* and *DEQUEUE* operations, indistinguishable from the following:

$$s = [6, 2, 7, 4, 2]$$
$$i = 3$$

The specification thus distinguishes states that are behaviourally indistinguishable, biasing subsequent refinements and implementations [31].

Proof Obligations and Rigorous Proof

VDM-SL is a highly expressive language. Note, for example, that some data types such as $\mathbb{N}$ are unbounded, although individual elements are required to be of finite size. Invariants, preconditions and post-conditions are all arbitrarily complex logical expressions. As a consequence, it is not possible to determine statically (in general) that a model is internally consistent. The aspects of model consistency that cannot be checked statically give rise to *proof obligations*, stated as conjectures in the proof theory. For example, there is a *satisfiability* obligation on implicit operation specifications. This requires that the operation's postcondition defines a result of the correct type for any (input, state) pair satisfying the precondition. For the *DEQUEUE* operation, this is stated formally as follows:

$$\forall \overleftarrow{qb} \in Queueb \cdot pre\text{-}DEQUEUE(\overleftarrow{qb}) \Rightarrow$$
$$\exists qb \in Queueb, e \in Qel \cdot post\text{-}DEQUEUE(\overleftarrow{qb}, qb, e)$$

Proof obligations also arise during refinement, when it is necessary to show the soundness of design steps in which a relatively abstract model is related to a more concrete counterpart.

	from $\overleftarrow{qb} \in Queueb, pre\text{-}DEQUEUE(\overleftarrow{qb})$	
1	**let** $i = \overleftarrow{i} + 1$	
2	**let** $qb = mk\text{-}Queueb(\overleftarrow{s}, i)$	
3	$\overleftarrow{i} < $ **len** $\overleftarrow{s}$	h2
4	$i \le $ **len** $\overleftarrow{s}$	$\mathbb{N}$,3,1
5	$inv\text{-}Queueb(qb)$	4,2,$inv\text{-}Queueb$
6	$qb \in Queueb$	5, $Queueb$
7	**let** $e = \overleftarrow{s}(i)$	
8	$e \in Qel$	7,4,**len**
9	$i = \overleftarrow{i} + 1 \wedge e = \overleftarrow{s}(i)$	$\wedge$-I(1,7)
10	$post\text{-}DEQUEUE(\overleftarrow{qb}, qb, e)$	$post\text{-}DEQUEUE$(9)
	infer $\exists qb \in Queueb, e \in Qel \cdot post\text{-}DEQUEUE(\overleftarrow{qb}, qb, e)$	$\exists$-I(6,8,10)

Fig. 2. Rigorous proof of satisfiability of *DEQUEUE* in the style of [30]

A proof of the satisfiability of *DEQUEUE* is shown in Fig. 2. The proof itself proceeds from hypotheses on the "**from**" line to a conclusion on the 'infer' line by a series of intermediate steps. Each step either introduces a local definition or follows by the application of reasoning from preceding lines. In the latter case, the line has a *justification* to the right. Justifications may appeal to the expressions on other lines by giving the line number as a reference. Since several expressions may appear as hypotheses on a '**from**' line, the reference "hn" is used to refer to the nth hypothesis. For example, line 3 appeals to the second hypothesis (h2), and line 4 appeals to the general theory of the type $\mathbb{N}$, and the expressions on lines 3 and 1. In general '**from** ... **infer**' sub-proofs may be nested within a larger proof.

It should be remembered that, when Jones was writing in the late 1980s, proof in VDM was primarily about writing arguments that helped to expose weaknesses in a model, and were detailed but nonetheless convincing to a human reader. Readability tended to win out over full formality at the level of detail needed to support automatic proof generation or checking. The proof in Fig. 2 is not formal – it could not be checked by a machine. Some of the justifications appeal to general properties of a data type (e.g. the reference to the properties of natural numbers on line 4). Some are references to symbols defined elsewhere (e.g. the reference to the definition of the invariant of *Queueb* on line 5). Some of the justifications, however, refer to precisely defined rules of inference, for example the rule for introduction of $\wedge$ ($\wedge$-Introduction) used on line 9 is defined as follows:

$$\boxed{\wedge\text{-I}}\ \frac{E_1;\ldots;E_n}{E_1 \wedge \ldots \wedge E_n}$$

The rule for the introduction of an existential quantifier is defined as follows:

$$\boxed{\exists\text{-I}}\ \frac{s \in X;\, E(s/x)}{\exists x \in X \cdot E(x)}$$

We have so far concentrated on proof as an activity conducted primarily by a human, often with 'pencil and paper'. Before exploring the formal proof theory in depth, it is useful to consider the ways in which automated tool support for VDM has evolved since the late 1980s.

2.4 Formalisation: Influence of Standardisation and Tool Support

Work on tool support brought semantic issues into clearer focus. From the late 1980s, there had been tool support for more than just typesetting the language. Bloomfield and Froome had experimented with Prolog-based animation of a VDM model [13], and went on to develop one of the most prominent early tools, SpecBox [14], which provided syntax checking, basic semantic checking and pretty printing for a version of the language that was close to the final ISO standard version. IFAD (Institute for Applied Datatechniques) in Denmark began a long and productive involvement with VDM, building on Larsen's contributions to the standardisation process, and developing the VDM Toolbox based on an executable subset of the modelling language (then called Meta-IV [42]). The Toolbox later evolved into VDMTools, the most robust set of support tools for VDM-SL, incorporating facilities for management of modular structuring, syntax and semantic checking, proof obligation generation, animation, batch mode testing and coverage analysis.

Figure 3 shows the *Queueb* model in the syntax of VDM-SL as it is supported by VDMTools. Comparing this with Fig. 1, a significant difference is the use of the interchange (ASCII-based) syntax. This was originally included in the ISO standard in order to promote transfer of models between tools.[3]

---

[3] A contemporary standard would probably have used XML.

Fitzgerald, Larsen and others have since tended to use this interchange syntax in training and industrial work, as it appears to present a lower barrier to practitioners more familiar with programming notations [22, 23].

```
types

Qel = token;

state Queueb of
  s : seq of Qel
  i : nat
inv mk_Queueb(s,i) == i <= len s
end

operations

ENQUEUE(e:Qel)
ext wr s : seq of Qel
post s = s~ ^ [e];

DEQUEUE()e:Qel
ext rd s : seq of Qel
    wr i : nat
pre i < len s
post i = i~+1 and e = s(i)
```

Fig. 3. The *Queueb* model in interchange syntax for VDMTools

VDMTools promotes the analysis of models in a lightweight way, by means of syntax and type checking, and testing through execution. The need to be able to execute the model tends to bias models to a more explicit style in which behaviour is described in a functional or even imperative programming style. An executable version of the *Queueb* model suitable for use with VDMTools might take the form shown in Fig. 4, in which the operations are expressed as functions over the data type denoting the state. An alternative presentation, supported by ISO standard VDM-SL and VDMTools, might be as a state-based model, with operations that are allowed to have side-effects (Fig. 5).

Tool development and increasing industrial engagement have motivated various additions to the capabilities of the modelling language. The EC-funded Afrodite project aimed to provide object-oriented and real-time extensions to VDM-SL and created VDM++ [19]. Later projects extended the coverage of the IFAD tools to VDM++, creating a bidirectional link to the object-oriented UML modelling tool Rational Rose, allowing multiple views of a common underlying model [23]. The development of real-time features has gathered pace with recent work on the modelling of timed communication in

```
types

Qel = token;

Queueb :: s : seq of Qel
           i : nat
inv mk_Queueb(s,i) == i <= len s;

functions

EnQueue: Qel * Queueb -> Queueb
EnQueue(e,mk_Queueb(s,i)) == mk_Queueb(s^[e],i);

DeQueue: Queueb -> Queueb * Qel
DeQueue(mk_Queueb(s,i)) == mk_( mk_Queueb(s,i+1), s(i) )
pre i < len s
```

Fig. 4. An executable function-based version of the *Queueb* model.

```
types

Qel = token;

state Queueb of
  s : seq of Qel
  i : nat
inv mk_Queueb(s,i) == i <= len s
end

operations

ENQUEUE: Qel ==> ()
ENQUEUE(e) ==
(
  s := s ^ [e]
);

DEQUEUE: () ==> Qel
DEQUEUE() ==
(
i := i+1;
return s(i);
)
pre i < len s
```

Fig. 5. An operational version of the executable *Queueb* model

the object model and a separate notion of deployment of processes to abstract processors [51].

The VDMTools technology was sold in 2004 to CSK Corporation, Japan, which continues to develop and promote the tool set.[4] At the time of writing, the community-based Overture initiative to develop a more loosely coupled and extensible set of tools for VDM had also begun [24].[5]

Although VDM-SL has been standardised, its community has generally sought to avoid it being packaged in a limiting methodology [28, 32, 5]. As a result of the IFAD VDMTools work, guidelines for VDM-based system modelling and analysis were developed and form part of the approach advocated in [22, 23] which stresses the construction of models as a cooperative process between engineers and domain experts; proof has a role to play in this process, even at the rigorous, rather than fully formal, level [21]. Experience in industrial studies suggests that the use of a modelling technology has significant effects on this dialogue [40]. As a result, much of the technological development around VDM since the mid 1990s has concerned modelling rather than specification, and tools for the exploration of models rather than proof. However, advances in proof and model checking technology, as well as interoperability of tools have made it worth considering the role that automated support for formal proof can play.

Formal Proof in VDM

The notion of proof as a means of exploring the properties of models is sometimes difficult to reconcile with the requirement for automation in reasoning about sophisticated models. The IPSE 2.5 project in the late 1980s and early 1990s aimed to address this by developing a prototype proof support environment that mimicked the exploratory style of rigorous reasoning, but with formal support. The main products were the *mural* tool [37] and formal theories of the typed logic that underpins VDM [10].

A formal proof of the *DEQUEUE* satisfiability conjecture in the *mural* style is shown in Fig. 6. There are several points of contrast between the formal proof and the rigorous argument shown in Fig. 2. The most obvious difference is the length and apparent complexity of the formal proof. However, it should be noted that the structure of the formal proof is basically the same as that of its rigorous counterpart. The main difference is that every line is justified by reference to an inference rule or folding/unfolding of a syntactic definition.

The formal proof is required to contain more detailed bookkeeping information than does the rigorous version. For example, the rigorous proof introduces local variables i and s (and their "before state" versions $\overleftarrow{i}$ and $\overleftarrow{s}$) by means of an informal "let" expression. In contrast, the formal proof

---

[4] http://www.csk.com/support_e/vdm/index.html

[5] http://www.overturetool.org.

from $\overleftarrow{qb} \in Queueb,\ pre\text{-}DEQUEUE(\overleftarrow{qb})$

1	$\overleftarrow{qb}.i < \mathbf{len}\ \overleftarrow{qb}.s$	unfolding(h2)
2	$\overleftarrow{qb}.i\colon \mathbb{N}$	i-form(h1)
3	$\overleftarrow{qb}.s\colon Qel^*$	s-form(h1)
4	$\mathbf{len}\ \overleftarrow{qb}.s\colon \mathbb{N}$	**len**-form(3)
5	$\overleftarrow{qb}.i + 1 \le \mathbf{len}\ \overleftarrow{qb}.s$	$<\to\le(2,4,1)$
6	$\overleftarrow{qb}.i + 1\colon \mathbb{N}_1$	$\mathbb{N}\to\mathbb{N}_1(2)$
7	$\overleftarrow{qb}.s(\overleftarrow{qb}.i + 1)\colon Qel$	$appl\text{-}form\text{-}seq(3,6,5)$
8	$inv\text{-}Queueb(\overleftarrow{qb}.s,\ \overleftarrow{qb}.i + 1)$	folding(5)
9	$mk\text{-}Queueb(\overleftarrow{qb}.s,\ \overleftarrow{qb}.i + 1)\colon Queueb$	$mk\text{-}Queueb\text{-}form(3,6,8)$
10	$mk\text{-}Queueb(\overleftarrow{qb}.s,\ \overleftarrow{qb}.i + 1).i = \overleftarrow{qb}.i + 1$	i-defn(9)
11	$\overleftarrow{qb}.s(mk\text{-}Queueb(\overleftarrow{qb}.s,\ \overleftarrow{qb}.i + 1).i)\colon Qel$	$=$-subs-left(a)(7,10,7)
12	$\overleftarrow{qb}.s(mk\text{-}Queueb(\overleftarrow{qb}.s,\ \overleftarrow{qb}.i + 1).i) =$	
	$\overleftarrow{qb}.s(mk\text{-}Queueb(\overleftarrow{qb}.s,\ \overleftarrow{qb}.i + 1).i)$	$=$-self-I(11)
13	$\overleftarrow{qb}.s(mk\text{-}Queueb(\overleftarrow{qb}.s,\ \overleftarrow{qb}.i + 1).i) = \overleftarrow{qb}.i + 1\wedge$	
	$\overleftarrow{qb}.s(mk\text{-}Queueb(\overleftarrow{qb}.s,\ \overleftarrow{qb}.i + 1).i) =$	
	$\overleftarrow{qb}.s(mk\text{-}Queueb(\overleftarrow{qb}.s,\ \overleftarrow{qb}.i + 1).i)$	$\wedge$-I(10,12)
14	$post\text{-}DEQUEUE(\overleftarrow{qb},\ mk\text{-}Queueb(\overleftarrow{qb}.s,\ \overleftarrow{qb}.i + 1),$	
	$\overleftarrow{qb}.s(mk\text{-}Queueb(\overleftarrow{qb}.s,\ \overleftarrow{qb}.i + 1).i))$	folding(13)
15	$\exists e\colon Qel \cdot post\text{-}DEQUEUE(\overleftarrow{qb},\ mk\text{-}Queueb(\overleftarrow{qb}.s,\ \overleftarrow{qb}.i + 1),\ e)$	
		$\exists$-I(11,14)

infer $\exists qb \in Queueb,\ e \in Qel \cdot post\text{-}DEQUEUE(\overleftarrow{qb},\ qb,\ e)$ $\qquad$ $\exists$-I(9,15)

Fig. 6. Formal proof of satisfiability of $DEQUEUE$ in the style of [10]

refers properly to the state variable qb, with i and s treated as selector functions. Formation and definition axioms are used in the justifications of the expressions introducing $\overleftarrow{qb}.i$ and $\overleftarrow{qb}.s$ at lines 2 and 3 of the formal proof. We give examples of such axioms in Sect. 5.

The requirement that justifications must appeal directly to defined rules of inference means that substantial theories of the underlying data types must be constructed. For example, consider line 4 of the rigorous proof in Fig. 2:

$$4 \quad i \leq \text{len } \overset{\backprime}{s} \qquad\qquad \mathbb{N},3,1$$

$$\dots$$

The justification of this line appeals to the general theory of natural numbers. In the formal proof, the inference is done at line 5 by appealing to a specific lemma:

$$\boxed{<\rightarrow\leq} \cfrac{i:\mathbb{N};\, n:\mathbb{N};\, i < n}{i+1 \leq n}$$

Most of the justifications in the rest of the proof refer to such rules.

The *mural* work concentrated on user-guided proof, specifically on the production of what might be considered "convincing" arguments in support of conjectures made about VDM models. The proof theory developed for *mural* was designed to have intuitive appeal and was aimed at largely manual use. A contrasting view, stressing the value of largely automatic proof production, motivated another strand of work, on experiments using the PVS and HOL theorem provers to discharge proof obligations automatically generated by VDMTools. Whichever approach is preferred, it is necessary to develop theories to underpin reasoning about VDM models, including properties about data types like the natural number examples above.

In Sects. 3 and 4, we consider typed LPF, and in Sect. 5, the theories that must be developed for reasoning about VDM models in the logic. In Sect. 6, we examine the forms of proof support that have been developed to date and the underlying theory itself.

Terminology and Notation

Since we take a "lightweight" view of formal methods in this context, we will tend to use the neutral term "model" to describe formal artefacts constructed in VDM-SL, rather than refer to them as specifications or designs, implying a particular development process. Models and model fragments in VDM-SL are presented using the mathematical syntax from the ISO standard [7], as this provides for a concise presentation.

3 A Proof Framework for VDM

This section introduces the logical framework for proof developed in the *mural* project [10, 37], which was based upon Jones's adaptation of the Natural Deduction style. Here, the elements of the framework are introduced in enough detail to discuss the representation of typed LPF and VDM.

3.1 Constants and Expressions

Three kinds of symbol are admitted: *variables, constants* and *binders*. Variables range over collections of values. Constants represent value and type constructors such as the empty set { }, the singleton sequence [_] or the finite-set type constructor _-**set**. Each constant has a fixed arity (x, y), where x is the number of value arguments it takes and y the number of type arguments (e.g. the arity of [_] is $(1, 0)$ and the constant _-**set** is of arity $(0, 1)$). Binary operators such as sequence concatenation $^\frown$, which expects two sequences as arguments (arity $(2, 0)$) will often be written using an infix form, for example $z ^\frown y$. Binders introduce and bind new variables, limiting their scope. The usual quantifiers of first-order predicate logic ($\forall, \exists$) and comprehension expression forms such as $\{\_ : \_ \mid \_\}$ are treated as binders.

An *expression* is either a variable symbol, or a constant symbol with the correct number of arguments instantiated, or a binder binding a variable in another expression. The *mural* logical framework also exploited a special notation for subtypes. The expression $\langle\langle x : \mathbb{N} \mid x < 10 \rangle\rangle$ denotes the subtype of natural numbers less than 10. In the remainder of this chapter, we will be liberal about the syntax, admitting infix versions of binary operators and omitting parentheses for commutative/associative operators.

3.2 Rules of Inference

Inference rules are given in a Hilbert-style system. An inference rule consists of a set of hypotheses, shown above a horizontal line, and a conclusion shown below the line. A name for the rule may be given in a box to the left of the line. For example, the following rule has one hypothesis and one conclusion:

$$\boxed{\_ + \text{1-form}} \frac{n : \mathbb{N}}{(n+1) : \mathbb{N}}$$

The symbol $\mathbb{N}$ in the rule $\_ + \text{1-form}$ is a constant, but the symbol n may be instantiated by an expression in a proof. Such a symbol is termed a *meta-variable*. On application in a proof, the meta-variables in a rule are consistently instantiated by expressions. It should be noted that meta-variables can take arguments, as in the following rule (we separate hypotheses by semicolons):

$$\boxed{=\text{-subs}} \frac{a = b; P(a)}{P(b)}$$

In using this rule, P could be instantiated by an expression which contains *placeholders* representing the argument. For example, $P(\_)$ could be $\forall x : \mathbb{N} \cdot \_ = x \lor x > \_$. Renaming avoids capture of free variables.

Axioms are distinguished by "Ax" to the right of the rule, thus:

$$\boxed{\text{0-form}}\ \frac{}{0:\mathbb{N}}\text{Ax}$$

3.3 Proofs

Proofs are represented as arguments from hypotheses to the conclusion. Consider a proof of the following conjecture:

$$\boxed{\text{Conj1}}\ \frac{ns:\mathbb{N}^*}{[0]\ ^\frown ns:\mathbb{N}^*}$$

The proof might have the following form:

	from $ns:\mathbb{N}^*$	
1	$0:\mathbb{N}$	0-form
2	$[0]:\mathbb{N}^*$	singl-form(1)
	infer $[0]\ ^\frown ns:\mathbb{N}^*$	$^\frown$-form(2,h1)

Each proof is organised into blocks bounded by **from** and **infer** lines. Each block limits the scope of the hypotheses stated on the **from** line. Within each block, inference steps are represented as numbered lines, each bearing a formula and a justification. Each justification is an appeal to an inference rule or a folding/unfolding of a syntactic definition.

The block structuring of proofs enables localised assumptions, permitting the discharging of sequent hypotheses, indicated by the turnstile symbol $\vdash$. For example, consider a proof based on the following rules from classical logic:

$$\boxed{\text{deduction}}\ \frac{e_1 \vdash e_2}{e_1 \Rightarrow e_2}$$

$$\boxed{\text{modus ponens}}\ \frac{e_1;\ e_1 \Rightarrow e_2}{e_2}$$

A proof using deduction discharges the sequent hypothesis in a sub-proof:

	from $P \Rightarrow Q;\ Q \Rightarrow R$	
1	**from** P	
1.1	Q	modus ponens(1.h1,h1)
2	**infer** R	modus ponens(1.1,h2)
	infer $P \Rightarrow R$	deduction(1)

The framework supports syntactic definitions of constants, for example

$$e_1 \wedge e_2 \triangleq \neg\,(\neg\, e_1 \vee \neg\, e_2)$$

This allows justifications by folding or unfolding across the definition, with expressions matching the meta-variables in the definition, for example:

$$\ldots$$

5	$\neg((A \wedge B) \vee \neg C)$	
6	$\neg(\neg(\neg A \vee \neg B) \vee \neg C)$	unfolding(5)
7	$(\neg A \vee \neg B) \wedge C$	folding(6)

$$\ldots$$

3.4 Theories

In the *mural* framework, a *theory* is a collection of constant and binder definitions, axioms and derived results *and their proofs*. A *theory store* is then a collection of theories in an inheritance structure. This structuring into theories was intended to promote reuse and to help to limit the scope of searches for applicable inference rules. No information-hiding mechanisms were proposed in the original *mural* project, but were suggested subsequently [20].

In order to support VDM modelling, theories were built for propositional LPF, and then typed predicate LPF with equality (see Sect. 4 for an introduction to the content of these core theories). This has been inherited into theories describing the base types (such as natural numbers) that are present in the modelling language, and the type constructors such as sets, sequences and mappings. These theories have then been inherited by a single theory that gathers together results sufficient to support proofs of properties of specific models (Sect. 5).

4 The Typed Logic of Partial Functions

Partial functions are commonplace in computing, at the implementation and specification levels. There is a long history of research into logics that handle the undefined terms resulting from the application of such functions. We will not describe the competing approaches here, but refer the reader to papers by Cheng and Jones setting out the view that underpins VDM [17, 34].

Partial functions and operators arise frequently in VDM models. Even in the simple biased-queue model presented in Fig. 1, a partial operator arises in the postcondition of the *DEQUEUE* operation, namely the indexing into a sequence $\overleftarrow{s}(i)$, which is defined only if i is in the set of indices for the sequence $\overleftarrow{s}$. Thus, the operation's precondition $i < \mathbf{len}\, s$ ensures the definedness of this expression.

The Logic of Partial Functions (LPF) is a first-order predicate logic which admits undefined terms resulting from the application of partial functions or operators. In the context of VDM, LPF was first introduced in the untyped propositional form by Barringer, Cheng and Jones in 1984 [9], and then in the predicate form by Cheng in 1986 [16]. A typed version of LPF was presented by Jones and Middelburg [36], and the *mural* group extended the basic predicate logic with types and operators specifically designed to support VDM [10].

4.1 Propositional LPF

Aside from the logical values **true** and **false**, LPF admits undefined terms. Within the proof theory, there is no need to assign a model theory to LPF which then includes a value $\perp_\mathbb{B}$ intended to denote undefined terms. The truth tables for propositional disjunction and negation (Fig. 7) may be thought of as describing a parallel lazy evaluation of the operands. For example, the expression $A \vee B$ evaluates to **true** if either disjunct evaluates to **true**, even if the other disjunct is undefined.

$\vee$	true	false	$\perp_\mathbb{B}$
true	true	true	true
false	true	false	$\perp_\mathbb{B}$
$\perp_\mathbb{B}$	true	$\perp_\mathbb{B}$	$\perp_\mathbb{B}$

$\neg$	
true	false
false	true
$\perp_\mathbb{B}$	$\perp_\mathbb{B}$

Fig. 7. Example truth tables for propositional LPF

The axiomatisation of propositional LPF may be defined from the constants **true**, $\vee$ and $\neg$. The axioms (Fig. 8) are similar to those of classical propositional logic except for the absence of the law of the excluded middle:

$$\text{Excl-Mid} \frac{}{e \vee \neg e}$$

Note that the third value present in the model theory is not actually required in the proof theory, and is often referred to as a 'gap' or absence of a value, rather than as a special value.

Several operators are introduced by syntactic definition:

$$\textbf{false} \overset{\triangle}{=} \neg \textbf{true}$$
$$e_1 \wedge e_2 \overset{\triangle}{=} \neg(\neg e_1 \vee \neg e_2)$$
$$e_1 \Rightarrow e_2 \overset{\triangle}{=} \neg e_1 \vee e_2$$
$$e_1 \Leftrightarrow e_2 \overset{\triangle}{=} e_1 \Rightarrow e_2 \wedge e_2 \Rightarrow e_1$$

A consequence of losing the excluded middle is that the classical Deduction Theorem does not hold:

$$\text{Deduction} \frac{e_1 \vdash e_2}{e_1 \Rightarrow e_2}$$

To see this, consider the possibility that e_1 and $e2$ are the same expression, say e. Certainly we can prove $e \vdash e$, but $e \Rightarrow e$ does not hold in LPF as it unfolds to

$$\boxed{\textbf{true-I}} \; \frac{}{\textbf{true}}\text{-Ax}$$

$$\boxed{\vee\text{-I-R}} \; \frac{e_1}{e_1 \vee e_2}\text{-Ax}$$

$$\boxed{\vee\text{-I-L}} \; \frac{e_2}{e_1 \vee e_2}\text{-Ax}$$

$$\boxed{\vee\text{-E}} \; \frac{e_1 \vee e_2; \; e_1 \vdash e; \; e_2 \vdash e;}{e}\text{-Ax}$$

$$\boxed{\neg\neg\text{-I}} \; \frac{e}{\neg\neg e}\text{-Ax}$$

$$\boxed{\neg\neg\text{-E}} \; \frac{\neg\neg e}{e}\text{-Ax}$$

$$\boxed{\text{contr}} \; \frac{e_1; \; \neg e_1}{e_2}\text{-Ax}$$

$$\boxed{\neg\text{-}\vee\text{-I}} \; \frac{\neg e_1; \; \neg e_2}{\neg(e_1 \vee e_2)}\text{-Ax}$$

$$\boxed{\neg\text{-}\vee\text{-E-L}} \; \frac{\neg(e_1 \vee e_2)}{\neg e_2}\text{-Ax}$$

$$\boxed{\neg\text{-}\vee\text{-E-R}} \; \frac{\neg(e_1 \vee e_2)}{\neg e_1}\text{-Ax}$$

Fig. 8. Axioms of propositional LPF

the excluded middle ($\neg e \vee e$). In order to recover the full power of classical logic for propositions and predicates that are well defined, a definedness judgement is added:

$$\delta e \triangleq e \vee \neg e$$

This leads to derived rules for the introduction and elimination of δ:

$$\boxed{\delta\text{-I}} \; \frac{e}{\delta e}$$

$$\boxed{\delta\text{-I-}\neg} \; \frac{\neg e}{\delta e}$$

$$\boxed{\delta\text{-E}} \; \frac{\delta e_1; \; e_1 \vdash e; \; \neg e_1 \vdash e}{e}$$

These allow the derivation of the qualified version of the Deduction Theorem that holds in LPF:

$$\boxed{\Rightarrow \text{-I}} \frac{\delta e_1;\ e_1 \vdash e_2}{e_1 \ \Rightarrow \ e_2}$$

In general, theorems of classical logic can be formed into theorems of LPF by adding the necessary δ hypotheses.

4.2 Typed Predicate LPF with Equality

Predicate LPF introduces the possibility of terms denoting values, and hence also the possibility that these terms may be undefined. Logical expressions of the form $e\colon T$ are *typing judgements* and assert that the expression e denotes a value belonging to a type T. Expressions that are undefined are termed *non-denoting* and do not represent values in any data type. Thus, we do not use special symbols or values to denote undefined terms, just as, in the propositional logic, we did not require the 'bottom' value in the axiomatisation.

The logical framework treats quantifiers as binders, with a type restricting the bound variable. Consequently, the rules for quantifiers often contain type judgements. For example, the axiom for introduction of the existential quantifier requires that the witness value is denoting:

$$\boxed{\exists \text{-I}} \frac{a\colon A;\ P(a)}{\exists x\colon A \cdot P(x)} \text{Ax}$$

The corresponding elimination axiom is a generalisation of $\vee$-Elimination:

$$\boxed{\exists \text{-E}} \frac{\exists x\colon A \cdot P(x);}{e} \text{Ax}$$

The subscript under the sequent indicates the variable bound in the sequent. If the same variable name occurs free in e, it must be renamed on instantiation of the rule.

The axiomatisation for predicate LPF is, by analogy with propositional LPF, given in terms of existential quantification and negation. Just as rules for $\neg$-$\vee$-Introduction and Elimination are required, so there are corresponding axioms at the quantifier level:

$$\boxed{\neg\text{-}\exists\text{-I}} \frac{x\colon A \vdash_x \neg P(x)}{\neg \exists y\colon A \cdot P(y)} \text{Ax}$$

$$\boxed{\neg\text{-}\exists\text{-E}} \frac{a\colon A, \neg \exists y\colon A \cdot P(y)}{\neg P(a)} \text{Ax}$$

Universal quantification is introduced by syntactic definition:

$$\forall x\colon A \cdot P(x) \triangleq \neg \exists x\colon A \cdot \neg P(x)$$

This leads to the expected introduction and elimination rules:

$$\boxed{\forall\text{-I}}\ \frac{y\colon A \vdash_y P(y)}{\forall x\colon A \cdot P(x)}$$

$$\boxed{\forall\text{-E}}\ \frac{a\colon A; \forall x\colon A \cdot P(x)}{P(a)}$$

When are quantified expressions defined? Consider the existentially quantified expression $\exists x\colon A \cdot P(x)$. If a witness value a can be produced for the predicate P, the existential expression is true by $\exists$-I, and so $(\delta(\exists x\colon A \cdot P(x)))$ is certainly defined, even if P is undefined for some values in A. Similarly, if it can be shown that no witness value exists, the quantified expression is false and likewise is defined. A third possibility is that, although P is known to be defined everywhere on A, there is not enough information to prove or refute the existence of a witness value. A further axiom covers this weaker case:

$$\boxed{\delta\text{-}\exists\text{-inherit}}\ \frac{x\colon A \vdash_x \delta P(x)}{\delta(\exists x\colon A \cdot P(x))}\text{Ax}$$

This extends in the expected way to $\forall$.

Equality has to be treated with some care where undefinedness is possible. LPF equality is *weak* in that it is only defined over denoting terms:

$$\boxed{\delta\text{-=-I}}\ \frac{a\colon A; b\colon A}{\delta(a = b)}\text{Ax}$$

This leads to an abundance of typing hypotheses in the rules relating to equality. Even the simple reflexivity axiom requires one:

$$\boxed{\text{=-self-I}}\ \frac{a\colon A}{a = a}\text{Ax}$$

Substitution of equals is done through inference rules, rather than building weak equality directly into the logical framework. For example,

$$\boxed{\text{=-subs-right(a)}}\ \frac{a\colon A; a = b; P(a)}{P(b)}\text{Ax}$$

Different combinations of typing hypotheses, $P(a)$ and $P(b)$ lead to a quartet of substitution rules which prove to be rather clumsy to select and use in practice. Other features, such as inequality ($\neq$), unique existential quantification ($\exists!$), unique choice (ι) and conditionals (**if** ... **then** ... **else** ...) are defined using the basic constructs of typed predicate LPF with the equality described here.

5 Theories Supporting VDM-SL

In order to use LPF to reason about the elements of a VDM model, it is necessary to provide theories that embody the properties of the constructs available in the language. Chief among these are the type constructors, and in particular those used to build collection types including finite sets, sequences and mappings. General theories are provided for these type constructors. Certain other constructors, such as records, are better handled on a per-model basis, translated into definitions and axiom sets in terms of the constructs in the VDM theories. Below, we show how both kinds of construct are handled. Section 5.1 describes the general theory of sets, while Sect. 5.2 shows how record structures are handled.

5.1 Theories for Generic VDM Features

In order to give a flavour of the theories describing generic VDM features, consider a simple example: the theory of finite sets. The axiomatisation is given in terms of constructors introduced as constants. In the case of sets these are the empty set ($\{\,\}$) and an *add* operator. Other operators, including the conventional operators on sets such as union and intersection, are introduced as constants and then defined either inductively or by syntactic definition. The majority of operators have *formation* rules which allow the introduction of typing judgements, for example

$$\boxed{\{\,\}\text{-form}}\ \frac{}{\{\,\}\colon A\text{-}\mathbf{set}}\text{Ax}$$

$$\boxed{add\text{-form}}\ \frac{a\colon A;\ s\colon A\text{-}\mathbf{set}}{add(a,s)\colon A\text{-}\mathbf{set}}\text{Ax}$$

Properties of operators are usually defined inductively over the constructors. For example, set membership has the following rules:

$$\boxed{\{\,\}\text{-is-empty}}\ \frac{a\colon A}{a\notin\{\,\}}\text{Ax}$$

$$\boxed{\in\text{-}add\text{-defn}}\ \frac{a\colon A;\ b\colon A;\ s\colon A\text{-}\mathbf{set}}{a\in add(b,s)\ \Leftrightarrow\ a=b\lor a\in s}\text{Ax}$$

The constructors form the basis of the induction rule:

$$\boxed{\text{set-indn}}\ \frac{s\colon A\text{-}\mathbf{set};\ P(\{\,\})}{a\colon A,\ s_1\colon A\text{-}\mathbf{set},\ P(S_1),\ a\notin s_1\vdash_{s,s_1}\ P(add(a,s_1))}{P(s)}\text{Ax}$$

Collections in VDM-SL (sets, sequences and mappings) are finite. This complicates the axiomatisation slightly, in that it is necessary to ensure finiteness in building comprehension expressions. For example, naive versions of the set comprehension formation and definition axioms might be as follows:

$$\overline{\{x\colon A \mid P(x)\}\colon A\text{-}\mathbf{set}}$$

$$\frac{a\colon A}{a \in \{x\colon A \mid P(x)\} \iff P(a)}$$

Finiteness is ensured by adding hypotheses requiring that there exists a valid set containing all the members of the newly constructed set:

$$\frac{\exists s\colon A\text{-}\mathbf{set} \cdot \forall y\colon A \cdot P(y) \implies y \in s}{\{x\colon A \mid P(x)\}\colon A\text{-}\mathbf{set}}$$

$$\frac{a\colon A;\, \exists s\colon A\text{-}\mathbf{set} \cdot \forall y\colon A \cdot P(y) \implies y \in s}{a \in \{x\colon A \mid P(x)\} \iff P(a)}$$

This is further complicated by the need to handle undefinedness. The characteristic predicate must be total:

$$\frac{\forall x\colon A \cdot \delta P(x)}{\exists s\colon A\text{-}\mathbf{set} \cdot \forall y\colon A \cdot P(y) \implies y \in s}{\{x\colon A \mid P(x)\}\colon A\text{-}\mathbf{set}}$$

$$\frac{\forall x\colon A \cdot \delta P(x)}{a\colon A;\, \exists s\colon A\text{-}\mathbf{set} \cdot \forall y\colon A \cdot P(y) \implies y \in s}{a \in \{x\colon A \mid P(x)\} \iff P(a)}$$

The more general form of set comprehension available in VDM-SL allows the construction of expressions from the elements satisfying the characteristic predicate, for example

$$\{f(x) \mid x\colon A \cdot P(x)\}$$

Here again, the finiteness and consistency requirements must be taken into account, with the additional constraint that the elements of the constructed set should be denoting:

$$\text{set-comp-form}\;\frac{\forall x\colon A \cdot \delta P(x)}{x\colon A, P(x) \vdash_x f(x)\colon B}{\exists s\colon B\text{-}\mathbf{set} \cdot \forall y\colon A \cdot P(y) \implies f(y) \in s}{\{f(x) \mid x\colon A \cdot P(x)\}\colon B\text{-}\mathbf{set}}$$

$$\in\text{-set-comp-defn} \quad \frac{\begin{array}{c} b\colon B \\ \forall x\colon A \cdot \delta P(x) \\ x\colon A, P(x) \vdash_x f(x)\colon B \\ \exists s\colon B\text{-}\mathbf{set} \cdot \forall y\colon A \cdot P(y) \;\Rightarrow\; f(y) \in s \end{array}}{b \in \{f(x) \mid x\colon A \cdot P(x)\} \;\Leftrightarrow\; \exists a\colon A \cdot P(a) \wedge b = f(a)}$$

5.2 Model-specific Theories

In the proof framework that was developed for *mural*, each construct had a fixed arity. It was not therefore possible to give a generic theory for constructs that have variable numbers of component parts: these are translated into definitions and axioms. The best example of this approach is the handling of composite types, or records. Consider, for example, the following VDM type definition from our *Queueb* example (for the moment omitting consideration of the invariant):

$$\begin{array}{lll} Queueb :: & s & : Qel^* \\ & i & : \mathbb{N} \end{array}$$

This is translated into a type name *Queueb*, a constructor *mk-Queueb* expressed as a two-argument constant, and two selectors, $\_.s$ and $\_.i$, each taking one argument. Axioms of formation and definition link the components. For example, the formation and definition axioms for the selector $\_.s$ are

$$s\text{-form} \quad \frac{q\colon Queueb}{q.s\colon Qel^*}\text{Ax}$$

$$s\text{-defn} \quad \frac{mk\text{-}Queueb(x,y)\colon Queueb}{mk\text{-}Queueb(x,y).s = x}\text{Ax}$$

The axioms for the constructor take the following form:

$$mk\text{-}Queueb\text{-form} \quad \frac{s\colon Qel^*;\, i\colon \mathbb{N}}{mk\text{-}Queueb(s,i)\colon Queueb}\text{Ax}$$

$$mk\text{-}Queueb\text{-defn} \quad \frac{q\colon Queueb}{mk\text{-}Queueb(q.s, q.i)\colon Queueb}\text{Ax}$$

These rules have been seen applied in the formal proof in Fig. 6. In the presence of invariants, the rules are complicated slightly by the need to ensure that the invariant is respected on formation of the composite value, and an axiom is added to allow the invariant to be introduced:

$$mk\text{-}Queueb\text{-form} \quad \frac{s\colon Qel^*;\, i\colon \mathbb{N};\, inv\text{-}Queueb(s,i)}{mk\text{-}Queueb(s,i)\colon Queueb}\text{Ax}$$

$$\boxed{inv\text{-}Queueb\text{-}I}\ \frac{mk\text{-}Queueb(x,y)\colon Queueb}{inv\text{-}Queueb(x,y)}\text{Ax}$$

Note that the invariant is introduced here as a binary constant and defined by a syntactic definition:

$$inv\text{-}Queueb(x,y) \stackrel{\triangle}{=} x \leq \textbf{len}\ y$$

5.3 Choices and Trade-offs

The main choices and trade-offs that have to be made in developing theories representing VDM-SL concepts within the *mural* logical framework have been discussed in depth elsewhere [25]. However, it is worth mentioning briefly two areas in which compromises were made. First, the syntactic definition mechanism does not support side conditions on the folding and unfolding of terms. Where such side conditions are required, it is necessary to use axiomatic definition. In particular, if a polymorphic term, for example including an equality, is included in the definition of a term not intended to be polymorphic, the whole defining expression can have a meaning outside its intended scope. Second, as already indicated, the decision to fix the arities of constants made reasoning about some VDM-SL constructs which have a variable number of components, such as record types (Cartesian products with field designators), quite unwieldy. This might be seen as a rather harsh criticism, bearing in mind that many formalisms avoid such constructions in the first place.

Some aspects of VDM-SL itself add to the complexity of the proof theory. The effect of requiring finiteness has already been indicated. Similar complexity arises when function types are introduced. VDM-SL provides for the restricted use of types of total functions, their elements being denoted by lambda expressions. Restrictions are imposed on the combination of function types with other type constructors such as sets (sets of functions are not permitted), and these can surface as still further typing hypotheses.

Loose specification is particularly challenging for modelling languages that aim to support abstract specification. VDM-SL admits loose specification via choice constructs. For example, the 'let ... be such that' expression:

let $x\colon A$ **be s.t.** $P(x)$ **in** $Q(x)$

incorporates some degree of choice. This expression implicitly specifies x as any value of type A that satisfies the condition P. If more than one value in A satisfies P, the expression's semantics becomes problematic. One might try to give the semantics in terms of a deterministic (Hilbert) choice operator ε:

$$\boxed{\varepsilon\text{-form}}\ \frac{\exists x\colon A \cdot P(x)}{(\varepsilon\, x\colon A \cdot P(x))\colon A}\text{Ax}$$

$$\boxed{\varepsilon\text{-I}}\ \frac{\exists x\colon A \cdot P(x)}{P(\varepsilon\, x\colon A \cdot P(x))}\text{Ax}$$

$$\frac{\exists x\colon A \cdot P(x);\ E(\varepsilon x\colon A \cdot P(x))\colon B}{(\textbf{let } x\colon A \textbf{ be s.t. } P(x) \textbf{ in } E(x)) = E(\varepsilon\, x\colon A \cdot P(x))}$$

However, this does not match the semantics of loose expressions in VDM-SL. The ε-form rule and the reflexivity of equality (=-self-I), allow us to conclude the following:

$$\frac{\exists x\colon A \cdot P(x)}{(\varepsilon\, x\colon A \cdot P(x)) = (\varepsilon\, x\colon A \cdot P(x))}$$

This is at odds with the semantics of loose expressions in VDM function definitions. Such definitions denote deterministic functions. Function definitions containing loose choice expressions are treated as *under-determined*. That is, they specify deterministic functions, but the specification does not constrain the particular deterministic function chosen from the range allowed by the choice operator. In contrast, VDM operations are non-deterministic. The use of a loose choice expression in an operation is treated as non-determinism: the same expression may denote different results at each occurrence. Thus, if the same loose expression occurs in different places in a VDM-SL model, it may denote different values. Consider, for example, the following fragment [39]:

$f : () \to \mathbb{N}$

$f() \quad \triangleq \quad \textbf{let } x\colon \mathbb{N} \textbf{ be s.t. } x \in \{1, 2\} \textbf{ in } x$

$g : () \to \mathbb{N}$

$g() \quad \triangleq \quad \textbf{let } x\colon \mathbb{N} \textbf{ be s.t. } x \in \{1, 2\} \textbf{ in } x$

The looseness in the definitions means that a valid implementation of f may always return the value 1, while a valid implementation of g may always return 2. However, our proof rules based on ε, along with reflexivity of equality over denoting terms, allow us to conclude $f() = g()$. In order to deal with this while retaining the basic equality rules, it becomes necessary to add context information differentiating the occurrences of expressions containing *varepsilon*. Larsen [39, 41] has explored the addition of this context information in some depth, in order to derive some more general rules for loose expressions. He went on to develop proof rules for recursive definitions incorporating looseness, utilising a determinism predicate which augments inference rules that introduces new equalities.

Loose specification is potentially a valuable feature. It contributes to compositional refinement, since different occurrences may be treated differently in a refinement step. However, there is a price to be paid, because of the need to tag expressions with contextual information.

6 Three Approaches to Supporting Logic in VDM

As discussed in Sect. 2, the provision of strong tool support has been a dominant theme in the VDM community in recent years. In this section we examine three approaches to the provision of support for reasoning about VDM models with partial functions. Each is characterised by a different understanding of the potential uses and users of the tools. First, in Sect. 6.1 we examine the implementation of support for user-led proof of obligations and conjectures about models, directly implementing LPF in the logical framework of Sect. 3. The second approach that we describe, in Sect. 6.2, is that taken in VDM-Tools, in which the logic is used indirectly and the tool support is geared primarily to the needs of a developer wishing to explore a model through approaches familiar from conventional software engineering, particularly testing. Third, in Sect. 6.3 we examine the use of automated proof support and the adaptation of general provers to LPF and VDM.

6.1 The "Pencil and Paper" Metaphor: the *mural* Approach

The *mural* tool was aimed at users with some expertise in structuring a formal proof. A basic specification support environment provided some rudimentary facilities for constructing models, and generating model-specific theories from them in the manner outlined in Sect. 5.2. Proof obligations would be added as unproven conjectures to a theory store which had been pre-populated with definitions and theorems for typed LPF. Users would complete proofs of obligations and manually added validation conjectures within a proof support environment that aimed to provide lightweight tools to assist with the book-keeping tasks involved in proof, as well as in the selection of applicable rules.

As an example of this style of reasoning, consider the proof of the inference rule for $\forall$-Introduction:

$$\boxed{\forall\text{-I}}\ \frac{y\colon A \vdash_y P(y)}{\forall x\colon A \cdot P(x)}$$

In *mural*, the rule would initially have an 'unproved' status within the theory store. Upon selection, a proof display opens in a window looking like a sheet of paper with the hypotheses at the top and the conclusion at the bottom:

from $y\colon A \vdash_y P(y)$

$\ \ \ ...$

infer $\forall x\colon A \cdot P(x)$ $\qquad\qquad\qquad\qquad\qquad$ $\langle$?? justify ?? $\rangle$

Note that the conclusion line is flagged as unjustified. The user is free to decide how to approach the problem, by working backwards from the goal or forwards from the knowns. Tools are supplied to search the theory store for applicable rules that can be matched to the knowns or goals. However, the expert user will often want to select a specific rule for application, and the *mural* 'justification tool' in this case manages the pattern-matching of the rule to the expressions in the proof. For example, the user may choose to work backwards from the conclusion by using the fact that $\forall$ is defined syntactically in terms of $\neg \exists$. With the aid of the justification tool, the proof is updated:

$$\textbf{from } y\colon A \vdash_y P(y)$$
$$\cdots$$

a $\neg \exists y\colon A \cdot P(y)$ $\langle$?? justify ?? $\rangle$
   $\textbf{infer } \forall x\colon A \cdot P(x)$ folding(a)

Rules with sequent hypotheses lead to the establishment of sub-proofs and, again, the *mural* tools can handle the bookkeeping:

$$\textbf{from } y\colon A \vdash_y P(y)$$

b $\textbf{from } z\colon A$

$$\cdots$$

   $\textbf{infer } \neg (\neg P(z))$ $\langle$?? justify ?? $\rangle$
a $\neg \exists y\colon A \cdot P(y)$ $\neg\text{-}\exists\text{-I}(b)$
   $\textbf{infer } \forall x\colon A \cdot P(x)$ folding(a)

The proof is completed by forward reasoning within the sub-proof (and renumbering lines to clean up the presentation):

$$\textbf{from } y\colon A \vdash_y P(y)$$

1    $\textbf{from } z\colon A$
1.1 $P(z)$ sequent h1 (1.h1)
   $\textbf{infer } \neg (\neg P(z))$ $\neg\neg\text{-I}(1.1)$
2    $\neg \exists y\colon A \cdot P(y)$ $\neg\text{-}\exists\text{-I}(1)$
   $\textbf{infer } \forall x\colon A \cdot P(x)$ folding(2)

Note some of the characteristics of this approach to implementing LPF in VDM. The user is assumed to have some knowledge of proof construction. The tools are specialised engines that provide a lightweight form of assistance to basic proof construction tasks, and the stress is on the crafting of a satisfying human-readable proof rather than a machine-readable proof script as is the case with some high-automation approaches. Other than the justification tool, the prototype tools supported the use of decision procedures and the application of tactics. All the tools operated on the underlying presentation of the proof.

The *mural* logical framework is similar to that used in Sect. 3 and was designed to be capable of adaptation to several logics. Apart from its instantiation for typed LPF, it has been applied to higher-order logics, modal logics and Hoare logic [37]. The generic character of the logical framework means that the handling of partial functions is done through the theory held in the tool's theory store. The user is faced directly with the problem of handling definedness.

Other VDM-specific characteristics of Typed LPF, such as finiteness and underspecification, must be understood by the *mural* user. The complexity of doing so taxed the *mural* logical framework and tools. In fact, the developers of the Typed LPF theory in [10] did not implement a solution to the underspecification problem. Certain styles of reasoning were not so well supported, notably chains of equalities, inequalities and implications, associative/commutative reasoning etc. However, some experimental tactic-like tools were built to help support reasoning in these cases.

In spite of some limitations, the *mural* environment provided for a faithful implementation of LPF and introduced the possibility of user-guided argument construction. Alan Wills' speculative but prescient appendix to the book on *mural* [37] entitled "The Theorem Prover's House" presented a vision of the future in which a theorem prover is emphatically not a computer program, but a skilled human. Wills's prover has access to on-line theory stores, specialist proof engines and intuitive interfaces. He does not prove every line himself, as the *mural* user had to do, but he does remain in control of the argument.

6.2 Logic in VDMTools

In contrast with *mural*'s very proof-focused tool set, the industry-developed VDMTools is driven by the "lightweight formal methods" paradigm. These tools are designed to encourage modelling and the exploration of models, often in collaboration with a domain expert. The targeted user of VDMTools is not necessarily a formalist with training in proof at all, but is assumed to be a competent software engineer. The tools correspond to those of a design or programming support environment: syntax and type checking, pretty printing, interpretation, batch mode testing and test coverage analysis. Models may be expressed in the classical "flat" VDM-SL language or its object-oriented extension VDM^{++}. For the latter, there is an explicit link with UML modelling tools.

The objective in the development of VDMTools has been on supplying forms of analysis that are familiar to the software engineering practitioner, and proof has not been a high priority. Nevertheless, the influence of the logic is present from the type-checking tools and along the rest of the chain. For example, type checking is not decidable in general for VDM, because of the arbitrary complexity of data type invariants. The approach taken is to offer two levels of type checking: possibly correct (*pos*) and definitely correct (*def*) [48]. The *pos* check is precise in that it only raises errors that are surely errors. The *def* check is imprecise but safe in the sense that it raises an error message for any situation in which an error may occur. The *def* checking process has been extended to generate proof obligations automatically for each case. The tools support user "sign-off" of each obligation, on the basis of inspection. Models which pass the syntax check may be executed in the VDMTools interpreter. Consequently, the interpreter has to take a position with respect to the evaluation of Boolean formulae written in VDM. Given the infeasibility of implementing parallel evaluation of the kind required for a faithful LPF interpretation of such formulae, the VDMTools interpreter treats propositional operators in VDM models as their McCarthy conditional counterparts based on a left-to-right evaluation, as taken in the RAISE Specification Language (RSL) [49, 50].

6.3 Use of Automation: PVS and HOL Support

VDM was not developed specifically for implementation in a proof support tool. It is therefore a considerable challenge to develop a useful embedding of the language in such a tool. There have been various attempts to date.

Shallow embeddings involve a translation from the concepts of the source language to those of the theorem prover. There are several superficial similarities between PVS and VDM, making it appealing to attempt a shallow embedding and explore the extent to which proof support might be automated. The implementation reported by Agerholm, Bicarregui and Maharaj [1, 2] takes this form. Each formal model is hand-translated to PVS. This approach has yielded a considerable reduction in the effort spent on handling tedious applications of associative/commutative principles. On the down side, PVS does not handle partial functions directly for Typed LPF. Handling of underspecification is not clean. PVS requires that each occurrence of a choice expression should yield the same result. Thus, as indicated in [2], the translation of genuine non-determinism in operation specifications to PVS choice operators is not correct.

Agerholm and Frost presented an embedding of Typed LPF in Isabelle [3, 4] as part of a larger scheme to extend the capabilities of the IFAD VDM-SL Toolbox (as it was then known). It is a straightforward embedding of the logic represented in [10], including therefore the handling of undefinedness. This approach has been successful, though limited by the "ad hoc" nature of the collection of rules in the initial sets of theories.

A subsequent implementation of Typed LPF in HOL98 within the PROSPER project [18] included the realisation of a much more sophisticated user interface which aimed to present proof-level expressions to the user within the specification formalism, rather than requiring the user to switch mentally between the model and the theorem prover. The PROSPER theories supporting VDM were structured into rule sets to aid efficient proof, and a more sophisticated set of tactics were developed. The link to VDMTools supported automatic generation and discharging of proof obligations, achieving around 90% automation. An interface was developed for limited user guidance of proof construction in cases where the obligation could not be discharged automatically. However, this received only limited experimental use. The PROSPER tools were limited to a subset of VDM models that stayed within a two-valued logic. Proof obligations were generated to ensure adherence to this requirement. Loose specification was handled using the Hilbert choice operator, so reflexivity of equality could be preserved. The PROSPER team, which included the author at various points, took the view that these restrictions were worth tolerating in order to produce a first integrated tool set.

7 Conclusions and Future Directions

We have attempted to characterise the Typed Logic of Partial Functions as it is used to support reasoning about models in VDM. In the earlier sections of the chapter, we painted a relatively simple picture of the underlying logic, in particular its features for handling undefined terms. The basic logic was extended with features to support VDM directly, including definitions of types and operators present in the modelling language. This attempt to accommodate features such as finiteness of data values and looseness poses a first set of challenges to the logical framework.

Once one begins to consider the requirements for robust, highly capable tool support, the picture becomes rather less clear because of the need to resolve conflicting aims, for example handling undefinedness in a way that is clean for both execution (as in VDMTools) and proof (as in *mural*). It remains an open question to see if a proof support environment can be developed that works in conjunction with VDMTools but also provides greater faithfulness to LPF than was the case in the PROSPER embedding.

This chapter has sought to make one critical point in regards to logics for formal modelling languages: it is a mistake to design or analyse a logic for formal modelling in isolation. The logic is just one of several interdependent elements (modelling language, static and dynamic semantics, proof theory, interpreter, analysis tools etc.) of a useful formal method. A decision to simplify one element usually has effects on others. For example, we could try to deal with undefinedness in VDM by prohibiting potentially undefined expressions in the modelling language in the first place. This is, in some sense, moving responsibility for handling undefinedness from the logic to the specification support tools. A motto for LPF might be that "there's no such thing as a free lunch."

A similar argument holds as we move from abstract specification to running systems via refinement. While it may be possible to sweep undefined expressions away at an abstract level, undefinedness must be faced in implementations, as must the resolution of loose specification and finiteness of representations. Exactly where specific responsibilities lie is a critical factor in determining the utility of a formal method. It is reasonable to expect that large-scale formal developments might employ a variety of related formalisms, and hence logical systems, at different stages. This trend is becoming all the stronger as work on tools moves away from monolithic solutions such as the current VDMTools towards collections of interoperable tools such as those envisaged in Overture and the fault-tolerance-focused RODIN project.[6]

---

[6] http://rodin.cs.ncl.ac.uk.

Several technological developments will have a significant influence on how we apply logics for specification languages in the future. Many of the core technologies needed to realise the *mural* vision of human-led proof are beginning to become available [11]. These include network-enabled capabilities such as shared work-spaces for developing specifications and theorems, access to searchable large-scale on-line theory libraries, remote access to reasoners and proof tools, and shared visualisation. These technologies have the potential to revolutionise our approach to advanced proof-based validation and verification as much as to increase the efficiency of provers and model checkers.

We have observed the challenge posed to automated proof by the handling of partial functions in VDM, as evidenced in the work to date on PVS, Isabelle and HOL98. Along the same lines, Chalin [15] has attacked the mismatches between the logics that underpin run-time assertion checking in programs and those supported in program verification tools. He reports a survey which suggests that programmers would prefer verification technology that provides an interpretation of terms consistent with that already used in run-time assertion checking. LPF is one possible candidate logic, and an interesting research topic is the use of LPF variants in assertion-based environments akin to ESC [38] and Spec# [8].

Acknowledgements

This chapter is based on material prepared for the 2004 CoLogNET Summer School on Logics of Formal Software Specification Languages. For personal reasons it was not possible to deliver the lectures, so I am particularly grateful to Dines Bjørner and Martin Henson for the opportunity to contribute this chapter, and for their forbearance during its preparation. I am grateful to Jeremy Bryans, Cliff Jones and Peter Gorm Larsen for many detailed and helpful comments, and for stimulating discussions on the topics covered. LPF's realisation in VDM has been pioneered by many colleagues, with whom it has been a pleasure to collaborate, including Peter Lindsay, Richard Moore, Juan Bicarregui, Brian Ritchie, Lockwood Morris, Sten Agerholm, Kim Sunesen and Paul Mukherjee.

References

1. S. Agerholm. Translating specifications in VDM-SL to PVS. In J. von Wright, J. Grundy, and J. Harrison, editors, *Proceedings of the 9th International Conference on Theorem Proving in Higher Order Logics (TPHOLs'96)*, volume 1125 of *Lecture Notes in Computer Science*, pages 1–16. Springer, 1996.
2. S. Agerholm, J. Bicarregui, and S. Maharaj. On the Verification of VDM Specifications and Refinement with PVS. In J.C. Bicarregui, editor, *Proof in VDM: Case Studies*, FACIT. Springer, 1998.

3. S. Agerholm and J. Frost. Towards an Integrated CASE and Theorem Proving Tool for VDM-SL. In J.S. Fitzgerald, C.B. Jones, and P. Lucas, editors, *FME'97: Industrial Applications and Strengthened Foundations of Formal Methods (Proceedings of the 4th Internatinal Symposium of Formal Methods Europe, Graz, Austria, September 1997)*, volume 1313 of Lecture Notes in Computer Science, pages 278–297. Springer, 1997.

4. S. Agerholm and J. Frost. Supporting Proof in VDM-SL using Isabelle. In J.C. Bicarregui, editor, *Proof in VDM: Case Studies*, FACIT. Springer, 1998.

5. S. Agerholm and P.G. Larsen. A Lightweight Approach to Formal Methods. In *Proceedings of the International Workshop on Current Trends in Applied Formal Methods*, Boppard, Germany, Springer, 1998.

6. M. Mac an Airchinnigh. Tutorial Lecture Notes on the Irish School of the VDM. In S. Prehn and W.J. Toetenel, editors, *VDM'91 – Formal Software Development Methods*, volume 552 of *Lecture Notes in Computer Science*, pages 141–237. Springer, October 1991.

7. D.J. Andrews, editor. *Information Technology – Programming Languages, Their Environments and System Software Interfaces: Vienna Development Method – Specification Language – Part 1: Base Language*. International Organization for Standardization, December 1996. International Standard ISO/IEC 13817-1.

8. M. Barnett, R. DeLine, B. Jacobs, M. Fähndrich, K. R. M. Leino, W. Schulte, and H. Venter. The Spec# Programming System: Challenges and Directions. In *Proceedings of the International Conference on Verified Software: Theories, Tools, Experiments*, 2005. http://vstte.ethz.ch/papers.html.

9. H. Barringer, J.H. Cheng, and C.B. Jones. A Logic Covering Undefinedness in Program Proofs. *Acta Informatica*, 21:251–269, 1984.

10. J. C. Bicarregui, J. S. Fitzgerald, P. A. Lindsay, R. Moore, and B. Ritchie. *Proof in VDM: A Practitioner's Guide*, FACIT. Springer, 1994.

11. J.C. Bicarregui, D. MacRandal, B. Matthews, and B. Ritchie. Return to the Theorem Prover's House: Application of the Learning Grid to Formal Methods. In S. Curtis and M. Green, editors, *Proceedings of the Workshop on Teaching Formal Methods: Practice and Experience*, pages 82–90, December 2003. http://cms.brookes.ac.uk/tfm2003/.

12. D. Bjørner and C. B. Jones, editors. *Formal Specification and Software Development*. Prentice-Hall International, 1982.

13. R. Bloomfield and P. Froome. The Application of Formal Methods to the Assessment of High Integrity Software. *IEEE Transactions on Software Engineering*, SE-12(9):988–993, September 1986.

14. R. Bloomfield, P. Froome, and B. Monahan. SpecBox: A Toolkit for BSI-VDM. *SafetyNet*, 5:4–7, 1989.

15. P. Chalin. Logical Foundations of Program Assertions: What do Practitioners Want? In Bernhard K. Aichernig and Bernhard Beckert, editors, *Proceedings of the 3rd International Conference on Software Engineering and Formal Methods (SEFM'05)*, pages 383–393. IEEE Computer Society Press, September 2005.

16. J.H. Cheng. *A Logic for Partial Functions*. PhD thesis, Department of Computer Science, University of Manchester, 1986. UMCS-86-7-1.

17. J.H. Cheng and C.B. Jones. On the Usability of Logics Which Handle Partial Functions. In C. Morgan and J. Woodcock, editors, *Proceedings of the Third Refinement Workshop*. Springer, 1990.

18. L. A. Dennis, G. Collins, M. Norrish, R. Boulton, K. Slind, G. Robinson, M. Gordon, and T. Melham. The PROSPER Toolkit. In *Proceedings of the 6th International Conference on Tools and Algorithms for the Construction and Analysis of Systems*, volume 1785 of *Lecture Notes in Computer Science*. Springer, 2000.

19. E.H. Dürr and N. Plat (editors). *VDM++ Language Reference Manual*. Afrodite (ESPRIT-III project number 6500), Cap Volmac, August 1995.

20. J. S. Fitzgerald. *Modularity in Model-Oriented Formal Specifications and its Interaction with Formal Reasoning*. PhD thesis, Department of Computer Science, University of Manchester, November 1991. Technical Report UMCS-91-11-2.

21. J. S. Fitzgerald and C. B. Jones. Proof in the Analysis of a Model of a Tracking System. In J.C. Bicarregui, editor, *Proof in VDM: Case Studies*, Formal Approaches to Computing and Information Technology, pages 1–29. Springer, 1998.

22. J. S. Fitzgerald and P. G. Larsen. *Modelling Systems – Practical Tools and Techniques in Software Development*. Cambridge University Press, 1998.

23. J. S. Fitzgerald, P. G. Larsen, P. Mukherjee, N. Plat, and M. Verhoef. *Validated Designs for Object-oriented Systems*. Springer, London, 2005. ISBN 1-85233-881-4.

24. J. S. Fitzgerald, P. G. Larsen, and N. Plat, editors. *Towards Next Generation Tools for VDM: Contributions to the First International Overture Workshop*, Newcastle, July 2005. Technical Report CS-TR-969, School of Computing Science, Newcastle University, June 2006.

25. J. S. Fitzgerald and R. Moore. Experiences in Developing a Proof Theory for VDM Specifications. In D. J. Andrews, J. F. Groote, and C. A. Middelburg, editors, *Proceedings of the International Workshop on Semantics of Specification Languages*. Springer, 1994.

26. W. Henhapl and C.B. Jones. The Block Concept and Some Possible Implementations, with Proofs of Equivalence. Technical Report 25.104, IBM Laboratory, Vienna, April 1970.

27. J. Hörl and B. K. Aichernig. Validating Voice Communication Requirements Using Lightweight Formal Methods. *IEEE Software*, May 2000.

28. D. Jackson and J. Wing. Lightweight Formal Methods. *IEEE Computer*, 29(4):22–23, April 1996.

29. C. B. Jones. *Software Development: A Rigorous Approach*. Prentice-Hall International, 1980.

30. C. B. Jones. *Systematic Software Development Using VDM*. Prentice-Hall International, 1986.

31. C. B. Jones. *Systematic Software Development Using VDM*, 2nd edition. Prentice-Hall International, 1990.

32. C. B. Jones. A Rigorous Approach to Formal Methods. *IEEE Computer*, 29(4):20–21, April 1996.

33. C. B. Jones. Scientific Decisions which Characterize VDM. In J.M. Wing, J.C.P. Woodcock, and J. Davies, editors, *FM'99: Formal Methods*, volume 1708 of *Lecture Notes in Computer Science*, pages 28–47. Springer, 1999.

34. C. B. Jones. Reasoning About Partial Functions in the Formal Development of Programs. *Electronic Notes in Theoretical Computer Science*, 145:3–25, January 2006.

35. C. B. Jones and P. Lucas. Proving correctness of Implementation Techniques. In E. Engeler, editor, *A Symposium on Algorithmic Languages*, volume 188 of *Lecture Notes in Computer Science*, pages 178–211. Springer, 1971.

36. C. B. Jones and C. A. Middelburg. A Typed Logic of Partial Functions Reconstructed Classically. *Acta Informatica*, 31(5):399–430, 1994.
37. C.B. Jones, K.D. Jones, P.A. Lindsay, and R. Moore, editors. *mural: A Formal Development Support System*. Springer, 1991.
38. J. R. Kiniry, P. Chalin, and C. Hurlin. Integrating Static Checking and Interactive Verification: Supporting Multiple Theories and Provers in Verification. In *Proceedings of the International Conference on Verified Software: Theories, Tools, Experiments*, 2005. http://vstte.ethz.ch/papers.html.
39. P. G. Larsen. *Towards Proof Rules for VDM-SL*. PhD thesis, Technical University of Denmark, Department of Computer Science, March 1995. ID-TR:1995-160.
40. P. G. Larsen, J. S. Fitzgerald, and T. Brookes. Applying Formal Specification in Industry. *IEEE Software*, 13(3):48–56, May 1996.
41. P. G. Larsen and B. S. Hansen. Semantics for underdetermined expressions. *Formal Aspects of Computing*, 8(1):47–66, January 1996.
42. P. G. Larsen and P. B. Lassen. An Executable Subset of Meta-IV with Loose Specification. In *VDM '91: Formal Software Development Methods*. VDM Europe, Springer, 1991.
43. P. Lucas. Two constructive realizations of the block concept and their equivalence. Technical Report 25.085, IBM Laboratory, Vienna, 1968.
44. P. Lucas. Note on strong meaning of logical operators. Technical Report 25.3.051, IBM Laboratory, Vienna, 1969.
45. P. Lucas and K. Walk. On the formal description of PL/I. *Annual Review of Automatic Programming Part 3*, 6(3), 1969.
46. Z. Manna and J. McCarthy. Properties of Programs and Partial Function Logic. In B. Meltzer and D. Michie, editors, *Machine Intelligence 5*, pages 27–37. Edinburgh University Press, 1969.
47. J. McCarthy. A Basis for a Mathematical Theory of Computation. In P. Braffort and D. Hirschberg, editors, *Computer Programming and Formal Systems*, pages 33–70. North-Holland, 1967.
48. P. Mukherjee. Computer-aided Validation of Formal Specifications. *Software Engineering Journal*, pages 133–140, July 1995.
49. The RAISE Language Group. *The RAISE Specification Language*. The BCS Practitioner Series. Prentice Hall, 1992.
50. The RAISE Language Group. *The RAISE Development Method*. The BCS Practitioner Series. Prentice Hall, 1995.
51. M. Verhoef, P. G. Larsen, and J. Hooman. Modeling and Validating Distributed Embedded Real-Time Systems with VDM++. In J. Misra and T. Nipkow, editors, *FM 2006*, volume 4085 of *Lecture Notes in Computer Science*. Springer, 2006. To appear.

VDM Indexes

Symbol Index

0-form, 466

Concept Index

Z Logic and Its Applications

Martin C. Henson[1], Moshe Deutsch[1] and Steve Reeves[2]

[1] Department of Computer Science, University of Essex, Wivenhoe Park, Colchester, Essex CO4 3SQ, UK, {hensm,mdeuts}@essex.ac.uk
[2] Department of Computer Science, University of Waikato, Private Bag 3105, Hamilton, New Zealand, stever@cs.waikato.ac.nz

Summary. We provide an introduction to the specification language Z from a logical perspective. The possibility of presenting Z in this way is a consequence of a number of joint publications on Z logic that Henson and Reeves have co-written since 1997. We provide an informal as well as a formal introduction to Z logic and show how it may be used, and extended, to investigate issues such as equational logic, the logic of preconditions, operation and data refinement, and monotonicity.

1 Introduction

This chapter describes an approach to the *logic* of the specification language Z – it is relatively unconcerned with the *semantics* of Z, except insofar as the existence of a non-trivial model is useful for establishing the consistency of the logic. The approach attempts neither to replicate nor to extend the excellent work on the standardisation of Z that led to ISO standard 13568.[1] It is, rather, complementary, seeking to explore and express the logical preliminaries of Z[2] and aiming to describe those uncontroversial properties of the major elements of the language, in particular, the language of *schemas* and its *calculus*.

The approach to Z logic taken here is based mainly on three papers [35,38, 39]; these remain the comprehensive technical resource for two separate though related approaches (we make some reference to the distinction in Sect. 3.5). Our objective in this chapter is to provide a more accessible overview of that work and to highlight some more advanced related work beyond specification,

---

[1] The Z Standard does not provide a logic. The strategic decision to exclude a logic was reported in [44]. An inconsistency [32] was discovered in the (unfinished) draft logic submitted as part of the ISO Committee Draft 1.2 of the Z standard in 1995.

[2] Although beginning from its logical first principles, we do not begin Z itself from first principles. The reader is assumed to be familiar with Z notation and concepts as described in one of the better textbooks, for example [68].

in particular in the theory of refinement, that becomes possible by virtue of the Z logic that we describe.

The present work is structured into three parts. The first is the least formal and most accessible: it explores initial considerations concerning the formalisation of vernacular[3] Z with particular reference to the novel features (those that take Z beyond higher-order logic, at least in expressivity.) concerning *schema types* and *bindings*. The second part is a more formally presented account of Z logic (the logic $\mathcal{Z}_C$) and how that logic may be extended by means of a series of conservative extensions to more comprehensive logical systems with wider coverage. The chapter is by no means encyclopaedic, and the earlier papers referred to above contain more detail and a more formal account. The final part contains the most advanced material: it looks beyond Z as a specification language and $\mathcal{Z}_C$ as a logic for reasoning about specification. It demonstrates the further utility of such a logic by showing how various theories of equality, operation and data refinement can be integrated with, and issues such as monotonicity explored within, the base logic in a smooth and systematic manner: something made possible with a logic in place. We end with some concluding remarks, our acknowledgements and relevant references to the literature.

2 Initial Considerations

We take it as self-evident that any formal specification should permit precise consequences to be obtained: the emphasis in the term *formal method* should fall on the second word and not the first. A language, even one with a semantics, is impoverished if there is no logic: it would provide no means for obtaining those consequences in a methodical, reproducible and agreed fashion. In this first part, we reintroduce the key features of specification in Z from a logical perspective. Our objective is to describe the motivation for, and introduce the basic principles of, the logic $\mathcal{Z}_C$, and to explain why this core logic is sufficient for capturing a range of Z concepts.

2.1 Z Schemas and Bindings

At the heart of Z is the *schema*. Schemas are usually used in two ways: for describing the *state space* of a system and for describing *operations* which the system may perform.

Example 1. The informal state space is a jug of water of capacity 250ml having a current volume and a current temperature. As a schema, this can be written as follows:

---

[3] By *vernacular* Z we mean Z as it has been used in practice and as it is reported in informal and semi-formal accounts in the literature.

$$\boxed{\begin{array}{l} \underline{\ Jug\ } \\ volume : \mathbb{N} \\ temp : \mathbb{N} \\ \hline volume \leq 250 \\ temp \leq 100 \end{array}}$$

Written in linear form, this would be

$$Jug =_{df} [volume : \mathbb{N};\ temp : \mathbb{N} \mid volume \leq 250 \wedge temp \leq 100]$$

This schema has the name *Jug* and introduces two *observations*, *volume* and *temp*, which have some natural number value (i.e. drawn from the set $\mathbb{N}$) in each system state.[4] The states which comprise a schema are called *bindings*; each binding belonging to a schema is a legitimate state of the system. In this example, the bindings associate values (of the correct type) with the observations named *volume* and *temp*. We use the word "observations" and *never* call them "variables". If one pursues the "schemas as sets of bindings" interpretation (which has been quite standard), then these are constants, not variables. Most informal accounts run into immediate difficulty in this area.[5] We shall write bindings like this:[6]

$$\langle\!| \ volume \Rrightarrow n, temp \Rrightarrow m \ |\!\rangle$$

where, in this case, $n, m \in \mathbb{N}$. Naturally, it *should* follow that, for example,

$$\langle\!| \ volume \Rrightarrow 100, temp \Rrightarrow 20 \ |\!\rangle \in Jug$$

and also

$$\langle\!| \ volume \Rrightarrow 100, temp \Rrightarrow 200 \ |\!\rangle \notin Jug$$

It is possible to extract the values associated with observations from bindings. This is called *binding selection*. For example, we should be able to show that

$$\langle\!| \ volume \Rrightarrow 100, temp \Rrightarrow 20 \ |\!\rangle.volume = 100$$

In order to capture these ideas, we begin by introducing the idea of a *schema type*:

$$[\cdots \mathbf{z}_i^{T_i} \cdots]$$

This is an unordered sequence of typed (indicated by superscripts) observations (the $\mathbf{z}_i$). Then *schemas* are either *schema sets*:

---

[4] Note that the schema describes a *state space*, that is, a set of legitimate system states. This is worth stressing because some informal accounts give a mixed message, sometimes suggesting that a schema describes a *particular* state.

[5] See, for example, [68]. In chapter 11, page 149 of that book, they are "variables"; by page 154 they are "components" (constants).

[6] ISO Z uses == rather than $\Rrightarrow$, a notation which dates back to [56,57].

$$[\cdots \mathbf{z}_i : C_i^{\mathbb{P}\,T_i} \cdots]$$

or *atomic schemas*:

$$[\,S \mid P\,]$$

where the C_i are sets, S is a schema and P is a predicate.

Of particular note are the *carrier sets* of the various types. These are formed by closing

$$\mathbb{N} =_{df} \{z^{\mathbb{N}} \mid true\}$$

under the Cartesian product, power type and schema type operations.[7] No ambiguity results from the overloading of the symbol $\mathbb{N}$ here: types appear only as superscripts – all other uses denote the carrier set.

We have remarked that schemas are *sets of bindings*. So the logic of schemas can be obtained from the logic of sets and bindings. In $\mathcal{Z}_C$, for sets, we have

$$\frac{P[z/t]}{t \in \{z \mid P\}} \;(\{\}^+) \qquad \frac{t \in \{z \mid P\}}{P[z/t]} \;(\{\}^-)$$

Note that $\mathcal{Z}_C$ is strongly typed, so these (typed) set comprehensions present no technical difficulties. See Sect. 3 for further details.

For bindings, $\mathcal{Z}_C$ has

$$\frac{}{(\!|\cdots \mathbf{z}_i \Rrightarrow t_i \cdots |\!).\mathbf{z}_i = t_i} \;(\Rrightarrow_0^=) \qquad \frac{}{(\!|\cdots \mathbf{z}_i \Rrightarrow t.\mathbf{z}_i \cdots |\!) = t^{[\cdots \mathbf{z}_i^{T_i} \cdots]}} \;(\Rrightarrow_1^=)$$

The first of these establishes what information may be extracted from bindings; the second confirms that these values are *all* that the binding contains.

The logical rules for schemas flow from the following $\mathcal{Z}_C$ definitions:

$$[\cdots \mathbf{z}_i : C_i \cdots] =_{df} \{x \mid \cdots \wedge x.\mathbf{z}_i \in C_i \wedge \cdots\}$$

and

$$[\,S \mid P\,] =_{df} \{z \in S \mid z.P\}$$

The *binding selection* operator, introduced in the object logic for selection from bindings (that is, $\mathcal{Z}_C$ terms such as $z.\mathrm{x}$), is generalised into a meta-language substitution over terms (that is, meta-terms such as $z.t$) and over propositions (meta-terms such as $z.P$).[8] This is essentially a straightforward structural recursive generalisation of binding selection, and appears in more detail in Sect. 3 below.

The rules for *schema sets* are then derivable in $\mathcal{Z}_C$:

$$\frac{\cdots \quad t_i \in C_i \quad \cdots}{(\!|\cdots \mathbf{z}_i \Rrightarrow t_i \cdots |\!) \in [\cdots \mathbf{z}_i : C_i \cdots]} \;(\![]^+) \qquad \frac{t \in [\cdots \mathbf{z}_i : C_i \cdots]}{t.\mathbf{z}_i \in C_i} \;(\![]^-)$$

---

[7] In fact $\mathbb{N}$ is only one possible base type. See Sect. 3 for further details.

[8] This is modelled to some extent on the more complex *object language* substitution operator *frogspawn* to be found in the faulty logic presented in [50]. A thorough analysis of frogspawn terms is presented in [35].

and, for *atomic schemas*,

$$\frac{t \in S \quad t.P}{t \in [S \mid P]} \ (S^+) \qquad \frac{t \in [S \mid P]}{t \in S} \ (S_0^-) \qquad \frac{t \in [S \mid P]}{t.P} \ (S_1^-)$$

Then, for example, writing b for $\langle\!\langle \ volume \Rrightarrow 100, temp \Rrightarrow 20 \ \rangle\!\rangle$, we have

$$\frac{\dfrac{\vdots}{100 \in \mathbb{N} \wedge 20 \in \mathbb{N}}}{\dfrac{b \in [volume : \mathbb{N}, temp : \mathbb{N}]}{b \in Jug}} \ (\langle\rangle^+) \qquad \frac{\vdots}{100 \leq 250 \wedge 20 \leq 100} \ (S^+)$$

as expected, with the trivial steps omitted.

The elimination rules allow us to determine properties of specifications. For example, taking the product of the temperature and the volume as a rudimentary measure of the thermal energy of the water, we can show that this is never bigger than 25 000:

$$\frac{\dfrac{\dfrac{\overline{b \in Jug} \ 1, (S_1^-)}{b.volume \leq 250 \wedge b.temp \leq 100}}{b.volume * b.temp \leq 25000}}{\forall b \in Jug \bullet b.volume * b.temp \leq 25000} \ 1$$

2.2 Schema Algebra and Filtered Bindings

Having now considered simple schemas, we shall move on immediately to consider an operator from the schema calculus: *schema conjunction*.

In order to provide a logical account of schema conjunction, we need to introduce a concept crucial to $\mathcal{Z}_C$: the *type restriction of a binding* (this is also called *filtering*). Roughly, the bindings we expect in the schema $S_0 \wedge S_1$ are those common to S_0 and S_1. But the story is more complicated: the *types* of S_0 and S_1 (say T_0 and T_1) need not necessarily be the same. In order for $S_0 \wedge S_1$ to be well-defined, these types must *agree on their overlap*. We shall write $T_0 \curlyvee T_1$ (in the meta-theory) for the *compatible type union* (it is not defined if they are incompatible) of T_0 and T_1. Then, more precisely, the bindings in $S_0 \wedge S_1$ will be *all* the bindings z in $T_0 \curlyvee T_1$ so that z restricted to T_0 is a member of S_0, and z restricted to T_1 is a member of S_1. Note that when the types are disjoint, this is effectively a *union* operation.

We write $z \upharpoonright T$ for the $\mathcal{Z}_C$ term called the *restriction* (or *filtering*) of the binding z to the type T. Naturally it is only well-formed when the type of z is an extension of T. For example, in $\mathcal{Z}_C$ we can prove

$$\langle\!\langle \ x \Rrightarrow 3, y \Rrightarrow 4 \ \rangle\!\rangle \upharpoonright [x^{\mathbb{N}}] = \langle\!\langle \ x \Rrightarrow 3 \ \rangle\!\rangle$$

We shall write $T_0 \preceq T_1$ in the meta-theory when T_0 is a schema subtype of T_1 in this sense. The critical $\mathcal{Z}_C$ rule which effects restricted bindings is this:

$$\frac{t^{T_0}.\mathbf{z}_i = t_i}{(t \upharpoonright T_1).\mathbf{z}_i = t_i} \ (\upharpoonright^=) \qquad T_1 \preceq T_0 \text{ and } \mathbf{z} \in \alpha T_1$$

The meta-term αT refers to the (meta-)set of observations occurring in T (the *alphabet* of T, see Sect. 3.

A natural generalisation of membership is useful, when $T_1 \preceq T_0$:

$$z^{T_0} \dot{\in} S^{\mathbb{P}\, T_1} =_{df} z \upharpoonright T_1 \in S$$

This idea can also be applied to equality:

$$t_0^{T_0} \doteq t_1^{T_1} =_{df} t_0 \upharpoonright (T_0 \curlywedge T_1) = t_1 \upharpoonright (T_0 \curlywedge T_1)$$

Here we have written $T_0 \curlywedge T_1$ for schema type intersection. The notation is most usefully employed when $T_1 \preceq T_0$ or $T_0 \preceq T_1$. More generally, we have

$$t_0^{T_0} =_T t_1^{T_1} =_{df} t_0 \upharpoonright T = t_1 \upharpoonright T$$

This notation is most usefully employed when $T \preceq T_0$ *and* $T \preceq T_1$.

With all this in place, we can define schema conjunction by translating the informal description above into a $\mathcal{Z}_C$ definition,

$$S_0^{\mathbb{P}\, T_0} \wedge S_1^{\mathbb{P}\, T_1} =_{df} \{z^{T_0 \curlyvee T_1} \mid z \upharpoonright T_0 \in S_0 \wedge z \upharpoonright T_1 \in S_1\}$$

which leads immediately to the following rules:

$$\frac{t \dot{\in} S_0 \quad t \dot{\in} S_1}{t \in S_0 \wedge S_1} \ (S_\wedge^+) \qquad \frac{t \in S_0 \wedge S_1}{t \dot{\in} S_0} \ (S_{\wedge_0}^-) \qquad \frac{t \in S_0 \wedge S_1}{t \dot{\in} S_1} \ (S_{\wedge_1}^-)$$

Example 2. Now let us move on to consider operations which change the state. Adding water to the jug is represented as:

```
┌─ AddWater ──────────────────────────────────
│ ΔJug
│ more? : [v : ℕ, t : ℕ]
├─────────────────────────────────────────────
│ volume′ = volume + more?.v
│ temp′ = (volume * temp + more?.v * more?.t) div volume′
└─────────────────────────────────────────────
```

where a primed observation, for example $volume'$, refers to a value in the state *after* the operation has been performed, while an unprimed observation refers to a value in the state *before* the operation has been performed. The declaration in this case amounts to the schema:

$$Jug \wedge Jug' \wedge [more? : [v : \mathbb{N}, t : \mathbb{N}]]$$

Given this observation, no modification of the interpretation of our definition for atomic state schemas is necessary. For example, using the rules already provided (together with other unexceptional rules of equality and propositions) we can prove:

$$b \in AddWater$$

where b is the binding

$$\langle\!| \ volume \Rrightarrow 50, temp \Rrightarrow 25, more? \Rrightarrow m, volume' \Rrightarrow 150, temp' \Rrightarrow 41 \ |\!\rangle$$

and m is the binding

$$\langle\!| \ v \Rrightarrow 100, t \Rrightarrow 50 \ |\!\rangle$$

We have

$$
\cfrac{
  \cfrac{b \stackrel{.}{\in} Jug \quad b \stackrel{.}{\in} Jug'}{b \stackrel{.}{\in} Jug \wedge Jug'}\,(S_\wedge^+)
  \qquad
  b \stackrel{.}{\in} [more? : [v : \mathbb{N}, t : \mathbb{N}]]
}{b \in Jug \wedge Jug' \wedge [more? : [v : \mathbb{N}, t : \mathbb{N}]]}\,(S_\wedge^+)
$$

where we have written P for $150 = 50 + 100 \wedge 41 = (50*25 + 100*50) \ \mathrm{div} \ 150$ and where, for example, δ is

$$
\cfrac{
  b \stackrel{.}{=} \langle\!| \ more? \Rrightarrow m \ |\!\rangle
  \qquad
  \cfrac{\cfrac{100 \in \mathbb{N} \quad 150 \in \mathbb{N}}{m \in [v : \mathbb{N}, t : \mathbb{N}]}}{\langle\!| \ more? \Rrightarrow m \ |\!\rangle \in [more? : [v : \mathbb{N}, t : \mathbb{N}]]}
}{b \stackrel{.}{\in} [more? : [v : \mathbb{N}, t : \mathbb{N}]]}
$$

Example 3. This operation simply takes the temperature of the water in the jug:

```
┌─ TakeTemp ─────────────────────────────
│ Ξ Jug
│ read! : ℕ
├────────────────────────────────────────
│ read! = temp
└────────────────────────────────────────
```

This is, as is well known, shorthand for

```
┌─ TakeTemp ─────────────────────────────
│ Δ Jug
│ read! : ℕ
├────────────────────────────────────────
│ read! = temp
│ θ Jug = θ Jug'
└────────────────────────────────────────
```

According to the definition given above, this is interpreted as the following set of bindings in $\mathcal{Z}_C$:

$$\{z \in \Delta Jug \wedge [more? : [v : \mathbb{N}, t : \mathbb{N}] \wedge [read! : \mathbb{N}]] \ | $$
$$z.(read! = temp \wedge \theta Jug = \theta Jug') \ \}$$

An explanation of θ-terms is missing from our account: in the *unprimed* case,

$$\theta S^{\mathbb{P}[\cdots z_i^{T_i}\cdots]} =_{df} \langle\!\langle \cdots z_i \Rrightarrow z_i \cdots \rangle\!\rangle$$

Thus $z^{T_0}.\theta S^{\mathbb{P}\, T_1} = z \restriction T_1$ whenever $T_1 \preceq T_0$. In the *primed* case, we have $\theta S' = \theta' S$, where

$$\theta' S^{\mathbb{P}[\cdots z_i^{T_i}\cdots]} =_{df} \langle\!\langle \cdots z_i \Rrightarrow z_i' \cdots \rangle\!\rangle$$

The second of these suggests, correctly, that in fact we have an operation (called θ') on S rather than S'. Indeed, we have not yet provided a precise explanation of the priming of schemas; θ' is, in fact, the more fundamental concept:

$$\big[\cdots x_i : T_i \cdots\big]' =_{df} \big[\cdots x_i' : T_i \cdots\big]$$

and

$$\big[\, S \mid P \,\big]' =_{df} \big[\, S' \mid \theta' S.P \,\big]$$

The special Z term θ has a history of notoriously poor and incomplete explanation. The introduction of *characteristic bindings* in [68] was a step forward. Integrating this with a comprehensive logic, adding a proper analysis of terms such as $\theta S'$, in particular the role of the rule $(\Rrightarrow_1^=)$ (see above), provides a complete description of its function and the circumstances in which it is properly typed.

2.3 Schema Algebra and Promotion

Promotion is a Z idiom which seeks to bring uniformity (and so security and likelihood of correctness) to a common situation when one is building models of systems. A similar idea is found with *mapping* (and its generalisations), as we find in functional programming languages.[9]

In addition to schema conjunction, schema existential quantification (hiding) also makes an appearance in promotion.

Further details of existential quantification appear in Sect. 3 below. For now, we note that this idea can be formalised in $\mathcal{Z_C}$ and that the rules for reasoning about such schema expressions are

$$\frac{t \in S}{t \,\dot\in\, \exists z \in T \bullet S} \ (S_\exists^+)$$

$$\frac{t \in \exists z \in T \bullet S \quad y \in S, y \,\dot=\, t \vdash P}{P} \ (S_\exists^-)$$

where y must not appear free in P, S or t or in any other assumption (we often refer to this sort of condition as "the usual" side-condition, or sum it up by saying that y must be an eigenvariable of the rule).

Let us illustrate promotion by examining the simplest of examples.

---

[9] Once again we assume familiarity with practical Z. Promotion is introduced and very well explored in, for example, [5, 68].

Example 4. Consider the following trivial operation:

```
┌─ Inc ──────────────────────────────
│ v, v' : ℕ
├─────────────────────────────────────
│ v' = v + 1
└─────────────────────────────────────
```

We wish to promote this operation, which is over the local state $\mathbb{N}$, to an operation over the global state $\mathbb{N} \times \mathbb{N}$. The global operation simply generalises the local operation by applying it to the first of the pair. The promotion schema, as usual, explains *how* the local and global state spaces are to be connected:

```
┌─ ΦPair ─────────────────────────────
│ v, v' : ℕ
│ w, w' : ℕ × ℕ
├─────────────────────────────────────
│ w.1 = v
│ w'.1 = v'
│ w'.2 = w.2
└─────────────────────────────────────
```

And the global operation is

$$PairInc \mathrel{\widehat{=}} \exists\, v, v' : \mathbb{N} \bullet Inc \wedge \Phi Pair$$

We should, for example, be able to prove that

$$\langle\!|\ w \Rrightarrow (3, 5),\ w' \Rrightarrow (4, 5)\ |\!\rangle \in PairInc$$

We shall write this binding as b_0, and the extended binding

$$\langle\!|\ v \Rrightarrow 3,\ v' \Rrightarrow 4,\ w \Rrightarrow (3, 5),\ w' \Rrightarrow (4, 5)\ |\!\rangle$$

as b_1. This is straightforward:

$$
\begin{array}{ccc}
\delta_0 & & \delta_1 \\
\vdots & & \vdots \\
\end{array}
$$

$$
\cfrac{
  \vdots \qquad
  \cfrac{
    b_0 \mathrel{\dot{=}} b_1 \qquad
    \cfrac{
      \cfrac{b_1 \mathrel{\dot{\in}} Inc \quad b_1 \mathrel{\dot{\in}} \Phi Pair}{b_1 \in Inc \wedge \Phi Pair}\ (S_\wedge^+)
    }{b_1 \mathrel{\dot{\in}} PairInc}\ (S_\exists^+)
  }{b_0 \in PairInc}
}{}
$$

Let b_2 be $\langle\!|\ x \Rrightarrow 3,\ x' \Rrightarrow 4\ |\!\rangle$, then δ_0 is

$$
\cfrac{
  \vdots \qquad
  \cfrac{
    b_1 \mathrel{\dot{=}} b_2 \qquad
    \cfrac{
      \cfrac{3 \in \mathbb{N} \quad 4 \in \mathbb{N}}{b_2 \in [v, v' : \mathbb{N}]} \quad \overline{4 = 3 + 1}
    }{b_2 \in Inc}
  }{b_1 \mathrel{\dot{\in}} Inc}
}{}
$$

and δ_1 is

$$\frac{b_1 \in [v, v' : \mathbb{N}, w, w' : \mathbb{N} \times \mathbb{N}] \quad 3 = 3 \wedge 4 = 4 \wedge 5 = 5}{b_1 \dot\in \varPhi Pair}$$

Here we omit all trivial steps, and those previously illustrated. Naturally, this proof illustrates the direct use of the basic rules for schema expressions, schemas and the base logic itself. As with all logics, it is in practice necessary to develop further derived rules to streamline derivation.

One can, of course, also reason *from* complex expressions (using the elimination rules). The following example shows that the second part of the global state is always unchanged. This trivial example is a prototype for the general policy of determining general properties that complex specifications possess.

Example 5. Consider the following property:

$$\forall\, b \in PairInc \bullet b.w.2 = b.w'.2$$

And the proof, which uses the elimination rules for existential, conjunctive and atomic schemas, is

$$\frac{b \in PairInc \;\; ^1 \quad \dfrac{y \doteq b \;\; ^2 \quad \dfrac{\dfrac{\dfrac{}{y \in Inc \wedge \varPhi Pair}\;^2}{y \dot\in \varPhi Pair} \quad \dfrac{y.w.1 = y.v \wedge t.w'.1 = y.v' \wedge y.w.2 = y.w'.2}{y.w.2 = y.w'.2}}{b.w.2 = b.w'.2}}{b.w.2 = b.w'.2}\;^{2,(S_{\exists}^{-})}}{\forall\, b \in PairInc \bullet b.w.2 = b.w'.2}\;^1$$

3 The Specification Logic $\mathcal{Z}_{\mathcal{C}}$

$\mathcal{Z}_{\mathcal{C}}$ is an extension of higher-order logic with the addition of the *schema types* that we introduced above.

3.1 The Types of $\mathcal{Z}_{\mathcal{C}}$

We begin with the language of types.

$$T ::= \varUpsilon \mid \mathbb{P}\,T \mid T \times T \mid [\cdots z^T \cdots]$$

Types of the form $\varUpsilon$ are the names of *free types* and are given by equations of the form

$$\Upsilon ::= \cdots \mid c_i \langle\!\langle \cdots \Upsilon_{ij} \cdots \rangle\!\rangle \mid \cdots$$

In order to permit recursion, any of the Υ_{ij} may be Υ. Also, $\langle\!\langle \cdots \Upsilon_{ij} \cdots \rangle\!\rangle$ may be omitted. An important example is

$$\mathbb{N} ::= zero \mid succ \langle\!\langle \mathbb{N} \rangle\!\rangle$$

This class of free types is quite simple, but has the virtues of covering many practical cases and ensuring the existence of trivial set-theoretic models. We do not permit *mutual* recursion here, but the generalisation is straightforward.[10]

Types of the form $[\cdots z_i^{T_i} \cdots]$ (the order is not important) are called *schema types*. We write $\alpha[\cdots z_i^{T_i} \cdots]$ for the alphabet set (in the meta-language) of observations $\{\cdots z_i \cdots\}$. No observation may occur more than once in such a type. The symbols $\preceq$, $\curlywedge$, $\curlyvee$ and $-$ denote the *schema subtype* relation, and the operations of *schema type intersection*, *schema type union* and *schema type subtraction*. All these relations and operations are defined only for schema types, and so any future definition which makes use of them is well defined only when the types in question are schema types. Schema type union imposes an additional constraint, since it is defined only when its schema type arguments are *compatible* (common observations agree on their type).

The last important operation on types is *priming*. First we associate with every observation z its *co-observation* z', where $z'' = z$. Then we set $[\cdots z \cdots]'$ to be $[\cdots z' \cdots]$. This is not a convention of vernacular Z but turns out to be extremely useful in Z logic, especially when combined with pattern-matching syntax in definitions.[11]

All further syntactic categories of the language of $\mathcal{Z}_{\mathcal{C}}$ must be well formed with respect to these types. Types are indicated by superscripting and omitted whenever possible.

We now move on to describe the languages of terms and propositions and their corresponding logical rules. The judgements of $\mathcal{Z}_{\mathcal{C}}$ have the form $\Gamma \vdash P$, where Γ is a set of formulae. The logic is presented as a natural deduction system in sequent form. We shall omit all data (entailment symbol, contexts, type, etc.) which remain unchanged by any rule.

3.2 The Terms of $\mathcal{Z}_{\mathcal{C}}$

First, we have variables, bindings, pairs and their projections:[12]

---

[10] For the reader interested in pursuing the technical issues concerning free types, see [3,55] for example.

[11] Much use of the idea of treating priming as an operation, rather than a diacritical, is made in Sect. 4.8 (the definition of composition), especially in connection with data refinement and the definitions of simulations.

[12] The reader may already have noticed, from the examples in Sect. 2, that we carefully distinguish between *observation meta-variables* and *variable meta-variables*.

$$t^T \quad ::= x^T \mid t^{[\cdots z^{\mathsf{T}}\cdots]}.\mathbf{z} \mid t^{T \times T_1}.1 \mid t^{T_0 \times T}.2$$
$$t^{T_0 \times T_1} ::= (t^{T_0}, t^{T_1})$$
$$t^{[\cdots z^{\mathsf{T}}\cdots]} ::= \langle\!\langle \cdots \mathbf{z} {\Rightarrow} t^T \cdots \rangle\!\rangle$$

These terms are characterised by various logical rules:

$$\frac{}{\langle\!\langle \cdots \mathbf{z}_i {\Rightarrow} t_i \cdots \rangle\!\rangle.\mathbf{z}_i = t_i} \ (\Rightarrow^{=}_{0}) \qquad \frac{}{\langle\!\langle \cdots \mathbf{z}_i {\Rightarrow} t.\mathbf{z}_i \cdots \rangle\!\rangle = t^{[\cdots z_i^{\mathsf{T}}\cdots]}} \ (\Rightarrow^{=}_{1})$$

$$\frac{}{(t_0, t_1).1 = t_0} \ (()^{=}_{0}) \qquad \frac{}{(t_0, t_1).2 = t_1} \ (()^{=}_{1}) \qquad \frac{}{(t.1, t.2) = t} \ (()^{=}_{2})$$

Second, we have the filtered (restricted) bindings:

$$t^{T_0} \ ::= t^{T_1} \upharpoonright T_0 \quad \text{where } T_0 \preceq T_1$$

As we have seen, the rule for these is

$$\frac{t^{T_0}.\mathbf{z}_i = t_i}{(t \upharpoonright T_1).\mathbf{z}_i = t_i} \ (\upharpoonright^{=}) \qquad T_1 \preceq T_0 \text{ and } \mathbf{z} \in \alpha T_1$$

Third, the values of free-type are

$$t^{\Upsilon} \ ::= c_i \cdots t^{\Upsilon_{ij}} \cdots$$

The logic of free types permits the introduction of values in the type, equality reasoning and finally, elimination (generally by induction):

$$\frac{\cdots z_{ij} \in \Upsilon_{ij} \cdots}{c_i \cdots z_{ij} \cdots \in \Upsilon} \ (\Upsilon^{+}) \qquad \frac{\cdots z_{ij} \in \Upsilon_{ij} \cdots \qquad \cdots z_{kl} \in \Upsilon_{kl} \cdots}{c_i \cdots z_{ij} \cdots \neq c_k \cdots z_{kl} \cdots} \ (\Upsilon_{\neq})$$

$$\frac{c_i \cdots z_{ij} \cdots = c_i \cdots y_{ij} \cdots}{z_{ij} = y_{ij}} \ (\Upsilon_{=})$$

$$\frac{\cdots \quad \cdots z_{ij} \in \Upsilon_{ij} \cdots, \cdots P[z/y_k] \cdots \vdash P[z/c_i \cdots z_{ij} \cdots] \quad \cdots}{z \in \Upsilon \vdash P} \ (\Upsilon^{-})$$

where the y_k are all those variables occurring in the z_{ij} with type Υ.
Finally, we have sets

$$t^{\mathbb{P} T} \ ::= \{z^T \mid P\}$$

These are governed by

In the *object language*, we do not make any distinction. The latter is quite standard in vernacular Z and the former ensures that the potential ambiguity is resolved at the level of the syntax.

$$\frac{P[z/t]}{t \in \{z \mid P\}} \;(\{\}^+) \qquad \frac{t \in \{z \mid P\}}{P[z/t]} \;(\{\}^-)$$

For clarity of presentation we shall use the meta-variable C (etc.) for sets (terms of power type), and S (etc.) for sets of schema type. The latter are, as we have seen, the *schemas*.

We employ the notation $b.P$ and $b.t$ (generalising binding selection), which is adapted from [67]. Suppose that $\{\cdots z_i \cdots\}$ is the alphabet set of t; the following equation then holds:

$$t.P = P[\cdots z_i \cdots / \cdots t.z_i \cdots]$$

3.3 The Formulae of $\mathcal{Z}_C$

The formulae of $\mathcal{Z}_C$ delineate a typed bounded predicate logic:

$$P ::= \mathit{false} \mid t^T = t^T \mid t^T \in C^{\mathbb{P}\,T} \mid \neg P \mid P \vee P \mid \exists z^T \in C^{\mathbb{P}\,T} \bullet P$$

The logic of $\mathcal{Z}_C$ is classical, so the remaining logical operations are available by definition. We also, as usual, abbreviate $\neg\,(t \in C)$ to $t \notin C$.

A crucial observation is the *unicity of types*: every term of $\mathcal{Z}_C$ has a unique type. We can make great use of this observation. It enables us to remove type decoration in most circumstances.

The logic for the propositions is then standard:

$$\frac{P_0}{P_0 \vee P_1} \;(\vee_0^+) \qquad \frac{P_1}{P_0 \vee P_1} \;(\vee_1^+) \qquad \frac{P_0 \vee P_1 \quad P_0 \vdash P_2 \quad P_1 \vdash P_2}{P_2} \;(\vee^-)$$

$$\frac{P \vdash \mathit{false}}{\neg P} \;(\neg^+) \qquad \frac{P \quad \neg P}{\mathit{false}} \;(\mathit{false}^+) \qquad \frac{\neg\neg P}{P} \;(\neg^-) \qquad \frac{\mathit{false}}{P} \;(\mathit{false}^-)$$

$$\frac{P[z/t] \quad t \in C}{\exists z \in C \bullet P} \;(\exists^+) \qquad \frac{\exists z \in C \bullet P_0 \quad y \in C, P_0[z/y] \vdash P_1}{P_1} \;(\exists^-)$$

The eigenvariable y may, as usual, occur free neither in $C, P_0 \, nor \, P_1$ nor in any other assumption.

$$\frac{}{\Gamma, P \vdash P} \;(\mathit{ass}) \qquad \frac{}{t = t} \;(\mathit{ref}) \qquad \frac{t_0 = t_1 \quad P[z/t_0]}{P[z/t_1]} \;(\mathit{sub})$$

$$\frac{t_0 \equiv t_1}{t_0 = t_1} \;(\mathit{ext})$$

where

$$t_0 \equiv t_1 =_{df} \forall z \in t_0 \bullet z \in t_1 \wedge \forall z \in t_1 \bullet z \in t_0$$

The transitivity of equality and numerous *equality congruence* rules for the various term-forming operations are all derivable in view of the rule (sub). In particular, we can prove that set equality in $\mathcal{Z}_C$ is extensional.

As an example of the rules for free types, we can give the following specialisations for $\mathbb{N}$, as defined above:

$$\frac{}{zero \in \mathbb{N}} \qquad \frac{n \in \mathbb{N}}{succ\ n \in \mathbb{N}} \qquad \frac{n \in \mathbb{N}}{zero \neq succ\ n}$$

$$\frac{succ\ n = succ\ m}{n = m} \qquad \frac{P[n/zero] \quad m \in \mathbb{N}, P[n/m] \ \vdash \ P[n/succ\ m]}{n \in \mathbb{N} \vdash P}$$

The following weakening rule is admissible and is incorporated within the system:

$$\frac{\Gamma \ \vdash \ P_1}{\Gamma, P_0 \ \vdash \ P_1} \ (wk)$$

Finally, a term of type T always belongs to the carrier set of T:

$$t^T \in T$$

3.4 Consistency

The only interesting issue is the interpretation of schema types and bindings, including binding selection and filtering.

Let B be an I-indexed family of sets over a suitable universe U.[13] We can define a *dependent function space* which is suitable for our purposes as follows:

$$\Pi_{(i \in I)}.B(i) =_{df} \{f \in I \to U \mid (\forall i \in I)(f(i) \in B(i))\}$$

We can harness this to interpret the schema types of $\mathcal{Z}_C$:

$$\left[\!\left[[\cdots \mathbf{z}_i^{T_i} \cdots] \right]\!\right] =_{df} \Pi_{(x \in I)}.B(x)$$

where $I =_{df} \{\cdots \mathbf{z}_i \cdots\}$ and $B(\mathbf{z}_i) =_{df} [\![T_i]\!]$. The observations $\mathbf{z}_i$ can be modelled in ZF in any number of ways, for example as finite ordinals. The only important point is that they must be distinguishable from one another. Then bindings, binding projection and filtered terms are defined as follows:

$$
\begin{array}{ll}
[\!\![(\!| \cdots \mathbf{z}_i \Rightarrow t_i \cdots |\!)]\!\!] & =_{df} f_0 \\
[\!\![t.\mathbf{z}]\!\!] & =_{df} [\![t]\!](\mathbf{z}) \\
[\!\![t \upharpoonright T]\!\!] & =_{df} f_1
\end{array}
$$

where $f_0 \in \left[\!\left[[\cdots \mathbf{z}_i^{T_i} \cdots] \right]\!\right]$, $f_0(\mathbf{z}_i) = [\![t_i]\!]$, $f_1 \in [\![T]\!]$ and $f_1(\mathbf{z}) = [\![t]\!](\mathbf{z})$ when $\mathbf{z} \in \alpha[D]$. Further detail is provided in [38] and (for free types) in [35].

---

[13] $F(\omega)$ is a suitable universe: see [38] for further details.

3.5 An Alternative Approach

The system we have described is a "Church-style" theory, in which the syntax formation rules are controlled by typing considerations and where terms explicitly carry their types. The unicity of types does simplify matters, permitting types to be omitted in most circumstances. The meta-language is imposed upon to carry the burden of this. Naturally, a machine implementation of the logic would need to consider these issues explicitly.

An alternative "Curry-style" approach was described in [38, 39]. In that presentation neither terms nor propositions were type-controlled. The logic, in that context, comprises two linked theories of typing and inference. This has the effect of making the logic as a whole considerably more complex, though the added explicit information might well be more convenient as a basis for a machine implementation.

In the "Curry-style" system one has additional judgements of the form $\Gamma \triangleright P \; prop$ and $\Gamma \triangleright t : T$. There are then typing rules such as

$$\frac{t_0 : T \quad t_1 : T}{t_0 = t_1 \; prop} \; (C_=) \qquad \frac{t : T \quad C : \mathbb{P}\,T}{t \in C \; prop} \; (C_\in)$$

These rules ensure that well-formed equality statements are between terms of the same type and that well-formed membership propositions are also appropriately typed.

We also have rules for non-atomic propositions such as

$$\frac{P_0 \; prop \quad P_1 \; prop}{P_0 \vee P_1 \; prop} \; (C_\vee) \qquad \frac{x : T \triangleright P \; prop}{\exists\, x : T \bullet P \; prop} \; (C_\exists)$$

With these in place, the logical rules can be stated. These typically make reference to typing judgements. For example,

$$\frac{\Gamma \vdash P_0 \quad \Gamma^- \triangleright P_1 \; prop}{\Gamma \vdash P_0 \vee P_1} \; (\vee_o^+)$$

and

$$\frac{\Gamma \vdash P[z/t] \quad \Gamma^- \triangleright t : T}{\Gamma \vdash \exists\, z : T \bullet P} \; (\exists^+)$$

In these rules, the context Γ^- represents the restriction of the context Γ to its typing assertions only.

In this version of the logic, one has the following critical result concerning *syntactic consistency*:

$$\text{If } \Gamma \vdash P \text{ then } \Gamma^- \triangleright P \; prop$$

This is proved by induction on the structure of the derivation $\Gamma \vdash P$.

4 Conservative Extensions

The base logic $\mathcal{Z}_C$ contains only rudimentary features of Z (schema types and bindings). We have, in Sect. 2, indicated in overview how $\mathcal{Z}_C$ can host more advanced features by means of conservative extensions. This approach is simple and attractive; in particular, the question of the consistency of more complex features is automatic.

4.1 Schema Sets and Atomic Schemas

Let $T = [\cdots \mathbf{z}_i^{T_i} \cdots]$. The syntax of basic schemas is

$$S^{\mathbb{P}\,T} ::= [\cdots \mathbf{z}_i : C_i^{\mathbb{P}\,T_i} \cdots] \mid [S^{\mathbb{P}\,T} \mid P]$$

These are the *schema sets* and *atomic schemas*, respectively. As usual, we shall write schemas of the form $[[\cdots \mathbf{z}_i : C_i \cdots] \mid P]$ as $[\cdots \mathbf{z}_i : C_i \cdots \mid P]$. We allow the obvious generalisation of our alphabet operator to atomic state schemas and state schema sets: $\alpha[S \mid P] =_{df} \alpha S$ and $\alpha[\cdots \mathbf{z}_i : C_i^{\mathbb{P}\,T_i} \cdots] =_{df} \alpha[\cdots \mathbf{z}_i^{T_i} \cdots]$. Then these two basic schemas can be interpreted in $\mathcal{Z}_C$ as follows:[14]

$$[\cdots \mathbf{z}_i : C_i \cdots] =_{df} \{x \mid \cdots \wedge x.\mathbf{z}_i \in C_i \wedge \cdots\}$$

and

$$[S \mid P] =_{df} \{z \in S \mid z.P\}$$

As we have already seen, the rules for *schema sets* are

$$\frac{\cdots \quad t_i \in C_i \quad \cdots}{\langle\!\langle \cdots \mathbf{z}_i \Rrightarrow t_i \cdots \rangle\!\rangle \in [\cdots \mathbf{z}_i : C_i \cdots]} \; (\lbrack\rbrack^+) \qquad \frac{t \in [\cdots \mathbf{z}_i : C_i \cdots]}{t.\mathbf{z}_i \in C_i} \; (\lbrack\rbrack^-)$$

and, for *atomic schemas*,

$$\frac{t \in S \quad t.P}{t \in [S \mid P]} \; (S^+) \qquad \frac{t \in [S \mid P]}{t \in S} \; (S_0^-) \qquad \frac{t \in [S \mid P]}{t.P} \; (S_1^-)$$

There is an important point to be made regarding the interpretation of schemas: *the proposition P appearing in a schema is drawn from a more permissive grammar of propositions than that established for $\mathcal{Z}_C$*. In particular, propositions in that context can contain *observations as terms*. A simple example will suffice to illustrate this.

---

[14] Strictly speaking, we should indicate (both here and below) the translation explicitly, writing for example

$$[\![[S \mid P]]\!] =_{df} \{z \in [\![S]\!] \mid z.P\}$$

We shall not bother with this as the intention is always quite obvious, and the use of the extra brackets is notationally very burdensome.

Example 6. Consider the following schema:

$$\boxed{\begin{array}{l} \underline{\quad Inc \quad\qquad\qquad\qquad\qquad\qquad} \\ v, v' : \mathbb{N} \\ \hline v' = v + 1 \end{array}}$$

Consultation of the syntax of $\mathcal{Z}_\mathcal{C}$ will reveal that the proposition $v' = v + 1$ is not a $\mathcal{Z}_\mathcal{C}$ proposition, because the observations v and v' are not terms of $\mathcal{Z}_\mathcal{C}$. This generality in the specification language is perfectly acceptable in view of the interpretation of schemas. Pursuing this example, the $\mathcal{Z}_\mathcal{C}$ interpretation is

$$\{z^{[v^{\mathbb{N}}, v'^{\mathbb{N}}]} \mid z.(v' = v + 1)\}$$

which simplifies to

$$\{z^{[v^{\mathbb{N}}, v'^{\mathbb{N}}]} \mid z.v' = z.v + 1\}$$

Note that $z.v' = z.v + 1$ is a bona fide proposition in $\mathcal{Z}_\mathcal{C}$. In all cases, a schema proposition P becomes $z.P$ under the interpretation and $z.P$ will always be well defined.

4.2 θ-Terms

The special Z term θ is interpreted as described in Sect. 2.2:

$$\theta S^{\mathbb{P}[\cdots z_i^{T_i} \cdots]} =_{df} \langle\!\langle \cdots z_i \Rrightarrow z_i \cdots \rangle\!\rangle$$

In the *primed* case we have $\theta S' = \theta' S$, where

$$\theta' S^{\mathbb{P}[\cdots z_i^{T_i} \cdots]} =_{df} \langle\!\langle \cdots z_i \Rrightarrow z_i' \cdots \rangle\!\rangle$$

It is also worth noting that these special terms are not in themselves $\mathcal{Z}_\mathcal{C}$ terms, but will translate under the interpretation appropriately. Another example is the following.

Example 7. Consider the following schemas:

$$\boxed{\begin{array}{l} \underline{\quad Example \quad\qquad\qquad\qquad\qquad\qquad\qquad} \\ \Delta S \\ \hline \theta S = \theta S' \end{array}}$$

where

$$\boxed{\begin{array}{l} \underline{\quad S \quad\qquad\qquad\qquad\qquad\qquad\qquad\qquad} \\ v : \mathbb{N} \end{array}}$$

Under the above interpretation, we have

$$\{z^{[v^{\mathbb{N}}, v'^{\mathbb{N}}]} \mid z.(\theta S = \theta S')\}$$

and this simplifies to

$$\{z^{[v^{\mathbb{N}}, v'^{\mathbb{N}}]} \mid z.v = z.v'\}$$

This is as expected, and the proposition $z.v = z.v'$ contains well-formed $\mathcal{Z}_C$ terms.

4.3 Schema Disjunction

When the schemas S_0 and S_1 have the types $\mathbb{P} \, T_0$ and $\mathbb{P} \, T_1$, the schema expression $S_0 \vee S_1$ has the type $\mathbb{P}(T_0 \curlyvee T_1)$. The definition of schema disjunction in $\mathcal{Z}_C$ is

$$S_0^{\mathbb{P} \, T_0} \vee S_1^{\mathbb{P} \, T_1} =_{df} \{z^{T_0 \curlyvee T_1} \mid z \in S_0 \vee z \in S_1\}$$

This leads to the following rules:

$$\frac{t \in S_0}{t \in S_0 \vee S_1} \, (S_{\vee_0}^+) \qquad \frac{t \in S_1}{t \in S_0 \vee S_1} \, (S_{\vee_1}^+)$$

$$\frac{t \in S_0 \vee S_1 \quad t \in S_0 \vdash P \quad t \in S_1 \vdash P}{P} \, (S_\vee^-)$$

4.4 Schema Conjunction

When the schemas S_0 and S_1 have the types $\mathbb{P} \, T_0$ and $\mathbb{P} \, T_1$, the schema expression $S_0 \wedge S_1$ has the type $\mathbb{P}(T_0 \curlyvee T_1)$. The definition of schema conjunction in $\mathcal{Z}_C$ is, as we have seen,

$$S_0^{\mathbb{P} \, T_0} \wedge S_1^{\mathbb{P} \, T_1} =_{df} \{z^{T_0 \curlyvee T_1} \mid z \in S_0 \wedge z \in S_1\}$$

and the rules are

$$\frac{t \in S_0 \quad t \in S_1}{t \in S_0 \wedge S_1} \, (S_\wedge^+) \qquad \frac{t \in S_0 \wedge S_1}{t \in S_0} \, (S_{\wedge_0}^-) \qquad \frac{t \in S_0 \wedge S_1}{t \in S_1} \, (S_{\wedge_1}^-)$$

4.5 Schema Negation

Schema negation is straightforward:

$$\neg S^{\mathbb{P} \, T} =_{df} \{z^T \mid z \notin S\}$$

These rules follow:

$$\frac{t \notin S}{t \in \neg S} \, (S_\neg^+) \qquad \frac{t \in \neg S}{t \notin S} \, (S_\neg^-)$$

4.6 Schema Inclusion

In addition, our notion of atomic schemas combines with schema conjunction to provide an immediate treatment of *schema inclusion* by interpreting the separation of declarations in a schema as schema conjunction. For example, the schema $[\mathbf{z} : T;\ S \mid P]$ is just $[[\mathbf{z} : T] \wedge S \mid P]$, and so on.

4.7 Schema Existential Hiding

If the schema S has the type $\mathbb{P}\, T_1$ and $[\mathbf{z}^{T_0}] \preceq T_1$, then the type of the schema expression $\exists \mathbf{z} : T_0 \bullet S$ is $\mathbb{P}(T_1 - [\mathbf{z}^{T_0}])$. Existentially quantified schemas are interpreted in $\mathcal{Z}_{\mathcal{C}}$ as follows:

$$\exists \mathbf{z} : T_0 \bullet S^{\mathbb{P}\, T_1} =_{df} \{ x \in T_1 - [\mathbf{z}^{T_0}] \mid \exists y \in T_1 \bullet y \in S \wedge x = y \upharpoonright (T_1 - [\mathbf{z}^{T_0}]) \}$$

These logical rules then follow:

$$\frac{t \in S}{t \mathrel{\dot{\in}} \exists \mathbf{z} : T \bullet S} \ (S_{\exists}^+)$$

$$\frac{t \in \exists \mathbf{z} : T \bullet S \quad y \in S, y \mathrel{\dot{=}} t \vdash P}{P} \ (S_{\exists}^-)$$

with the usual side-conditions on y.

4.8 Schema Composition

In this and the next section, we shall consider operation schemas, that is, those schemas whose type is $\mathbb{P}\, T$, where T has the form $T^{in} \curlyvee T^{out'}$, and where T^{in} contains declarations of all *before* observations and $T^{out'}$ contains declarations of all *after* observations. We shall also need to refer to T^{out}, the co-type of $T^{out'}$. We shall use the meta-variable U when we are specifically referring to operation schemas.

Note that the types T^{in} and $T^{out'}$ are always disjoint. We can therefore write the bindings belonging to U in the form $t_0 \star t_1'$, where t_0 has the type T^{in}, t_1' has the type $T^{out'}$, and the star represents *binding concatenation*, which will be defined only in circumstances in which its arguments have non-overlapping types. This operation can be raised to sets:

$$C_0 \star C_1 =_{df} \{ z_0 \star z_1 \mid z_0 \in C_0 \wedge z_1 \in C_1 \}$$

For schema composition, we present only a special case. For the general case (which is substantially more complex) and for related operations, such as schema piping, see [35]. Suppose $T_0^{out} = T_1^{in}$. Then,

$$U_0^{\mathbb{P}(T_0^{in} \curlyvee T_0^{out'})} \mathbin{\fatsemi} U_1^{\mathbb{P}(T_1^{in} \curlyvee T_1^{out'})} =_{df} \{ (z_0 \star z_1')^{T_0^{in} \curlyvee T_1^{out'}} \mid$$
$$\exists y^{T_0^{out'}} \bullet z_0 \star y' \in U_0 \wedge y \star z_1' \in U_1 \}$$

The rules are then

$$\frac{t_0 \star t_2' \in U_0 \quad t_2 \star t_1' \in U_1}{t_0 \star t_1' \in U_0 \, \S \, U_1} \ (U_\S^+)$$

$$\frac{t_0 \star t_1' \in U_0 \, \S \, U_1 \quad t_0 \star y' \in U_0, y \star t_1' \in U_1 \vdash P}{P} \ (U_\S^-)$$

The usual side-conditions apply to the eigenvariable y.

4.9 Schema Preconditions

We can introduce the idea of the *precondition* of an operation schema (essentially the domain of the partial relation that the schema denotes).
    Let $T^{in} \preceq V$. Then,

$$Pre \ U \ x^V =_{df} \exists z \in U \bullet x =_{T^{in}} z$$

This leads to the following rules:

$$\frac{t_0 \in U \quad t_0 =_{T^{in}} t_1}{Pre \ U \ t_1} \ (Pre^+) \qquad \frac{Pre \ U \ t \quad y \in U, y =_{T^{in}} t \vdash P}{P} \ (Pre^-)$$

with the usual side-conditions on y.

    For later convenience, the notion of a precondition is introduced as a predicate. In vernacular Z, the precondition is a schema (a set of bindings). This is easily recovered when necessary as $\{ z^{T^{in}} \mid Pre \ U \ z \}$.

    The reader interested in pursuing these issues in more depth, for example for more general operations such as schema-level quantification and generic schemas, should consult [35, 38, 39] which contain more detail.

4.10 Pause for Breath ...

We now move into the final, though the largest, part of this chapter: First covering applications of the logic and then investigating a range of topics which build still further on the mathematical basis. Once Z has been established as a specification logic, it becomes possible to address new issues and characteristic properties in a systematic and integrated manner. We shall begin with the equational logic of Z and the precondition logic for schema expressions. After this, we tackle the crucial topic of refinement. With all this in place, it becomes possible to investigate the monotonicity (or otherwise) of the schema calculus operators with respect to refinement.

5 Equational Logic

It is interesting to note that the fundamental relation of Z is, in fact, *equality*. So far as schemas are concerned, this is essentially equality of the *partial relations* which schemas denote.

In the absence of a logic, the informal explanation of schema operators has often been given in terms of certain equalities.

Example 8. It is the case that

$$[T_0 \mid P_0] \wedge [T_1 \mid P_1] = [T_0 \curlyvee T_1 \mid P_0 \wedge P_1]$$

Note that this equality is *not* definitional. In the context of the logic, it should be (and indeed is) derivable. This, and all other expected schema equations, are derivable in the schema logic described in Sect. 3. By way of example, consider the expected equation for negated schemas,

$$\neg[T \mid P] = [T \mid \neg P]$$

This is the proof: the result follows, by the rule (*ext*), from these two derivations:

$$
\cfrac{
  \cfrac{
    \cfrac{
      \cfrac{t \in \neg[T \mid P]}{t \notin [T \mid P]}\ (S_\neg^-)
    }{\neg(t \in T \wedge t.P)}
  }{t \notin T \vee \neg t.P}
  \qquad
  \cfrac{\cfrac{\overline{t \notin T}\ (1) \quad \overline{t^T \in T}}{false}}{t \in [T \mid \neg P]}
  \qquad
  \cfrac{\cfrac{\overline{\neg t.P}\ (1) \quad \overline{t^T \in T}}{t \in [T \mid \neg P]}\ (S^+)}{}\ (1)
}{t \in [T \mid \neg P]}
$$

and

$$
\cfrac{
  \cfrac{\cfrac{t \in [T \mid \neg P]}{\neg t.P}\ (S_1^-) \qquad \cfrac{t \in [T \mid P]}{t.P}\ (S_1^-)}{false}
}{\cfrac{t \notin [T \mid P]}{t \in \neg[T \mid P]}\ (S_\neg^+)}
$$

6 Precondition Logic

We considered the concept of schema preconditions in Sect. 4.9. That general logical account can be combined with the logic of the schema calculus to provide a logic of schema preconditions for all compound schemas.

6.1 The Precondition for Conjunction Schemas

In general, the precondition of a conjunction of operations is not the conjunction of the preconditions of the individual constituents [64]. This is a direct consequence of the underlying "postcondition only" approach that Z takes (in contrast to other notations such as B [1] and the Refinement Calculus [48]).

Let $i \in \{0,1\}$; the following elimination rule is then derivable for the precondition of conjoined schemas:

$$\frac{Pre\ (U_0 \wedge U_1)\ t}{Pre\ U_i\ t}\ (Pre_{\wedge_i}^-)$$

6.2 The Precondition for Disjunction Schemas

The analysis of the precondition of disjoined operations is more straightforward. Let $i \in \{0,1\}$; the following introduction and elimination rules for the precondition of the disjunction of schemas are then derivable:

$$\frac{Pre\ U_i\ t}{Pre\ (U_0 \vee U_1)\ t}\ (Pre_{\vee_i}^+)$$

$$\frac{Pre\ (U_0 \vee U_1)\ t \quad Pre\ U_0\ t \vdash P \quad Pre\ U_1\ t \vdash P}{P}\ (Pre_{\vee}^-)$$

With these in place, we can easily prove the full distributivity of the precondition over disjunction:

$$Pre\ (U_0 \vee U_1)\ t \Leftrightarrow Pre\ U_0\ t \vee Pre\ U_1\ t$$

6.3 The Precondition for Composition

We shall deal with instances of composition where the operation schema expression $U_0 \,_9^9\, U_1$ has the type $\mathbb{P}(T_0 \curlyvee T_1')$ and where U_0 is of type $\mathbb{P}(T_0 \curlyvee T_2')$ and U_1 is of type $\mathbb{P}(T_2 \curlyvee T_1')$. The following introduction and elimination rules for the precondition of composed operation schemas are derivable:

$$\frac{t_0 \star t_1' \in U_0 \quad Pre\ U_1\ t_1}{Pre\ (U_0 \,_9^9\, U_1)\ t_0}\ (Pre_9^+)$$

$$\frac{Pre\ (U_0 \,_9^9\, U_1)\ t_0 \quad Pre\ U_1\ y, t_0 \star y' \in U_0 \vdash P}{P}\ (Pre_9^-)$$

The usual side-conditions apply to the eigenvariable y.

The following additional rule is derivable for the precondition of a composition.

Lemma 1.

$$\frac{Pre\ (U_0 \,_9^9\, U_1)\ t_0}{Pre\ U_0\ t_0}$$

$\square$

6.4 The Precondition for the Existential Quantifier

In this case we consider the simultaneous hiding of an observation and its co-observation in an operation. Let z (and z') have the type T^z. Then we can derive the following rules:

$$\frac{Pre\ U\ t}{Pre\ (\exists\, z, z' : T^z \bullet U)\ t}\ (Pre_{\exists}^{+})$$

$$\frac{Pre\ (\exists\, z, z' : T^z \bullet U)\ t \quad Pre\ U\ y, y \doteq t \vdash P}{P}\ (Pre_{\exists}^{-})$$

Note that the usual side-conditions apply to the eigenvariable y. Further detail, including a treatment of other schema operations, can be found in [24].

7 Operation Refinement

After introducing a conservative extension of $\mathcal{Z}_C$ within which to undertake our analysis, we provide four distinct notions of refinement and then compare them. This serves to illuminate them all, particularly the notion based on what we shall call the *Woodcock completion* which is the de facto standard for Z.

7.1 The Theory $\mathcal{Z}_C^{\perp}$

The standard total correctness theory of refinement (also permitting weakening of preconditions) involves the process of relational completion (see, for example, Chapter 16 of [68]). This completion is often called the *lifted totalisation* and introduces an additional element, usually written $\perp$ (see Sect. 7.4 below). Such a value must be separated from the interpretation of Z, and this is easily achieved by introducing a simple $\mathcal{Z}_C$ theory which we call $\mathcal{Z}_C^{\perp}$. In this extended theory, we introduce new constants $\perp^T$ for every type T: types thus equipped are usually called "lifted" types. There are, additionally, a number of axioms which ensure that all the new $\perp^T$ values interact properly:

$$\overline{(\!|\ z_0 \Rightarrow \perp^{T_0} \cdots z_n \Rightarrow \perp^{T_n}\ |\!)} = \perp^{[z_0^{T_0} \cdots z_n^{T_n}]}$$

$$\overline{(\perp^{T_0}, \perp^{T_1}) = \perp^{T_0 \times T_1}}$$

$$\overline{\{z^T \mid z = \perp^T\} = \perp^{\mathbb{P}\,T}}$$

For example,

$$\perp^{[z_0^{T_0} \cdots z_n^{T_n}]}.z_i = \perp^{T_i} \qquad (0 \le i \le n)$$

These are the *only* axioms concerning these terms; hence, the term-forming constructions are *non-strict* with respect to the $\perp^T$ values.

Natural carriers for each type (sets which exclude $\perp$) are then easily defined by closing,

$$\Upsilon =_{df} \{z^{\Upsilon} \mid z \neq \perp\}$$

under the type-forming operations. These are then used to establish the ($\perp$-free) schema logic, as described in Sect. 3 above. When we are working in this more general framework, we sometimes need the following lemma.

Lemma 2.

$$\frac{\perp \in U}{false} \qquad \frac{Pre \ U \ t}{t \neq \perp}$$

$\square$

Further details, including the fact that the theory $\mathcal{Z}_{\mathcal{C}}^{\perp}$ is conservative over $\mathcal{Z}_{\mathcal{C}}$, can be found in [23].

7.2 F-Refinement

To a logician, a specification resembles a theory; so a natural question is: what are the models of the theory? A computer scientist may ask a closely related question: when is a program an implementation of the specification? We shall, in this section, consider deterministic programs and model them as (total) functions. We do this via a standard expedient of introducing a special value $\perp$, which might represent some sort of unwelcome behaviour. Such behaviour might be non-termination but it need not, and nothing we shall do with this value commits us to that interpretation. We shall pronounce $\perp$ the *abortive* value. In [68] it is referred to as *undefined*, which is, we feel, unfortunate in the context of partial relations; we shall have much more to say about this in Sect. 8.6. In order to introduce this value into the analysis, the technical development below takes place in the extended theory $\mathcal{Z}_{\mathcal{C}}^{\perp}$.

From the logical perspective, we are interested in all the models of a theory, so given a putative model g and a theory U, we would be inclined to write

$$g \models U$$

to represent the statement that g is a model of U. Within our application area in computer science, we might prefer to read this as a relation of *implementation*. To signal this interpretation, we shall in fact write this judgement as

$$g \Subset U$$

to be pronounced "g implements (is an implementation of) U".

Now, an operation schema has been modelled as a partial relation (think of each binding in the schema as being one "tuple" of the relation – it may be that not all possible bindings for the type occur and, hence, as a relation, the schema, a set of bindings, should be considered as partial), and so we need to consider how an implementation behaves outside the precondition of the schema (the domain of the underlying relation). There are degrees of freedom, but here we shall permit what we call *chaotic models*.[15] More exactly, we understand silence in the specification to be permission for an implementation to behave in any arbitrary manner, including the abortive behaviour $\perp$. In other respects, we shall expect a model (an implementation) to produce a result which is in the relation whenever it is supplied with an input inside the precondition. This leads to the following definition of the modelling (implementing) relation.

Definition 1.

$$g \in_f U =_{df} (\forall z \in T_{\perp}^{in} \bullet Pre\ U\ z \Rightarrow z \star (g\ z)' \in U) \wedge g \in T_{\perp}^{in} \to T_{\perp}^{out'}$$

We can then prove the following.

Proposition 1. *The following introduction and elimination rules are derivable:*

$$\frac{z \in T_{\perp}^{in}, Pre\ U\ z \vdash z \star (g\ z)' \in U \quad g \in T_{\perp}^{in} \to T_{\perp}^{out'}}{g \in_f U} \ (\in_f^+)$$

where z is a fresh variable, and

$$\frac{g \in_f U \quad Pre\ U\ t \quad t \in T_{\perp}^{in}}{t \star (g\ t)' \in U} \ (\in_{f_o}^-) \qquad \frac{g \in_f U}{g \in T_{\perp}^{in} \to T_{\perp}^{out'}} \ (\in_{f_1}^-)$$

$\square$

This is sufficient technical development to allow us to explore refinement: when is U_0 a refinement of U_1? A reasonable answer is: when any implementation of U_0 is also an implementation of U_1. After all, we wish to be able to replace any specification U_1 by a refinement U_0, and if all potential implementations of the latter are implementations of the former, we are quite safe. Thus we are led to the following definition.

Definition 2.

$$\widehat{U} =_{df} \{z \mid z \in_f U\}$$

We then have F-refinement ("F" for function).

Definition 3.

$$U_0 \sqsupseteq_f U_1 =_{df} \widehat{U_0} \subseteq \widehat{U_1}$$

Obvious introduction and elimination rules for F-refinement follow from this definition.

---

[15] There is an obvious alternative, based on *abortive models* or what in [28] is effectively the *partial model*. This is a large and separate topic; there is no more on this here.

7.3 S-Refinement

In this section we introduce a purely proof-theoretic characterisation of refinement, which is closely connected to refinement as introduced by Spivey in, for example, [56] and as discussed in [45, 52]. In those contexts we do not so much have an alternative notion of refinement as two sufficient conditions (essentially the premises of the introduction rule in Proposition 2 below). By adding the two elimination rules we add necessary conditions, and thus formalise an independent theory. There is also a connection with Theorem 3.1.2 of [40] (page 77), although that analysis concerns the two-predicate *designs* of UTP or Refinement Calculus (syntactic preconditions) rather than the single-predicate specifications of a language such as Z (logical preconditions).

This notion is based on two basic observations regarding the properties one expects in a refinement: first, that a refinement may involve the reduction of non-determinism, and second, that a refinement may involve the expansion of the domain of definition. Put another way, we have a refinement providing that *postconditions do not weaken* (we do not permit an increase in non-determinism in a refinement) and that *preconditions do not strengthen* (we do not permit requirements in the domain of definition to disappear in a refinement).

This notion can be captured by forcing the refinement relation to hold *exactly* when these conditions apply. S-refinement, named for Mike Spivey, is written $U_0 \sqsupseteq_s U_1$ and is given by the definition that leads directly to the following rules.

Proposition 2. *Let* z, z_0, z_1 *be fresh variables.*

$$\frac{Pre\ U_1\ z \vdash Pre\ U_0\ z \quad Pre\ U_1\ z_0, z_0 \star z_1' \in U_0 \vdash z_0 \star z_1' \in U_1}{U_0 \sqsupseteq_s U_1} \ (\sqsupseteq_s^+)$$

$$\frac{U_0 \sqsupseteq_s U_1 \quad Pre\ U_1\ t}{Pre\ U_0\ t} \ (\sqsupseteq_{s_0}^-)$$

$$\frac{U_0 \sqsupseteq_s U_1 \quad Pre\ U_1\ t_0 \quad t_0 \star t_1' \in U_0}{t_0 \star t_1' \in U_1} \ (\sqsupseteq_{s_1}^-)$$

□

This theory does not depend on, and makes no reference to, the value $\perp$. It can be formalised in the core theory $\mathcal{Z}_C$.

7.4 W•-Refinement

Our third notion of refinement is taken directly from the literature [68]. It is based on a relational completion operator due to Woodcock. For notational convenience we shall write T^* for the set $T_\perp^{in} \star T_\perp^{out'}$. The *lifted totalisation* of a set of bindings (Woodcock completion) can be defined as follows.

Definition 4.

$$\overset{\bullet}{U} =_{df} \{z_0 \star z_1' \in T^* \mid Pre\ U\ z_0 \Rightarrow z_0 \star z_1' \in U\}$$

Proposition 3. *The following introduction and elimination rules are derivable for lifted totalised sets:*

$$\frac{t_0 \star t_1' \in T^* \quad Pre\ U\ t_0 \vdash t_0 \star t_1' \in U}{t_0 \star t_1' \in \overset{\bullet}{U}} \ (\bullet^+)$$

and

$$\frac{t_0 \star t_1' \in \overset{\bullet}{U} \quad Pre\ U\ t_0}{t_0 \star t_1' \in U} \ (\bullet_\circ^-) \qquad \frac{t_0 \star t_1' \in \overset{\bullet}{U}}{t_0 \star t_1' \in T^*} \ (\bullet_1^-)$$

□

Note that it is sometimes useful to use the following version of the rule $(\bullet_\circ^-)$, which is based upon disjunction elimination, rather than implication elimination.

Proposition 4.

$$\frac{t_0 \star t_1' \in \overset{\bullet}{U} \quad \neg\ Pre\ U\ t_0 \vdash P \quad t_0 \star t_1' \in U \vdash P}{P} \ (\bullet_\circ^-)$$

□

Lemma 3. *The following are derivable:*

$$\frac{}{U \subseteq \overset{\bullet}{U}} \ (i) \qquad \frac{}{\bot \in \overset{\bullet}{U}} \ (ii) \qquad \frac{\neg Pre\ U\ t_0 \quad t_0 \in T^{in}_\bot \quad t_1' \in T^{out'}_\bot}{t_0 \star t_1' \in \overset{\bullet}{U}} \ (iii)$$

Proof (i) is trivial. For (ii), consider the following derivation:

$$\frac{\dfrac{}{\bot \in T^*} \quad \dfrac{\dfrac{Pre\ U\ \bot}{(1)} \quad \dfrac{\dfrac{\overline{y \in U}\ (2) \quad \overline{y =_{T^{in}} \bot}\ (2)}{false}}{\dfrac{\bot \in U}{\ }\ (2)}}{\bot \in U}\ (1)}{\bot \in \overset{\bullet}{U}}$$

For (iii), consider the following derivation:

$$\frac{\dfrac{t_0 \in T^{in}_\bot \quad t_1' \in T^{out'}_\bot}{t_0 \star t_1' \in T^*} \quad \dfrac{\dfrac{\neg Pre\ U\ t_0 \quad \overline{Pre\ U\ t_0}\ (1)}{false}}{t_0 \star t_1' \in U}\ (1)}{t_0 \star t_1' \in \overset{\bullet}{U}}$$

□

Lemmas 3(i), (ii) and (iii) demonstrate that Definition 4 is consistent with the intentions described in [68] chapter 16: the underlying partial relation is contained in the completion, the abortive element is present in the relation and, more generally, each value outside the precondition maps to every value in the co-domain of the relation. Furthermore, the following rules, which are derived from Lemma 3(iii), embody *non-strict* lifting with respect to the abortive element and the fact that everything outside the precondition is mapped onto the abortive value (as well as everything else in the co-domain of the relation).

Corollary 1.

$$\frac{t' \in T_\perp^{out'}}{\perp \star t' \in \overset{\bullet}{U}} \ (i) \qquad \frac{\neg \ Pre \ U \ t \quad t \in T_\perp^{in}}{t \star \perp' \in \overset{\bullet}{U}} \ (ii)$$

□

$W_\bullet$-*refinement*, written $U_0 \sqsupseteq_{w_\bullet} U_1$, and named for Jim Woodcock, is defined as follows.

Definition 5.

$$U_0 \sqsupseteq_{w_\bullet} U_1 =_{df} \overset{\bullet}{U_0} \subseteq \overset{\bullet}{U_1}$$

Obvious introduction and elimination rules follow from this.

7.5 WP-Refinement

Our final theory of refinement is based on a *weakest precondition* interpretation.[16] In order to formalise this, we begin by introducing a notion of a *postcondition* to complement the precondition we introduced earlier.

Definition 6.

$$Post \ U \ z_0 =_{df} \{z_1' \mid z_0 \star z_1' \in U\}$$

---

[16] A weakest precondition semantics for Z is provided in [14], a paper based on the semantics of Z to be found in the (then) draft Z standard [13] (now superseded by [61]). It would be very interesting to investigate the relationship between the two approaches, but that is beyond the scope of the current work. In passing we note that the authors provide an interpretation over the syntax of Z (atomic operation schema expressions), whereas we opt for one over the partial relational semantics (sets of bindings). Generality (an interpretation over *all* schema expressions) is obtained in two significantly different ways: in our approach it follows because all schema expressions denote sets of bindings through the semantics; [14], on the other hand, relies on the fact that all schema expressions may be written in the form of an atomic schema. That, in turn, relies on the standard equational logic of schemas. These considerations will become even more significant when we examine monotonicity issues in Sect. 20.

Note that this introduces a set, rather than a predicate. With this in place we can introduce the weakest precondition interpretation of an operation schema. Again, the specified postcondition (C in the definition below) is expressed as a set rather than as a predicate.

Definition 7.

$$wp\ U\ C =_{df} \{z \mid Pre\ U\ z \wedge Post\ U\ z \subseteq C\}$$

The reason why we choose to work with sets, rather than predicates, is simply that it casts the technical material in a style similar to that of the models we introduced earlier for F-refinement and $W_\bullet$-refinement, which also construct sets from the underlying partial relations.

Proposition 5. *The following introduction and elimination rules for the weakest precondition of U are derivable:*

$$\frac{Pre\ U\ t \quad z' \in Post\ U\ t \vdash z' \in C}{t \in wp\ U\ C}$$

where z is a fresh variable, and

$$\frac{t \in wp\ U\ C}{Pre\ U\ t} \qquad \frac{t_0 \in wp\ U\ C \quad t_1' \in Post\ U\ t_0}{t_1' \in C}$$

□

We can now define WP-refinement.

Definition 8.

$$U_0 \sqsupseteq_{wp} U_1 =_{df} \forall C^{\mathbb{P}\ T^{out'}} \bullet wp\ U_1\ C \subseteq wp\ U_0\ C$$

Proposition 6. *The following introduction and elimination rules for WP-refinement are derivable:*

$$\frac{z \in wp\ U_1\ C \vdash z \in wp\ U_0\ C}{U_0 \sqsupseteq_{wp} U_1} \quad (\sqsupseteq_{wp}^+)$$

where z and C are fresh variables, and

$$\frac{U_0 \sqsupseteq_{wp} U_1 \quad t \in wp\ U_1\ C}{t \in wp\ U_0\ C} \quad (\sqsupseteq_{wp}^-)$$

□

Lemma 4.

$$\frac{Pre\ U\ t}{t \in wp\ U\ (Post\ U\ t)}$$

Proof.

$$\frac{\overline{Pre\ U\ t\quad z' \in Post\ U\ t}\ (1)}{t \in wp\ U\ (Post\ U\ t)}\ (1)$$

□

The reverse direction always holds, and so we have established that $t \in wp\ U\ (Post\ U\ t)$ and $Pre\ U\ t$ are equivalent.

□

These interpretations will be familiar from accounts such as [48], although it is unusual to provide a proof-theoretic presentation in terms of introduction and elimination rules. In addition, in [48], the preconditions and postconditions of specification statements are syntactic (explicitly given), rather than logical (implicitly given) as they are in Z. Note that our interpretation does not involve the value ⊥, and could therefore be formalised in $\mathcal{Z}_C$.

7.6 Questions ...

What is the relationship between these four notions of refinement? In particular, can an exploration of that question shed any light on why the Woodcock completion has been defined in just the way it has? What, in particular, is the role of the value ⊥? Why is the lifting process non-strict with respect to the "abortive" value? We shall begin with the first of these questions.

8 Four Equivalent Theories

In this section we demonstrate that our four theories of refinement are all equivalent. In doing this we shall see clearly the critical role that the value ⊥ plays. We shall show that all judgements of refinement in one theory among the refinements sanctioned by another. Such results will always be established proof-theoretically. Specifically we shall show that the refinement relation of a theory T_0 satisfies the elimination rule (or rules) for refinement of another theory T_1. Since the elimination rules and introduction rules of a theory possess the usual symmetry property, this is sufficient to show that all T_0-refinements are also T_1-refinements.[17]

---

[17] An alternative strategy would be to show that a similar property holds for the introduction rule. In the refinement theories that we consider, there is only ever a single introduction rule, and this suggests that this might be a more efficient approach. However, there are as many premises to the introduction rule as there are distinct elimination rules, so in the end the amount of work involved is essentially the same. Moreover, by considering the elimination rules separately, we can in some cases (see for example Sects. 8.4 and 8.6) isolate particular properties and reasons underlying equivalence (or non-equivalence in other circumstances) which highlight particular issues of interest.

8.1 F-Refinement and $W_\bullet$-Refinement are Equivalent (in $\mathcal{Z}_c^\perp +$ AC)

R-Refinement

We begin this analysis by defining, by way of an intermediate stage, the set of total functions compatible with an operation schema. This forms a bridge between F-refinement and $W_\bullet$-refinement.

Definition 9.

$$\overline{U} =_{df} \{ z \in T_\perp^{in} \to T_\perp^{out'} \mid z \subseteq \overset{\bullet}{U} \}$$

Then we have:

Definition 10. *R-refinement is:*

$$U_0 \sqsupseteq_r U_1 =_{df} \overline{U_0} \subseteq \overline{U_1}$$

with the usual introduction and elimination rules. We also define

$$g \in_r U =_{df} g \in \overline{U}$$

for later use.

8.2 R-Refinement and $W_\bullet$-Refinement are Equivalent

We begin by showing that R-refinement satisfies the $W_\bullet$-refinement elimination rule.

Proposition 7. *The following rule is derivable:*

$$\frac{U_0 \sqsupseteq_r U_1 \quad t \in \overset{\bullet}{U_0}}{t \in \overset{\bullet}{U_1}}$$

Proof. The proof requires the axiom of choice (see the step labelled (AC) below).

$$\cfrac{\cfrac{t \in \overset{\bullet}{U_0}}{\exists g \in T_\perp^{in} \to T_\perp^{out'} \bullet t \in g \wedge g \subseteq \overset{\bullet}{U_0}}\ (AC) \qquad \begin{matrix} \delta \\ \vdots \\ t \in \overset{\bullet}{U_1} \end{matrix}}{t \in \overset{\bullet}{U_1}}\ (1)$$

where δ is

$$\cfrac{U_0 \sqsupseteq_r U_1 \quad \cfrac{\cfrac{y \in T_\perp^{in} \to T_\perp^{out'}}{} (1) \quad \cfrac{y \subseteq \overset{\bullet}{U_0}}{} (1)}{y \in \overline{U_0}}}{\cfrac{\cfrac{y \in \overline{U_1}}{y \subseteq \overset{\bullet}{U_1}} \qquad \cfrac{}{t \in y} (1)}{t \in \overset{\bullet}{U_1}}}$$

□

From this we have the following theorem.

Theorem 1.

$$\frac{U_0 \sqsupseteq_r U_1}{U_0 \sqsupseteq_{w_\bullet} U_1}$$

Proof. This follows immediately, by $(\sqsupseteq_{w_\bullet}^+)$, from Proposition 7.[18]

□

We now show that $W_\bullet$-refinement satisfies the R-refinement elimination rule.

Proposition 8.

$$\frac{U_0 \sqsupseteq_{w_\bullet} U_1 \quad g \in \overline{U_0}}{g \in \overline{U_1}}$$

Proof.

$$\frac{g \in \overline{U_0} \quad \dfrac{\dfrac{g \in \overline{U_0}}{g \subseteq \mathring{U}_0} \quad \overline{t \in g}}{\dfrac{U_0 \sqsupseteq_{w_\bullet} U_1 \quad t \in \mathring{U}_0}{\dfrac{t \in \mathring{U}_1}{g \subseteq \mathring{U}_1}} \ (1)}}{g \in \overline{U_1}}$$

□

Theorem 2.

$$\frac{U_0 \sqsupseteq_{w_\bullet} U_1}{U_0 \sqsupseteq_r U_1}$$

□

Theorems 1 and 2 together demonstrate that $W_\bullet$-refinement and R-refinement are equivalent.

8.3 R-Refinement and F-Refinement are Equivalent

In this case we show that the notions of *implementation* (rather than refinement) are equivalent by the same strategy involving elimination rules. We first establish that F-implementation implies R-implementation.

Proposition 9. *The following rules are derivable:*

$$\frac{g \in_f U}{g \subseteq \mathring{U}} \qquad \frac{g \in_f U}{g \in T_\perp^{in} \to T_\perp^{out'}}$$

---

[18] The proofs of such theorems are always automatic by the structural symmetry between introduction and elimination rules. We shall not give them in future.

Proof.

$$\cfrac{\cfrac{\cfrac{g \in_f U}{g \in T^{in}_\perp \to T^{out'}_\perp} \quad \cfrac{}{z_0 \star z'_1 \in g}\,(1)}{z_0 \star z'_1 \in T^*} \quad \cfrac{\delta_0 \atop \vdots}{z_0 \star z'_1 \in U}\,(2)}{\cfrac{z_0 \star z'_1 \in \overset{\bullet}{U}}{g \subseteq \overset{\bullet}{U}}\,(1)}$$

where δ_0 is

$$\cfrac{g \in_f U \quad \cfrac{Pre\ U\ z_0}{z_0 \star (g\ z_0)' \in U}\,(2) \quad \cfrac{\cfrac{Pre\ U\ z_0}{z_0 \in T^{in}_\perp}\,(2)}{z_0 \in T^{in}_\perp} \quad \cfrac{\delta_1 \atop \vdots}{z'_1 = (g\ z_0)'}}{z_0 \star z'_1 \in U}$$

and δ_1 is

$$\cfrac{\cfrac{g \in_f U}{g \in T^{in}_\perp \to T^{out'}_\perp} \quad \cfrac{}{z_0 \star z'_1 \in g}\,(1)}{z'_1 = (g\ z_0)'}$$

The second rule is immediate.

□

Theorem 3.

$$\frac{g \in_f U}{g \in_r U}$$

□

Now we show that R-implementation implies F-implementation.

Proposition 10.

$$\frac{g \in_r U \quad Pre\ U\ t \quad t \in T^{in}_\perp}{t \star (g\ t)' \in U} \qquad \frac{g \in_r U}{g \in T^{in}_\perp \to T^{out'}_\perp}$$

Proof.

$$\cfrac{\cfrac{g \in_r U}{g \subseteq \overset{\bullet}{U}} \quad \cfrac{\cfrac{g \in_r U}{g \in T^{in}_\perp \to T^{out'}_\perp} \quad t \in T^{in}_\perp}{t \star (g\ t)' \in g}}{\cfrac{t \star (g\ t)' \in \overset{\bullet}{U} \qquad Pre\ U\ t}{t \star (g\ t)' \in U}}$$

The second rule is immediate.

□

Theorem 4.

$$\frac{g \in_r U}{g \in_f U}$$

□

From Theorems 3 and 4, we see that the two notions of implementation are equivalent. Hence, so are the two notions of refinement.

8.4 $W_\bullet$-Refinement and S-Refinement are Equivalent

We begin by showing that $W_\bullet$-refinement satisfies the two S-refinement elimination rules. First, the rule for preconditions is the following.

Proposition 11. *The following rule is derivable:*

$$\frac{U_0 \sqsupseteq_{w_\bullet} U_1 \quad Pre \ U_1 \ t}{Pre \ U_0 \ t}$$

Proof. Consider the following derivation:

$$
\cfrac{U_0 \sqsupseteq_{w_\bullet} U_1 \qquad \cfrac{\cfrac{}{\neg Pre \ U_0 \ t}\ (1) \quad \cfrac{Pre \ U_1 \ t}{t \in T_\bot^{in}}}{t \star \bot' \in \overset{\bullet}{U_0}}\ (1(ii))}{\cfrac{t \star \bot' \in \overset{\bullet}{U_1}}{\cfrac{\cfrac{t \star \bot' \in U_1}{false}\ (2)}{Pre \ U_0 \ t}\ (1)} \qquad\qquad Pre \ U_1 \ t}
$$

□

Turning now to the second elimination rule in S-refinement, we have the following.

Proposition 12. *The following rule is derivable:*

$$\frac{U_0 \sqsupseteq_{w_\bullet} U_1 \quad Pre \ U_1 \ t_0 \quad t_0 \star t_1' \in U_0}{t_0 \star t_1' \in U_1}$$

Proof.

$$
\cfrac{U_0 \sqsupseteq_{w_\bullet} .\, U_1 \qquad \cfrac{t_0 \star t_1' \in U_0}{t_0 \star t_1' \in \overset{\bullet}{U_0}}\ (3(i))}{\cfrac{t_0 \star t_1' \in \overset{\bullet}{U_1} \qquad\qquad Pre \ U_1 \ t_0}{t_0 \star t_1' \in U_1}}
$$

□

Theorem 5.

$$\frac{U_0 \sqsupseteq_{w_\bullet} U_1}{U_0 \sqsupseteq_s U_1}$$

□

We now show that S-refinement satisfies the $W_\bullet$-elimination rule.

Proposition 13.

$$\frac{U_0 \sqsupseteq_s U_1 \quad t_0 \star t_1' \in \overset{\bullet}{U_0}}{t_0 \star t_1' \in \overset{\bullet}{U_1}}$$

Proof.

$$\cfrac{\cfrac{t_0 \star t'_1 \in \overset{\bullet}{U_0} \qquad \cfrac{U_0 \sqsupseteq_s U_1 \quad \overline{Pre\ U_1\ t_0}}{t_0 \star t'_1 \in T^\star}}{t_0 \star t'_1 \in T^\star} \quad \cfrac{t_0 \star t'_1 \in \overset{\bullet}{U_0} \quad \cfrac{U_0 \sqsupseteq_s U_1 \quad \cfrac{U_0 \sqsupseteq_s U_1 \quad \overline{Pre\ U_1\ t_0}^{(1)}}{Pre\ U_0\ t_0}}{t_0 \star t'_1 \in U_0}}{t_0 \star t'_1 \in U_1}^{(1)}}{t_0 \star t'_1 \in \overset{\bullet}{U_1}}$$

$\square$

Theorem 6.

$$\cfrac{U_0 \sqsupseteq_s U_1}{U_0 \sqsupseteq_{w_\bullet} U_1}$$

$\square$

Theorems 5 and 6 together establish that the theories of S-refinement and $W_\bullet$-refinement are equivalent.

8.5 WP-Refinement and S-Refinement are Equivalent

We begin by showing that WP-refinement satisfies the two S-refinement elimination rules. In these results we shall often use the fact that $t'_1 \in Post\ U\ t_0$ and $t_0 \star t'_1 \in U$ are equivalent without further comment. First we have the rule for preconditions.

Proposition 14.

$$\cfrac{U_0 \sqsupseteq_{wp} U_1 \quad Pre\ U_1\ t}{Pre\ U_0\ t}$$

Proof. Consider the following derivation:

$$\cfrac{\cfrac{U_0 \sqsupseteq_{wp} U_1 \quad \cfrac{Pre\ U_1\ t}{t \in wp\ U_1\ (Post\ U_1\ t)}^{(4)}}{t \in wp\ U_0\ (Post\ U_1\ t)}}{Pre\ U_0\ t}$$

$\square$

Now we have the second elimination rule.

Proposition 15. *The following rule is derivable:*

$$\cfrac{U_0 \sqsupseteq_{wp} U_1 \quad Pre\ U_1\ t_0 \quad t_0 \star t'_1 \in U_0}{t_0 \star t'_1 \in U_1}$$

Proof. Consider the following derivation:

$$\frac{U_0 \sqsupseteq_{wp} U_1 \quad \dfrac{Pre\ U_1\ t_0}{t_0 \in wp\ U_1\ (Post\ U_1\ t_0)}\ (4)}{\dfrac{t_0 \in wp\ U_0\ (Post\ U_1\ t_0)}{t_0 \star t_1' \in U_1} \qquad t_0 \star t_1' \in U_0}$$

$\square$

Theorem 7.

$$\frac{U_0 \sqsupseteq_{wp} U_1}{U_0 \sqsupseteq_s U_1}$$

$\square$

We now show that every S-refinement is a WP-refinement.

Proposition 16.

$$\frac{U_0 \sqsupseteq_s U_1 \quad t \in wp\ U_1\ C}{t \in wp\ U_0\ C}$$

Proof. Consider the following derivation:

$$\frac{U_0 \sqsupseteq_s U_1 \quad \dfrac{t \in wp\ U_1\ C}{Pre\ U_1\ t}}{\dfrac{Pre\ U_0\ t}{t \in wp\ U_0\ C}} \quad t \in wp\ U_1\ C \qquad \dfrac{U_0 \sqsupseteq_s U_1 \quad \dfrac{t \in wp\ U_1\ C}{Pre\ U_1\ t} \quad t \star t_0' \in U_0}{\dfrac{t \star t_0' \in U_1}{t_0' \in C}\ (1)}\ (1)$$

$\square$

Theorem 8.

$$\frac{U_0 \sqsupseteq_s U_1}{U_0 \sqsupseteq_{wp} U_1}$$

$\square$

Theorems 7 and 8 establish that WP-refinement and S-refinement are equivalent.

8.6 Review

The model of schemas introduced in $W_\bullet$-refinement totalises the schema as a set of bindings and also introduces the value $\bot$, extending the domains and co-domains accordingly. The totalisation stipulates chaotic behaviour outside the precondition and additionally for the value $\bot$. Why is it necessary to include the new values? What are the consequences of totalisation *without* lifting?

In [68], these questions are explicitly discussed.[19] By way of explanation the following particular schema

$$
\begin{array}{|l}
\hline
\;\kappa \underline{\hspace{8cm}} \\
\quad x, x' : \mathbb{N} \\
\hline
\quad x' = 0 \\
\hline
\end{array}
$$

is considered. This denotes a total constant relation in the model. The authors of [68] then illustrate carefully the fact that lifting ensures that schema composition is *strict* with respect to chaotic behaviour.[20] On the other hand, totalisation without lifting leads to non-strict recovery from chaos. First we introduce the chaotic specification.

Definition 11.

$$Chaos =_{df} [T \mid false]$$

Now we describe the *non-lifted* totalisation, by ensuring that the values are drawn only from the natural carrier set rather than the extension including the abortive value.

Definition 12.

$$\overset{\diamond}{U} =_{df} \{z \in T \mid Pre\ U\ z \Rightarrow z \in U\}$$

Proposition 17 (due to Woodcock and Davies).

$$(i)\quad \overset{\bullet}{Chaos}\ {}_{\S}\overset{\bullet}{\kappa} =_{df} \overset{\bullet}{Chaos}$$
$$(ii)\quad \overset{\diamond}{Chaos}\ {}_{\S}\overset{\diamond}{\kappa} =_{df} \kappa$$

Proof. See [68], page 238.
□

It should be noted that the second of these results is contingent on the particular choice κ: it is not true in general. But this observation notwithstanding, the interpretation of the results requires care. *Chaos* is described as representing undefinedness, or a run-time error being encountered whatever the initial value. This is odd, since, in particular, *Chaos* permits the input $\bot$ to result in a well-defined output (lifting is non-strict with respect to $\bot$). *Chaos*, as is indicated by our nomenclature, is a relation that permits a chaotic relationship between input and output. It is the relation $\{z_0 \star z_1' \in T^\star \mid z_1 =\bot\}$ that would be closer to what the authors of [68] have in mind (since they refer to $\bot$ as the undefined value).

---

[19] The authors of [68] call the value $\bot$ "undefined", which is perhaps unfortunate since this is also used with reference to values outside the domain of definition of particular schemas. We shall continue to call it the "abortive" value for the time being.

[20] Note that this is strictness with respect to chaos, not the abortive value.

W.-refinement is defined as the subset on the Woodcock completion; since *Chaos* is the whole of T^*, *every schema refines it.* In particular the identity relation refines it, and this is the identity for composition. Hence we have[21]

$$\kappa = Identity \, \overset{\circ}{,} \, \kappa \sqsupseteq Chaos \, \overset{\circ}{,} \, \kappa$$

for *any* κ, and this would appear not to be recovery from a run-time error, but a natural consequence of the general permissiveness inherent in *Chaos*, indeed, a natural consequence of the fact that the Woodcock completion is non-strict with respect to the abortive value.

Our analysis has, on the other hand, provided a very clear mathematical explanation for lifting: with non-lifted totalisation it is not possible to prove Proposition 11 (which requires explicit use of the value $\perp$). Indeed, we can do better: the following is an explicit counterexample.

Definition 13.
$$True =_{df} [T \mid true]$$

Proposition 18.
$$\overset{\diamond}{True} = \overset{\diamond}{Chaos}$$

□

It is an immediate consequence that the more permissive notion of refinement does not, for example, insist that preconditions do not strengthen.

We have, however, only begun to provide answers to the natural questions that arise. For example, although lifting appears to be necessary, why does it have to be non-strict with respect to $\perp$? Proposition 18 also raises a question: why is there a distinction between *implicit* (*Chaos*) and *explicit* (*True*) permission to behave? Note that in the Woodcock completion, $\overset{\bullet}{True} \neq \overset{\bullet}{Chaos}$.

9 The Non-lifted Totalisation

In the previous section, we noted the asymmetry between implicit and explicit chaos. Implicit chaos is more extensive; it permits abortive behaviour that explicit chaos does not allow. This asymmetry seems inevitable if one is to obtain a reasonable theory of refinement.[22] This is, as we have shown, indeed the case, unless we re-examine the nature of preconditions.

It seemed only natural to identify the notion of the precondition of a schema with the domain of definition of the underlying relation. There is, however, an alternative approach. Instead of taking a value to be in the precondition when it *is* related to at least one element of the co-domain of the

---

[21] At least when κ is, for example, total, and so when composition can be guaranteed to be monotonic.

[22] One might take S-refinement to establish *minimal* conditions.

underlying relation, we could take the condition to be that a value *is not* related to at least one element of the co-domain of the *completed* relation. This anticipates the idea that a value which is not in the domain of definition of the underlying relation will be related to *all* values in the co-domain *after* the relation is completed: it excludes from the precondition values in the underlying relation which are *already* related to all values in the co-domain.

Surprisingly, this leads to a theory which can be formalised entirely in $\mathcal{Z}_C$ (it does not require lifting at all) and which is equivalent to the theories of the previous section. In this way we show that, for operation refinement at least, *lifting* of relations is not necessary if one wishes to establish a relational completion semantics for refinement.

9.1 Preconditions Revisited

In this section we refer to the standard definition of a precondition as Pre_0 in order to contrast it clearly with a new definition.

Definition 14. *Let* $T^{in} \preceq V$.

$$Pre_1 \ U \ z^V =_{df} \exists x_0', x_1' \in T^{out'} \bullet z \restriction T^{in} \star x_0' \notin U \wedge z \restriction T^{in} \star x_1' \in U$$

There is a similarity to (but not quite an equivalence with) the *total model* described in [28] (page 45). The interpretation of specifications as predicates in that model makes use of a concept of a precondition similar to Pre_1, although this is not made explicit.

Proposition 19. *The following introduction and elimination rules are derivable for preconditions:*

$$\frac{t \star t_0' \notin U \quad t \star t_1' \in U \quad t_0' \in T^{out'}}{Pre_1 \ U \ t} \ (Pre_1^+)$$

$$\frac{Pre_1 \ U \ t \quad t \restriction T^{in} \star y_0' \notin U, t \restriction T^{in} \star y_1' \in U, y_0' \in T^{out'} \vdash P}{P} \ (Pre_1^-)$$

where y_0 *and* y_1 *are eigenvariables.*

□

The new notion of preconditions implies the old one.

Lemma 5. *The following rule is derivable:*

$$\frac{Pre_1 \ U \ t}{Pre_0 \ U \ t}$$

□

9.2 W$_\diamond$-Refinement

The *totalisation* (non-lifted) of a set of bindings can be defined as follows.

Definition 15.

$$\mathring{U} =_{df} \{z_0 \star z_1' \in T \mid Pre_1\ U\ z_0 \Rightarrow z_0 \star z_1' \in U\}$$

Proposition 20. *The following rules are derivable:*

$$\frac{t_0 \star t_1' \in T \quad Pre_1\ U\ t_0 \vdash t_0 \star t_1' \in U}{t_0 \star t_1' \in \mathring{U}}\ (\diamond^+)$$

$$\frac{t_0 \star t_1' \in \mathring{U} \quad Pre_1\ U\ t_0}{t_0 \star t_1' \in U}\ (\diamond_0^-) \qquad \frac{t_0 \star t_1' \in \mathring{U}}{t_0 \star t_1' \in T}\ (\diamond_1^-)$$

□

Notice that the values in this completion range over the natural carrier set of the type T.

Lemma 6.

$$\frac{}{U \subseteq \mathring{U}}\ (i) \qquad \frac{}{\mathring{U} \subseteq \mathring{U}}\ (ii) \qquad \frac{\neg\ Pre_0\ U\ t_0 \quad t_0 \in T^{in} \quad t_1' \in T^{out'}}{t_0 \star t_1' \in \mathring{U}}\ (iii)$$

Proof. For (ii), consider the following derivation:

$$
\cfrac{
\cfrac{
\cfrac{t_0 \star t_1' \in \mathring{U} \quad t_0 \star t_1' \notin U}{t_0 \star t_1' \in T}\ {}^{(2)}
}{t_0 \star t_1' \in T^*}
\qquad
\cfrac{
\cfrac{
\cfrac{t_0 \star t_1' \in \mathring{U} \quad Pre_1\ U\ t_0}{t_0 \star t_1' \in U}
}{false}\ {}^{(2)}
}{t_0 \star t_1' \in U}\ {}^{(1)}
}{t_0 \star t_1' \in \mathring{U}}
$$

where δ is

$$
\cfrac{
\cfrac{}{Pre_0\ U\ t_0}\ {}^{(1)}
\qquad
\cfrac{
t_0 \star t_1' \notin U\ {}^{(2)} \qquad
\cfrac{t_0 \star y' \in U \qquad \cfrac{\cfrac{t_0 \star t_1' \in \mathring{U}}{t_0 \star t_1' \in T}}{t_1' \in T^{out'}}}{Pre_1\ U\ t_0}\ {}^{(3)}
}{Pre_1\ U\ t_0}\ {}^{(3)}
}{}
$$

□

W$_\diamond$-refinement is then defined as follows.

Definition 16.

$$U_0 \sqsupseteq_{w_\diamond} U_1 =_{df} \mathring{U}_0 \subseteq \mathring{U}_1$$

Obvious introduction and elimination rules are derivable.

9.3 $W_\diamond$-Refinement and S_1-Refinement are Equivalent

As we have seen, the abortive value was critical in showing that $W_\bullet$-refinement and S-refinement are equivalent. Naturally, we need to assure ourselves that $W_\diamond$-refinement and a modified version of S-refinement are equivalent. Let S_1-refinement be S-refinement in which all instances of Pre_0 are replaced by Pre_1. We shall content ourselves with showing that $W_\diamond$-refinement satisfies the S_1-refinement elimination rule concerning preconditions. The remaining elimination rule, and indeed the other direction of the equivalence proof, is not significantly different from the proofs we provided earlier in Sect. 8.4.

Proposition 21. *The following rule is derivable:*

$$\frac{U_0 \sqsupseteq_{w_\diamond} U_1 \quad Pre_1\ U_1\ t}{Pre_1\ U_0\ t}$$

Proof. Consider the following derivation:

$$
\cfrac{Pre_1\ U_1\ t \quad \cfrac{\cfrac{\delta \atop \vdots \quad \overline{t \star y_0' \notin U_1}\ (2)}{\cfrac{t \star y_0' \in U_1}{false}} \quad \overline{t \star y_1' \in U_1}\ (2)}{\cfrac{t \star y_1' \notin U_1 \qquad\qquad false}{\cfrac{false}{Pre_1\ U_0\ t}\ (1)}\ (2)}}
$$

where δ is

$$
\cfrac{U_0 \sqsupseteq_{w_\diamond} U_1 \quad \cfrac{\cfrac{}{\neg\ Pre_1\ U_0\ t}\ (1) \quad \cfrac{Pre_1\ U_1\ t}{t \in T^{in}} \quad \overline{y_0' \in T^{out'}}\ (2)}{t \star y_0' \in \overset{\diamond}{U_0}}\ (6(iii))}{\cfrac{t \star y_0' \in \overset{\diamond}{U_1} \qquad\qquad\qquad Pre_1\ U_1\ t}{t \star y_0' \in U_1}}
$$

$\square$

9.4 $W_\diamond$-Refinement and $W_\bullet$-Refinement are Equivalent (in $\mathcal{Z_C}$)

We begin by showing that $W_\diamond$-refinement satisfies the $W_\bullet$-refinement elimination rule, for bindings that range over the natural carrier set.

Proposition 22. *Let $t_0 \star t_1'$ be a binding with the property that*

$$t_0 \star t_1' \in T$$

The following rule is then derivable:

$$\frac{U_0 \sqsupseteq_{w_\diamond} U_1 \quad t_0 \star t_1' \in \overset{\bullet}{U}_0}{t_0 \star t_1' \in \overset{\bullet}{U}_1}$$

Proof. Consider the following derivation:

$$\frac{U_0 \sqsupseteq_{w_\diamond} U_1 \quad \dfrac{t_0 \star t_1' \in T \quad \dfrac{t_0 \star t_1' \in \overset{\bullet}{U}_0 \quad \dfrac{Pre_1\ U_0\ t_0 \quad (1)}{Pre_0\ U_0\ t_0}\ (5)}{t_0 \star t_1' \in U_0}\ (1)}{t_0 \star t_1' \in \overset{\diamond}{U}_0}}{\dfrac{t_0 \star t_1' \in \overset{\diamond}{U}_1}{t_0 \star t_1' \in \overset{\bullet}{U}_1}\ (6(ii))}$$

$\square$

Theorem 9. *When* $W_\bullet$*-refinement is understood to range over the natural carriers, we have*

$$\frac{U_0 \sqsupseteq_{w_\diamond} U_1}{U_0 \sqsupseteq_{w_\bullet} U_1}$$

$\square$

Likewise, we can show that $W_\bullet$-refinement satisfies the $W_\diamond$-refinement elimination rule.

Proposition 23. *The following rule is derivable:*

$$\frac{U_0 \sqsupseteq_{w_\bullet} U_1 \quad t_0 \star t_1' \in \overset{\diamond}{U}_0}{t_0 \star t_1' \in \overset{\diamond}{U}_1}$$

Proof. Consider the following derivation:

$$\frac{\dfrac{t_0 \star t_1' \in \overset{\diamond}{U}_0}{t_0 \star t_1' \in T} \quad \dfrac{U_0 \sqsupseteq_{w_\bullet} U_1 \quad \dfrac{t_0 \star t_1' \in \overset{\diamond}{U}_0}{t_0 \star t_1' \in \overset{\bullet}{U}_0}\ (6(ii))}{t_0 \star t_1' \in \overset{\bullet}{U}_1} \quad \dfrac{Pre_1\ U_1\ t_0 \quad (1)}{Pre_0\ U_1\ t_0}\ (5)}{\dfrac{t_0 \star t_1' \in U_1}{t_0 \star t_1' \in \overset{\diamond}{U}_1}\ (1)}$$

$\square$

In this case, a term cannot satisfy the premise $t_0 \star t_1' \in \overset{\diamond}{U}_0$ without belonging to the natural carrier, so no extra condition is necessary in this direction.

Theorem 10.

$$\frac{U_0 \sqsupseteq_{w_\bullet} U_1}{U_0 \sqsupseteq_{w_\circ} U_1}$$

$\square$

For terms ranging over the natural carriers, then, the non-lifted and lifted models are equivalent. Since $W_\circ$-refinement can be formalised in $\mathcal{Z}_C$, and since the carrier sets of $\mathcal{Z}_C$ are the natural carriers of $\mathcal{Z}_C^\perp$, we may conclude that we can formalise a form of W-refinement in $\mathcal{Z}_C$ without moving to an extended theory and introducing lifting. The penalty for this is the need for a novel notion of a precondition.

10 The Strictly-Lifted Totalisation

A second question arising from our review was this: why is it necessary to permit recovery from the abortive value in completing the relation? In order to investigate this, we consider a final relational completion in which the relation is lifted and totalised, but is strict with respect to abortive behaviour: $\perp$ maps only to $\perp$.

Definition 17.

$$\overset{\ominus}{U} =_{df} \{ z_0 \star z_1' \in T^* \mid Pre\ U\ z_0 \Rightarrow z_0 \star z_1' \in U \wedge z_0 =\perp \Rightarrow z_1' =\perp' \}$$

We obtain obvious introduction and elimination rules, which in this case we shall not state explicitly. In addition, we have what are by now fairly standard properties, as follows.

Lemma 7.

$$\frac{}{U \subseteq \overset{\ominus}{U}}\ (i) \qquad \frac{}{\overset{\ominus}{U} \subseteq \overset{\bullet}{U}}\ (ii) \qquad \frac{}{\perp \in \overset{\ominus}{U}}\ (iii)$$

$$\frac{\neg\ Pre\ U\ t \quad t \in T^{in}_\perp}{t \star \perp' \in \overset{\ominus}{U}}\ (iv) \qquad \frac{\neg Pre\ U\ t_0 \quad t_0 \in T^{in} \quad t_1' \in T^{out'}_\perp}{t_0 \star t_1' \in \overset{\ominus}{U}}\ (v)$$

Notice that in (v), t_0 ranges over the natural carrier set, rather than the extended carrier.

$\square$

We now introduce $W_\ominus$-refinement.

Definition 18.

$$U_0 \sqsupseteq_{w_\ominus} U_1 =_{df} \overset{\ominus}{U_0} \subseteq \overset{\ominus}{U_1}$$

Again, we shall not state the obvious rules.

10.1 $W_\ominus$-Refinement and $W_\bullet$-Refinement are Equivalent

In the usual manner, we shall show that $W_\ominus$-refinement satisfies the elimination rule of $W_\bullet$-refinement.

Proposition 24. *The following rule is derivable:*

$$\frac{U_0 \sqsupseteq_{w_\ominus} U_1 \quad t_0 \star t_1' \in \overset{\bullet}{U_0}}{t_0 \star t_1' \in \overset{\bullet}{U_1}}$$

Proof. Consider the following derivation:

$$
\cfrac{
\cfrac{t_0 \star t_1' \in \overset{\bullet}{U_0}}{t_0 \star t_1' \in T^\star} \qquad
\cfrac{
\cfrac{\delta_0}{\vdots} \quad U_0 \sqsupseteq_{w_\ominus} U_1 \quad t_0 \star t_1' \in \overset{\ominus}{U_0}
}{t_0 \star t_1' \in \overset{\ominus}{U_1}} \quad \overline{Pre\ U_1\ t_0} \ {(1)}
}{t_0 \star t_1' \in \overset{\ominus}{U_1}} \ {(1)}
$$

where δ_0 is

$$
\cfrac{
t_0 \star t_1' \in \overset{\bullet}{U_0} \qquad
\cfrac{
\cfrac{
\cfrac{
\cfrac{\delta_1}{\vdots} \quad U_0 \sqsupseteq_{w_\ominus} U_1 \quad t_0\star \perp' \in \overset{\ominus}{U_0}
}{t_0\star \perp' \in \overset{\ominus}{U_1}} \quad \overline{Pre\ U_1\ t_0}\ {(1)}
}{\cfrac{t_0\star \perp' \in U_1}{false}\ {(2)}}
}{t_0 \star t_1' \in \overset{\ominus}{U_0}} \qquad
\cfrac{\cfrac{t_0 \star t_1' \in U_0}{t_0 \star t_1' \in \overset{\ominus}{U_0}}\ {(7(i))}}{}\ {(2)}
}{t_0 \star t_1' \in \overset{\ominus}{U_0}} \ {(2)(4)}
$$

and where δ_1 is

$$
\cfrac{
\overline{\neg\ Pre\ U_0\ t_0}\ {(2)} \qquad
\cfrac{
\cfrac{t_0 \star t_1' \in \overset{\bullet}{U_0}}{t_0 \star t_1' \in T^\star}
}{t_0 \in T_\perp^{in}}\ {(7(iv))}
}{t_0\star \perp' \in \overset{\ominus}{U_0}}
$$

Notice the use of the second version of the rule $(\bullet_0^-)$ (Proposition 4) in δ_0.
□

Theorem 11.

$$\frac{U_0 \sqsupseteq_{w_\ominus} U_1}{U_0 \sqsupseteq_{w_\bullet} U_1}$$

□

Likewise, we prove that $W_\bullet$-refinement implies $W_\ominus$-refinement by proving that $W_\bullet$-refinement satisfies the elimination rule of $W_\ominus$-refinement.

Proposition 25. *The following rule is derivable:*

$$\frac{U_0 \sqsupseteq_{w_\bullet} U_1 \quad t_0 \star t_1' \in \overset{\ominus}{U_0}}{t_0 \star t_1' \in \overset{\ominus}{U_1}}$$

Proof. Consider the following derivation:

$$
\cfrac{
\cfrac{t_0 \star t_1' \in \overset{\ominus}{U_0}}{t_0 \star t_1' \in T^\star} \quad
\cfrac{t_0 \star t_1' \in \overset{\bullet}{U_1} \quad \overline{Pre\ U_1\ t_0}}{t_0 \star t_1' \in U_1}{}^{(1)} \quad
\cfrac{t_0 \star t_1' \in \overset{\ominus}{U_0} \quad \overline{t_0 = \perp}}{t_1' = \perp'}{}^{(1)}{}^{(1)}
}{t_0 \star t_1' \in \overset{\ominus}{U_1}}
$$

with δ above $t_0 \star t_1' \in \overset{\bullet}{U_1}$

where δ is

$$
\cfrac{
U_0 \sqsupseteq_{w_\bullet} U_1 \qquad
\cfrac{t_0 \star t_1' \in \overset{\ominus}{U_0} \quad
\cfrac{U_0 \sqsupseteq_{w_\bullet} U_1 \quad \overline{Pre\ U_1\ t_0}}{Pre\ U_0\ t_0}{}^{(1)}{}^{(11)}
}{
\cfrac{t_0 \star t_1' \in U_0}{t_0 \star t_1' \in \overset{\bullet}{U_0}}{}^{(3(i))}
}
}{t_0 \star t_1' \in \overset{\bullet}{U_1}}
$$

□

Theorem 12.

$$\frac{U_0 \sqsupseteq_{w_\bullet} U_1}{U_0 \sqsupseteq_{w_\ominus} U_1}$$

□

11 Data Refinement (Forward)

The methods of data refinement in state-based systems are well established. The conditions under which a transformation is a correct refinement step can be summarised by two simulation-based refinement techniques: *forward simulation* and *backward simulation* [17]. In this section, we revise these and introduce some essential material underlying our investigation.

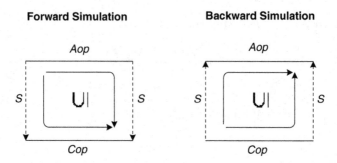

Fig. 1: Forward-simulation and backward-simulation refinement techniques. *Aop* and *Cop* represent the abstract and concrete operations, respectively, whereas S represents the simulation. Note that a forward simulation is oriented (by composition) from the abstract to the concrete data space, and a backward simulation is oriented in the opposite direction

A data simulation [68, 70] is a relation between an abstract data space and a concrete counterpart. Data simulations[23] underlie two refinement techniques which enable us to verify data refinement, as shown by the two semi-commuting diagrams in Fig. 1. Both the forward- and the backward-simulation[24] refinement techniques are known to be sound, but neither of them is singly complete. However, they are known to be *jointly complete* [69].

In what follows, U_0 will always be concrete and U_1 abstract. We adopt the approach taken in [16]: our concrete type is $\mathbb{P}(T_0 \curlyvee T_0')$ and the abstract type is $\mathbb{P}(T_1 \curlyvee T_1')$. A forward simulation (abstract to concrete) is of type $\mathbb{P}(T_1 \curlyvee T_0')$. In this way, a simulation is modelled as a set of bindings like any other operation schema.

We shall need to incorporate the value $\perp$ into a simulation used with lifted-totalised operations (see Sect. 7.1 and [23, 25]). Naturally, Woodcock's chaotic totalisation [68] is unacceptable here, as this might enforce a link between abstract and concrete states that are not supposed to be linked. The

---

[23] The notion of simulation is overloaded in the literature. Various authors use it to denote a certain refinement technique, whereas others use it to denote the *retrieve relation* used in a certain refinement technique. In this chapter we use the word "simulation" to specifically denote a retrieve relation. It will be explicitly stated when it is used in other contexts.

[24] Forward and backward simulations are also respectively known as *downward* and *upward* simulations [17, 18, 30] owing to to their directions in the commuting diagrams in Fig. 1.

conventional approach [18,68] is to (non-strictly) lift[25] $\perp$ in the input set of the simulation, thus retaining its partiality. This leads to the following definition.

Definition 19 (Non-Strictly Lifted Forward Simulation).

$$S^{\mathbb{P}(\overset{\circ}{T_1 \curlyvee T_0'})} =_{df} \{z_1 \star z_0' \in T_{1_\perp} \star T_{0_\perp}' \mid z_1 \neq \perp \Rightarrow z_1 \star z_0' \in S\}$$

The following introduction and elimination rules are then derivable.

Proposition 26.

$$\frac{t_1 \star t_0' \in T_{1_\perp} \star T_{0_\perp}' \quad t_1 \neq \perp \vdash t_1 \star t_0' \in S}{t_1 \star t_0' \in \overset{\circ}{S}} \ (\circ^+) \qquad \frac{t_1 \star t_0' \in \overset{\circ}{S} \quad t_1 \neq \perp}{t_1 \star t_0' \in S} \ (\circ_\circ^-)$$

$$\frac{t_1 \star t_0' \in \overset{\circ}{S}}{t_1 \star t_0' \in T_{1_\perp} \star T_{0_\perp}'} \ (\circ_1^-)$$

$\square$

Lemma 8. *The following additional rules are derivable for non-strictly lifted simulations:*

$$\frac{}{S \subseteq \overset{\circ}{S}} \ (i) \qquad \frac{}{\perp \in \overset{\circ}{S}} \ (ii) \qquad \frac{t' \in T_{0_\perp}'}{\perp \star t' \in \overset{\circ}{S}} \ (iii) \qquad \frac{t_1 \star \perp' \in \overset{\circ}{S}}{t_1 = \perp} \ (iv)$$

$\square$

Lemmas 8(i—iv) demonstrate that Definition 19 is consistent with the intentions described in [18, 68]: the underlying partial relation is contained in the lifting, the value $\perp$ is present in the relation and is mapped onto every after-state, and no other initial state is so. This raises an immediate question: why does the lifting of the simulation have to be non-strict with respect to $\perp$? This issue was not explored in [18,68], where the non-strict lifting of the simulation is taken as self-evident. We shall gradually provide an answer to this question in the remainder of this chapter. To do this, we shall need a definition of a strictly-lifted forward simulation.

Definition 20 (Strictly-lifted Forward Simulation).

$$S^{\mathbb{P}(\overrightarrow{T_1 \curlyvee T_0'})} =_{df} \{z_1 \star z_0' \in T_{1_\perp} \star T_{0_\perp}' \mid (z_1 \neq \perp \Rightarrow z_1 \star z_0' \in S) \wedge$$
$$(z_1 = \perp \Rightarrow z_0' = \perp')\}$$

---

[25] Lifting signifies mapping the value $\perp$ of the input set of the relation onto all the states of its output set. In general, the notion of strictness discussed here is with respect to $\perp$; therefore, strict lifting denotes mapping $\perp$ onto only its output counterpart.

Obvious introduction and elimination rules follow from this.

Lemma 9. *The following additional rules are derivable for strictly-lifted simulations:*

$$\frac{}{S \subseteq \vec{S}} \ (i) \qquad \frac{}{\vec{S} \subseteq \overset{\circ}{S}} \ (ii) \qquad \frac{}{\bot \in \vec{S}} \ (iii)$$

$$\frac{t_1 \star \bot' \in \vec{S}}{t_1 = \bot} \ (iv) \qquad \frac{t_1 \star t_0' \in \vec{S} \quad t_0' \neq \bot'}{t_1 \star t_0' \in S} \ (v)$$

$\square$

Lemmas 9(iv) and (v) embody the strictness captured by definition 20: if the after-state is $\bot$ then the initial state must also be $\bot$, and if the after-state is not $\bot$ then the initial state is not either.

12 Four (Forward) Theories

In Sect. 7 (see also [23, 25]) we investigated operation refinement (that is the degenerate case of data refinement in which simulations are identity functions) for specifications whose semantics is given by partial-relation semantics. We compared three characterisations of *operation refinement*: S-refinement, a proof-theoretic characterisation closely connected to refinement as introduced by Spivey [56]; $W_{\bullet}$-refinement, based on Woodcock's relational completion operator [68]; and $W_{\ominus}$-refinement, based on a strict relational completion operator (see Sect. 10). We proved that all these refinement theories are equivalent. The investigation also illuminated the crucial role of $\bot$ in the topic of total-correctness operation refinement.

In this section, we provide four distinct notions of data refinement, based on the notions of operation refinement described above and generalised to forward-simulation data refinement. We shall then go on to compare them, thus providing an investigation complementary to that given in Sect. 7 (see also [23, 25]).

12.1 SF-Refinement

In this section, we introduce a purely proof-theoretic characterisation of forward-simulation refinement, which is closely connected to the sufficient refinement conditions introduced by, for example, Josephs [43], King [45], Woodcock [68, p. 260] (referred to there as "F-corr") and Derrick and Boiten [18, p. 90]. These conditions correspond to the premises of our introduction rule for SF-refinement.

This generalisation of S-refinement (Sect. 7.3) is based on two properties expected in a refinement: that *postconditions do not weaken* (we do not permit an increase in non-determinism in a refinement) and that *preconditions do not strengthen* (we do not permit requirements in the domain of definition to disappear in a refinement). In this case these two properties must hold in the presence of a simulation.

This notion can be captured by forcing the refinement relation to hold *exactly* when these conditions apply. SF-refinement is written $U_0 \sqsupseteq_{sf}^{s} U_1$ (U_0 SF-refines U_1 with respect to the simulation S)[26] and is given by the following $\mathcal{Z}_C$ definition.

Definition 21.

$$U_0 \sqsupseteq_{sf}^{s} U_1 =_{df} (\forall z_0, z_1 \bullet z_1 \star z_0' \in S \wedge Pre\ U_1\ z_1 \Rightarrow Pre\ U_0\ z_0) \wedge$$
$$(\forall z_2, x_0, x_1 \bullet Pre\ U_1\ x_1 \wedge x_0 \star z_2' \in U_0 \wedge x_1 \star x_0' \in S$$
$$\Rightarrow \exists y \bullet x_1 \star y' \in U_1 \wedge y \star z_2' \in S)$$

This leads directly to the following rules.

Proposition 27. *Let x_0, x_1, z_0, z_1, z_2 be fresh variables.*

$$\frac{\begin{array}{l} z_1 \star z_0' \in S, Pre\ U_1\ z_1 \qquad\qquad\qquad \vdash Pre\ U_0\ z_0 \\ Pre\ U_1\ x_1, x_0 \star z_2' \in U_0, x_1 \star x_0' \in S \vdash x_1 \star t' \in U_1 \\ Pre\ U_1\ x_1, x_0 \star z_2' \in U_0, x_1 \star x_0' \in S \vdash t \star z_2' \in S \end{array}}{U_0 \sqsupseteq_{sf} U_1} \quad (\sqsupseteq_{sf}^{+})$$

$$\frac{U_0 \sqsupseteq_{sf} U_1 \qquad Pre\ U_1\ t_1 \qquad t_1 \star t_0' \in S}{Pre\ U_0\ t_0} \quad (\sqsupseteq_{sf_0}^{-})$$

$$\frac{\begin{array}{l} U_0 \sqsupseteq_{sf} U_1 \\ Pre\ U_1\ t_1 \\ t_0 \star t_2' \in U_0 \\ t_1 \star t_0' \in S \\ t_1 \star y' \in U_1, y \star t_2' \in S \vdash P \end{array}}{P} \quad (\sqsupseteq_{sf_1}^{-})$$

The usual side-conditions apply to the eigenvariable y.
□

This theory does not depend on, and makes no reference to, the value $\bot$; it is formalised in the theory $\mathcal{Z}_C$. We take SF-refinement as *normative*: this is our prescription for data refinement, and another theory is acceptable providing it is at least sound with respect to it.

---

[26] We shall omit the superscript S from now on, in this and other notions of refinement that depend upon a simulation, although we shall keep it in definitions in order that these will be well formed.

12.2 Relational Completion-based Refinement

We now introduce three forward-simulation refinement theories in the extended framework $\mathcal{Z}_{\mathcal{C}}^{\perp}$. These are based on the two distinct notions of lifted totalisation set out in Sects 7.4 and 10. Each of them captures, schematically, the forward-simulation commuting diagram in Fig. 1 and is based on *schema* or, more generally, *relational composition* (see Sect. 4.8).

WF$_\bullet$-Refinement

This notion of refinement is also discussed in [68, p. 246] and [17]. It is written $U_0 \stackrel{s}{\sqsupseteq}_{wf_\bullet} U_1$ and is defined as follows.

Definition 22.
$$U_0 \stackrel{s}{\sqsupseteq}_{wf_\bullet} U_1 =_{df} \stackrel{\circ}{S} \,\mathbin{\raisebox{0.3ex}{\scriptsize 9}}\, \stackrel{\bullet}{U_0} \subseteq \stackrel{\bullet}{U_1} \,\mathbin{\raisebox{0.3ex}{\scriptsize 9}}\, \stackrel{\circ}{S}$$

The following introduction and elimination rules are then immediately derivable for WF$_\bullet$-refinement.

Proposition 28. *Let* z_0, z_1 *be fresh.*

$$\frac{z_1 \star z_0' \in \stackrel{\circ}{S} \,\mathbin{\raisebox{0.3ex}{\scriptsize 9}}\, \stackrel{\bullet}{U_0} \vdash z_1 \star z_0' \in \stackrel{\bullet}{U_1} \,\mathbin{\raisebox{0.3ex}{\scriptsize 9}}\, \stackrel{\circ}{S}}{U_0 \stackrel{}{\sqsupseteq}_{wf_\bullet} U_1} \; (\sqsupseteq^+_{wf_\bullet})$$

$$\frac{U_0 \sqsupseteq_{wf_\bullet} U_1 \quad t_1 \star t_0' \in \stackrel{\circ}{S} \,\mathbin{\raisebox{0.3ex}{\scriptsize 9}}\, \stackrel{\bullet}{U_0}}{t_1 \star t_0' \in \stackrel{\bullet}{U_1} \,\mathbin{\raisebox{0.3ex}{\scriptsize 9}}\, \stackrel{\circ}{S}} \; (\sqsupseteq^-_{wf_\bullet})$$

$\square$

WF$_\phi$-Refinement

The natural generalisation of W$_\ominus$-refinement (see Sect. 10 and [23]), at least in the light of the standard literature, is to use strictly-lifted totalised operations, yet a non-strictly lifted simulation. We name this WF$_\phi$-refinement; it is defined as follows.

Definition 23.
$$U_0 \stackrel{s}{\sqsupseteq}_{wf_\phi} U_1 =_{df} \stackrel{\circ}{S} \,\mathbin{\raisebox{0.3ex}{\scriptsize 9}}\, \stackrel{\ominus}{U_0} \subseteq \stackrel{\ominus}{U_1} \,\mathbin{\raisebox{0.3ex}{\scriptsize 9}}\, \stackrel{\circ}{S}$$

Obvious introduction and elimination rules follow from this.

WF$_\ominus$-Refinement

Our third characterisation of refinement is motivated by the query raised in Sect. 11. Establishing a refinement theory in which both the operations and the simulation are strictly lifted provides a point of reference which will aid us in investigating two important matters: first, whether the strict and non-strict relational completion operators are still interchangeable underlying generalisations of data refinement; and second, whether the non-strict lifting of the simulation is an essential property. We name this theory WF$_\ominus$-refinement; it is defined as follows.

Definition 24.

$$U_0 \sqsupseteq^s_{wf_\ominus} U_1 =_{df} \overrightarrow{S} \,\overset{\ominus}{;}\, \overset{\ominus}{U_0} \subseteq \overset{\ominus}{U_1} \,\overset{\ominus}{;}\, \overrightarrow{S}$$

Obvious introduction and elimination rules follow from this definition.

13 Three Equivalent Theories

In this section, we demonstrate that three of the refinement theories are equivalent, whereas the fourth theory, WF$_\ominus$-refinement, is sound (but not complete) with respect to the others. We shall clearly see the critical role that the value $\perp$ plays in model-theoretic refinement, in general, and the consequences of strict lifting, in particular.

13.1 WF$_\bullet$-Refinement and SF-Refinement are Equivalent

We begin by showing that WF$_\bullet$-refinement implies SF-refinement by proving that WF$_\bullet$-refinement satisfies both of the SF-refinement elimination rules. First, we consider the rule for preconditions.

Proposition 29. *The following rule is derivable:*

$$\frac{U_0 \sqsupseteq_{wf_\bullet} U_1 \quad Pre\ U_1\ t_1 \quad t_1 \star t_0' \in S}{Pre\ U_0\ t_0}$$

Proof.

$$\frac{\begin{array}{c} \delta \\ \vdots \\ t_1\star \perp' \in \overset{\bullet}{U_1} \,\overset{\circ}{;}\, \overset{\circ}{S} \end{array} \quad \dfrac{\dfrac{\dfrac{}{t_1 \star y' \in \overset{\bullet}{U_1}}\ {\scriptstyle (2)} \quad \dfrac{\dfrac{}{y \star \perp' \in \overset{\circ}{S}}\ {\scriptstyle (2)}}{y = \perp}\ {\scriptstyle (L.\ 8(iv))}}{t_1\star \perp' \in \overset{\bullet}{U_1}} \quad \dfrac{\dfrac{}{t_1\star \perp' \in U_1}\ \quad Pre\ U_1\ t_1}{false}\ {\scriptstyle (L.\ 2)}}{\begin{array}{c} t_1\star \perp' \in U_1 \\ \hline false \end{array}\ {\scriptstyle (2)}}}{\dfrac{false}{Pre\ U_0\ t_0}\ {\scriptstyle (1)}}$$

where δ is

$$
\cfrac{U_0 \sqsupseteq_{wf_\bullet} U_1 \qquad \cfrac{\cfrac{t_1 \star t_0' \in S}{t_1 \star t_0' \in \overset{\circ}{S}}\ (L.\,8(i)) \qquad \cfrac{\overline{\neg Pre\ U_0\ t_0}\ (1) \qquad \cfrac{t_1 \star t_0' \in S \quad \cfrac{t_0 \in T_0}{t_0 \in T_{0_\perp}}}{t_0 \star \perp' \in \overset{\bullet}{U_0}}\ (C.\,1(ii))}{t_1 \star \perp' \in \overset{\circ}{S} \, \overset{\circ}{\,{}_9\,} \overset{\bullet}{U_0}}}{t_1 \star \perp' \in \overset{\bullet}{U_1} \, {}_9 \overset{\circ}{S}}
$$

□

Notice the explicit use of $\perp$ in the proof. This is reminiscent of our earlier investigation of operation refinement, in which the explicit use of $\perp$ is critical for proving that $W_\bullet$-refinement satisfies the precondition elimination rule for S-refinement (proposition 11). Much the same observation can be made here, the only difference being that the use of Lemmas 3(iii) *and* 8(iv) in the proof suggests that *both* the lifted totalisation of the operations and the lifting of the simulation are essential for showing that $WF_\bullet$-refinement guarantees that preconditions do not strengthen in the presence of the simulation. Turning now to the second elimination rule in SF-refinement, we have the following.

Proposition 30. *The following rule is derivable:*

$$
\cfrac{U_0 \sqsupseteq_{wf_\bullet} U_1 \quad Pre\ U_1\ t_1 \quad t_0 \star t_2' \in U_0 \quad t_1 \star t_0' \in S \quad t_1 \star y' \in U_1, y \star t_2' \in S \vdash P}{P}
$$

where the usual conditions apply to the eigenvariable y.

Proof.

$$
\cfrac{\cfrac{U_0 \sqsupseteq_{wf_\bullet} U_1 \qquad \cfrac{\cfrac{t_1 \star t_0' \in S}{t_1 \star t_0' \in \overset{\circ}{S}}\ (L.\,8(i)) \qquad \cfrac{t_0 \star t_2' \in U_0}{t_0 \star t_2' \in \overset{\bullet}{U_0}}\ (L.\,3(i))}{t_1 \star t_2' \in \overset{\circ}{S} \, {}_9 \overset{\bullet}{U_0}}}{t_1 \star t_2' \in \overset{\bullet}{U_1} \, {}_9 \overset{\circ}{S}} \qquad \cfrac{\delta}{\vdots \atop P}}{P}\ (1)
$$

where δ is

$$
\cfrac{\cfrac{\cfrac{}{t_1 \star y' \in \overset{\bullet}{U_1}}\ (1) \qquad Pre\ U_1\ t_1}{t_1 \star y' \in U_1} \qquad \cfrac{\cfrac{}{y \star t_2' \in \overset{\circ}{S}}\ (1)}{y \star t_2' \in S} \qquad \cfrac{\cfrac{}{t_1 \star y' \in \overset{\bullet}{U_1}}\ (1) \qquad Pre\ U_1\ t_1}{\cfrac{t_1 \star y' \in U_1}{y \neq \perp}\ (L.\,2)}}{\cfrac{t_1 \star y' \in U_1 \wedge y \star t_2' \in S}{\vdots \atop \dot{P}}}
$$

□

Theorem 13.

$$U_0 \sqsupseteq_{wf_\bullet} U_1 \Rightarrow U_0 \sqsupseteq_{sf} U_1$$

Proof. This follows immediately, by $(\sqsupseteq_{sf}^+)$, from Propositions 29 and 30.
□

We now show that SF-refinement satisfies the WF$_\bullet$-elimination rule.

Proposition 31. *The following rule is derivable:*

$$\frac{U_0 \sqsupseteq_{sf} U_1 \quad t_1 \star t_0' \in \overset{\circ}{S} \, \overset{\circ}{\mathbin{\text{\textbf{?}}}} \, \overset{\bullet}{U_0}}{t_1 \star t_0' \in \overset{\bullet}{U_1} \, \overset{\circ}{\mathbin{\text{\textbf{?}}}} \, \overset{\circ}{S}}$$

Proof.

$$
\begin{array}{c}
\delta_0, \delta_1 \\
\vdots
\end{array}
$$

$$
\cfrac{t_1 \star t_0' \in \overset{\circ}{S} \, \mathbin{\text{\textbf{?}}} \, \overset{\bullet}{U_0} \qquad \cfrac{\cfrac{\rule{0pt}{1em}}{Pre\ U_1\ t_1 \vee \neg\ Pre\ U_1\ t_1}\ (LEM) \qquad t_1 \star t_0' \in \overset{\bullet}{U_1} \, \mathbin{\text{\textbf{?}}} \, \overset{\circ}{S}}{t_1 \star t_0' \in \overset{\bullet}{U_1} \, \mathbin{\text{\textbf{?}}} \, \overset{\circ}{S}}\ (2)}{t_1 \star t_0' \in \overset{\bullet}{U_1} \, \mathbin{\text{\textbf{?}}} \, \overset{\circ}{S}}\ (1)
$$

where δ_0 is

$$
\cfrac{U_0 \sqsupseteq_{sf} U_1 \quad \cfrac{\rule{0pt}{1em}}{Pre\ U_1\ t_1}\ (2) \qquad
\begin{array}{c}\beta_0 \\ \vdots \\ y \star t_0' \in U_0\end{array} \qquad
\cfrac{\cfrac{\rule{0pt}{1em}}{t_1 \star y' \in \overset{\circ}{S}}\ (1) \qquad \cfrac{Pre\ U_1\ t_1}{t_1 \neq \bot}\ (2)}{t_1 \star y' \in S} \qquad \begin{array}{c}\beta_1 \\ \vdots\end{array}}{t_1 \star t_0' \in \overset{\bullet}{U_1} \, \mathbin{\text{\textbf{?}}} \, \overset{\circ}{S}}\ (3)
$$

Here, β_0 stands for the following branch:

$$
\cfrac{\cfrac{\rule{0pt}{1em}}{y \star t_0' \in \overset{\bullet}{U_0}}\ (1) \qquad \cfrac{U_0 \sqsupseteq_{sf} U_1 \quad \cfrac{\rule{0pt}{1em}}{Pre\ U_1\ t_1}\ (2) \qquad \cfrac{\cfrac{\rule{0pt}{1em}}{t_1 \star y' \in \overset{\circ}{S}}\ (1) \quad \cfrac{Pre\ U_1\ t_1}{t_1 \neq \bot}\ (2)}{t_1 \star y' \in S}\ (L.\ 2)}{Pre\ U_0\ y}}{y \star t_0' \in U_0}
$$

β_1 is

$$
\cfrac{\cfrac{\cfrac{\rule{0pt}{1em}}{t_1 \star w' \in U_1}\ (3)}{t_1 \star w' \in \overset{\bullet}{U_1}}\ (L.\ 3(i)) \qquad \cfrac{\cfrac{\rule{0pt}{1em}}{w \star t_0' \in S}\ (3)}{w \star t_0' \in \overset{\circ}{S}}\ (L.\ 8(i))}{t_1 \star t_0' \in \overset{\bullet}{U_1} \, \mathbin{\text{\textbf{?}}} \, \overset{\circ}{S}}
$$

and δ_1 is

$$\cfrac{\cfrac{\neg\, Pre\ U_1\ t_1}{t_1\star \perp' \in \overset{\bullet}{U_1}}\ (2) \qquad \cfrac{\cfrac{\dfrac{\overline{\qquad\qquad}\ (1)}{t_1 \star y' \in \overset{\circ}{S}}}{\dfrac{t_1 \star y' \in T_{1_\perp} \star T'_{0_\perp}}{t_1 \in T_{1_\perp}}}\ (C.\,1(ii)) \qquad \cfrac{\dfrac{\overline{\qquad\qquad}\ (1)}{\dfrac{y \star t'_0 \in \overset{\bullet}{U_0}}{\dfrac{y \star t'_0 \in T_{0_\perp} \star T'_{0_\perp}}{t'_0 \in T'_{0_\perp}}}}}{\perp \star t'_0 \in \overset{\circ}{S}}\ \spadesuit\,(L.\,8(iii))}{t_1 \star t'_0 \in \overset{\bullet}{U_1}\ {}_9^{\circ}\ \overset{\circ}{S}}$$

$\square$

Notice that this proof depends on the use of the *law of the excluded middle* (see, for example, [60]). We suspect that this result is strictly classical, and there appear to be many other examples of this in refinement theory; so abandoning the *constructive approach* that was taken in [36] may be inevitable.

Theorem 14.

$$U_0 \sqsupseteq_{sf} U_1 \Rightarrow U_0 \sqsupseteq_{wf_\bullet} U_1$$

$\square$

Theorems 13 and 14 together establish that the theories of SF-refinement and WF$_\bullet$-refinement are equivalent.

13.2 WF$_\phi$-Refinement and SF-Refinement are Equivalent

We now show that WF$_\phi$-refinement and SF-refinement are equivalent. Proving that WF$_\phi$-refinement satisfies both of the SF-elimination rules leads to proofs identical to those of Propositions 29 and 30, modulo substitution of $\sqsupseteq_{wf_\phi}$ for $\sqsupseteq_{wf_\bullet}$, $\overset{\ominus}{U}$ for $\overset{\bullet}{U}$, applications of $(\ominus_0^-)$ for $(\bullet_0^-)$, and Lemmas 7(iv) and 7(i) in place of Lemmas 1(ii) and 3(i), respectively. Likewise, proving that SF-refinement satisfies the WF$_\phi$-elimination rule is very similar to the proof of Proposition 31. In this case, we require the same general substitutions as above, in addition to applications of $(\ominus_1^-)$ for $(\bullet_1^-)$. From this we immediately obtain implication in both directions.

Theorem 15.

$$U_0 \sqsupseteq_{wf_\phi} U_1 \Leftrightarrow U_0 \sqsupseteq_{sf} U_1$$

$\square$

Despite their superficial dissimilarity, SF-, WF$_\bullet$- and WF$_\phi$-refinement are each equivalent to one another. This reinforces the results from Sect. 7 (see also [23,25]) showing clearly the significance of $\perp$ (Proposition 29). In addition, we have shown that strict lifting of the operations is sufficient for introducing a model-based refinement theory that preserves the very natural properties of SF-refinement.

The fact that, given the appropriate substitutions, the proofs in this section are identical to the ones in Sect. 13.1 suggests that the *minimal* mathematical properties of the lifted-totalised models that are essential for establishing

Theorems 13 and 14 are those of $\overset{\ominus}{U}$. To be more specific, the use of Lemma 1(ii) (Propositions 29 and 31) indicates that everything outside the precondition of the underlying operation, *including* $\bot$, should be mapped onto the value $\bot$ of the output state space. This observation is precisely the property of strictly-lifted totalised relations within a non-strict framework, as there is no evidence requiring a property which expresses the non-strict lifting of the operations.

13.3 WF$_\ominus$-Refinement is Sound with Respect to SF-Refinement

Section 13.2 and [23] demonstrate that the strict and non-strict relational completion operators are interchangeable. In order to examine whether a similar observation can be made for strict and non-strict lifting of the simulation, we need to investigate the relationship between WF$_\ominus$-refinement and SF-refinement.

In order to show that WF$_\ominus$-refinement implies SF-refinement, we need to make use of the same substitutions in and amendments to the proofs of Propositions 29 and 30 as we made use of in Theorem 15, except that $\sqsupseteq_{wf_\ominus}$ replaces $\sqsupseteq_{wf_\bullet}$, $\vec{S}$ replaces $\overset{\circ}{S}$ and we apply Lemmas 9(i) and 9(iv) in place of Lemmas 8(i) and 8(iv), respectively. Moreover, applications of $(\overset{\rightarrow}{\circ})$ replace $(\circ_\circ^-)$. From this we have the following theorem.

Theorem 16.
$$U_0 \sqsupseteq_{wf_\ominus} U_1 \Rightarrow U_0 \sqsupseteq_{sf} U_1$$

□

The other direction of implication (completeness) fails. In fact, given the above substitutions in the proof of proposition 31, we can see exactly why: it fails in the proof step labelled ♠ (δ_1 branch): the application of Lemma 8(iii) does not have a counterpart substitution in a strict framework, because it involves the non-strict lifting of the simulation. This unsuccessful proof attempt aids us in devising the representative counterexample shown in Fig. 2. This complements the mathematical analysis and clearly illustrates the failure. Each of the diagrams in Fig. 2 constitutes an extension of the forward-simulation commuting diagram in Fig. 1, showing the (lifted-totalised) operations and the (lifted) simulation. Since a model-theoretic refinement can be captured diagrammatically, WF$_\bullet$-refinement represents SF-refinement (to which it is equivalent: see Theorems 13 and 14 in Sect. 13.1). Both diagrams capture the data that we have in the δ_1 branch of Proposition 31. In the case of WF$_\bullet$-refinement, we have three pieces of information: $t_1 \star y' \in \overset{\circ}{S}$, $y \star t'_0 \in \overset{\bullet}{U_0}$ (which denotes a path from t_1 to t'_0 through the simulation via an intermediate state y) and $\neg\ Pre\ U_1\ t_1$, from which we need to establish a commuting path in the other direction. As shown in the proof, and illustrated in the diagram on the left, the fact that t_1 (being outside the precondition of U_1) is (also) mapped

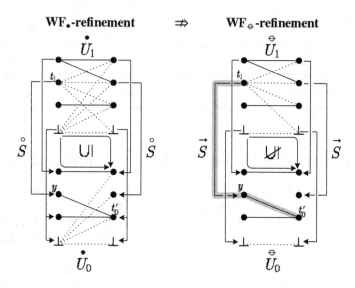

Fig. 2: A counterexample: WF$_\ominus$-refinement is not complete with respect to SF-refinement

onto $\perp$ and that the simulation is non-strictly lifted allows a commuting path from t_1 through $\perp$ in $\overset{\bullet}{U}_1$ and then, via the simulation, to t_0'. This is not the case with WF$_\ominus$-refinement, because the highlighted path is not associated with a path in the other direction: the subset relation fails.

Abstractly, we can observe that both diagrams illustrate a classic case of *weakening the precondition* in the presence of forward simulation: t_1 is outside the precondition of the abstract operation, yet its concrete counterpart y is in the precondition of the concrete operation, and they are both linked by the simulation. This is, naturally, a valid case of WF$_\bullet$-refinement, but not of WF$_\ominus$-refinement, precisely because of the strict lifting of the simulation, as we can see in the diagram on the right. This illuminates the significance of $\perp$ in sanctioning preconditions to weaken as well as in preventing them from strengthening (Proposition 29) throughout forward-simulation refinement (we shall reinforce this observation in Sect. 14). Furthermore, we can easily see, from both the mathematical analysis and the counterexample, that the strictly-lifted totalisation of the operations has nothing to do with the fact that SF-refinement fails to imply WF$_\ominus$-refinement.

In conclusion, WF$_\ominus$-refinement is an acceptable theory of refinement because it is sound with respect to SF-refinement (Theorem 16). However, it is not complete, because the strict lifting of forward simulation has a restrictive effect: under certain circumstances WF$_\ominus$-refinement *prevents weakening of preconditions* and hence narrows the diversity of possible design decisions.

14 The Non-lifted Totalisation underlying Data Refinement

In Sect. 9.1 (see also [23]) we presented Pre_1 as a distinct semantics for the notion of the precondition of an operation. This notion underlies $W_\diamond$-refinement, a model-theoretic operation refinement theory based on *non-lifted totalisation* (denoted $\overset{\diamond}{U}$) of the underlying operations. We demonstrated that $W_\diamond$-refinement is equivalent to S_1-refinement, a *normative* characterisation of refinement which is identical to S-refinement (Sect. 7.3) with all occurrences of Pre_0 substituted by Pre_1. This allows us to obtain an acceptable model-theoretic characterisation of operation refinement, without having to use the value $\perp$.

In this section we shall show that this is not the case under the generalisation to data refinement, highlighting the inevitability of using the value $\perp$ in both the lifting (of the simulation) and the relational completion models (of the operations) underlying forward-simulation refinement.

We begin by introducing $WF_\diamond$-refinement as a generalisation of $W_\diamond$-refinement (Sect. 9.2) with forward simulation. Since the totalisation of the operations is not lifted, we neither lift the simulation nor do we totalise it, for reasons discussed in Sect. 11. Therefore, $WF_\diamond$-refinement is defined as follows.

Definition 25.
$$U_0 \overset{s}{\sqsupseteq}_{wf_\diamond} U_1 =_{df} S \mathbin{\overset{\circ}{,}} \overset{\diamond}{U_0} \subseteq \overset{\diamond}{U_1} \mathbin{\overset{\circ}{,}} S$$

Obvious introduction and elimination rules for $WF_\diamond$-refinement follow from this definition.

In Sect. 9.4 (see also [23]) we proved that $W_\diamond$-refinement and $W_\bullet$-refinement are equivalent for bindings that range over the *natural carrier set*.[27] We can make a similar observation for forward refinement because the following proposition is provable using the same side-condition.

Proposition 32. *Let $t_1 \star t_0'$ be a binding with the property that $t_1 \star t_0' \in T$. The following rule is then derivable:*

$$\frac{U_0 \sqsupseteq_{wf_\diamond} U_1 \quad t_1 \star t_0' \in \overset{\circ}{S} \mathbin{\overset{\bullet}{,}} \overset{\bullet}{U_0}}{t_1 \star t_0' \in \overset{\bullet}{U_1} \mathbin{\overset{\circ}{,}} \overset{\circ}{S}}$$

□

From this we can easily establish the soundness of $WF_\diamond$-refinement with respect to $WF_\bullet$-refinement for all bindings that range over the natural carrier set, and therefore conclude that $WF_\diamond$-refinement is an acceptable refinement

---

[27] Natural carrier sets in $\mathcal{Z}_C^\perp$ explicitly exclude bindings that contain at least one observation bound to $\perp$.

theory. But it would be inappropriate to base our judgement on the observation above, because at this stage we do not know what exactly the side-condition in Proposition 32 means. In Sect. 9.4 (see also [23]) we concluded that a similar side-condition means that the (chaotic) lifted totalisation and the non-lifted totalisation coincide in a "$\bot$-less" framework, under the interpretation of Pre_1. However, that followed noting that $W_\diamond$-refinement is an acceptable refinement theory: it is sound (as well as complete) with respect to the normative theory of S_1-refinement. Clearly we need to take the same approach here: SF_1-refinement (that is, SF-refinement with all instances of Pre_0 substituted by Pre_1) would be our normative characterisation, guaranteeing the two properties expected in a forward-simulation refinement (Sect. 12.1), under the interpretation of Pre_1. Notice that we can prove that SF-refinement satisfies both of the SF_1-refinement elimination rules. This is a straightforward consequence of Lemma 5. From this we immediately obtain the following theorem.

Theorem 17.

$$U_0 \sqsupseteq_{sf} U_1 \Rightarrow U_0 \sqsupseteq_{sf_1} U_1$$

$\square$

We start with completeness: $WF_\diamond$-refinement is *not complete* with respect to SF_1-refinement, since SF_1-refinement fails to satisfy the $WF_\diamond$-elimination rule. The proof attempt is essentially very similar to the one that leads to the counterexample in Fig. 2; thus it fails for similar reasons. This induces the counterexample shown in Fig. 3.

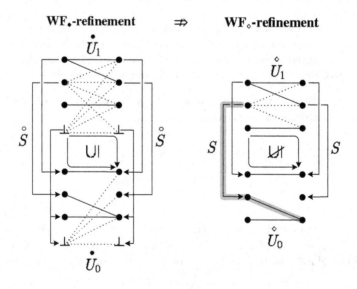

Fig. 3: A counterexample: $WF_\diamond$-refinement is not complete with respect to SF_1-refinement

Notice that the refinement case presented in Fig. 3[28] is very similar to the one in Fig. 2 because it depicts a similar observation: under certain circumstances, $WF_\diamond$-refinement *prevents weakening of preconditions*.

A more severe phenomenon is that $WF_\diamond$-refinement is *not sound* with respect to SF_1-refinement. Employing the same proof strategy involving elimination rules, we start by proving that $WF_\diamond$-refinement satisfies the SF_1-elimination rule for postconditions.

Proposition 33. *The following rule is derivable:*

$$\frac{\begin{array}{l} U_0 \sqsupseteq_{wf_\diamond} U_1 \\ Pre_1\ U_1\ t_1 \\ t_0 \star t_2' \in U_0 \\ t_1 \star t_0' \in S \\ t_1 \star y' \in U_1, y \star t_2' \in S \vdash P \end{array}}{P}$$

where the usual conditions apply to the eigenvariable y.

$\square$

The structure of the proof is very similar to that of proposition 30. From this we can deduce that $WF_\diamond$-refinement *guarantees that postconditions do not weaken*. Nevertheless, it cannot guarantee that *preconditions do not strengthen*, because it fails to satisfy the SF_1-elimination rule for preconditions. If we attempt to prove Proposition 29 with $\sqsupseteq_{wf_\diamond}$ replacing $\sqsupseteq_{wf_\bullet}$ and Pre_1 in place of Pre_0, we immediately learn that, unlike the proof of Proposition 29, we cannot derive a contradiction from the assumption that t_0 is *not* in the precondition of U_0. This is precisely because the non-lifted totalisation does not involve the value $\perp$ which, ultimately, leads to the contradiction in Proposition 29. We exhibit a counterexample in Fig. 4, which manifests this observation. This is a classic case of *strengthening the precondition* in the presence of forward simulation, something that is naturally prohibited by $WF_\bullet$-refinement (again, representing the normative theory) owing to a path (highlighted in the diagram on the right) linking t_1 to $\perp$ via t_0, which is not associated with a path in the other direction, because t_1 is in the precondition of U_1 and thus is not mapped onto $\perp$. As we can see in the diagram on the left, this is not the case in $WF_\diamond$-refinement, which allows requirements to disappear from the domain of specification.

In conclusion, the fact that $WF_\diamond$-refinement is not sound with respect to SF_1-refinement is a sufficient argument for stipulating that it is an unacceptable refinement theory.

We would like to highlight the significance of using a normative characterisation of refinement as a common foundation for such investigations: it

---

[28] We can use $WF_\bullet$-refinement to represent an SF_1-refinement in the counterexample, because we have Theorem 17 and we know that SF-refinement and $WF_\bullet$-refinement are equivalent.

WF$_\diamond$-refinement $\Rightarrow$ **WF$_\bullet$-refinement**

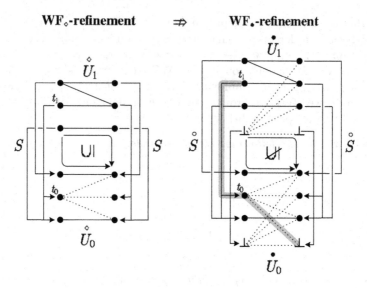

Fig. 4: A counterexample: WF$_\diamond$-refinement is not sound with respect to SF$_1$-refinement

enables us to pinpoint the source of the problem in terms of the two basic properties concerning preconditions and postconditions (for example Fig. 4), and it also overrules excessively strong results (for example, Proposition 32) that, in contrast to Sect. 9.4 (and [23]), constitute a very partial picture when a generalisation to forward-simulation data refinement is involved. Moreover, it is interesting to observe that, since WF$_\diamond$-refinement is also incomplete with respect to the normative theory, Figs. 3 and 4 jointly demonstrate that under certain circumstances WF$_\diamond$-refinement guarantees that *preconditions do not weaken*. This is, of course, the converse of the basic property permitted in a refinement.

15 Data Refinement (Backward)

We turn now to backward-simulation data refinement. We begin with the completion for simulations.

Definition 26 (Non-Strictly Lifted Backward Simulation).

$$\overset{\circ}{S} =_{df} \{z_0 \star z_1' \in T_{0_\perp} \star T_{1_\perp}' \mid z_0 \neq \perp \Rightarrow z_0 \star z_1' \in S\}$$

The following introduction and elimination rules are then derivable.

Proposition 34.

$$\frac{t_0 \star t_1' \in T_{0_\perp} \star T_{1_\perp} \quad t_0 \neq \perp \vdash t_0 \star t_1' \in S}{t_0 \star t_1' \in \overset{\circ}{S}} \ (\circ^+)$$

$$\frac{t_0 \star t_1' \in \overset{\circ}{S} \quad t_0 \neq \perp}{t_0 \star t_1' \in S} \ (\circ_\circ^-) \qquad \frac{t_0 \star t_1' \in \overset{\circ}{S}}{t_0 \star t_1' \in T_{0_\perp} \star T_{1_\perp}} \ (\circ_1^-)$$

□

Lemma 10. *The following additional rules are derivable for non-strictly lifted simulations:*

$$\frac{}{S \subseteq \overset{\circ}{S}} \ (i) \qquad \frac{}{\perp \in \overset{\circ}{S}} \ (ii) \qquad \frac{t \in T_{1_\perp}}{\perp \star t' \in \overset{\circ}{S}} \ (iii)$$

$$\frac{t_0 \star \perp' \in \overset{\circ}{S}}{t_0 = \perp} \ (iv)$$

□

Lemmas 10(i—iv) demonstrate that Definition 26 is consistent with the intentions described in [18, 68]: the underlying partial relation is contained in the lifting, the value $\perp$ is mapped onto every after state, and no other initial state is so. This raises an immediate question: why does the lifting of the simulation have to be non-strict with respect to $\perp$? This issue was not explored in [18, 68], where the non-strict lifting of the simulation is taken as self-evident. We shall gradually provide an answer to this question in the remainder of this chapter. To do this, we need the definition of a strictly-lifted backward simulation.

Definition 27 (Strictly-Lifted Backward Simulation).

$$\overrightarrow{S} =_{df} \{z_0 \star z_1' \in T_{0_\perp} \star T_{1_\perp} \mid (z_0 \neq \perp \Rightarrow z_0 \star z_1' \in S) \land (z_0 = \perp \Rightarrow z_1 = \perp)\}$$

Obvious introduction and elimination rules follow from this.

Lemma 11. *The following additional rules are derivable for strictly lifted simulations:*

$$\frac{}{S \subseteq \overrightarrow{S}} \ (i) \qquad \frac{}{\overrightarrow{S} \subseteq \overset{\circ}{S}} \ (ii) \qquad \frac{}{\perp \in \overrightarrow{S}} \ (iii)$$

$$\frac{t_0 \star t_1' \in \overrightarrow{S} \quad t_1 = \perp}{t_0 = \perp} \ (iv) \qquad \frac{t_0 \star t_1' \in \overrightarrow{S} \quad t_1 \neq \perp}{t_0 \star t_1' \in S} \ (v)$$

□

Lemmas 11(iv) and (v) embody the strictness captured by Definition 20: if the after-state is $\perp$ then the initial state must also be $\perp$, and if it is not $\perp$, then the initial state was not either.

16 Four (Backward) Theories

In this section, we provide four distinct notions of data refinement, generalising operation refinement, based on backward simulation. We shall then compare them, providing a an investigation complementary to that in Sect. 7 et seq. (see also [22, 25]) in the more general setting of data refinement and partial relation semantics.

16.1 SB-Refinement

In this section, we introduce a purely proof-theoretic characterisation of backward-simulation refinement, which is closely connected to the sufficient refinement conditions introduced by Woodcock [68, p. 270] (referred to there as "B-corr") and by Derrick and Boiten [18, p. 93]. These conditions correspond to the premises of our introduction rule for SB-refinement.

This generalisation of S-refinement (Sect. 7.3) is based on two properties expected in a refinement: that *postconditions do not weaken* (we do not permit an increase in non-determinism in a refinement) and that *preconditions do not strengthen* (we do not permit requirements in the domain of definition to disappear in a refinement). In this case, these two properties must hold in the presence of a simulation.

This notion can be captured by forcing the refinement relation to hold *exactly* when these conditions apply. SB-refinement is written $U_0 \stackrel{s}{\sqsupseteq}_{sb} U_1$ and is given by a definition that leads directly to the following rules.

Proposition 35. *Let* x, x_0, x_1, z, z_0 *be fresh variables.*

$$
\frac{
\begin{array}{c}
x \star z' \in S \Rightarrow Pre\ U_1\ z \vdash Pre\ U_0\ x \\
z_0 \star z' \in S \Rightarrow Pre\ U_1\ z, x_0 \star x_1' \in S, z_0 \star x_0' \in U_0 \vdash \\
z_0 \star t' \in S \\
z_0 \star z' \in S \Rightarrow Pre\ U_1\ z, x_0 \star x_1' \in S, z_0 \star x_0' \in U_0 \vdash \\
t \star x_1' \in U_1
\end{array}
}{
U_0 \sqsupseteq_{sb} U_1
} \ (\sqsupseteq_{sb}^+)
$$

$$
\frac{U_0 \sqsupseteq_{sb} U_1 \quad t \star z' \in S \vdash Pre\ U_1\ z}{Pre\ U_0\ t} \ (\sqsupseteq_{sb_0}^-)
$$

$$
\frac{
\begin{array}{c}
t_0 \star z' \in S \vdash Pre\ U_1\ z \\
t_1 \star t_2' \in S \quad t_0 \star t_1' \in U_0 \\
U_0 \sqsupseteq_{sb} U_1 \quad t_0 \star y' \in S, y \star t_2' \in U_1 \vdash P
\end{array}
}{
P
} \ (\sqsupseteq_{sb_1}^+)
$$

The usual side-conditions apply to the eigenvariable y.
□

This theory does not depend on, and makes no reference to, the value $\perp$. We take SB-refinement as *normative*: this is our prescription for data refinement, and another theory is acceptable providing it is at least sound with respect to it.

16.2 Relational Completion-based Refinement

We now introduce three backward-simulation refinement theories. These are based on the two distinct notions of the lifted totalisation. Each of them captures, schematically, the backward simulation commuting diagram in Fig. 1 and is based on relational composition.

WB$_\bullet$-Refinement

This notion of refinement is also discussed in [68, p. 247] and [17]. It is defined as follows.

Definition 28.

$$U_0 \sqsupseteq^s_{wb_\bullet} U_1 =_{df} \overset{\bullet}{U_0} \mathbin{\mathring{\mathfrak{g}}} \overset{\circ}{S} \subseteq \overset{\circ}{S} \mathbin{\mathring{\mathfrak{g}}} \overset{\bullet}{U_1}$$

The following rules are then derivable for WB$_\bullet$-refinement.

Proposition 36. *Let* z_0, z_1 *be fresh.*

$$\frac{z_0 \star z_1' \in \overset{\bullet}{U_0} \mathbin{\mathring{\mathfrak{g}}} \overset{\circ}{S} \vdash z_0 \star z_1' \in \overset{\circ}{S} \mathbin{\mathring{\mathfrak{g}}} \overset{\bullet}{U_1}}{U_0 \sqsupseteq_{wb_\bullet} U_1} \quad (\sqsupseteq^+_{wb_\bullet})$$

$$\frac{U_0 \sqsupseteq_{wb_\bullet} U_1 \qquad t_0 \star t_1' \in \overset{\bullet}{U_0} \mathbin{\mathring{\mathfrak{g}}} \overset{\circ}{S}}{t_0 \star t_1' \in \overset{\circ}{S} \mathbin{\mathring{\mathfrak{g}}} \overset{\bullet}{U_1}} \quad (\sqsupseteq^-_{wb_\bullet})$$

□

WB$_\Phi$-Refinement

The natural generalisation of W$_\ominus$-refinement (Sect. 9.2 and [22]), at least in the light of the standard literature, is to use strictly-lifted totalised operations, but a non-strictly-lifted simulation. We name this WB$_\Phi$-refinement and define it as follows.

Definition 29.

$$U_0 \sqsupseteq^s_{wb_\Phi} U_1 =_{df} \overset{\ominus}{U_0} \mathbin{\mathring{\mathfrak{g}}} \overset{\circ}{S} \subseteq \overset{\circ}{S} \mathbin{\mathring{\mathfrak{g}}} \overset{\ominus}{U_1}$$

Obvious introduction and elimination rules follow from this.

$WB_\ominus$-Refinement

Our third characterisation of refinement is motivated by some issues raised in Sect. 11. Establishing a refinement theory in which both the operations and the simulation are strictly lifted provides a point of reference which will aid us in investigating two important matters: first, whether the strict and non-strict relational completion operators are still interchangeable underlying generalisations of data refinement; second, whether the non-strict lifting of the simulation is an essential property. We name this theory $WB_\ominus$-refinement, written $U_0 \stackrel{s}{\sqsupseteq}_{wb_\ominus} U_1$; it is defined as follows.

Definition 30.

$$U_0 \stackrel{s}{\sqsupseteq}_{wb_\ominus} U_1 =_{df} \stackrel{\ominus}{U_0} \,\mathbin{\mathring{9}}\, \vec{S} \subseteq \vec{S} \,\mathbin{\mathring{9}}\, \stackrel{\ominus}{U_1}$$

Obvious introduction and elimination rules follow from this definition.

17 Four Equivalent Theories

In this section, we demonstrate that all four of these theories of refinement are equivalent, and we shall clearly see the critical role that the value $\perp$ plays in the three model-theoretic approaches.

17.1 $WB_\bullet$-Refinement and SB-Refinement are Equivalent

We begin by showing that $WB_\bullet$-refinement implies SB-refinement, by proving that $WB_\bullet$-refinement satisfies both of the SB-refinement elimination rules. First we consider the rule for preconditions.

Proposition 37. *The following rule is derivable:*

$$\frac{U_0 \sqsupseteq_{wb_\bullet} U_1 \quad t \star z' \in S \vdash Pre\ U_1\ z}{Pre\ U_0\ t}$$

Proof.

$$
\cfrac{
\cfrac{
t\star \perp' \in \stackrel{\circ}{S} \,\mathbin{\mathring{9}}\, \stackrel{\bullet}{U_1} \quad false
}{
\cfrac{false}{Pre\ U_0\ t}\ (1)
}\ (2)
}{}
\qquad
\begin{array}{c}\delta_0 \\ \vdots \end{array}
\qquad
\begin{array}{c}\delta_1 \\ \vdots \end{array}
$$

where δ_0 is

$$
\cfrac{
\cfrac{
U_0 \sqsupseteq_{wb_\bullet} U_1 \qquad
\cfrac{
\cfrac{\neg\ Pre\ U_0\ t}{}\ (1) \quad \cfrac{\overline{t \in T_0}}{t \in T_{0_\perp}}\ (T)
}{
t\star \perp' \in \stackrel{\bullet}{U_0}
}\ (C.\ 1(ii)) \quad \cfrac{}{\perp \in \stackrel{\circ}{S}}
}{
t\star \perp' \in \stackrel{\bullet}{U_0} \,\mathbin{\mathring{9}}\, \stackrel{\circ}{S}
}
}{
t\star \perp' \in \stackrel{\circ}{S} \,\mathbin{\mathring{9}}\, \stackrel{\bullet}{U_1}
}
$$

and δ_1 is

$$
\dfrac{
\dfrac{\rule{2cm}{0.4pt}\;(2)}{t \star y' \in \overset{\circ}{S}}
\qquad
\dfrac{t \in T_0}{t \neq \bot}\;(T)
}{t \star y' \in S}
$$

$$
\dfrac{
\dfrac{\rule{2cm}{0.4pt}\;(2)}{y \star \bot' \in \overset{\bullet}{U_1}}
\qquad
\begin{array}{c}\vdots \\ Pre\; U_1\, y\end{array}
}{
\dfrac{y \star \bot' \in U_1}{false}
}
$$

□

There are two observations that we can make from this proof. First, note that the ability to distinguish between $\mathcal{Z}_C$ and $\mathcal{Z}_C^{\bot}$ types is a crucial factor: the proof steps labelled (T) denote the use of Proposition 2.3 of [35] (see also Sect. 3.3). This is an admissible axiom for $\mathcal{Z}_C$, in which every term of type T is a member of the corresponding *carrier set*[29]. It is not admissible for $\mathcal{Z}_C^{\bot}$, as terms may involve the value $\bot$. Hence, this proof step is valid because SB-refinement is defined in $\mathcal{Z}_C$ (Sect. 7.3). Second, notice the explicit use of $\bot$ in the proof. This is reminiscent of our earlier investigation of operation refinement, in which the explicit use of $\bot$ is critical for proving that $W_\bullet$-refinement satisfies the precondition elimination rule for S-refinement (Proposition 11). Much the same observation can be made here, the only difference being that the use of Lemmas 1(ii) and 10(ii) in the proof suggests that *both* the lifted totalisation of the operations *and* the lifting of the simulation are essential for showing that $WB_\bullet$-refinement guarantees that preconditions do not strengthen in the presence of the simulation.

We turn now to the second elimination rule in SB-refinement.

Proposition 38. *The following rule is derivable:*

$$
\dfrac{
U_0 \sqsupseteq_{wb\bullet} U_1 \quad
\begin{array}{c}
t_0 \star z' \in S \vdash Pre\; U_1\, z \\
t_1 \star t_2' \in S \quad t_0 \star t_1' \in U_0 \\
t_0 \star y' \in S, y \star t_2' \in U_1 \vdash P
\end{array}
}{P}
$$

where the usual conditions apply to the eigenvariable y.

Proof.

$$
\dfrac{
U_0 \sqsupseteq_{wb\bullet} U_1 \quad
\dfrac{
\dfrac{\dfrac{t_0 \star t_1' \in U_0}{t_0 \star t_1' \in \overset{\bullet}{U_0}}\,(L.\,3(i)) \quad
\dfrac{t_1 \star t_2' \in S}{t_1 \star t_2' \in \overset{\circ}{S}}\,(L.\,10(i))}
{t_0 \star t_2' \in \overset{\bullet}{U_0}\,\fatsemi\, \overset{\circ}{S}}
}{t_0 \star t_2' \in \overset{\circ}{S}\,\fatsemi\,\overset{\bullet}{U_1}}
\quad
\begin{array}{c}\delta_0 \\ \vdots \\ P\end{array}
}{P}\;(1)
$$

---

[29] In $\mathcal{Z}_C^{\bot}$ these *natural carrier sets* explicitly exclude bindings that contain at least one observation bound to $\bot$ (see Sect. 7.1 for further detail).

Here, δ_0 is:

$$
\cfrac{
\cfrac{\rule{2cm}{0.4pt}}{t_0 \star y' \in \overset{\circ}{S}}\ (1) \quad \cfrac{t_0 \star t_1' \in U_0}{t_0 \neq \perp}\ (L.\,2)
}{t_0 \star y' \in S} \qquad
\begin{array}{c}\delta_1 \\ \vdots \\ y \star t_2' \in U_1\end{array}
$$

$$
\cfrac{t_0 \star y' \in S \wedge y \star t_2' \in U_1}{\begin{array}{c}\vdots \\ P\end{array}}
$$

where δ_1 is

$$
\cfrac{
\cfrac{
\cfrac{\rule{2cm}{0.4pt}}{t_0 \star y' \in \overset{\circ}{S}}\ (1) \quad \cfrac{t_0 \star t_1' \in U_0}{t_0 \neq \perp}\ (L.\,2)
}{t_0 \star y' \in S}
}{}
$$

$$
\cfrac{
\cfrac{\rule{2cm}{0.4pt}}{y \star t_2' \in \overset{\bullet}{U_1}}\ (1) \qquad \begin{array}{c}\vdots \\ Pre\ U_1\ y\end{array}
}{y \star t_2' \in U_1}
$$

□

Theorem 18. $U_0 \sqsupseteq_{wb_\bullet} U_1 \Rightarrow U_0 \sqsupseteq_{sb} U_1$

Proof. This follows immediately, by $(\sqsupseteq_{sb}^+)$, from Propositions 37 and 38.
□

We now show that SB-refinement satisfies the WB$_\bullet$-elimination rule.

Proposition 39.

$$
\cfrac{U_0 \sqsupseteq_{sb} U_1 \qquad t_0 \star t_1' \in \overset{\bullet}{U_0}\,\mathbin{\mathstrut_{\!9}}\overset{\circ}{S}}{t_0 \star t_1' \in \overset{\circ}{S}\,\mathbin{\mathstrut_{\!9}}\overset{\bullet}{U_1}}
$$

Proof. Let ϕ be $\forall z \bullet t_0 \star z' \in S \Rightarrow Pre\ U_1\ z \vee \exists z \bullet t_0 \star z' \in S \wedge \neg\ Pre\ U_1\ z$
We then have

$$
\cfrac{
t_0 \star t_1' \in \overset{\bullet}{U_0}\,\mathbin{\mathstrut_{\!9}}\overset{\circ}{S} \qquad
\cfrac{\overset{\displaystyle \overline{\phi}}{}\ (LEM) \quad \begin{array}{c}\delta_0 \\ \vdots \\ t_0 \star t_1' \in \overset{\circ}{S}\,\mathbin{\mathstrut_{\!9}}\overset{\bullet}{U_1}\end{array} \quad \begin{array}{c}\delta_1 \\ \vdots \\ t_0 \star t_1' \in \overset{\circ}{S}\,\mathbin{\mathstrut_{\!9}}\overset{\bullet}{U_1}\end{array}}{t_0 \star t_1' \in \overset{\circ}{S}\,\mathbin{\mathstrut_{\!9}}\overset{\bullet}{U_1}}\ (2)
}{t_0 \star t_1' \in \overset{\circ}{S}\,\mathbin{\mathstrut_{\!9}}\overset{\bullet}{U_1}}\ (1)
$$

where δ_0 is

$$
\cfrac{U_0 \sqsupseteq_{sb} U_1 \qquad \cfrac{\rule{3cm}{0.4pt}}{\forall z \bullet t_0 \star z' \in S \Rightarrow Pre\ U_1\ z}\ (2) \qquad \begin{array}{ccc}\beta_0 & \beta_1 & \beta_2 \\ \vdots & \vdots & \vdots\end{array}}{t_0 \star t_1' \in \overset{\circ}{S}\,\mathbin{\mathstrut_{\!9}}\overset{\bullet}{U_1}}\ (3)
$$

and where β_0, β_1 and β_2 are, respectively

$$\cfrac{\cfrac{}{t_0 \star y' \in \overset{\bullet}{U_0}}\;(1) \quad \cfrac{U_0 \sqsupseteq_{sb} U_1 \quad \overline{\forall z \bullet t_0 \star z' \in S \Rightarrow Pre\,U_1\,z}\;(2)}{Pre\,U_0\,t_0}}{t_0 \star y' \in U_0}$$

and

$$\beta_0 \atop \vdots$$

$$\cfrac{\cfrac{}{y \star t_1' \in \overset{\circ}{S}}\;(1) \quad \cfrac{t_0 \star y' \in U_0}{y \neq \bot}\;(L.\,2)}{y \star t_1' \in S}$$

and

$$\cfrac{\cfrac{\cfrac{t_0 \star w_0' \in S}{\,}\;(3)}{t_0 \star w_0' \in \overset{\circ}{S}}\;(L.\,10(i)) \quad \cfrac{\cfrac{w_0 \star t_1' \in U_1}{\,}\;(3)}{w_0 \star t_1' \in \overset{\bullet}{U_1}}\;(L.\,3(i))}{t_0 \star t_1' \in \overset{\circ}{S}\;\mathbin{\overset{\circ}{\mathrm{9}}}\;\overset{\bullet}{U_1}}$$

δ_1 is

$$\alpha_0 \atop \vdots$$

$$\cfrac{\cfrac{}{\exists z \bullet t_0 \star z' \in S \wedge \neg\,Pre\,U_1\,z}\;(2) \quad t_0 \star t_1' \in \overset{\circ}{S}\;\mathbin{\overset{\circ}{\mathrm{9}}}\;\overset{\bullet}{U_1}}{t_0 \star t_1' \in \overset{\circ}{S}\;\mathbin{\overset{\circ}{\mathrm{9}}}\;\overset{\bullet}{U_1}}\;(4)$$

where α_0 is

$$\cfrac{\cfrac{\cfrac{t_0 \star w_1' \in S \wedge \neg\,Pre\,U_1\,w_1}{t_0 \star w_1' \in S}\;(4)}{t_0 \star w_1' \in \overset{\circ}{S}}\;(L.\,10(i)) \qquad \begin{array}{c}\alpha_1 \\ \vdots \\ w_1 \star t_1' \in \overset{\bullet}{U_1}\end{array}}{t_0 \star t_1' \in \overset{\circ}{S}\;\mathbin{\overset{\circ}{\mathrm{9}}}\;\overset{\bullet}{U_1}}$$

α_1 is

$$\cfrac{\cfrac{t_0 \star w_1' \in S \wedge \neg\,Pre\,U_1\,w_1}{\neg\,Pre\,U_1\,w_1}\;(4) \quad \begin{array}{c}\alpha_3 \\ \vdots \\ w_1 \in T_{1_\bot}\end{array} \quad \cfrac{\cfrac{\cfrac{}{y \star t_1' \in \overset{\circ}{S}}\;(1)}{y \star t_1' \in T_{0_\bot} \star T_{1_\bot}'}}{t_1 \in T_{1_\bot}}\;(L.\,3(iii))}{w_1 \star t_1' \in \overset{\bullet}{U_1}}$$

and α_3 is

$$\cfrac{\cfrac{\cfrac{\cfrac{t_0 \star w_1' \in S \wedge \neg\,Pre\,U_1\,w_1}{t_0 \star w_1' \in S}\;(4)}{w_1 \in T_1}}{w_1 \in T_{1_\bot}}}{}\;(\clubsuit)$$

$\square$

Notice that this proof depends on use of the *law of the excluded middle* (see, for example, [60, p. 47] and [54, p. 105]). We suspect that this result is strictly classical, and there appear to be many other examples of this in refinement theory.

Theorem 19.

$$U_0 \sqsupseteq_{sb} U_1 \Rightarrow U_0 \sqsupseteq_{wb_\bullet} U_1$$

$\square$

Theorems 18 and 19 together establish that the theories of SB-refinement and $WB_\bullet$-refinement are equivalent.

17.2 WB_ϕ-, $WB_\ominus$- and SB-Refinement are Equivalent

We now show that WB_ϕ-refinement and $WB_\ominus$-refinement are both equivalent to SB-refinement. Proving that WB_ϕ-refinement satisfies both SB-elimination rules leads to proofs identical to Propositions 37 and 38, modulo substitution of $\sqsupseteq_{wb_\phi}$ for $\sqsupseteq_{wb_\bullet}$, $\overset{\ominus}{U}$ for $\overset{\bullet}{U}$, applications of $(\ominus_0^-)$ for $(\bullet_0^-)$, and Lemmas 7(iv) and 7(i) in place of Lemmas 3(iii) and 3(i), respectively. Likewise, proving that SB-refinement satisfies the WB_ϕ-elimination rule is very similar to the proof of Proposition 39. In this case, we require the same general substitutions as above, in addition to a modification in the proof branch labelled α: applying Lemma 7(iv) in place of Lemma 3(iii) requires the variable w_1 to range over a $\bot$-free set; hence, the proof step labelled (♣) is redundant here. From this we have the following theorem.

Theorem 20.

$$U_0 \sqsupseteq_{wb_\phi} U_1 \Leftrightarrow U_0 \sqsupseteq_{sb} U_1$$

$\square$

A similar situation arises when we consider $WB_\ominus$-refinement. SB-refinement constitutes our common ground, and again we need to make use of the substitutions in and amendments to the proofs of Propositions 37, 38 and 39 as we did for Theorem 20, except that $\sqsupseteq_{wb_\ominus}$ replaces $\sqsupseteq_{wb_\bullet}$, $\vec{S}$ replaces $\overset{\circ}{S}$, and we apply Lemmas 11(i) and 11(iii) in place of Lemmas 10(i) and 10(ii), respectively. Moreover, applications of $(\rightarrow_0^-)$ and $(\rightarrow_1^-)$ replace $(\circ_0^-)$ and $(\circ_1^-)$, respectively. From this we immediately obtain implication in both directions.

Theorem 21.

$$U_0 \sqsupseteq_{wb_\ominus} U_1 \Leftrightarrow U_0 \sqsupseteq_{sb} U_1$$

$\square$

Despite their superficial dissimilarity, all four theories are equivalent. In establishing this, we reinforce the results of Sect. 7 et seq. (see also [22, 25]) showing clearly the significance of $\bot$ (Proposition 37). Additionally we have shown that *strict lifting of both the operations and the simulation is sufficient* for introducing a model-based refinement theory that preserves the natural properties of SB-refinement.

The fact that, given the appropriate substitutions, the proofs in this section are identical to those of Sect. 17.1 suggests that the *minimal* mathematical properties of the models that are essential for establishing theorems 18 and 19 are those $\overset{\ominus}{U}$ and $\vec{S}$. To be more specific, the use of Lemma 1(ii) (Proposition 37) indicates that everything outside the preconditions of the underlying operation, *including* $\bot$, should be mapped onto the value $\bot$ of the output set; and the use of the proof step labelled ($\clubsuit$) in conjunction with Lemma 3(iii) (Proposition 39) indicates that everything outside the preconditions *that is not* $\bot$ should be mapped onto everything in the output set. These observations are precisely the properties of strictly-lifted totalised relations within a non-strict framework. A similar observation can be made for the simulation: the only lemma concerning the lifting of the simulation used in the proofs is Lemma 10(ii) (Proposition 37); there is no evidence for requiring Lemma 10(iii), which expresses the non-strict lifting.

18 The Non-lifted Totalisation underlying Data Refinement

In Sect. 9 (see also [22]), we presented Pre_1 as a distinct semantics for the notion of the precondition of an operation. This notion underlies $W_\diamond$-refinement, a model-theoretic operation refinement theory based on *non-lifted totalisation*[30] (denoted $\overset{\diamond}{U}$) of the underlying operations. We demonstrated that $W_\diamond$-refinement is equivalent to S_1-refinement, a *normative* characterisation of refinement which is identical to S-refinement (Sect. 7.3) with all occurrences of Pre_0 substituted by Pre_1. This allows us to obtain an acceptable model-theoretic characterisation of operation refinement, without having to use the value $\bot$.

In this section, we shall show that this is not the case under the generalisation to data refinement, highlighting the inevitability of using the value $\bot$ in both the lifting (of the simulation) and the relational completion models (of the operations) underlying backward-simulation refinement.

We begin by introducing $WB_\diamond$-refinement as a generalisation of $W_\diamond$-refinement (Sect. 9.2 and [22]) with backward simulation. Since the totalisation of the operations is not lifted, we do not lift the simulation either; nor do we totalise it, for reasons discussed in Sect. 11. Therefore, $WB_\diamond$-refinement is defined as follows.

Definition 31.

---

[30] The definitions of Pre_1 and of non-lifted totalisation can be found in Sect. 9. Moreover, in this section, we shall refer to the standard definition of the precondition as Pre_0 in order to distinguish it from the new notion.

$$U_0 \stackrel{s}{\sqsupseteq}_{wb_\diamond} U_1 =_{df} \stackrel{\diamond}{U_0} \,{}_9^\circ\, S \subseteq S \,{}_9^\circ\, \stackrel{\diamond}{U_1}$$

Obvious introduction and elimination rules for $WB_\diamond$-refinement follow. This definition raises an immediate question: is $WB_\diamond$-refinement an acceptable theory of refinement? If not, what are the reasons for that? In Sect. 9 (and in [22]) we concluded that the (chaotic) lifted totalisation and the non-lifted totalisation coincide in a "$\bot$-less" framework, under the interpretation of Pre_1. However, that followed noting that $W_\diamond$-refinement is an acceptable refinement theory: it is sound (as well as complete) with respect to the normative theory of S_1-refinement. Clearly, we need to take the same approach here: SB_1-refinement (that is, SB-refinement with all instances of Pre_0 substituted by Pre_1) would be our normative characterisation, guaranteeing the two properties expected in a backward-simulation refinement (Sect. 16.1), under the interpretation of Pre_1. Notice that we can prove that SB-refinement satisfies both of the SB_1-refinement elimination rules. This is a straightforward consequence of Lemma 5 (Sect. 9). From this, we immediately obtain the following theorem.

Theorem 22.

$$U_0 \sqsupseteq_{sb} U_1 \Rightarrow U_0 \sqsupseteq_{sb_1} U_1$$

$\square$

We start with completeness: $WB_\diamond$-refinement is *complete* with respect to SB_1-refinement since SB_1-refinement satisfies the elimination rule for $WB_\diamond$-refinement.

Proposition 40. *The following rule is derivable:*

$$\frac{U_0 \sqsupseteq_{sb_1} U_1 \quad t_0 \star t_1' \in \stackrel{\diamond}{U_0} \,{}_9^\circ\, S}{t_0 \star t_1' \in S \,{}_9^\circ\, \stackrel{\diamond}{U_1}}$$

The structure of the proof is very similar to that of Proposition 39.
$\square$

The following theorem is then immediate.

Theorem 23.

$$U_0 \sqsupseteq_{sb_1} U_1 \Rightarrow U_0 \sqsupseteq_{wb_\diamond} U_1$$

$\square$

An example of this is given in Fig. 5, where each of the diagrams constitutes an extension of the backward-simulation commuting diagram in Fig. 1, showing the (completed) operations and the (lifted in the case of $WB_\bullet$-refinement) simulation. We can use $WB_\bullet$-refinement to represent an SB_1-refinement in such examples, because we have theorem 22 and we know that SB-refinement and $WB_\bullet$-refinement are equivalent (Theorems 18, 19). We can observe that

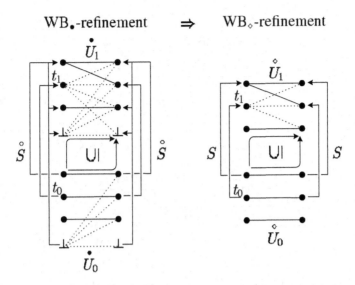

Fig. 5: An example: WB$_\diamond$-refinement is complete with respect to SB$_1$-refinement

both diagrams illustrate a classic case of *weakening the precondition* in the presence of backward simulation: t_1 is outside the precondition of the abstract operation, yet its concrete counterpart t_0 is in the precondition of the concrete operation, and they are both linked by the simulation. This property is, naturally, sanctioned by SB$_1$-refinement and, owing to Theorem 23, also by WB$_\diamond$-refinement. However, does WB$_\diamond$-refinement guarantee that preconditions do not strengthen? In order to answer this, we need to investigate whether WB$_\diamond$-refinement is *sound* with respect to SB$_1$-refinement.

Employing the same proof strategy involving elimination rules, we start by proving that WB$_\diamond$-refinement satisfies the SB$_1$-elimination rule for postconditions.

Proposition 41. *The following rule is derivable:*

$$
\frac{
\begin{array}{c}
t_0 \star z' \in S \vdash Pre_1\, U_1\, z \\
t_1 \star t_2' \in S \quad t_0 \star t_1' \in U_0 \\
U_0 \sqsupseteq_{wb_\diamond} U_1 \quad t_0 \star y' \in S, y \star t_2' \in U_1 \vdash P
\end{array}
}{P}
$$

where the usual side-conditions apply to the eigenvariable y.

Proof.

$$\cfrac{\cfrac{\cfrac{t_0 \star t_1' \in U_0}{t_0 \star t_1' \in \overset{\circ}{U_0}}\ (L.\ 6(i))}{U_0 \sqsupseteq_{wb_\circ} U_1 \qquad \cfrac{t_0 \star t_1' \in \overset{\circ}{U_0}}{t_0 \star t_2' \in \overset{\circ}{U_0}\ {}_{\mathfrak{g}}\ S}\quad t_1 \star t_2' \in S}{\cfrac{t_0 \star t_2' \in S\ {}_{\mathfrak{g}}\ \overset{\circ}{U_1}}{P}} \qquad \cfrac{\delta}{\underset{P}{\vdots}}}{P}\ (\mathbf{1})$$

where δ is

$$\cfrac{\cfrac{}{t_0 \star y' \in S}\ (\mathbf{1}) \qquad \cfrac{\cfrac{}{y \star t_2' \in \overset{\circ}{U_1}}\ (\mathbf{1}) \qquad \cfrac{\overset{\displaystyle \cfrac{}{t_0 \star y' \in S}\ (\mathbf{1})}{\vdots}}{Pre_1\ U_1\ y}}{y \star t_2' \in U_1}}{\underset{\underset{\dot{P}}{\vdots}}{t_0 \star y' \in S \wedge y \star t_2' \in U_1}}$$

□

From this we can deduce that WB$_\circ$-refinement *guarantees that postconditions do not weaken*. Nevertheless, it cannot guarantee that *preconditions do not strengthen*, because it fails to satisfy the SB$_1$-elimination rule for preconditions. If we attempt to prove Proposition 37 with $\sqsupseteq_{wb_\circ}$ replacing $\sqsupseteq_{wb_\bullet}$ and Pre_1 in place of Pre_0, we immediately learn that, unlike the proof of Proposition 37, we cannot derive a contradiction from the assumption that t is *not* in the precondition of U_0. This is precisely because the non-lifted totalisation does not involve the value $\bot$ which, ultimately, leads to the contradiction required in the proof of Proposition 37. We exhibit a counterexample in Fig. 6, which manifests this observation. Both diagrams capture the data that we have in the proof of Proposition 37. In the case of WB$_\bullet$-refinement (again, representing the normative theory), we have two pieces of information: $\neg\ Pre\ U_0\ t$ and $\bot \in \overset{\circ}{S}$. These denote a path (highlighted in the diagram on the right) from t to $\bot$ through the simulation via an intermediate state $\bot$. But this path is not associated with a path in the other direction: the subset relation fails. This is a classic case of *strengthening the precondition* in the presence of backward simulation, something that is naturally prohibited by WB$_\bullet$-refinement. As we can see in the diagram on the left, this is not the case in WB$_\circ$-refinement, which allows requirements to disappear from the domain of specification, in the presence of the simulation.

In conclusion, the fact that WB$_\circ$-refinement is not sound with respect to SB$_1$-refinement makes it an *unacceptable refinement theory*.

We would again like to highlight the significance of using a normative characterisation of refinement as a common foundation for such investigations: it enables us to pinpoint the source of the problem in terms of the two basic properties concerning preconditions and postconditions and to construct representative counterexamples that illustrate the problem (for example, Fig. 6).

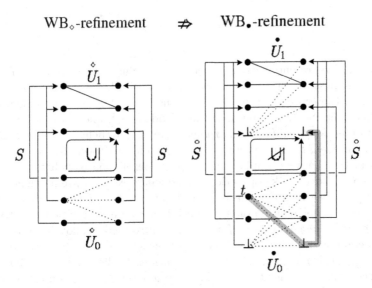

Fig. 6: A counterexample: $\text{WB}_\diamond$-refinement is not sound with respect to SB_1-refinement

19 Discussion

The non-lifted totalisation underlying refinement introduces a variety of problems. Woodcock [68, p. 237–238] provides a motivation for an explanation, to some extent. We discussed this matter thoroughly in Sect. 8.6 (see also [22] (section 4.4)), where, at the end, we raised a question: why is there a distinction between *implicit* (*Chaos*) and *explicit* (*True*) permission to behave in a lifted totalised framework and not in a non-lifted totalised one? In this section we shall gradually answer this question, and secure the observations that we made in Sect. 18.

A useful way to examine the essence of a relational completion model is by scrutinising it under *extreme specifications* (see, for example, chapter 3 of [28]). This enables us to observe and explain phenomena that might not emerge otherwise. In this spirit, we revisit two such specifications which respectively denote explicit and implicit "permission to behave".

Definition 32.

$$(i)\quad True \ =_{df} \ \{z \in T \star T' \mid true\}$$
$$(ii)\quad Chaos \ =_{df} \ \{z \in T \star T' \mid false\}$$

By applying the (chaotic) lifted totalisation and the non-lifted totalisation to these specifications we immediately obtain the following.

Lemma 12.

$$(i)\ \overset{\diamond}{True} = \overset{\diamond}{Chaos} \quad (ii)\ \overset{\bullet}{True} \neq \overset{\bullet}{Chaos}$$

□

Lemma 12(i) represents a counterexample, in which *augmentation of undefinedness* is possible in a refinement based on non-lifted totalisation, under the standard interpretation of preconditions (Sect. 4.9). This is remedied by $W_\bullet$-refinement (Sect. 7.4) because the Woodcock-completion [68] imposes a distinction between *implicit* and *explicit* permission to behave (Lemma 12(ii)). The alternative Pre_1 interpretation of preconditions (Sect. 9), under which the distinction between implicit and explicit permission to behave collapses, leads to a Woodcock-like operation refinement theory, $W_\diamond$-refinement (Sect. 9.2 and [22]), in which the relations need not be lifted. This theory is simply defined as a subset relation of the (non-lifted) totalised relations, where the subset *prevents augmentation of non-determinism* and the non-lifted totalisation, in conjunction with the subset, plays the same role as its lifted counterpart in *preventing augmentation of undefinedness*. Therefore, $W_\diamond$-refinement is an acceptable refinement theory that guarantees these two elementary properties without utilising the value $\perp$. So, why does the non-lifted totalisation have no future underlying model-theoretic refinement? More specifically, we are asking: why does it not work for data refinement?

The answer concerns data simulations and the properties of *composition*. Consider the example in Fig. 7, where we present the specification $True^{31}$ as a refinement of a certain specification U_1, under both $WB_\diamond$-refinement and $WB_\bullet$-refinement. This is *not* a case of weakening the postcondition, because the simulation links the first output state in U_1 with *all* the output states in $True^{32}$; thus, it is a sensible case of data refinement. Yet in a non-lifted totalised operation, it is impossible to indicate whether an input state is mapped onto *all* output states as a result of not being mapped onto anything, or being mapped onto everything in the underlying operation. For this reason, the specifications *True* and *Chaos* are *indistinguishable* in this model and therefore the $WB_\diamond$-refinement case in Fig. 7 also holds for *Chaos*, as we can see in Fig. 8. Naturally, it is unacceptable that a chaotic specification refines some other specification that is *not chaotic*. This means that undefinedness has been augmented, as a result of *a strengthening of preconditions*. Indeed, as we have seen in Sect. 18, $WB_\diamond$-refinement sanctions this feature and is therefore unacceptable as a refinement theory. This case is prohibited by $WB_\bullet$-refinement, precisely because the lifted totalisation maps input states outside the precondition of the underlying operation onto $\perp$, as well as everything else in the output set. Thus, $WB_\bullet$-refinement fails in Fig. 8, since none of the highlighted paths leading to $\perp$ are associated with paths in the other direction. Notice

---

[31] Here, as usual, *True* belongs to $\mathbb{P}(T_0 \star T_0')$ and U_1 to $\mathbb{P}(T_1 \star T_1')$.

[32] Recall that, although $WB_\diamond$-refinement is unacceptable as a refinement theory, it still guarantees that postconditions do not weaken (Proposition 41). This is certainly the case for $WB_\bullet$-refinement, as it is equivalent to SB-refinement.

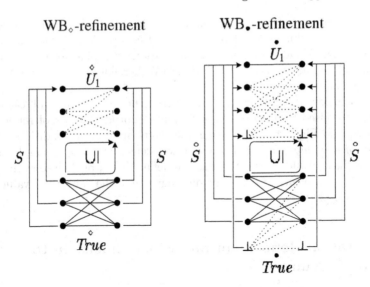

Fig. 7: An example: the specification *True* refines the specification U_1

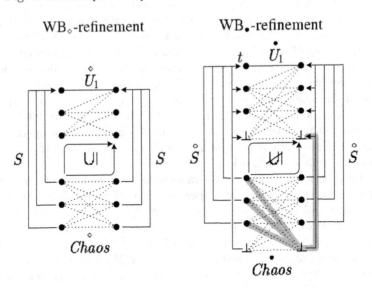

Fig. 8: A counterexample: the specification *Chaos* constitutes a valid WB$_\circ$-refinement case of the specification U_1

that the only way to establish these paths is through a link between t and $\bot$ in $\overset{\bullet}{U_1}$: this does not exist, because t is in the precondition of U_1.

What we have discussed here also follows from consideration of forward-simulation data refinement. If one reverses the direction of the simulation relation in Figs. 7 and 8, one obtains illustrations of similar examples similar based on WF$_\diamond$-refinement and its relation to WF$_\bullet$-refinement (or, equivalently, SF-refinement).

In conclusion, $\perp$ underlies the distinction between *True* and *Chaos* in the lifted totalised framework. This prevents imprudent cases of refinement such as that in Fig. 8 by prohibiting a strengthening of preconditions *in the presence of a simulation*. For this reason we prefer to refer to $\perp$ simply as the "distinguished" value, rather than as "undefined" [68] or "non-termination" [14,28,31,47], or even our own previous suggestion, the "abortive" value (see Sect. 7.6 and [22]).

20 Operation Refinement and Monotonicity in the Schema Calculus

The major advantage of Z, in contrast to other paradigms such as Refinement Calculus and even B [1], is its potential for expressing modular specifications using schema operators. However, in order to properly exploit modularity and in particular to undertake specification refinement, it is vital that the various schema operators of the language are monotonic. When monotonicity holds, the components of a composite specification can be refined independently of the remainder of the specification (see [27] which also contains analyses similar to some of the material developed in this section); refinement can then be performed in a modular manner. Unfortunately, it is well-known folklore that the Z schema calculus operators have very poor monotonicity properties; this has a major effect on their usefulness, for example, in the context of program development from Z specifications.

In this section, we analyse the monotonicity properties of four of the most interesting schema calculus operators (conjunction, disjunction, existential hiding and composition) with respect to S-refinement and two modifications which we now describe. We provide examples of monotonicity (or non-monotonicity) and establish side-conditions, as "healthiness conditions" on specifications, in order to attain monotonicity. We also discuss the usefulness of these side-conditions in the context of the various refinement theories that we consider.

20.1 SP-Refinement

This is an alternative proof-theoretic characterisation of refinement, which is closely connected to refinement in the *behavioural* [18] or *firing condition* [59] approach. This special case of S-refinement may involve reduction of non-determinism but insists on the *stability of the precondition*. SP-refinement is written $U_0 \sqsupseteq_{sp} U_1$ and is given by a definition that leads directly to the following rules.

Proposition 42. *Let* z, z_0, z_1 *be fresh variables.*

$$\frac{Pre\ U_1\ z \vdash Pre\ U_0\ z \quad z_0 \star z_1' \in U_0 \vdash z_0 \star z_1' \in U_1}{U_0 \sqsupseteq_{sp} U_1}\ (\sqsupseteq_{sp}^+)$$

$$\frac{U_0 \sqsupseteq_{sp} U_1 \quad Pre\ U_1\ t}{Pre\ U_0\ t}\ (\sqsupseteq_{sp_0}^-) \qquad \frac{U_0 \sqsupseteq_{sp} U_1 \quad t_0 \star t_1' \in U_0}{t_0 \star t_1' \in U_1}\ (\sqsupseteq_{sp_1}^-)$$

□

We showed in [25] that SP-refinement is equivalent to several other characterisations of refinement, for example $W_\square$-refinement, which is based on the *abortive* relational completion model discussed in [10, 18].

20.2 SC-Refinement

SC-refinement is our third alternative proof-theoretic characterisation of refinement. It is written $U_0 \sqsupseteq_{sc} U_1$ and is given by a definition that leads directly to the following rules.

Proposition 43. *Let* z_0, z_1 *be fresh variables.*

$$\frac{z_0 \star z_1' \in U_1 \vdash z_0 \star z_1' \in U_0 \quad Pre\ U_1\ z_0, z_0 \star z_1' \in U_0 \vdash z_0 \star z_1' \in U_1}{U_0 \sqsupseteq_{sc} U_1}\ (\sqsupseteq_{sc}^+)$$

$$\frac{U_0 \sqsupseteq_{sc} U_1 \quad t_0 \star t_1' \in U_1}{t_0 \star t_1' \in U_0}\ (\sqsupseteq_{sc_0}^-)$$

$$\frac{U_0 \sqsupseteq_{sc} U_1 \quad Pre\ U_1\ t_0 \quad t_0 \star t_1' \in U_0}{t_0 \star t_1' \in U_1}\ (\sqsupseteq_{sc_1}^-)$$

□

Lemma 13. *The following extra rule is derivable for SC-refinement:*

$$\frac{U_0 \sqsupseteq_{sc} U_1 \quad Pre\ U_1\ t}{Pre\ U_0\ t}$$

□

SC-refinement is introduced for technical reasons which inform the analysis to follow. This notion, in which the precondition may weaken, but in which the postcondition is stable, is not otherwise of much pragmatic interest.

20.3 Refinement for Conjunction

We do not have an introduction rule for the precondition of conjoined operations (see Sect. 6.1). Consequently, schema conjunction is not monotonic with respect to S-refinement. Here is a simple counterexample. Consider the following schemas:

$$U_0 \mathrel{\hat{=}} [\,x, x' : \mathbb{N} \mid x' = 8\,] \quad U_1 \mathrel{\hat{=}} [\,x, x' : \mathbb{N} \mid x' < 10\,] \quad U_2 \mathrel{\hat{=}} [\,x, x' : \mathbb{N} \mid x' = 2\,]$$

We note that U_1 is a non-deterministic operation that can be refined by strengthening its postcondition, for example to U_0. However, when conjoining the operations, we have the following schemas:

$$U_0 \wedge U_2 = [\,x, x' : \mathbb{N} \mid \textit{false}\,] \qquad U_1 \wedge U_2 = [\,x, x' : \mathbb{N} \mid x' = 2\,]$$

In Sect. 7.6 (see also [23, 25]), we define the chaotic specification $\textit{Chaos} =_{df}$ $[T \mid \textit{false}]$. A chaotic specification cannot constitute a refinement of any other specification, because this would signify *augmentation of undefinedness* and would therefore violate any sensible notion of refinement.[33] Thus, $U_0 \wedge U_2 \not\sqsupseteq_s U_1 \wedge U_2$.

The counterexample also shows the reason for the failure: strengthening the postcondition might create a chaotic specification, owing to both the "postcondition only" (single predicate) approach that Z takes [49, 63, 65] and the definition of schema conjunction. This motivates us to add the following side-condition. It is perhaps not surprising that this is precisely the missing introduction rule for the precondition of conjoined operations.

Proposition 44. *Let z be a fresh variable and let U_0, U_1, U_2 be operation schemas with the property that*

$$\textit{Pre } U_0 \, z \wedge \textit{Pre } U_2 \, z \Rightarrow \textit{Pre } (U_0 \wedge U_2) \, z$$

The following rule is then derivable:

$$\frac{U_0 \sqsupseteq_s U_1}{U_0 \wedge U_2 \sqsupseteq_s U_1 \wedge U_2}$$

Proof.

$$\frac{U_0 \sqsupseteq_s U_1 \quad \dfrac{\dfrac{\textit{Pre } (U_1 \wedge U_2)\, z}{\textit{Pre } U_1\, z}^{(1)}}{}}{\dfrac{\textit{Pre } U_0\, z \qquad \dfrac{\dfrac{\textit{Pre } (U_1 \wedge U_2)\, z}{\textit{Pre } U_2\, z}^{(1)}}{}}{\dfrac{\textit{Pre } U_0\, z \wedge \textit{Pre } U_2\, z}{\vdots}}}$$

$$\frac{\textit{Pre } (U_0 \wedge U_2)\, z \qquad\qquad\qquad \begin{array}{c}\delta\\ \vdots\\ z_0 \star z_1' \in U_1 \wedge U_2\end{array}}{U_0 \wedge U_2 \sqsupseteq_s U_1 \wedge U_2}^{(1)}$$

---

[33] See [23, Sect. 4.4] for further details.

where δ is

$$\cfrac{U_0 \sqsupseteq_s U_1 \qquad \cfrac{\overline{Pre\,(U_1 \wedge U_2)\,z_0}\;\;(1)}{Pre\,U_1\,z_0}}{z_0 \star z_1' \dot{\in} U_1} \qquad \cfrac{\cfrac{\overline{z_0 \star z_1' \in U_0 \wedge U_2}\;\;(1)}{z_0 \star z_1' \dot{\in} U_0} \qquad \cfrac{\overline{z_0 \star z_1' \in U_0 \wedge U_2}\;\;(1)}{z_0 \star z_1' \dot{\in} U_2}}{z_0 \star z_1' \in U_1 \wedge U_2}$$

$\square$

Much the same observation can be made for SP-refinement: since non-monotonicity follows by the reduction of non-determinism, SP-refinement and S-refinement coincide. Proposition 44 with $\sqsupseteq_s$ substituted by $\sqsupseteq_{sp}$, holds for SP-refinement; the proof is similar.

SC-refinement guarantees that no reduction of non-determinism is possible, thus ensuring that schema conjunction is monotonic with respect to SC-refinement.

Proposition 45. *The following rule is derivable:*

$$\frac{U_0 \sqsupseteq_{sc} U_1}{U_0 \wedge U_2 \sqsupseteq_{sc} U_1 \wedge U_2}$$

Proof.

$$\cfrac{\cfrac{U_0 \sqsupseteq_{sc} U_1 \qquad \cfrac{\overline{z_0 \star z_1' \in U_1 \wedge U_2}\;\;(1)}{z_0 \star z_1' \dot{\in} U_1}}{z_0 \star z_1' \dot{\in} U_0} \qquad \cfrac{\overline{z_0 \star z_1' \in U_1 \wedge U_2}\;\;(1)}{z_0 \star z_1' \dot{\in} U_2}}{U_0 \wedge U_2 \sqsupseteq_{sc} U_1 \wedge U_2}\;\;(1)$$

where δ is the branch δ of the proof of Proposition 44 (with $\sqsupseteq_s$ substituted by $\sqsupseteq_{sc}$).

$\square$

Note that, although the non-monotonicity of conjunction with respect to S-refinement and SP-refinement is a direct consequence of the ability to strengthen the postcondition, the side-condition used in Proposition 44 is applied in the proof branch concerning the precondition. This is not surprising, because if one attempts to prove the refinement of the conjoined schemas given in the counterexample, one discovers that the branch for the postcondition is provable, owing to the *false* antecedent of the implication, whereas the branch for the precondition fails for the opposite reason (a *false* consequent). Thus, one can expect an application of the side-condition in this branch of the proof at some point.

We would like to highlight the value of insights gained from both counterexamples and formal proofs. One of the benefits of a precise investigation is the ability to deduce or suggest various results as a direct consequence of these. The side-condition above can be calculated through a direct attempt to prove Proposition 44.

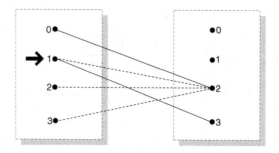

Fig. 9: The solid lines represent the partial relation denoted by the schema $U_1 \vee U_2$, and the dotted lines represent the additional behaviours in the schema $U_0 \vee U_2$. Note the point (marked with a right arrow) which represents *weakening of the postcondition* with respect to $U_1 \vee U_2$. Hence $U_0 \vee U_2 \not\sqsubseteq_s U_1 \vee U_2$

20.4 Refinement for Disjunction

Schema disjunction is not monotonic with respect to S-refinement. In contrast to the analysis of schema conjunction in Sect. 20.3, the reason for non-monotonicity in this case is the fact that S-refinement enables us to weaken the precondition. Weakening the precondition of (at least) one component specification might extend the domain of the disjunction of the two components, leading to an *increase in non-determinism* and thus a failure of refinement. For example, consider the following schemas:

$$U_0 \cong \left[\, \mathsf{x}, \mathsf{x}' : \mathbb{N} \mid \mathsf{x}' = 2 \,\right] \qquad U_1 \cong \left[\, \mathsf{x}, \mathsf{x}' : \mathbb{N} \mid \mathsf{x} = 0 \wedge \mathsf{x}' = 2 \,\right]$$

$$U_2 \cong \left[\, \mathsf{x}, \mathsf{x}' : \mathbb{N} \mid \mathsf{x} = 1 \wedge \mathsf{x}' = 3 \,\right]$$

The specification U_1 is partial and, therefore, can be refined to U_0 by weakening its precondition. However, disjoining the schemas above yields the following specifications:

$$U_0 \vee U_2 = \left[\, \mathsf{x}, \mathsf{x}' : \mathbb{N} \mid \mathsf{x}' = 2 \vee \mathsf{x} = 1 \wedge \mathsf{x}' = 3 \,\right]$$

$$U_1 \vee U_2 = \left[\, \mathsf{x}, \mathsf{x}' : \mathbb{N} \mid \mathsf{x} = 0 \wedge \mathsf{x}' = 2 \vee \mathsf{x} = 1 \wedge \mathsf{x}' = 3 \,\right]$$

Clearly $U_0 \vee U_2 \not\sqsubseteq_s U_1 \vee U_2$. This is because the schema $U_0 \vee U_2$ permits the behaviour $\langle\!\langle\ \mathsf{x} \Rrightarrow 1, \mathsf{x}' \Rrightarrow 2\ \rangle\!\rangle$, which is prohibited by $U_1 \vee U_2$. This is a representative example: the only reason why S-refinement can fail in such a case is as a result of an augmentation of non-determinism with respect to the abstract disjunction; this is shown in Fig. 9. The analysis above suggests that the side-condition will be required in the proof branch concerning the postcondition; as we shall now see, this is the case.

Proposition 46. *Let z be fresh and let U_0, U_1, U_2 be operation schemas with the property that*

$$Pre\ U_0\ z \wedge Pre\ U_2\ z \Rightarrow Pre\ U_1\ z$$

The following rule is then derivable:

$$\frac{U_0 \sqsupseteq_s U_1}{U_0 \vee U_2 \sqsupseteq_s U_1 \vee U_2}$$

Proof.

$$\frac{\delta_0 \qquad\qquad \delta_1}{\vdots \qquad\qquad \vdots}$$

$$\frac{Pre\ (U_0 \vee U_2)\ z \quad z_0 \star z_1' \in U_1 \vee U_2}{U_0 \vee U_2 \sqsupseteq_s U_1 \vee U_2}\ (1)$$

Here, δ_0 stands for the following branch:

$$\frac{\dfrac{U_0 \sqsupseteq_s U_1 \quad \overline{Pre\ U_1\ z}}{Pre\ U_0\ z}\ ^{(2)}}{\dfrac{Pre\ (U_1 \vee U_2)\ z}{}\ ^{(1)} \quad \dfrac{Pre\ U_0\ z}{Pre\ (U_0 \vee U_2)\ z} \qquad \dfrac{\overline{Pre\ U_2\ z}\ ^{(2)}}{Pre\ (U_0 \vee U_2)\ z}}{Pre\ (U_0 \vee U_2)\ z}\ (2)$$

δ_1 is

$$\alpha$$
$$\vdots$$

$$\frac{\dfrac{U_0 \sqsupseteq_s U_1 \quad \dfrac{Pre\ U_1\ z_0 \quad z_0 \star z_1' \in U_0}{\quad}\ ^{(3)}}{z_0 \star z_1' \in U_1}}{\psi}$$

$$\frac{z_0 \star z_1' \in U_0 \vee U_2}{\quad}\ ^{(1)} \qquad \frac{\overline{z_0 \star z_1' \in U_2}\ ^{(3)}}{\psi}\ (3)$$

$$\frac{}{\psi}\ (3)$$

where we have written ψ for $z_0 \star z_1' \in U_1 \vee U_2$, and α is

$$\frac{\dfrac{\overline{z_0 \star z_1' \in U_0}\ ^{(3)}}{Pre\ U_0\ z_0} \qquad \overline{Pre\ U_2\ z_0}\ ^{(4)}}{Pre\ U_0\ z_0 \wedge Pre\ U_2\ z_0}$$

$$\vdots$$

$$\frac{\dfrac{Pre\ (U_1 \vee U_2)\ z_0}{}\ ^{(1)} \qquad \overline{Pre\ U_1\ z_0}\ ^{(4)} \qquad Pre\ U_1\ z_0}{Pre\ U_1\ z_0}\ (4)$$

□

Once again, the side-condition is determined by the proof: it is precisely the entailment of an otherwise unprovable proposition ($Pre\ U_1\ z_0$) from the available assumptions ($Pre\ U_0\ z_0$ and $Pre\ U_2\ z_0$).

The situation with SC-refinement is very similar since, as the counterexample illustrates, the critical factor leading to non-monotonicity in this case is the weakening of the precondition. SC-refinement sanctions this and, therefore, Proposition 46 holds with $\sqsupseteq_s$ substituted by $\sqsupseteq_{sc}$. The proof, given this substitution, is similar.

Schema disjunction is monotonic with respect to SP-refinement because weakening of the precondition is prohibited. The following rule is derivable.

Proposition 47.

$$\frac{U_0 \sqsupseteq_{sp} U_1}{U_0 \vee U_2 \sqsupseteq_{sp} U_1 \vee U_2}$$

Proof.

$$\frac{Pre\,(U_0 \vee U_2)\,z \quad z_0 \star z_1' \in U_1 \vee U_2}{U_0 \vee U_2 \sqsupseteq_{sp} U_1 \vee U_2}\;(1)$$

where δ_0 is identical to the precondition branch in the proof of Proposition 46 (with $\sqsupseteq_s$ substituted by $\sqsupseteq_{sp}$) and δ_1 stands for the following branch:

$$\frac{\dfrac{U_0 \sqsupseteq_{sp} U_1 \quad \dfrac{}{z_0 \star z_1' \in U_0}\,(3)}{z_0 \star z_1' \in U_1}}{\dfrac{z_0 \star z_1' \in U_1 \vee U_2}{z_0 \star z_1' \in U_1 \vee U_2}} \qquad \dfrac{\dfrac{}{z_0 \star z_1' \in U_2}\,(3)}{z_0 \star z_1' \in U_1 \vee U_2}\,(3)$$

$$\dfrac{z_0 \star z_1' \in U_0 \vee U_2}{}\,(1)$$

□

20.5 Refinement for Existential Quantification

There is, of course, an intimate relationship between disjunction and existential quantification. We might expect the monotonicity properties of schema existential quantification to be similar to those for schema disjunction. Indeed, schema existential quantification is not monotonic with respect to S-refinement, because weakening of the precondition might admit behaviours in the concrete operation that are unacceptable in the abstract operation. The reason is that schema existential quantification can hide an arbitrary observation and, in particular, observations that can lead to an augmentation of non-determinism. This is shown by the counterexample in Fig. 10.

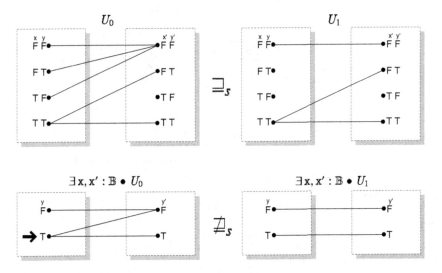

Fig. 10: A counterexample: schema existential quantification is not monotonic with respect to S-refinement

We now present the specifications U_0 and U_1, whose alphabets comprise the Boolean observations x, x', y and y'. The specifications $\exists\, x, x' : \mathbb{B} \bullet U_0$ and $\exists\, x, x' : \mathbb{B} \bullet U_1$ hide the pair of observations x and x' from U_0 and U_1. Note that the schema U_1 denotes a partial operation and U_0 S-refines it by weakening the precondition. Nevertheless, hiding those observations introduces a weakening of the postcondition (marked with an arrow in Fig. 10) of $\exists\, x, x' : \mathbb{B} \bullet U_0$ with respect to $\exists\, x, x' : \mathbb{B} \bullet U_1$. Hence, S-refinement fails.

Like the case of schema disjunction, the above counterexample also suggests that, in order to prove monotonicity of existential hiding, a side-condition is required in the proof branch concerning the postcondition. The side-condition here is stronger than the one used for disjunction because, unlike in the case of schema disjunction, we do not have an additional disjoined schema.

Proposition 48. *Let z be fresh and let U_0, U_1 be operation schemas with the property that*

$$Pre\ U_0\ z \Rightarrow Pre\ U_1\ z$$

The following rule is then derivable:

$$\frac{U_0 \sqsupseteq_s U_1}{\exists\, z : T^z \bullet U_0 \sqsupseteq_s \exists\, z : T^z \bullet U_1}$$

Proof.

$$\cfrac{\cfrac{\delta_0}{\vdots} \qquad \cfrac{\cfrac{z_0 \star z_1' \in \exists \mathbf{z} : T^{\mathbf{z}} \bullet U_0 \quad (1)}{\quad} \quad \cfrac{\delta_1}{\vdots} \quad z_0 \star z_1' \in \exists \mathbf{z} : T^{\mathbf{z}} \bullet U_1}{z_0 \star z_1' \in \exists \mathbf{z} : T^{\mathbf{z}} \bullet U_1} \ (3)}{Pre\,(\exists \mathbf{z} : T^{\mathbf{z}} \bullet U_0)\,z \qquad \qquad \qquad \qquad (1)}$$

$$\exists \mathbf{z} : T^{\mathbf{z}} \bullet U_0 \sqsupseteq_s \exists \mathbf{z} : T^{\mathbf{z}} \bullet U_1$$

where δ_0 is

$$\cfrac{\cfrac{}{Pre\,(\exists \mathbf{z} : T^{\mathbf{z}} \bullet U_1)\,z} \ (1) \qquad \cfrac{\cfrac{U_0 \sqsupseteq_s U_1 \quad \overline{Pre\,U_1\,y} \ (2)}{Pre\,U_0\,y}}{\cfrac{Pre\,(\exists \mathbf{z} : T^{\mathbf{z}} \bullet U_0)\,y}{Pre\,(\exists \mathbf{z} : T^{\mathbf{z}} \bullet U_0)\,z}} \qquad \overline{y \doteq z} \ (2)}{Pre\,(\exists \mathbf{z} : T^{\mathbf{z}} \bullet U_0)\,z} \ (2)$$

and δ_1 is

$$\cfrac{U_0 \sqsupseteq_s U_1 \quad \cfrac{\cfrac{\overline{w \in U_0} \ (3)}{Pre\,U_0\,w}}{\vdots \quad Pre\,U_1\,w} \quad \overline{w \in U_0} \ (3)}{\cfrac{\cfrac{w \in U_1}{w \in \exists \mathbf{z} : T^{\mathbf{z}} \bullet U_1} \qquad \overline{w \doteq z_0 \star z_1'} \ (3)}{z_0 \star z_1' \in \exists \mathbf{z} : T^{\mathbf{z}} \bullet U_1}}$$

□

Note that the above side-condition forces a "fixed-precondition" refinement, which is precisely SP-refinement. So it is an immediate consequence that existential hiding is monotonic with respect to SP-refinement.

Proposition 49. *The following rule is derivable:*

$$\cfrac{U_0 \sqsupseteq_{sp} U_1}{\exists \mathbf{z} : T^{\mathbf{z}} \bullet U_0 \sqsupseteq_{sp} \exists \mathbf{z} : T^{\mathbf{z}} \bullet U_1}$$

□

The proof is essentially identical to Proposition 48.

One might expect that the monotonicity properties of existential hiding with respect to S-refinement and SC-refinement would coincide. Indeed, the side-condition of Proposition 48 is required for proving monotonicity of schema existential hiding with respect to SC-refinement. However, since the side-condition guarantees stability of the precondition, and SC-refinement the stability of the postcondition, the result holds only when the abstract and concrete operations are *equivalent*, which is, of course, far from useful.

20.6 Refinement for Composition

It is not surprising that schema composition is not monotonic with respect to S-refinement, because composition in Z can be expressed in terms of conjunction and existential quantification. Consideration of the results of Sects.

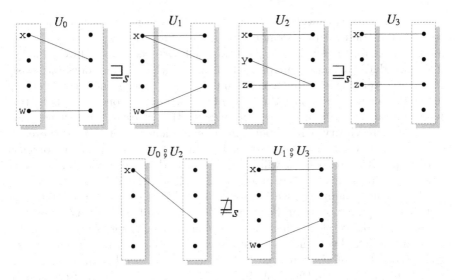

Fig. 11: A counterexample: schema composition is not monotonic with respect to refinement

20.3 and 20.5 suggests that both weakening the precondition and strengthening the postcondition of the component specifications will cause a problem. This is fairly intuitive, since reduction of non-determinism is *demonic* with respect to schema composition (since strengthening the postcondition on the *left* of the composition might demonically choose those after-states that do not connect with the precondition of the operation to the right of the composition). This results in losing requirements from the domain of the composed specifications. In addition, weakening the precondition on the *right* of the composition might demonically extend the specification domain in such a way that the composition will introduce unacceptable behaviours mapped from the original precondition.

The following counterexample illustrates the problems and suggests a solution by suggesting a side-condition. Consider the specifications in Fig. 11. We introduce two abstract specifications U_1 and U_3, and their respective S-refinements U_0 and U_2. We now show that the composition of the underlying concrete specifications does not constitute a refinement of the composition of their abstract counterparts. We label the before-states of each specification using the labels x, y, z and w (from the top).

The specification U_1 has two instances of non-determinism, and U_0 S-refines it by reducing both of these. However, this is demonic, so that the after-state mapped from w in U_0 does not compose with anything in the precondition of U_2; we therefore lose the before-state w from the domain of $U_0 \,\mathbin{;}\, U_2$, whereas it still exists in the domain of $U_1 \,\mathbin{;}\, U_3$. This is one of the reasons for non-refinement.[34] U_2 S-refines U_3 by weakening its precondition, so, in conjunction with the demonic reduction of non-determinism by U_0, the after-state mapped from x in U_0 is composed with the before-state y in U_2. This introduces a binding mapping from x in $U_0 \, \text{\textreferencemark} \, U_2$ which does not exist in $U_1 \, \text{\textreferencemark} \, U_3$, yet x is in the precondition of $U_1 \, \text{\textreferencemark} \, U_3$. This is the second reason for non-refinement. The fact that $(\sqsupseteq_s^+)$ fails for reasons concerning both the precondition and the postcondition suggests that neither the SP- nor the SC-refinement theory will support this monotonicity result. Furthermore, it suggests that a side-condition which is sufficient for proving monotonicity with respect to S-refinement will be needed in both the precondition and the postcondition branches of the proof; as we shall see, this is indeed the case.

The counterexample above and [28, p. 39–40],[35] suggest a remedy: if we insist that every after-state in the range of U_1 is mapped onto at least one value in the precondition of U_3, then, not only can strengthening of the postcondition (on the left) by U_0 never be demonic (as, in the presence of refinement, the precondition of U_2 is at least as large as that of U_3), but also weakening of the precondition (on the right) by U_2 can never introduce an after-state in $U_0 \, \text{\textreferencemark} \, U_2$ that is connected via an intermediate value that was not in the precondition of U_3.[36] This property is called *strong connectivity* and it is defined as follows.

Definition 33 (Strong Connectivity).

$$Sc \; U_0 \; U_1 =_{df} \forall z_0, z_1 \bullet z_0 \star z_1' \in U_0 \Rightarrow Pre \; U_1 \; z_1$$

We can prove that schema composition is monotonic with respect to all three refinement theories, providing $Sc \; U_1 \; U_3$ holds; but we can do better than that. Although strong connectivity is a very intuitive side-condition, there is a weaker condition which is also sufficient. We can be led to this condition by considering further counterexamples. We call it *forking connectivity*. Two specifications comply with this property if, for every non-deterministic before-state (forking point) in the first specification, either *all* the after-states mapped from it connect with some before-state in the *precondition* of the second specification, or *none* of them does.

Definition 34 (Forking Connectivity).

$$Fc \; U_0 \; U_1 =_{df} \forall z_0, z_1, z_2 \bullet (z_0 \star z_1' \in U_0 \land z_0 \star z_2' \in U_0 \land Pre \; U_1 \; z_1) \Rightarrow Pre \; U_1 \; z_2$$

---

[34] Note that had the precondition of U_3 not been weakened by U_2, we would have also lost the before-state x from the precondition of $U_0 \, \text{\textreferencemark} \, U_2$. This would have induced a chaotic specification $U_0 \, \text{\textreferencemark} \, U_2$.

[35] The author of [28] proposes a modified *definition* of composition, in which strong connectivity is embedded.

[36] Unless, of course, this is as a result of composing an after-state in U_0 that constitutes a new behaviour (as a consequence of weakening the precondition of U_1) with a before-state that is outside the precondition of U_3 but is inside the precondition of U_2. Such a case is not relevant in the present context.

Obvious introduction and elimination rules follow from this.

With this in place, we can now prove the monotonicity result. We shall provide only the proof for S-refinement.

Proposition 50. *Let U_0, U_1, U_2 and U_3 be operation schemas with the property that*

$$Fc\ U_1\ U_3$$

The following rule is then derivable:

$$\frac{U_0 \sqsupseteq_s U_1 \quad U_2 \sqsupseteq_s U_3}{U_0 \,\overset{\circ}{,}\, U_2 \sqsupseteq_s U_1 \,\overset{\circ}{,}\, U_3}$$

Proof.

$$\frac{\overset{\delta_0}{\vdots} \qquad \overset{\delta_1}{\vdots}}{Pre\,(U_0 \,\overset{\circ}{,}\, U_2)\, z \quad z_0 \star z_1' \in U_1 \,\overset{\circ}{,}\, U_3}{U_0 \,\overset{\circ}{,}\, U_2 \sqsupseteq_s U_1 \,\overset{\circ}{,}\, U_3}\ (1)$$

Here, δ_0 is

$$\frac{U_0 \sqsupseteq_s U_1 \quad \dfrac{\overline{Pre\,(U_1 \,\overset{\circ}{,}\, U_3)\, z}\ (1)}{Pre\ U_1\ z}}{Pre\ U_0\ z} \qquad \dfrac{\overline{z \star y_0' \in U_0}}{}\ (2) \qquad \dfrac{U_2 \sqsupseteq_s U_3 \quad \overset{\alpha_0}{\vdots}\ Pre\ U_3\ y_0}{Pre\ U_2\ y_0}}{Pre\,(U_0 \,\overset{\circ}{,}\, U_2)\, z}\ (2)$$
$$\overline{Pre\,(U_0 \,\overset{\circ}{,}\, U_2)\, z}\ (2)$$

where α_0 is

$$\frac{\overline{Pre\,(U_1 \,\overset{\circ}{,}\, U_3)\, z}\ (1) \quad \dfrac{Fc\ U_1\ U_3 \quad \overset{\gamma_0}{\vdots}\ z \star y_0' \in U_1 \quad \overline{z \star w_0' \in U_1}\ (3) \quad \overline{Pre\ U_3\ w_0}\ (3)}{Pre\ U_3\ y_0}\ (3)}{Pre\ U_3\ y_0}$$

where γ_0 is

$$\frac{U_0 \sqsupseteq_s U_1 \quad \overline{z \star y_0' \in U_0}\ (2) \quad \dfrac{\overline{Pre\,(U_1 \,\overset{\circ}{,}\, U_3)\, z}\ (1)}{Pre\ U_1\ z}}{z \star y_0' \in U_1}$$

and δ_1 is

$$\frac{\overline{z_0 \star z_1' \in U_0 \,\overset{\circ}{,}\, U_2}\ (1)}{\dfrac{U_0 \sqsupseteq_s U_1 \quad \dfrac{\overline{Pre\,(U_1 \,\overset{\circ}{,}\, U_3)\, z_0}\ (1)}{Pre\ U_1\ z_0} \quad \overline{z_0 \star y_1' \in U_0}\ (4) \quad \overset{\alpha_1}{\vdots}}{z_0 \star y_1' \in U_1} \quad \dfrac{z_0 \star z_1' \in U_1 \,\overset{\circ}{,}\, U_3}{}\ (4)}{z_0 \star z_1' \in U_1 \,\overset{\circ}{,}\, U_3}}$$

where α_1 is

$$\cfrac{U_2 \sqsupseteq_s U_3 \qquad \cfrac{\cfrac{}{Pre\,(U_1 \,\fatsemi\, U_3)\,z_0}\,{}^{(1)}}{Pre\,U_3\,y_1} \qquad \cfrac{\begin{array}{c}\beta_1\\\vdots\\Pre\,U_3\,y_1\end{array}}{}\,{}^{(5)}}{y_1 \star z_1' \in U_3} \qquad \cfrac{}{y_1 \star z_1' \in U_2}\,{}^{(4)}$$

where β_1 is

$$\cfrac{Fc\,U_1\,U_3 \qquad z_0 \star y_1' \in U_1 \qquad \cfrac{\begin{array}{c}\gamma_1\\\vdots\\z_0 \star w_1' \in U_1\end{array}}{}\,{}^{(5)} \qquad \cfrac{}{Pre\,U_3\,w_1}\,{}^{(5)}}{Pre\,U_3\,y_1}$$

and where γ_1 is

$$\cfrac{U_0 \sqsupseteq_s U_1 \qquad \cfrac{\cfrac{}{Pre\,(U_1 \,\fatsemi\, U_3)\,z_0}\,{}^{(1)}}{Pre\,U_1\,z_0} \qquad \cfrac{}{z_0 \star y_1' \in U_0}\,{}^{(4)}}{z_0 \star y_1' \in U_1}$$

$\square$

Finally, it is interesting to note that, since weakening the precondition causes a problem on the right and strengthening the postcondition causes a problem on the left, it is an immediate consequence that schema composition is *monotonic on the right* with respect to SP-refinement (because the precondition is fixed), and *monotonic on the left* with respect to SC-refinement (because the postcondition is fixed). Hence, the following rules are derivable.

Proposition 51.

$$\cfrac{U_0 \sqsupseteq_{sp} U_1}{U_2 \,\fatsemi\, U_0 \sqsupseteq_{sp} U_2 \,\fatsemi\, U_1} \qquad \cfrac{U_0 \sqsupseteq_{sc} U_1}{U_0 \,\fatsemi\, U_2 \sqsupseteq_{sc} U_1 \,\fatsemi\, U_2}$$

Proof. We provide only the proof for SP-refinement.

$$\cfrac{\cfrac{\cfrac{}{Pre\,(U_2 \,\fatsemi\, U_1)\,z}\,{}^{(1)}}{Pre\,(U_2 \,\fatsemi\, U_0)\,z}\quad\cfrac{\cfrac{}{z \star y' \in U_2}\,{}^{(2)} \qquad \cfrac{U_0 \sqsupseteq_{sp} U_1 \qquad \cfrac{}{Pre\,U_1\,y}\,{}^{(2)}}{Pre\,U_0\,y}}{Pre\,(U_2 \,\fatsemi\, U_0)\,z}\,{}^{(2)}}{U_2 \,\fatsemi\, U_0 \sqsupseteq_{sp} U_2 \,\fatsemi\, U_1}\quad\cfrac{\begin{array}{c}\delta\\\vdots\\{}\end{array}}{}\,{}^{(1)}$$

where δ is

$$\cfrac{\cfrac{}{z_0 \star z_1' \in U_2 \,\fatsemi\, U_0}\,{}^{(1)} \qquad \cfrac{\cfrac{}{z_0 \star y' \in U_2}\,{}^{(3)} \qquad \cfrac{U_0 \sqsupseteq_{sp} U_1 \qquad \cfrac{}{y \star z_1' \in U_0}\,{}^{(3)}}{y \star z_1' \in U_1}}{z_0 \star z_1' \in U_2 \,\fatsemi\, U_1}\,{}^{(3)}}{z_0 \star z_1' \in U_2 \,\fatsemi\, U_1}$$

$\square$

21 Distributivity Properties of the Chaotic Completion

The standard interpretation of refinement for Z in the literature (for example, [18, 68]) is what we have called $W_\bullet$-refinement (Sect. 7.4 and [23, 25]). It is important to note that the definition concerns the partial-relation interpretation of schema *expressions*. That is, the interpretation of schemas, and of *all* the operations for building modular specifications, are logically *prior* to the theory of refinement.

$W_\bullet$-refinement is, as we have already remarked, equivalent to S-refinement, the theory we used in the previous section. So everything we have established so far also applies to $W_\bullet$-refinement. It is, however, often illuminating to consider matters through distinct though equivalent formulations; this section is devoted to that, mainly through a consideration of lifted totalisation as an operator in its own right.

One way of illustrating the failure of monotonicity, as it arises in the $W_\bullet$-refinement framework, is to take a look at how the lifted totalisation interacts directly with the schema operators. For example, if the following full distributivity property held,

$$(U_0 \stackrel{\bullet}{\wedge} U_1) = \stackrel{\bullet}{U_0} \wedge \stackrel{\bullet}{U_1} \quad \text{✗}$$

then schema conjunction *would* be fully monotonic with respect to refinement. That is, we would have

$$\frac{U_0 \sqsupseteq_{w_\bullet} U_2 \quad U_1 \sqsupseteq_{w_\bullet} U_3}{U_0 \wedge U_1 \sqsupseteq_{w_\bullet} U_2 \wedge U_3} \quad \text{✗}$$

with a proof:

$$\cfrac{\cfrac{\cfrac{\cfrac{}{z \in (U_0 \stackrel{\bullet}{\wedge} U_1)} \,(1)\;\text{✗}}{z \in \stackrel{\bullet}{U_0} \wedge \stackrel{\bullet}{U_1}}}{U_0 \sqsupseteq_{w_\bullet} U_2 \quad z \in \stackrel{\bullet}{U_0}}{z \in \stackrel{\bullet}{U_2}} \qquad \cfrac{\cfrac{\cfrac{\cfrac{}{z \in (U_0 \stackrel{\bullet}{\wedge} U_1)} \,(1)\;\text{✗}}{z \in \stackrel{\bullet}{U_0} \wedge \stackrel{\bullet}{U_1}}}{U_1 \sqsupseteq_{w_\bullet} U_3 \quad z \in \stackrel{\bullet}{U_1}}{z \in \stackrel{\bullet}{U_3}}}{\cfrac{\cfrac{z \in \stackrel{\bullet}{U_2} \wedge \stackrel{\bullet}{U_3}}{z \in (U_2 \stackrel{\bullet}{\wedge} U_3)} \;\text{✔}}{U_0 \wedge U_1 \sqsupseteq_{w_\bullet} U_2 \wedge U_3} \,(1)}$$

Here, the annotations of the proof indicate the problem: only half of the full distributivity equation holds. Put another way, for full (unconditioned) monotonicity, *we needed the equation at the level of the total-relation semantics, but in Z we have it only at the level of the partial-relation semantics* (this is the usual equational logic to be found in textbooks).

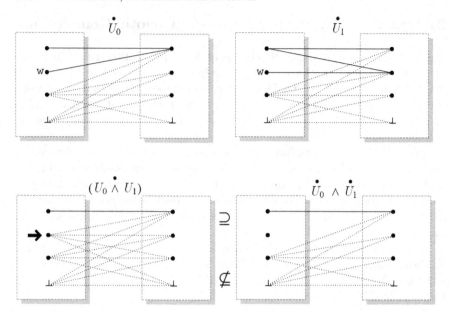

Fig. 12: Lifted totalisation does not fully distribute over schema conjunction

The situation is similar for every schema operator. In this section we shall analyse in detail the reasons why full distributivity of the lifted totalisation operator fails with respect to each of the schema calculus operators investigated in Sect. 20. We shall introduce side-conditions that are sufficient to attain *full-distributivity equations* and then analyse their usefulness and their relationship to the side-conditions introduced in Sect. 20.

21.1 Distributivity for Conjunction

The problem with distributing the lifted totalisation operator over schema conjunction arises when identical before-states of the two component specifications do not agree on their after-states. This leads only to a distributivity in-equation and not to full equivalence. This case is illustrated in Fig. 12. The figure illustrates two specifications, U_0 and U_1, which share the before-state w, but map it to distinct after-states. Conjoining these two specifications removes w from the domain, and the completion operator interprets partiality as *chaos*: anything is possible (marked with an arrow in Fig. 12). This contrasts with the result of conjoining the completions of the specifications, which introduces partiality at the level of the refinement theory. Here the partiality looks more like *infeasibility*. General infeasibility is often known (for example, in two-predicate frameworks such as Refinement Calculus and VDM [41, 42]) as *magic*:[37] an extreme specification whose precondition is *true* and whose postcondition is *false* (it is guaranteed to terminate, yet must establish an impossible outcome). In the figure, the infeasibility is localised: we shall refer to this as *local magical behaviour*.

As we can see in Fig. 12, distributing the relational completion operator over schema conjunction may cause local magical behaviour whenever distinct after-states are mapped from the same before-state (w in this case) in the two component specifications, prior to the lifted totalisation. This behaviour results in partiality, in a similar fashion to the two-predicate-based frameworks (including the approach taken in [34, 37]). Note that Z, a *single-predicate* framework, is capable of modelling only two of the extreme specifications: *chance* and *chaos*, in which the preconditions and postconditions are simultaneously true and false, respectively. For this reason, we have a distributivity *in*-equation.

Proposition 52. *The following rule is derivable:*

$$\frac{t_0 \star t_1' \in \overset{\bullet}{U_0} \wedge \overset{\bullet}{U_1}}{t_0 \star t_1' \in \overset{\bullet}{(U_0 \wedge U_1)}}$$

□

The only way to ensure that distributivity holds in the other direction is by preventing such contentious states in the component specifications: that is, preventing local magical behaviour. This is achieved by insisting that the conjunction of the two specifications will, at least, retain the precondition of their *disjunction*:

Definition 35 (Properly Conjoined Operation Schemas).

$$Pc \ U_0 \ U_1 =_{df} \forall z \bullet Pre \ (U_0 \vee U_1) \ z \Rightarrow Pre \ (U_0 \wedge U_1) \ z$$

Proposition 53. *Let U_0 and U_1 be operation schemas with the property that*

$$Pc \ U_0 \ U_1$$

The following rule is then derivable:

$$\frac{t_0 \star t_1' \in \overset{\bullet}{(U_0 \wedge U_1)}}{t_0 \star t_1' \in \overset{\bullet}{U_0} \wedge \overset{\bullet}{U_1}}$$

□

---

[37] For a complete account of extreme specifications see, for example, [28, 48, 65, 66].

21.2 Distributivity for Disjunction

The lifted totalisation operator does not distribute fully over schema disjunction because completing component specifications that have different preconditions may induce chaotic behaviour in their disjunction, but non-chaotic behaviour when the component specifications are disjoined and then completed. Fig. 13 illustrates this.

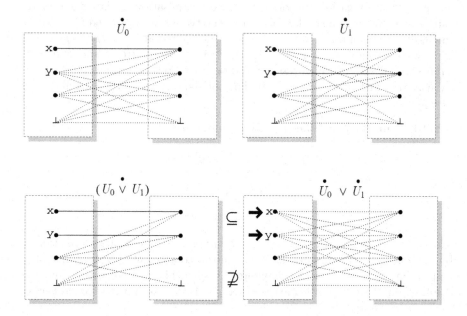

Fig. 13: Lifted totalisation does not fully distribute over schema disjunction

The specification U_0 has just one after-state mapped from x, and the specification U_1 has just one after-state mapped from y. Disjoining these partial relations, prior to completion, results in those two after-states (mapped from x and y in $U_0 \vee U_1$) and chaotic behaviour everywhere else. However, applying the lifted totalisation to U_0 and U_1 (individually), gives rise to chaotic behaviour mapped from y in $\overset{\bullet}{U_0}$ and similarly for x in $\overset{\bullet}{U_1}$. Thus, $\overset{\bullet}{U_0} \vee \overset{\bullet}{U_1}$ is chaotic from these two before-states (marked with arrows); hence, we have an in-equation rather than a full equivalence.

Proposition 54. *The following rule is derivable:*

$$\frac{t_0 \star t_1' \in (U_0 \overset{\bullet}{\vee} U_1)}{t_0 \star t_1' \in \overset{\bullet}{U_0} \vee \overset{\bullet}{U_1}}$$

□

We observed, in Fig. 13, that full distributivity fails because of distinctions in the preconditions of the specifications U_0 and U_1. Therefore, insisting that the component specifications have identical preconditions guarantees full distributivity.

Definition 36 (Stable Preconditions).

$$Sp\ U_0\ U_1 =_{df} \forall z \bullet Pre\ U_0\ z \Leftrightarrow Pre\ U_1\ z$$

Proposition 55. *Let U_0 and U_1 be operation schemas with the property that*

$$Sp\ U_0\ U_1$$

The following rule is then derivable:

$$\frac{t_0 \star t_1' \in \overset{\bullet}{U_0} \vee \overset{\bullet}{U_1}}{t_0 \star t_1' \in (U_0 \overset{\bullet}{\vee} U_1)}$$

□

21.3 Distributivity for Existential Quantification

Full distribution of the relational completion operator over schema existential hiding fails. This follows because hiding observations after applying lifted totalisation can introduce chaotic behaviour that will not always arise when observations are hidden before lifted totalisation. This is shown in Fig. 14. We present a specification U whose alphabet comprises the Boolean observations x, x', y and y'. Hiding the observations x and x' yields a *total* specification $\exists x, x' : \mathbb{B} \bullet U$. The only effect of lifted totalisation on this will be the mapping of $\perp$ onto all after-states. Yet, hiding the same observations after lifted totalisation introduces chaotic behaviour from the before-state **T** (marked with an arrow) in the specification $\exists x, x' : \mathbb{B} \bullet \overset{\bullet}{U}$. This is a consequence of mapping the before-state **FT** (which is outside the precondition of U) onto all the after-states in $\overset{\bullet}{U}$ (including $\perp$). As a result, hiding the observations x and x' in $\overset{\bullet}{U}$ leaves the remainder of this state sanctioning every possible outcome. For this reason, we have only a distributivity in-equation.

Proposition 56. *The following rule is derivable:*

$$\frac{t \in (\exists z : T^z \overset{\bullet}{\bullet} U)}{t \in \exists z : T^z \bullet \overset{\bullet}{U}}$$

□

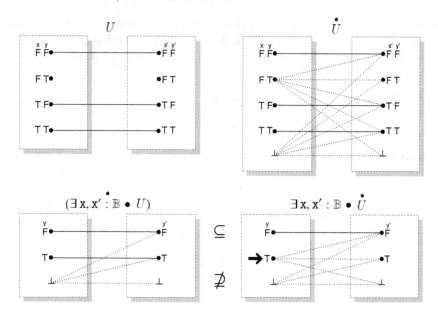

Fig. 14: Lifted totalisation does not fully distribute over schema existential quantification

Since existential quantification is a generalisation of disjunction, it is not surprising that the failure of the converse in-equation is reminiscent of the case for schema disjunction (Sect. 21.2), although here we have one specification rather than two: the difference described by Fig. 14 arises because distinct before-states, which involve the same hidden observation in the specification, have a different *precondition status*.[38]

Naturally, the remedy is very similar to "stable preconditions" (Definition 36), though here we have only a single specification: we need to ensure that any before-state in the precondition of $\exists z : T^z \bullet U$ is equivalently in the precondition of U. One direction is merely $(Pre_{\exists}^+)$ (see Sect. 6.4); thus all we need is the following property.

Definition 37 (Weak Binding).

$$Wb\ U =_{df} \forall x \bullet Pre\ (\exists z : T^z \bullet U)\ x \Rightarrow Pre\ U\ x$$

Proposition 57. *Let U be operation schema with the property that*

$$Wb\ U$$

The following rule is then derivable:

---

[38] One before-state is in the precondition and one is outside the precondition of the specification.

$$t \in \exists z : T^z \bullet \overset{\bullet}{U}$$
$$\overline{}$$
$$t \in (\exists z : \overset{\bullet}{T^z} \bullet U)$$

□

21.4 Distributivity for Composition

The lifted totalisation operator distributes over schema composition (but not conversely) because composing a non-deterministic specification (on the left) with a partial specification (on the right) may give rise to local chaos in the composition of their (individual) completions, but this might not arise in the completion of their composition. This is illustrated in Fig. 15.

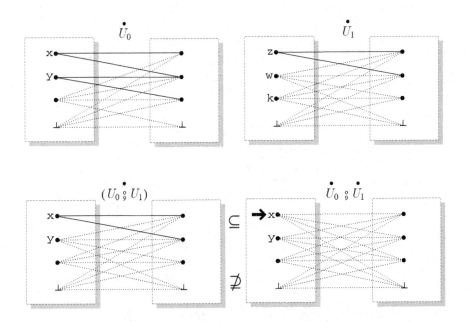

Fig. 15: Lifted totalisation does not fully distribute over schema composition

An observation, such as w, outside the precondition of U_1 plays no part in linking before-states of U_0 and after-states of U_1 in the composition $U_0 \,\fatsemi\, U_1$ (nor in its lifted totalisation). Thus x, in $U_0 \,\fatsemi\, U_1$, is associated with the two after-states, mapped from z in U_1. However, applying the relational completion operator to U_0 and U_1 separately results in chaotic behaviour mapped from w in $\overset{\bullet}{U_1}$ and, consequently, chaotic behaviour (marked with an arrow) from x in $\overset{\bullet}{U_0} \,\fatsemi\, \overset{\bullet}{U_1}$. Therefore, we have only the following in-equation. We provide the proofs in this case.

Proposition 58. *The following rule is derivable:*

$$\frac{t_0 \star t_1' \in (U_0 \,\overset{\bullet}{\,{}_9\,} U_1)}{t_0 \star t_1' \in \overset{\bullet}{U_0} \,{}_9\, \overset{\bullet}{U_1}}$$

Proof.

$$\frac{t_0 \star t_1' \in (U_0 \,\overset{\bullet}{\,{}_9\,} U_1) \quad t_0 \star t_1' \in \overset{\bullet}{U_0} \,{}_9\, \overset{\bullet}{U_1} \quad t_0 \star t_1' \in \overset{\bullet}{U_0} \,{}_9\, \overset{\bullet}{U_1}}{t_0 \star t_1' \in \overset{\bullet}{U_0} \,{}_9\, \overset{\bullet}{U_1}} \,\heartsuit\,(1)$$

with δ_0 and γ above the first and third premises respectively.

where δ_0 is

$$\frac{\dfrac{}{\neg\, Pre\,(U_0 \,{}_9\, U_1)\, t_0}\,(1)}{\dfrac{\neg\, Pre\, U_0\, t_0 \vee (\forall z \bullet t_0 \star z' \in U_0 \Rightarrow \neg\, Pre\, U_1\, z) \quad t_0 \star t_1' \in \overset{\bullet}{U_0} \,{}_9\, \overset{\bullet}{U_1}}{t_0 \star t_1' \in \overset{\bullet}{U_0} \,{}_9\, \overset{\bullet}{U_1}}\,(2)}$$

with δ_1, δ_2 above.

and δ_1 is

$$\frac{\neg\, Pre\, U_0\, t_0 \,(2) \quad \dfrac{\dfrac{t_0 \star t_1' \in (U_0 \,\overset{\bullet}{\,{}_9\,} U_1)}{\dfrac{t_0 \star t_1' \in T_{0\perp}^{in} \star T_{1\perp}^{out'}}{t_0 \in T_{0\perp}^{in}}\,(C.\,1(ii))}{t_0 \star \perp' \in \overset{\bullet}{U_0}} \quad \dfrac{\dfrac{t_0 \star t_1' \in (U_0 \,\overset{\bullet}{\,{}_9\,} U_1)}{\dfrac{t_0 \star t_1' \in T_{0\perp}^{in} \star T_{1\perp}^{out'}}{t_1' \in T_{1\perp}^{out'}}\,(C.\,1(i))}{\perp \star t_1' \in \overset{\bullet}{U_1}}}{t_0 \star t_1' \in \overset{\bullet}{U_0} \,{}_9\, \overset{\bullet}{U_1}}$$

and δ_2 is

$$\frac{\dfrac{}{Pre\, U_0\, t_0 \vee \neg\, Pre\, U_0\, t_0}\,(LEM) \quad t_0 \star t_1' \in \overset{\bullet}{U_0} \,{}_9\, \overset{\bullet}{U_1}}{t_0 \star t_1' \in \overset{\bullet}{U_0} \,{}_9\, \overset{\bullet}{U_1}}\,(3)$$

with α_0, β_1 above the right premise.

and α_0 is

$$\frac{Pre\, U_0\, t_0\,(3) \quad \dfrac{\dfrac{\dfrac{t_0 \star w' \in U_0}{t_0 \star w' \in \overset{\bullet}{U_0}}\,(L.\,3(i)) \quad w \star t_1' \in \overset{\bullet}{U_1}}{t_0 \star t_1' \in \overset{\bullet}{U_0} \,{}_9\, \overset{\bullet}{U_1}}}{}\,(4)}{t_0 \star t_1' \in \overset{\bullet}{U_0} \,{}_9\, \overset{\bullet}{U_1}}$$

with (4) above $t_0 \star w' \in U_0$ and β_0 above $w \star t_1' \in \overset{\bullet}{U_1}$.

and β_0 is

$$\cfrac{\cfrac{\cfrac{\cfrac{\overline{t_0 \star w' \in U_0}\ (4)}{t_0 \star w' \in T_0^{in} \star T_1^{in'}}}{w \in T_1^{in}}}{w \in T_{1\perp}^{in}} \qquad \cfrac{\cfrac{\cfrac{t_0 \star t_1' \in (U_0 \mathbin{\overset{\bullet}{\text{\fontsize{6}{6}\selectfont 9}}} U_1)}{t_0 \star t_1' \in T_{0\perp}^{in} \star T_{1\perp}^{out'}}}{t_1' \in T_{1\perp}^{out'}}}{}\ (L.\ 3(iii))}{w \star t_1' \in \overset{\bullet}{U_1}}$$

with α_1 and $\neg\ Pre\ U_1\ w$ on the left branch.

and α_1 is

$$\cfrac{\cfrac{\overline{\forall\, z \bullet t_0 \star z' \in U_0 \Rightarrow \neg\ Pre\ U_1\ z}\ (2)}{t_0 \star w' \in U_0 \Rightarrow \neg\ Pre\ U_1\ w} \qquad \overline{t_0 \star w' \in U_0}\ (4)}{\neg\ Pre\ U_1\ w}$$

and β_1 is identical to δ_1 modulo substitution of the label (3) for the label (2). Finally, γ is

$$\cfrac{\overline{t_0 \star t_1' \in U_0 \mathbin{\text{\fontsize{6}{6}\selectfont 9}} U_1}\ (1) \qquad \cfrac{\cfrac{\cfrac{\overline{t_0 \star y' \in U_0}\ (5)}{t_0 \star y' \in \overset{\bullet}{U_0}}\ (L.\ 3(i)) \qquad \cfrac{\overline{y \star t_1' \in U_1}\ (5)}{y \star t_1' \in \overset{\bullet}{U_1}}\ (L.\ 3(i))}{t_0 \star t_1' \in \overset{\bullet}{U_0} \mathbin{\overset{\bullet}{\text{\fontsize{6}{6}\selectfont 9}}} \overset{\bullet}{U_1}}}{}\ (5)}{t_0 \star t_1' \in \overset{\bullet}{U_0} \mathbin{\overset{\bullet}{\text{\fontsize{6}{6}\selectfont 9}}} \overset{\bullet}{U_1}}$$

□

There are two observations we can make about this proof. First, note that the proof step labelled $\heartsuit$ denotes an application of $(\bullet^-)$ but where Definition 7.4 is expressed using disjunction (in the obvious way) in place of implication, leading to a single disjunctive elimination rule. This rule is also used in the proofs of Propositions 54 and 56. Second, the proof depends on use of the *law of the excluded middle*. Once again, we suspect that the result is strictly classical, as are many others in refinement theory (for example, [19–21]).

Fig. 15 demonstrates that distributivity fails in the other direction precisely because the two after-states mapped from x in U_0 coincide with two before-states in U_1 with a different precondition status. We can see that the forking point y in U_0 does not constitute a problem, since w and k are both outside the precondition of U_1; thus y is associated with chaotic behaviour in both $(U_0 \mathbin{\overset{\bullet}{\text{\fontsize{6}{6}\selectfont 9}}} U_1)$ and $\overset{\bullet}{U_0} \mathbin{\overset{\bullet}{\text{\fontsize{6}{6}\selectfont 9}}} \overset{\bullet}{U_1}$. Furthermore, had we had w in the precondition of U_1, we would have obtained the same (non-chaotic) behaviour associated with x in both cases. This suggests that a side-condition guaranteeing full distributivity would insist on associating all the after-states, mapped from a certain *non-deterministic before-state* in U_0, with some before-states in U_1 – all of which have the same precondition status. This is, indeed, the *forking connectivity* property used to ensure monotonicity of schema composition with respect to S-refinement (Sect. 20.6).

Proposition 59. *Let U_0 and U_1 be operation schemas, with the property that*

$$Fc\ U_0\ U_1$$

The following rule is then derivable:

$$\frac{t_0 \star t_1' \in \overset{\bullet}{U_0} \,\mathring{,}\, \overset{\bullet}{U_1}}{t_0 \star t_1' \in (U_0 \,\mathring{,}\, U_1)^{\bullet}}$$

Proof.

$$\frac{\dfrac{\beta}{\vdots} \quad \dfrac{\dfrac{}{y \star t_1' \in \overset{\bullet}{U_1}} \,(1) \quad Pre\ U_1\ y}{y \star t_1' \in U_1}}{\dfrac{t_0 \star y' \in U_0 \qquad y \star t_1' \in U_1}{t_0 \star t_1' \in U_0 \,\mathring{,}\, U_1}} \qquad \dfrac{\dfrac{\delta}{\vdots} \quad t_0 \star t_1' \in \overset{\bullet}{U_0} \,\mathring{,}\, \overset{\bullet}{U_1}}{t_0 \star t_1' \in T_{0\perp}^{in} \star T_{1\perp}^{out'}}\,(2)}{\dfrac{\psi \qquad \qquad \qquad t_0 \star t_1' \in (U_0 \,\mathring{,}\, U_1)^{\bullet}}{t_0 \star t_1' \in (U_0 \,\mathring{,}\, U_1)^{\bullet}}\,(1)}$$

where we have written ψ for $t_0 \star t_1' \in \overset{\bullet}{U_0} \,\mathring{,}\, \overset{\bullet}{U_1}$, and δ is

$$\frac{\dfrac{}{Pre\ (U_0 \,\mathring{,}\, U_1)\ t_0}\,(2) \qquad \dfrac{Fc\ U_0\ U_1 \quad t_0 \star y' \in U_0 \quad \dfrac{}{Pre\ U_1\ w}\,(3) \quad \dfrac{}{t_0 \star w' \in U_0}\,(3)}{Pre\ U_1\ y}}{Pre\ U_1\ y}\,(3)$$

and β is

$$\frac{\dfrac{}{t_0 \star y' \in \overset{\bullet}{U_0}}\,(1) \qquad \dfrac{\dfrac{Pre\ (U_0 \,\mathring{,}\, U_1)\ t_0}{Pre\ U_0\ t_0}\,(2)}{Pre\ U_0\ t_0}\,(L.1)}{t_0 \star y' \in U_0}$$

□

21.5 Discussion

The side-conditions that we have isolated, either for ensuring full distributivity or for establishing monotonicity directly, are not similar to the syntactic side-conditions routinely associated with logical rules, such as $\exists$-elimination. Syntactic side-conditions are decidable, so it can always be determined when a rule applies. The side-conditions that we have formulated are proof-theoretically more complex and, in fact, only semi-decidable. From a practical point of view, this is not very satisfactory. Moreover, most make mention of the *concrete* specification in addition to the abstract specification. This is unfortunate because it reduces the practical use of the refinement rules when used *calculationally*, to *construct* the concrete specification. The exceptions to this are the two connectivity principles used in the case of composition. And one could in fact avoid mention of the concrete specification, in the case of disjunction, by omitting one of the antecedent propositions, thereby obtaining a condition which is purely abstract, but which is, of course, somewhat less applicable. It could be argued that these side-conditions are reasonable only if they refer *exclusively* to either the abstract or the concrete specifications [62]. In this way the true spirit of *abstraction* (in which the internal structure of the abstract specification is not to be disclosed) is upheld. Overall, the lack of monotonicity is a distinct drawback which such proof-theoretic side-conditions do not address satisfactorily from a practical perspective.

Our analysis has of course concentrated on only two (equivalent) notions of refinement: S-refinement and $W_\bullet$-refinement. Possibly there are other formulations of refinement which would be better behaved. And, as we know, there are several alternative approaches:

- *Weakest-precondition refinement* – it is possible to reinterpret the partial relations in terms of a weakest-precondition semantics and to characterise refinement in the standard way in that regime.
- *Sets of implementation* – in the spirit of constructive theories of program development, for example Martin-Löf type theory [46] (though in the setting of classical logic) it is possible to reinterpret specifications as sets of permissible implementations. Refinement in this case is simply set inclusion.
- *strictly-lifted totalisation* – it is possible to modify the lifted totalisation so that the lifting is strict (abortive) rather then non-strict (chaotic).
- *Non-lifted totalisation* – it is possible to totalise the partial relations without lifting if one is prepared to exclude fully chaotic behaviour from the notion of a precondition.

We demonstrated in Sect. 7 et seq. (see also [23]) that all of these theories of refinement are equivalent to the standard lifted-totalised account. As a consequence, all suffer from the same weaknesses in terms of their (lack of) monotonicity properties. Naturally, one could ask: are there still others which have yet to be discovered? In addressing this question, we would need to find some *principles* which distinguish a relation worthy of the name "refinement" from any arbitrary binary relation on specifications. After all, the schema operators are all fully monotonic with respect to *equality*, but equality is evidently *not* a notion of refinement. In capturing the general principles, one would be led to the properties described by S-refinement or SP-refinement. A notion of refinement ought to be at least *sound* with respect to one or other of those. Our analysis has already demonstrated the limits of modular reasoning with respect to these notions.

Our analysis of distributivity does provide an interesting clue that motivates us to make some final remarks. This is the observation that we have an equational logic at the level of the underlying *partial* relations, but not at the level of the *total* relations involved in refinement, suggesting an alternative approach: instead of developing a schema calculus at the level of partial relations and only then introducing total relational refinement, we could introduce that calculus afterwards. This would naturally lead to a fully monotonic schema calculus, because refinement would then simply become the subset relation on the modified relational model. Of course, it would obviously lead to a distinct schema calculus with quite different properties. Such a trajectory has led to a new specification language νZ, in the Z tradition but offering a very interesting and distinct mathematical, pragmatic and methodological approach. Early research on this has been reported in [33].

22 Conclusions

The current work addresses two aims: first, to provide an accessible introduction to the Z logic based on $\mathcal{Z}_C$, and second, to survey a range of more advanced applications of this logic with references to the relevant literature.

The reader will have noticed one or two occasions on which some concepts here differ from vernacular Z (and indeed ISO Z). It is worth reflecting a little on the reasons for these differences. Z was originally introduced not as a theory, but rather as a notation or language. The early formal work on Z concentrated on semantics (see [57] in particular). This emphasis did not naturally lead to an increase in the level of formality for future investigations: a logic permits direct reasoning in the language, whereas reasoning in the semantics is hardly a practical (nor even a desirable) matter. It should not be too surprising, therefore, to discover opportunities and difficulties when a language, which has to a great extent developed independently of its mathematical foundations, is considered in a logical context. These tensions are very much a part of some previous work to which we have already referred: whilst [35] is largely devoted to vernacular Z, [38,39] explicitly ask questions about vernacular Z which arise as a consequence of a logical analysis. In this chapter, the deviations (apart from trivial notational differences) are modest but present: priming considered as a bijective operation between observations and co-observations (Sect. 3.1) and a hint in the direction of novelty in connection with θ-terms of the form $\theta S'$ (Sect. 2.2). The papers [38,39] are more revisionary, as their titles suggest.

A second theme that we wish to highlight concerns our survey of more advanced areas: the fact that the logic permits the formalisation of associated conceptual apparatus alongside the specification language itself. Of particular note is the wide variety of refinement theories that we have presented. In addition to the material discussed here, it is also possible to formalise programming notations within the logic, and relationships between programs and specifications. This is covered in [34,37]; again, all the formalisation and analysis takes place within a single framework.

23 Acknowledgements

We have discussed Z, Z logic, and associated theories of refinement and program development with more people than we can possibly list without running a risk of serious omission. There is no excuse, however, for failing to mention Rob Arthan, Eerke Boiten, Jonathan Bowen, John Derrick, Lindsay Groves, Greg Reeve, Ray Turner (who provided much inspiration in the form of an earlier attempt to provide a logic for Z), Mark Utting and Jim Woodcock.

References

1. J.R. Abrial. *The B-Book*. Cambridge University Press, 1996.
2. K. Araki, A. Galloway and K. Taguchi, editors. *Integrated Formal Methods, Proceedings of the 1st International Conference on Integrated Formal Methods*. Springer, 1999.
3. R.D. Arthan. On free type definitions in Z. In *[51]*, pages 40–58.
4. D. Azada and P. Muenchaisri, editors. *APSEC 2003: 10th Asia-Pacific Software Engineering Conference*. IEEE Computer Society Press, 2003.
5. R. Barden, S. Stepney and D. Cooper. *Z in Practice*. Prentice Hall, 1994.
6. D. Bert, J.P. Bowen, S. King, and M. Waldén, editors. *2nd International Workshop on Refinement of Critical Systems: Methods, Tools and Developments*, 2003.
7. D. Bert, J.P. Bowen, S. King, and M. Waldén, editors. *ZB 2003: Formal Specification and Development in Z and B, Third International Conference of B and Z Users*, volume 2651 of Lecture Notes in Computer Science. Springer, 2003.
8. D. Bjørner, C.A.R. Hoare and H. Langmaack, editors. *VDM '90, VDM and Z: Formal Methods in Software Development, Third International Symposium of VDM Europe*, volume 428 of Lecture Notes in Computer Science. Springer, 1990.
9. E. Boiten, J. Derrick, J. von Wright and J. Woodcock, editors. *REFINE 2002: The BCS FACS Refinement Workshop*. Elsevier, 2002.
10. C. Bolton, J. Davies, and J.C.P. Woodcock. On the refinement and simulation of data types and processes. In *[2]*, pages 273–292.
11. J.P. Bowen, S. Dunne, A. Galloway and S. King, editors. *ZB 2000: Formal Specification and Development in Z and B, First International Conference of B and Z Users*, volume 1878 of Lecture Notes in Computer Science. Springer, 2000.
12. J.P. Bowen and M. G. Hinchey, editors. *The Z Formal Specification Notation, 9th International Conference of Z Users*, volume 967 of Lecture Notes in Computer Science. Springer, 1995.
13. S.M. Brien and J.E. Nicholls. *Z Base Standard Version 1.0*. Technical Monograph PRG-107. Oxford University Computing Laboratory, 1992.
14. A. Cavalcanti and J.C.P. Woodcock. A weakest precondition semantics for Z. *The Computer Journal*, 41(1):1–15, 1998.
15. L.J. Cohen, editor. *Logic, Methodology and Philosophy of Science VI*. North Holland, 1982.
16. W.P. de Roever and K. Engelhardt. *Data Refinement: Model-Oriented Proof Methods and Their Comparison*. Prentice Hall International, 1998.
17. J. Derrick and E.A. Boiten. Calculating upward and downward simulations of state-based specifications. *Information and Software Technology*, 41:917–923, July 1999.

18. J. Derrick and E.A. Boiten. *Refinement in Z and Object-Z: Foundations and Advanced Applications,*. Formal Approaches to Computing and Information Technology, FACIT. Springer, 2001.

19. M. Deutsch and M.C. Henson. An analysis of backward simulation data refinement for partial-relation semantics. In *[4]*, pages 38–48.

20. M. Deutsch and M. C. Henson. An analysis of forward simulation data refinement. In *[7]*, pages 148–167.

21. M. Deutsch and M. C. Henson. An analysis of total correctness refinement models for partial relation semantics II. *Logic Journal of the IGPL*, 11(3):319–352, 2003.

22. M. Deutsch and M. C. Henson. Four theories for backward-simulation data refinement. In *[6]*.

23. M. Deutsch, M. C. Henson, and S. Reeves. An analysis of total correctness refinement models for partial relation semantics I. *Logic Journal of the IGPL*, 11(3):287–317, 2003.

24. M. Deutsch, M. C. Henson, and S. Reeves. Operation refinement and monotonicity in the schema calculus. In *[7]*, pages 103–126.

25. M. Deutsch, M. C. Henson, and S. Reeves. Results on formal stepwise design in Z. In *[58]*, pages 33–42.

26. G. Goos and J. Hartmanis, editors. *European Symposium on Programming '86*, volume 213 of Lecture Notes in Computer Science. Springer, 1986.

27. L.J. Groves. Refinement and the Z schema calculus. In *[9]*, pages 70–93.

28. J. Grundy. *A Method of Program Refinement*. PhD thesis, University of Cambridge, 1993.

29. J. Grundy, M. Schwenke and T. Vickers, editors. *International Refinement Workshop and Formal Methods Pacific 1998*, Springer Series in Discrete Mathematics and Theoretical Computer Science. Springer, 1998.

30. J. He, C.A.R Hoare, and J.W. Sanders. Data refinement refined. In *[26]*, pages 187–196.

31. J. He, C.A.R Hoare, and J.W. Sanders. Prespecification in data refinement. *Information Processing Letters*, 25(2):71–76, 1987.

32. M. C. Henson. The standard logic of Z is inconsistent. *Formal Aspects of Computing*, 10(3):243–247, 1998.

33. M.C. Henson, M. Deutsch, and B. Kajtazi. The specification language νZ. *Formal Aspects of Computing*, 18(3):364–395, 2006.

34. M. C. Henson and S. Reeves. A logic for schema-based program development. *Formal Aspects of Computing*, 15(1):84–99, 2003.

35. M. C. Henson and S. Reeves. Investigating Z. *Journal of Logic and Computation*, 10(1):43–73, 2000.

36. M. C. Henson and S. Reeves. New foundations for Z. In *[29]*, pages 165–179, 1998.

37. M. C. Henson and S. Reeves. Program development and specification refinement in the schema calculus. In *[11]*, pages 344–362.

38. M. C. Henson and S. Reeves. Revising Z: I – logic and semantics. *Formal Aspects of Computing*, 11(4):359–380, 1999.

39. M. C. Henson and S. Reeves. Revising Z: II – logical development. *Formal Aspects of Computing*, 11(4):381–401, 1999.

40. C.A.R. Hoare and J. He. *Unifying Theories of Programming*. Prentice Hall International, 1998.

41. C.B. Jones. *Software Development: A Rigorous Approach.* Prentice Hall International, 1980.

42. C.B. Jones. *Systematic Software Development using VDM (2nd edition).* Prentice Hall International, 1990.

43. M.B. Josephs. The data refinement calculator for Z specifications. *Information Processing Letters*, 27:29–33, 1988.

44. S. King. The standard logic for Z: a clarification. *Formal Aspects of Computing*, 11(4):472–473, 1999.

45. S. King. Z and the Refinement Calculus. In *[8]*, pages 164–188, 1990.

46. P. Martin-Löf. Constructive mathematics and computer programming. In *[15]*, pages 153–175.

47. R. Miarka, E.A. Boiten, and J. Derrick. Guards, preconditions, and refinement in Z. In *Z [11]*, pages 286–303.

48. C.C. Morgan. *Programming from specifications (2nd edition).* Prentice Hall International, 1994.

49. C.C. Morgan. The specification statement. *ACM Transactions on Programming Languages and Systems*, 10:403–419, 1988.

50. J.E. Nicholls, editor. *Z notation: version 1.2.* Z Standards Panel, 1995.

51. J.E. Nicholls, editor. *Z user workshop: proceedings of the sixth annual Z user meeting*, Workshops in Computing. Springer, 1992.

52. B. Potter, J. Sinclair, and D. Till. *An introduction to formal specification and Z (2nd edition).* Prentice Hall, 1996.

53. S. Prehn and W.J. Toetenel, editors. *Formal software development, 4th international symposium of VDM Europe*, volume 551 of Lecture Notes in Computer Science. Springer, 1991.

54. S. Reeves and M. Clarke. *Logic for Computer Science.* International Computer Science Series. Addison-Wesley, 1990.

55. J.M. Spivey. The consistency theorem for free type definitions in Z. *Formal Aspects of Computing*, 8(3):369–376, 1996.

56. J.M. Spivey. *The Z Notation: A Reference Manual (2nd edition).* Prentice Hall, 1992.

57. J.M. Spivey. *Understanding Z: A specification language and its formal semantics.* Cambridge University Press, 1988.

58. P. Strooper and P. Muenchaisri, editors. *9th Asia-Pacific Software Engineering Conference.* IEEE Computer Society Press, 2002.

59. B. Strulo. How firing conditions help inheritance. In *[12]*, pages 264–275.

60. N.W. Tennant. *Natural Logic (2nd edition).* Edinburgh University Press, 1990.

61. I. Toyn, editor. *Z Notation: Final Committee Draft, CD 13568.2.* Z Standards Panel, 1999.

62. M. Utting. Personal communication. Department of Computer Science, University of Waikato, Hamilton, New Zealand, June 2002.

63. J.C.P. Woodcock. An introduction to refinement in Z. In *[53]*, pages 96–117.

64. J.C.P. Woodcock. Calculating properties of Z specifications. *ACM SIGSOFT Software Engineering Notes*, 14(5):43–54, 1989.

65. J.C.P. Woodcock. The Refinement Calculus. In *[53]*, pages 80–95.

66. J.C.P. Woodcock. The rudiments of algorithm refinement. *The Computer Journal*, 35(5):441–450, 1992.

67. J.C.P. Woodcock and S.M. Brien. W: a logic for Z. In *[51]*, pages 77–96.

68. J.C.P. Woodcock and J. Davies. *Using Z: Specification, Refinement and Proof.* Prentice Hall, 1996.

69. J.C.P. Woodcock and C.C. Morgan. Refinement of state-based concurrent systems. In *[8]*, pages 340–351.

70. J.B. Wordsworth. *Software development with Z: a practical approach to formal methods in software engineering.* International Computer Science Series. Addison-Wesley, 1992.

Indexes

Symbol Index

implementation

F-implementations: $\widehat{U}$, 513

F-implements: $\in_f$, 513

implements: $\in$, 512

R-implementations: $\overline{U}$, 519

R-implements: $\in_r$, 519

logic

disjunction: $\vee$, 501

equality: $=$, 501

existential quantifier: $\exists$, 501

false: *false*, 501

filtered equality: $\doteq$, 494

filtered membership: $\dot{\in}$, 494

megation: $\neg$, 501

membership: $\in$, 501

models: $\models$, 512

restricted equality: $=_T$, 494

weakest precondition: wp, 517

monotonicity

forking connectivity: Fc, 574

properly conjoined: Pc, 579

stable preconditions: Sp, 581

strong connectivity: Sc, 574

weak binding: Wb, 582

refinement

F-refines: $\sqsupseteq_f$, 513

R-refines: $\sqsupseteq_r$, 519

S-refines (negation of): $\not\sqsupseteq_s$, 568

S-refines: $\sqsupseteq_s$, 514

SC-refines: $\sqsupseteq_{sc}^{s}$, 565

SF-refines: $\sqsupseteq_{sf}$, 537

W$_\bullet$-refinement: $\sqsupseteq_{w_\bullet}$, 516

W$_\circ$-refines: $\sqsupseteq_{w_\circ}$, 528

W$_\ominus$-refines: $\sqsupseteq_{w_\ominus}^{s}$, 531

WB$_\bullet$-refines: $\sqsupseteq_{wb_\phi}^{s}$, 551

WB$_\bullet$-refines: $\sqsupseteq_{wb_\bullet}^{s}$, 551

WB$_\circ$-refines: $\sqsupseteq_{wb_\circ}$, 557

WB$_\ominus$-refines: $\sqsupseteq_{wb_\ominus}^{s}$, 552

WF$_\phi$-refines: $\sqsupseteq_{wf_\phi}^{s}$, 538

WF$_\bullet$-refines: $\sqsupseteq_{wf_\bullet}^{s}$, 538

WF$_\circ$-refines: $\sqsupseteq_{wf_\circ}^{s}$, 545

WF$_\ominus$-refines: $\sqsupseteq_{wf_\ominus}^{s}$, 539

WP-refines: $\sqsupseteq_{wp}$, 517

relational completions

lifted totalisation: $\overset{\bullet}{U}$, 514

non-lifted totalisation: $\overset{\circ}{U}$, 525

non-strict lifting: $\overset{\circ}{S}$, 535

strictly-lifted totalisation: $\overset{\ominus}{U}$, 531

schema

chaos: *Chaos*, 525

composition: $\mathbin{\raise.3ex\hbox{$\scriptstyle\circ$}}_9$, 507

conjunction: $\wedge$, 506

delta schema: Δ, 494

disjunction: $\vee$, 506

existential quantification: $\exists$, 507

negation: $\neg$, 506

postcondition: *Post*, 516

precondition: *Pre*, 508

precondition: Pre_0, 527

Concept Index

Part III

Postludium

Part III

Reviews

Dines Bjørner[1,2] and Martin Henson[3] (editors)

[1] Department of Informatics and Mathematical Modelling, Technical University of Denmark, DK-2800 Kgs. Lyngby, Denmark. (bjorner@gmail.com)
[2] Department of Computer Science, University of Essex, Wivenhoe Park, Colchester, Essex CO4 3SQ, UK (hensm@essex.ac.uk)

Summary. In this chapter we present short commentaries of the specification languages whose logics are presented in this book. The brief "essays" are written by people closely related to the development and research of the individual languages.

1 Yuri Gurevich: ASM

We share our experience of using abstract state machines for teaching computation theory at the University of Michigan.

1.1 Introduction

Dines Bjørner asked me to write a short non-technical essay "taking its departure" in the chapter Abstract State Machines for the Classroom by Wolfgang Reisig. Well, I like Wolfgang's chapter very much. Let me use this opportunity to share some of my experience of teaching with ASMs at the University of Michigan. I was at Michigan from 1982 till 1998, most of the time (from 1984 on) with the Department of Electrical Engineering and Computer Science (EECS). The last few of those Michigan years I used ASMs in my teaching. To keep this essay short, let me restrict attention to the course on computation theory.

I taught the course often. At the Mathematics Department of Israel's Ben Gurion University, where I taught before coming to Michigan, undergraduate courses were up for grabs, and I enjoyed teaching and learning new courses. In EECS, the undergraduate curriculum was partitioned into feudal domains, and the small computer theory group owned few courses. Kevin Compton, my fellow theorist in EECS, said once: "I've taught that course so many times that I could do it in my sleep . . . and often have." In this connection, I tried each time a new angle in teaching the course, which partially explains why my frequent teaching of the course did not result in a book. Since 1998, I am with Microsoft Research. The engineering culture of Microsoft has rubbed off on me, and today my teaching would be different. But I would continue to use ASMs in my teaching; my confidence in ASMs has only grown.

The computation theory course was a part of the official curriculum of the Association for Computing Machinery (ACM), and it served as a prerequisite for some other courses. It was supported by the venerable 1979 "Introduction to Automata Theory, Languages, and Computation" by John Hopcroft and Jeffrey Ullman [3], and new excellent textbooks kept appearing. Nevertheless in the 1990s the course on finite state machines, pushdown automata and Turing machines seemed antiquated. Computing became so much broader: graphical user interfaces, parallel and distributed computing, networks, Web based computing and searching, communication and security protocols, and other forms of computing that didn't exist or weren't yet important in 1979. And computer science attracted more students than ever before, many of them mathematically challenged. Students (and their parents!) complained that they don't see much use for Turing machine programming. ASMs could describe arbitrary computations naturally and *without lowering the abstraction level*. That gave me an idea of using ASMs for teaching. But I had to be careful in fiddling with the computation theory course; it was a traditional undergraduate course, a part of the ACM curriculum and a prerequisite for other courses.

1.2 Finite State Machines and Context-Free Languages

The computation theory course consisted of three parts: (i) finite automata and regular languages, (ii) context-free languages and pushdown automata, and (iii) Turing machines, undecidability and complexity. The first two parts were similar from the point of view of the use of ASMs. They included numerous algorithmic constructions, for example the subset construction that turns a nondeterministic finite automaton into an equivalent deterministic one. The constructions would typically involve parallelism. You can write prose describing such a construction or give pseudocode for the construction. I programmed the constructions as ASMs and required the students to do the same. The ASM programs looked like pseudocode of a particular style to the students. But we were using of course a precise ASM computation model which allowed us to use strings as well as finite sets and sequences of arbitrary entities. A couple of ASM programs from that computation theory course appear, slightly modified, in [2 (Section 3)].

Typically the students would adapt to the "pseudocode" style rather quickly. One difficulty was related to the default parallelism of ASMs. In conventional programming languages, like C, commands listed in some order are executed in that order. In the ASM world, the default is parallel execution. If you want that commands be executed sequentially, you have to say so explicitly [2]. The students had programming experience in conventional languages and found default parallelism strange. I could circumvent the difficulty by making parallelism explicit and writing "do in parallel" in the appropriate places but I didn't want to clog the ASM code. More importantly, I wanted to break the sequential-by-default thinking and thus elevate the abstraction level of programming.

The primary beneficiaries of the ASM use in parts one and two of the computation theory course were mathematically challenged students scared of proofs. Programming was a different story. It was often their strong suit. ASMs allowed me to present proof assignments as largely programming assignments without lowering the abstraction level and with no unnecessary details.

Today I would use AsmL, the high-level specification/programming language developed in Microsoft Research [1], so that the students could execute their programs. (I would also show the students finite and pushdown automata that do something useful, e.g. the scanner of a lexical analyzer and a mini parser, respectively.)

1.3 Universal Computation Models

It is in the third part of the computation theory course that we really took advantage of ASMs. I would tell the students that they are already familiar with a universal computation model. The dramatic effect was lost on some as they had read about Turing machines or realized where I was going. But there were always some students who looked perplexed and were about to protest. At this point, I would explain that ASMs constitute a universal model, and we had been using the ASM computation model all along. I never dwelt on the greater universality of ASMs. That aspect of ASMs was beyond the scope of the course.

Of course Turing machines (TMs) were introduced as well. They are indispensable for undecidability proofs. So both ASMs and Turing machines were used. And there was a price to pay: to show that TMs can simulate ASMs. (The other way round is obvious.) This was done via random-access machines (RAMs). First show that TMs can simulate RAMs, and then show that RAMs can simulate ASMs. There are elegant forms of the first simulation in the literature, see [4] for example. The second simulation was recently simplified and made elegant in [5].

The price was worth paying. ASMs allowed us to avoid Turing programming. Consider for example the theorem that, for every nondeterministic TM that computes a function, there is a deterministic TM that computes the same function. The idea is simple — interleave all possible computations of the given nondeterministic TM, but the TM programming of the interleaving is a tedious task on a low abstraction level. Instead program the interleaving in the ASM language and then refer to the fact that TMs can simulate ASMs; the ASM programming of the interleaving is a programming exercise that can be assigned as a part of homework. Even proving an initial undecidability result is made easier by the use of ASMs.

Another advantage of using ASMs was that, contrary to Turing machines, ASMs could be actually used for various purposes. In fact, throughout the course, we used ASMs to program algorithms, many of them highly parallel. The reader may ask why not use a conventional programming language instead of ASMs for programming algorithms. The reason is that ASMs allow you to program algorithms without lowering the abstraction level.

Acknowledgments

Many thanks to Andreas Blass and Kevin Compton for their comments on a draft of this essay.

1. Abstract State Machine Language (AsmL), `http://research.microsoft.com/fse/asml/`
2. Yuri Gurevich, Margus Veanes and Charles Wallace, "Can Abstract State Machines Be Useful in Language Theory," Technical Report MSR-TR-2006-159, Microsoft Research, 2006.
3. John E. Hopcroft and Jeffrey D. Ullman, "Introduction to Automata Theory, Languages, and Computation," Addison-Wesley, 1979.
4. Christos H. Papadimitriou, "Computational Complexity", Addison-Wesley, 1994.
5. Comandur Seshadhri, Anil Seth and Somenath Biswas, "RAM Simulation of BGS Model of Abstract State Machines?"[3] Fundamentae Informaticae, IOS Press, vol. 77, nos. 1–2, 2007, pages 175–185.

2 Jean-Raymond Abrial: On B and event-B

The chapter on B and event-B written by Dominique Cansell and Dominique Méry in this book is certainly a tour de force, which I could not have written myself. I particularly appreciate the variety of examples they develop: B thus appears as what it is intended to be, namely nothing other than the use of *ordinary discrete mathematics* organized in a framework which makes it possible to use a *refining and proving* intellectual — as well as practical — tool at the disposal of the "formal engineer".

As mentioned in that chapter, B has been used in academic circles where regular B conferences are organized: it is certainly fundamental to develop a lively community that makes formal methods an active research area.

But B has been used in industry as well (this is also mentioned in the chapter) to develop the safety-critical parts of "real" train systems: line 14 of the Parisian Metro (driverless), Charles de Gaulle airport shuttle (driverless), the New York City Metro, the Barcelona Metro, the new project of Paris Metro line 1 (driverless), and so on. What is interesting here is not so much

---

[3] Proceedings of the 12th International Workshop on Abstract State Machines (ASM 2005), March 8-11, 2005, Paris, France, pages 377–386, www.univ-paris12.fr/lacl/dima/asm05/asm05-contents.html.

the use of B itself, but rather the fact that formal methods *with refinement and proofs* have entered the culture of certain industrial domains.

In these areas, the concerned industrialists have reached the conclusion that using a formal method with refinement and proofs can be mastered, does not require special skills beyond the ones that "normal" engineers have, and is clearly far more efficient financially (needless to say, technically) than classical methods using testing as their main verification process. Readers who do not believe me can contact the Parisian Metro Authority (RATP)!

For the sake of completeness, it is worth mentioning that other industrialists have said that they will never use B because it is totally useless! Needless to say, I did not try to convince them: this is a waste of time.

In fact, using this formal approach corresponds to a clear *mental revolution* on the part of the managers and technical people in charge of such real projects. It means that one can envisage developing *complex embedded systems* in such a way that they will be proved to be eventually *correct by construction*. Clearly, engineers in other, more mature, disciplines than ours would be very surprised that we, the computer people, have just discovered what they have been doing for many decades, but they do not remember probably their status while they were in their infancy!

Yes, it is possible to develop systems whose software parts interact with a dangerous environment in a satisfactory fashion. Notice, that I have not written in a 'correct' fashion nor in a 'zero-fault' fashion; this was done on purpose. The notion of correctness and thus the expression 'correct by construction' has to be manipulated with great care. It is a *relative* notion, relative to the assumptions which must have been clearly put forward to begin with. Outside such assumptions, nothing is guaranteed, of course.

But this raises now another problem concerning the consistency and completeness of such initially defined assumptions. Completeness will be immediately discarded as no formal (I mean "mathematical") approach can verify completeness: it depends on the professional skills of the engineers. Consistency is another matter. It is quite possible that the initial informal specifications prepared by the system engineers be inadequate or even inconsistent. Nothing prevents this happening presently except the usually extremely high professional caliber of system engineers.

It is my belief that formal methods with refinement and proofs can be used at this level with great profit: this is precisely the aim of Event-B, which consists at the same time in a drastic simplification with regard to "classical B" (as presented in the B-Book [1]) but also provides means to develop distributed systems *as a whole* (not only their software parts).

Dear reader, read *carefully and slowly* the chapter written by Dominique Cansell and Dominique Méry: if you encounter such material for the first time, it is certainly not something you can swallow in one afternoon. But once you feel comfortable, you can use the tool "click′n′Prove", it's fun. But you might be a bit frustrated by the emacs interface. Wait! We are preparing a new set of tools (sponsored by the European project Rodin), it works under Eclipse, it is completely free, and it will be stable within a few months.

1. J.-R. Abrial: *The B Book: Assigning Programs to Meanings* (Cambridge University Press, UK 1996)

3 Kokichi Futatsugi: Formal Methods and CafeOBJ

Formal methods are not "silver bullets", but are still expected to improve practices of constructions, analyses, and/or verifications of domain, requirement, and/or design specifications. Formal methods are based on formal specifications of realities, and a formal specification language plays an important role in any formal method. CafeOBJ is a formal specification language which is designed to be used in constructions/analyses/verifications of specifications.

3.1 Verification of High-Level Specifications

To create domain/requirement/design specifications and analyze/verify them as early phase as possible is one of the most important and challenging topics in the current software engineering. It is important because quite a few critical bugs are caused at the level of domains/requirements/designs. It is also important for the cases where no program codes are generated and specifications are analyzed/verified only for justifying models of realities. It is challenging because modeling of realities and its validation against the realities is the most challenging topic of formal methods (or of any science/technology).

For analyzing and/or verifying specifications, a balanced use of informal and formal specifications is inevitable. In the current practices of system development, informal specifications are dominating and formal specifications are not necessarily accepted or used in a proper way. This implies that only very limited analyses/verifications can be done in the phase of high-level specification development.

3.2 Interactive Modeling/Verification

The term 'verify' is used in a sentence like "verify a program against a specification". The term "validate" is used in a sentence like "validate specifications against the realities". This suggests that verification means showing by formal proof that some property holds against already established formal descriptions, and validation means showing by empirical/experimental means that some property hold against realities. This almost implies that only validation is possible for domain or requirement specifications, for there are no formal specifications for domains/requirements a priori.

One critical issue here is that the traditional theory/technology of validating informal specifications against reality by means of empirical/experimental ways does not meet the recent requirements of realizing more safe and secure systems. One of the main purposes of verification of high-level specifications is to overcome this situation by improving traditional verification technology to cope with "validation of domain/requirement specifications against realities".

To make verification meaningful as validation, it should be interactive, for validation against realities is better to be done by human stakeholders through interactions. The proof score approach with CafeOBJ [1,2] is a possible solution for more effective and usable verification/validation of high-level (i.e., domain, requirement, and/or design) specifications.

3.3 The Proof Score Approach

The goal of verification in software engineering is to increase confidence in the correctness of systems. For verification to be genuinely useful in software engineering, careful account must be taken of the context of actual use, including the capabilities and culture of users, and the available technology. Absolute certainty is not achievable in real applications.

Fully automatic theorem provers often fail to convey an understanding of their proofs, and they are generally unhelpful when they fail because of user errors in specifications or goals, or due to the lack of a necessary lemma or case split. It follows that one should seek to make optimal use of the respective abilities of humans and computers, so that computers do the tedious formal calculations, and humans do the high-level planning; the trade off between detail and comprehension should also be carefully balanced.

Proof score is a central concept in the CafeOBJ approach for meeting these goals; proof scores are instructions to a proof engine, such that when they are executed (or "played"), if everything evaluates as expected, then a desired theorem is proved. Proof scores hide the detailed calculations done by machines, while revealing the proof plan created by humans.

There is an important distinction between "system specifications" versus "property specifications". System specifications are specifications of systems which are supposed to be modeled and/or developed. Property specifications are specifications of properties which are supposed to be satisfied by systems. In the current proof score method in CafeOBJ, both system and property specifications are written in equational specifications.

CafeOBJ adopts the principle of executable specifications. System specifications are executable by interpreting equations as rewriting rules. This helps a lot in achieving clear and transparent constructions and verifications of high-level specifications.

3.4 CafeOBJ Logic and Methodology

Dr. Răzvan Diaconescu gives a beautiful introduction to CafeOBJ logic in his "A Methodological Guide to CafeOBJ Logic" (abbreviated as MGcafe in the following). He explains fundamental language constructs, methodologies, and semantics (or logic) of CafeOBJ in a mixture of informal narrative and formal mathematical styles. Mathematical definitions of important concepts are given in a course of narrative descriptions. Executable CafeOBJ codes are also given for helping to understand these definitions/descriptions. By doing this, he has succeeded in giving a clear and precise description of the CafeOBJ logic and language.

MGcafe also gives clear explanations of the following important and unique contributions of CafeOBJ to research on designs of formal specification languages.

- **Behavioral Specification:** CafeOBJ is the first formal specification language which adopts behavioral specification. By introducing behavioral specification, it has become possible to specify dynamic process types and static data types in a uniform way. Introduction of behavioral specification opens up many new application areas, and is the most important feature of CafeOBJ.
- **Rewriting Logic Specification:** Rewriting logic is a logic for state transitions. CafeOBJ's rewriting logic is a simplified version of the original one, but can provide succinct specifications and verifications of *declarative encoding of algorithms* as well as ordinary transition systems. A transition system can be a model for dynamic systems, and rewriting logic specification provides a secondary way for modeling dynamic systems in CafeOBJ.
- **Institutional Semantics:** Institutions provide a framework for giving unified semantics for a multilogic algebraic specification language like CafeOBJ. Serious adoption of institutional semantics is an important unique contribution of CafeOBJ to the semantics of algebraic specification languages.

As a result, MGcafe amounts to an excellent introduction to CafeOBJ from the standpoint of its underlining logic or semantics, even if some parts include heavily condensed explanations of semantics based on institutional/categorical concepts.

MGcafe says many things about CafeOBJ methodologies, but does not say much about recently developed methodologies for proof score writings like "systematic case splitting and lemma discovery" [2]. The theoretical frameworks of CafeOBJ which are explained in MGcafehave potential to give clear and precise semantics for the advance proof score methodology for high-level specifications, and it is desirable to see such research developments in the near future.

1. Kokichi Futatsugi. Verifying specifications with proof scores in CafeOBJ. In *ASE*, pages 3–10. IEEE Computer Society, 2006.
2. Kazuhiro Ogata and Kokichi Futatsugi. Some tips on writing proof scores in the OTS/CafeOBJ method. In Kokichi Futatsugi, Jean-Pierre Jouannaud, and José Meseguer, editors, *Essays Dedicated to Joseph A.*

Goguen, volume 4060 of *Lecture Notes in Computer Science*, pages 596–615. Springer, 2006.

4 Peter D. Mosses: A View of the CASL

> *Castles in the air – they are so easy to take refuge in.*
> *And so easy to build, too.*[4]

4.1 Background

CASL is the youngest of the specification languages whose logics are presented in this book. It was designed and constructed by members of CoFI,[5] the common framework initiative for algebraic specification and development of software. CoFI was originally conceived as a joint task of IFIP WG 1.3 (on *Foundations of System Specification*) and the ESPRIT Basic Research WG COMPASS. During the meeting of the 10th WADT with the 5th COMPASS workshop at S. Margherita, Italy, in 1994, I had asked, rather impertinently:

Why do we need so many different algebraic specification languages?

The languages that had been developed for algebraic specification of software included ACT ONE/ACT TWO, ASF, ASL, CLEAR, EXTENDED ML, LARCH, OBJ3, PLUSS, and SPECTRUM (there were more than 25 of them altogether). Although many of them shared various features and had similar foundations, they lacked uniformity of notation, libraries of standard specifications, and a generally accepted textbook. Various useful tools had been developed for particular languages, but these were not interoperable.

No satisfactory answer to my question was forthcoming, and I was asked to coordinate an investigation into the possibility of establishing a 'unifying framework' for algebraic specification. The topic was discussed further at a COMPASS satellite meeting at TAPSOFT'95 in Aarhus, and CoFI itself was born in 1995, at an IFIP WG 1.3 meeting held at Soria Moria, Norway, later the same year. Despite considerable general scepticism about the chances of success, it was encouraging to see how many leaders of research groups in algebraic specification joined the initiative. Although CoFI was sponsored by IFIP WG 1.3 and the COMPASS WG, participation was open to all, with the aim of reaching a broad consensus.

CoFI started by cataloguing the features of 12 existing languages. The aim was to base the intended unifying framework on a critical selection of the best features (rather than trying to combine all the features). Task groups were established for language design, semantics, tools, methodology, and specification of reactive systems. Mailing lists were set up, and many participants

---

[4] Henrik Ibsen, *The Master Builder*, 1892, act 3.
[5] http://www.cofi.info. CoFI is pronounced like 'coffee'.

wrote study notes regarding design choices for particular features of algebraic specifications. The collective experience and expertise of the participants provided a unique opportunity to achieve the aims of CoFI within a reasonably short time-span.

The main specification language of the unifying framework was given the name CASL: the Common Algebraic Specification Language. Combining the selected features together in a single language was however not at all straightforward. There was also the highly debated question of how rich to make CASL. Quite surprisingly, it was easy to reach agreement on the issue of partiality, which had previously been regarded as particularly contentious. Allowing full first-order logic for axioms was somewhat controversial, but familiar from LARCH. Other language design issues, such as those concerning subsorting and architectural specification, were considerably more troublesome, and their resolution involved research into novel variants of the features of existing specification languages – something which had not been foreseen when CoFI started.

4.2 Status

Apart from a few details, the CASL design was completed in 1998, and version 1.0 was released. The same year, CoFI obtained funding as an ESPRIT working group, and Don Sannella took over as overall coordinator. IFIP WG 1.3 approved the final design in April 2001. The current version (1.0.2) was adopted in October 2003, and no further revisions of the CASL design are anticipated. The CASL User Manual and Reference Manual were published in 2004 [1,3]. Various sub-languages of CASL were defined (inheriting their semantics from CASL), and several new languages have been approved as extensions of CASL: higher-order (HASCASL), co-algebraic (COCASL), reactive (CASL-LTL, CSP-CASL), and structural (HETCASL). The original CoFI task groups have terminated, although there is still coordination of activities concerning tool development.

The editors of this book have kindly invited me to reflect here on the current state of CASL. What has been achieved by the development of this new family of algebraic specification languages by CoFI? Has the initiative to provide a 'unifying framework' succeeded in its main aim?

It has to be admitted that the design of CASL is somewhat more innovative than CoFI had originally envisaged, and CASL itself does not correspond directly to any previous language – even at the level of basic specifications. Thus one might claim that by developing CASL, CoFI has simply added to the proliferation of different languages... However, it has been shown [2] that some of the major languages that preceded CASL (ACT ONE, ASF, LARCH, OBJ3, and the functional part of CAFEOBJ) do correspond closely to sub-languages of CASL regarding their features and foundations. Moreover, some novel languages have been developed as extensions of CASL, instead of as completely different languages. Thus the CASL *family* of languages can indeed be seen as providing a unifying framework. The fragmentation of work on algebraic specification has also been reduced by the developers of some previous languages dropping them in favour of CASL.

Some remaining languages (e.g. ASF+SDF, CAFEOBJ, MAUDE) are strongly linked to well-developed rewriting engines that support execution and analysis of specifications. One of the aims of CoFI was to support tool *interoperability* through the CASL family of languages. The Heterogeneous Tool Set HETS provides much tool support for the CASL languages themselves, together with interfaces to theorem provers, but a system providing CASL-based interfaces to the various rewriting engines is currently lacking. Although the design of the CASL languages themselves has been successful, further efforts are needed to fully realise the remaining the aims of CoFI – new participants are always welcome!

1. M. Bidoit and P.D. Mosses. CASL *User Manual – Introduction to Using the Common Algebraic Specification Language*, volume 2900 of *Lecture Notes in Computer Science*. Springer, 2004.
2. T. Mossakowski. Relating CASL with other specification languages: The institution level. *Theor. Comput. Sci.*, 286(2):367–475, 2002.
3. P.D. Mosses, editor. CASL *Reference Manual – The Complete Documentation of the Common Algebraic Specification Language*, volume 2960 of *Lecture Notes in Computer Science*. Springer, 2004.

5 Zhou Chaochen: Duration Calculus

I thank the editors for including Duration Calculus (DC) in this book and for asking me to write a non-technical but still academic essay about DC in addition to the excellent chapter written by Michael R. Hansen.

DC was introduced by Tony Hoare, Anders Ravn and myself in 1991 [1] for the ProCoS project, when we conducted a case study on a gas burner system. Since then, research on DC has covered the development of DC variants, their applications and tools. In 2004, Michael Hansen and I published a book [2] on DC and tried to present the existing research in a systematic way. Recently, the ongoing project AVACS (Automatic Verification and Analysis of Complex Systems) [3] aroused my interest in DC again. It combines CSP, OZ and DC into a uniform language with an ambition to specify and verify the European Train Control System. I wish the project great success in applying DC to real-world problems.

It is my understanding that from the logical point of view the main contribution of DC to formal specification of real-time systems, in particular real-time hybrid systems, is to

- adopt Interval Logic as a logical base, and

- introduce into specification languages a notion of the integral from continuous mathematics.

Interval Logic is a branch of Modal Logic. Given the Phase Transition System [4] as the computational model of a hybrid system, the choice of Interval Logic for hybrid systems can be well justified. Interval Logic has also been used by J.F. Allen, J. Halpern et al. in the areas of artificial intelligence, circuit design, etc. [5,6]. Moreover, in a personal communication, Tony Hoare drew my attention to the possible correspondence between the chop operator in Interval Logic and the separating (spatial) conjunction in Separation Logic [7]. I believe that Interval Logic deserves an important role in computing science.

DC includes an inference system for integration of Boolean-valued functions. Inclusion of more continuous mathematics such as differential and integral equations strengthens various specification languages to describe behaviour of hybrid systems [8,9]. Recent achievement of research on computational properties of hybrid systems (e.g. decidability of reachability of linear hybrid systems [10,11]) shows great promise in this respect. Not only do hybrid systems require continuous mathematics, a program element can also be specified using continuous mathematics if its variables are typed as reals. Along this line people reduce termination analysis, invariant generation and other problems to solutions of algebraic systems and then use computer algebra to verify programs [12,13,14]. This demonstrates support from continuous mathematics for formal verification of computing systems.

1. C. Zhou, C.A.R. Hoare, A.P. Ravn AP (1991) A Calculus of Durations. Information Processing Letters 40(5):269-276
2. C. Zhou, M.R. Hansen (2004) Duration Calculus: A Formal Approach to Real-Time Systems. Springer
3. The AVACS project page (2006) Transregional Collaborative Research Center 14 AVACS: http://www.avacs.org
4. Z. Manna, A. Pnueli (1993) Verifying Hybrid Systems. LNCS 736:4-35, Springer
5. J.F. Allen (1984) Towards a General Theory of Action and Time. Artificial Intelligence 23:123-154
6. J. Halpern, B. Moskowski, Z. Manna (1983) A Hardware Semantics Based on Temporal Intervals. LNCS 154:278-291, Springer
7. J.C. Reynolds (2002) Separation Logic: A Logic for Shared Mutable Data-structures. In Proceedings of IEEE Symposium, LICS
8. R. Alur, C. Courcoubetis, T. Henzinger, P.H. Ho (1993) Hybrid Automata: An Algorithmic Approach to the Specification and Verification of Hybrid Systems. LNCS 736:209-229, Springer
9. C. Zhou, J. Wang, A.P. Ravn (1996) A Formal Description of Hybrid Systems. LNCS 1066:511-530, Springer

10. G. Lafferriere, G.J. Pappas, S. Yovine (2001) Symbolic Reachability Computation for Families of Linear Vector Fields. J. Symbolic Computation 32(3)231-253
11. A. Tiwari (2003) Approximate Reachability for Linear Systems. LNCS 2623:514-525, Springer
12. A. Tiwari (2004) Termination of Linear Programs. LNCS 3114:70–82, Springer
13. S. Sankaranarayanan, H.B. Sipma, Z. Manna (2004) Non-linear Loop Invariant Generation Using Gröbner Bases. In ACM POPL'04:318–329
14. L. Yang, N. Zhan, B. Xia, C. Zhou (2005) Program verification by Using DISCOVERER. IFIP WG2.3 Working Conference on Verified Software, VSTTE'05: Tools, Techniques and Experiments, 10-13 October 2005: http://vstte.ethz.ch/, Zürich, Switzerland.

6 Klaus Havelund: RAISE in Perspective

6.1 The Contribution of RAISE

The RAISE [6] Specification Language, RSL, originated as a derivation of VDM [9] during a five-year effort involving several researchers. The purpose was to improve VDM by augmenting it with a module system, a process description language, a formal semantics standard, and tool support. A goal was to keep the language a wide spectrum language including high-level specification constructs as well as low-level programming constructs, allowing specification and program fragments to be mixed arbitrarily with each other without imposing a linguistically layered language. The effort resulted in a language inspired by, but in many ways different from VDM. A main deviation from VDM is the emphasis on an algebraic specification-style logic where a module consists of a signature and a set of axioms over the names introduced in the signature. Derived forms exist which reflect the classical VDM definitional style. Correspondingly, types can be abstract sorts as in algebraic specifications or they can be defined through type definitions as in VDM using what is normally referred to as a model-oriented style. The pure model-oriented style usually uses such explicit type definitions and a definitional style for functions. The pure algebraic style uses sorts and more liberal equations with arbitrary terms on the left-hand side as well as on the right-hand side. In the axiomatic style emphasis is on operations and how they relate to each other. In the model-oriented style the emphasis is on data types. When modeling a problem in VDM, the problem is usually first understood by writing down a set of type definitions. The same style is possible in RSL, although the added module system suggests the association of operations with types in a compartmentalized manner.

Although the language is completely uniform, RSL is often for pedagogical purposes presented as supporting three paradigms: functional, procedural with side effects on a state, and process algebraic. In addition each paradigm can be presented in an axiomatic style or in a model oriented definitional style, conceptually forming a 3-by-2 matrix. However, there is only one notion of function, which potentially can have side effects or communicate on channels, and which can be defined axiomatically, with a special case being a model-oriented definitional style. Considering this 3-by-2 matrix, the theoretical contribution of RSL was the algebraic specification of functions with side effects on state variables and channels, and the linguistic and semantic unification of all these concepts.

6.2 Relationship to Programming Languages

However, in spite of the axiomatic capabilities of RSL, the model-oriented definitional style seems more often used. For example the case study in the paper is mostly written in a such a style (first functional and then procedural, but both model-oriented). In essence, many specifications have the flavor of high-level programs. This observation might lead us to question what the relationship between specification languages and programming languages should be. Traditionally specification languages are seen as existing separately from programming languages, only connected with a translator from the specification language to the programming language in case the specification language contains an executable subset. This separation has some advantages and some disadvantages. A main advantage is clearly that the specification language can be used to describe systems independently of the final choice of programming language. The implementation can even be programmed in different programming languages, which is in fact typically the case. Another advantage is that the specification language is liberated from issues of executability. Specifications can be as abstract as required.

Amongst the disadvantages is the fact that a software project has to administer artifacts written in a specification language as well as in a programming language. One can imagine that some parts of the system have been implemented already in a programming language, while other parts have been captured in a specification language, resulting in a multilanguage situation. This problem seems even less necessary when considering that specification language and programming language often have many constructs in common. It is not always possible to rely on a translator from the specification language to the programming language. Typically such a translator will not yield code that is efficient enough. The programmer will not trust the complicated translation process and would be more comfortable with a real one-step compiler. Finally, the link between specification and program cannot in practice be formal. In theory it can be formalized, but it would require a formal semantics of the programming language and a proof that every specification is translated to a semantically equivalent program.

Whether one will argue for or against a separation between specification language and programming language, it is clear that there are advantages of combining specification and programming into one language. An interesting example is the now widely used scripting and programming language Python [5]. Python has built-in succinct notation for sets, lists and maps, and iterators over these, exactly the core data types of VDM and RSL. These concepts also exist in Java [3], although as libraries. Some programming language extensions incorporate specifications in a layered manner, where specifications are separated from the actual code, as axioms [2] or as pre-/post-conditions [1,4,7]. It is desirable that more ideas from formal specification languages "make it" into programming languages and that there is a more elaborate exchange of ideas between the two communities. The formal methods community has a lot to offer the programming language community, and vice versa.

RSL is not object oriented. For example, RSL objects are not values. Object orientation was yet not as fashionable when RSL was designed as it is today. Object orientation has, however, shown itself to be a useful way of encapsulating state. As an example, an object-oriented presentation of the case study without explicitly mentioning the state variable might be more succinct than the functional style where the state is passed as argument to all functions. In general, certain concepts have shown themselves to be useful in specification as well as programming, and hence could be considered candidates for integration into a programming language. These include object orientation, functional programming, algebraic data types generated with constructors and pattern matching over these, as well as succinct notation for operating sets, lists and maps, as well as logic-inspired constructs such as existential and universal quantification over finite sets. There is no reason why the concepts that have shown themselves most useful to express problems could not exist in one language. It is even conceivable that equational rewriting rules could be merged with traditional programming constructs in a programming language. Notation-wise this is allowed in RSL, however it is currently not supported by a computational model. The main point of the above discussion has been to emphasize that specification languages and programming languages overlap and that the gap between the two universes is not as big as one could believe. This observation should be utilized to design programming languages inspired by specification languages.

6.3 Verification Versus Testing

As a final point, it is worth mentioning the use of formal methods for testing. RAISE stands for "Rigorous Approach to Industrial Software Engineering". By "Rigorous" is meant that the correctness of a software artifact developed using the RAISE technology can be justified by a proof, relating formal artifacts. Rigor is an important and essential element of a formal method like RAISE. However, rigor comes with a price: generating proofs is hard. Testing still seems to be the most practical approach for large specifications. The testing method referred to in the paper resembles various unit testing methods found in programming. The user writes a set of tests, each of which performs a sequence of function calls, and then observes the result. A useful augmentation of this approach would consist of prefixing these tests with universal quantifications over data referred to in the tests, and then use random selection of data from the types quantified over for automated testing. Selection of data from the types could even be guided by additional strategies. A more uniform view would be to regard any equational axiom as a test case, hence avoiding introducing new concepts into the language. A specification should be directly usable for generating test cases. A special view on testing is run time verification [10], where a specification is used to monitor the execution of the final program. If specifications become part of the programmer's test arsenal, there is a bigger chance that specification technology will be adopted by practitioners.

1. Eiffel — www.eiffel.com
2. Extended ML — homepages.inf.ed.ac.uk/dts/eml
3. Java — java.sun.com
4. JML — www.cs.iastate.edu/~leavens/JML
5. Python — www.python.org
6. RAISE — www2.imm.dtu.dk/~db/raise
7. Spec# — research.microsoft.com/specsharp
8. Standard ML — en.wikipedia.org/wiki/Standard_ML
9. VDM — www.vdmportal.org
10. Runtime Verification Workshops — www.runtime-verification.org

7 Cliff B. Jones: VDM "Postludium"

This volume focuses on the logics used in well-known specification languages. John Fitzgerald's chapter addresses the use of "LPF" (the Logic of Partial Functions) which is used in many of the writings on VDM.

Let me first discuss some aspects of VDM itself. (I do not reproduce citations here where the VDM chapter has already set them in context.) As observed in Fitzgerald's chapter, there are various "schools" even within the VDM community; [4] was written in honour of Peter Lucas' retirement from the Technical University of Graz and traces some of the changes that occurred in the transition from the operational semantics (VDL) work on programming language semantics to VDM itself (as, for example, described in the first book on VDM [1]). The books cited in Fitzgerald's chapter trace the development of the VDM ideas as they apply to the specification and development of programs other than compilers.

One of the things that is extremely gratifying to the original VDM team is the influence that VDM has had on other specification languages. Clear acknowledgements of this influence are recorded by the authors of works on Larch, VVSL, RAISE, VDM++ and B (and thus Event-B). At a BCS-FACS (British Computer Society, Formal Aspects of Computing) meeting in London in January 2006, many of these influences were discussed — a record of both the panel position statements and the ensuing discussion is available as [2].

It is to be hoped that most people having studied this book will appreciate that it is the notion of modelling systems abstractly that is crucial. This is much more important than the fine details of one or another notation. To emphasise this point, let me relate two personal experiences. In 1979–81, I shared an office in Oxford with Jean-Raymond Abrial; we neither of us found any difficulty in discussing models of interesting systems with Jean-Raymond working in the then version of Z and me using the version of VDM used in my 1980 book.[6] I now have the pleasure to be working again with Jean-Raymond on the EU-funded project RODIN;[7] I have no difficulty in expressing most of my models in "Event-B" and benefit from the superb tools that his team in ETH have produced (of course, it would be highly desirable if it were to include rely and guarantee conditions!).

The preceding paragraph should not be seen as saying that the differences between specification languages are irrelevant. In fact they are very interesting and their logics are one of the areas of particular interest.

I'm delighted that Fitzgerald has written about LPF. His choice is not that surprising since he was a member of the team that built "mural" (a theorem proving assistant for which we explored interface ideas which have still to be bettered!). Fitzgerald's own books have also done a great deal to explore the role of proof in program development.

It is a cause of puzzlement to me that LPF is not more widely used. To be provocative, I am particularly surprised that RAISE did not use LPF. It is certainly true that LPF is one possible solution to the problem of "undefined" in specifications and designs of programs. It is not the only way around the thorny issue of the frequent occurrence of operators and functions which can be undefined. We have found that with tool support, one simply does not notice that the axiomatisation is non-standard; one rarely misses the "law of the excluded middle". Fitzgerald's chapter discusses mechanisation of LPF: the only real problem would appear to be the re-working of the concept of "resolution".

I sincerely hope that this book will widen researchers' awareness of those technical distinctions which are important (and deflect them from discussing less critical differences). In particular, I hope that the volume will serve to stimulate a focused debate on the logics underlying specification languages.

1. D. Bjørner and C.B. Jones, editors. *The Vienna Development Method: The Meta-language*, volume 61 of *Lecture Notes in Computer Science*. Springer-Verlag, 1978.

---

[6] The BCS-FACS meeting which is referred to above resulted in yet one more publication of the paper (which connects to the purpose of this volume): [3] highlights the main differences between Z and VDM.

[7] See http://rodin.cs.ncl.ac.uk

2. J.S. Fitzgerald. Perspectives on formal methods in the last 25 years. *Formal Aspects of Computing*, 2006(2):13–33, 2006.

3. I.J. Hayes, C.B. Jones, and J.E. Nicholls. Understanding the differences between VDM and Z. *FACS FACTS*, 2006(2):56–78, 2006.

4. C.B. Jones. The transition from VDL to VDM. *JUCS*, 7(8):631–640, 2001.

8 Leslie Lamport: The Specification Language TLA$^+$

Stephan Merz describes the TLA logic in great detail and provides about as good a description of TLA+ and how it can be used as is possible in a single chapter. Here, I give a historical account of how I developed TLA and TLA+ that explains some of the design choices, and I briefly discuss how TLA+ is used in practice.

Whence TLA

The logic TLA adds three things to the very simple temporal logic introduced into computer science by Pnueli [4]:

- Invariance under stuttering.
- Temporal existential quantification.
- Taking as atomic formulas not just state predicates but also action formulas.

Here is what prompted these additions.

When Pnueli first introduced temporal logic to computer science in the 1970s, it was clear to me that it provided the right logic for expressing the simple liveness properties of concurrent algorithms that were being considered at the time and for formalizing their proofs. In the early 1980s, interest turned from ad hoc properties of systems to complete specifications. The idea of specifying a system as a conjunction of the temporal logic properties it should satisfy seemed quite attractive [5]. However, it soon became obvious that this approach does not work in practice. It is impossible to understand what a conjunction of individual properties actually specifies. The only practical way to specify non-trivial systems is to describe them as abstract state machines. So, I started writing specifications as state machines, where the meaning of a state machine was a temporal logic formula that described the set of all its possible executions.

There is a basic problem with using a state machine as a specification. Consider an hour clock—a clock that displays only the hour. Ignoring the actual time that elapses between ticks, an hour clock is trivially specified by a state machine that increments the hour with each step. This specification, or any similar one, does not forbid the clock from showing minutes (or temperature or the phase of the moon). The specification should therefore be satisfied by a clock that shows both the hour and the minute. However, a naive state-machine specification of the hour clock asserts that the hour changes with every step, while an hour–minute clock changes the hour only on every 60th step. This problem is solved by requiring invariance under stuttering. The specification of the hour clock must allow any finite number of stuttering steps—ones that leave the hour unchanged—between successive changes to the hour. Steps of the hour–minute clock that change only the minute are then stuttering steps allowed by the hour clock's specification.

At the time, such state-machine specifications were criticized as being overly specific. The state-machine specification of a FIFO queue I would have written in those days would have been equivalent to the specification given by module *InternalFIFO* in Merz's Figure 4 (Section 3.5), though probably written in a pseudo-programming language. Critics pointed out that a specification should only mention the interface variables *in* and *out*. The variable *q* should not appear, since there is no reason why an implementation needs to implement the required behavior with an explicit queue. The only way to avoid all mention of *q* is to describe explicitly all the queue's possible behaviors. To see how difficult this is, I urge the reader to try to write an informal natural-language specification of a FIFO queue without mentioning the contents of the queue. However, the criticism remained valid: a specification of the queue should be in terms only of the variables *in* and *out*. The answer was to hide internal state variables. Hiding a variable is expressed in temporal logic by temporal existential quantification. The only (free) variables of the specification *Fifo* in module *FIFO* of Merz's Figure 4 are *in* and *out*.

The final step in the development of TLA came when I realized that taking action formulas as the atomic formulas in Pnueli's temporal logic made it easy to describe state machines with temporal logic formulas. There was no need to translate from a language for expressing state machines into temporal logic. The state machine could be written directly as a temporal logic formula.

TLA has allowed me to better understand and to formalize many concepts in concurrency. Merz discusses implementation as implication and composition as conjunction. The example that I find most compelling is reduction. Reduction is the process of proving properties of a concurrent algorithm by reasoning about a coarser-grained version. There are a number of theorems and folk theorems stating when this is possible. For example, one reduction folk theorem asserts that if shared variables are accessed only in mutually exclusive critical sections, then we can pretend that the execution of an entire critical section is a single atomic step. It was intuitively clear that these results were all variations on one basic idea, but it was only with the aid of TLA that I was able to understand reduction well enough to express that idea as a single theorem that encompasses those prior results [1].

Whence TLA$^+$

After deciding that TLA was the right way to describe and reason about concurrent systems, my next step was to develop a complete specification language based on it. Merz makes the simple idea of taking predicate logic and (untyped) set theory as the logic of actions for TLA seem natural and almost inevitable. In fact, it took me years to discard the usual concepts of computer science to achieve the simplicity of TLA+. Here are two examples.

Like most computer scientists, I thought that assignment statements were the natural way to describe state changes. I was skeptical when Jim Horning suggested that I write $x' = x + 1$ instead of $x := x + 1$. However, I tried it and found that it worked quite well. Unlike most computer scientists, I realized how much simpler $x' = x + 1$ is than $x := x + 1$. The assignment statement asserts that nothing but x changes—a concept that cannot be expressed mathematically in any simple way. (Since there are an infinite number of possible variables and a mathematical formula can mention only a finite number of them, a formula cannot assert that no variable other than x changes.) I was therefore happy to eliminate assignment statements. Upon seeing TLA+, almost every computer scientist suggests getting get rid of the UNCHANGED conjuncts, essentially by introducing assignment. Initially, I replied that this would gain little, since removing the UNCHANGED conjuncts would reduce the size of most real specifications by less than 5%. I now point out that the explicit UNCHANGED conjuncts provide valuable redundancy, allowing the model checker to detect the common error of forgetting to specify the new value of a variable.

Like most computer scientists, I assumed that a language should be typed. When I realized that I could eliminate traditional types and let type correctness be an invariant, Martín Abadi encouraged me to do so. Only after I took his advice and started writing untyped specifications did I realize how complicated and constraining types are [2].

When I first started to think about a specification language for TLA, I assumed it would need the usual kinds of programming-language constructs favored by computer scientists. However, I didn't know which ones. I therefore decided to start with only TLA and simple mathematics, and to add other constructs as I needed them. Somewhat to my surprise, I found that all I needed were:

- A few constructs for writing mathematics formally, such as definitions and an IF/THEN/ELSE operator.
- Variable declarations and name scoping, which led to the TLA+ module structure.

Using TLA$^+$

The initial motivation for TLA was to make completely formal, hierarchical correctness proofs of concurrent systems as simple as possible. The development of TLA+ was motivated by the needs of engineers building large systems, for which complete formal development is out of the question. Thus, the TLC model checker was written about 6 years ago, while a project to develop a mechanical proof checker for TLA+ is just starting. (This is in contrast to B, which was developed for the complete mechanical verification of relatively simple programs.)

The industrial TLA+ specifications I know of have mainly been high-level descriptions of concurrent algorithms or protocols. They have been written to debug the designs (with the aid of TLC) and to serve as documentation. TLA+ specifications have also been used to improve testing of implementations. Randomly generated tests are notoriously inefficient at finding errors in concurrent systems. It is much more effective to guide testing with behaviors generated by TLC from the TLA+ specification [6].

My fundamental objective is to improve the design of systems by getting engineers to think carefully about what they build. I have met with very limited success. Most engineers are looking for tools that can find bugs automatically without requiring any thought. Such tools are useful, but good systems are not built by removing the bugs from poorly designed ones. Thus far, hardware engineers have been the most eager users of TLA+. They are very concerned about errors and are accustomed to using formal tools.

A couple of years ago, I asked Brannon Batson, then a hardware designer at Intel, why he used TLA+. He replied:

> I get asked this question a lot. I randomly select between the following two answers:
> 1. It saves a lot of effort to use a high-level language which easily models operations on complex data structures—i.e., select the subset of elements in this set satisfying these conditions and apply this next state equation, etc. Most languages achieve readability of such operations through function encapsulation and other information hiding techniques. But information hiding is the last thing we want in a formal specification. TLA+ provides a powerful set of operators (borrowed from mathematics) which can be used to densely encode complex statements in a readable fashion, without hiding information.
> 2. The next big frontier in computer engineering is algorithmic complexity. In order to tackle this increasingly complex world, we need tools and languages which augment human thought, not supplant it. TLA+ is a language which connects engineers to the underlying mathematics of their design—providing insight which they otherwise wouldn't have.

For an idea of the problems that face designers of complex systems, I recommend trying to solve the Wildfire Challenge Problem [3].

1. Ernie Cohen and Leslie Lamport. Reduction in TLA. In David Sangiorgi and Robert de Simone, editors, *CONCUR'98 Concurrency Theory*, volume 1466 of *Lecture Notes in Computer Science*, pages 317–331. Springer-Verlag, 1998.

2. Leslie Lamport and Lawrence C. Paulson. Should your specification language be typed? *ACM Transactions on Programming Languages and Systems*, 21(3):502–526, May 1999.

3. Leslie Lamport, Madhu Sharma, Mark Tuttle, and Yuan Yu. The Wildfire Verification Challenge Problem. At URL `http://research.microsoft.com/users/lamport/tla/wildfire-challenge.html` on the World Wide Web. It can also be found by searching the Web for the 24-letter string `wildfirechallengeproblem`.

4. Amir Pnueli. The temporal logic of programs. In *Proceedings of the 18th Annual Symposium on the Foundations of Computer Science*, pages 46–57. IEEE, November 1977.

5. Richard L. Schwartz and P.M. Melliar-Smith. Temporal logic specification of distributed systems. In *Proceedings of the 2nd International Conference on Distributed Computing Systems*, pages 446–454. IEEE Computer Society Press, April 1981.

6. Serdar Tasiran, Yuan Yu, Brannon Batson, and Scott Kreider. Using formal specifications to monitor and guide simulation: Verifying the cache coherence engine of the Alpha 21364 microprocessor. In *Proceedings of the 3rd IEEE Workshop on Microprocessor Test and Verification, Common Challenges and Solutions*. IEEE Computer Society, 2002.

9 James C.P. Woodcock: Z Logic and Its Applications

The chapter by Henson, Deutsch, and Reeves on *Z logic and its applications* gives a suitably technical description of the Z notation from a logical viewpoint. It assumes that the reader is familiar with the language, and gives an authoritative account of the authors' formalisation of the logical foundations of Z and its theories of refinement. Having read this chapter and the rest of the book, the reader will be struck by the diversity of the different specification languages. So what more could I add as a reviewer asked to provide a non-technical essay, taking the chapter as its departure point? How about this?

In spite of their diversity, the specification languages in this book have more in common than apparently separates them.

My short essay offers some evidence to support this claim.

Tony Hoare recruited me to his embryonic Verifying Compiler project [3] when we lectured together at the Marktoberdorf Summer School in 2003. The project has gradually turned into the Grand Challenge in Verified Software [4], a worldwide association of researchers dedicated to advancing the scientific principles of programming. We believe that a mature scientific discipline should set its own agenda and pursue ideals of purity, generality, and accuracy far beyond current needs. Over the next 15 to 20 years, we want to collect a significant body of verified programs with precise external specifications, complete internal specifications, and machine-checked proofs of correctness. These programs will replace existing unverified ones, and will continue to evolve as verified code. This collection will constitute the *Verified Software Repository* [1]. At the end of the project it will be clear to everyone what kind of large industrial systems can be mechanically verified and how easily this can be done.

The research road map and the goals of the Repository are described elsewhere [2]. What I'd like to do is to describe briefly one of the experiments. In January 2006, we launched the first pilot project: a year-long exercise to demonstrate research collaboration and competition, and to generate artifacts to populate the Repository. The task was to verify a key property of the Mondex smart card for financial transactions, and in doing so to assess the current state of proof mechanisation.

Mondex is an electronic purse hosted on a smart card. It was developed to the high-assurance standard ITSEC Level E6 by a consortium led by NatWest, a UK high-street bank. These purses interact using a communications device, and strong guarantees are needed that transactions are secure. In spite of power failures and mischievous attacks, we must guarantee that electronic cash can't be counterfeited. The transactions are completely distributed: there is no centralised control, and all security measures locally implemented, without any real-time external audit logging or monitoring. The original verification was seriously security critical. Logica (with assistance from the University of Oxford) used Z for the development process. We produced formal models of the system and its abstract security policy, and made hand proofs that the system design possesses the required security properties. The abstract security policy specification is about 20 pages of Z and the concrete specification (of an n-step protocol) is about 60 pages. The verification is suitable for the independent evaluation needed for E6, and consists of about 200 pages of refinement proof, with a further 100 pages of derivation of refinement rules.

The original hand proof was vital in getting the required certification; it was also useful in finding and evaluating different models. In particular, the original team made a key modelling discovery: an abstraction that gave a precise description of the security property and that explained why the protocol is secure. It revealed a bug in the implementation of a secondary protocol, giving a convincing counterexample. The challenge was to take a publicly available version of the Mondex specification, designs, and proofs [5] and to investigate the degree of automation that can now be achieved in the correctness proofs. It was taken up by researchers working with specification languages described in this book: ASM (Augsburg), Event-B (Southampton), Raise (Macao/DTU), and Z (York). Other researchers used Alloy (MIT), OCL (Bremen), Perfect-Developer (Escher Technologies), and the π-calculus (Newcastle).

The ASM group used the KIV specification and verification system to produce an alternative formalisation of the communication protocol. They produced a mechanical verification of the full Mondex case study, except transcription of failure logs to a central archive, which is orthogonal to the money-transfer protocol. Their work was completed in just four weeks, although the existence of a (nearly) correct refinement relation helped. The Event-B group re-did the development from scratch using B4free. A key feature of this development is the use of nine refinement levels. These small steps led to larger numbers of verification conditions, but their resulting simplicity made their discharge automatic. The Raise group verified their RSL specifications using PVS. They created new models, viewing Mondex abstractly as a simple problem in accounting: no purses, no protocol messages, just bottom-line values and money-transfer operations. The first refinement level introduces abstract purses and concrete operations, but with no details of the mechanisms preserving the asserted invariant. At the concrete level there are full details of the value-transferring protocol. The Z group mechanised all the original models, refinements, and proofs faithfully, without changing anything. The objective was to show how the existing work could be automated without changing things just to make life easier.

All four groups spent about the same amount of time mechanising their developments, and they all found the same bugs in the system. These are mostly to do with some missing properties in the intermediate design, permitting operations involving inauthentic purses. The mechanisation of the proofs turns out not to be the biggest problem in a development of this kind. Instead, the biggest problem is *modelling*: finding the right abstractions and suitable invariants. And this was what united the eight groups working on Mondex; the differences between the logics was rarely discussed. Instead, the joint meetings during the project were exciting as 16 people got together to discuss their work, exchanging ideas, models, and invariants, not debating notational differences.

Future Repository projects will see different groups using each others' notations and tools as we learn that there's more uniting us than dividing us. It's the logical next step.

1. J. Bicarregui, C.A.R. Hoare, and J.C.P. Woodcock. The verified software repository: a step towards the verifying compiler. *Formal Aspects of Computing* **18**(2):143–151 2006.
2. *Verified Software Roadmap.* qpq.csl.sri.com/vsr.
3. C.A.R. Hoare. The verifying compiler: A grand challenge for computing research. *Journal of ACM* **50**(1):63–69 2003.
4. C.B. Jones, P.W. O'Hearn, and Jim Woodcock. Verified Software: A Grand Challenge. *IEEE Computer* **39**(4):93–95 (2006).
5. S. Stepney, D. Cooper, and J.C.P. Woodcock. *An Electronic Purse: Specification, Refinement, and Proof.* Technical Monograph PRG-126, Programming Research Group, Oxford University. (2000)

10 Closing: Dines Bjørner and Martin C. Henson

The reader who makes it to this point will wish, with us, to extend heartfelt thanks to all who made this book possible. Just now we must first say, to Yuri, Jean-Raymond, Kokichi, Peter, Zhou, Klaus, Cliff, Leslie and Jim: *thank you!* for your fascinating reflections.

The two weeks in Stara Lesna are now a three-year-old memory, but much remembered with affection. We hope the memory lives on in the heads and hearts of the wonderful students who attended. Each evening we celebrated a day well-spent on study with excellent food and, if not Pilsner, then something from a bottle brought by one of the participants (Irish whiskey from Dublin; honeyed chilli vodka from the Ukraine, and so on). We all, students, presenters and organizers alike, deserved it. And now, dear reader, so do you. Sit back, put your feet up, empty your mind of all thoughts of category theory, higher-order logic and the like, and sip on a *Stara Lesna*:

4-8 parts	lemon vodka	strong
1 part	lime cordial	sour
1 part	lemon juice	sour
1 part	triple sec	sweet
3	ice cubes	cold

Blend and shake well before serving. If you made it with us to the end of the book, then you *really do* deserve it!

K. Jensen
Coloured Petri Nets
Basic Concepts, Analysis Methods
and Practical Use, Vol. 1
2nd ed.

K. Jensen
Coloured Petri Nets
Basic Concepts, *Analysis Methods*
and Practical Use, Vol. 2

K. Jensen
Coloured Petri Nets
Basic Concepts, Analysis Methods
and *Practical Use*, Vol. 3

A. Nait Abdallah
The Logic of Partial Information

Z. Fülöp, H.Vogler
Syntax-Directed Semantics
Formal Models Based
on Tree Transducers

A. de Luca, S. Varricchio
**Finiteness and Regularity
in Semigroups
and Formal Languages**

E. Best, R. Devillers, M. Koutny
Petri Net Algebra

S.P. Demri, E.S. Orlowska
**Incomplete Information:
Structure, Inference, Complexity**

J.C.M. Baeten, C.A. Middelburg
Process Algebra with Timing

L.A. Hemaspaandra, L. Torenvliet
Theory of Semi-Feasible Algorithms

E. Fink, D. Wood
Restricted-Orientation Convexity

Zhou Chaochen, M.R. Hansen
Duration Calculus
A Formal Approach to Real-Time
Systems

M. Große-Rhode
**Semantic Integration
of Heterogeneous Software
Specifications**

H. Ehrig, K. Ehrig, U. Prange,
G. Taentzer
**Fundamentals of Algebraic
Graph Transformation**

W. Michiels, E. Aarts, J. Korst
**Theoretical Aspects
of Local Search**

D. Bjørner, M.C. Henson (Eds.)
Logics of Specification Languages

Texts in Theoretical Computer Science · An EATCS Series